AF544835

The 50 most
influential
street artists today

Street art
/today^2

The 50 most
influential
street artists today

Street art
/today²

Bjørn Van Poucke

LANNOO

INTRO-

It feels like the peak of street art's identity crisis is finally behind us and we're witnessing the re-birth of a new, reinvented scene.

THE HYPER-GLOBALISATION of the world in the 21st century has resulted in dynamics and trends that are hard to comprehend and categorise using existing tools and methods. Whether we're talking politics, economy, or culture, the transglobal mixing and merging – spiced up with the virtual allure of social media – has created hybrids which are regularly comprised of variety, sometimes incorporating opposing elements from different origins. In a converged world, everything has become a hard-to-read mishmash of stuff which sometimes just doesn't make sense any more.

Highly noticeable, relatable, and ultimately hyper-likable, street art has not been spared these developments. Just like other forms of urban culture such as music or skateboarding, the mainstream pretty much lost its well-calculated mind over these forms of youth culture expression. Seeing its immeasurable value as part of gentrification processes worldwide, borrowing elements to build their own credibility, or plainly (ab)using it for marketing or branding purposes, we've witnessed the creation of a monster in the recent years. But this isn't the first time that things are taking such turn, as similar scenarios happened to other rebellious-minded movements – and most of them are still alive and kicking. And in all honesty, it feels like the peak of street art's identity crisis is finally behind us and we're witnessing the re-birth of a new, reinvented scene.

Getting deep into this matter, I can't help thinking of Jeremy Rifkin's *Entropy: A New World View* and the way he relates the world's economic and social structures by using the second law of thermodynamics. First, energy cannot be created; it's only possible to change its form. Second, everything moves from a state of perfection towards chaos. Like all things existing in the universe, the street art culture is also part of this predetermined programme. What started as a spontaneous form of expression by individuals has evolved into a globally recognised movement with a number of different forms and conducts.

DUCTION

At the same time, the initial writing of statements and names evolved into the creation of the most elaborate, giant-scale murals in every corner of the globe, using classical art, technology, or anything else within its reach. And yes, a whole pile of decorative, Instagram-friendly work that is simply riding the same hype wave.

So yes, street art is still street, but not all of it is. As Escif stated in the interview I did with him for *Juxtapoz Magazine*, 'Actual street art is created by people who don't care about art: wall painters in Senegal, sign painters in Mexico, Pixadores in Brazil, political painters in Greece, homeless in United States and outsider people all around the world who really believe that what they are doing is a tool to change their context.' Those still exist, regardless of big festivals that took over gentrified areas of major cities everywhere, from Honolulu to Hong Kong. And so do the genuine street artists like Escif himself, or Blu, or countless others who are very much aware of how quickly tables can be turned and their 'tools to change their context' can ultimately be used for someone else's gain. The same goes for graffiti writers that are nurturing the vandalising aspect of the original movement. People like 1UP crew who are taking the marking of urban space to absolute extremes these days, risking their freedom and literally their lives while jumping trains and hanging off buildings in order to create the most insane and in-your-face illegal work we've witnessed to date.

Coming from a country that is usually not on the map of countries where big things happen, I've been following the introduction and evolution of street art in Croatia. It was interesting seeing the dynamics I've experienced elsewhere, watching them slowly taking place in my homeland, and observing a growing local interest. This has helped me step out of my bubble, in which I was aware of the ways the movement has been institutionalised (more or less successfully), labelled, bought and sold, or just transformed into Instagram likes. It made me realise that there will always be new generations and new regions where these forms of expressions are not familiar and people will appreciate them, or hate them, with a pure heart, without prejudice or inhibitions previous experiences.

So again, street art is still street, it just grew bigger in so many ways, from its universal recognition to its general artistic quality. And while it might not look or feel like it did a decade ago, there will always be a significant group of individuals that will come up with new concepts, new visuals, and new techniques, which will challenge the viewer and other creatives. Because that is precisely what was happening in the beginning and is still the root of it all, no matter how many likes a selfie-friendly mural of angel wings on a bustling street of London/ New York/ Rijeka gets.

Sasha Bogojev

Contributing editor at *Juxtapoz Magazine* / writer / curator

PREFACE

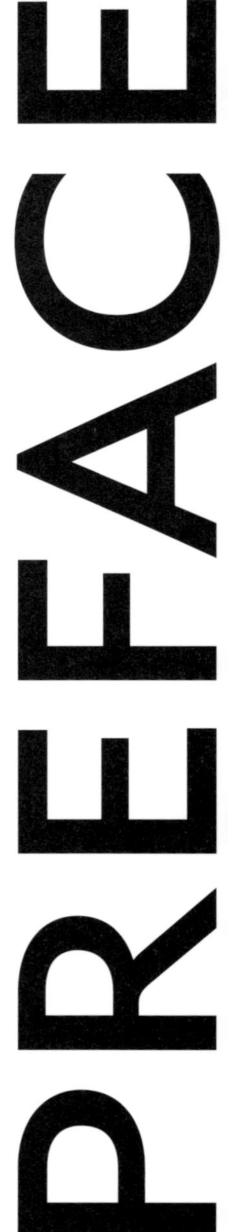

IN 2016 WE RELEASED *Street Art Today,* the first book in what was already set to become a series of publications, which aimed to retrace the history of art in public space and present the 50 most influential artists of that time. We had curated the volume, presenting categories of style in an attempt to impose some order on the writhing and morphing world of street art. Even when writing that first text, it was clear to us that these artists, these projects and the speed of the changing environment around us made it nearly impossible to document exactly. The pace of evolution made each pinpoint of time sprint away before we could finish any sentence.

Three years on, we are continuing the conversation. Here we present an update, a Chapter II, a return, a small glimpse back over the past three years into the world of street art through the eyes of the artists, the curators, the journalists and the groupies. So many projects have been born in the last 36 months that we cannot do them justice in these few pages. As we present a new group of the 50 most influential artists worldwide, you may notice some changes since the last edition. New names have popped up, and we are super-excited to share the work of some talented emerging artists. How lucky we are to see fresh and exciting works catch our eye around the globe! You may also notice that previous chapters on toyism / naive art and surrealism do not grace these pages.
That innovation will simplify the book's navigation for you, dear reader, but also relates to self-reflection. Aware of the polyvalence of all artists represented, we choose to broaden the themes in order to leave more breathing room for their creative minds to navigate.
It feels wrong to pigeonhole or 'freeze' any artist in a rigid style, especially in the fast-paced world of street art.

In this edition, we are very happy to put forward some new thoughts, projects and artists that represent what we see as growing trends,

Which leads us to the question: is street art still 'street'?

as well as some obvious themes that we feel it is important to discuss. The past few years have seen a rise in socially engaged art, with many artists across all styles and genres giving their voice, sometimes their screams, to raise awareness of climate change, discriminatory immigration policies, gender inequality, racism and violent governments. The rise in artists engaging in projects working directly with the community, often through not-for-profit organisations, is also important to note; we firmly believe in the power of public art to enable communities to engage in positive change.

When crafting this selection, we also found it important to address the question of gender inequality in street art and unfortunately in most creative networks, meaning by proxy across society at large. Though founded on notions of democracy, the street art world is not exempt from inequity, and even if we chose to promote a higher percentage of female artists than would typically be shown, women remain underrepresented in this field. It is important today to recognise this point, not in a voice of anger or defeat, but rather in celebration of all those brilliant minds that are creating environments of open discussion, addressing gender equality for artists and audience alike.

Technology is also considered an important element in public art production today. With accessible new gadgets popping up everywhere, and superfast programs being developed worldwide, artists are increasingly playing with installations, projection mapping, interactive artworks, and digital tech. Not only does this open the doors of creation, but it also increases our ability to disseminate works globally. It's a beautiful thing to be able to see the latest walls in Istanbul, the biggest pieces in Rio or the most hidden of ephemeral works. It's frightening, however, when we see artists sacrificing creativity for the ego game of cheap 'likes', hits or a competition about who can get the most 'followers'. Social media is becoming both innovation's best friend and creativity's worst enemy.

As street art is being slowly absorbed into academia, with accredited university degrees being promoted and endless studies conducted on urban visual history, we see more and more artists who hold university degrees. street art continues to grow and evolve towards a 'legitimate' art form, far from the grit and glamour of the American tagging crews of the early days of graffiti, which people still associate with public art. As more and more university-trained artists become actors in the urban landscape, the diversity of the group grows – and with most creatives not creating a 'pure street' body of work, the lines between contemporary art, street art and design are increasingly blurred.

Commercially, international street art festivals are becoming longer standing, better organised and highly sponsored. Simultaneously, public funding is increasingly focused on community identity and 'creative placemaking'. Today, street art is more educated, more accepted and more popular than ever. But in some cases, it is being unfoundedly appropriated, unjustly exploited, cleaned up, toned down, auto-censored, commercially focused and dryly institutionalised. Which leads us to question in this edition: is street art still 'Street'?

Bjørn Van Poucke

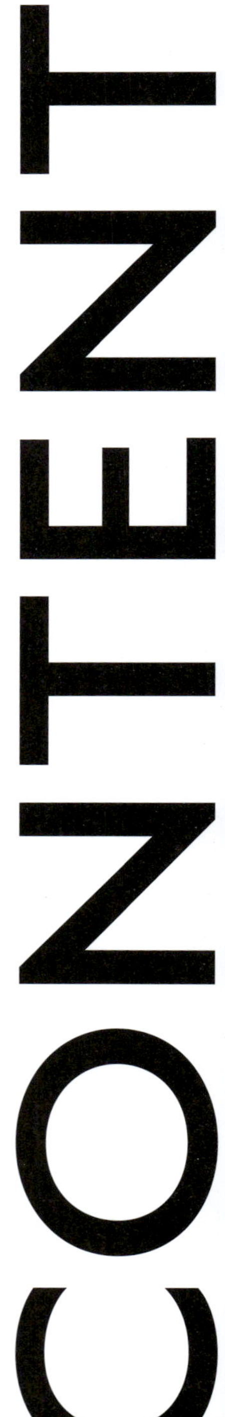

004 **INTRODUCTION /** by Sasha Bogojev

006 **PREFACE /** by Bjørn Van Poucke

020 **INTERVIEW /** Anne-Laure Lemaitre, Doug Gillen, Iryna Kanischeva & Martyn Reed

1/ ABSTRACT

038 INTRODUCTION
040 ELIAN
044 ELLEN RUTT - interview
054 FELIPE PANTONE
058 KRISTIN FARR
062 MADC
066 MOMO
070 MR. JUNE
074 NELIO
078 OKUDA
082 ROBERTO CIREDZ

2/ FIGURATIVE

086 INTRODUCTION
088 ALEX SENNA
092 ALICE PASQUINI
096 ANDREA WAN
100 ARYZ
104 BELIN
106 CINTA VIDAL
112 MILU CORRECH - interview
122 ESCIF
126 FAITH47
130 FINTAN MAGEE
134 HERAKUT
138 HYURO
142 JAZ
146 LOW BROS
150 PAOLA DELFIN
154 SAINER
158 SETH GLOBEPAINTER
162 SHERYO & YOK

3/
REALISM

166 INTRODUCTION
168 AXEL VOID
172 BOSOLETTI
176 CASE MACLAIM
180 GUIDO VAN HELTEN
184 LONAC
188 SEBAS VELASCO
192 ZOER & VELVET - interview

4/
URBAN INTERVENTIONISM

202 INTRODUCTION
204 AMPPARITO
208 BANKSY
212 CRYSTAL WAGNER
216 ERNEST ZACHAREVIC
220 ICY & SOT - interview
230 ISAAC CORDAL
234 JAUNE
238 JR
242 LEON KEER
246 PEJAC
250 SHEPARD FAIREY
254 SPY
258 STROOK
262 SWOON
266 WASTED RITA

» /

Bosoletti
Bonito, Italy, 2018
PHOTO BY THE ARTIST

Sebas Velasco & Zoer
Tolosa, Spain, 2019
PHOTO BY THE ARTIST

Aryz
Chongqing, China, 2016
PHOTO BY THE ARTIST

Okuda
Llanera, Spain, 2015
PHOTO BY THE ARTIST

Elian
Valencia, Spain, 2018
PHOTO BY THE ARTIST

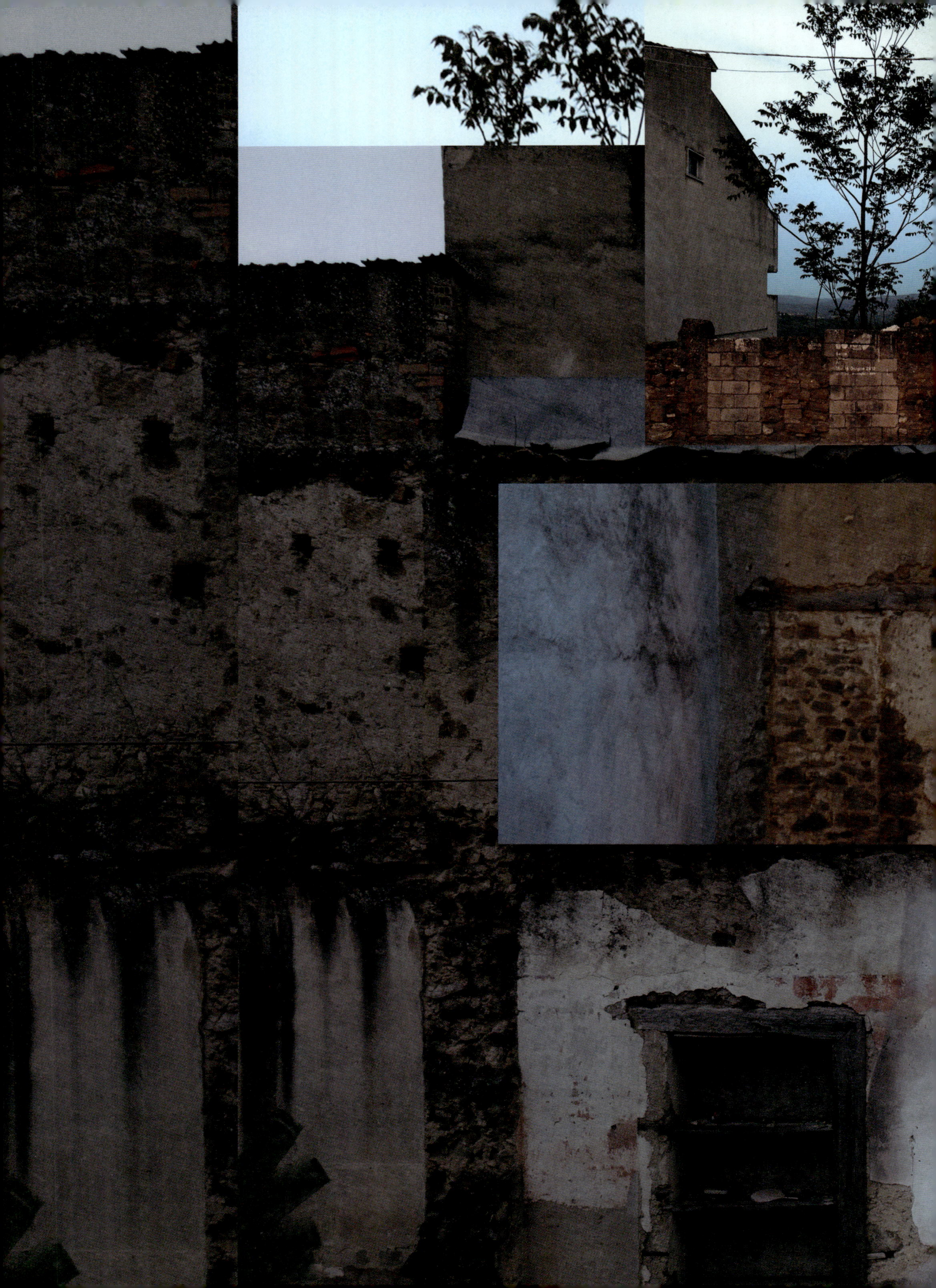

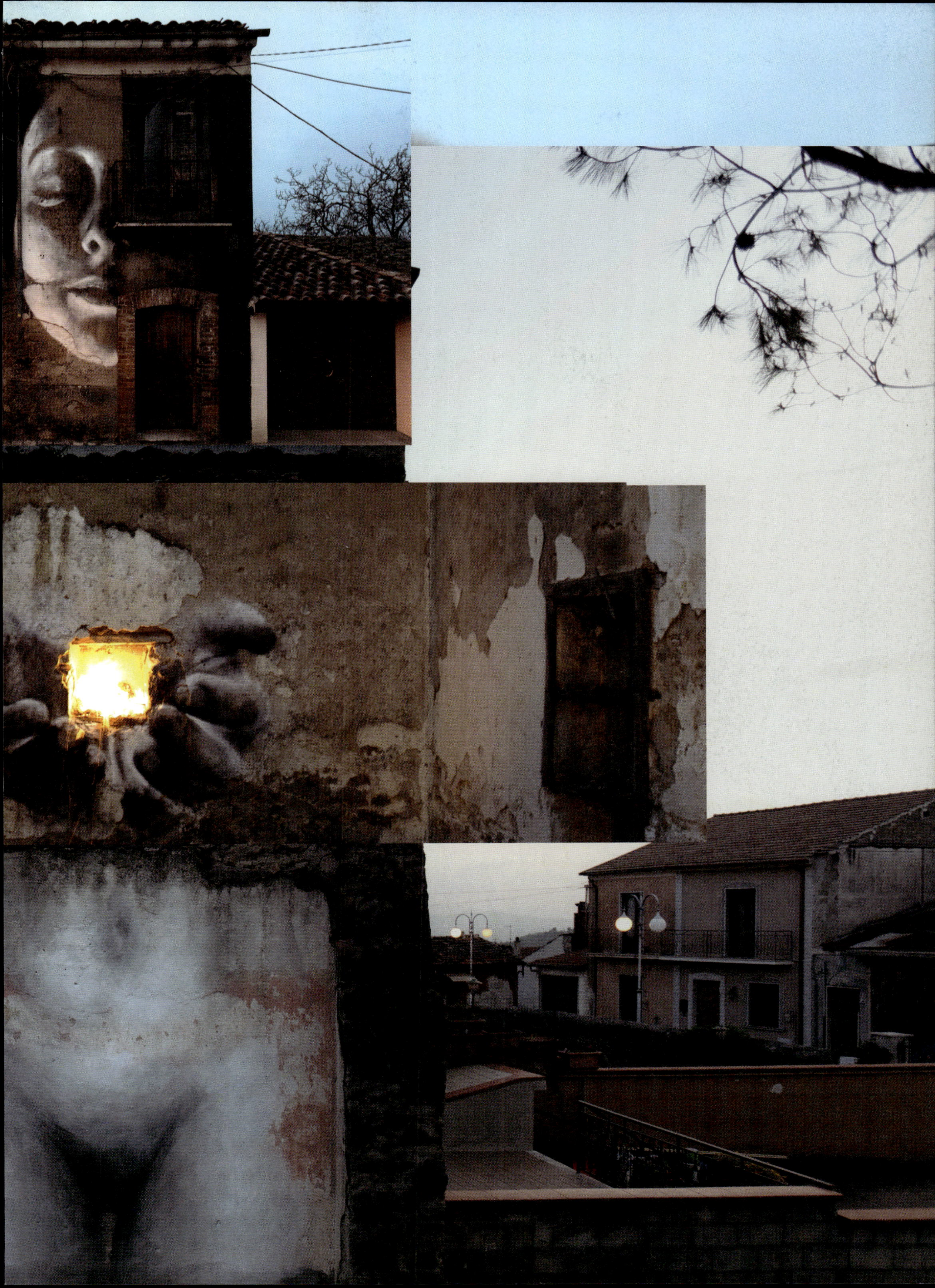

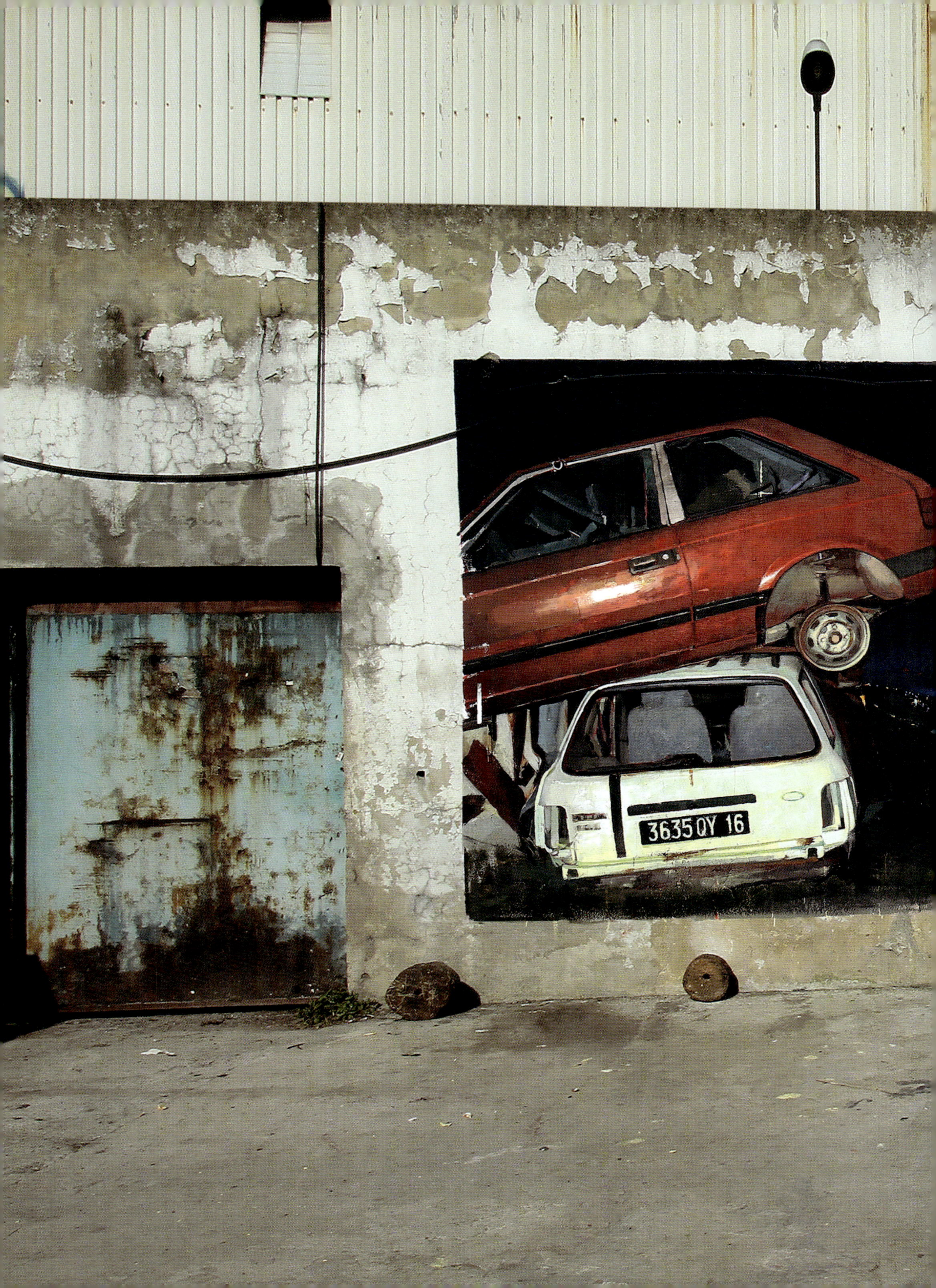
3635 QY 16

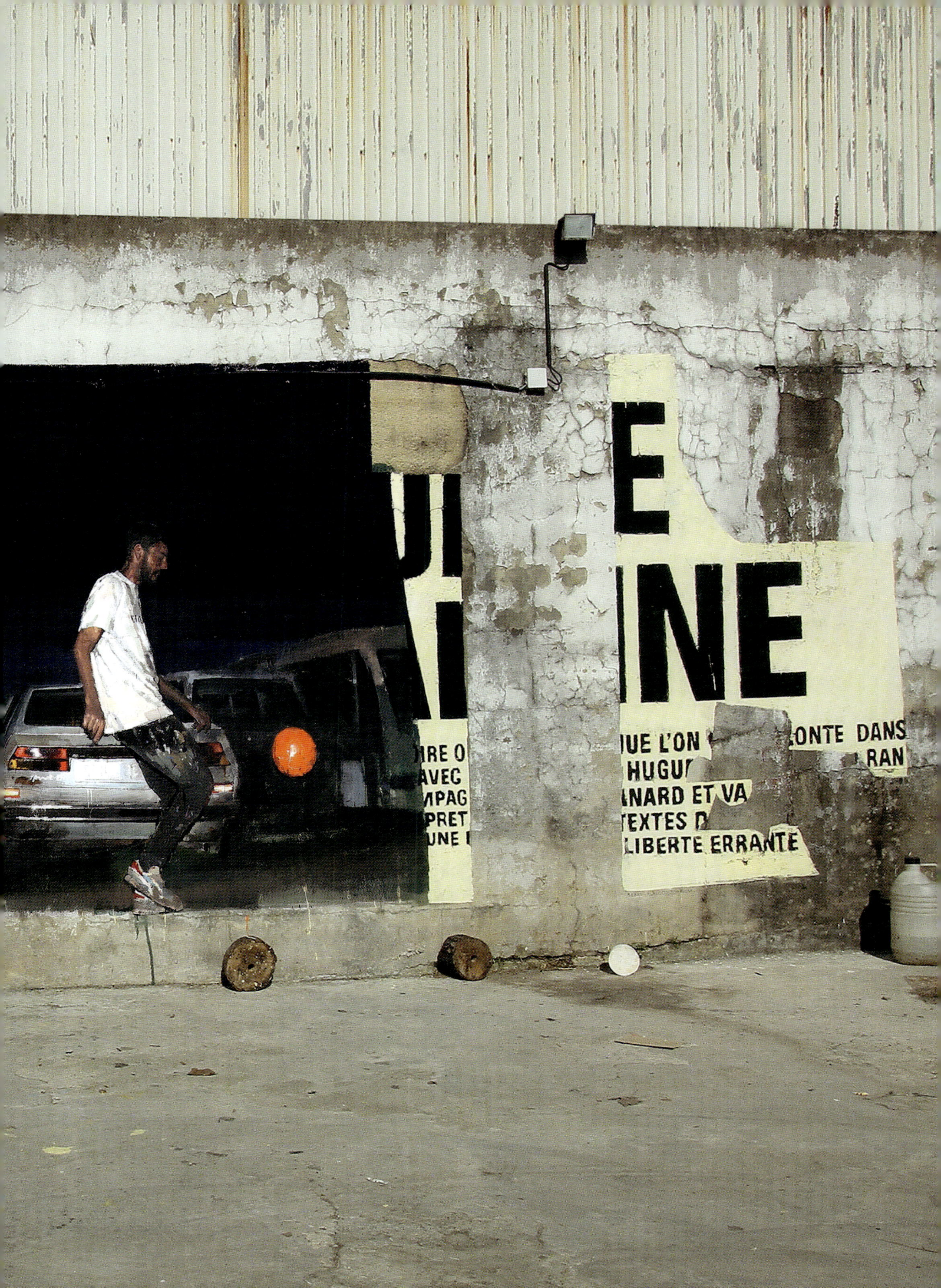

AVEC
UE L'ON
ONTE DANS
ANARD ET VA
TEXTES D
LIBERTE ERRANTE

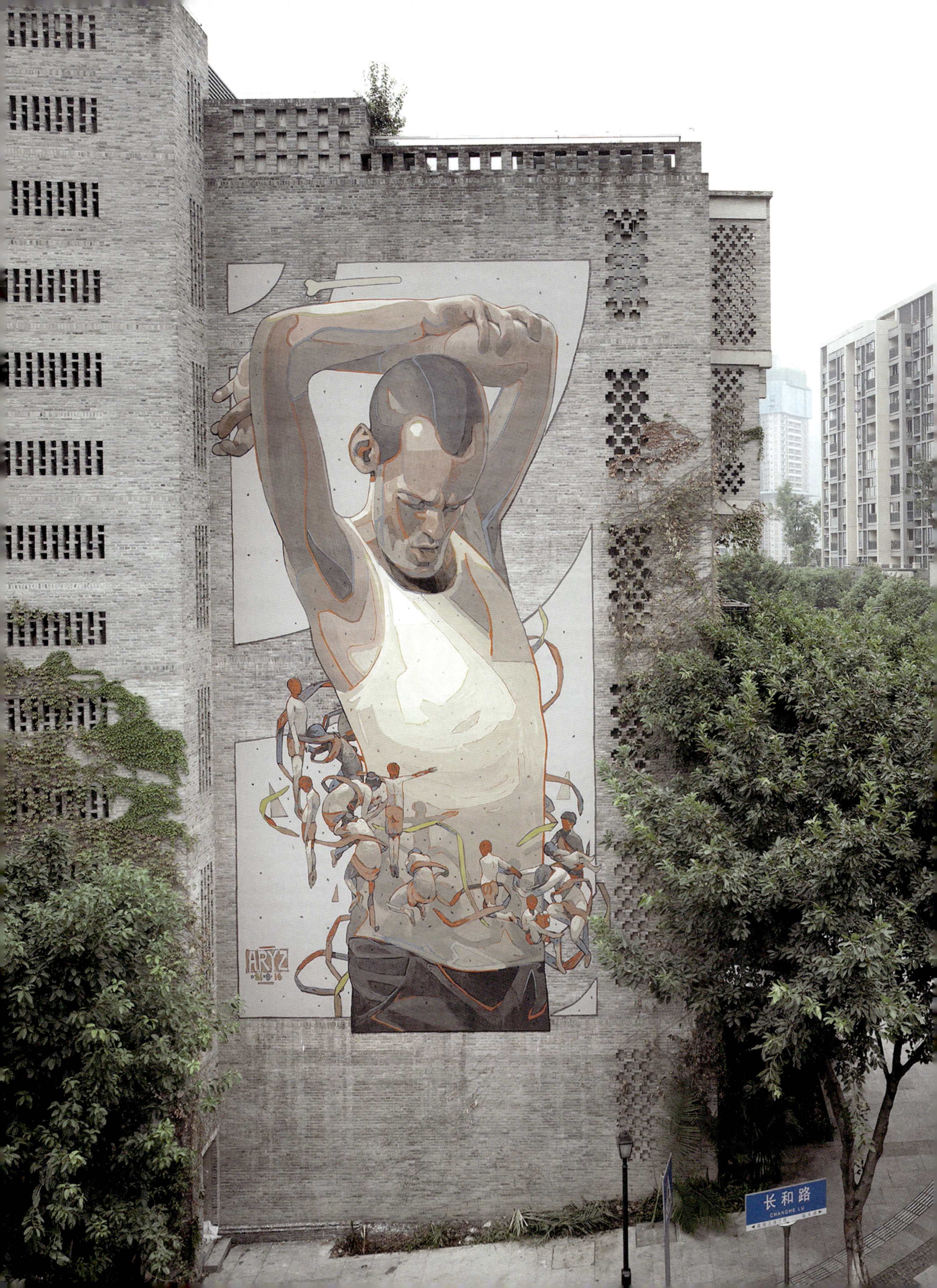
ARYZ
长和路
CHANGHE LU

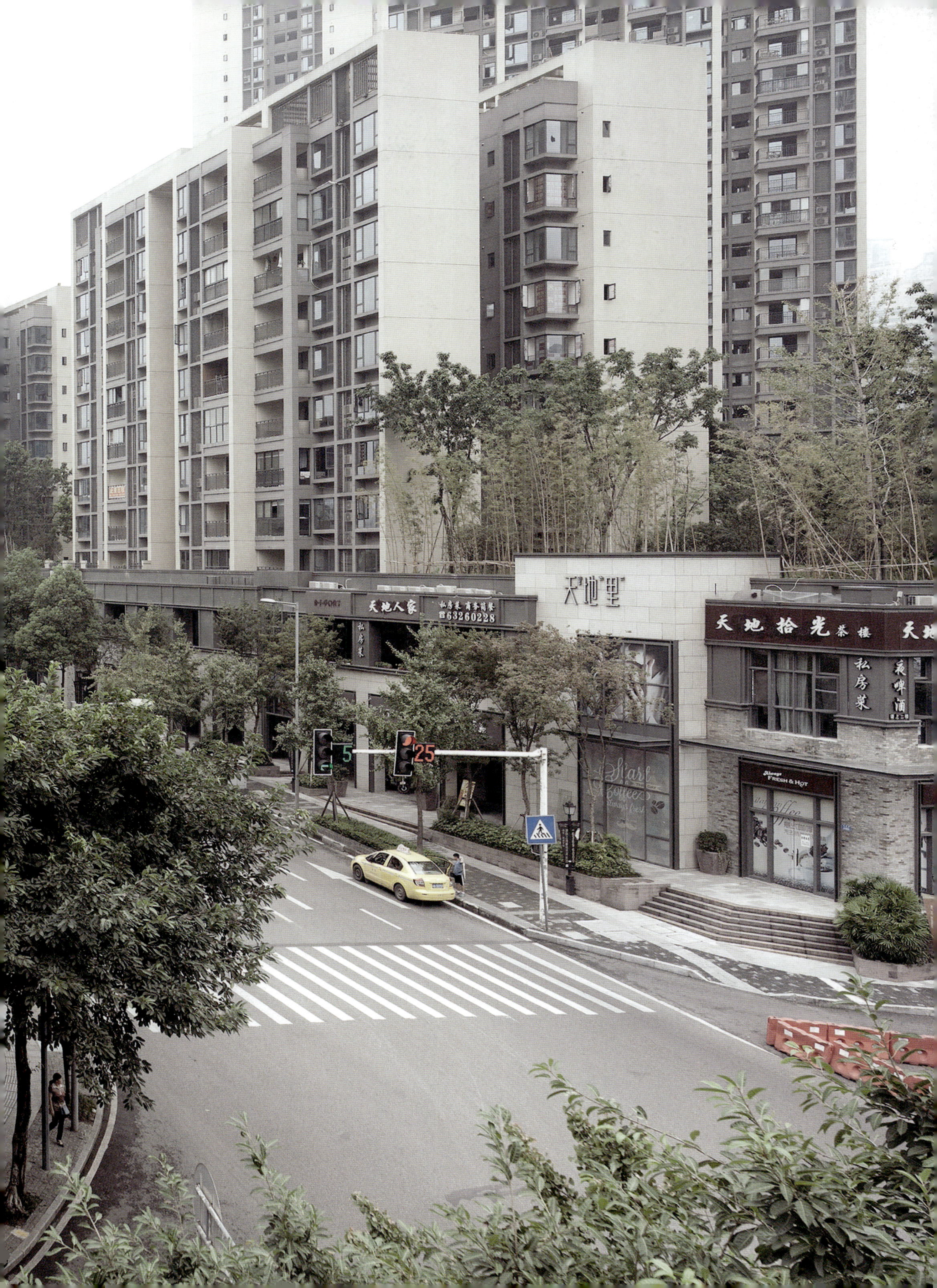
天地人家
私房菜 商务简餐
63260228
私房菜
天地里
天地拾光茶楼
私房菜
夜啤酒
Always FRESH & HOT

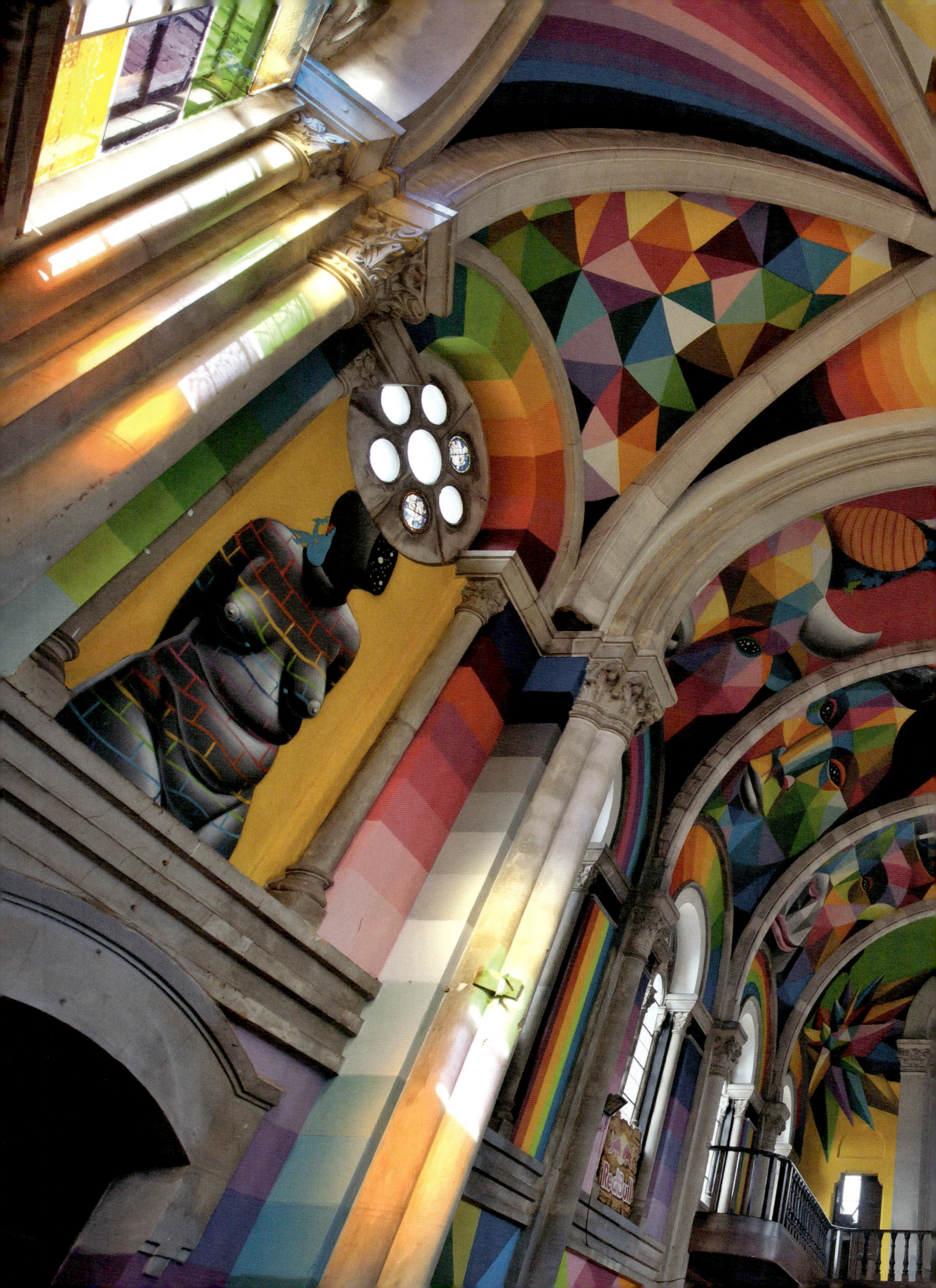
Red Bull

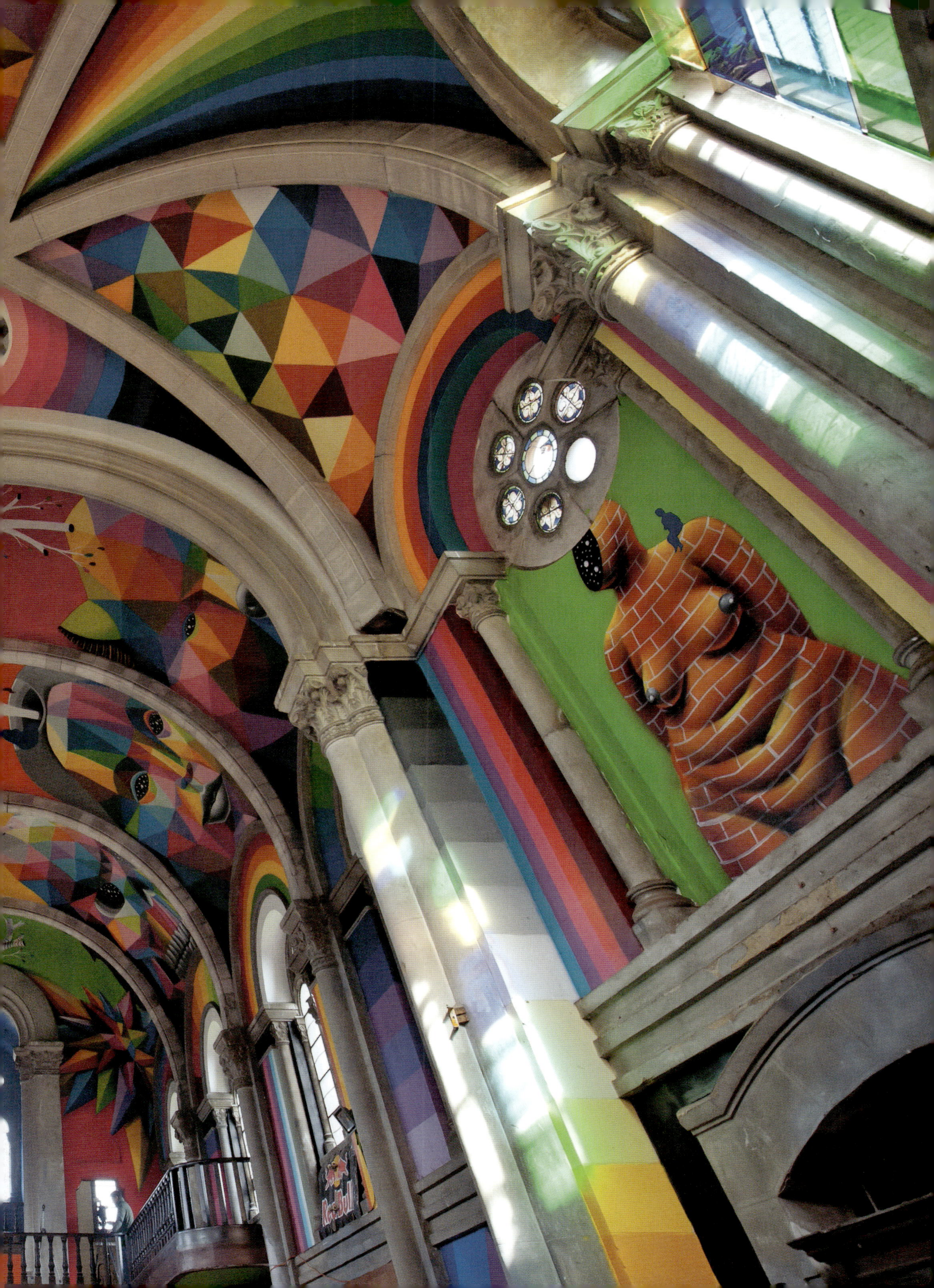
Red Bull

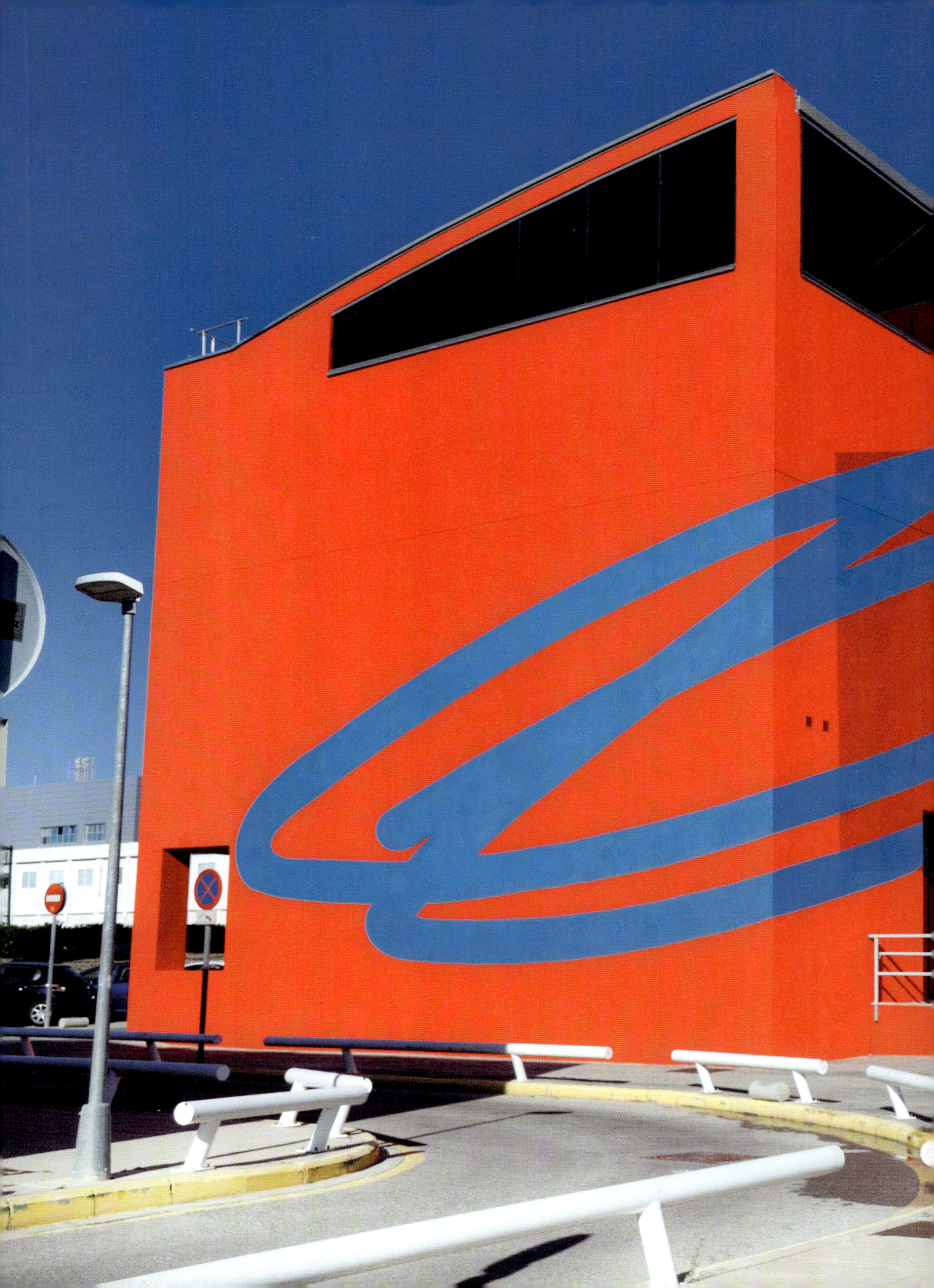

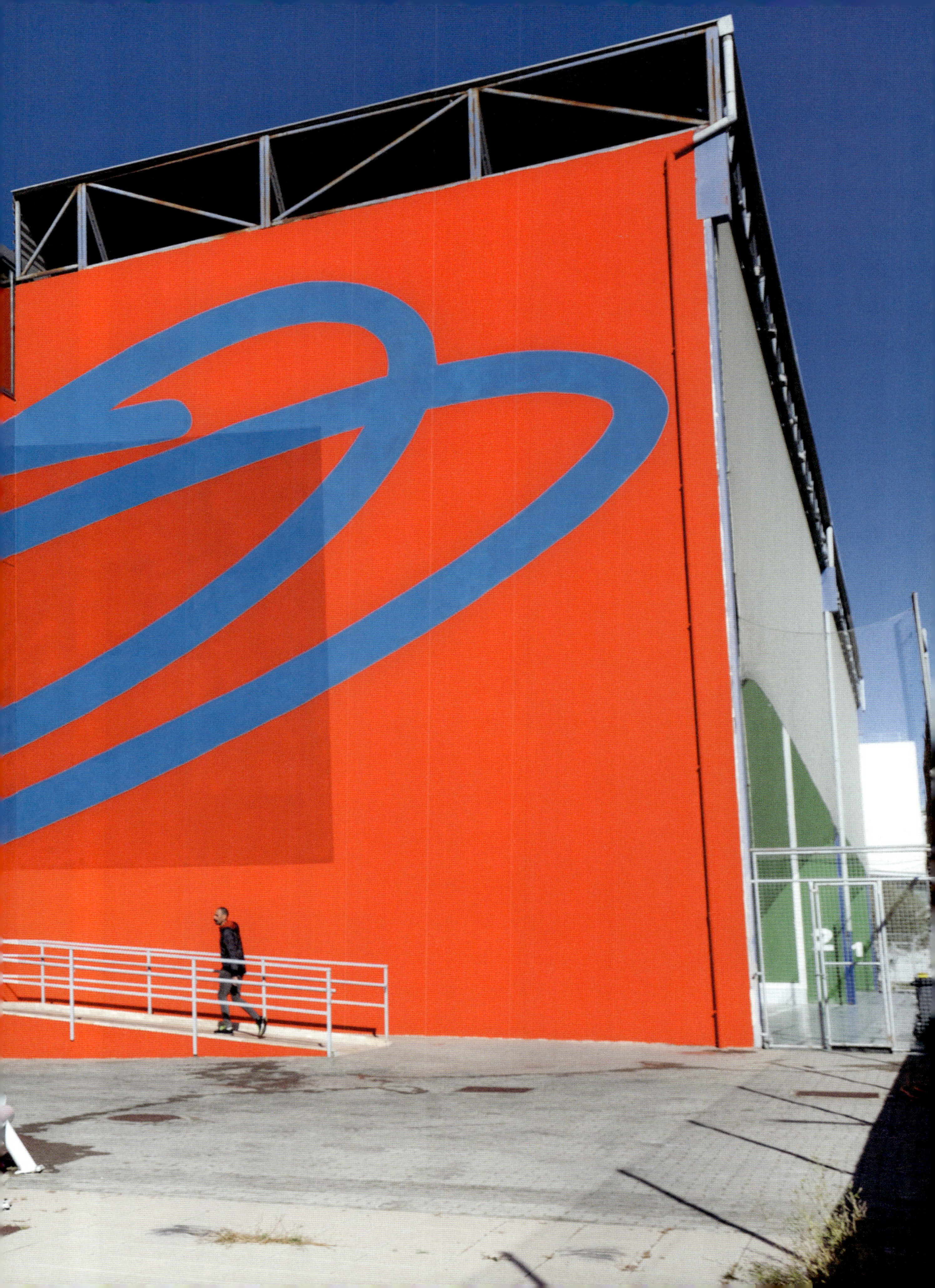

1

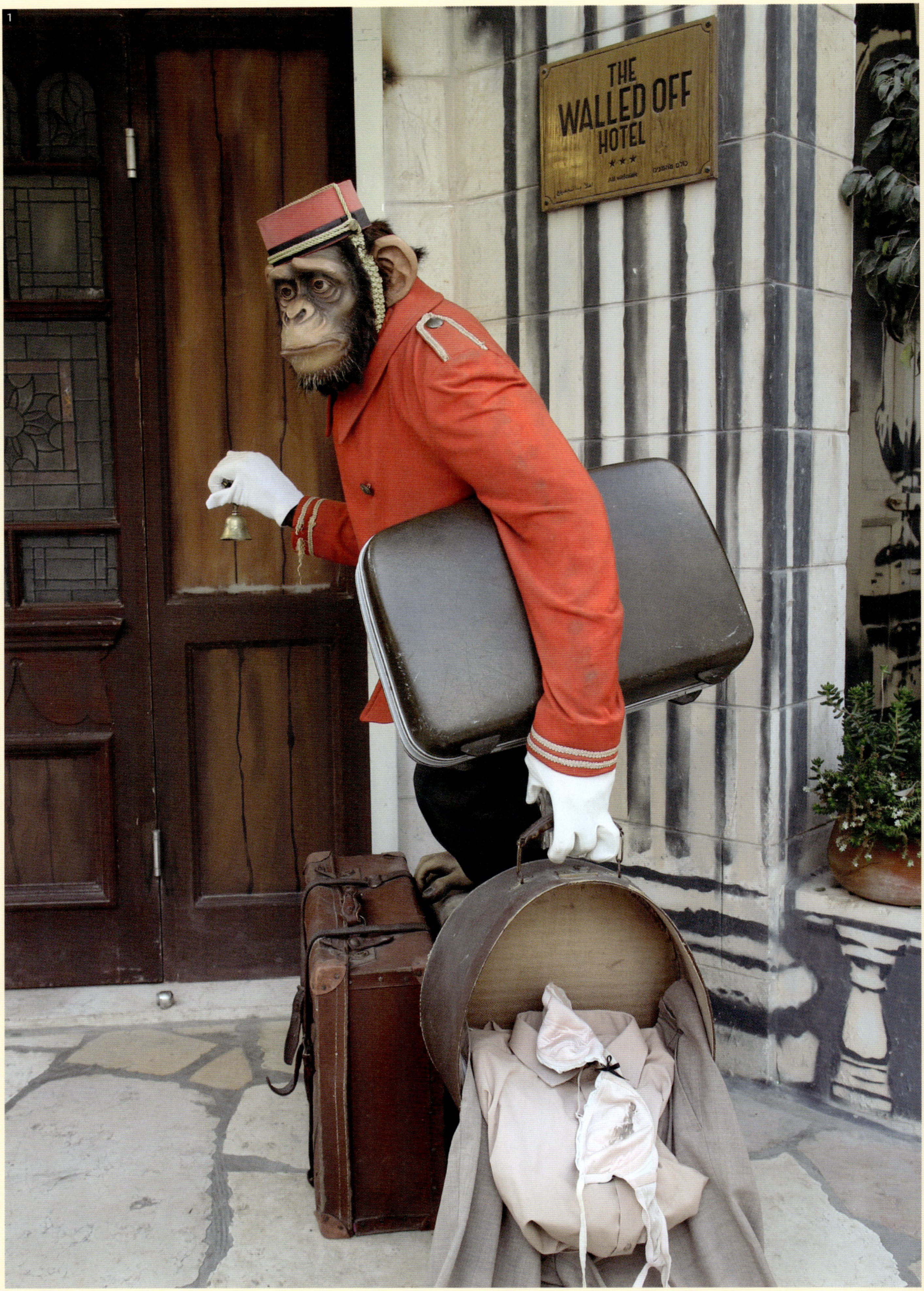

ANNE-LAURE LEMAITRE, DOUG GILLEN, IRYNA KANISHCHEVA & MARTYN REED

Interview

Has there ever been a more audacious project in the history of contemporary political art other than Banksy's Walled Off Hotel?

What have been the most inspiring projects in the past three years?
AL: Street art has experienced tremendous changes over the past 10-15 years, shifting from a niche alternative scene to an art form which is universally recognised and appreciated. This evolution allowed for a greater plurality of voices, techniques, and approaches, visually and conceptually diverse.
MR: I'd say the exponential growth of the monolithic mural as the default setting for municipal and corporate-sponsored "street art", alongside the expansion of the mural festival network and the dominance of large-scale decorative works in public space.
DG: Nothing has changed street art like the internet. From the smallest illegal paste-up to ground-breaking blockbuster festivals, art is being constantly showcased and available for consumption 24/7. This has changed the experience for the artist and the spectator like nothing else in history.

What have been the most inspiring projects in the past three years?
MR: If 'project' is something conceived with a beginning and an end that requires financial resources other than the artist's own, then it has to be Banksy's 'Walled Off Hotel in Bethlehem'. Has there ever been a more audacious project in the history of contemporary political art? It's second only to his Sotheby's prank with the 'Shredded Girl with Balloon'.
If on the other hand 'project' is a plan conceived and executed on the streets by someone who simply wants to make their mark on the world, then I'd have to salute every tagger, stencillist, writer and stickerist out there. I'm inspired every day by the tags I pass, that manage to turn the private to public in the most efficient way imaginable under a system that

1 /
Banksy
Bethlehem, Jerusalem, 2017
PHOTO BY SASHA BOGOJEV

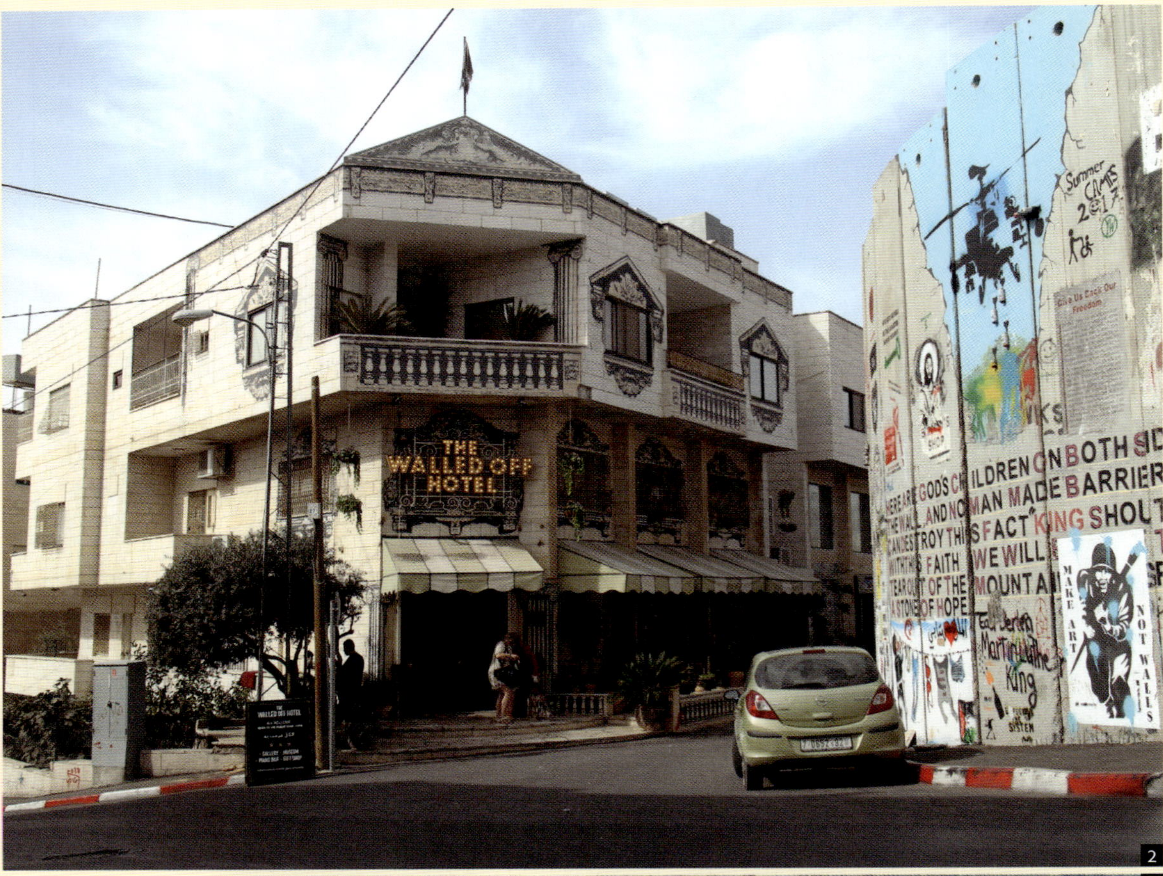

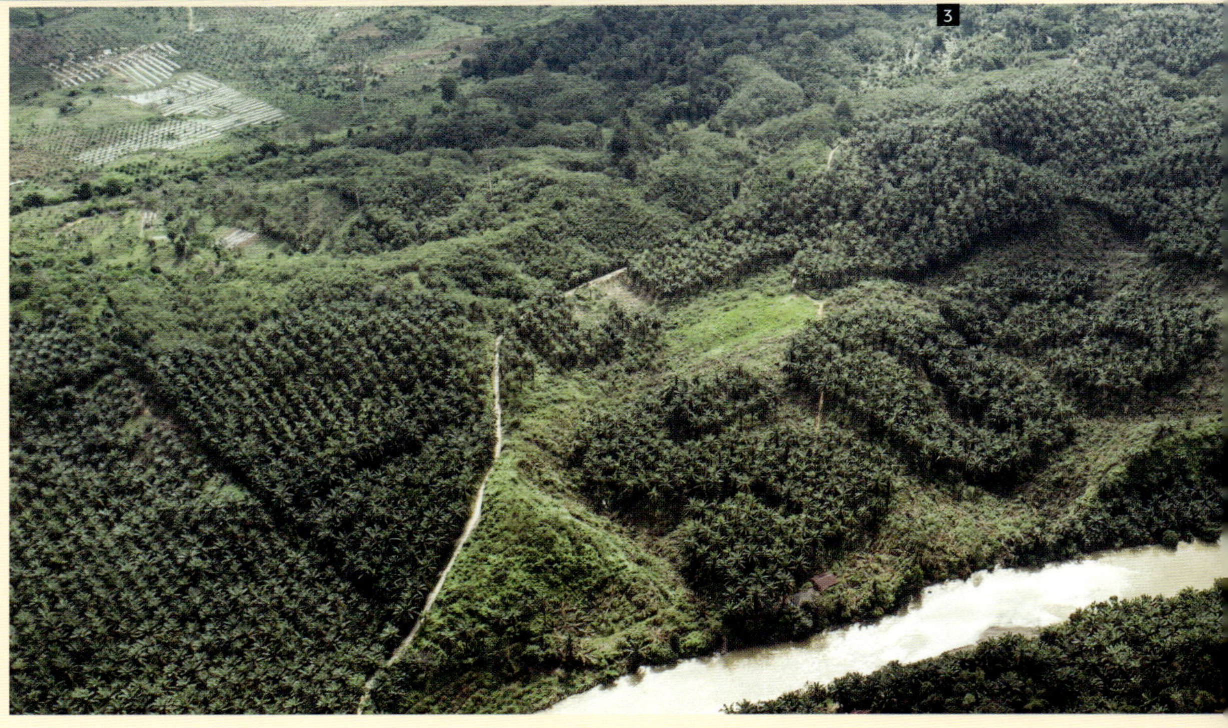

2 /
Banksy
Bethlehem, Jerusalem, 2017
PHOTO BY SASHA BOGOJEV

3 /
Ernest Zacharevic
Sumatra, Indonesia, 2018
PHOTO BY THE ARTIST

values property above all else. It's a constant reminder that there are people out there willing to transgress rules, to put their neck on the line, who don't do it for the income, but for the outcome. There's an important message for us all in that.
DG: Street art has gained an increased global presence over the last decade, accompanied by confidence in both artistic ambition and logistical support. Ernest Zacharevic's 'Splash and Burn' is a great example of what this kind of confidence can achieve. As a way of tackling the Indonesian palm-oil industry's negative impact on local wildlife and its dramatic contribution to poisonous carbon emissions, Ernest invited artists to the region to engage with this topic in various ways. In 2018 this culminated with the subproject 'Save Our Souls', which saw Ernest acquire a patch of plantation. They tore down the uninhabitable plantation trees to form the letters SOS, the acronym for international distress. The land was then repopulated with trees native to the area, encouraging the return of local wildlife.

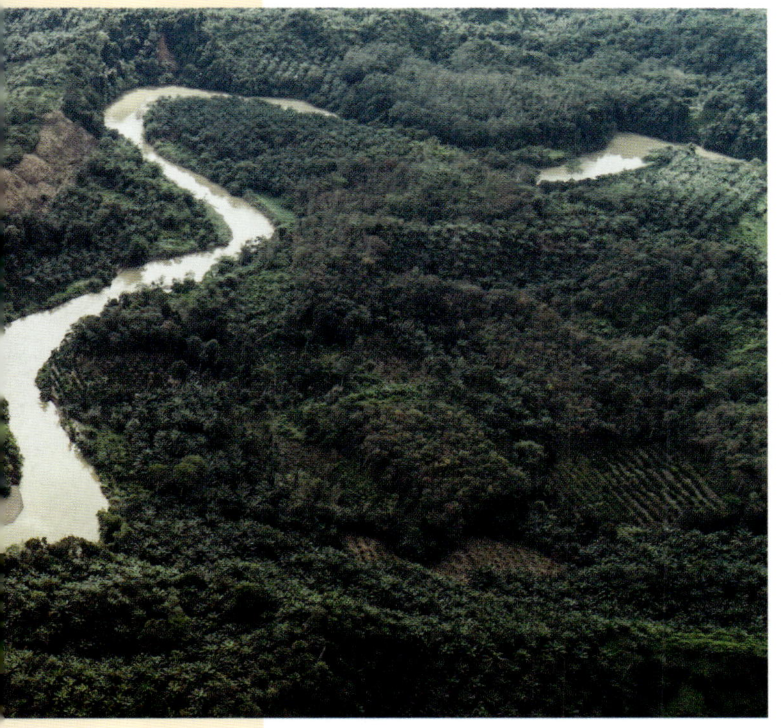

Street art is now offered as a subject in some universities as a theoretical course, but is rarely seen in fine arts courses. Why is that? Does street art belong in art schools? Does it belong in museums?
AL: I'm not sure why practical/technical street art 'classes' are not taught in school. I do believe in the virtue of education and shared knowledge, but then again I definitely don't think street art is simply about learning how to make art on a larger scale. Street art requires a genuine interest in producing site-specific works which will engage with their environment, the frame and their potential viewers. Part of what makes street artists so different from one another is their personal journey – outside of any common core curriculum or institution – towards choosing this field as their main mode of expression. Why they decided to take their work to 'the streets' and what they learned from the technical limitations and challenges they had to face along the way directly informs their style. Their expertise and skills were built from unique experiences, encounters, interests and discoveries gathered on that seminal path. I'm not sure how well this would truly translate as a curriculum or how one would recreate this journey in school.
As for street art in museums, I understand the willingness and importance of proceeding to a conservation of this movement's history,

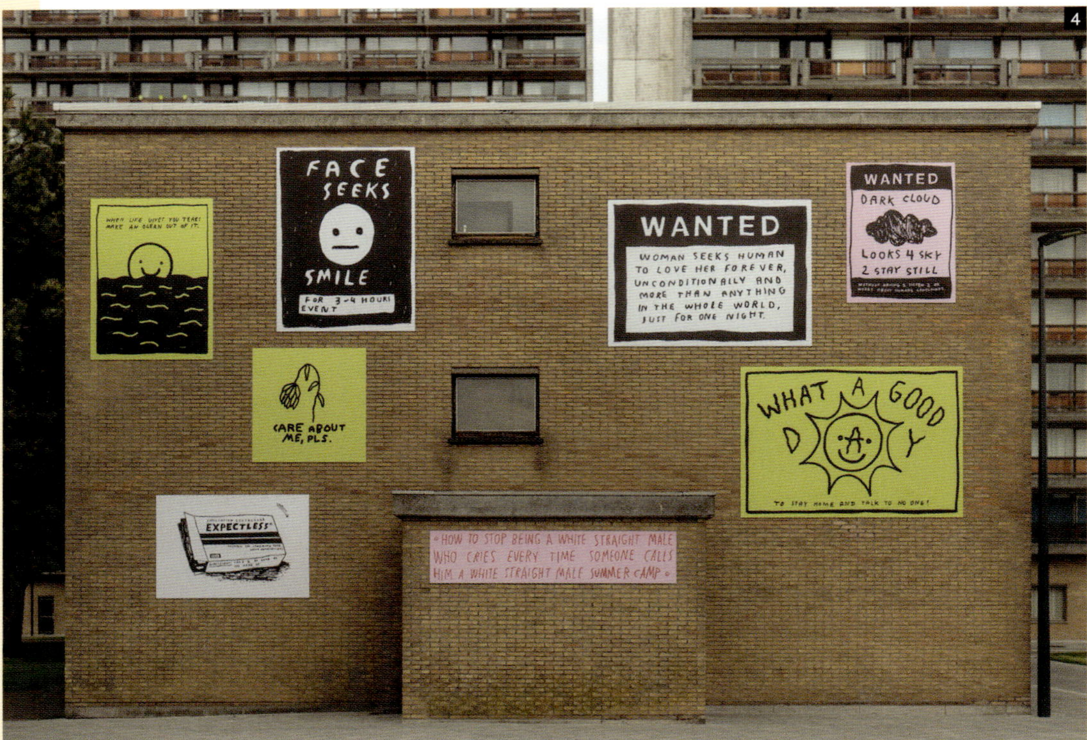

but I have yet to visit an institution that approached it in a way that truly made sense to me. Maybe it's because most of these dedicated spaces negate the ephemeral and contextual aspect inherent to street art and try to simply 'record' artists on a smaller scale, through removable canvases which often don't recount well the beauty of their public works.

IK: Street art must be taught in a course in fine art schools, not least because it is part of art history. The job of a street artist and public art curator is very relevant nowadays. Like any innovation that becomes widely accepted, street art needs comprehensive education. We are responsible for what we produce in the streets, how we educate the public and enhance the community. It's important to be familiar with the history of street art, but that hardly helps you to organise a new contemporary project. It takes time to conduct research, read publications and include them in a fine arts course.

As creative placemaking becomes an increasingly popular tool for governments and developers, has art in public space lost its rebellious edge?

AL: The lines between genuine artist-led creation and marketing stunt are definitely blurrier than ever, so it's difficult for the public to always understand the essence of what they are dealing with.

That being said, I do think artists, and especially artists who chose to work in the public space for its social impact, tend to know exactly how to flip the script and subvert in new and different ways, even sometimes within a corporate frame.

Is street art as a whole less 'outrageous' than tag and graffiti were at their prime in the '70s? Absolutely.

4 /
Wasted Rita
Ostend, Belgium, 2019
PHOTO BY THE ARTIST

It doesn't mean plenty of artists aren't using street art and the new territories it now occupies in other subversive and rebellious ways with the same energy that kids had back in the day.

DG: In many cities today, the space once occupied by artists has been re-packed to vaguely resemble the liberated idealism it previously exuded. The commodification of muralism has opened new avenues for developers, business and municipalities. Visual signifiers, such as large spray-painted murals, bars with exposed lighting, and endless streams of coffee shops, convey the allure of chic, urban living, allowing capitalist forces to quietly increase living expenses beyond the reach of the lower-income residents that, more often than not, happen to live at the epicentre of this change.

The incentive of paying rent on time is an alluring concept for artists trying to sustain a living within the confines of the developing city. Although, it could be argued that this comfortable slide into regular paid work comes at the expense of the kind of rebellious, free-spirited artwork artists on the breadline are known for.

Culture isn't something preserved in the back pockets of elders; it's organic, it grows, continuously finding form. For every commissioned mural, there's an artist with a fire extinguisher ready to scrawl their name on the side of a building.

Culture isn't something prereserved in the back pockets of elders; it's organic, it grows, continuously finding form.

Has the street art world become more competitive? Do you think it is easier for artists that work in the street to survive financially now than it was ten years ago?

DG: Today the street art world is comprised of 10-year-old kids learning stencils in their back garden, 90-year-old grandpas covering their towns in art, rock-star muralists paid to travel the world, graphic design students, former bankers and just about everyone in between. Defining the competitive aspect of street art is hard because with no unified goal connecting all the players. How would a winner be decided? The battle for wall space remains as competitive as ever; city walls are premium real estate. It's not uncommon to see your favourite work replaced, and it's even less uncommon now to see it replaced with 'hand-painted advertising'.

Being noticed doesn't require a physical audience like it once did; the real arena for attention exists on social media. Reposts and shares could result in your next job, go viral and who knows how many doors you might find open.

IK: 10 years ago, I believe, the purpose of creating murals was less pragmatic than it is now, and a curator's work was based on enthusiasm. Artists painted for free, slept in one room and created something together, with the spirit of freedom and belief in positive change. Today, nobody is shy to ask for good payment, negotiate on conditions, or sue a company that took a picture of an illegal graffiti piece. Everyone believes they're a great muralist, so we experience excess supply: the quantity demanded is less than the quantity supplied. The majority of artists are easily replaceable. In the conditions of perfect competition, artists are trying to apply new techniques and technologies to stand out from the crowd, be recognised and invited. In general, an artist is paid more for their work because of access to different budget sources,

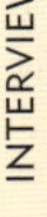

5

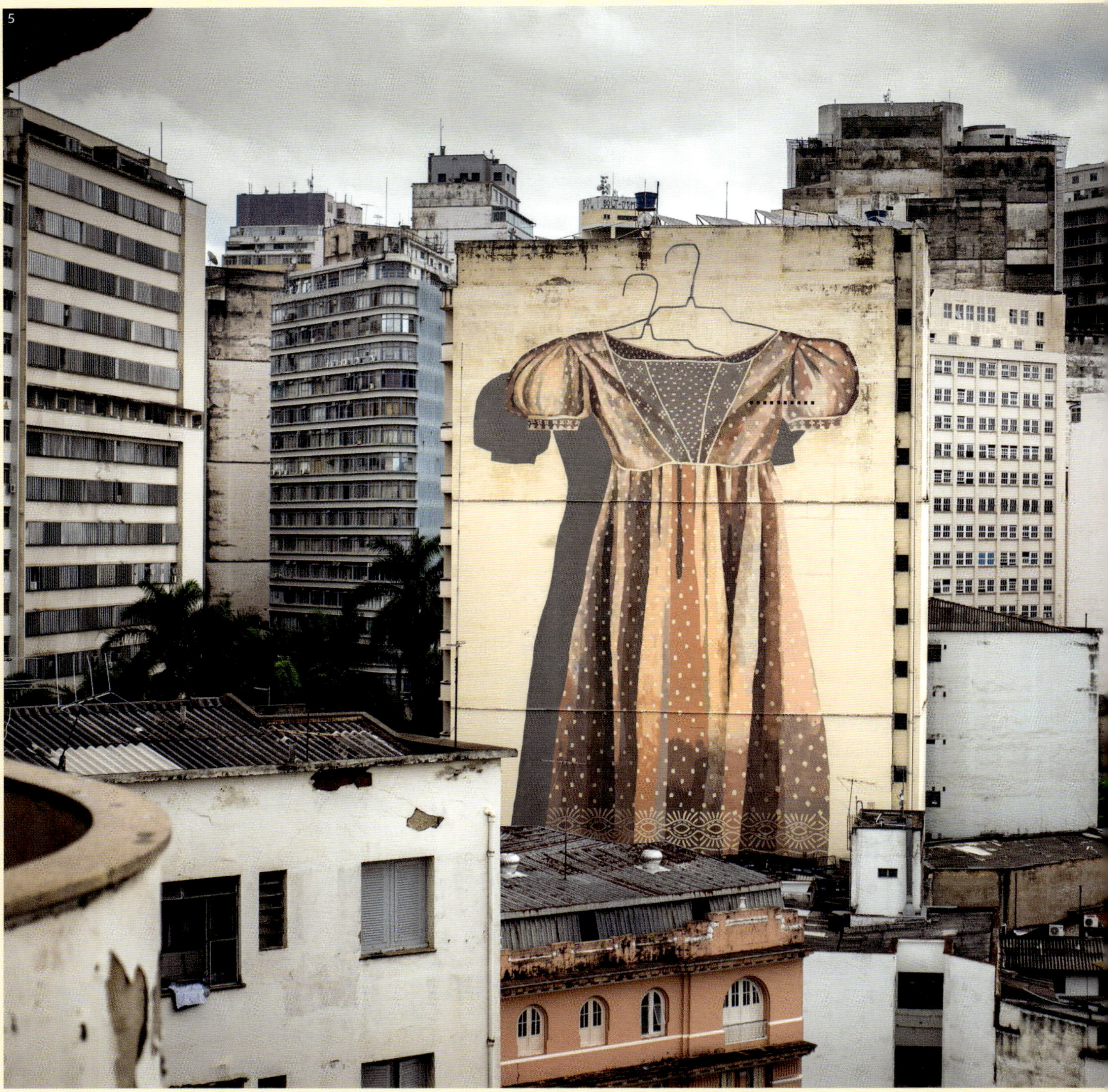

5 /
Hyuro
Belo Horizonte, Brazil, 2018
PHOTO BY THE ARTIST

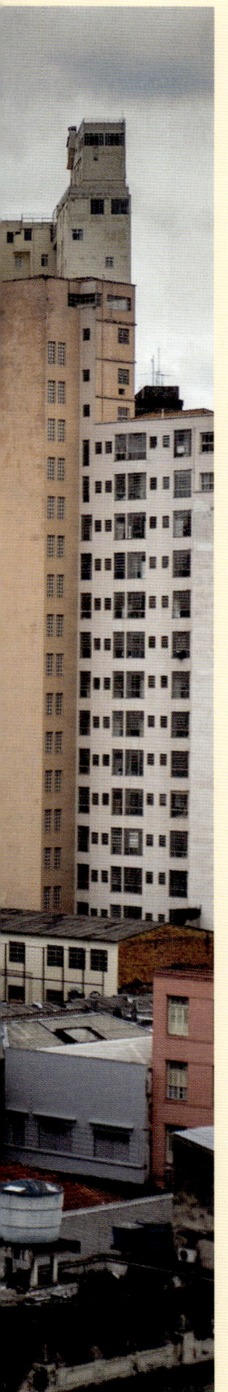

including the government. However, I can't say the same about artistic freedom. If you know any poor artist today, it is either because they are a jerk, or because they're an idealist that creates 'controversial art' – in other words, inflexible to market demand.

The past few years has seen huge political, social and environmental issues all across the globe. What is your opinion of artists expressing political views in public space?

AL: Social commentary has always been an active part of art, and street art is one of the visual art forms with the best ability to reach audiences at random. You can stumble on an artwork in the streets that will shift your aesthetic perception or your understanding of the world. You can be confronted by ideas you would have never even considered nor been exposed to otherwise. Street art, like any art form, holds as many approaches as it holds creators. Not all art has a deeper meaning or message, nor should it. But I do think street art's power comes from its impact and reach. Artists tend to be amongst the first to voice their opinion in times of crisis and use the power of their work as a weapon of change. Blu or Escif, amongst many others, have mastered how to evoke complex social dynamics in simple yet impactful ways on the streets, and I'm definitely there for all of it. I totally agree with Banksy's quote: 'Art should comfort the disturbed and disturb the comfortable.'

DG: There's nothing new about people, artists or not, utilising the public sphere to express political stances or grievances. From Middle Eastern uprisings to sectarian divisions in Ireland, examples of weaponised wall spaces can be found all over the world. Political art at times reflects the views of a community and at others infiltrates communities with unwanted views. I believe artists have a duty to challenge us, to showcase new ideals and to help us visualise our thoughts. The clever ones will ask us questions that we have to answer for ourselves, rather than making the mistake of telling us what to think.

Can street artists survive without social media?

DG: Yes, street artists can survive without social media, but few do. The Italian artist Blu has built a career around street art, but has never succumbed to the siren call of social media, though he sits in a very small pool of artists that follow suit; even the enigmatic Banksy relies on it. Social media is where artists are seen; it's where names are built and jobs are offered. Art isn't known for being the easiest career choice, so there's a lot to be said for using the tools available to help you climb that slippery ladder. That said, in the art world, rules are made to be broken.

AL: While social media has been instrumental in the recent rise of street art and in the sustainability of the number of street artists, I don't think it is essential to their survival. I know street artists who only have private profiles, and others who shut all off their channels but one and who are considering cutting that last tie loose as well. They are fine. Humans have been painting on walls since before Lascaux and street artists existed and lived off their work before social media was ever invented. An artist's practice would definitely be more insular and isolated nowadays without it, and I won't deny that my job finding talents would definitely be harder without social media, but I really don't believe it is the key to success in itself.

There seems to be an increase in female artists producing in public space. Why do you think that is?
AL: Women have been part of street art since its inception. Obviously not at the same ratio as men at all, but I think there's always been a few more women street artists than people seem to have been aware of. While the number of women street artists does seem to have been increasing substantially, which is great, they are probably also simply being given more opportunities and better visibility than they had before. Maybe it's a sign we're doing better as a society. What matters is that I now know little girls who truly believe they can do this when they grow up, because they see Faith47 doing her thing. Representation matters.
IK: The increase is in the number of artists in general and females accordingly. Also, the influence of other female artists and the popularity of feminism. However, if you look at some female artists' social media, it is not even clear what's the subject of their work as most of the content is focused on personal attractiveness. Another illustration of adjustment to public needs. Do all those followers like the art or pictures of women in bikinis?

How do you think street art and artists will evolve over the next decade?
IK: I think artists must become even more creative and start collaborating with engineers, because just a mural is not so impressive any more. An interactive mural with AR extension, lightning installation, projection mapping, app extension, and other 'whoa' effects is already in demand.
AL: There's obviously a big push towards immersive art and bringing a dimensionality to a field that was before mostly composed of murals. I think a lot of artists will explore how to bring their art to life in new ways.
Quite a few artists are talking about reclaiming ownership of their work by breaking away more regularly from the corporate commission/ gallery show/ festival cycle in order to focus on significant projects they want to accomplish for themselves.
DG: The street art scene itself is comprised of many sub-divisions, and each will evolve in their own unique way. I'd like to see the same support large-scale murals receive extended to artists operating on a more human scale. There is no question about the awe-inspiring effect a mural can have on a landscape, but at times they stand like nothing more than phallic impositions upon a surface, testaments to the artist's ego, soldiers of gentrification.
There is an intimacy in human-scale street art. The artist invites the viewer into a game in which the curious are rewarded in, a treasure hunt between strangers. I would like to see more invested into nurturing curiosity and activating spaces that encourage exploration. Bring communities to life with playful exchange rather than driving them apart for development.

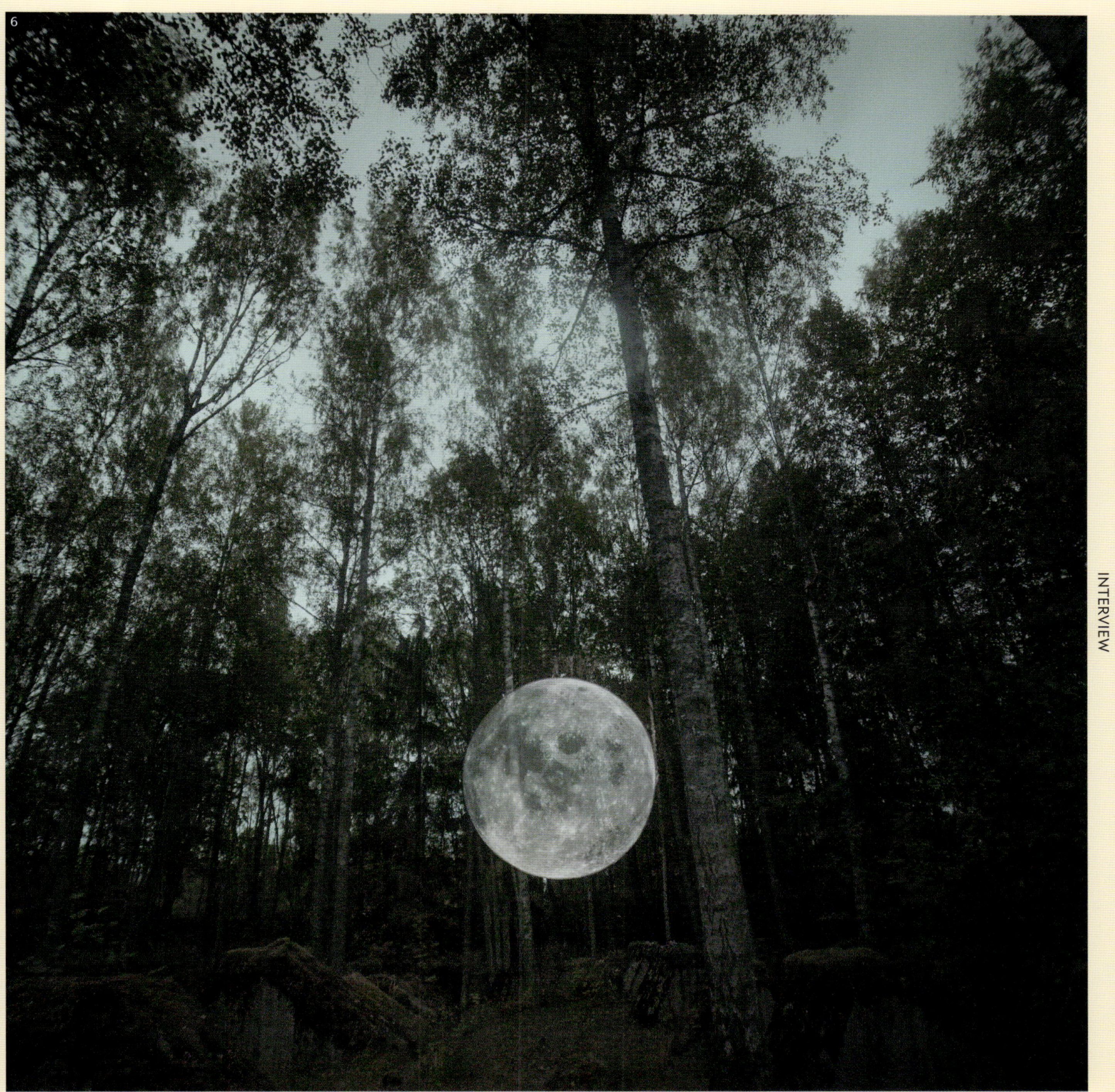

» /
Leon Keer
Valletta, Malta, 2015
PHOTO BY THE ARTIST

JR
Paris, France, 2019
PHOTO BY AGENCE VU

Jaz
Eugene, Oregon, USA, 2017
PHOTO BY THE ARTIST

6 /
Faith47
Värmland, Sweden, 2017
PHOTO BY THE ARTIST

Alex Senna
Schinveld, The Netherlands, 2017
PHOTO BY THE ARTIST

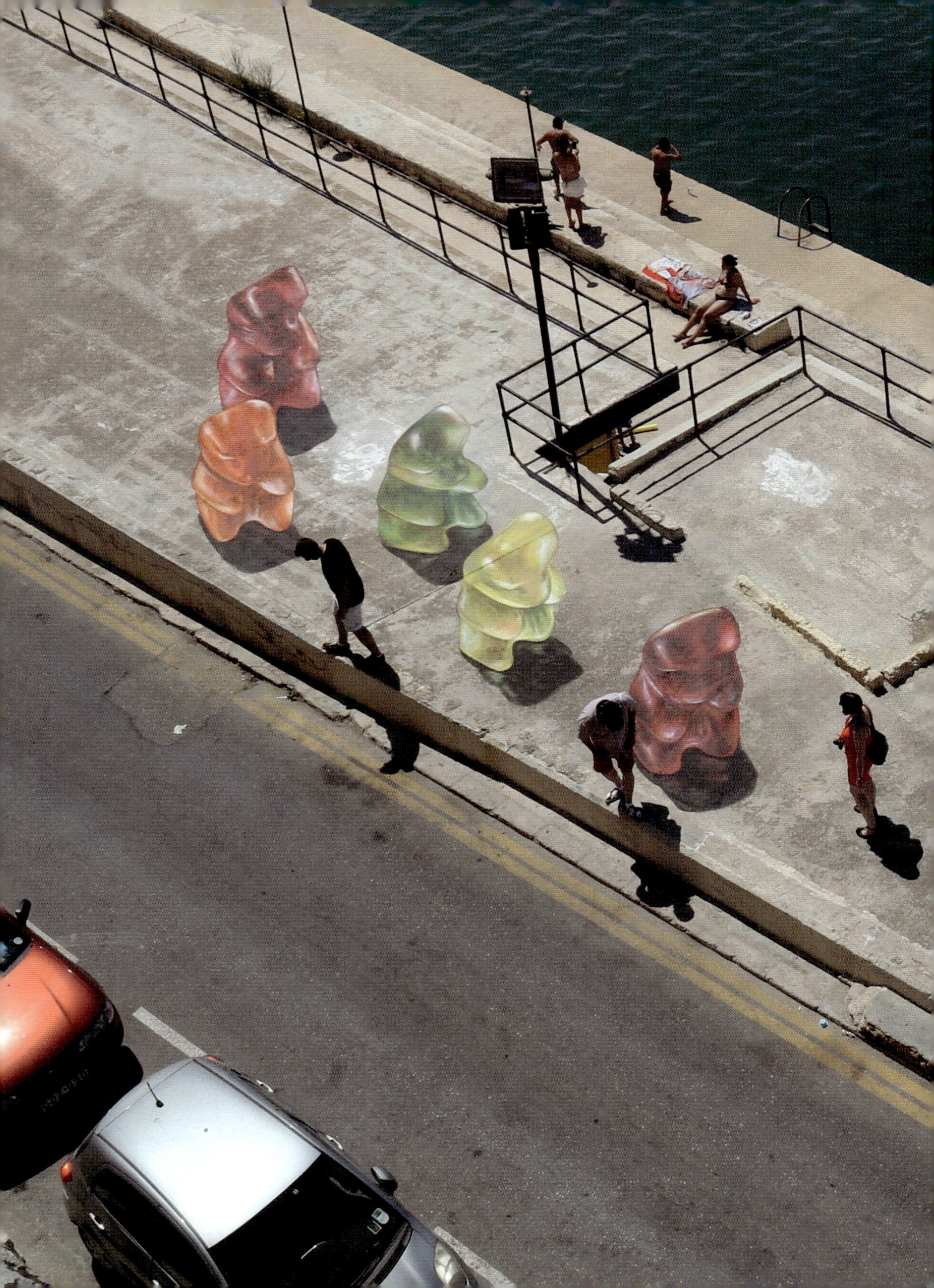

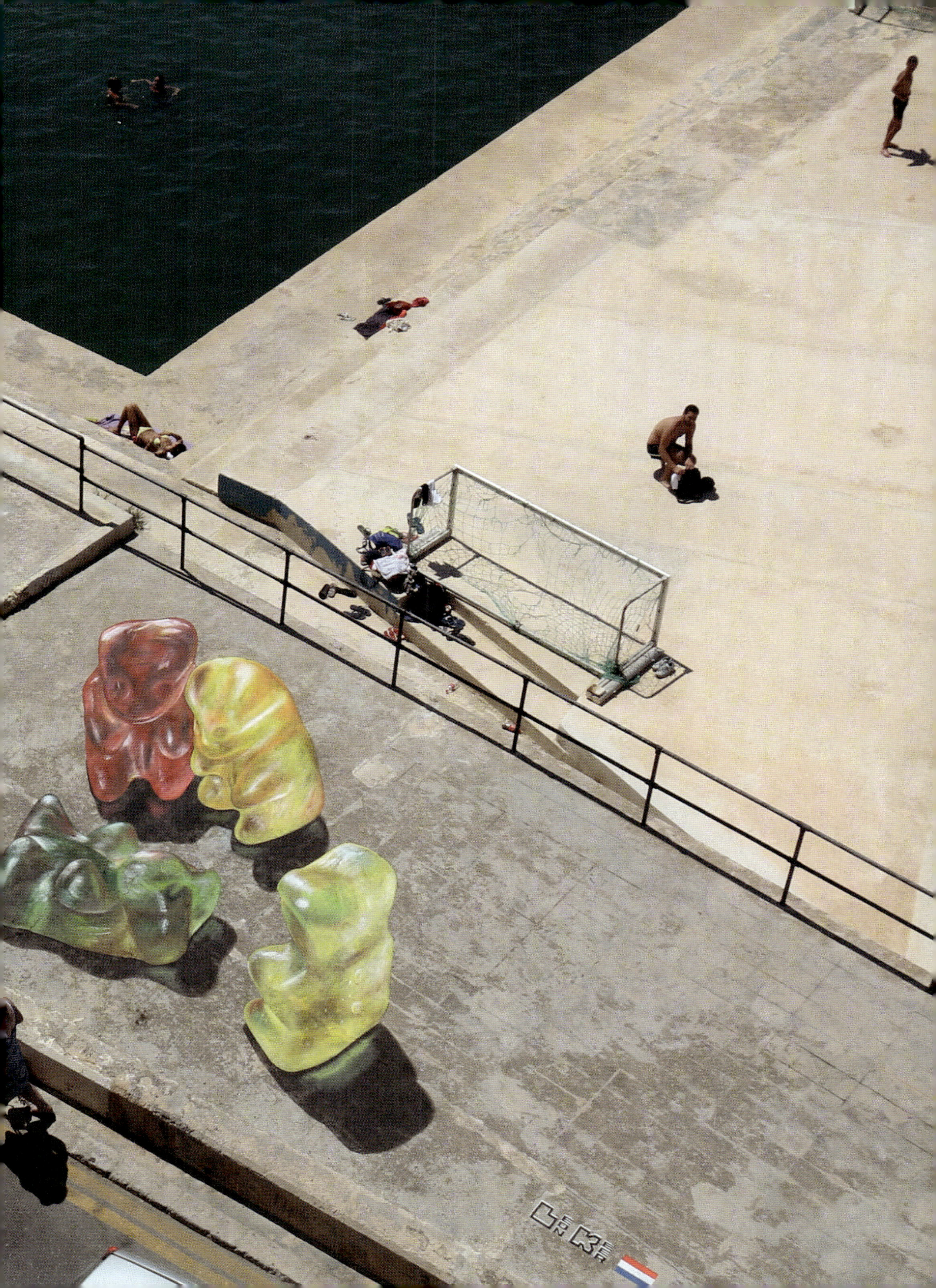
LEON KEER

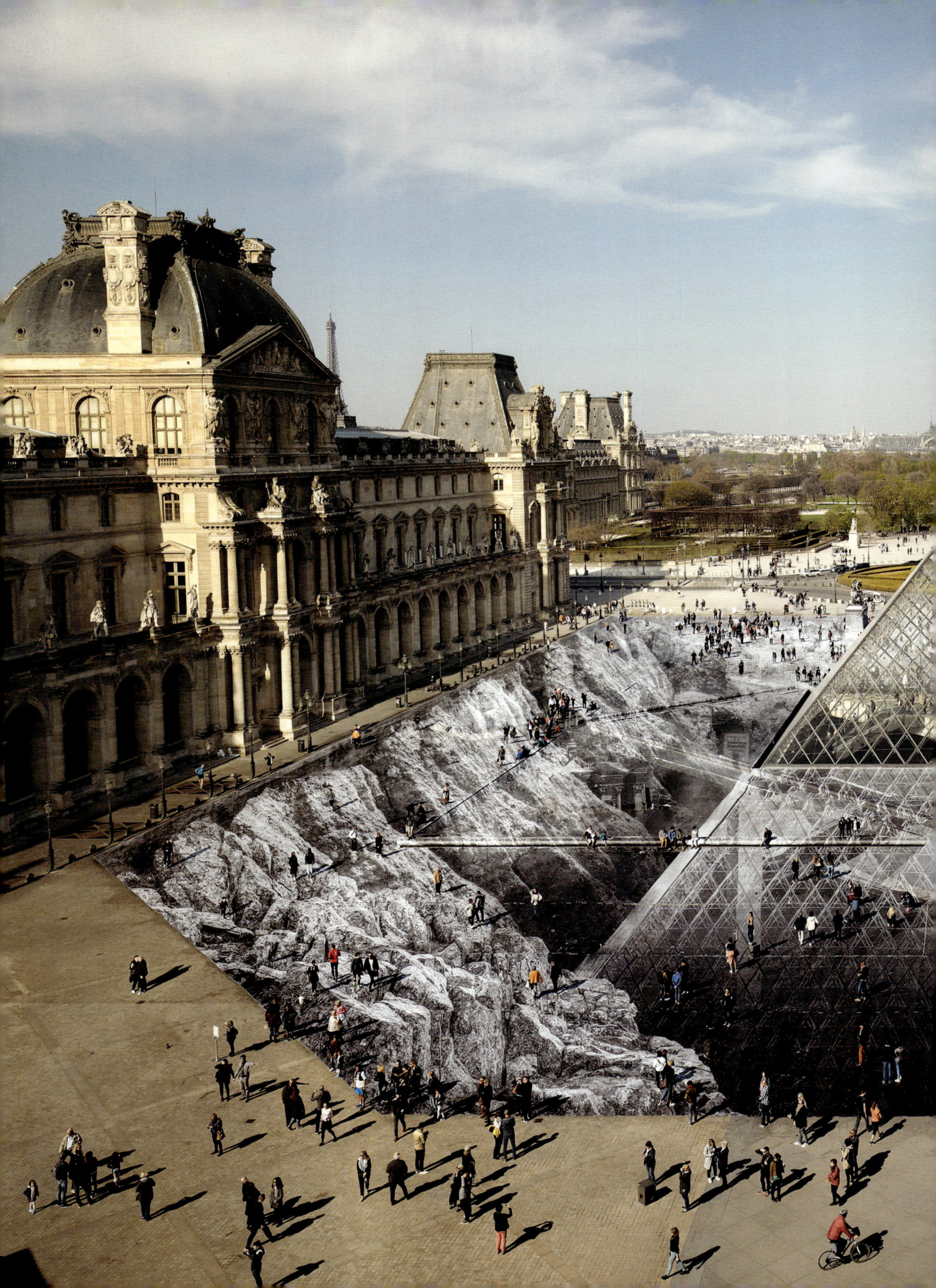

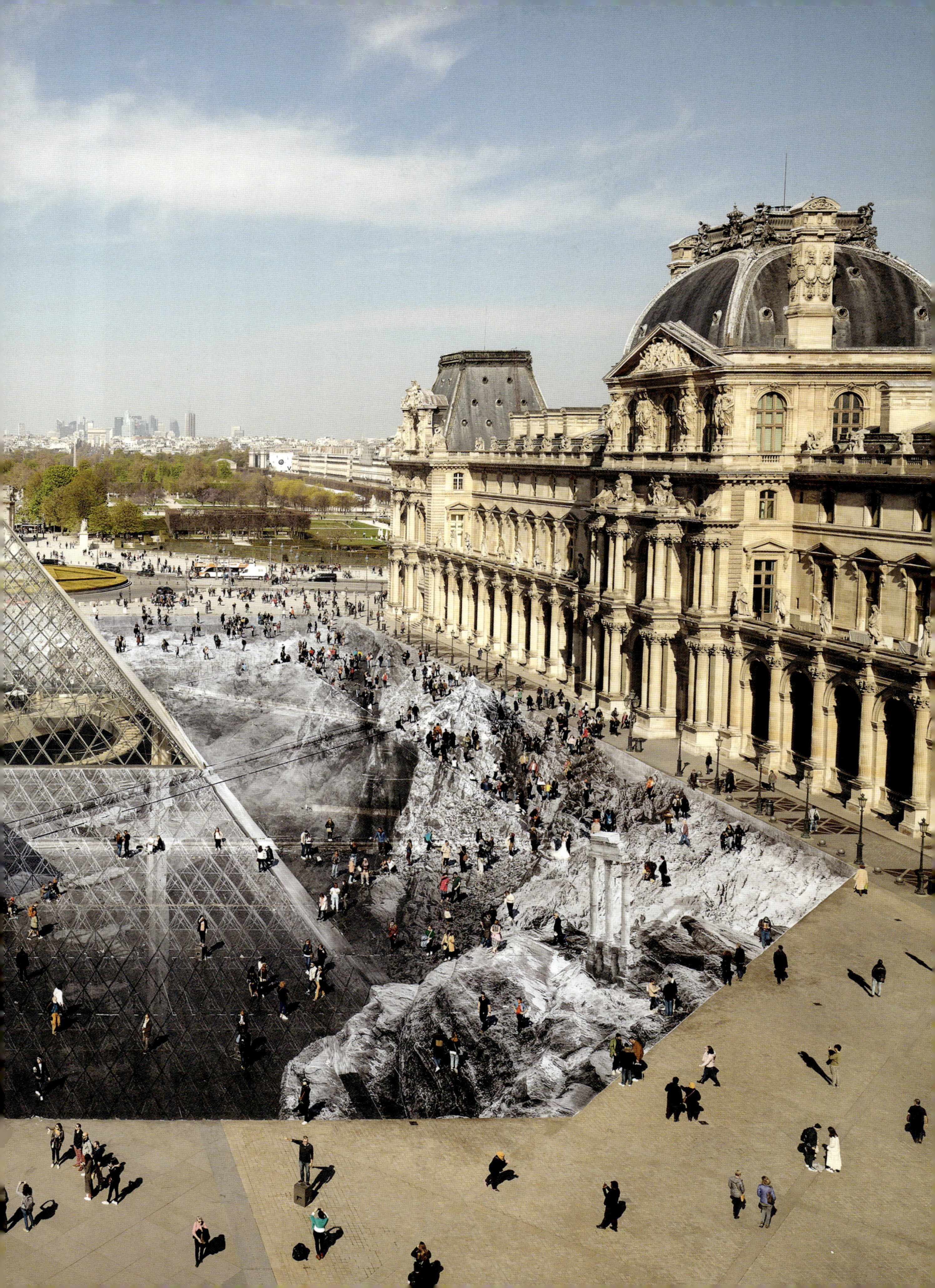

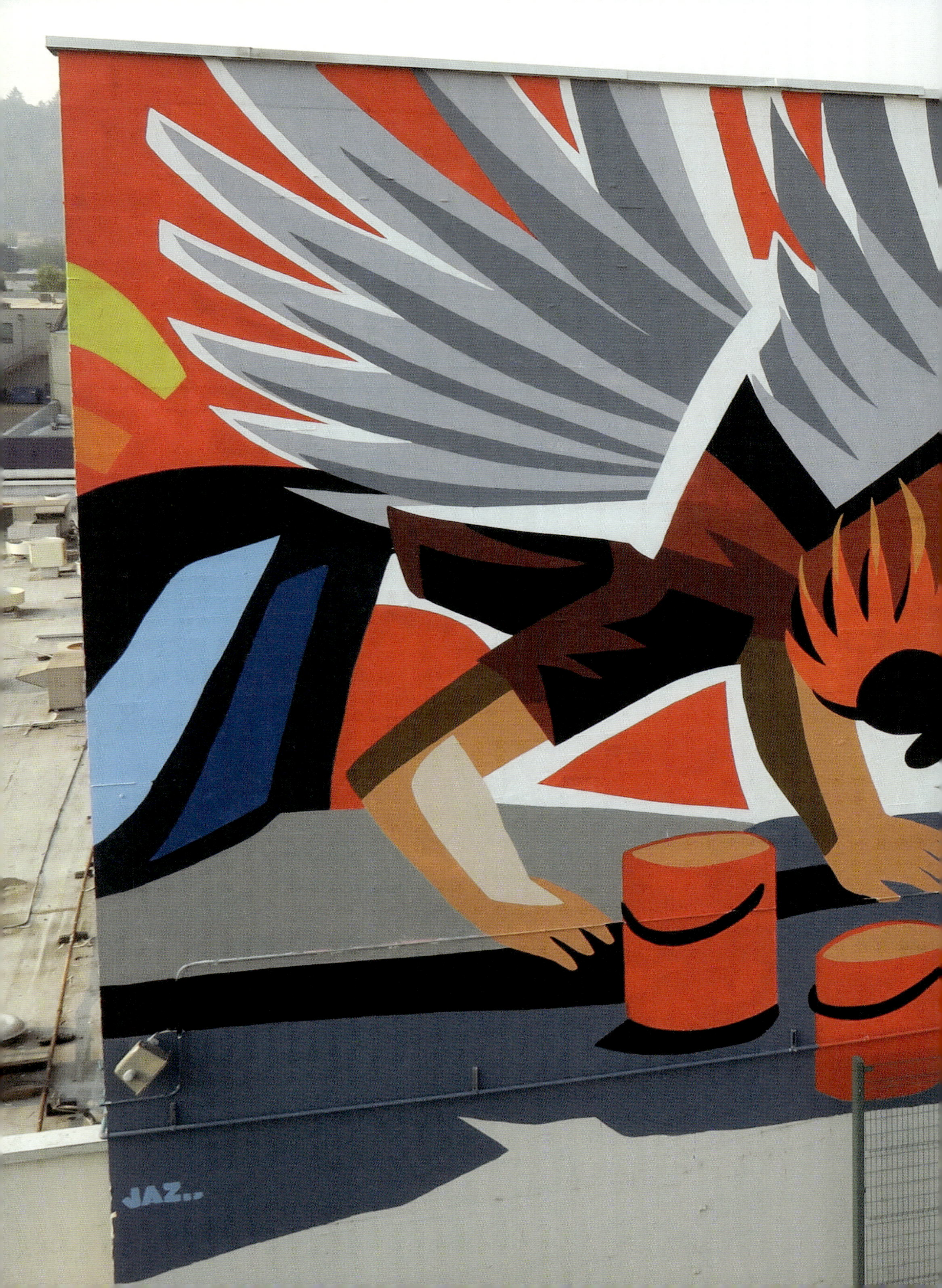
JAZ

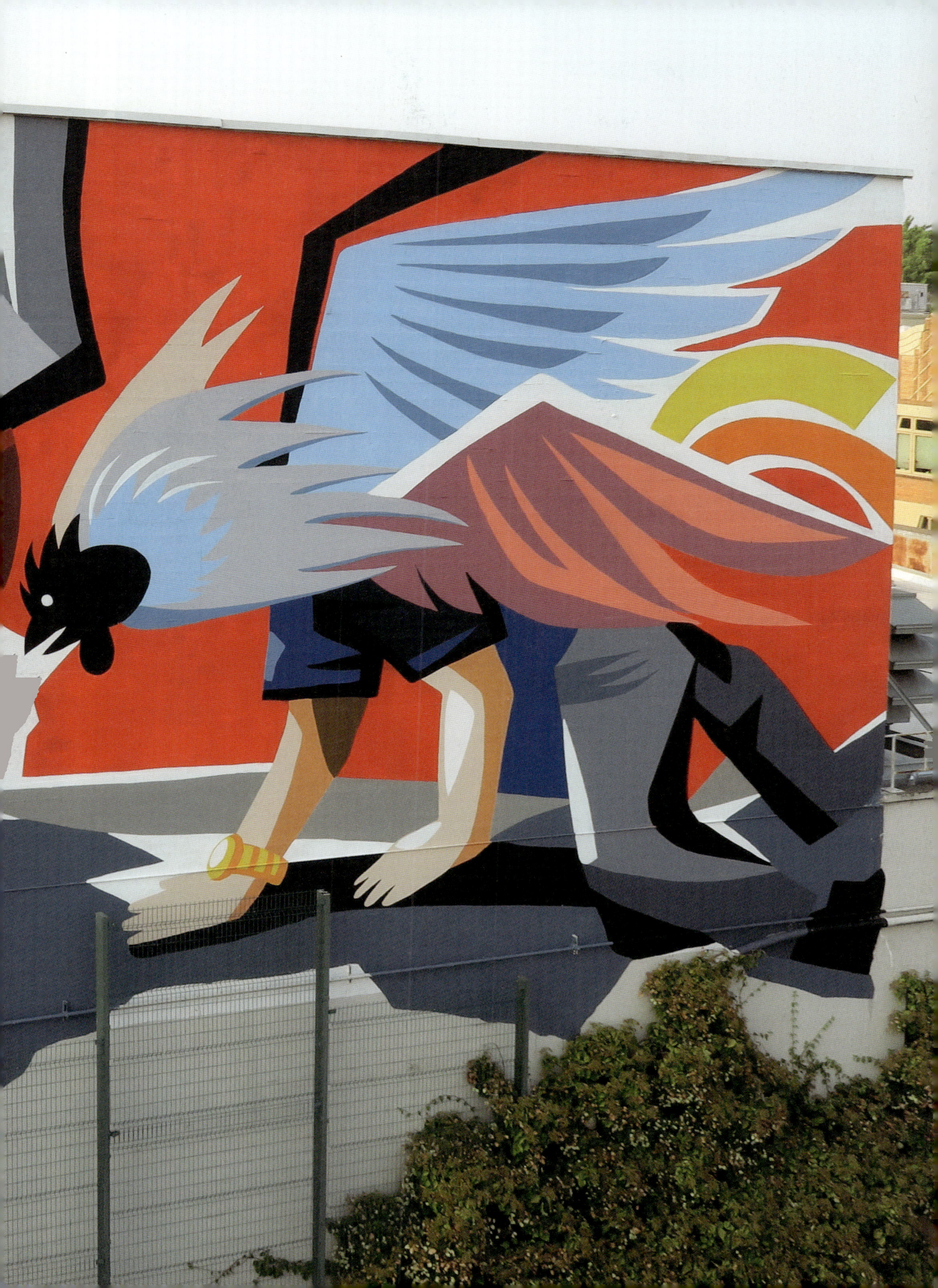

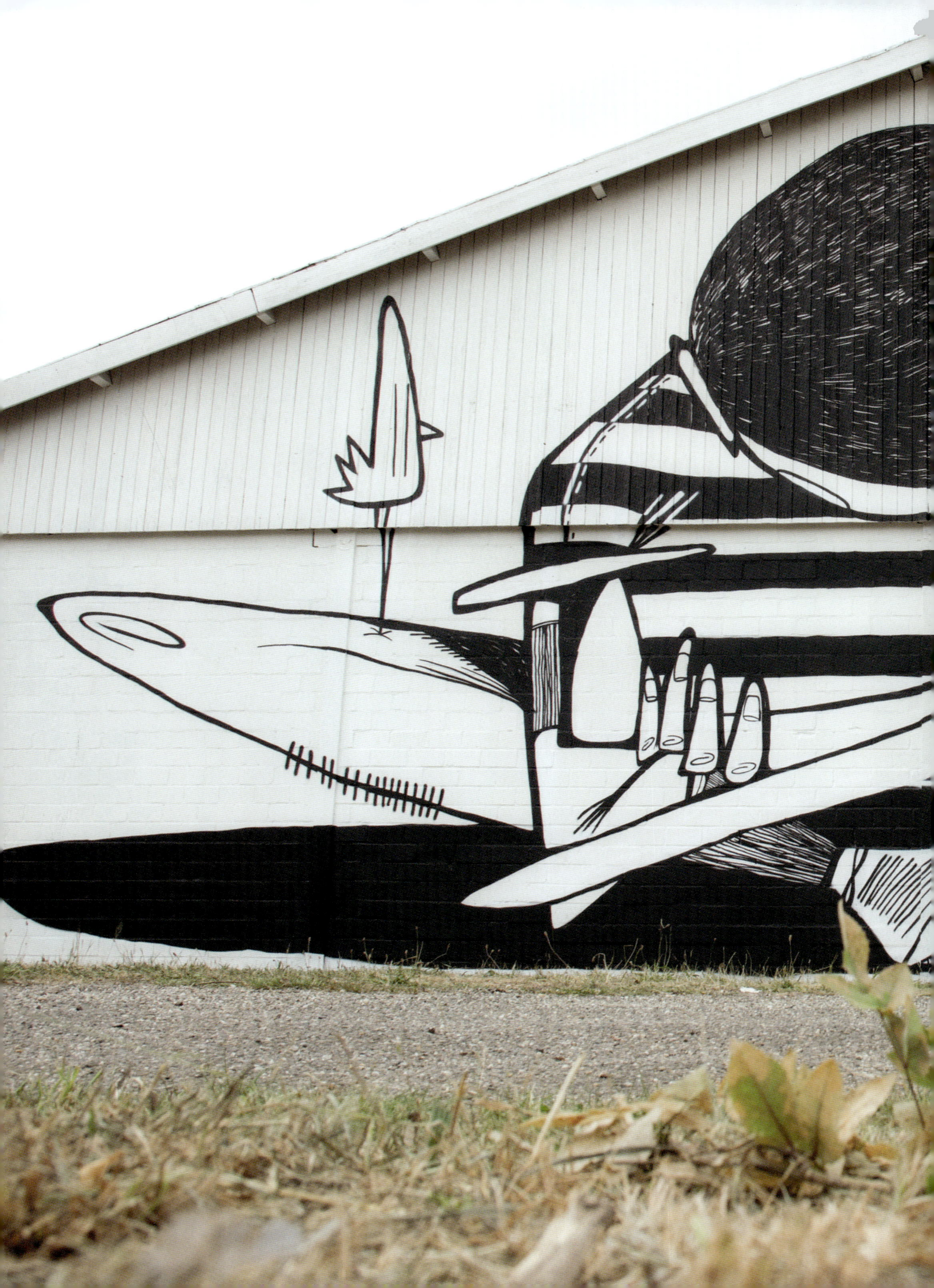

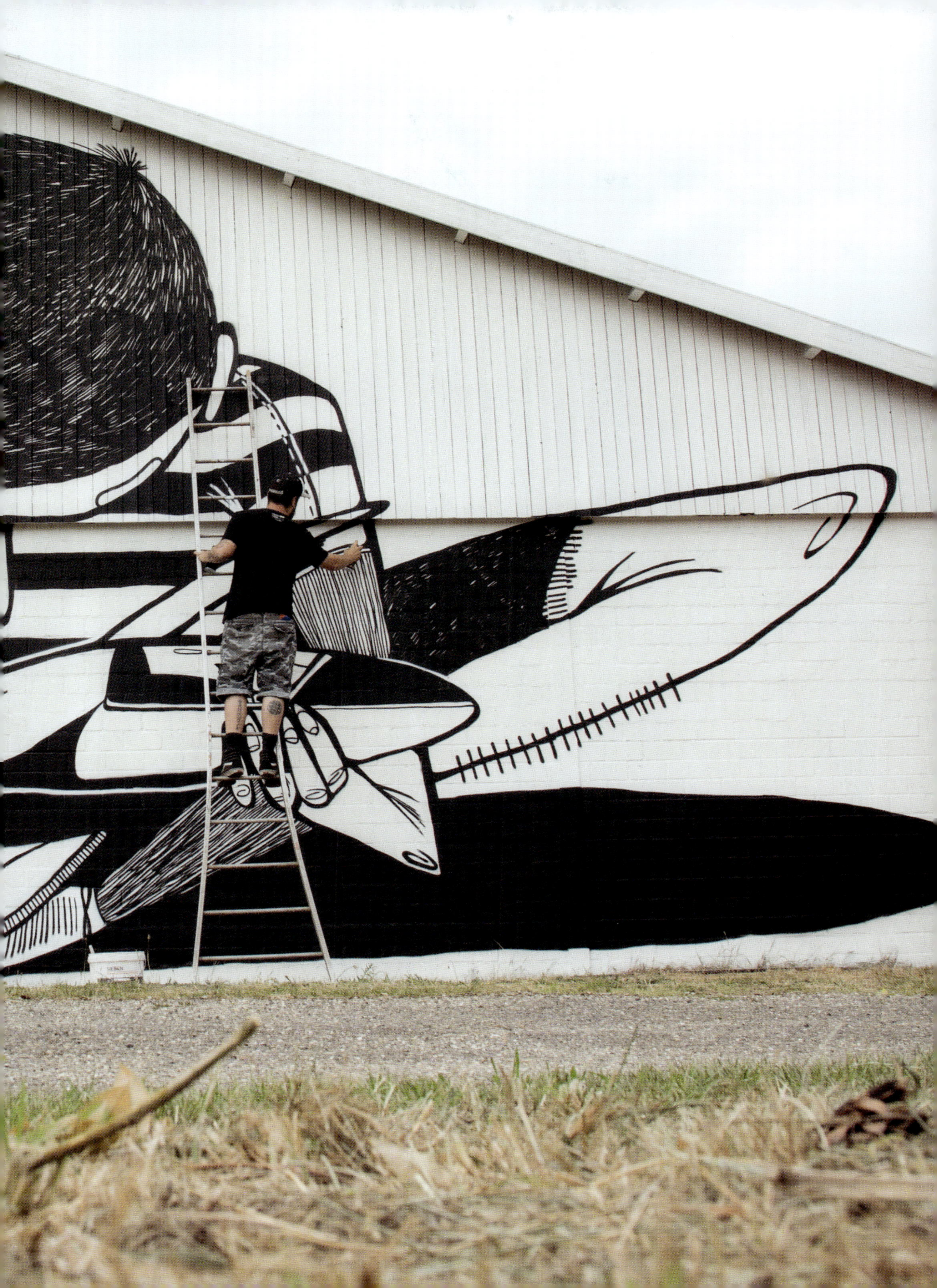

1/

ELIAN
ELLEN RUTT
FELIPE PANTONE
KRISTIN FARR
MADC
MOMO
MR. JUNE
NELIO
OKUDA
ROBERTO CIREDZ

AB-STRACT

ABSTRACT ART IN THE PUBLIC realm has proved to be incredibly dynamic and controversial over the past few years. A huge surge in public works leaning towards a non-figurative form has seen the selection for this chapter surge from three to ten since the previous edition. Simultaneous industry developments can be pinpointed to explain this rising interest. Firstly, a more fluid link to the worlds of contemporary art and fine art has been evolving through public works being presented in a more academic form. Second, a move towards more minimalist works from star post-graffiti art producers has seen street cred move towards abstraction. Lastly, and raising more challenging issues in the street art discussion, public works are being used for commercial branding, with many artists in this chapter producing for highly commercial design contracts.

Over the past few years, a growing number of artists have been gravitating to producing abstract works, showing a tendency to be active in the worlds of both contemporary art and street art, with most of them holding higher education degrees in fine art or design. It seems that street art is slowly being accepted (or perhaps absorbed?) into more academic environments, with many artists integrating an outdoor practice into a larger body of work. It is unexceptional today to see artists 'step out of the studio', and common to see street artists become teachers in design courses or art schools. Although other styles of public art producers are also commonly 'academically certified', it seems more common for abstract artists to have solid CVs of gallery shows and institutional recognition.

Today, we witness artists who use public space with non-representational works having greater ease in being active in the communities of both contemporary art and street art. Profiles like those of Nelio and Momo give seemingly equal importance to indoor and outdoor work. Although these bridges seem to be crossed more easily, there still remains a clear struggle between what is still seen as 'legitimate' or 'underground', both groups being responsible for and victim to a certain degree of snobbism. On the flip side, however, we see more established painters coming from the other end of the spectrum, artists like MadC representing a post-graffiti trajectory, their propositions coming from a long journey through tagging, graffiti lettering, exploration of colour and finally a minimalist approach. These old-schoolers are seen to strengthen the close community ties that street art has been typically rooted in, their work representing the possibilities of artist development, always with an origin of urban counterculture.

The relationship between public art and marketing has been brewing for many years. Previously, the vulgarisation of this relationship saw brands try to buy 'street cool', placing their products alongside famous artists' works in the hope that their audience would be naive enough to believe in their counterculture philosophy. Artists today seem to have taken stronger control, using their works to create their own design brands, collaborating with like-minded creators in fashion, object design and many other forms of commercial ventures. The positive repercussions include increased financial independence for artists, allowing them to control the use of their work and widening their potential audience. Some negatives can be seen as well, for example in productions made for purely commercial gain or to support marketing tactics.

It is these fine moments of balance and struggle that have seen abstract artists develop bigger, more engaging, more controversial pieces. Abstract street art is infiltrating the creative sector from all sides and corners of the globe.

ELIAN

/ Buenos Aires

Famous for his bright geometric murals, Argentinian artist Elian was featured in the last edition of *Street Art Today* as one of the leaders in abstract street art. His large-scale works have continued to dominate the international urban art world as he moves forward, developing his craft through sensitive observations of architectural and social context.

His interventions are the fruit of studied dialogue with the architectural lines. Though the bright colours are often breath-taking, he takes particular care in creating a harmonious environment for the passers-by. 'I find it interesting that a person in his usual routine becomes a spectator / user of a work of art. I think it is an unexpected encounter with creativity.'

1 2

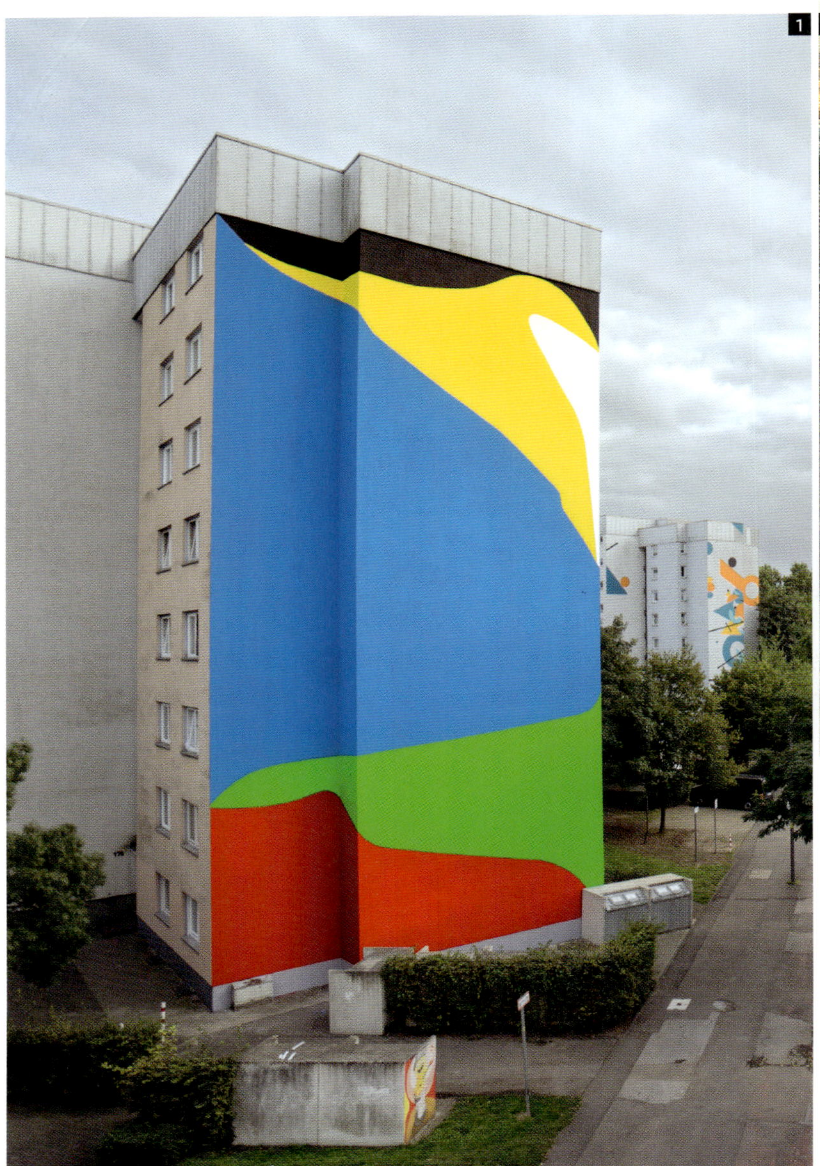

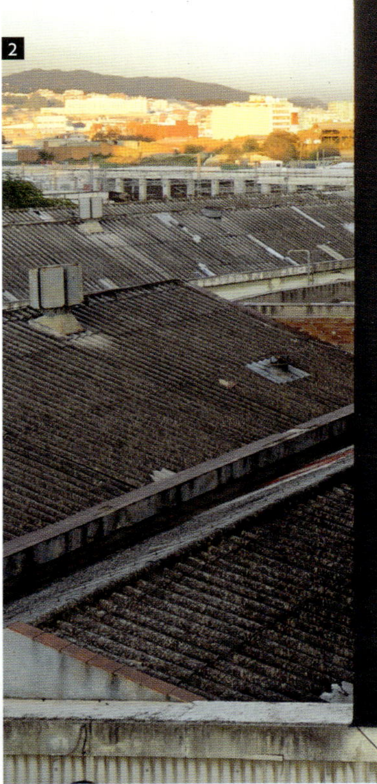

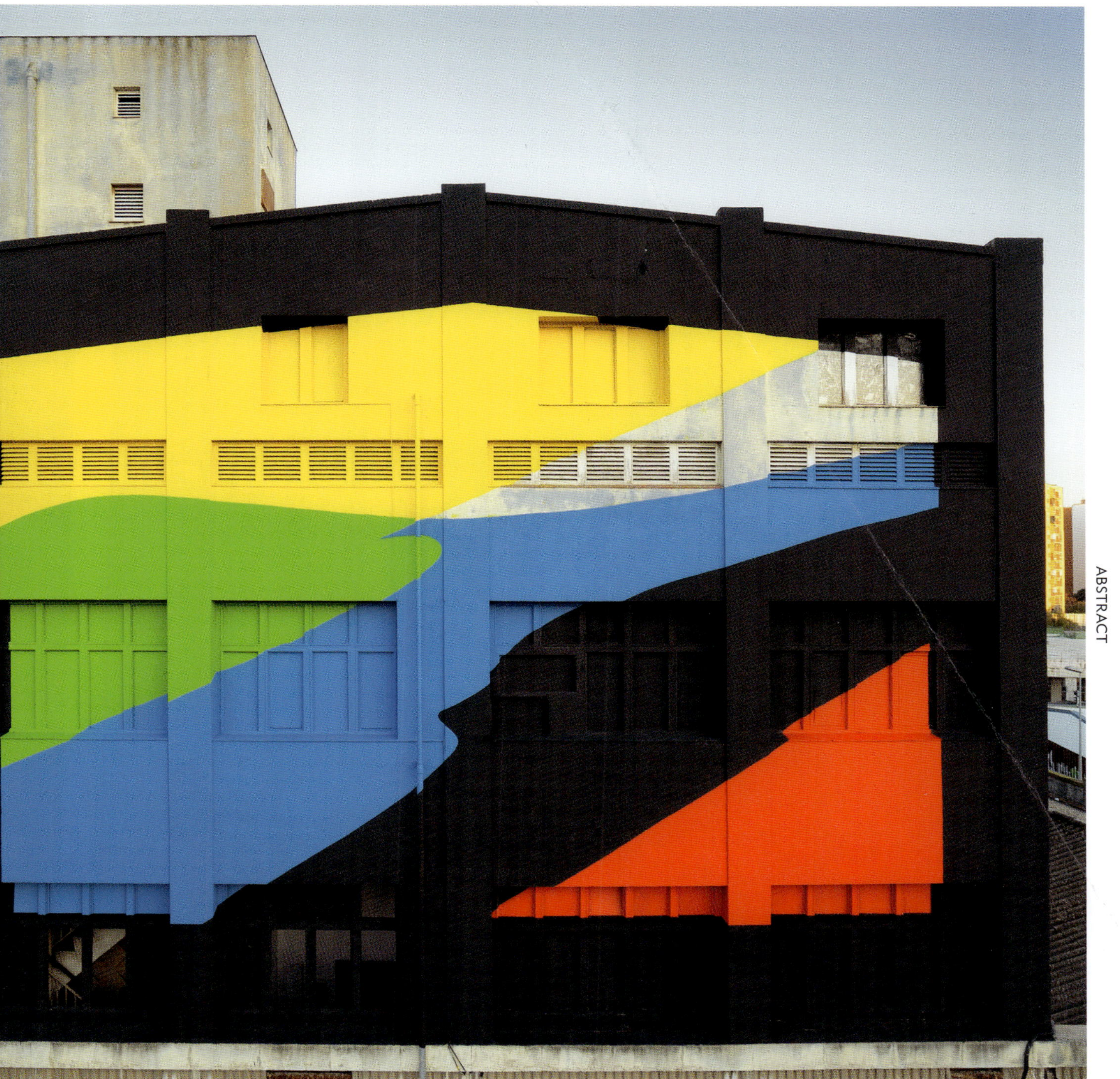

1 /
Cologne, Germany, 2017
PHOTO BY THE ARTIST

2 /
Barcelona, Spain, 2018
PHOTO BY THE ARTIST

I find it interesting that a person in his usual routine becomes a spectator / user of a work of art.

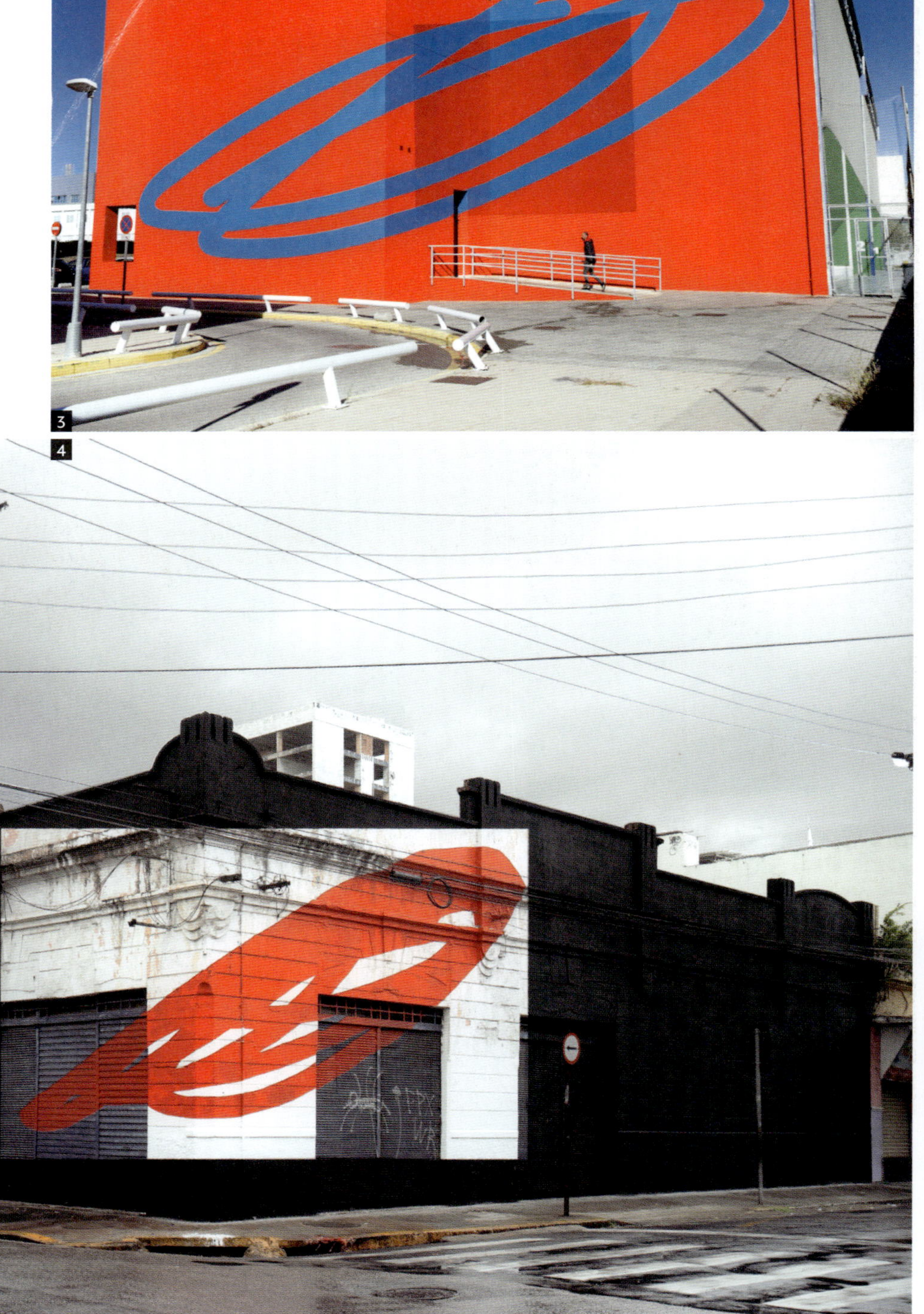

3

4

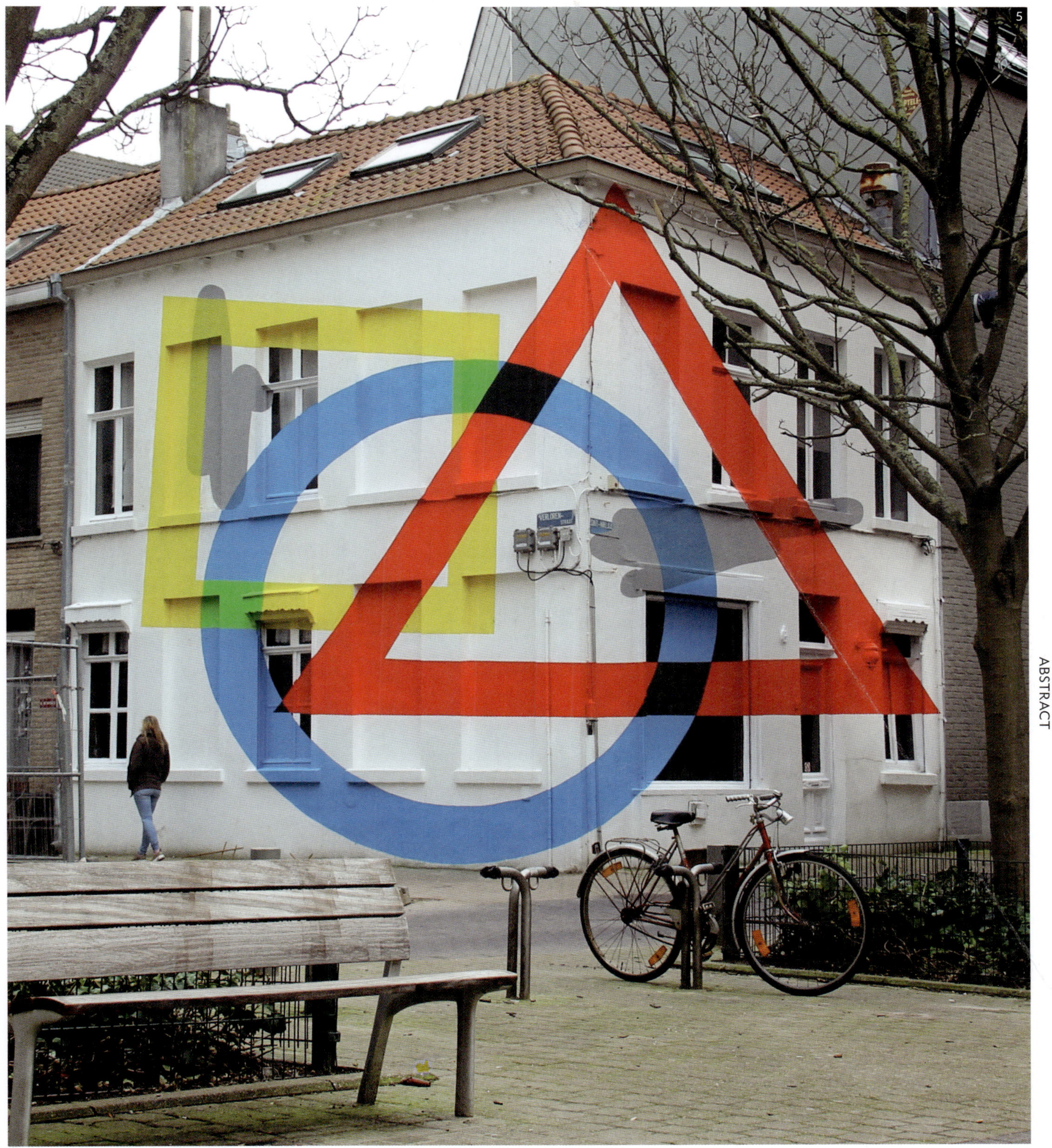

5

3 /
Valencia, Spain, 2018
PHOTO BY THE ARTIST

4 /
Fortaleza, Brazil, 2018
PHOTO BY THE ARTIST

5 /
Ostend, Belgium, 2016
PHOTO BY THE ARTIST

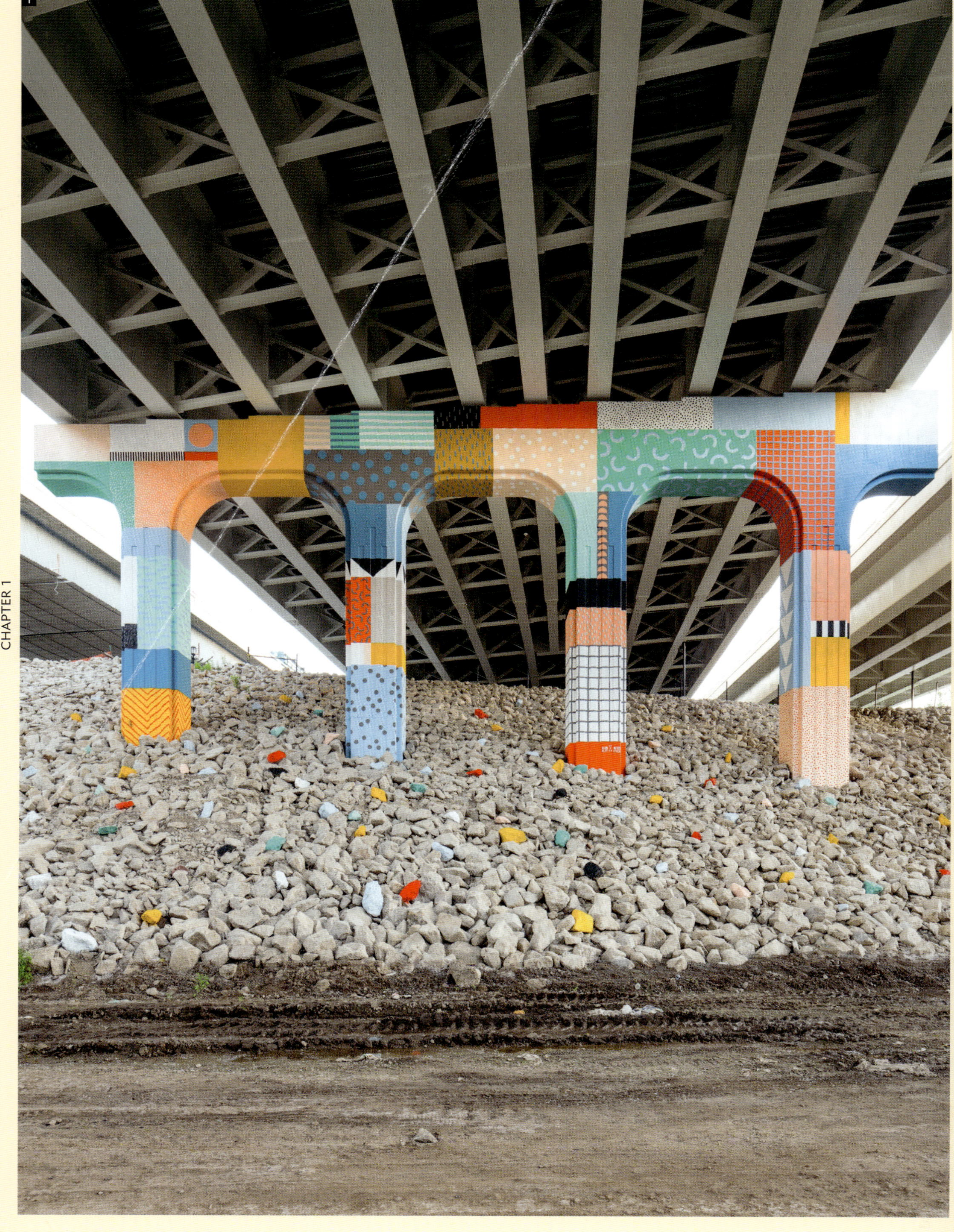

1 /
Cleveland, Ohio, USA, 2016
PHOTO BY THE ARTIST

ELLEN RUTT

/ Detroit

Painting murals dramatically changed the way I think about art in spaces.

Your work spans object design, video, fashion, collage, painting, sculpture, murals and more. Is there a medium that you feel most drawn to? What type of project do you enjoy the most?
My favourite projects are always outdoors, work that is part of a living environment. I am less connected with a specific medium, and more interested in the variety of ways that materials can be used to create experiences. I love it that I get to make work in studios, galleries, houses, office cubicles, public bathrooms, highway underpasses, city street corners, dirty alleyways and rural hilltops, and deep in lush, tropical forests. Working across various media, I use abstract shapes as a metaphor for different facets of our identity, and explore the way those facets impact on our movement through physical, social, and cultural spaces.

Throughout your career, you seem to be hopping over the lines of art and design. Do you think these worlds are colliding more and more? Or do you have to choose between either the 'artist' or the 'designer' hat for each project?
If art is more about the process of exploring an idea, and design aims to find visual solutions for a particular prompt, the 'artist' and 'designer' parts of my brain are in an endless battle between chaos and order! Of course, the territory between those two practices is infinite and offers a range of work that exists in both worlds, depending on the context in which it is viewed. My desire to plan ahead and my proclivity for improvisation are paradoxes that continue to frustrate and excite me.

You are often referred to as a Detroit artist. What does that mean? How has the city influenced your work?

ELLEN RUTT

I assume I am called a Detroit artist because I live and work in Detroit – unless there's some secret other reason that I don't know about. So many artists live in New York or LA, maybe naming my location becomes an easy differentiating descriptor. I am happy to identify as a Detroit artist for now, knowing that it could change in the future.

In 2012, when I first moved here, there weren't many galleries but there was abundant wall space, so I started painting murals, which allowed me to work at a fairly large scale pretty quickly. Painting murals dramatically changed the way I think about art in spaces, how we engage with space, who gets to experience the work and how. Making public art in Detroit has made me hyper-aware of community as a structure (place or identity) in which people feel a deep sense of belonging, and that anyone doing public artwork has a responsibility to ensure that their work doesn't undermine existing structures of belonging. This is particularly imperative in an era of commercially funded murals, where public art oftentimes becomes a tool of cultural or physical gentrification.

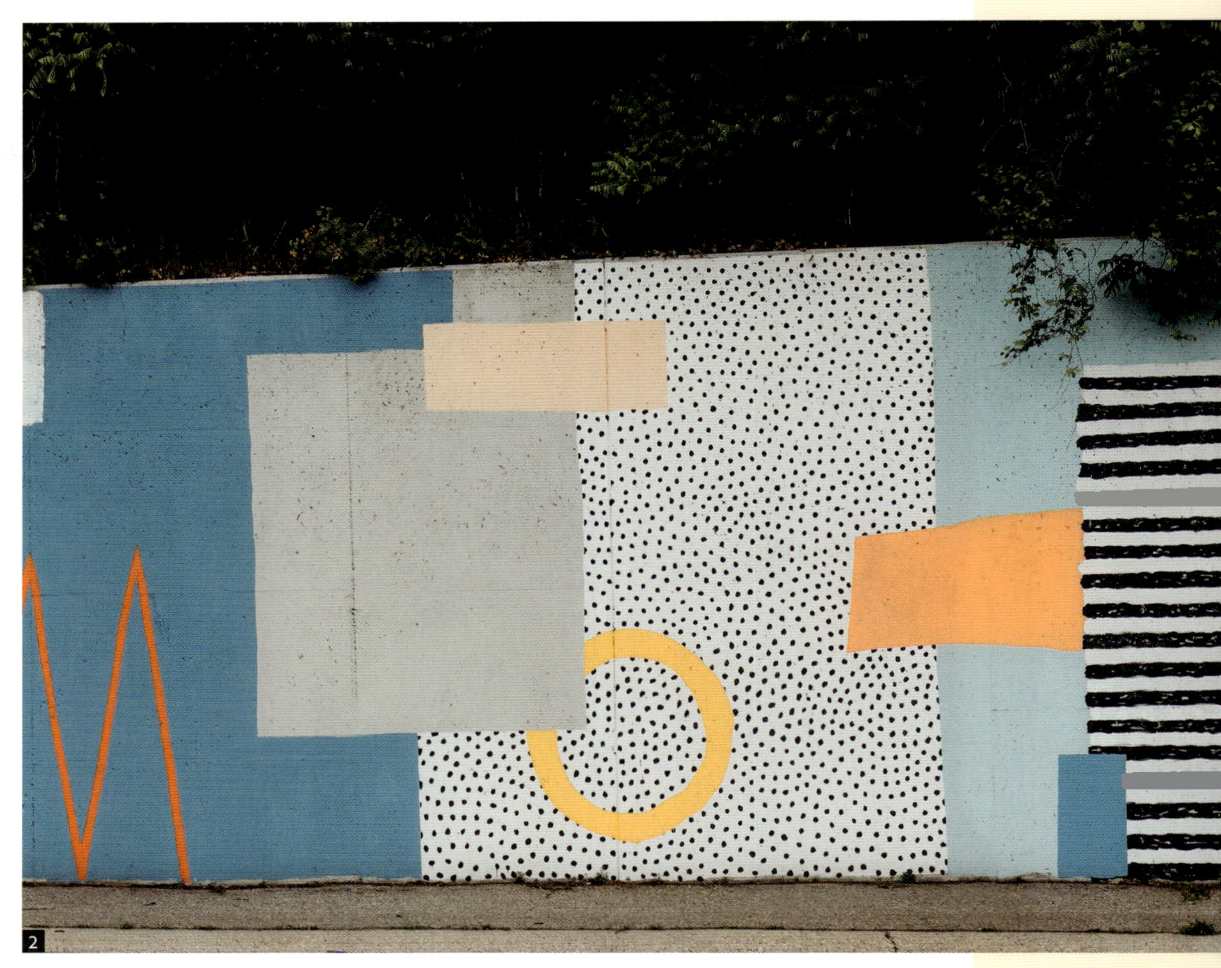
2

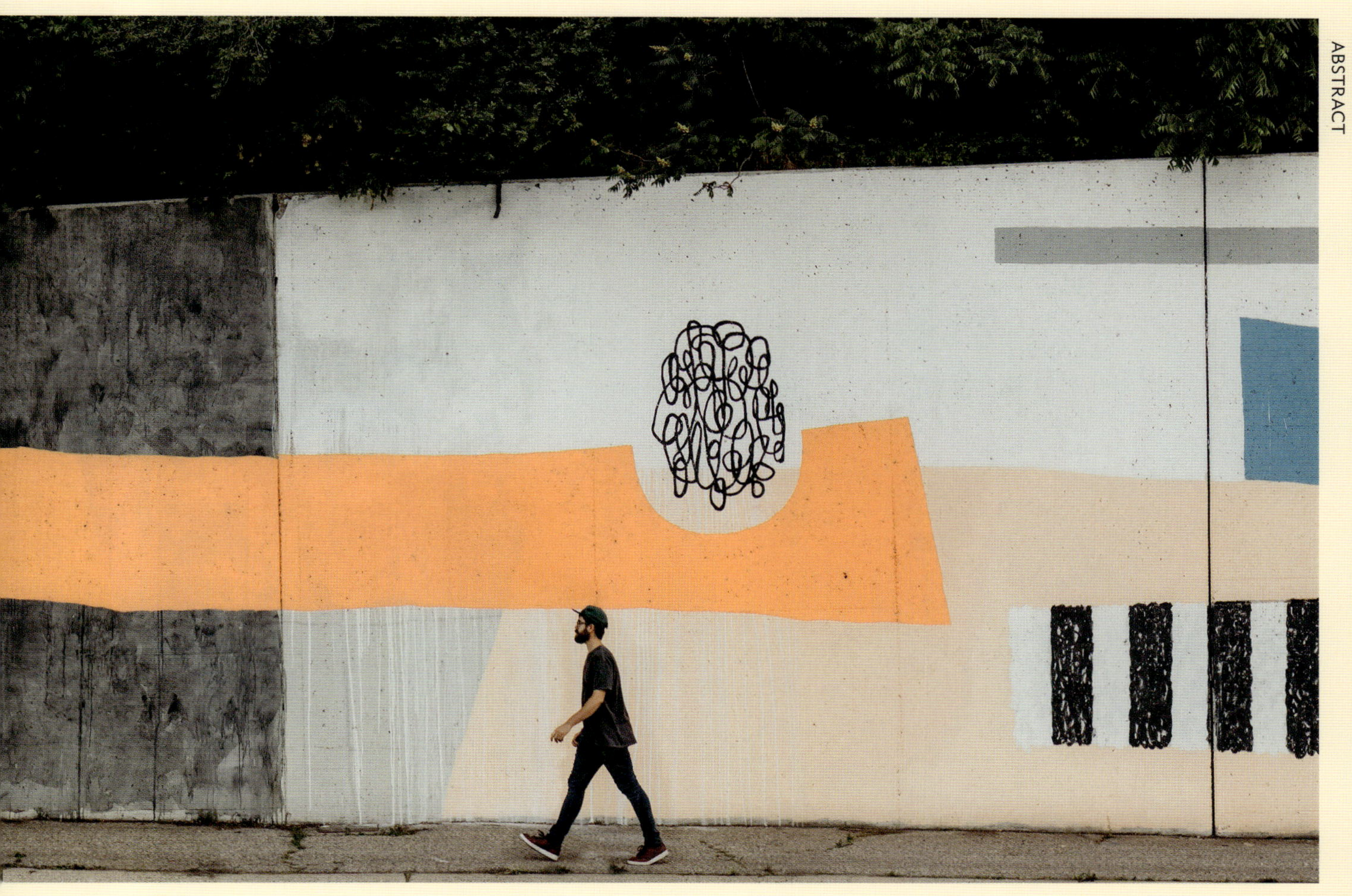

2 /
Grand Rapids, Michigan, USA, 2017
PHOTO BY THE ARTIST

–Unfortunately, we still live in a world of gender inequity. Have you felt handicapped being a woman in the creative industry? Does it feel like times are changing?
I don't think 'handicapped' is the right word, but I am definitely aware of the patriarchal systems that provide more opportunities for men than women, femme-identifying individuals and people of colour.

Times are changing as communities and artists bring the inequities into public discourse, but you don't have to look far to find predominantly male mural festivals, or galleries whose rosters feature mostly white men.

No matter the project or collaboration, you always bring your distinctive style and a recognisable colour palette. Can you tell us more about your choice of colours?
A few years ago, I was spending so much time choosing colours, it started to feel overwhelming. It's such a funny problem to have, like: too many colours, not enough time! So I decided to step back, and return to the primaries: red, yellow and blue. From there I expanded into tints and shades of those colours to include pinks, light blues and mustard. For the most part, restricting my palette gave me the constraints I needed to unify the work.

In past interviews you have likened mural painting to dancing. Do your works happen organically, with shapes coming forth themselves, or do you have a 'go to' kit of forms that you puzzle into each work?
Both, for sure! There are certainly some shapes and shape combos that show up many times, and others that are more unique to a specific piece. The shapes embody ideas (centeredness, mistakes, memory, fluidity) and qualities (soft, hard, rigid, loose, round, smooth, dense), and in composition they can act as symbols of broader structures.

What projects have made you excited over the past few years?
I hope I don't get too rambly on this one, but one of my favourite projects was 'Nothing Is Separate: a Collaboration with Nature' which began as an experimental, travelling installation during the Temple Children Artist Residency in Hilo, Hawaii, in 2017. By creating intuitive compositions of painted, repurposed wood shapes and costumes at several of the island's distinct and isolated terrains, I explored the complex relationship humans have with both natural and constructed environments.

I'm really excited about my newest body of work, 'This Must Be The Place,' which presents a new investigation at the intersection of performance and painting. How do we move through space? How do we contort our identities to fit in? How do we establish a deep sense of belonging in both the digital and the physical world? By tracing elements and textures from the physical environment and allowing overlooked aspects of the architecture and landscape to dictate the composition, I'm drawing connections between vastly different landscapes, calling attention to the interconnectivity of earth's systems. Through improvised movements and unconventional

3

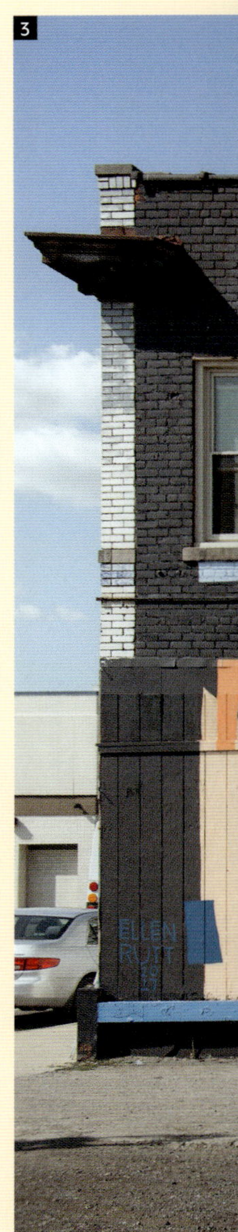

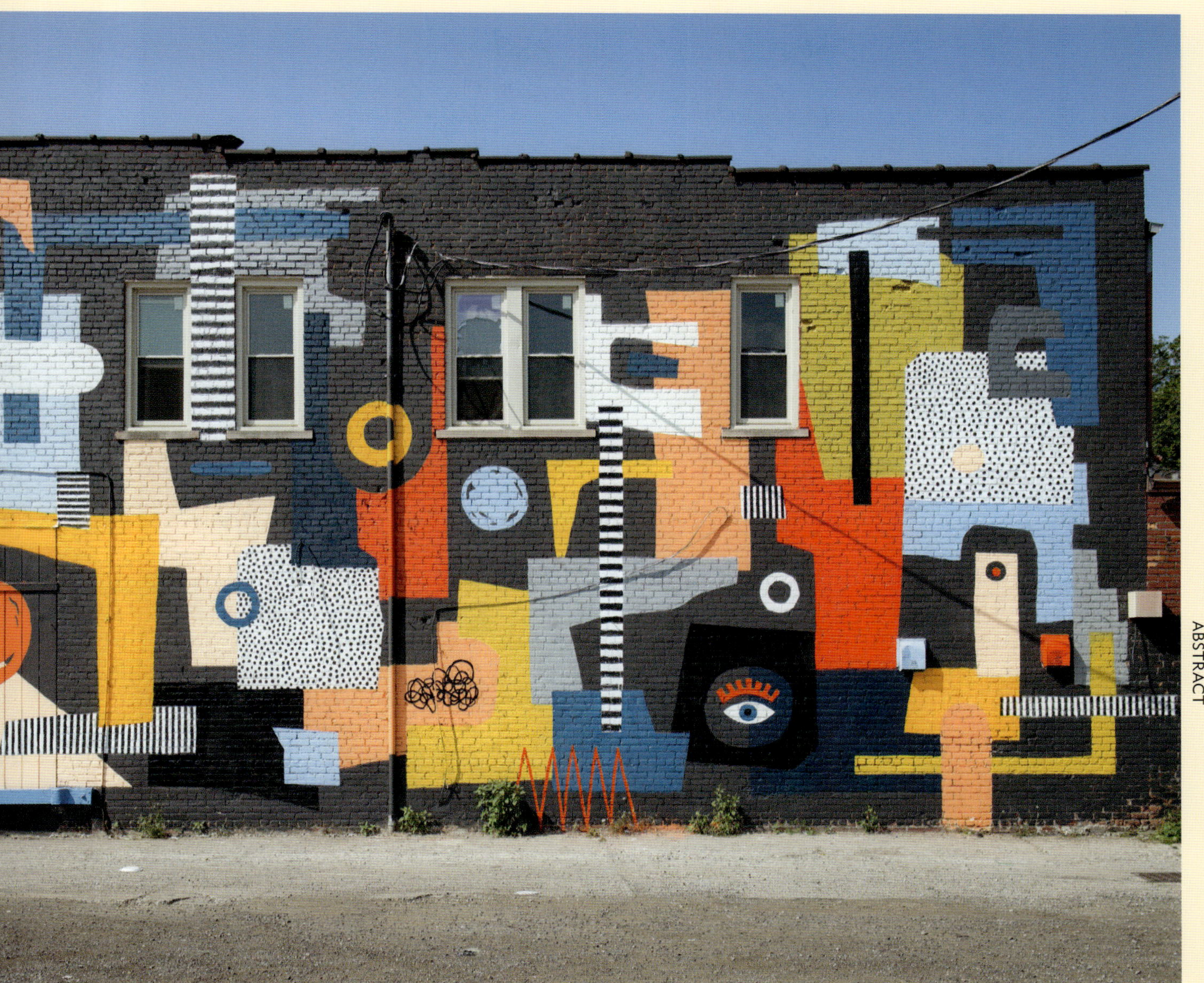

3 /
Detroit, Michigan, USA, 2017
PHOTO BY THE ARTIST

mark-making techniques cumulatively becoming 'Place Paintings,' I've been exploring alternative ways of noticing, engaging with new locations and developing a sustained inquiry into what it means to be alive and making work in the age of climate change.

What are your thoughts on artists working with brands?
That's a huge question. How do we – as artists, activists, people – fight capitalism while simultaneously existing within the current economic structure? How do we shift culture away from a hyper-consumption model while also supporting our day-to-day needs? Which brands are actually paying their workers fair wages and making efforts to make sustainability a critical aspect of their business, and which ones are just greenwashing? How are my own behaviours problematic and hypocritical, and how can I use my relative privilege to support the issues that are relevant, important and urgent? Maybe the question is how we work with brands, and making sure that we aren't letting companies sanitize or silence difficult issues.

Making public art in Detroit has made me hyper-aware of community as a structure.

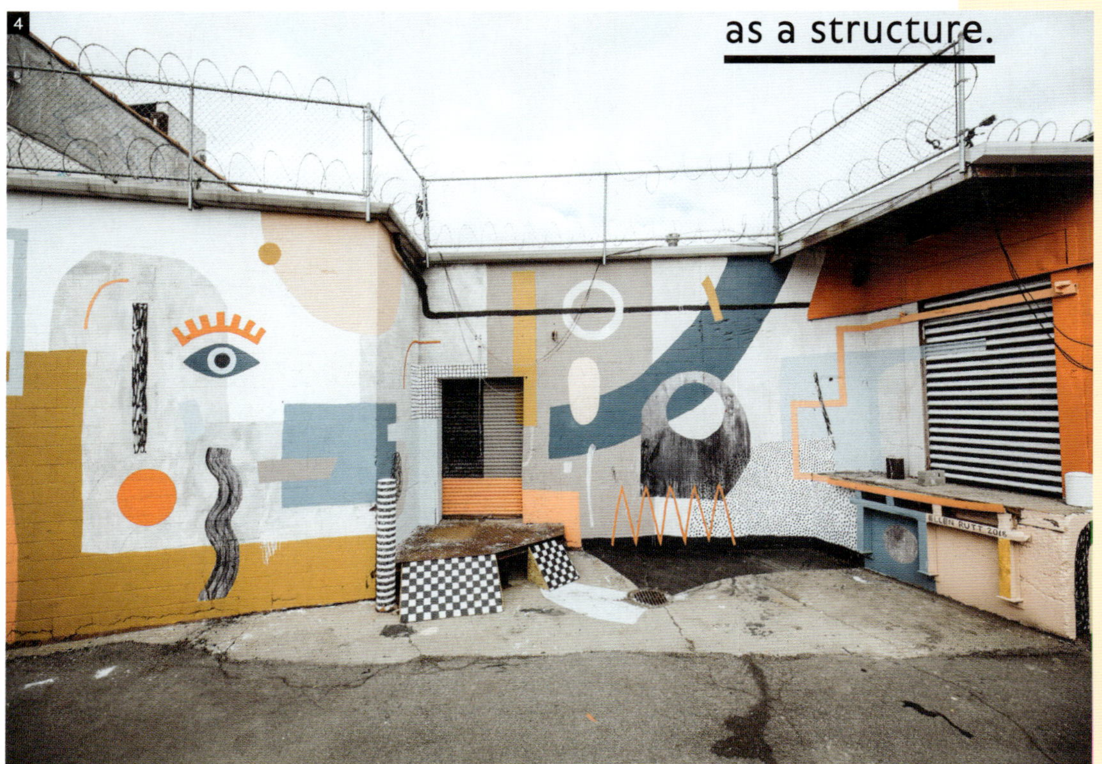

4 / Detroit, Michigan, USA, 2018
PHOTO BY THE ARTIST

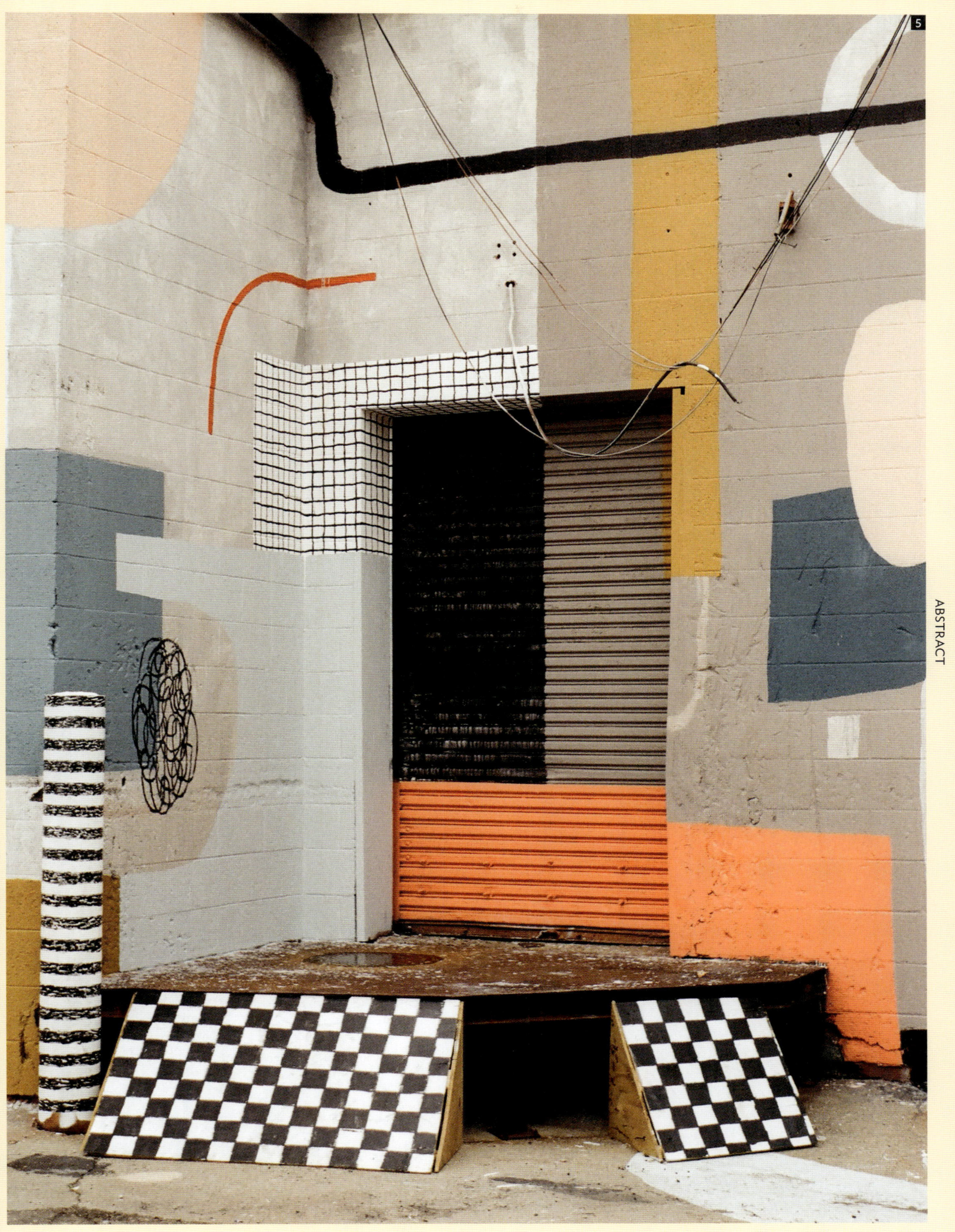

5 /
Detroit, Michigan, USA, 2018
PHOTO BY THE ARTIST

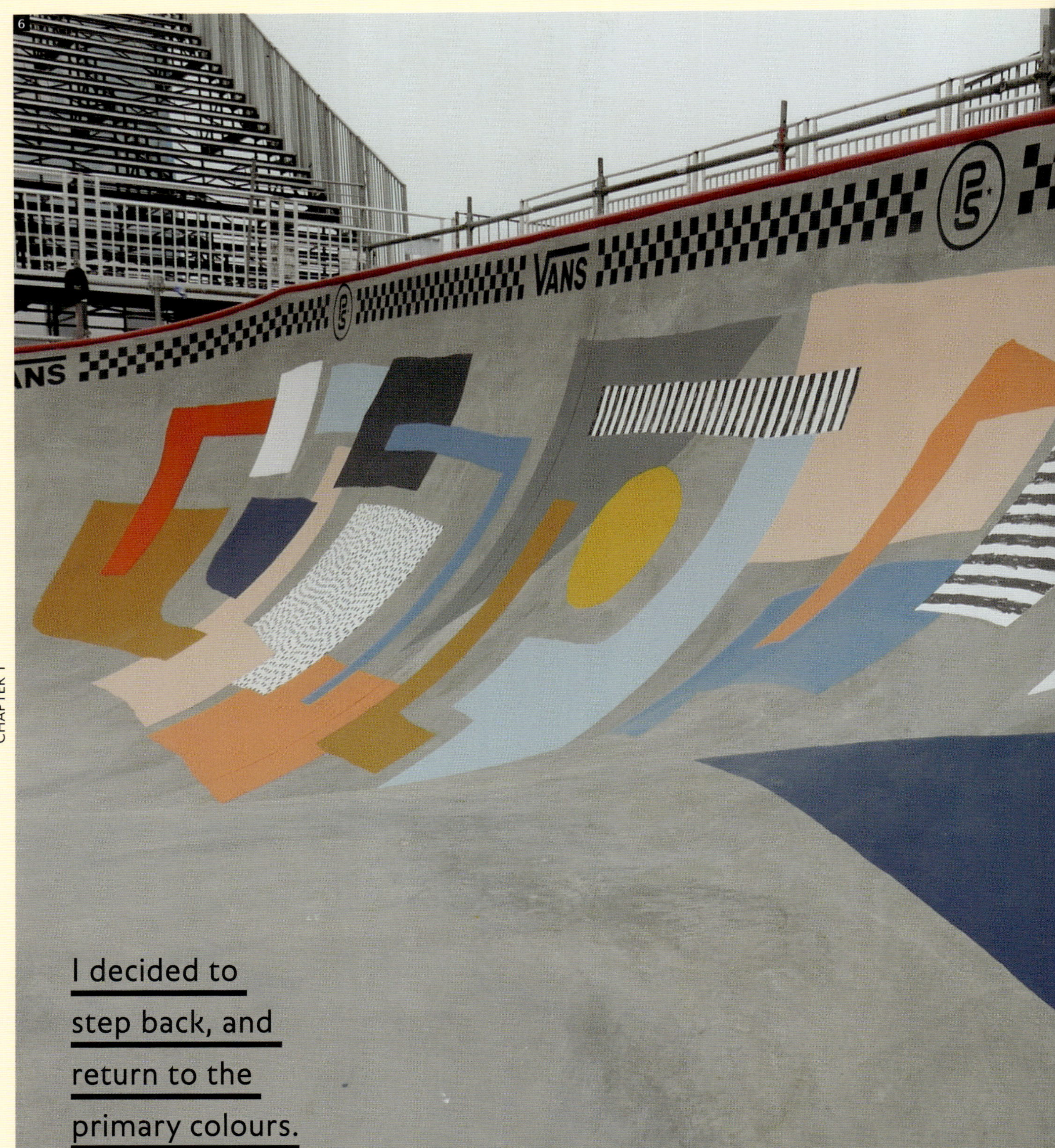

I decided to step back, and return to the primary colours. From there it expanded into tints and shades.

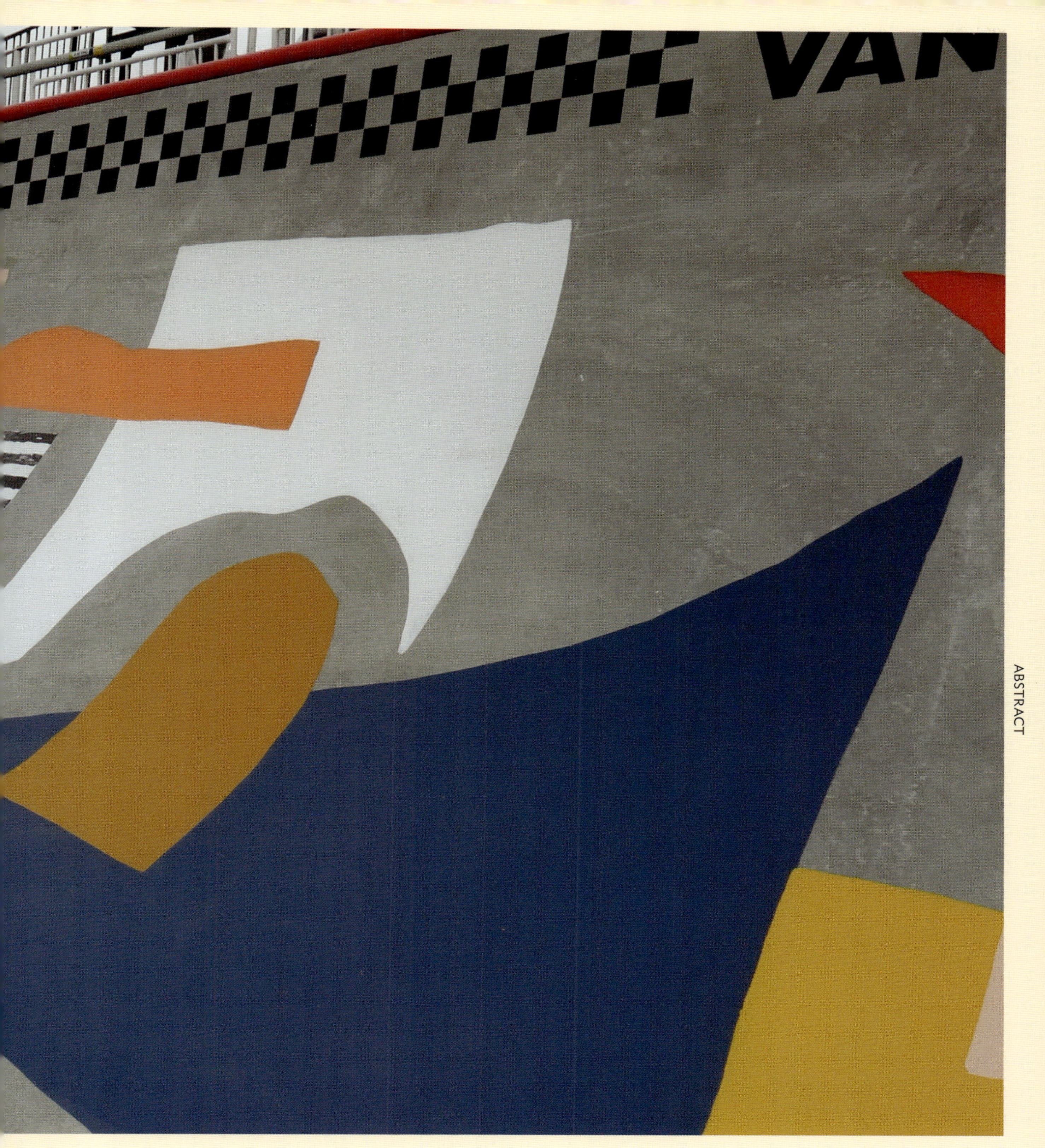

6 /
Huntington Beach, California, USA, 2018
PHOTO BY THE ARTIST

FELIPE PANTONE

/ Valencia

Felipe Pantone, the Spanish-based child of the internet, has covered the globe with colossal murals as well as huge volumes of installations and a score of exhibition and design collaborations. Impossible to miss, his neon gradients, harsh geometric lines and mural glitches explore contemporary consumption of colour and light through the screens and computers of the digital world.

With a passion for graffiti and imagery of the internet age, Felipe draws inspiration from the infinite and insatiable concept of programmed visuals. Creating huge works in public space reminds us of the infiltration of the synthetic into the tactile world: a wake-up call with a retro wink, as neons and thunderbolts create visual noise.

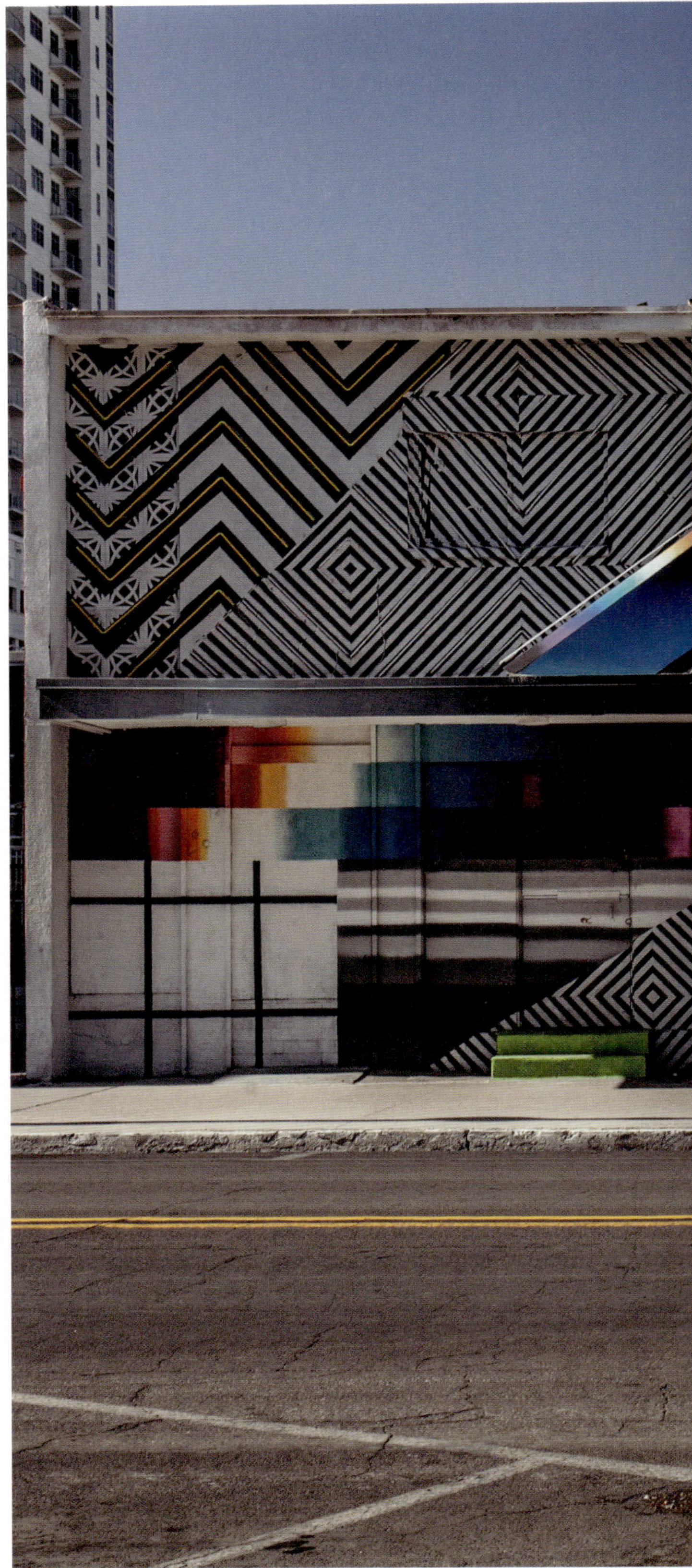

Felipe draws inspiration from the infinite and insatiable concept of programmed visuals.

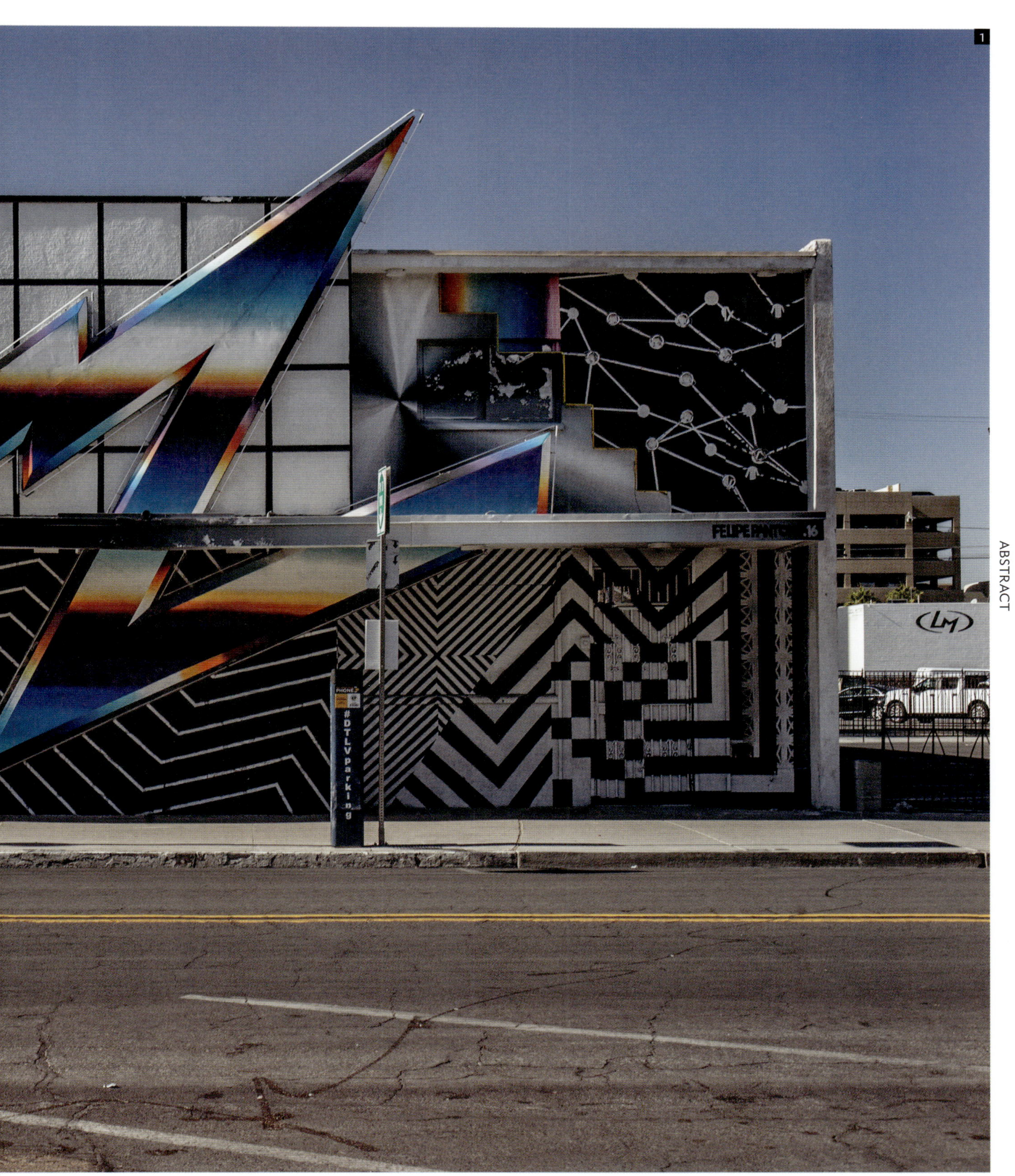

1 /
Las Vegas, Nevada, USA, 2017
PHOTO BY BIRDMAN

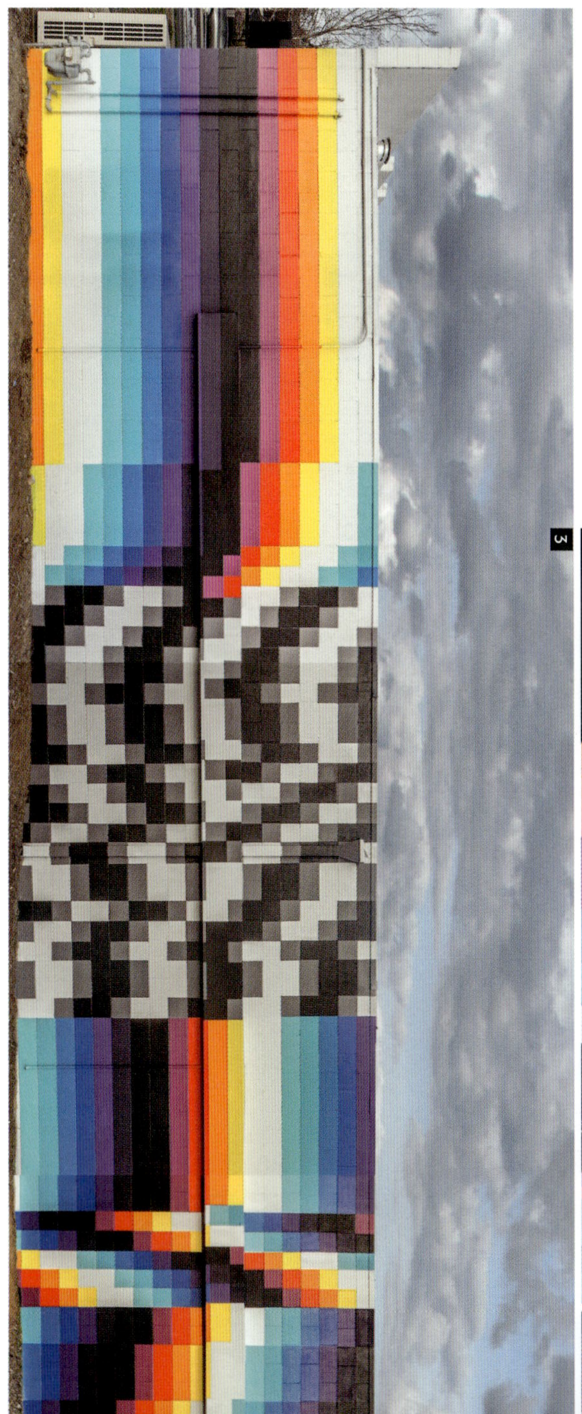

3

2

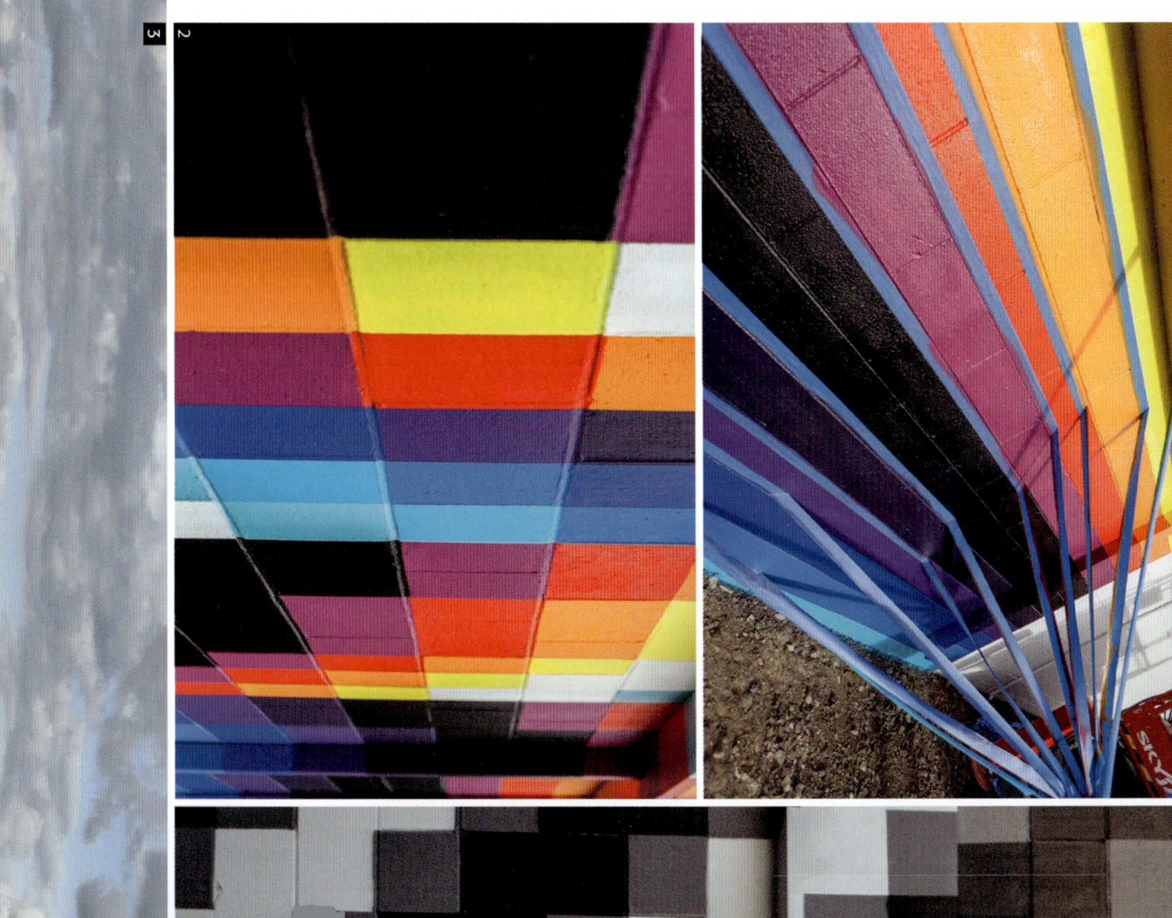

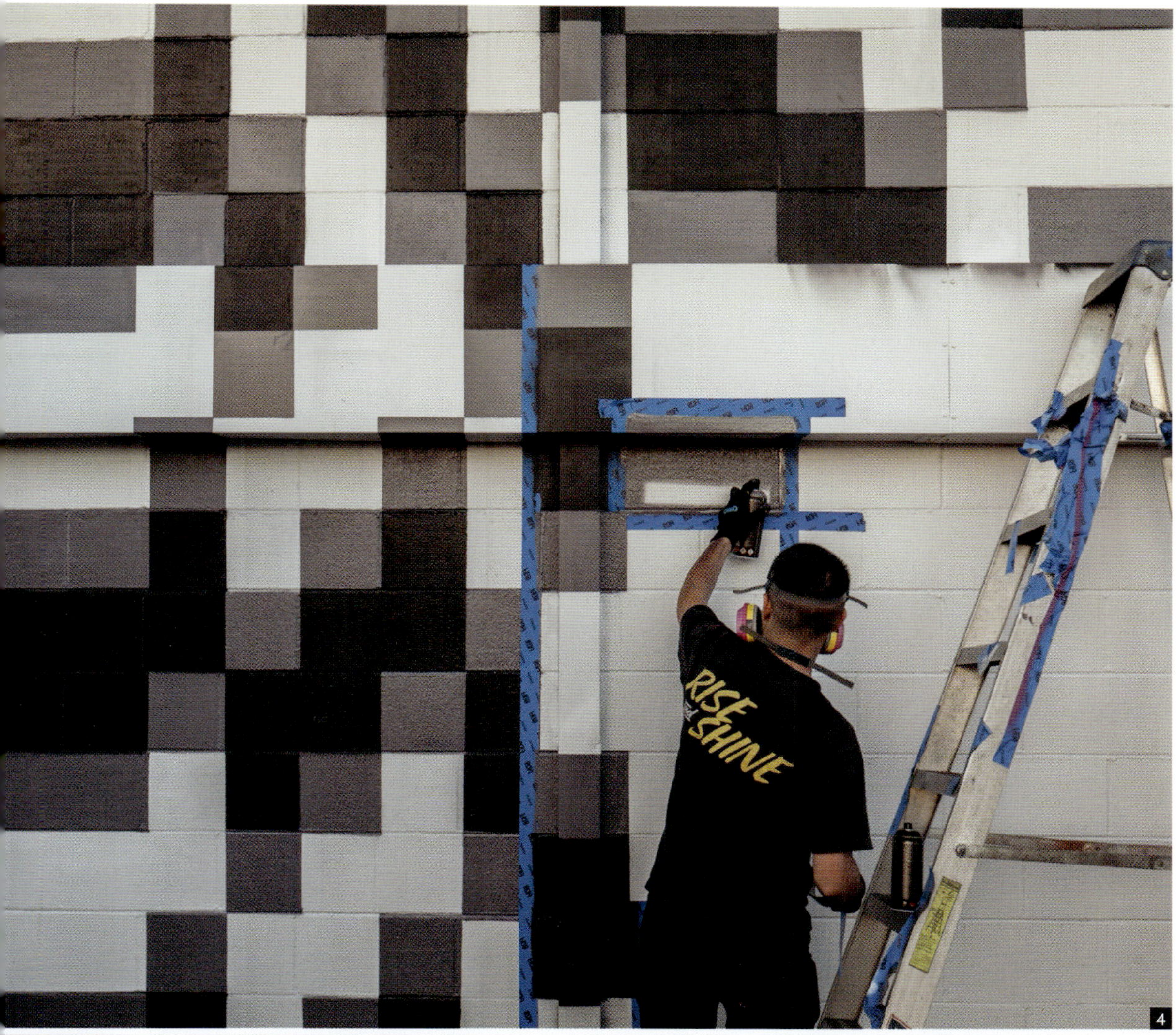

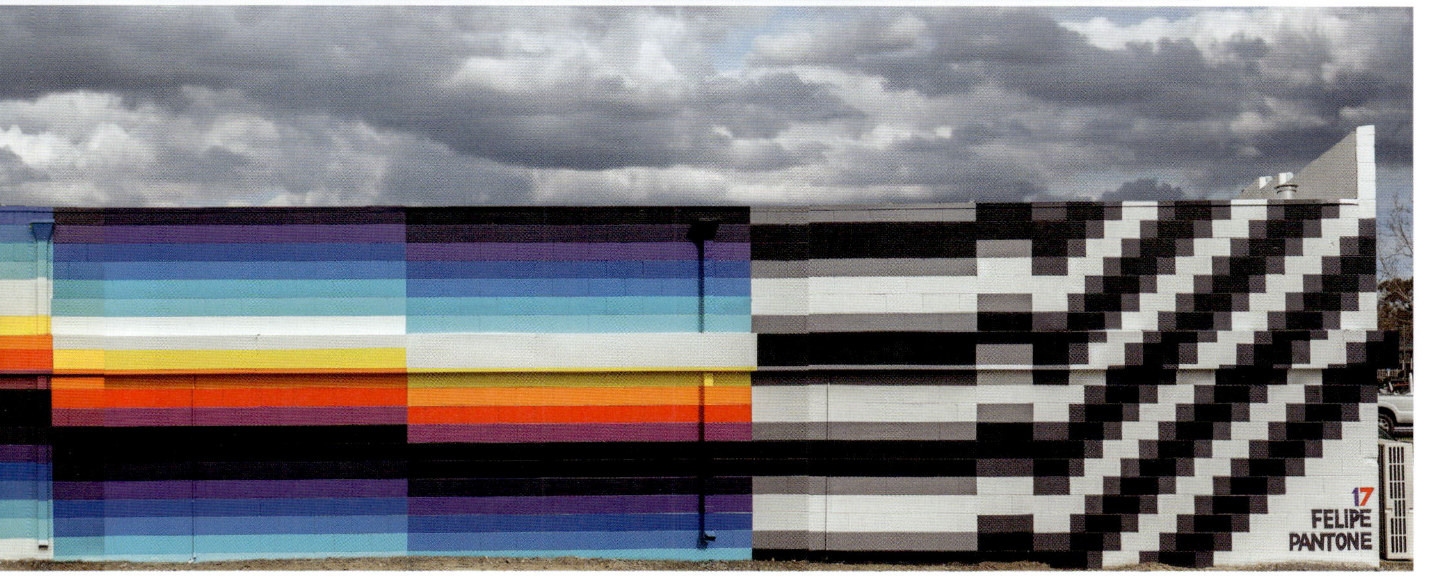

2 / 3 / 4
Napa, California, USA, 2017
PHOTO BY BIRDMAN

KRISTIN FARR

/ San Francisco

San-Fran-based artist, curator and editor Kristin Farr floats through the online and tactile art world with a playful and unique vision of creative production and artists' place in the world. Creator of the KQED Art School video series, editor of the famous *Juxtapoz* magazine and curator of Facebook's Artist in Residence programme, Kristin juggles many exciting roles. Her own art practice has an infallible style, however. The bright, multicoloured, geometric works show strong influences from folk art, specifically the hex signs that were used to decorate barns in Pennsylvania, which were first seen as early as the 19th century. Exuding addictive positivity, her geometric rainbows can now be seen splayed over walls, canvases and various design projects across the globe.

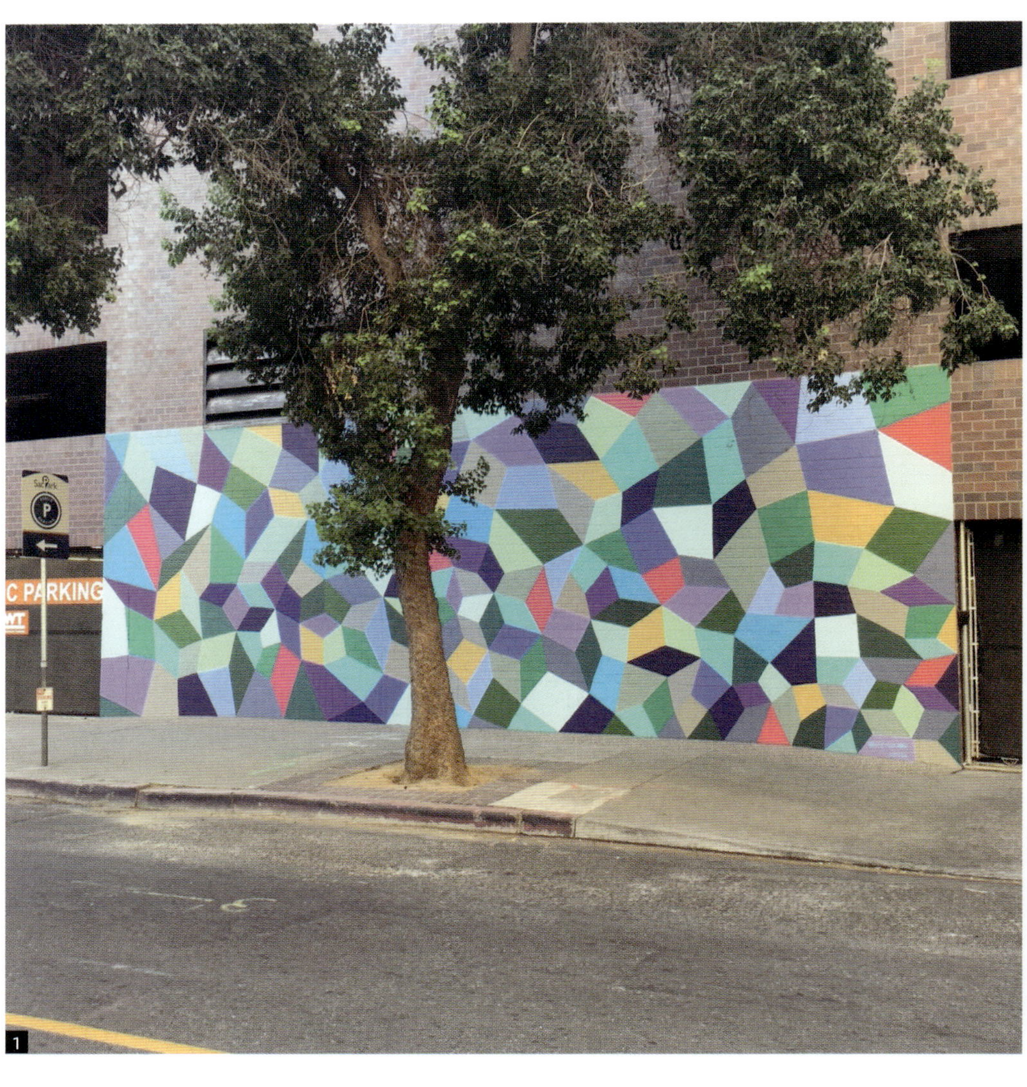

1 /
Sacramento, California, USA, 2016
PHOTO BY THE ARTIST

2 /
Manchester, Tennessee, USA, 2018
PHOTO BY THE ARTIST

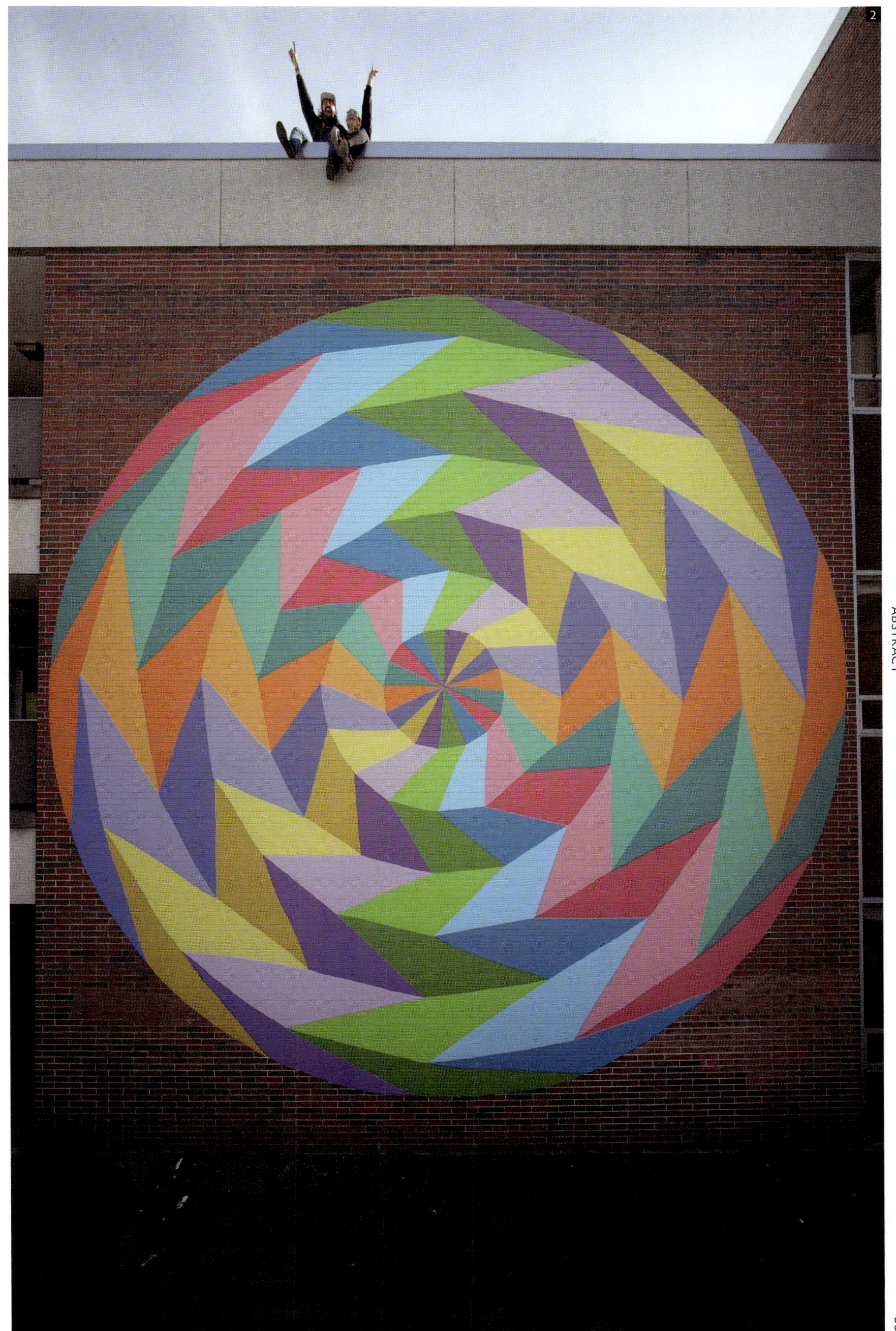

2

3

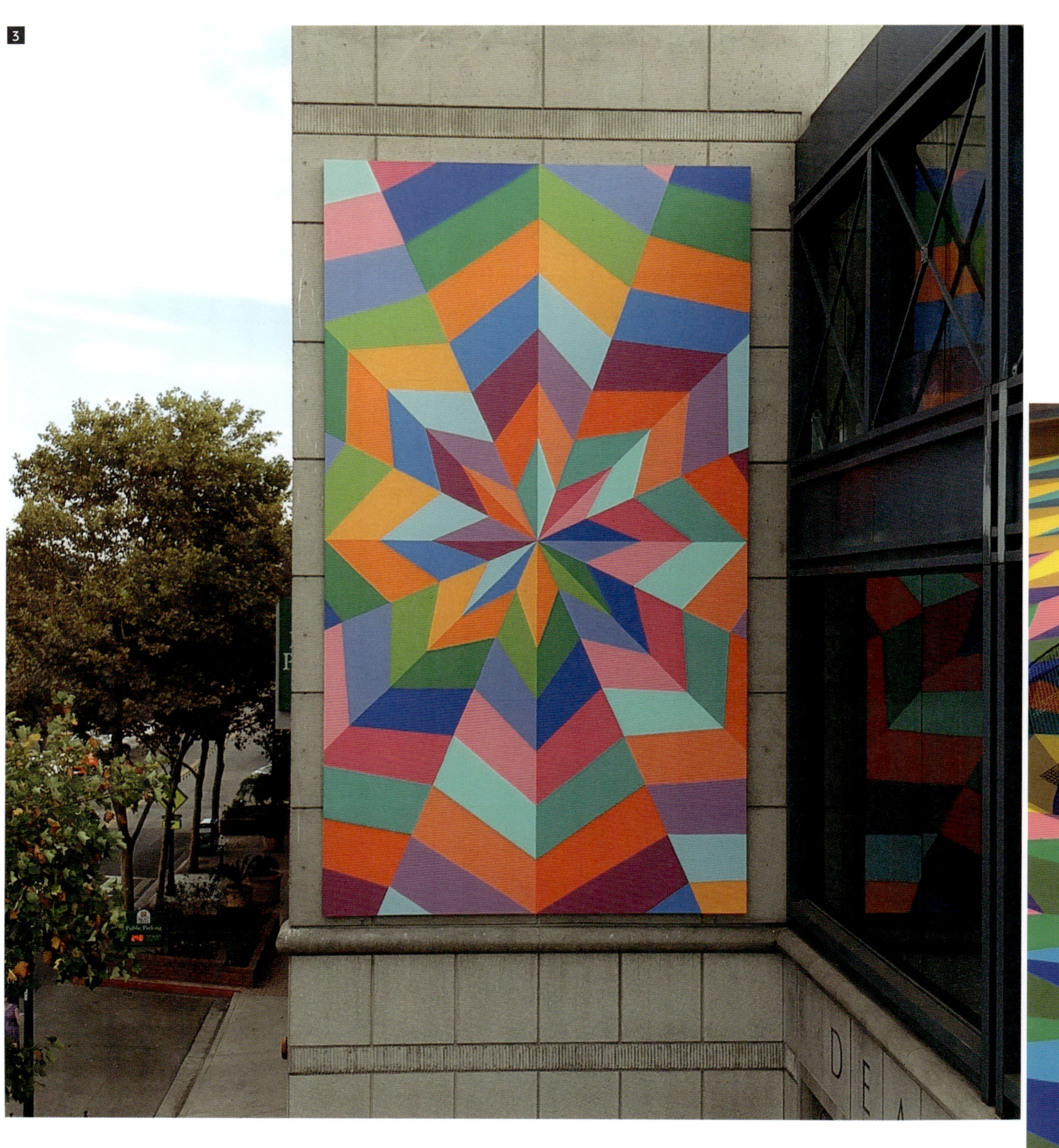

The bright, multicoloured, geometric works show strong influences from folk art.

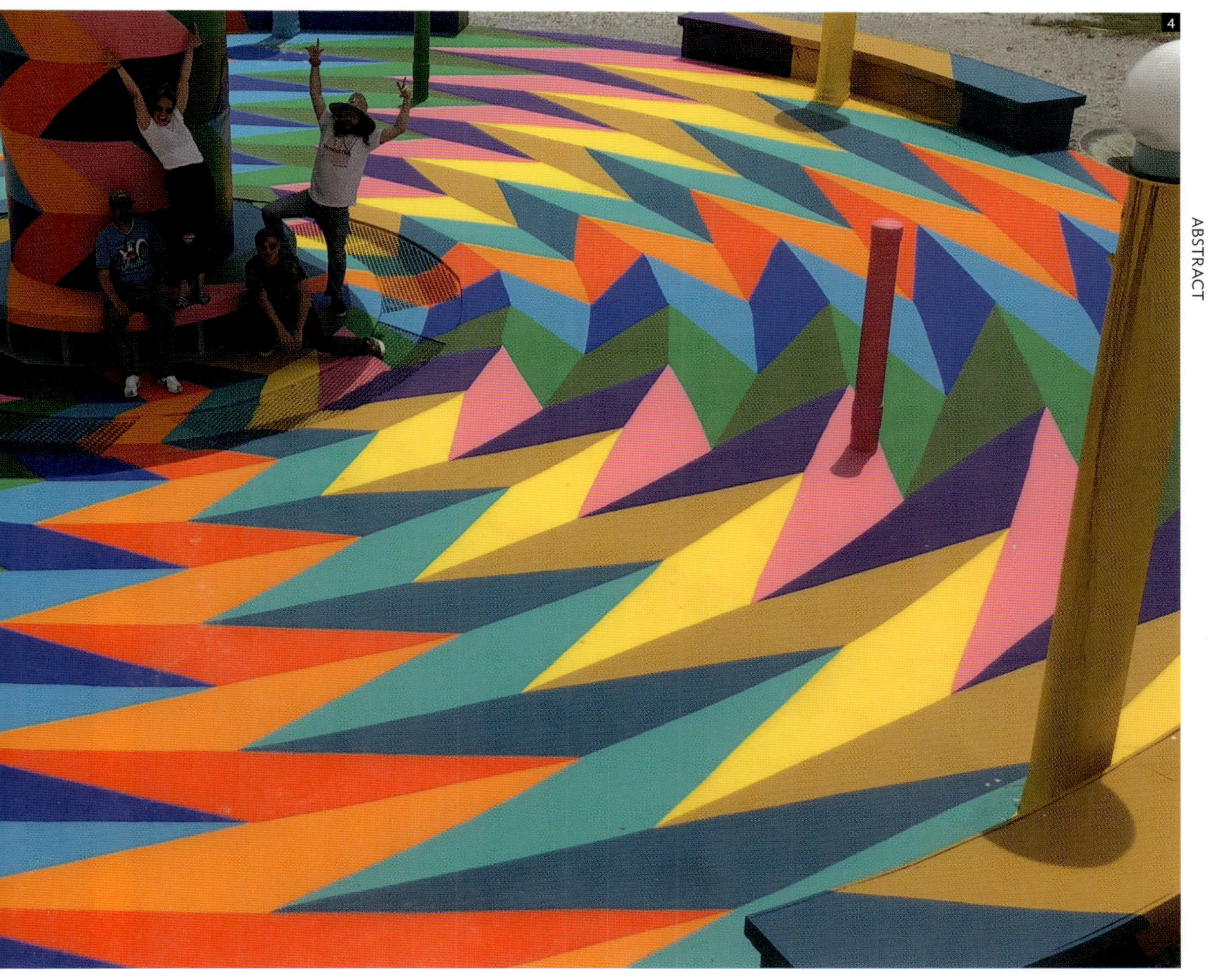

3 /
Walnut Creek, California, USA, 2018
PHOTO BY THE ARTIST

4 /
Manchester, Tennessee, USA, 2018
PHOTO BY THE ARTIST

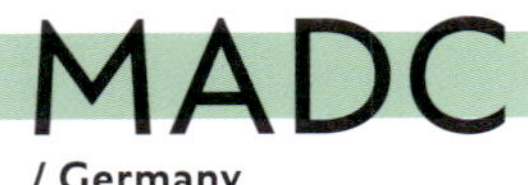

MADC

/ Germany

Twenty-three years into her career since she painted her first graffiti piece in '96, German artist MadC (aka Claudia Walde) can be admired for many aspects of her trajectory. Not only does she exhibit a mastery of lettering and technique, but she has also achieved dominance in a male-focused industry, and shown her dedication to the community though research and publication of street art books.

The last few years for MadC have seen her colour palette brighten and lean towards more gestural, abstract murals. However, the clear lines and dynamic compositions show off her roots in wildstyle lettering. Whether she is working on huge murals or canvas design, each project is a pure expression of street influence.

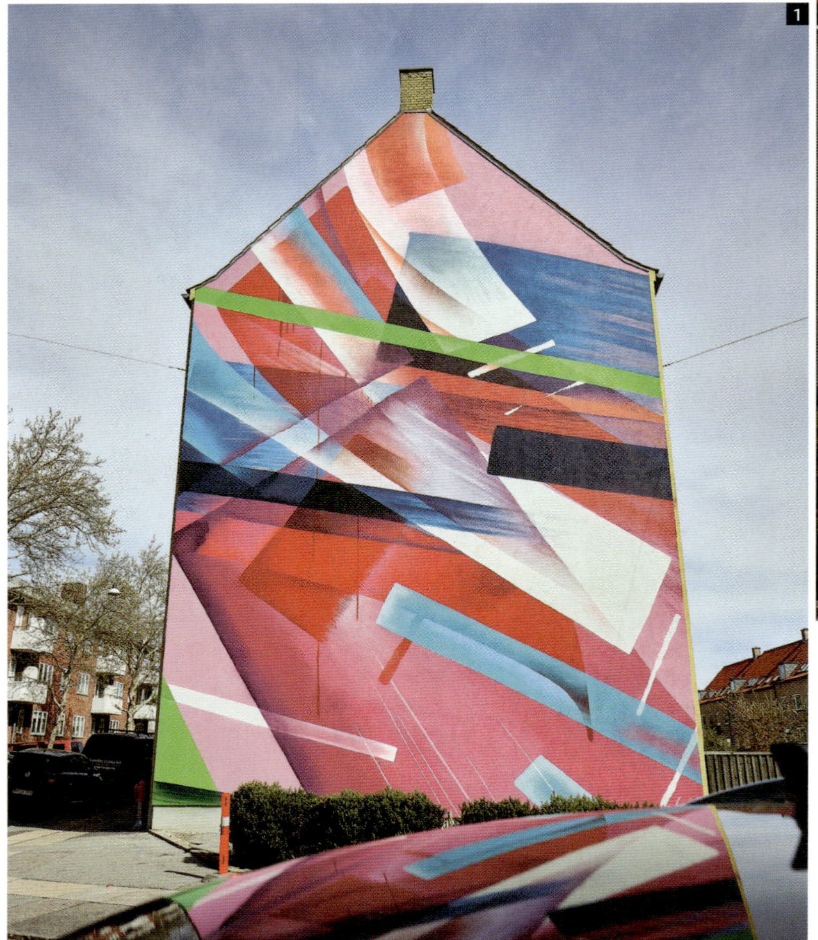

1

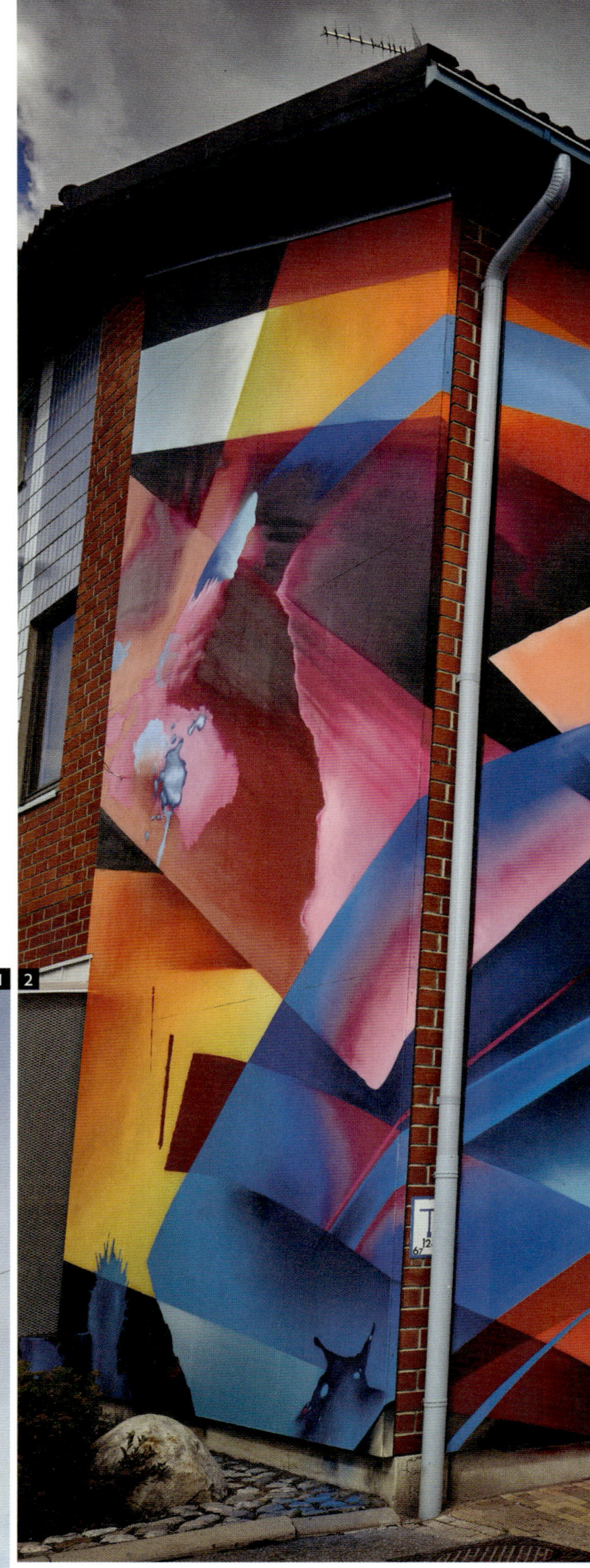

2

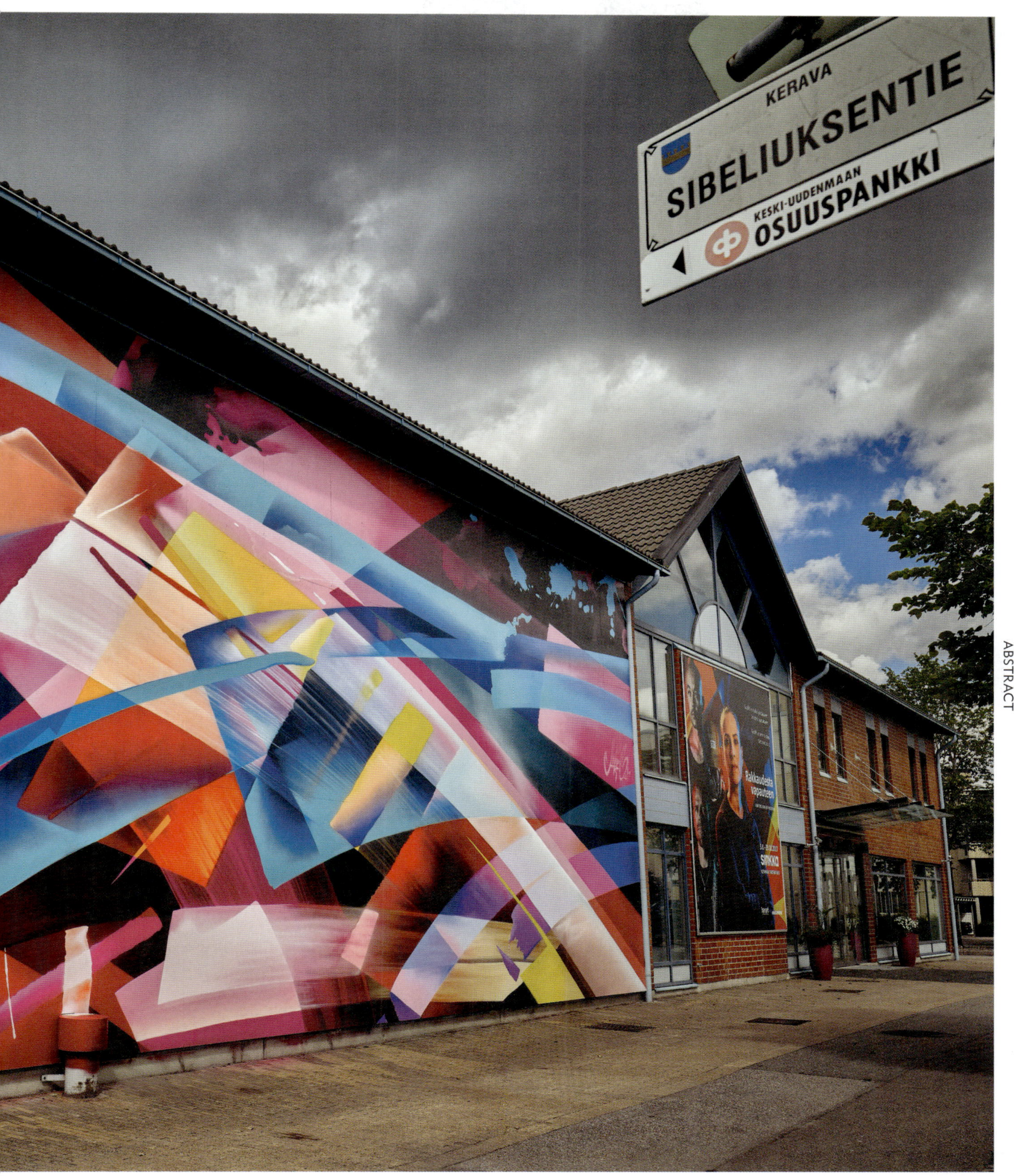

1 /
Copenhagen, Denmark, 2019
PHOTO BY THE ARTIST

2 /
Kerava, Finland, 2017
PHOTO BY THE ARTIST

The clear lines and dynamic compositions show off her roots in wildstyle lettering.

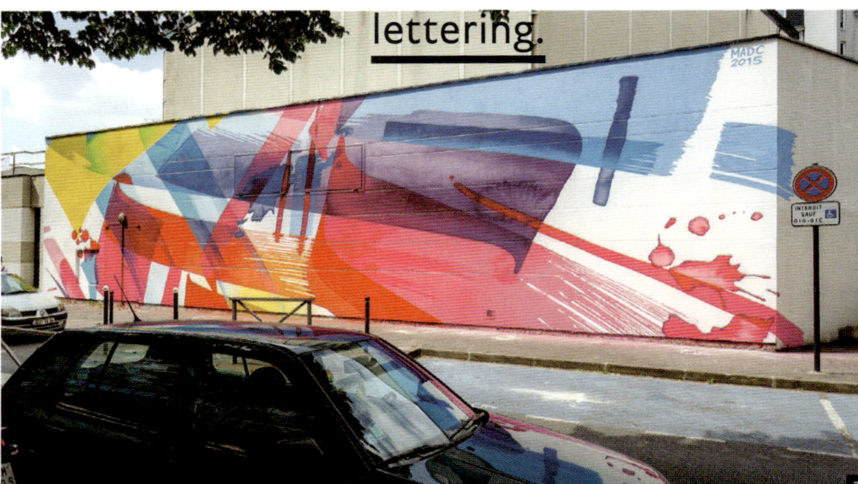

3 5

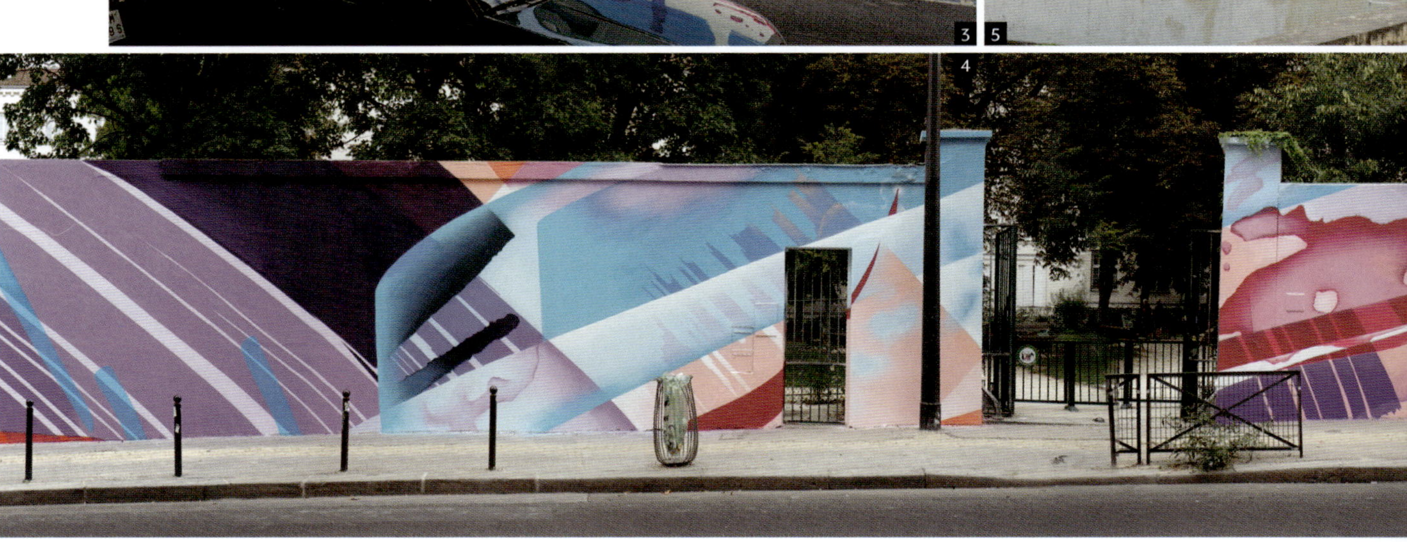

4

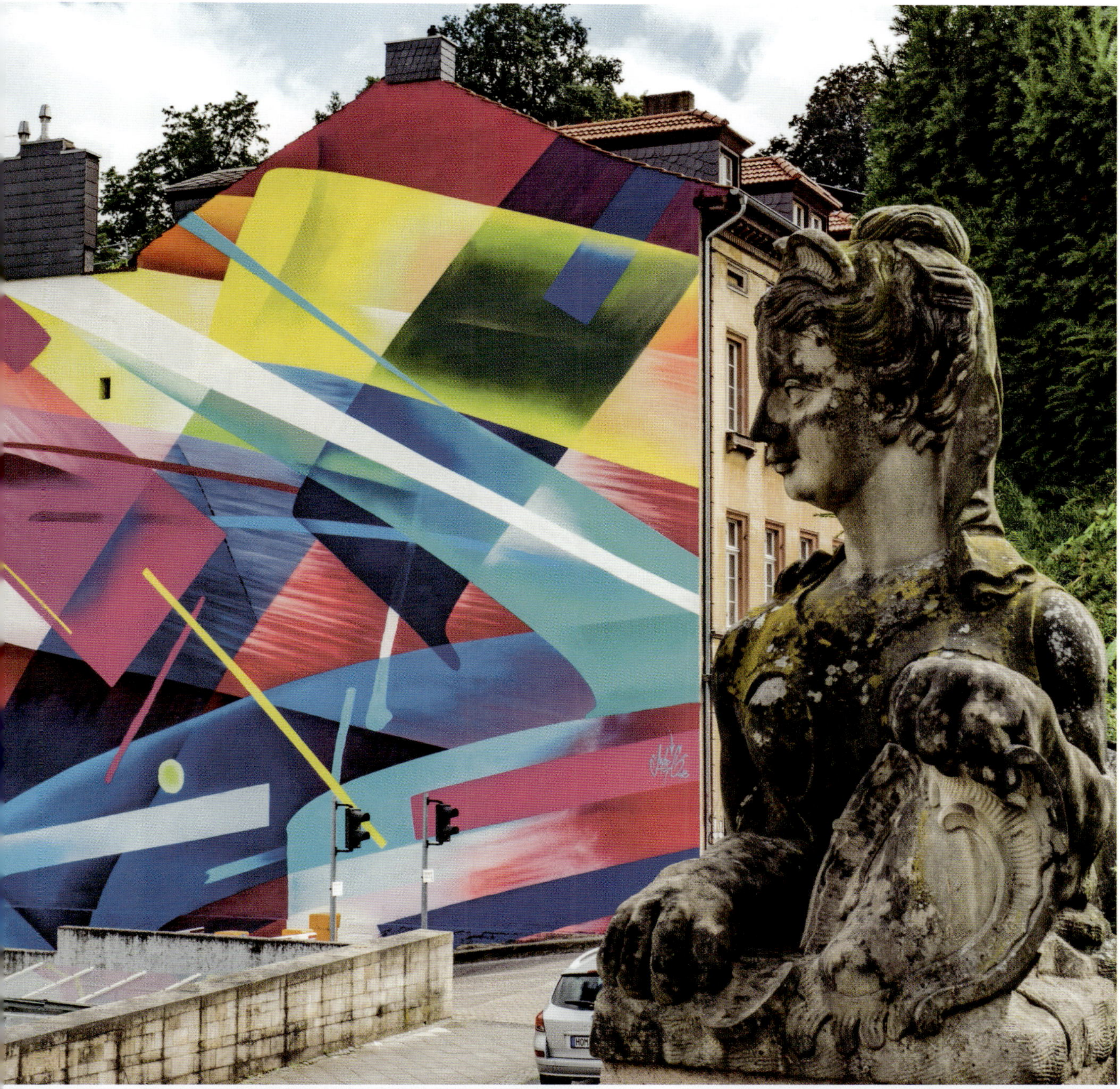

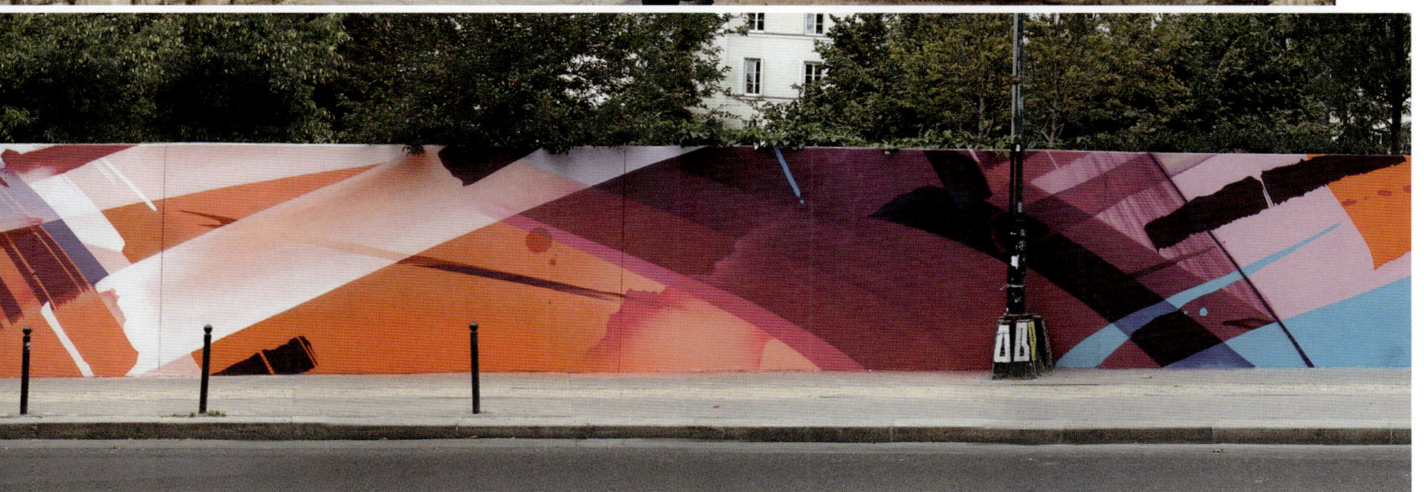

3 / 4
Paris, France, 2015
PHOTO BY THE ARTIST

5 /
Saarbrücken, Germany, 2018
PHOTO BY THE ARTIST

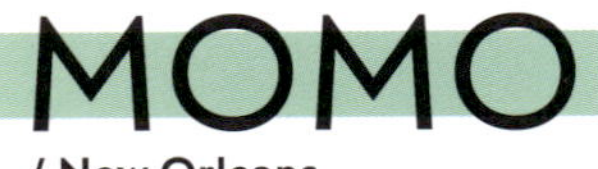

MOMO

/ New Orleans

American artist Momo is often found on the fringes of what is considered street art. Featuring highly experimental and abstract works, his paintings and collages are more often found in institutes and galleries, with his muralism complementing his larger body of studio practice. His oeuvre includes elements of chance and randomness, allowing each unique piece a degree of spontaneity.

Also cited as part of the post-graffiti movement, he was chosen alongside Maya Hayuk, Swoon and Faile to inaugurate the Millennium Iconoclast Museum of Art in Brussels in 2016, with installations on display over five floors of the former brewery space.

Momo creates highly experimental and abstract works.

1

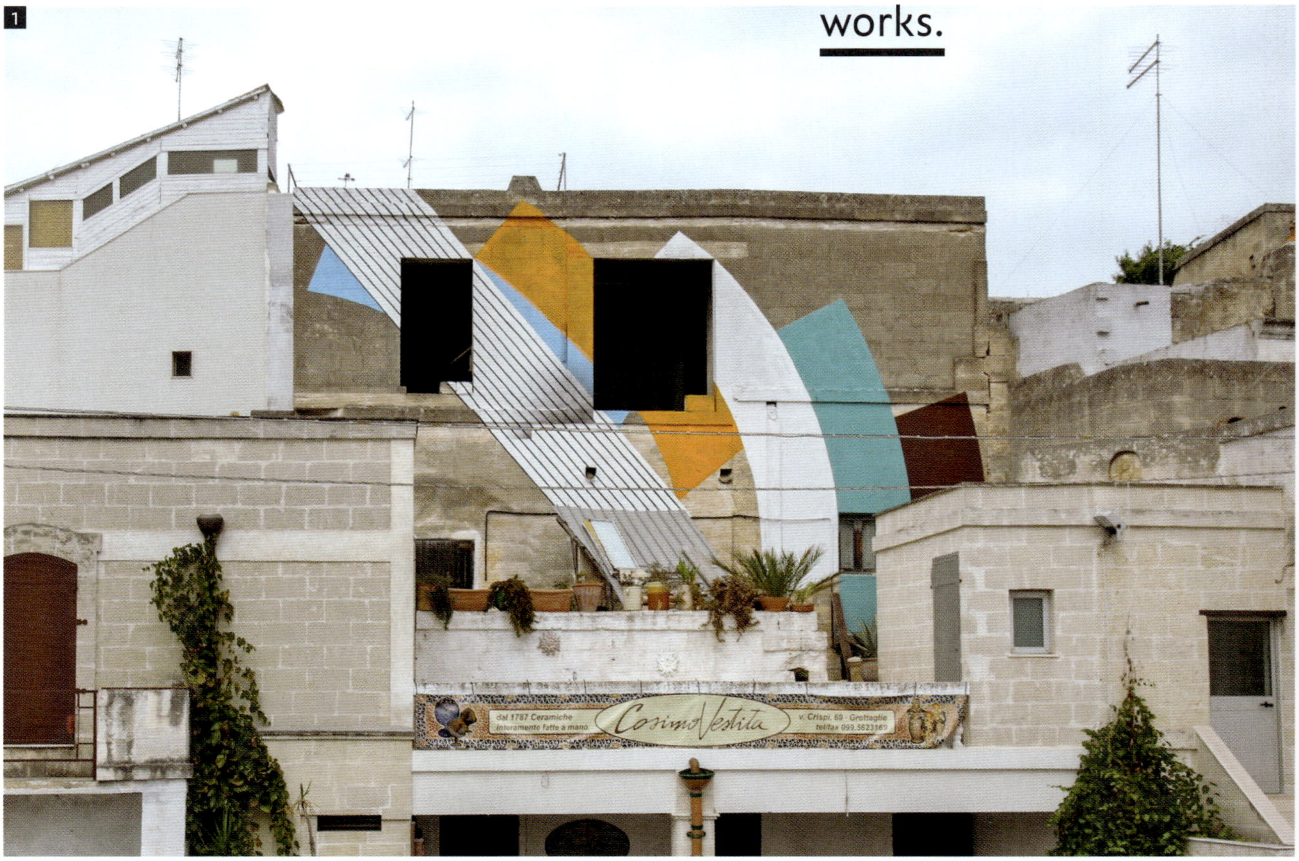

1 /
Grottaglie, Italy, 2012
PHOTO BY HENRIK HAVEN

2 /
Grottaglie, Italy, 2012
PHOTO BY HENRIK HAVEN

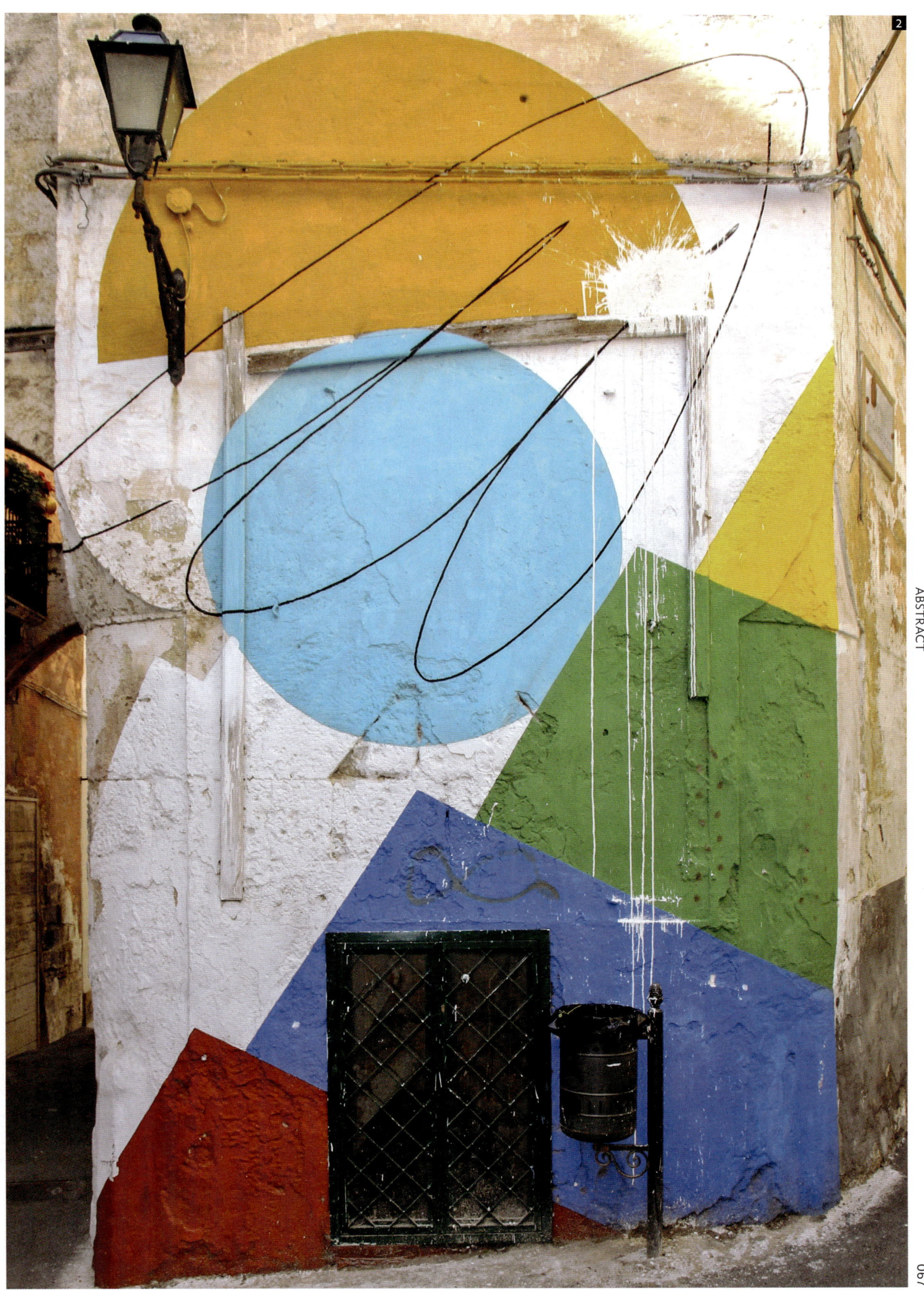

2

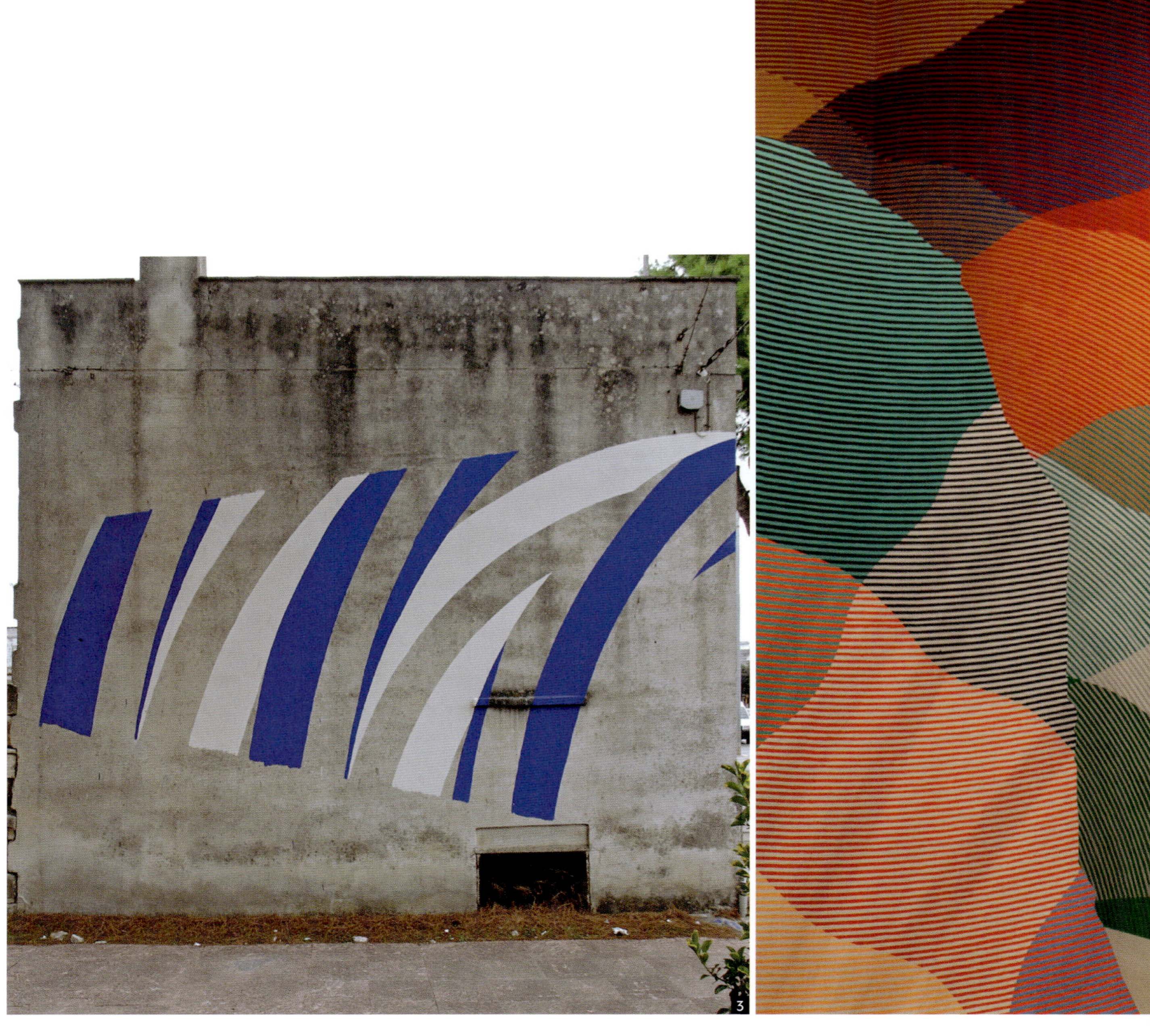

His oeuvre includes elements of chance and randomness.

3 /
Grottaglie, Italy, 2012
PHOTO BY HENRIK HAVEN

4 / 5
Brussels, Belgium, 2016
PHOTO BY VINNY CORNELLI

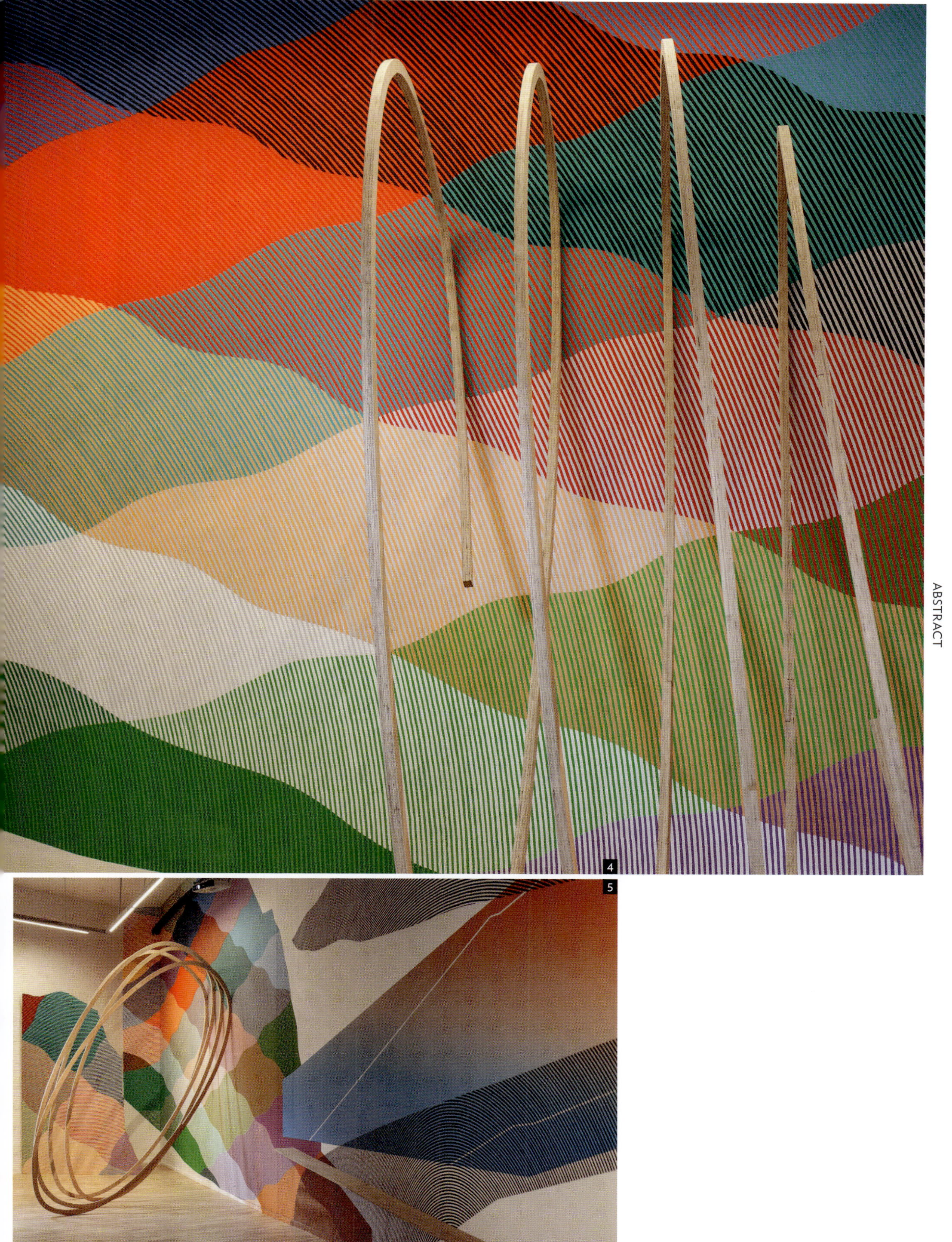

4

5

MR. JUNE

/ Amsterdam

Mr. June (aka David Louf) has traversed many a creative role since his entrance into the urban arts landscape in the mid-1980s. From old-school hip hop to bboying and break, he later experimented with graffiti, discovering an undying love for typography that would lead him to study graphic design at HKU University of the Arts Utrecht, where he would later return to teach.

But first, a rebellious career in commercial graphic design, where he broke free of his art-director role to form his own agency in 2000, called Out Of Order. This 'no-boss' freedom allowed him to invest time in developing his creative skills, quickly becoming a pioneer in the placement of illusionist abstract works. His background in fine arts and graffiti roots result in visuals that border on illusionism.

Very early in his career, he was invited to participate in major international street art festivals, exhibiting outdoor work combining his infatuation for typography with masterful graphic manipulation. After years of practice, Mr. June became a powerful reference for many painters interested in street art.

Mr. June became a powerful reference for many painters interested in street art.

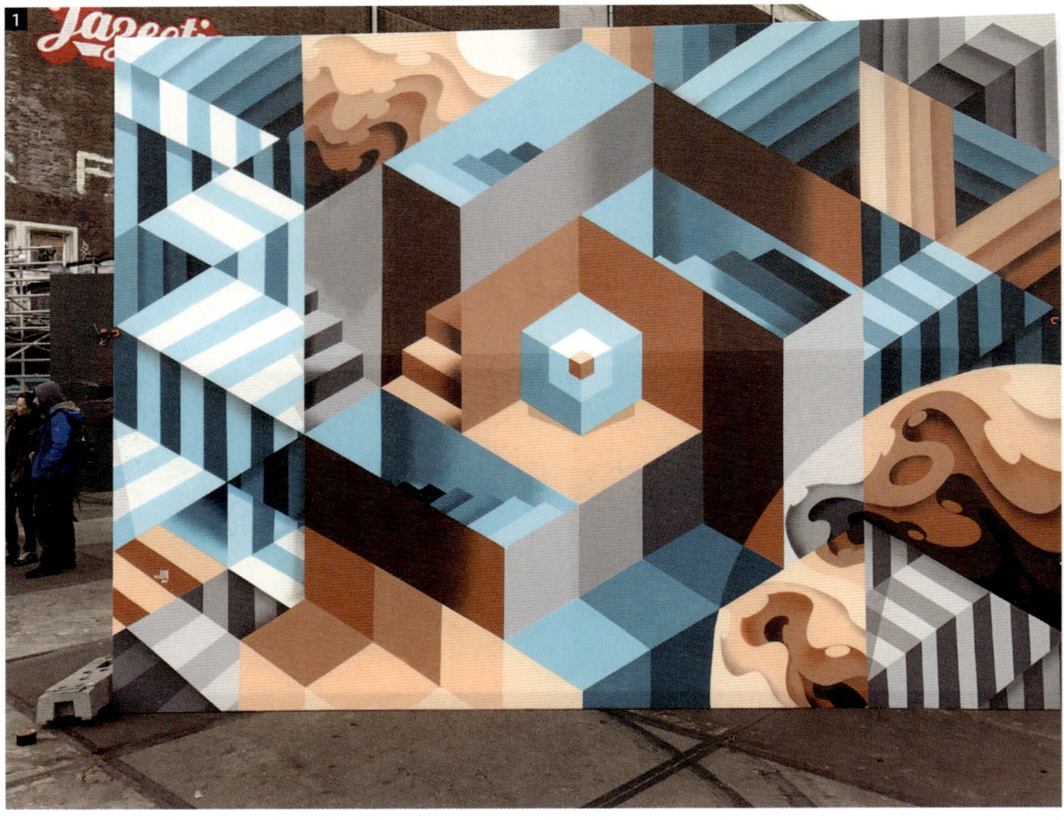

1 /
Amsterdam, The Netherlands, 2017
PHOTO BY THE ARTIST

2 /
Miami, Florida, USA, 2018
PHOTO BY THE ARTIST

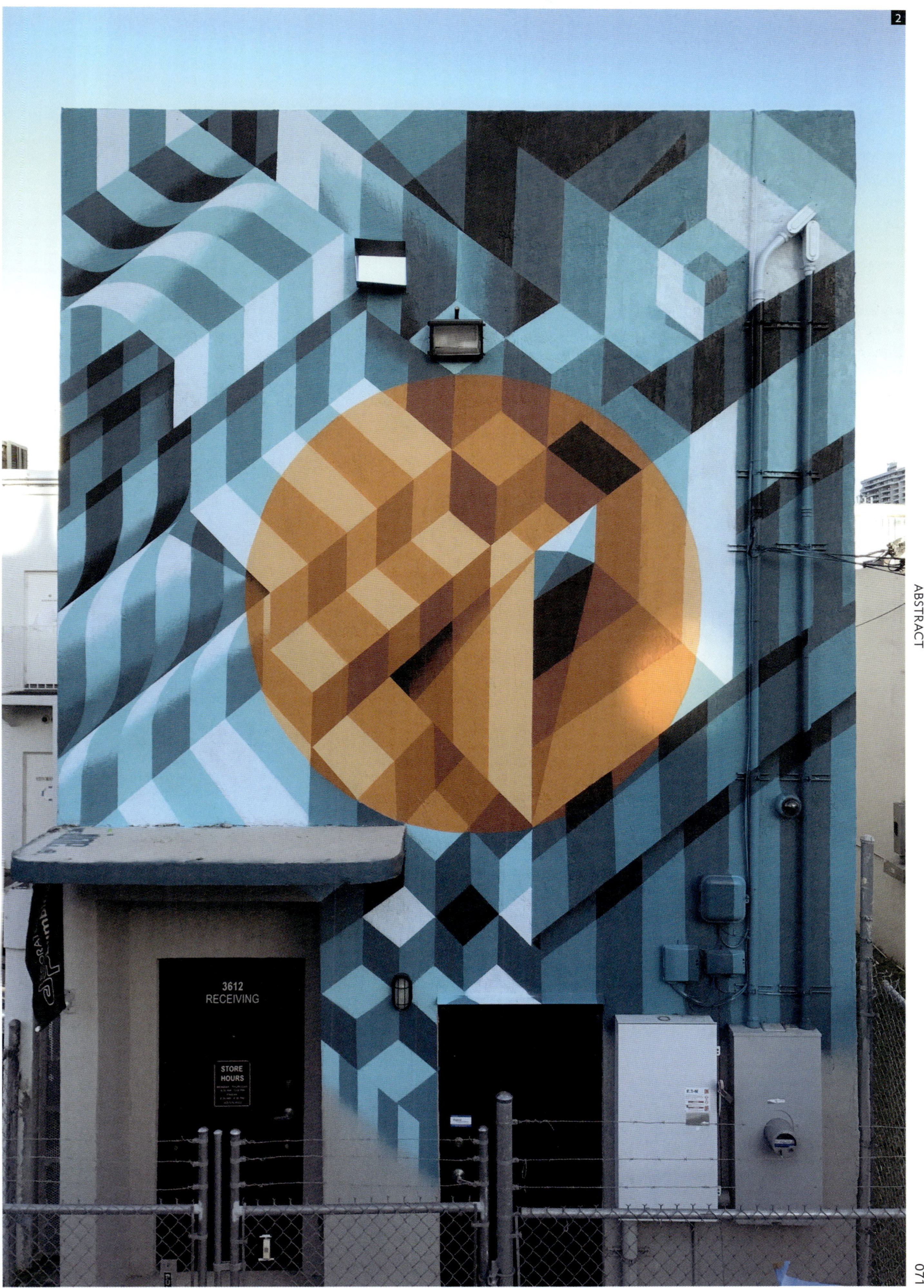
3612
RECEIVING
STORE
HOURS

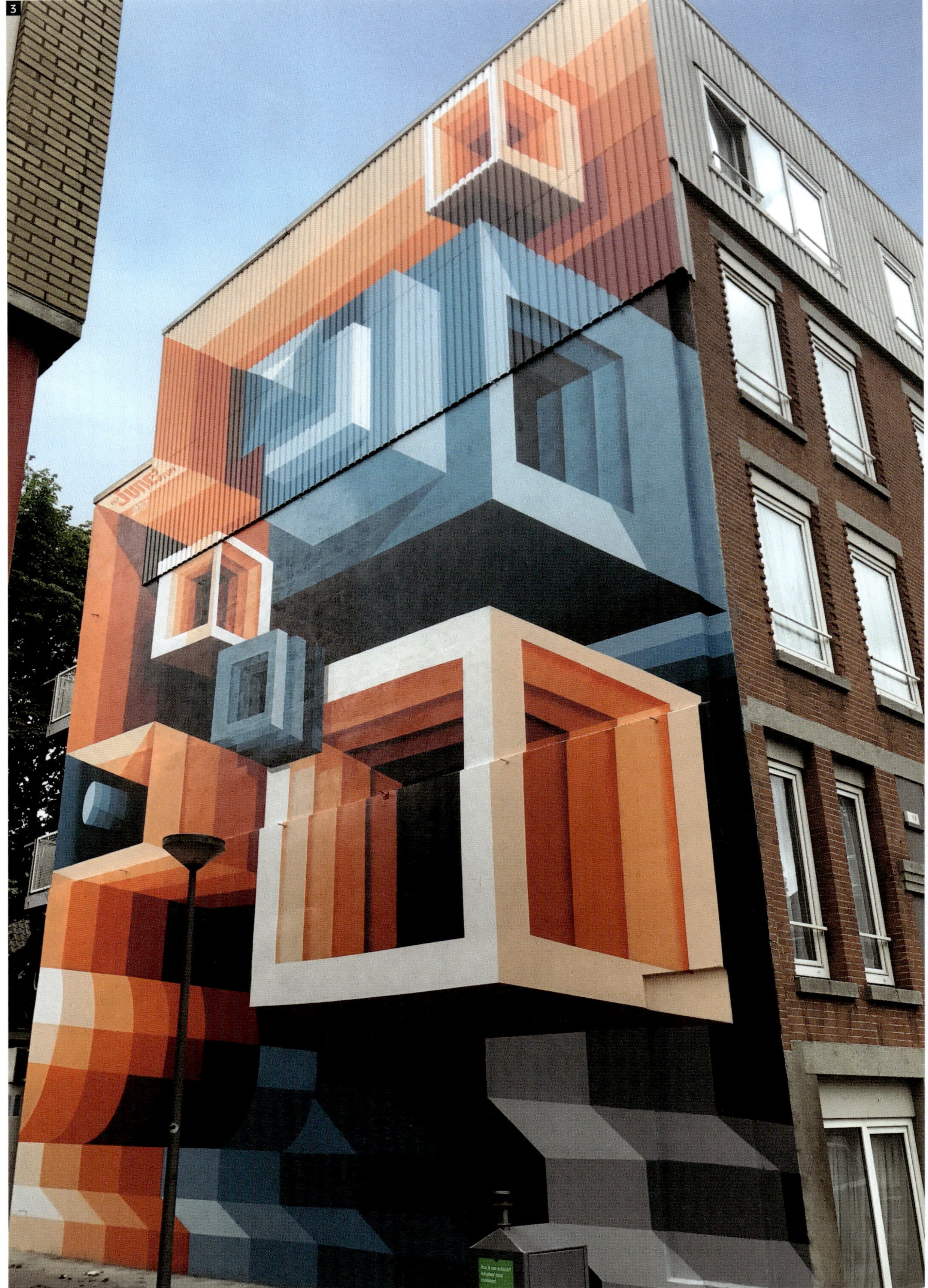

3

His background in fine arts and graffiti roots result in visuals that border on illusionism.

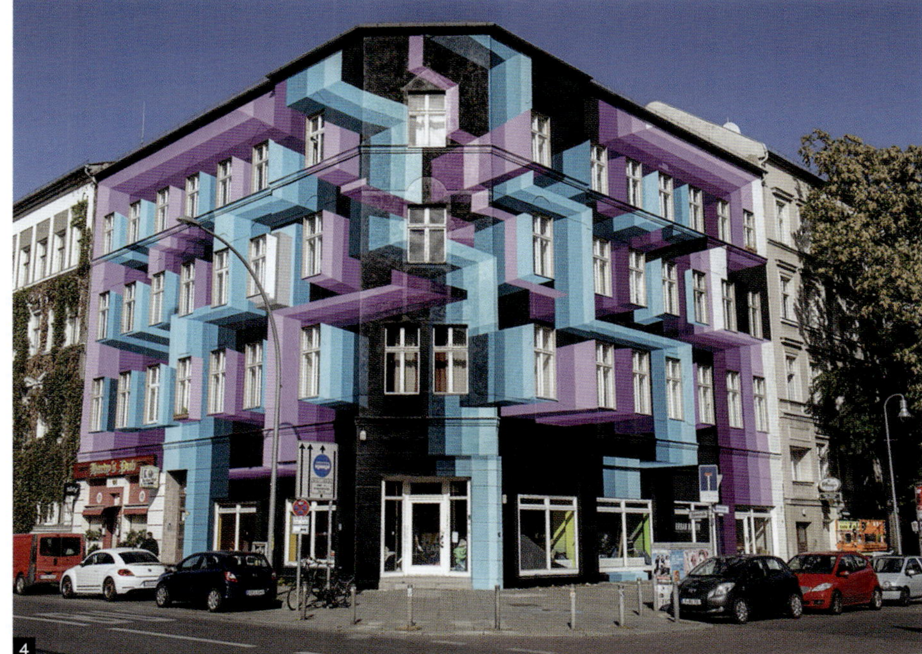

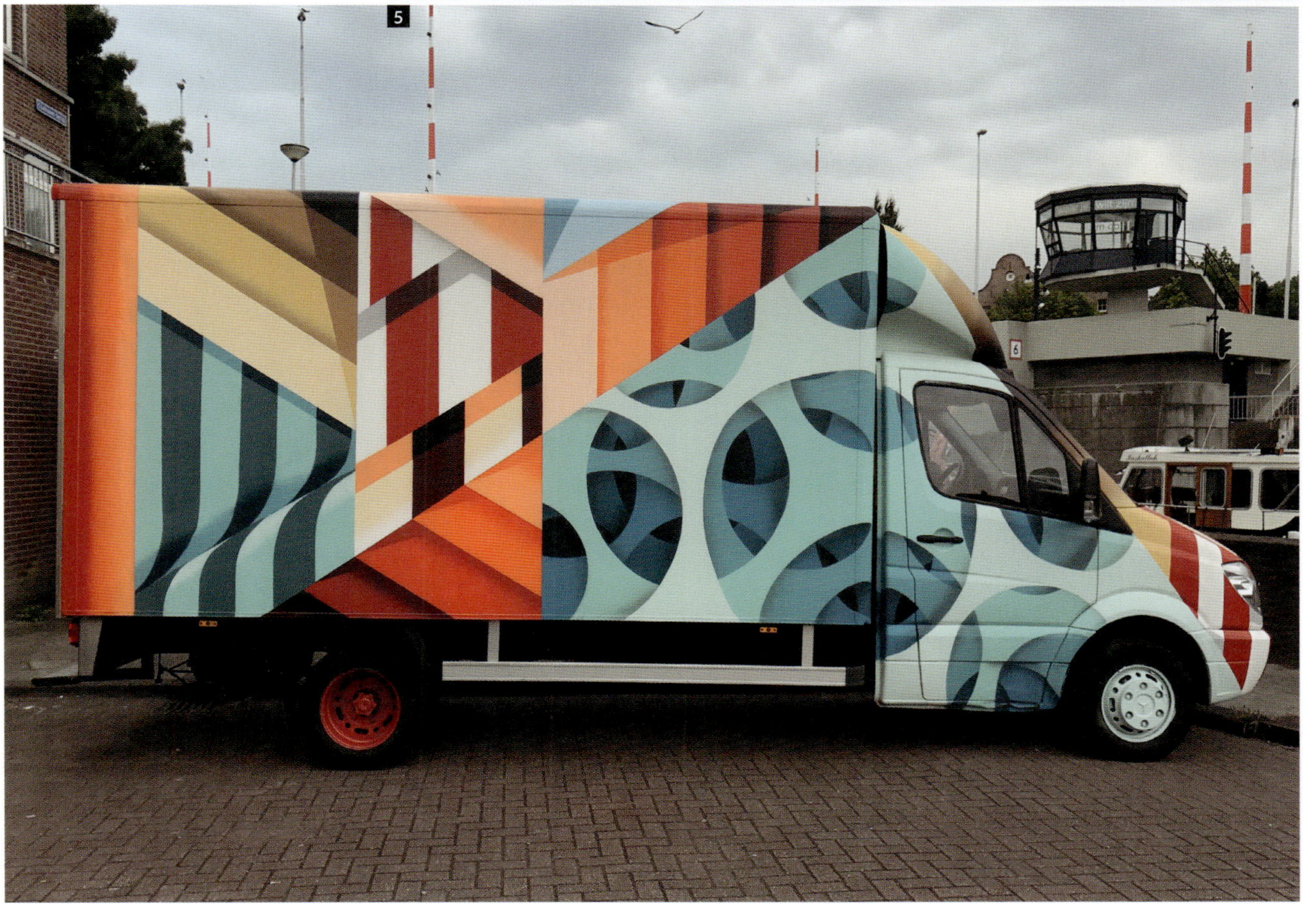

4

5

4 /
Berlin, Germany, 2018
PHOTO BY THE ARTIST

3 /
Rotterdam, The Netherlands, 2017
PHOTO BY THE ARTIST

5 /
Rotterdam, The Netherlands, 2017
PHOTO BY THE ARTIST

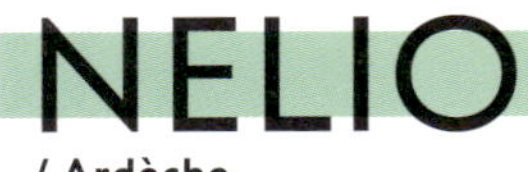

/ Ardèche

Nelio was born in France in 1982. Mainly influenced by graffiti, abstract painting, graphic design, screen-printing and architecture, this self-taught artist has developed a unique artistic approach. His early letter-based style and figurative works slowly evolved into a purely abstract universe, where primary geometric forms and unstructured lines contrast today in well-balanced compositions. Part of the specificity of Nelio's work is his unusual use of different colour palettes, from monochromatic tones to intense polychromatic compositions. Another feature is the way he mixes flat and 3D elements, creating embedded spaces that play with movement and perception.

1

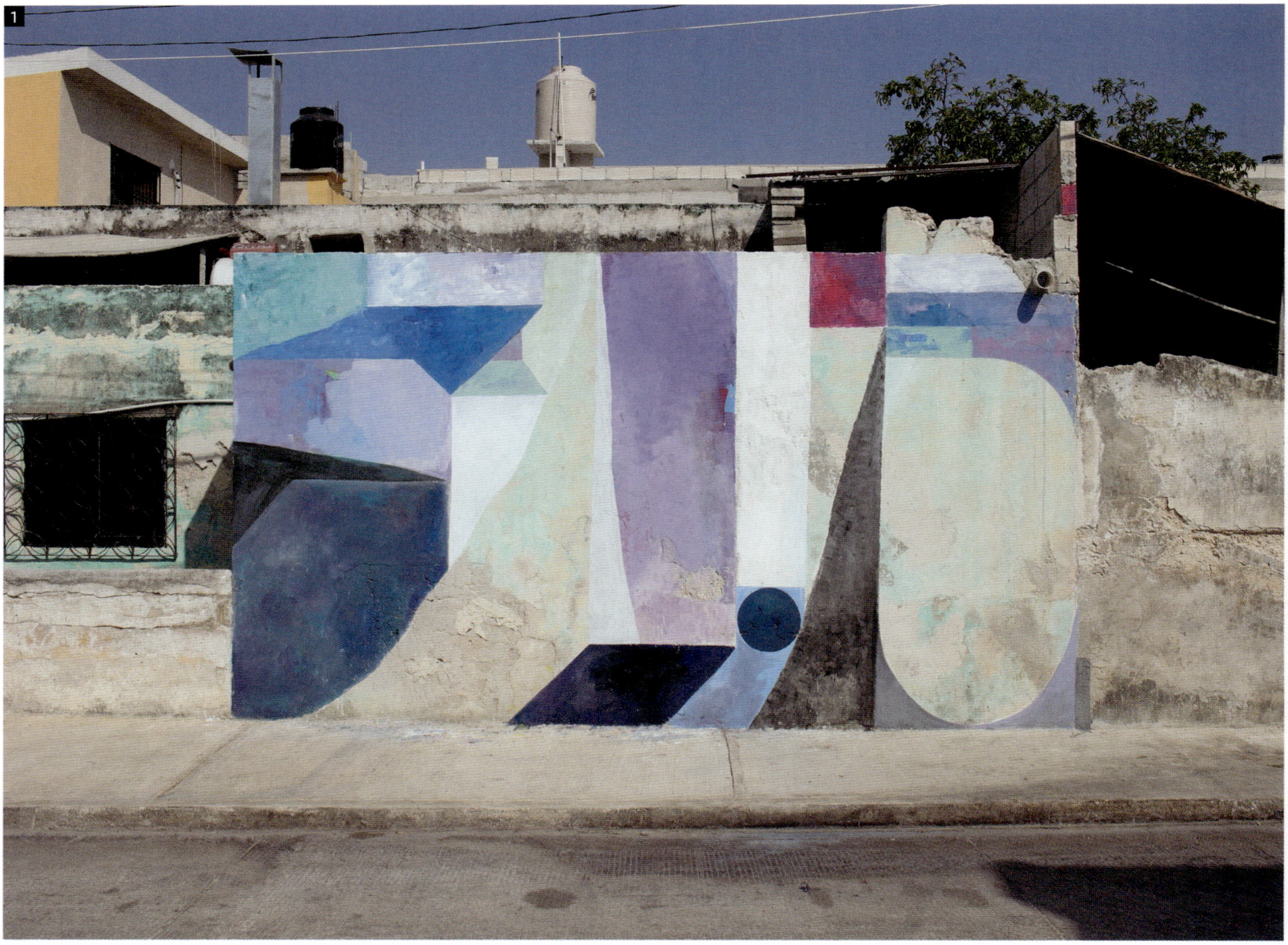

2

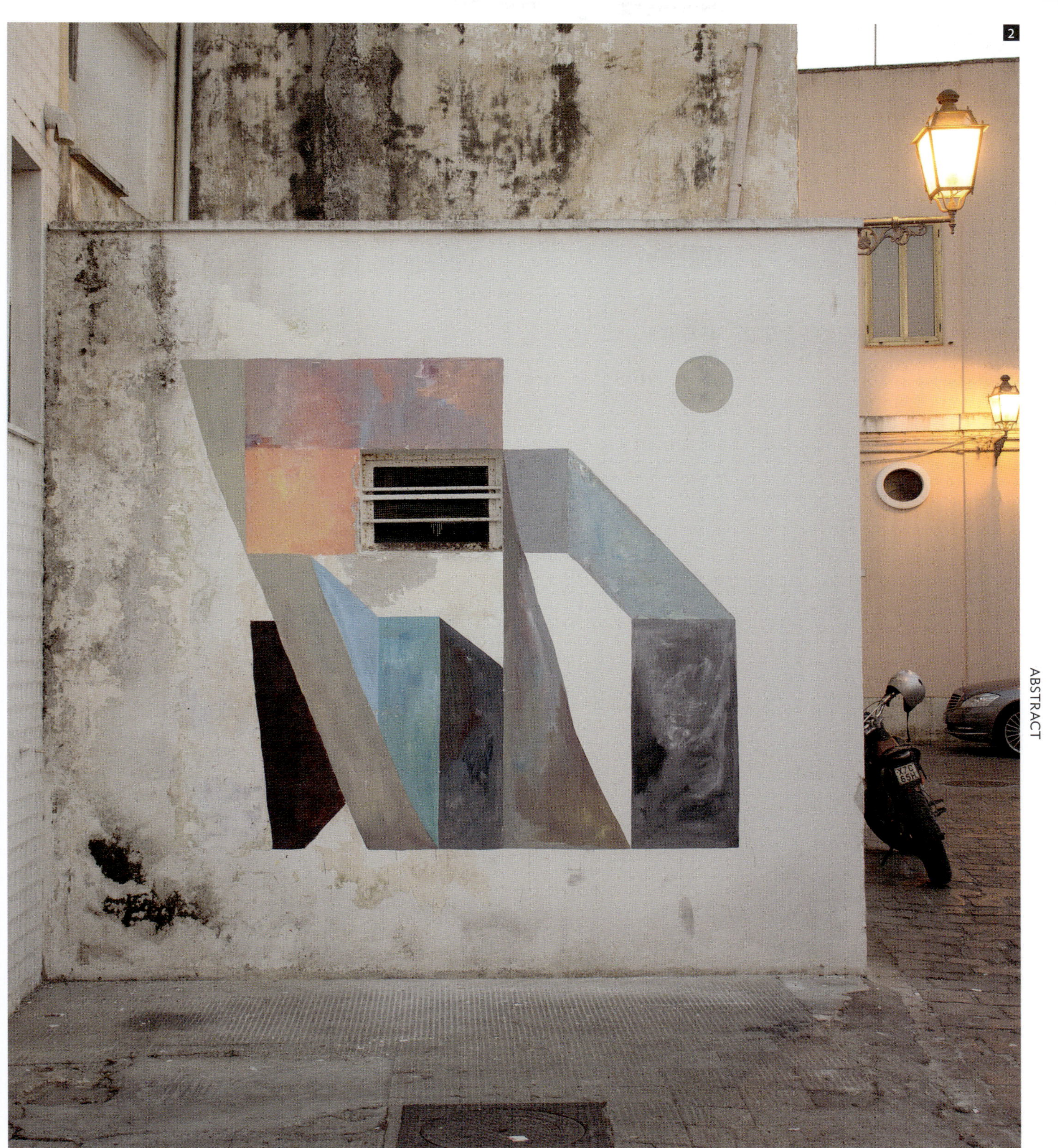

1 /
Campeche, Mexico, 2017
PHOTO BY THE ARTIST

2 /
Racale, Italy, 2017
PHOTO BY THE ARTIST

Early letter-based style and figurative works slowly evolved into a purely abstract universe.

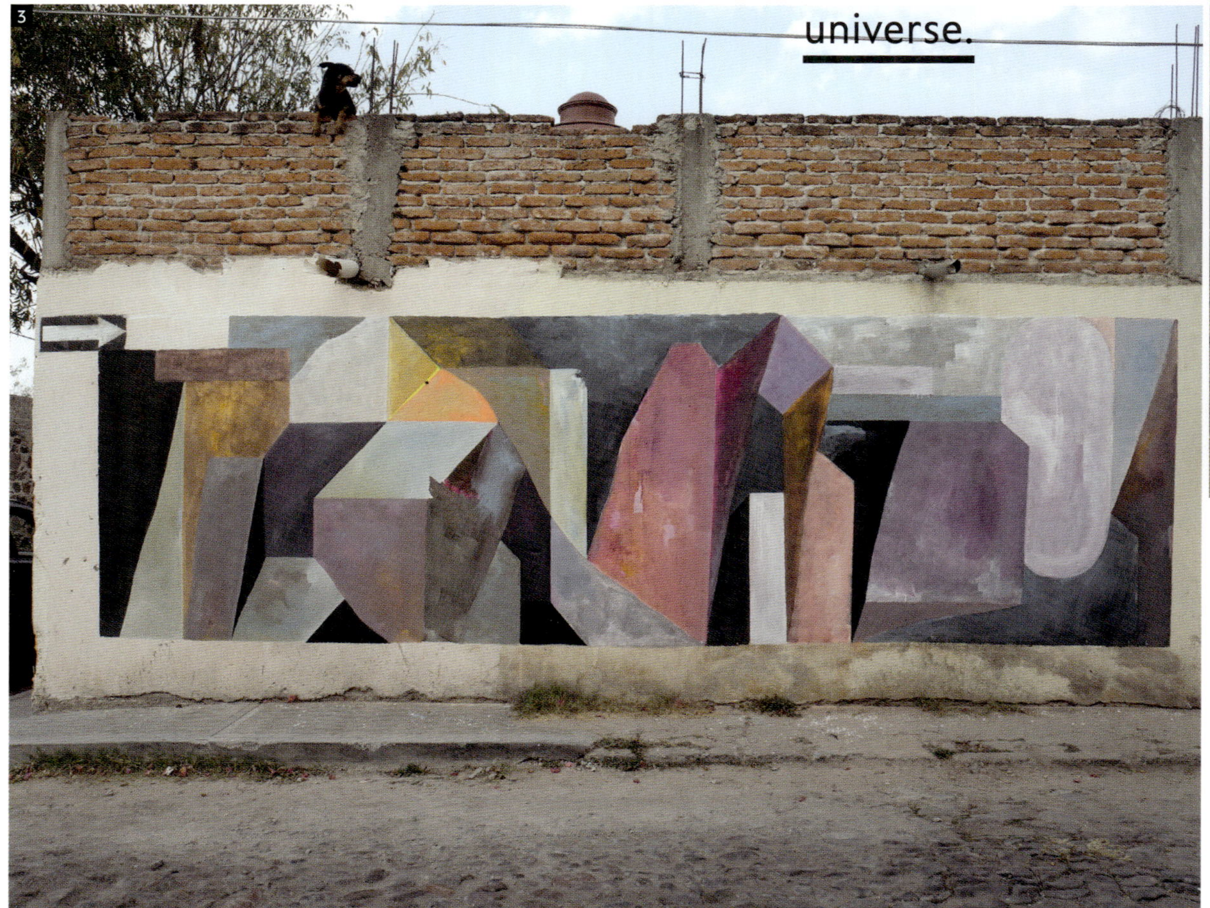

3

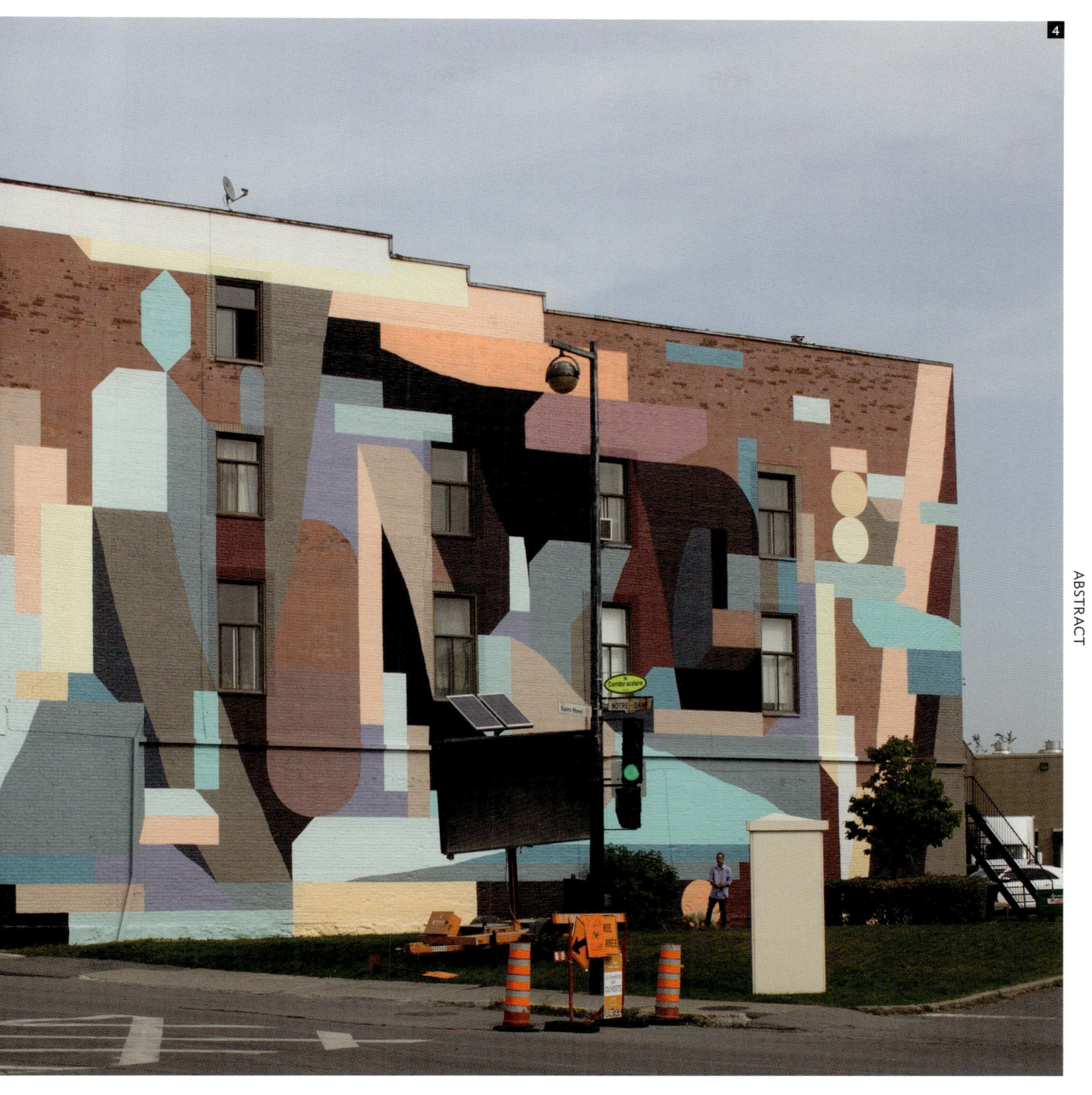

3 /
San Miguel de Allende, Mexico, 2017
PHOTO BY THE ARTIST

4 /
Montreal, Canada, 2017
PHOTO BY THE ARTIST

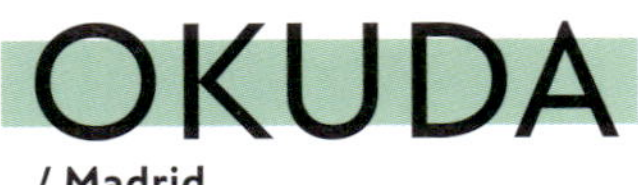

OKUDA

/ Madrid

The rainbow-coloured fireball that is Spanish artist Okuda gained some serious kudos after completing the Kaos Temple in Asturias in 2015. The 'Sistine chapel of skateboarding' was entirely covered in his signature pop-cubist characters, with the skate park becoming a pilgrimage for the street community of the region.

Over the past few years, Okuda has seemed to somehow become brighter and (if possible) even more flamboyant, with his works continuing to cover unconventional religious and public spaces. An exciting, strong development into volume-based pieces has also seen his presence in public squares and parks. The rainbows of geometric and organic shapes create a weird parallel universe: deceptively naive, and disconcertingly loud.

His works create a weird parallel universe: deceptively naive, and disconcertingly loud.

1

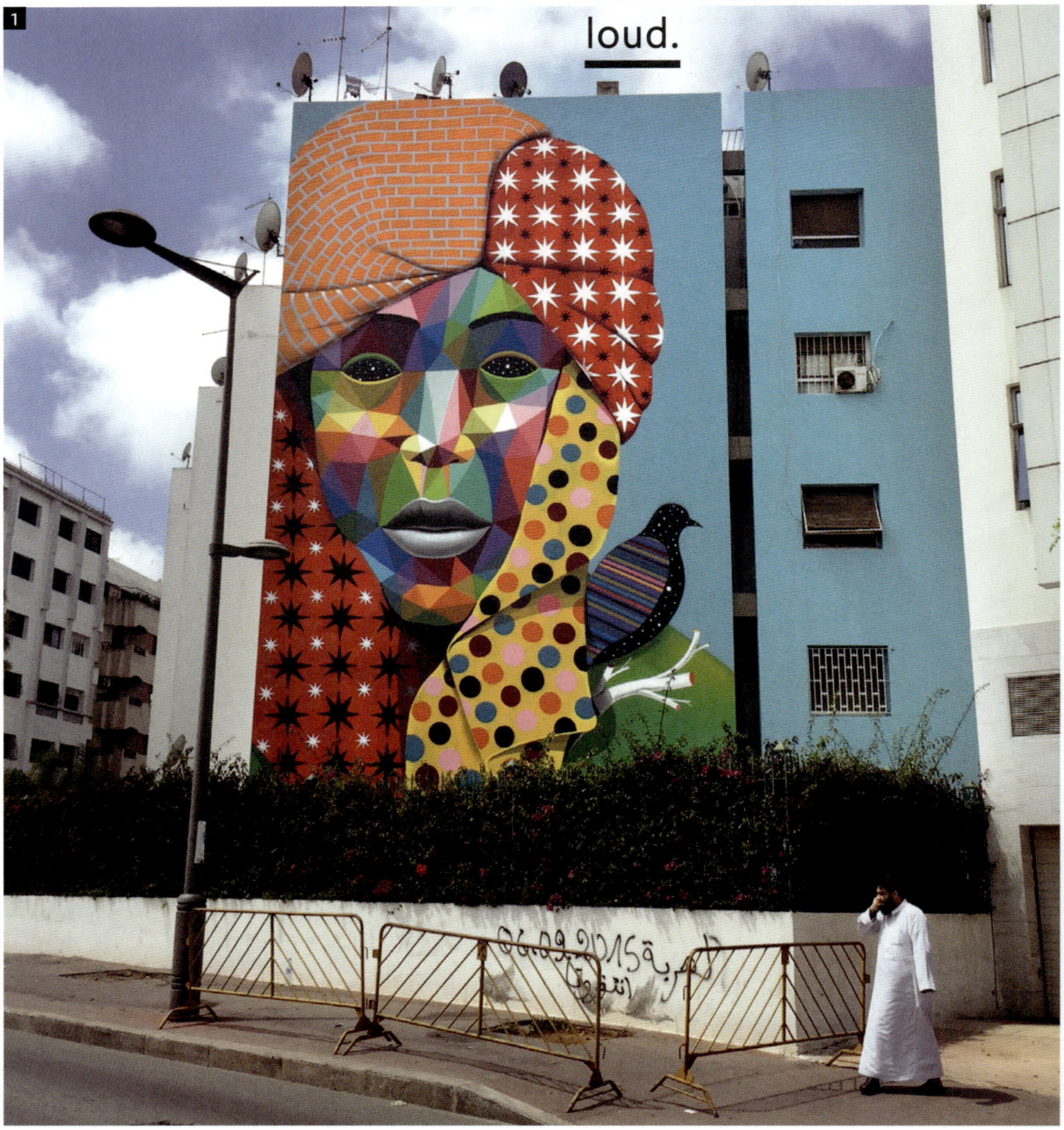

1 /
Rabat, Morocco, 2016
PHOTO BY THE ARTIST

2 /
Toronto, Canada, 2018
PHOTO BY THE ARTIST

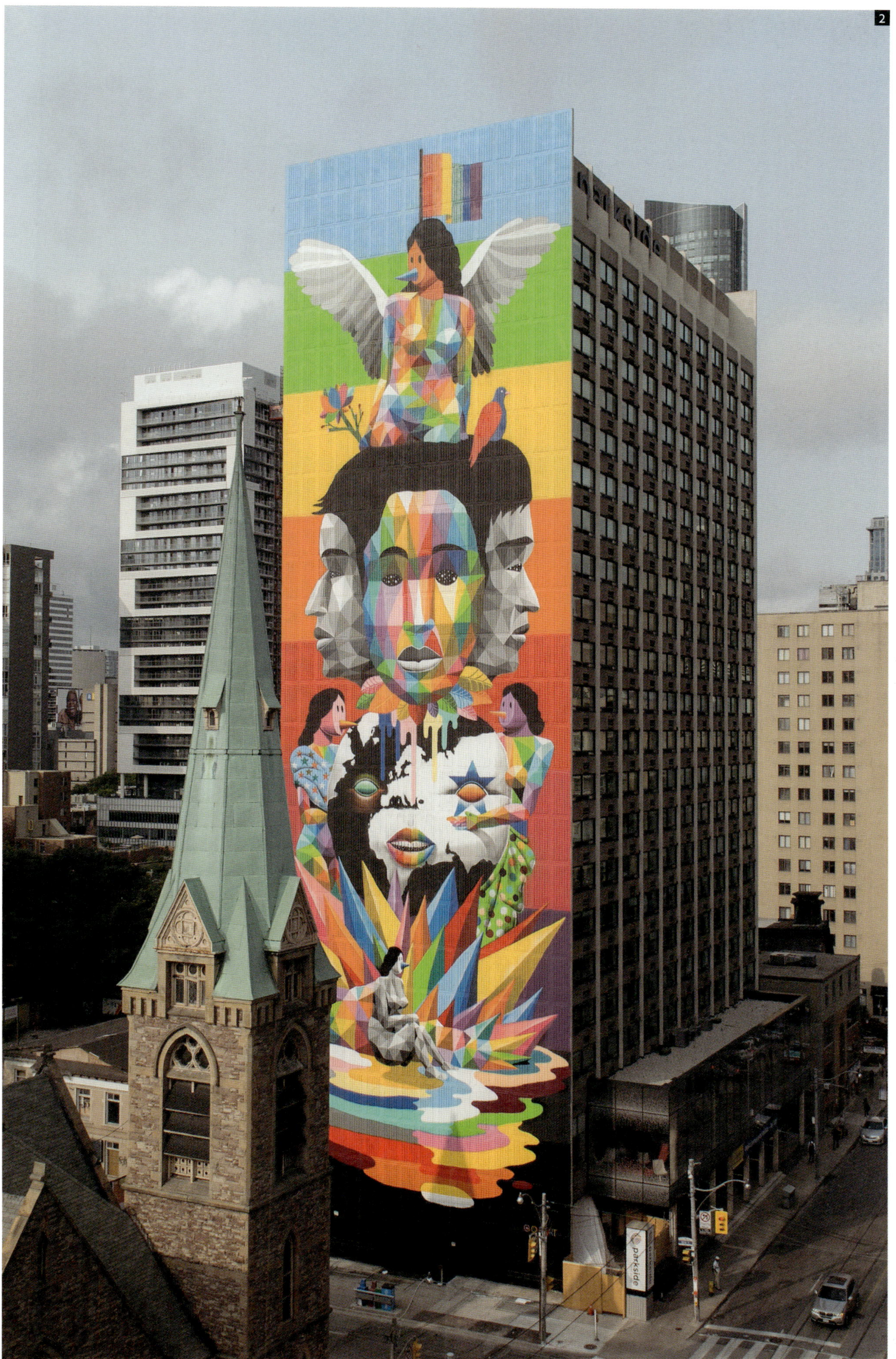
2
parkside

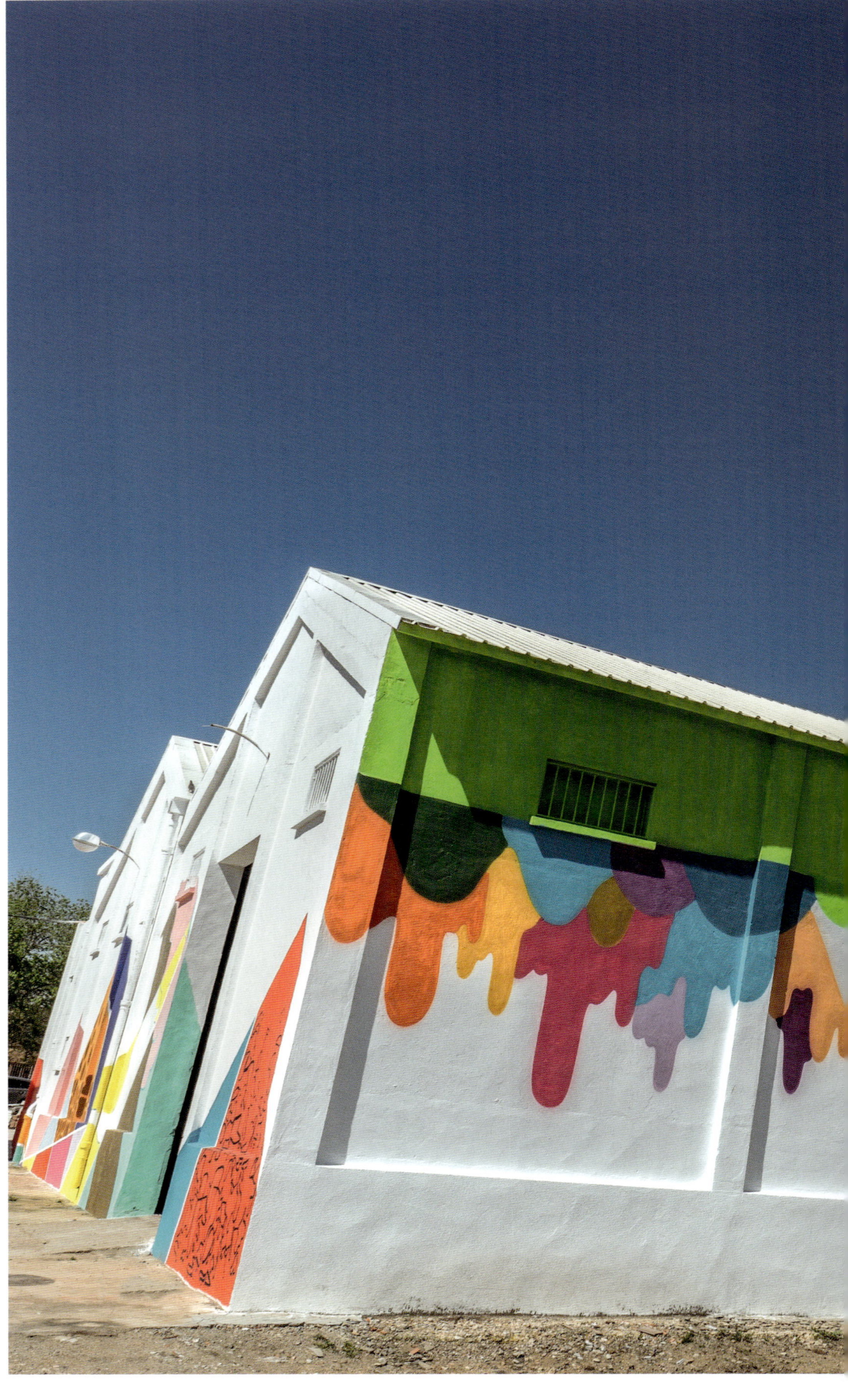

3 /
Calzada de Calatrava, Spain, 2019
PHOTO BY THE ARTIST

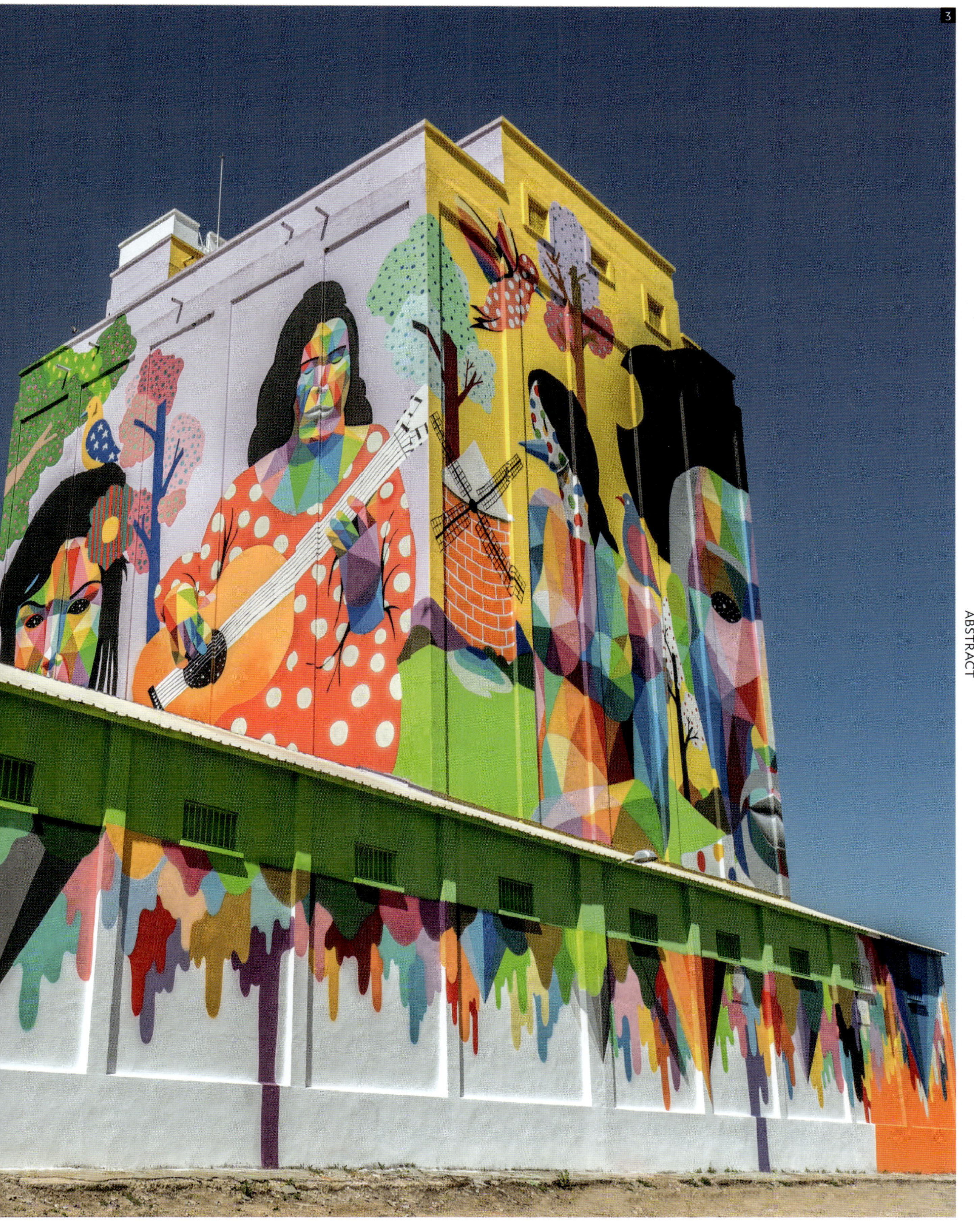

3

ABSTRACT

ROBERTO CIREDZ

/ Sardinia

Roberto's unique approach to observing space has seen him move drastically away from his previously figurative style to a systematic, near-scientific analysis of topography and the natural environment. He observes and analyses shapes and textures, reproducing colour schemes present in the organic and transforming them into a visual language of geometry and monochromatic panels.

The relationship between humans and nature is central to Roberto's work. With a special interest in materials, he ponders urban (originally organic) materials such as stone and cement to inform his work. Predominantly working on murals, he also produces installations and sculptures, both in urban settings and isolated landscapes.

The relationship between humans and nature is central to Roberto's work.

1

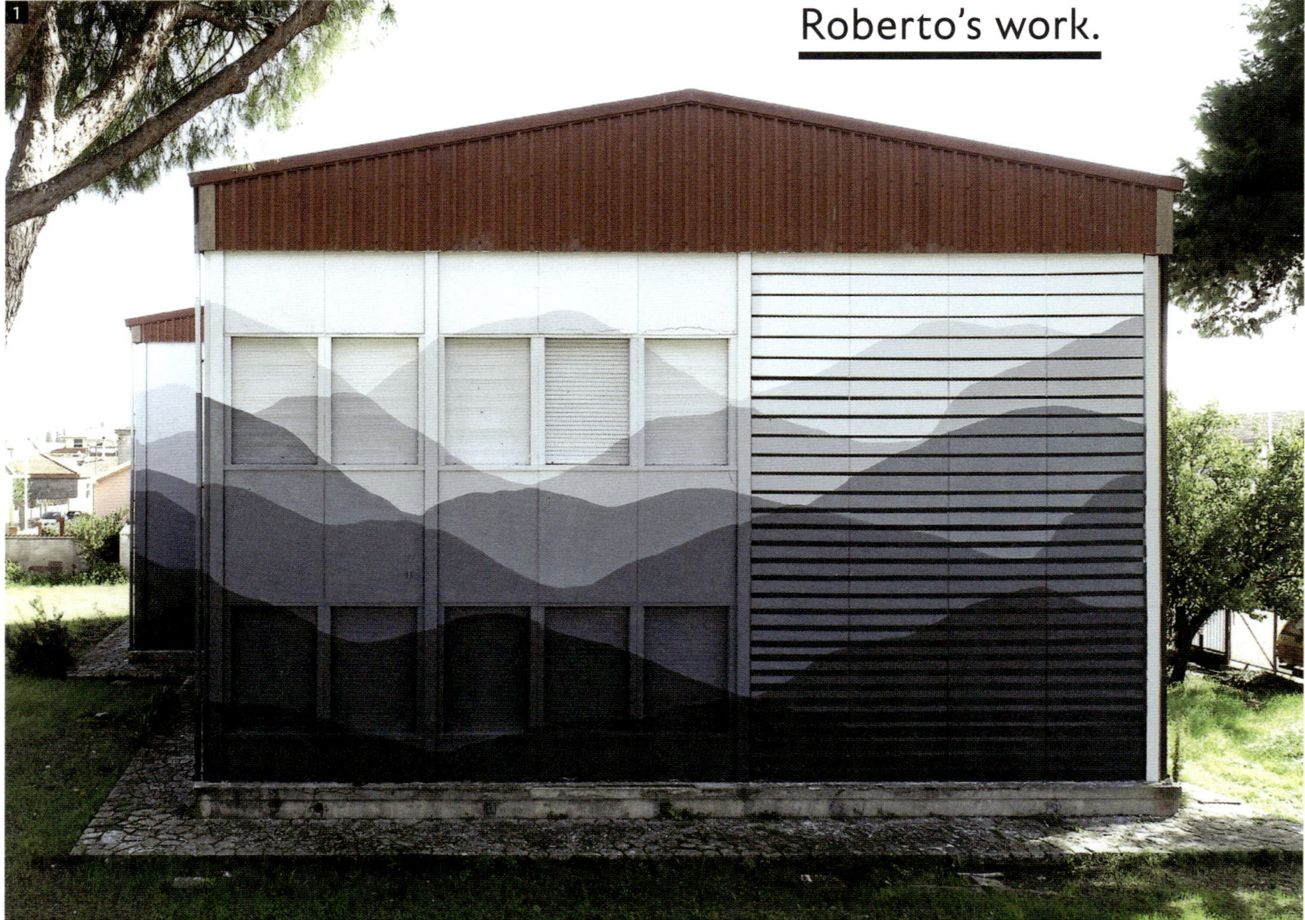

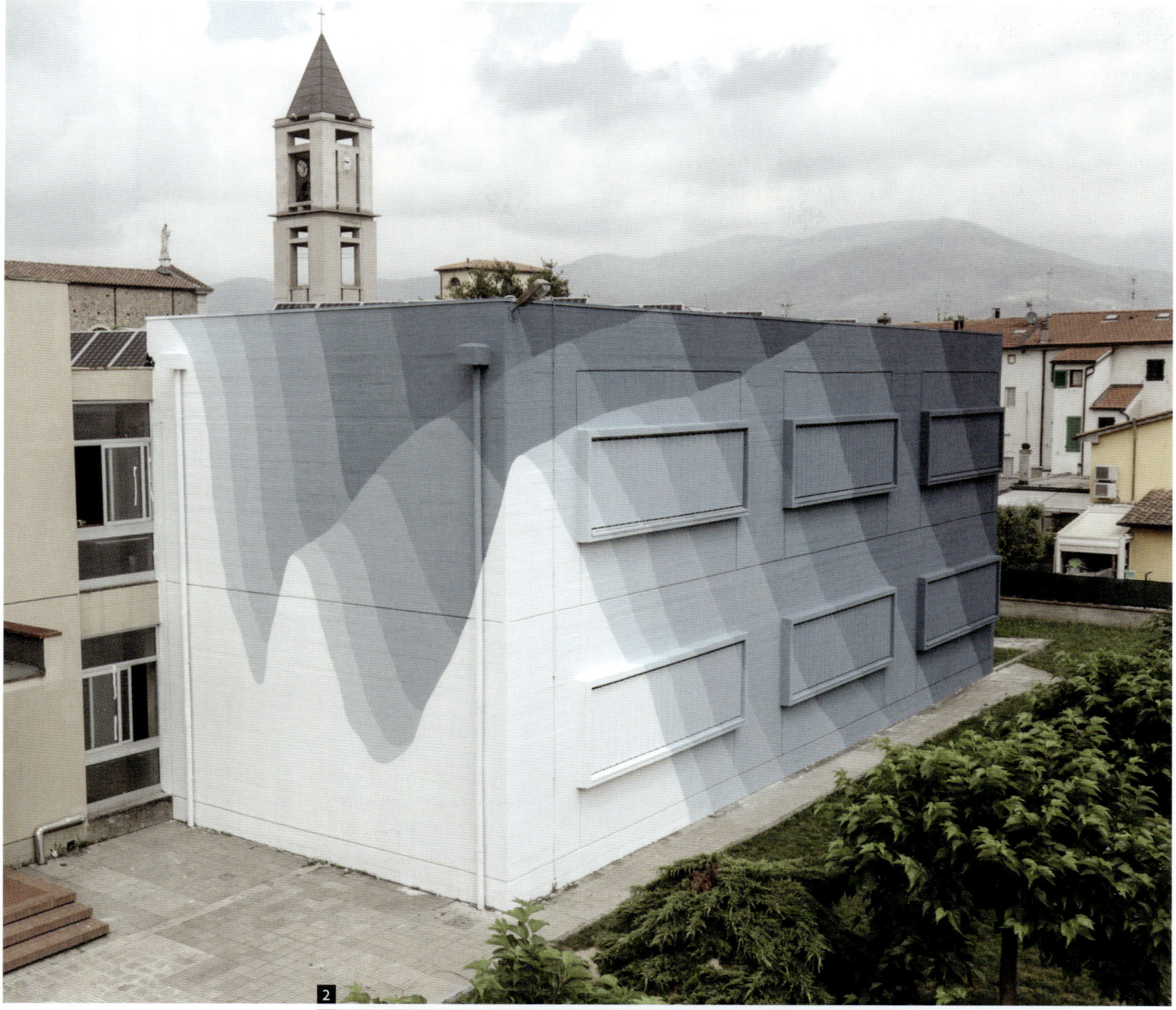

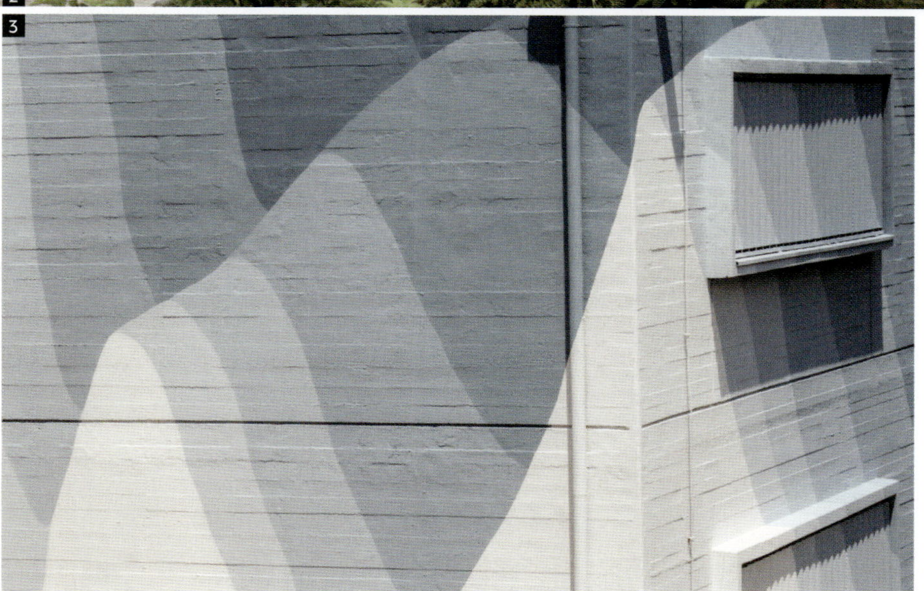

1 /
San Gavino Monreale, Italy, 2018
PHOTO BY THE ARTIST

2 / 3
Agliana, Italy, 2018
PHOTO BY THE ARTIST

With a special interest in materials, he ponders urban materials such as stone and cement to inform his work.

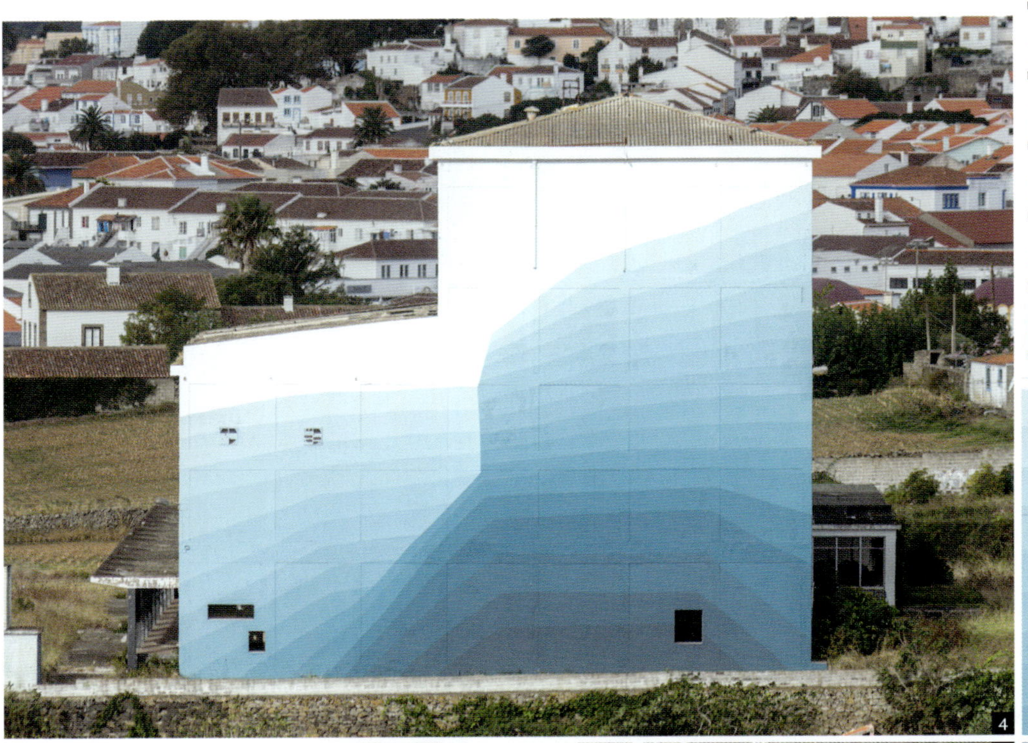

4

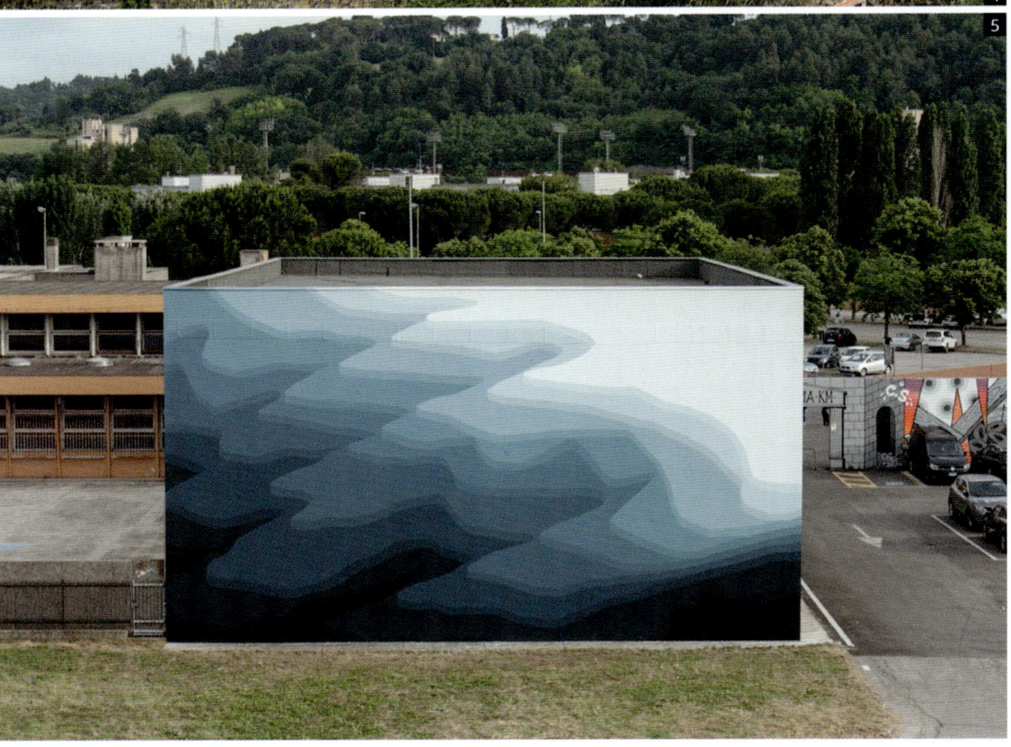

5

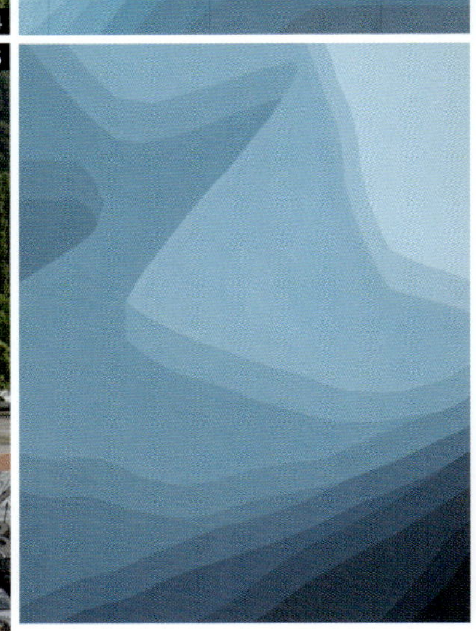

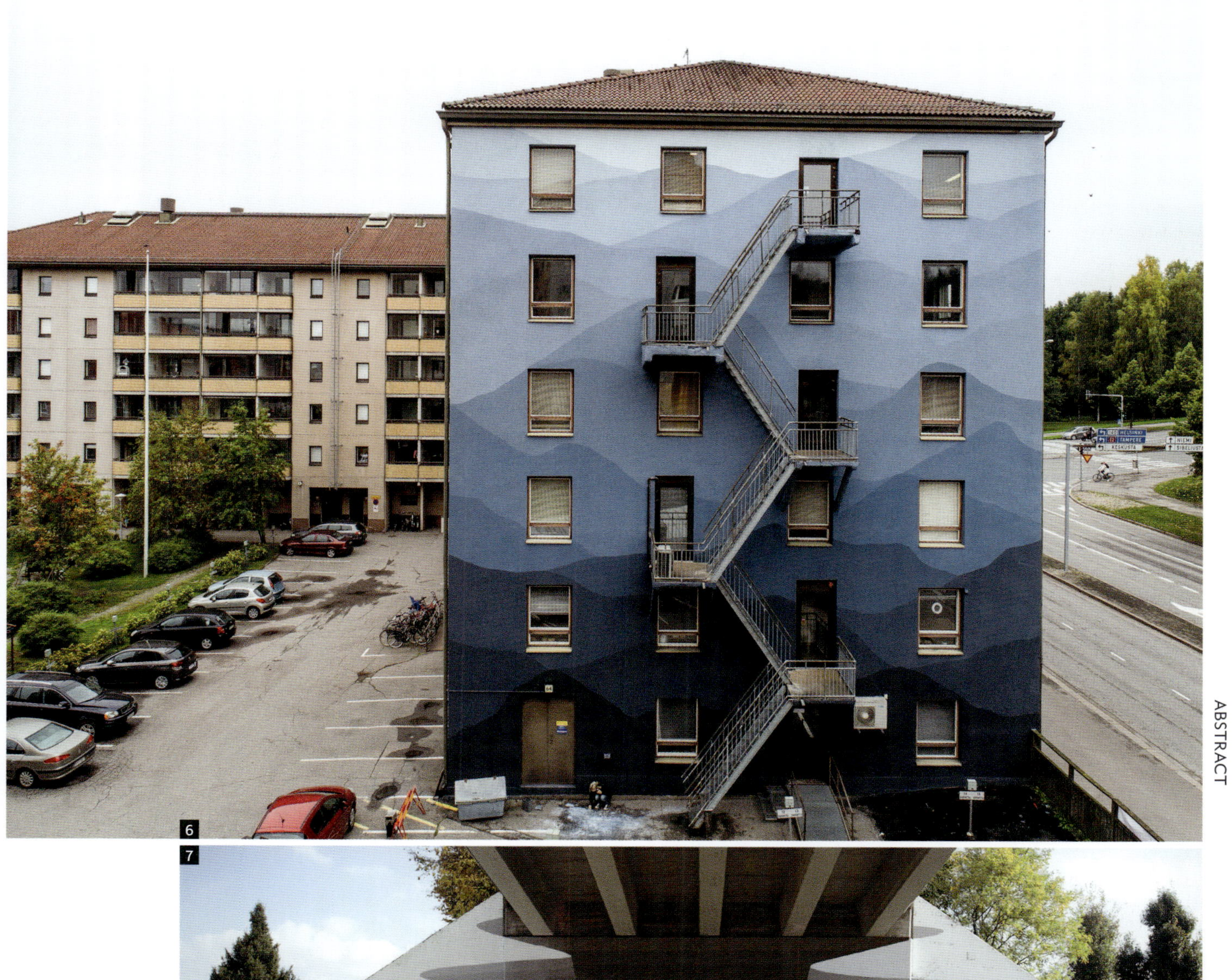

4 / 5
Angra do Heroísmo, Italy, 2017
PHOTO BY THE ARTIST

6 /
Lahti, Italy, 2017
PHOTO BY THE ARTIST

7 /
Lahti, Italy, 2017
PHOTO BY THE ARTIST

2/

FIGU- RATIVE

ALEX SENNA
ALICE PASQUINI
ANDREA WAN
ARYZ
BELIN
CINTA VIDAL
MILU CORRECH
ESCIF
FAITH47
FINTAN MAGEE
HERAKUT
HYURO
JAZ
LOW BROS
PAOLA DELFÍN
SAINER
SETH GLOBEPAINTER
SHERYO & YOK

FIGURATION, OFTEN POISED at the opposite end of the spectrum from abstract art, is understood as creative output that makes direct reference to reality – be it an object, landscape or person. Since the beginning of art production, figuration has been a common rite of passage for most artists, not only as a means of developing technique but also in order to articulate the process of appropriation and representation. By observing, translating and presenting a take on reality, artists position themselves in the art landscape, engaging in meaningful discussions with their audience and the world around them.

In the public domain, contemporary figurative art takes on a huge variety of forms, from 'classic' painterly portraiture in the cases of Fintan Magee or Hyuro, to Cinta Vidal's recomposed urbanscapes, to Jaz's man/beast creations. Representational artists often hold discourse on social issues, directly representing the community concerned in their works and therefore easily communicating messages to the greater public.

A group of 18 strong artists are presented here in the chapter on figurative art. Our largest group, and debatably the most established in terms of career narrative, these artists display with spectacular force the creative variations possible in the street art world. We continue to be impressed by the innovative trajectory of the long-running stars, with Faith47 taking a fresh route towards experimental collaborations, Aryz continuing to reinvent his technique with incredible detail and class, and of course Low Bros, Fintan Magee, Escif and Sainer, all long-standing creative pioneers whom we look up to for their constant development of style.

In this particular selection, you will notice a ratio of women that is much higher than the norm, with more than half of the artists female. It would be a fine world if we did not have to point this out, but the industry of art is still one of disparity between genders. Our selection highlights, through the voices of Milu Correch and Hyuro, an attempt to contribute to a global movement towards gender equality in the industry. We believe this grows more and more possible as industry leaders demand more equitable practice and these incredible artists become strong role models for the younger generations of creatives.

ALEX SENNA

/ Sao Paulo

Few artists today aspire to such sincerity and genuine compassion for his fellow human as does Alex Senna. His illustration-style black-and-white street sketches portray people in the everyday. With positively endearing snippets of love, embrace, romance and tenderness, he demonstrates kindness and empathy. Rumoured to be colour-blind, Alex is self-taught and hardworking, having painted in the streets, galleries and studio for over ten years.

Often drawing inspiration from narratives of family and friends, Alex also presents wider concerns of the São Paulo community, one of disparity and contrast. His characters often take a larger-than-life presence with the simple use of shadowing, rendering an everyday scene suddenly spectacular. Alex talks of universal emotions, reminding us of the extraordinary in the ordinary and of moments that unite us all as human.

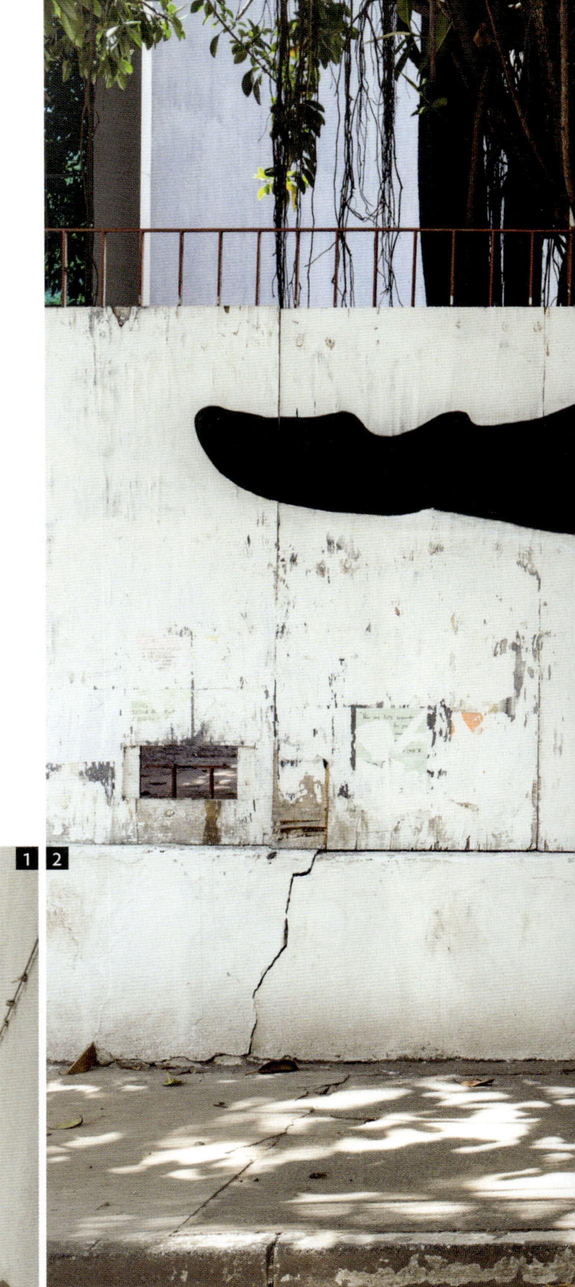

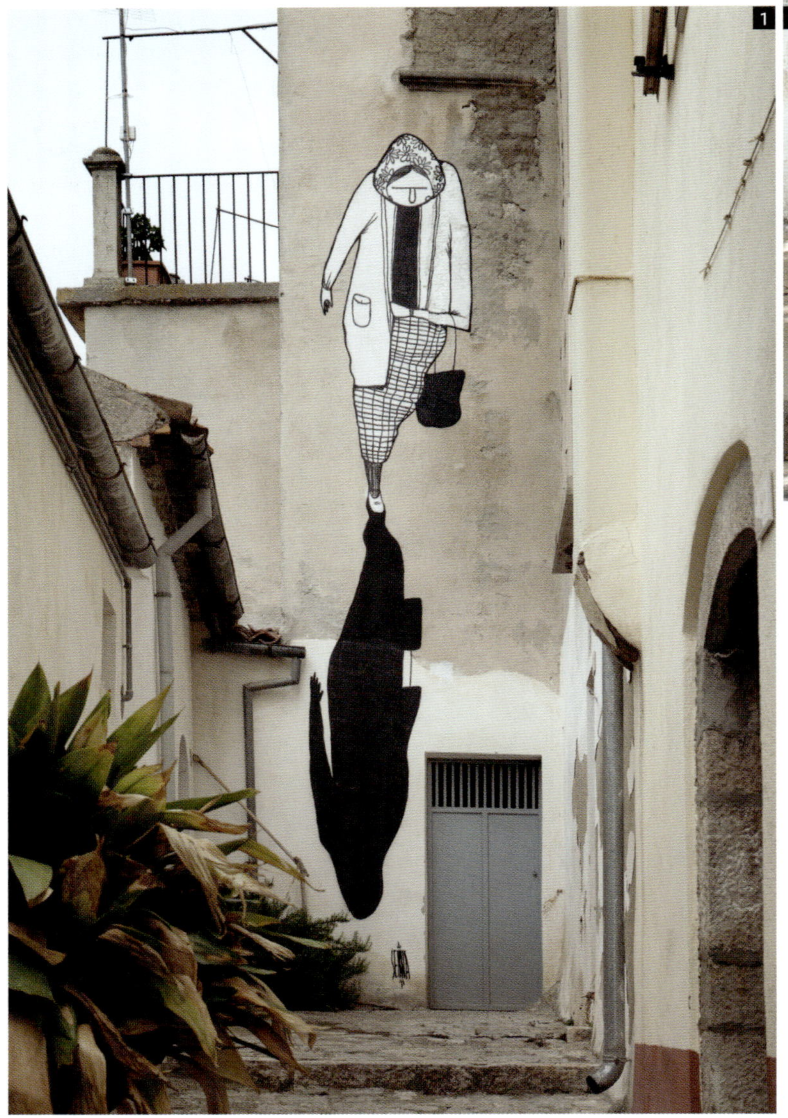

1 2

1 /
Civita Campomarano, Molise, Italy, 2017
PHOTO BY THE ARTIST

2 /
Civita Campomarano, Molise, Italy, 2017
PHOTO BY RODRIGO ERIB

3 /
Civita Campomarano, Molise, Italy, 2019
PHOTO BY THE ARTIST

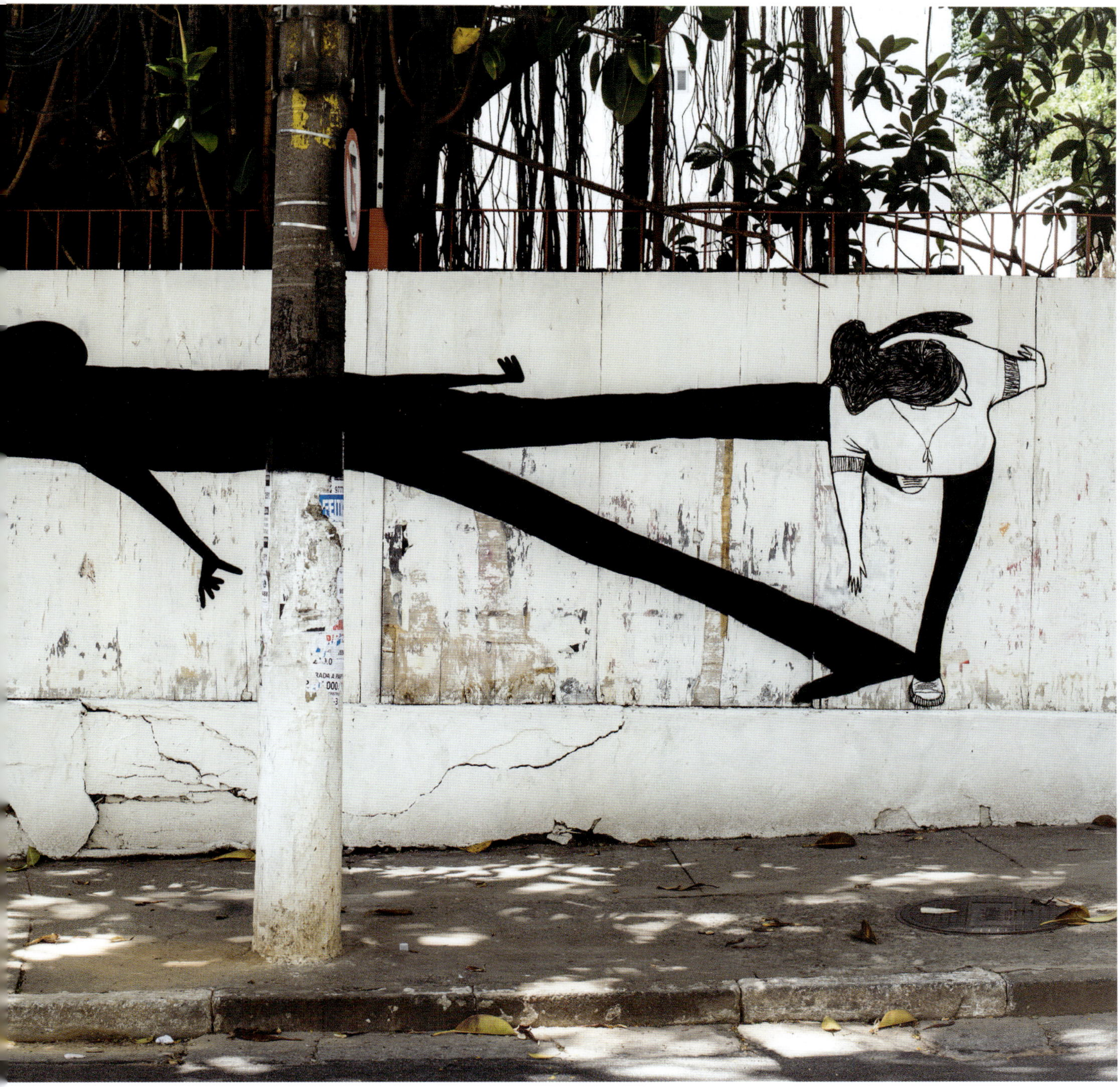

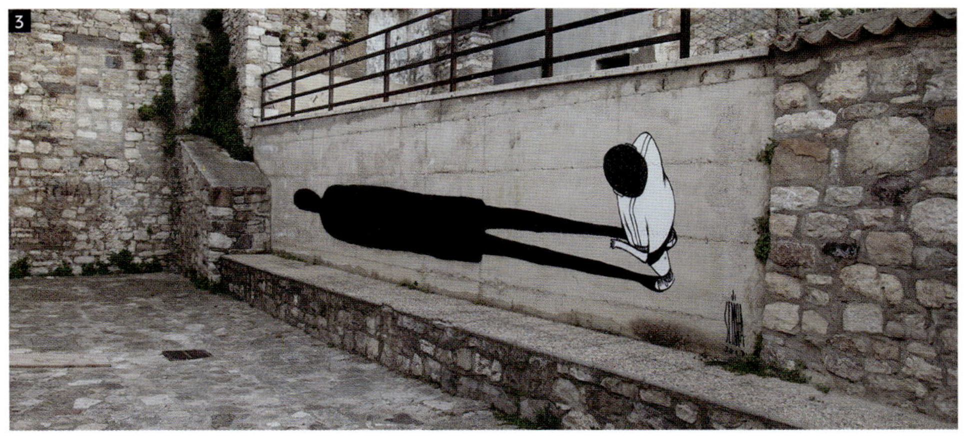

3

His characters often take a larger-than-life presence with the simple use of shadowing.

4

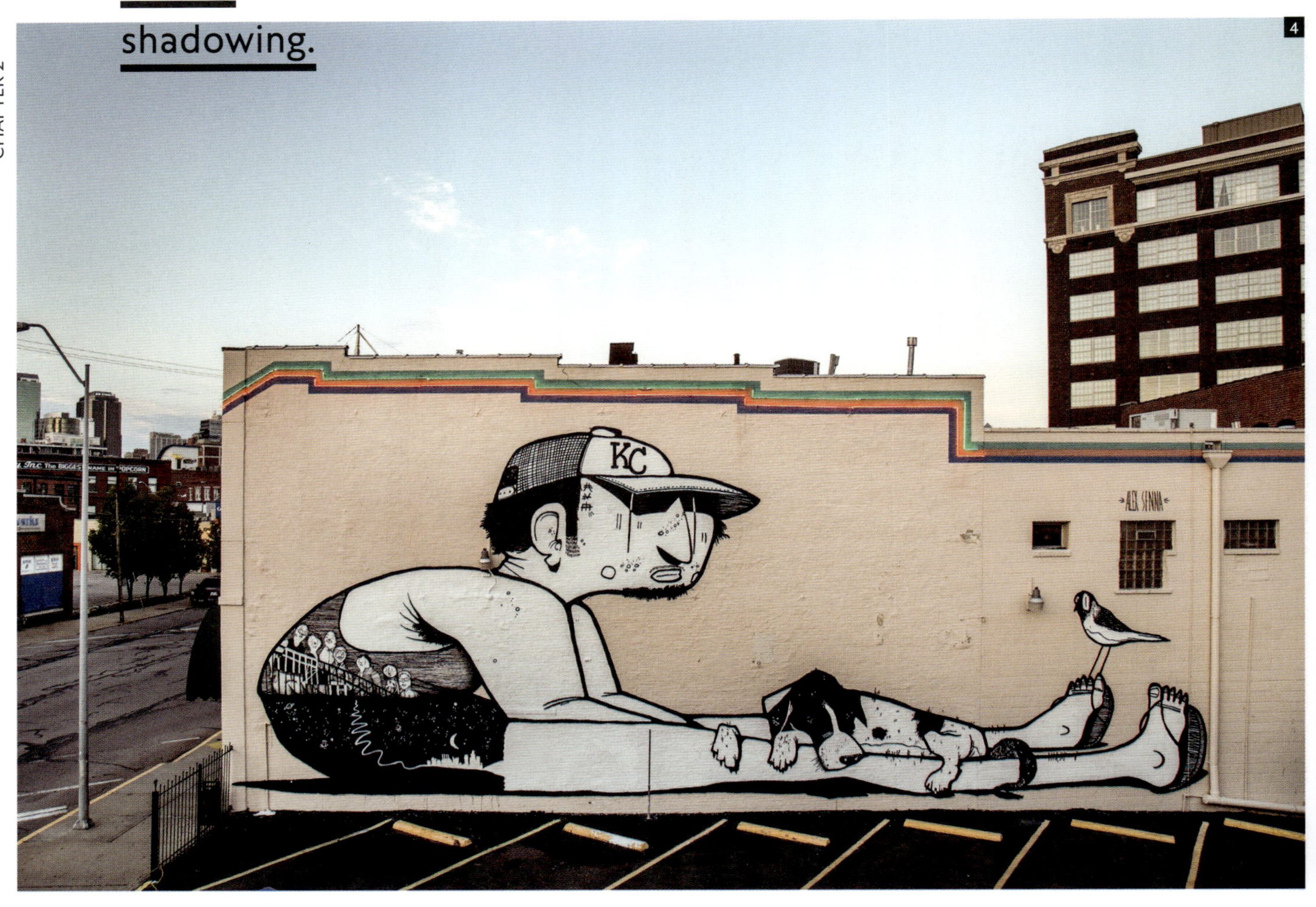

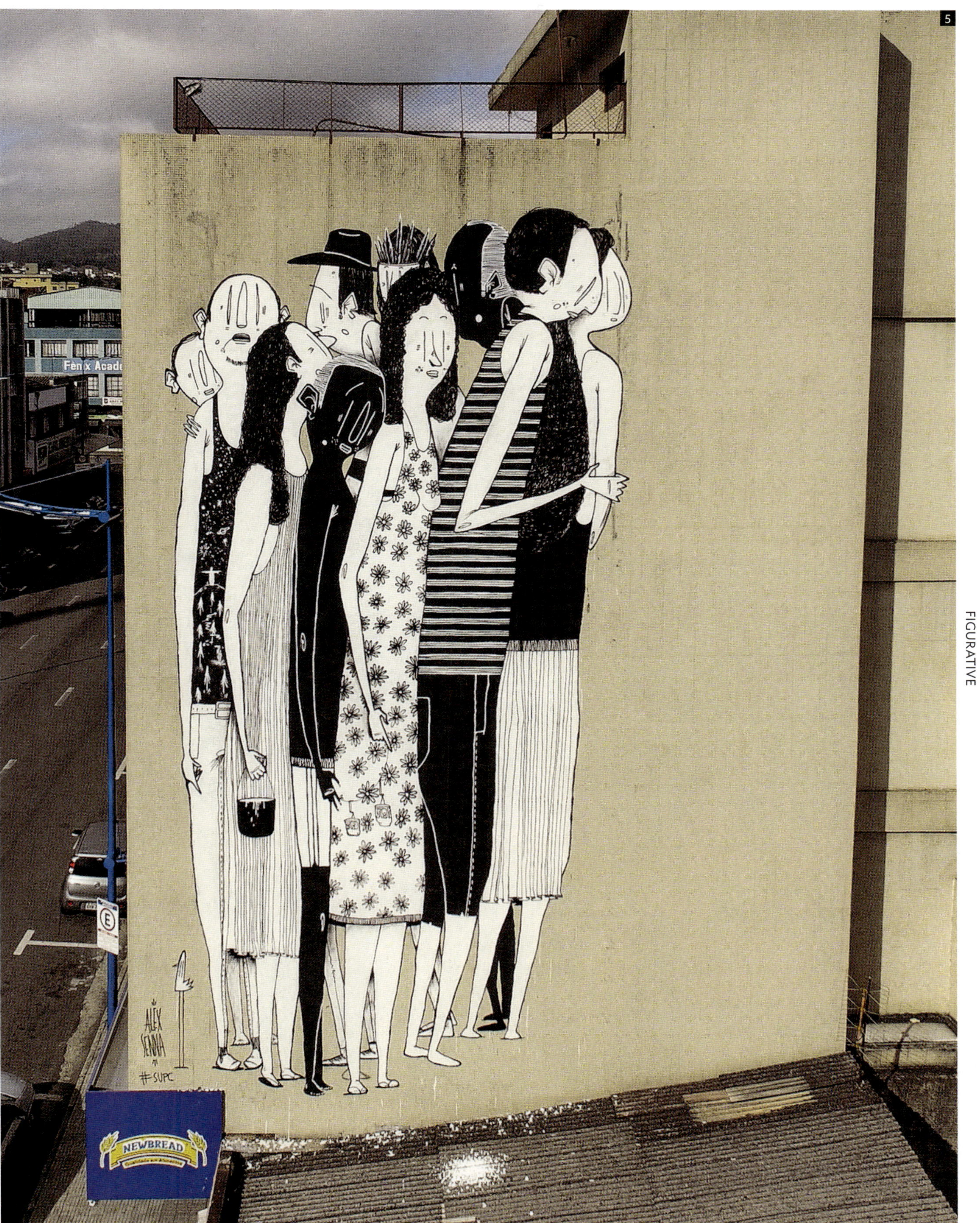

4 /
Kansas City, Missouri, USA, 2018
PHOTO BY THE ARTIST

5 /
Poços de Caldas, Brazil, 2018
PHOTO BY THE ARTIST

ALICE PASQUINI

/ Rome

Alice Pasquini first developed her work in an academic context, spending many years in art schools. With a master's degree in art criticism behind her, she rebelled against the elitist approach of her professors and made the move from classroom to street. With hundreds of works spread across the globe, Alice sees herself as a contextual artist, making careful consideration of the textural and architectural placement of her pieces.

Exploring portraiture primarily, Alice is interested in everyday moments, casual encounters and the human emotions that transcend geography and time.

1

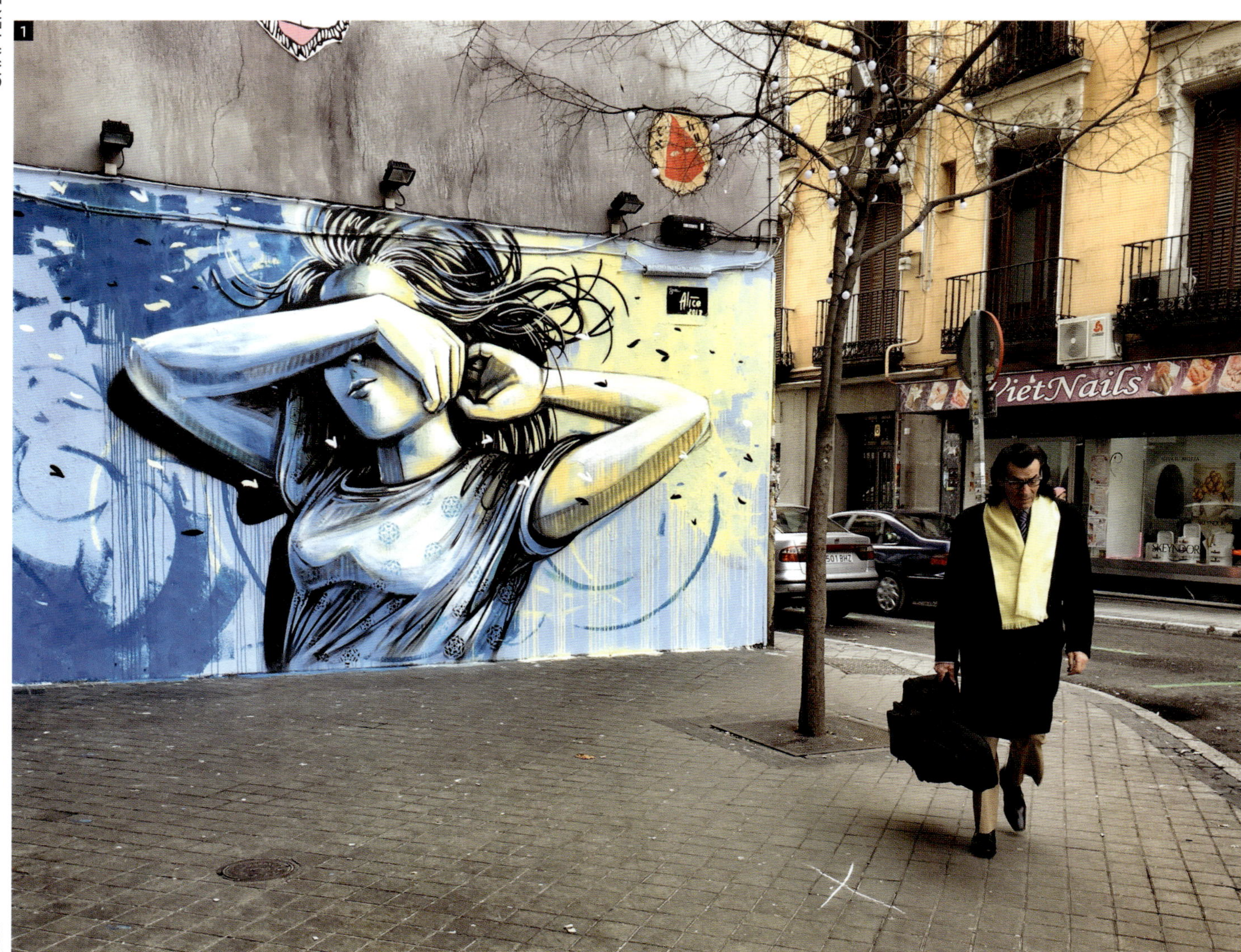

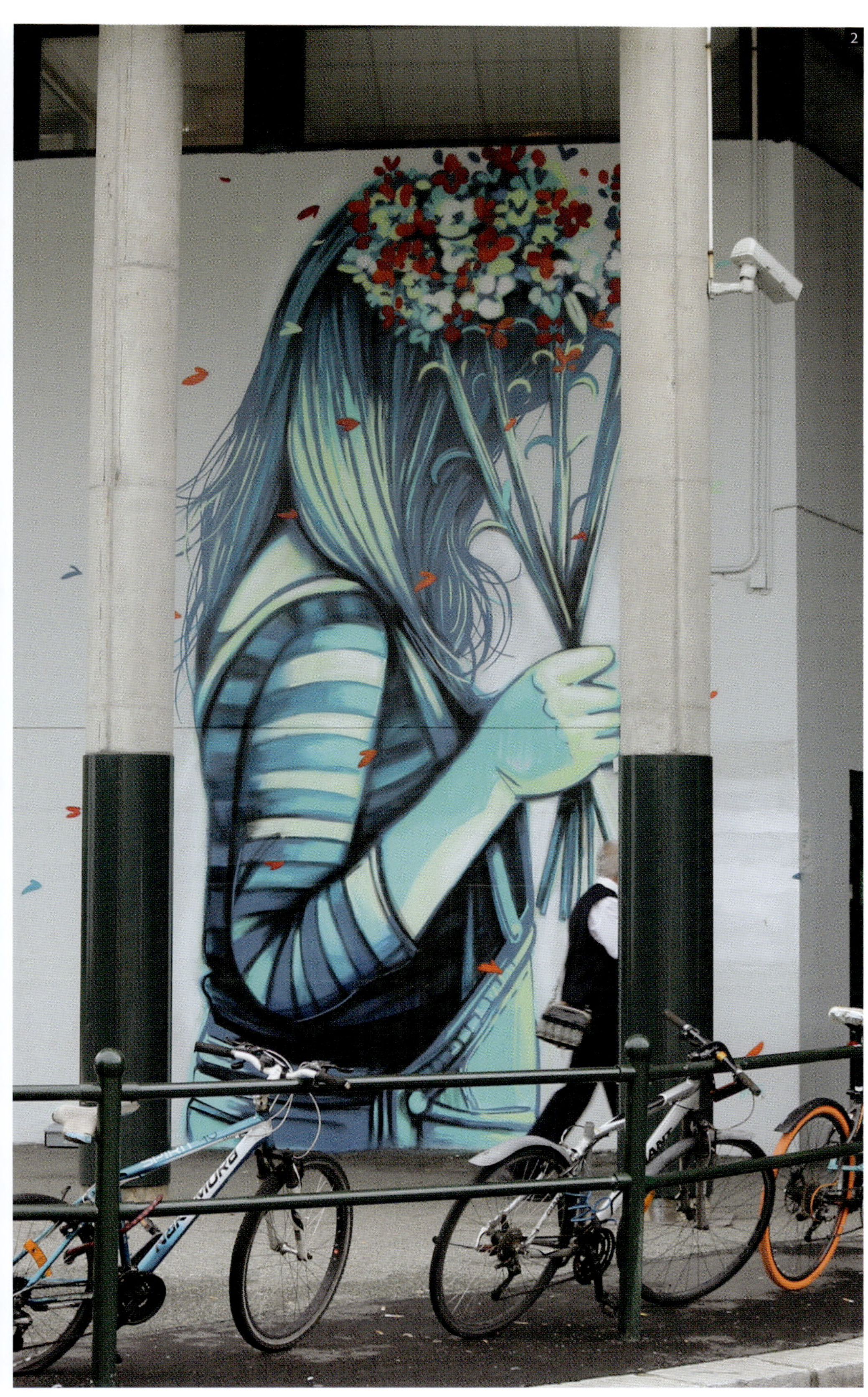

1 /
Madrid, Spain, 2017
PHOTO BY THE ARTIST

2 /
Stavanger, Norway, 2018
PHOTO BY THE ARTIST

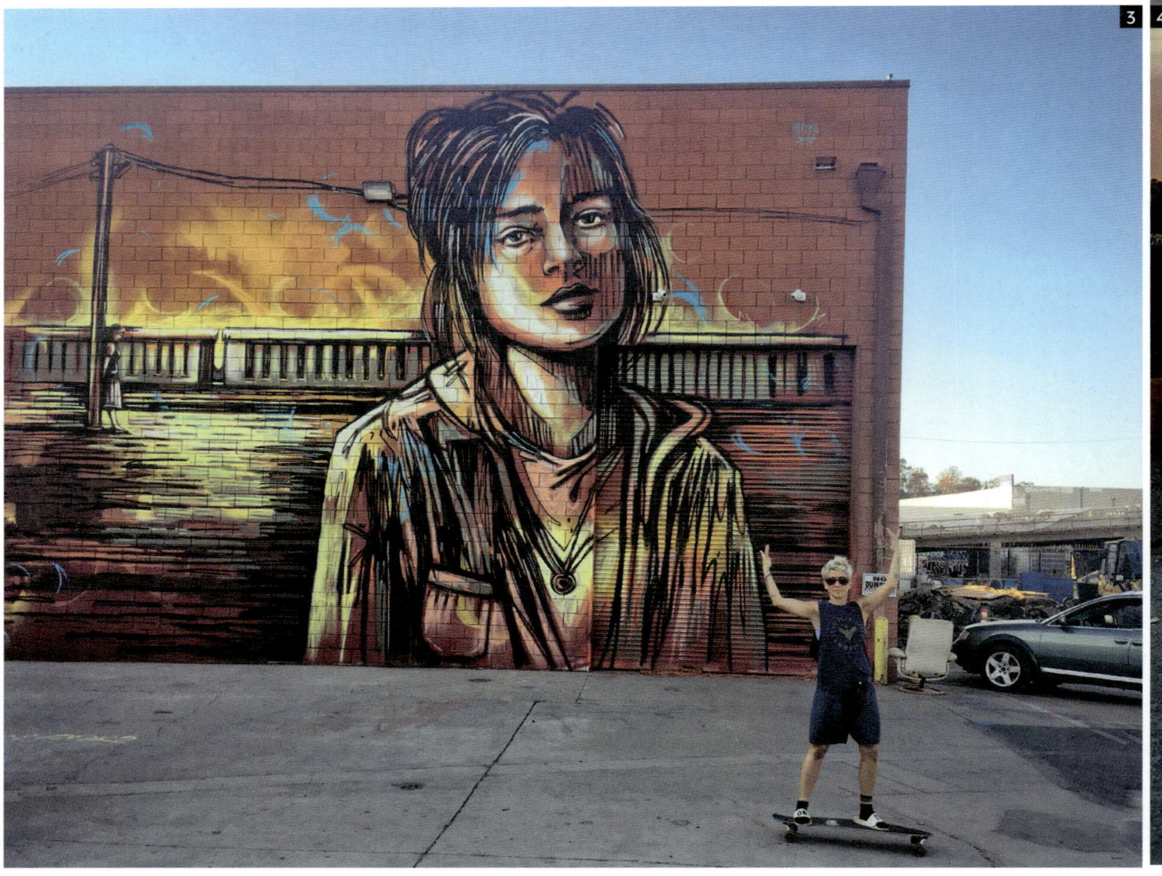

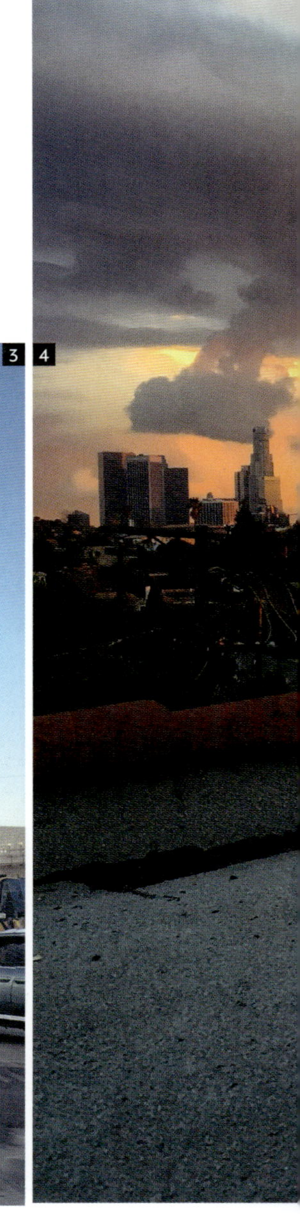

3 /
Los Angeles, California, USA, 2017
PHOTO BY THE ARTIST

4 /
Silver Lake, Los Angeles, USA, 2019
PHOTO BY THE ARTIST

5 /
Hamburg, Germany, 2016
PHOTO BY THE ARTIST

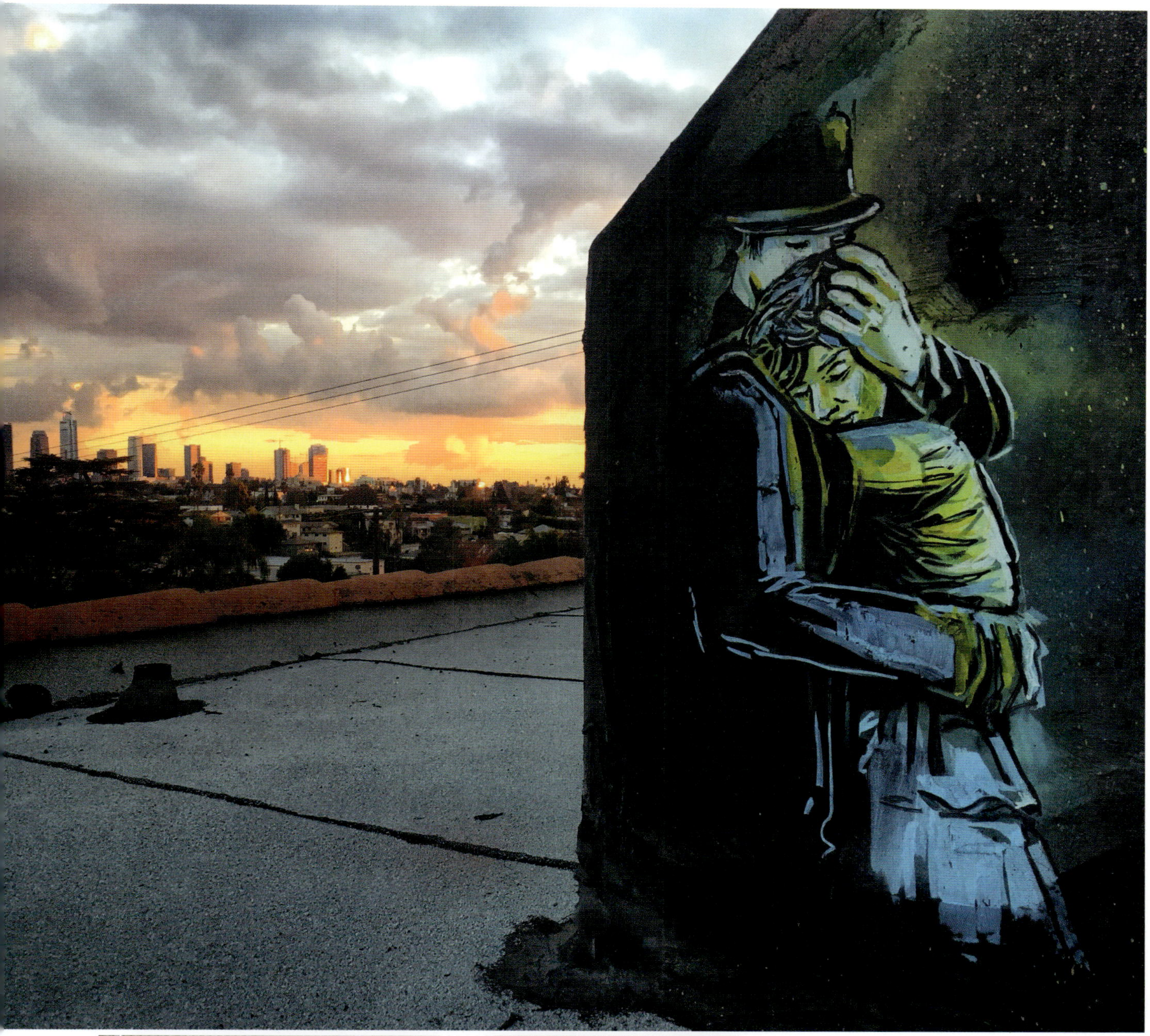

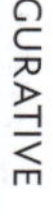

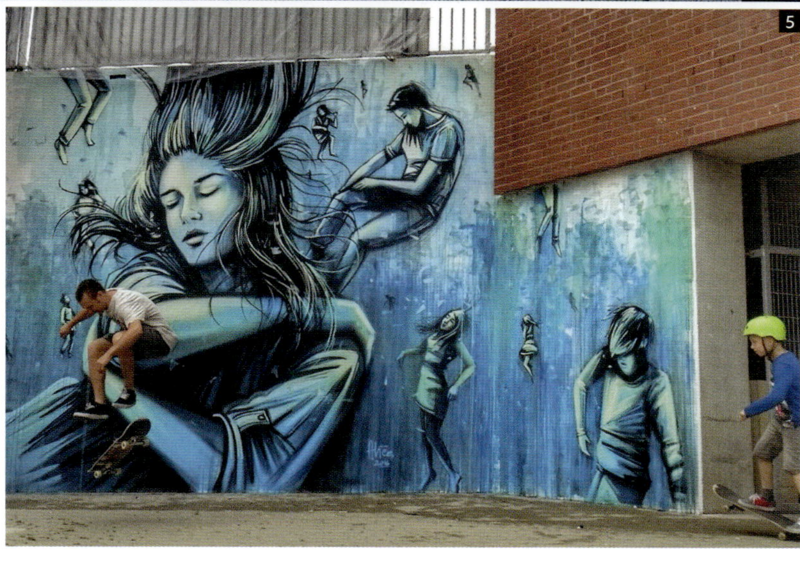

5

ANDREA WAN

/ Berlin

The world of Andrea Wan balances personal subconscious with contemporary surrealism and fable-influenced narrative. Her work testifies to contrasting re(dis)-locations drawn from a childhood in Hong Kong, a coming of age in Vancouver and now a flourishing career in the Berlin art scene.

Educated as an animation illustrator, her work meanders through ink-based studio production to digital or product design and distinctive murals, all with a refreshing coherent and recognisable style. Her use of fluid curves and a nostalgic colour palette are distinctly feminine. Via her universe, we are guided through surreal landscapes, where brain cells turn to stars and staircases run from mushrooms to merry-go-rounds.

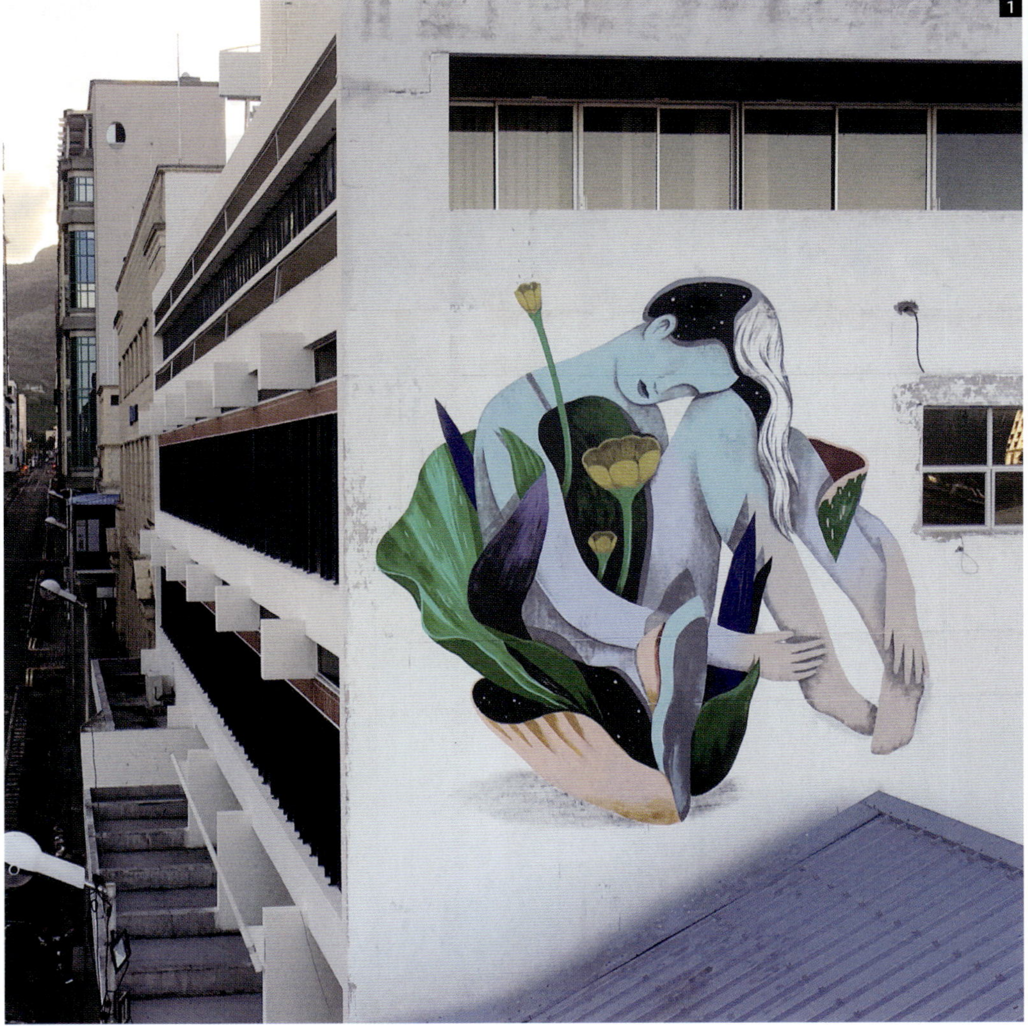

1

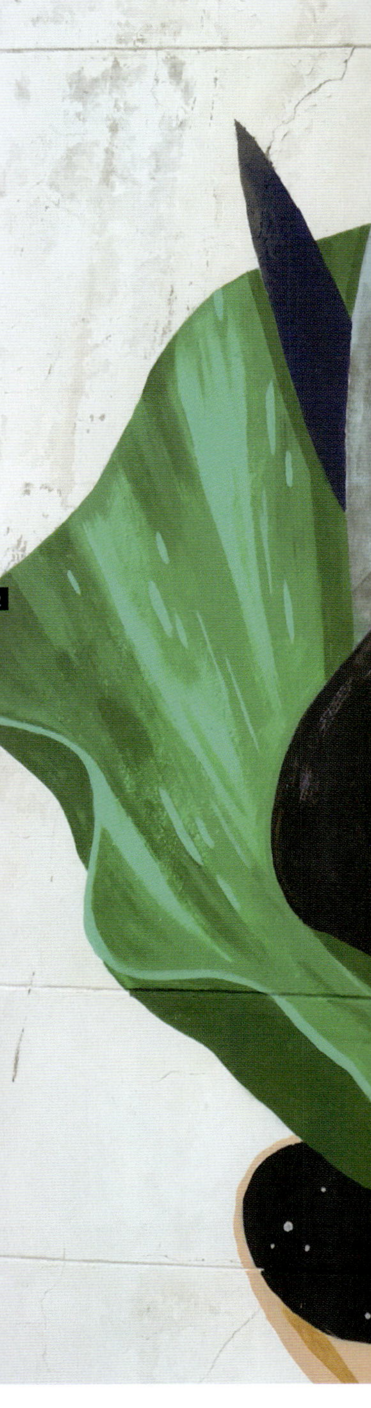

2

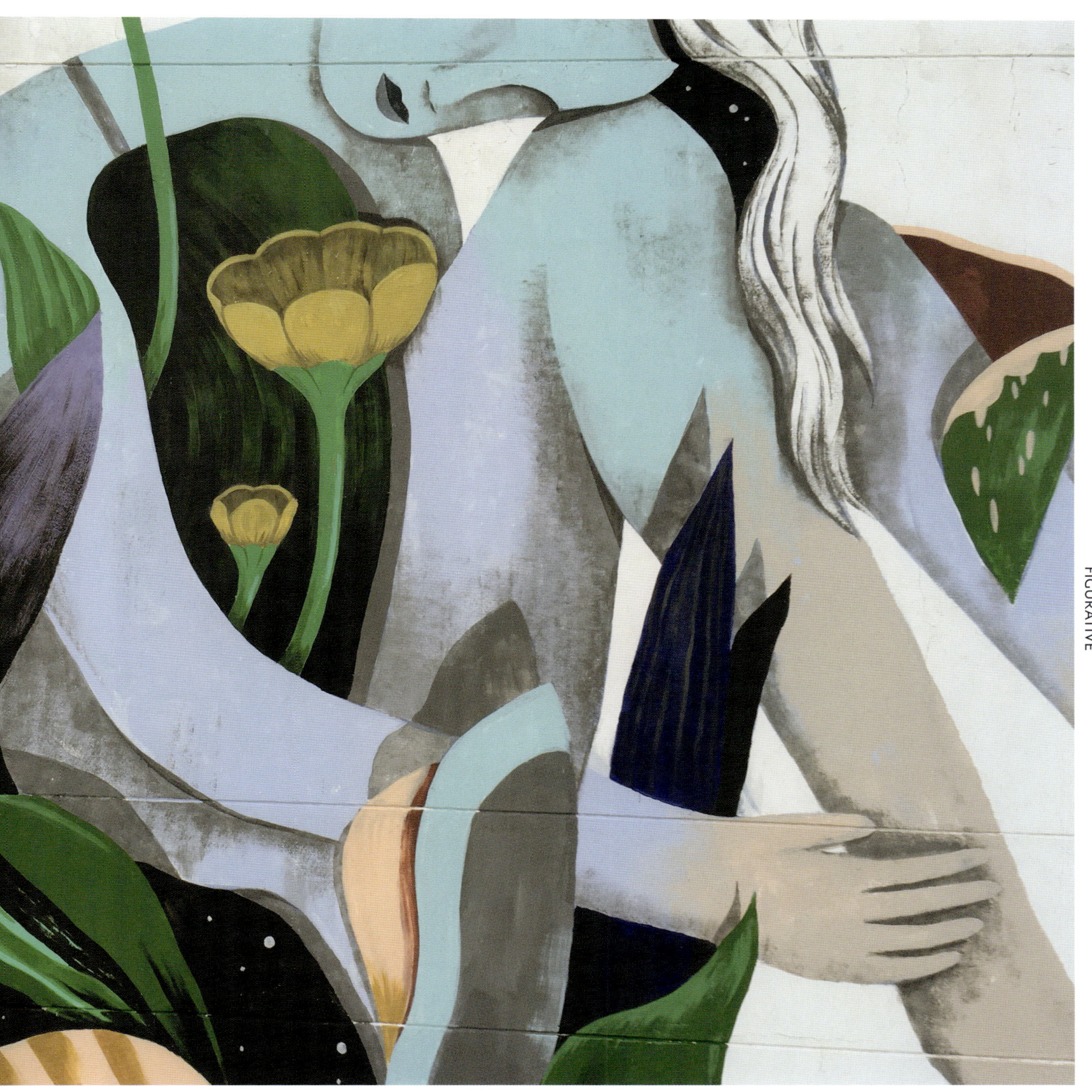

1 / 2
Port Louis, Mauritius, 2017
PHOTO BY THE ARTIST

3

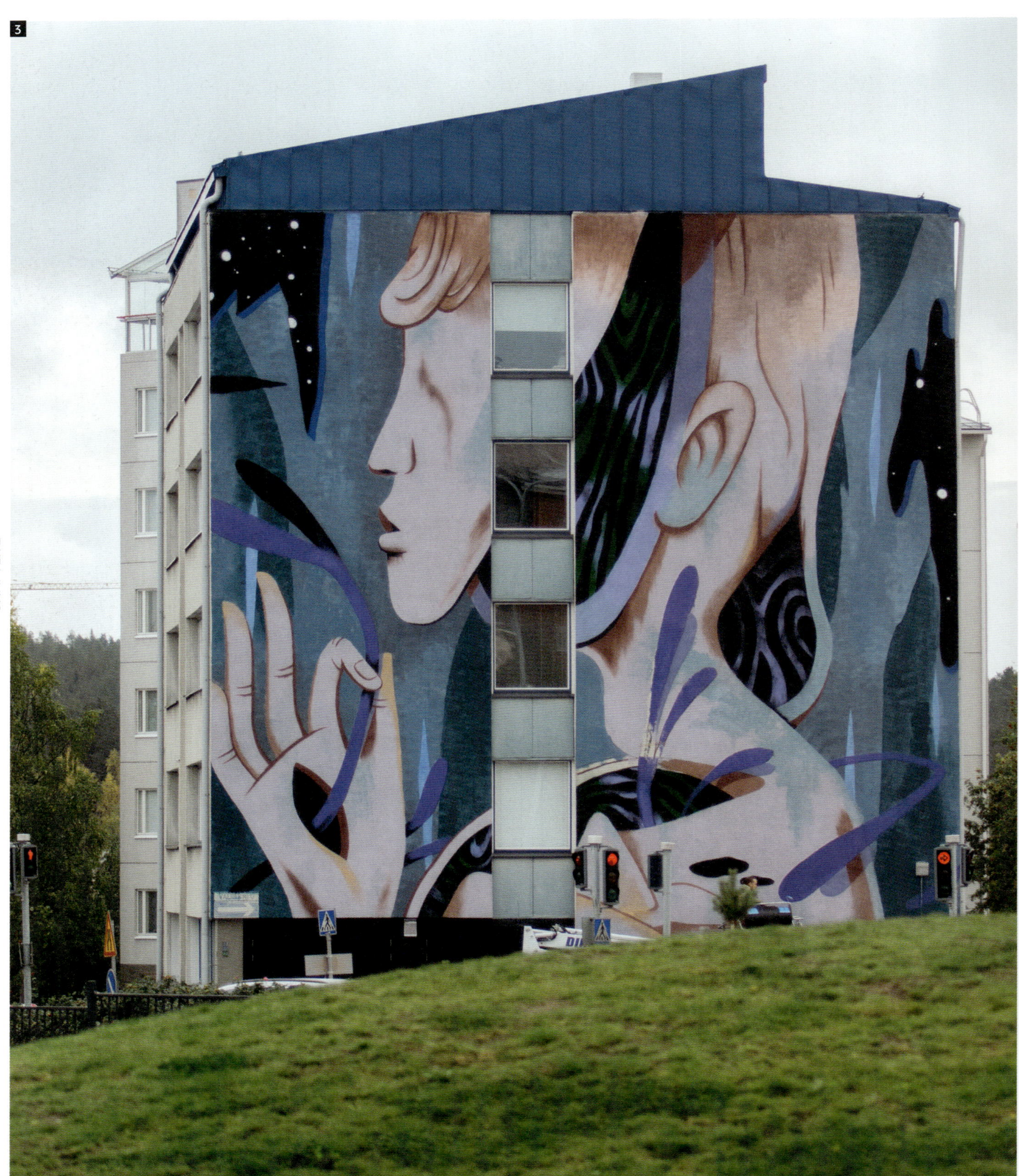

4

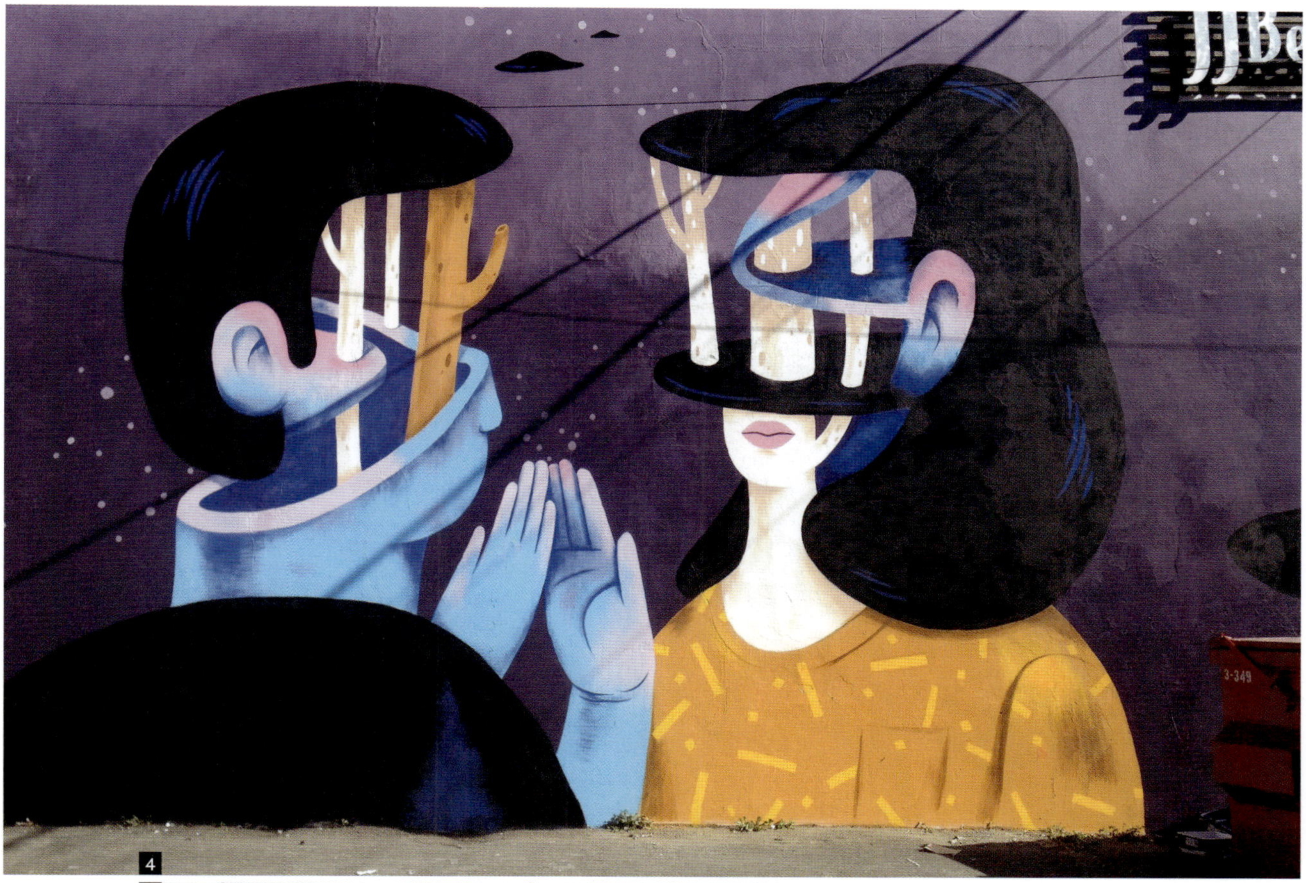

5

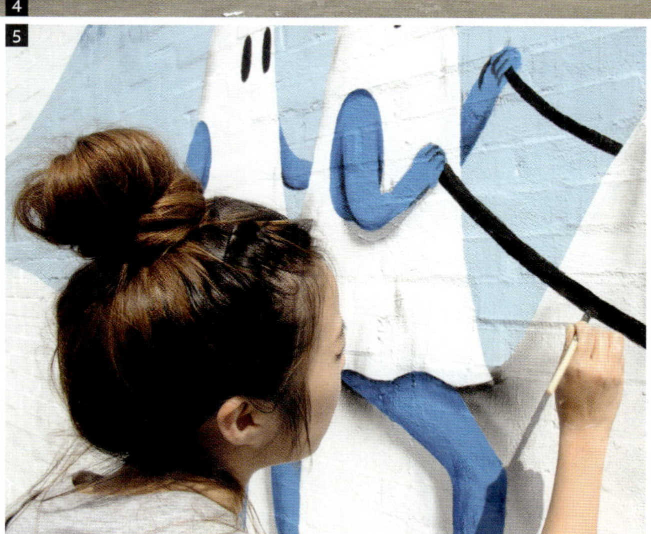

Surreal landscapes, where brain cells turn to stars and staircases run from mushrooms to merry-go-rounds.

3 /
Rovaniemi, Finland, 2017
PHOTO BY THE ARTIST

4 /
Vancouver, Canada, 2016
PHOTO BY THE ARTIST

5 /
Horsens, Finland, 2015
PHOTO BY THE ARTIST

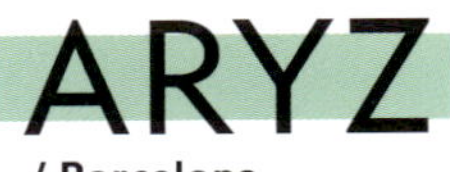

ARYZ

/ Barcelona

Young Spanish painter Aryz is very much an artist's artist. His distinctive style of expressive yet realistic portraiture and still lifes, his unique use of colour and his mammoth-scaled works make him a common reference for fellow creatives, who look to him as a pioneer in his field.
An inspiringly active painter, his works can be seen all over the globe, each project uniquely formed with a hugely diverse range of subject matter and integration techniques.

The past few years have seen Aryz gravitate to a simplified primary colour palette, exploring new techniques of spatial expression, always keeping the Old Masters as a reference, though with a new and contemporary pop art feel.

1

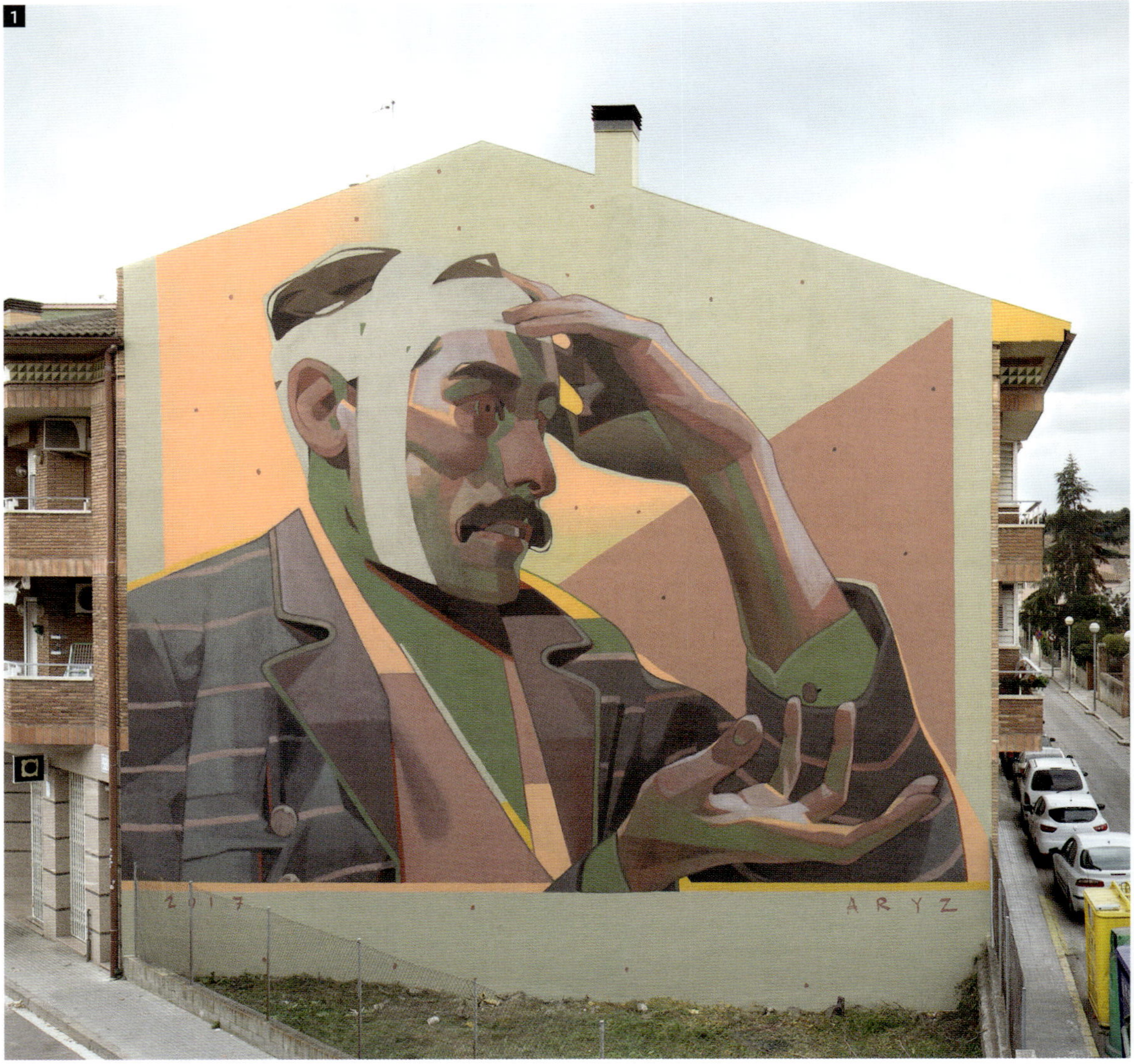

1 /
Cardedeu, Spain, 2017
PHOTO BY THE ARTIST

2 /
Manresa, Catalunya, Spain, 2018
PHOTO BY THE ARTIST

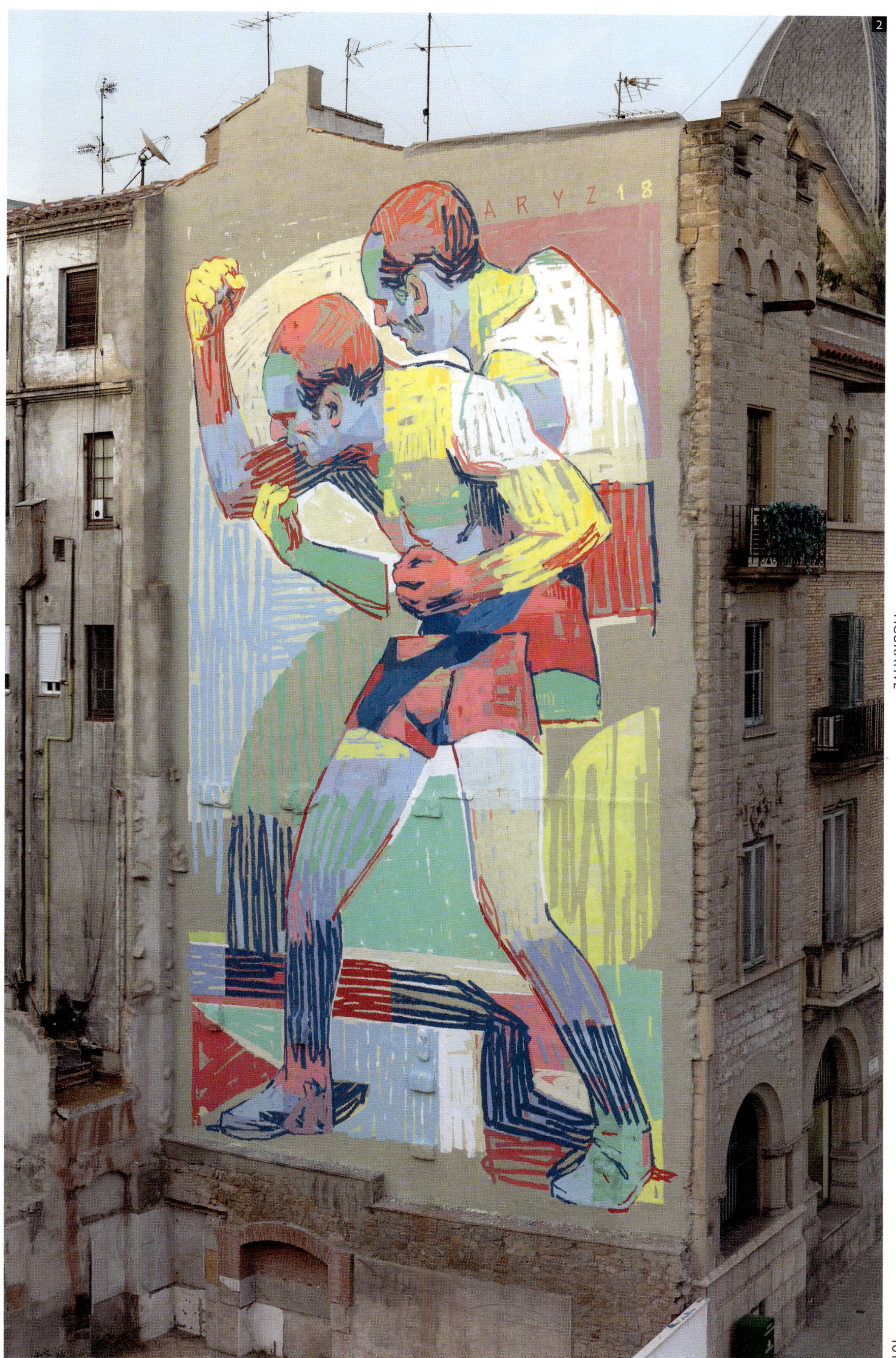

2

FIGURATIVE

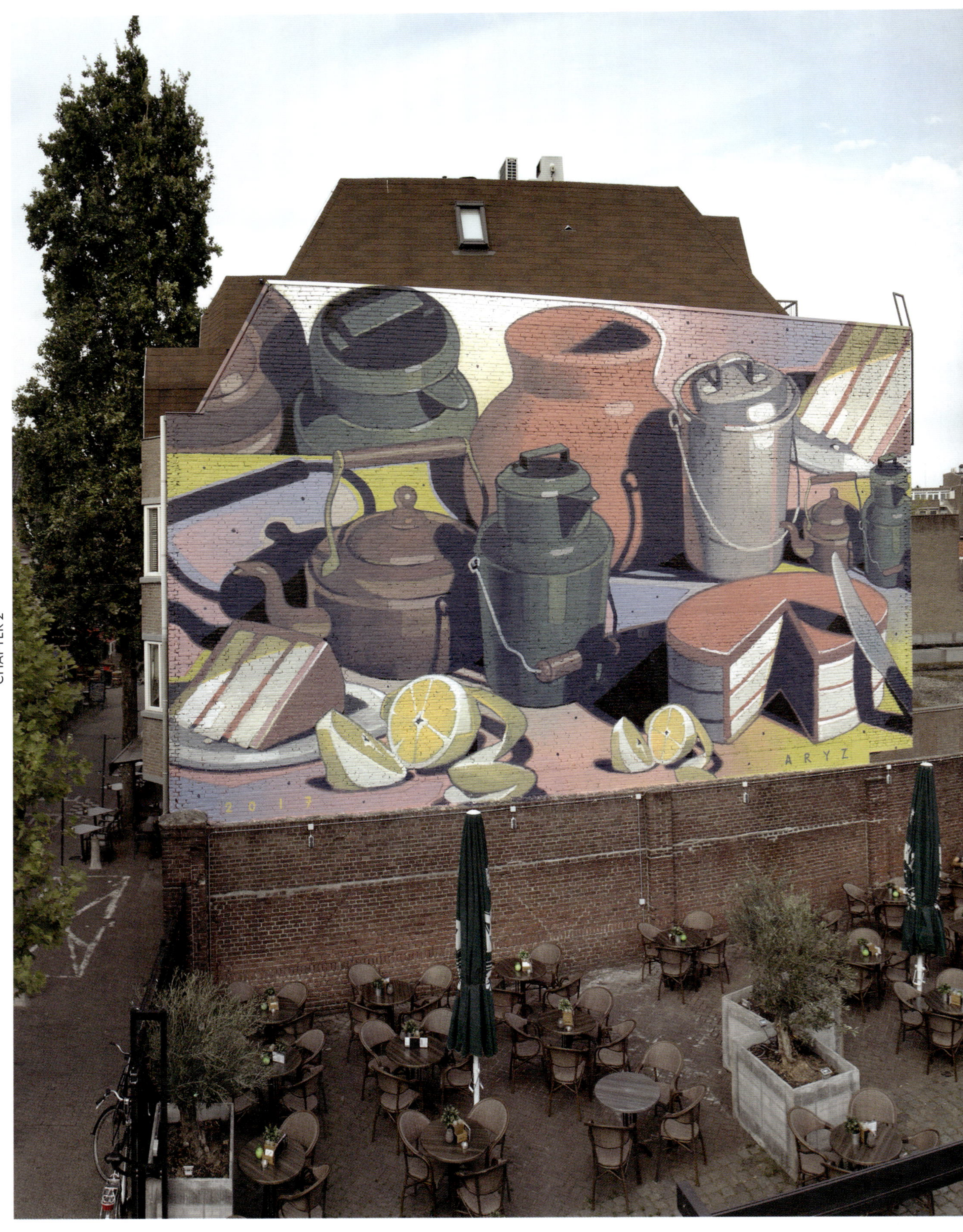
ARYZ
2017

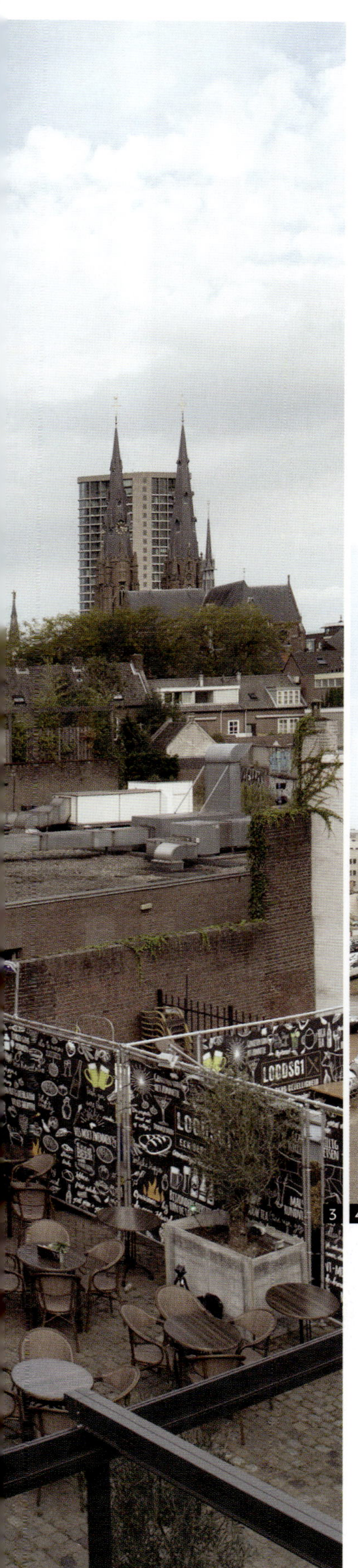

Keeping the Old Masters as a reference, though with a new and contemporary pop art feel.

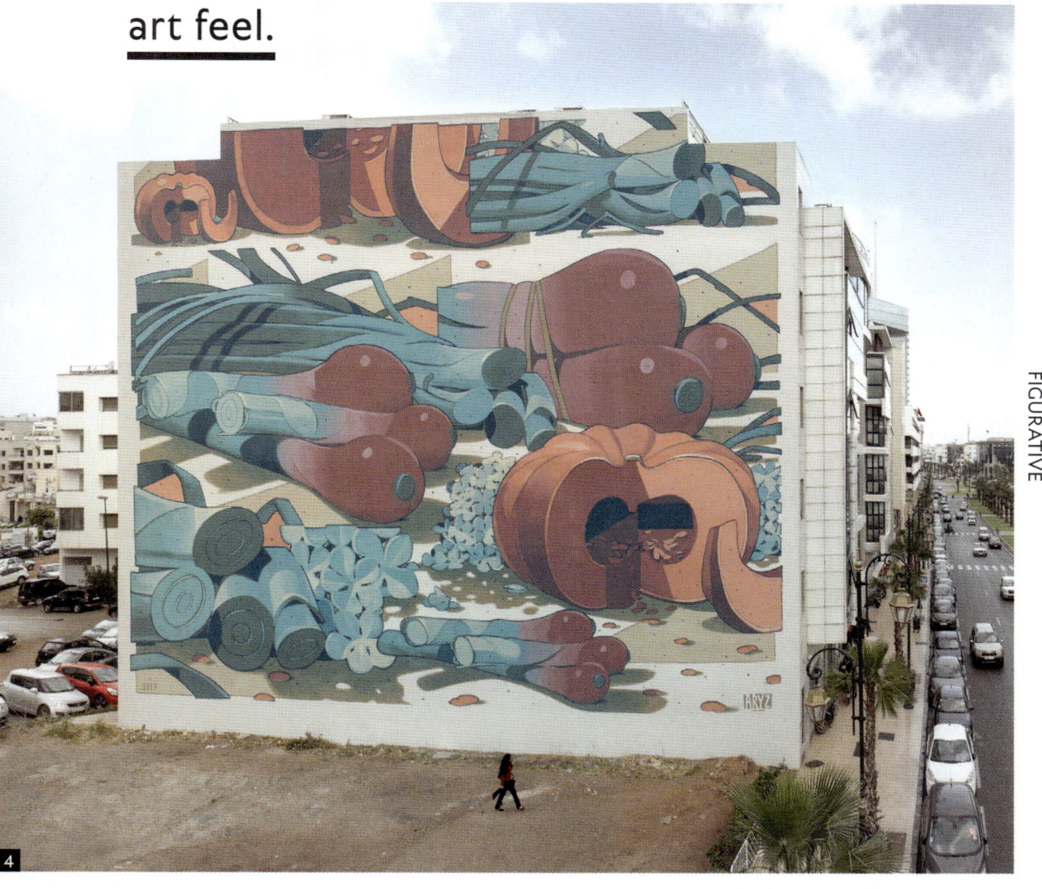

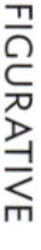

3 /
Eindhoven, The Netherlands, 2017
PHOTO BY THE ARTIST

4 /
Rabat, Morocco, 2014
PHOTO BY THE ARTIST

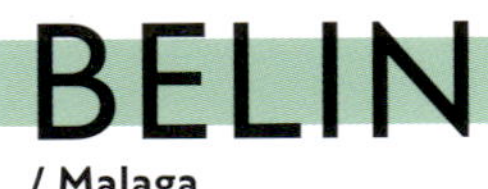

BELIN

/ Malaga

Spanish artist Miguel Ángel Belinchón Bujes, aka Belin, made an impressive shift in his work when he moved from a mastery of photorealism to integrate cubist influences into his portraiture. He now refers to his distinctive style as 'post-neo-cubism': a self-declared tribute to fellow Spaniard and godfather of cubism Pablo Picasso. Often based on the personalities of loved ones, his portraits deconstruct normal perspective in order to recompose the configurations into barely recognisable caricatures. His bright colour scheme and strong use of geometric lines are complemented by elements of photorealism, allowing each portrait to live in a representation that is simultaneously abstract and precise.

Without disregarding his clear fine art influences, Belin insists on the importance of fun and collaboration, inspired by the lightness of the everyday around him. Today his work can be seen in streets and galleries around the world, from neighbourhood walls to museums and galleries.

1

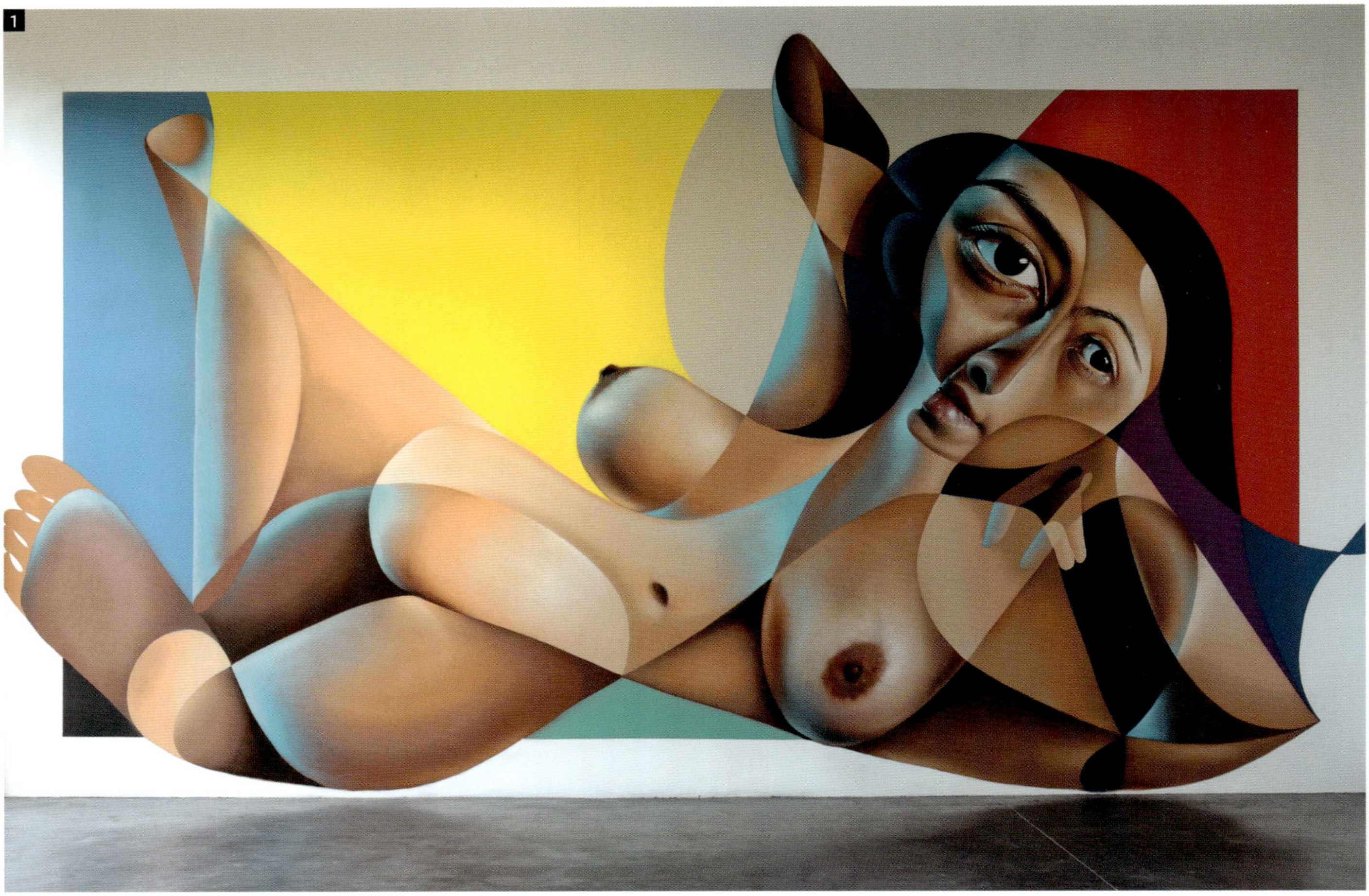

1 /
Rouen, France, 2018
PHOTO BY THE ARTIST

2 /
Córdoba, Spain, 2018
PHOTO BY THE ARTIST

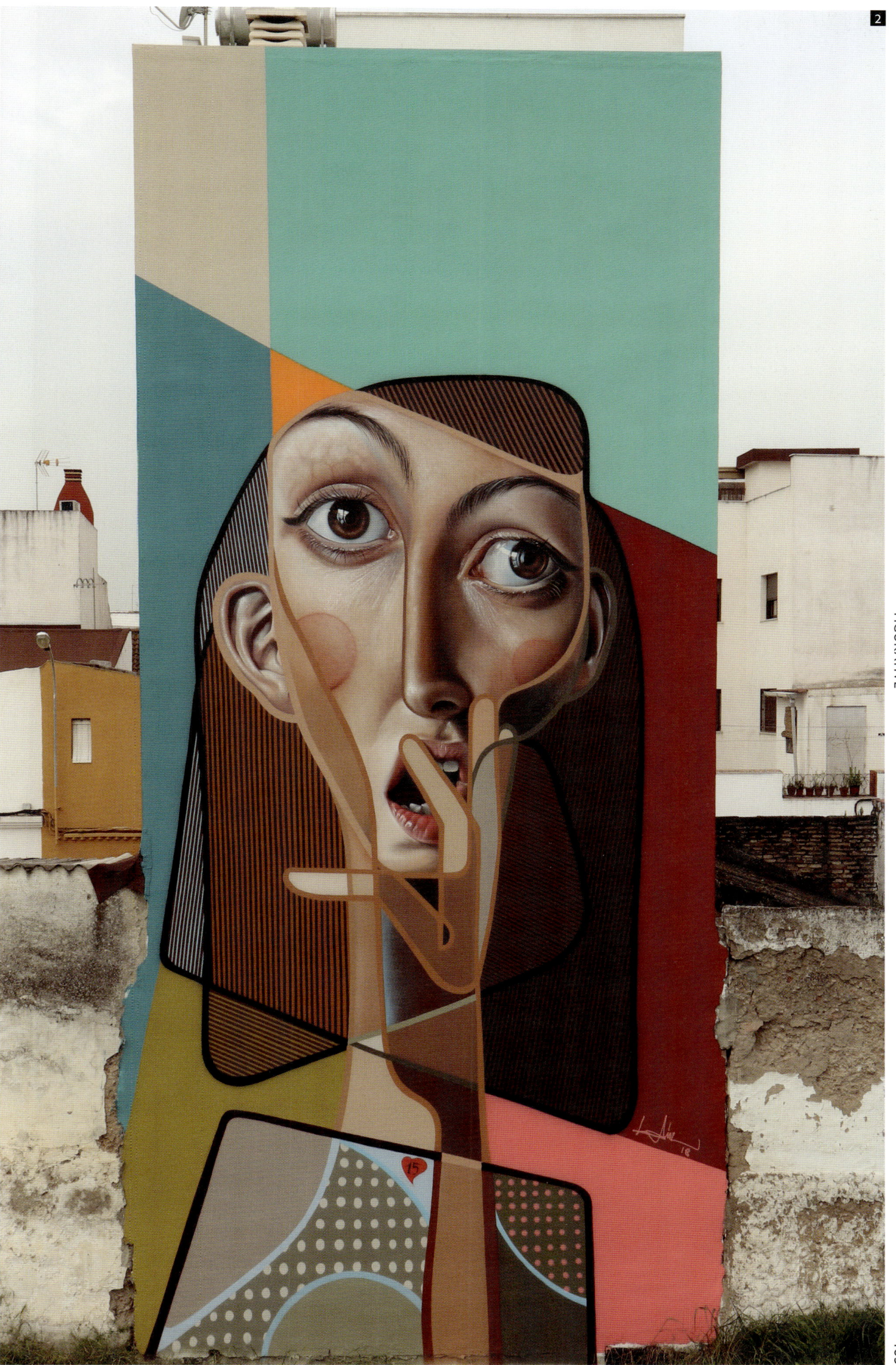

2

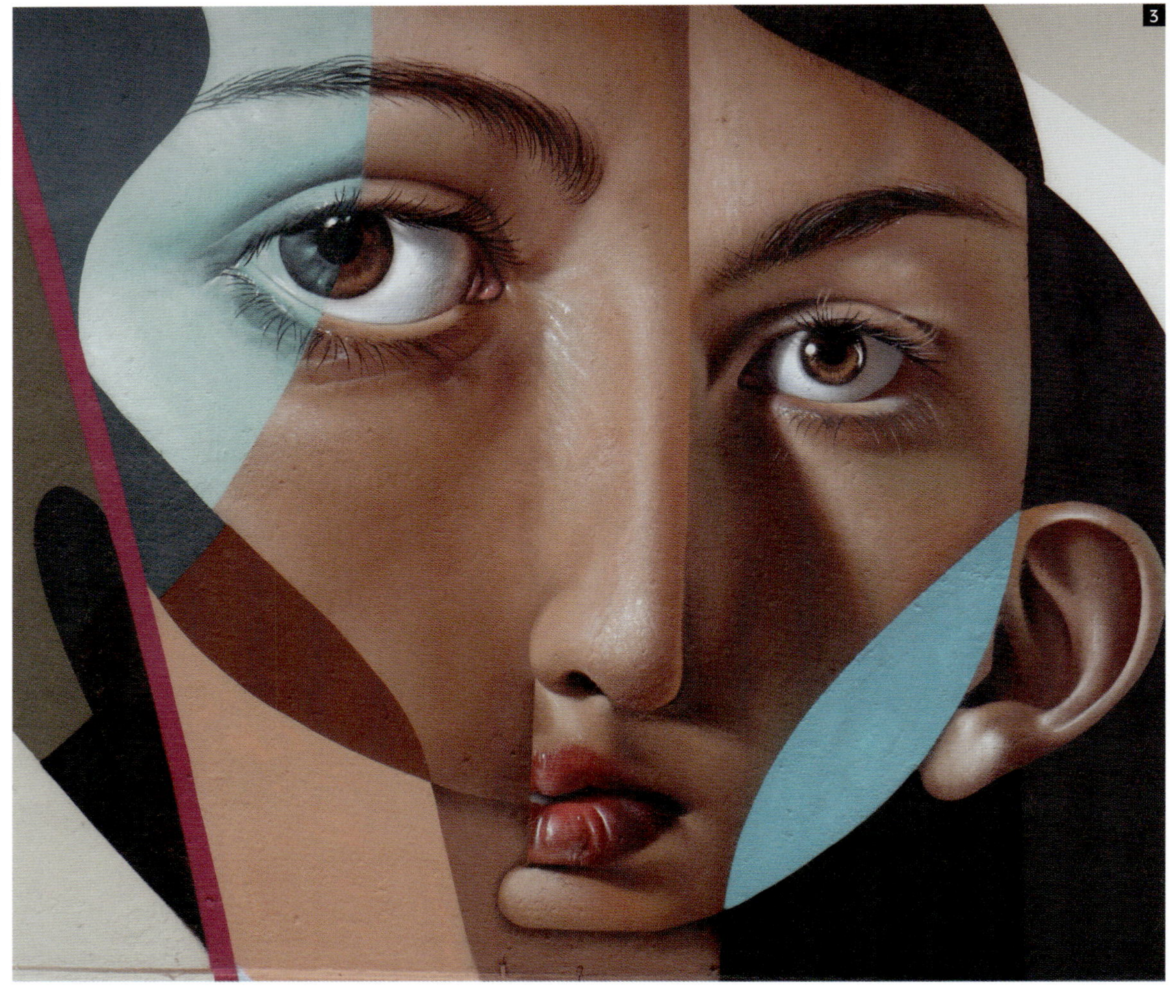

3 4

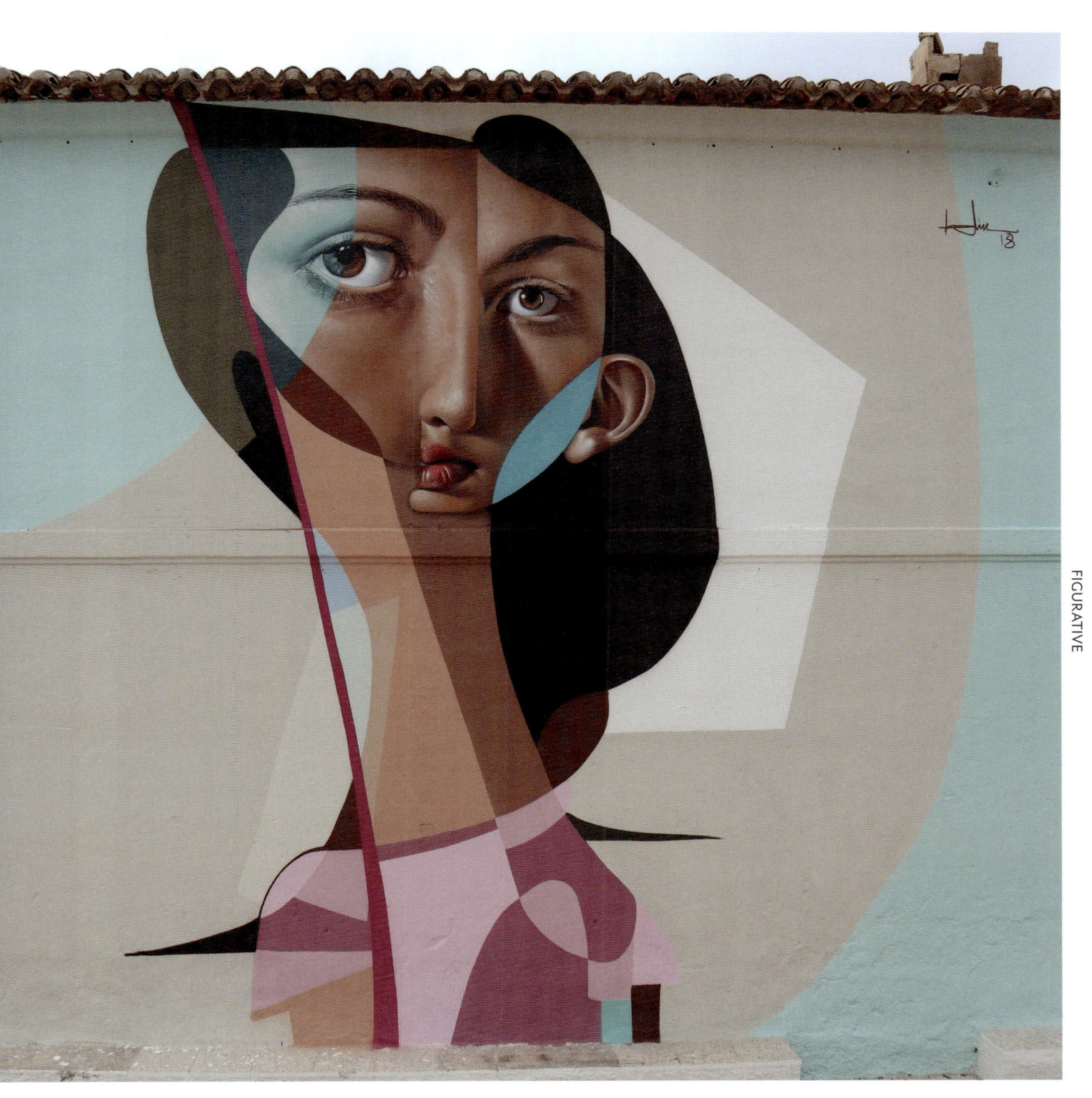

3 /
Vera, Spain, 2018
PHOTO BY THE ARTIST

4 /
Vera, Spain, 2018
PHOTO BY THE ARTIST

CINTA VIDAL

/ Barcelona

Spanish painter Cinta Vidal followed an a-typical path to become the artist she is today. After studying art in Barcelona's Escola Massana, she developed her painting craft as a scenography apprentice, creating pieces for theatre, opera and performance. This experience developed her strength in manipulation of scale and perspective, giving her a unique vision when representing space and narrative.

She creates gravity-defying universes, but her incorporation of everyday objects and recurrent use of 'homely' images suggest her interest in the shifting perspective of the everyday. With flying sofas, floating gardens and never-ending staircases, her quirky landscapes seem familiar, yet hint playfully at a possible but outlandish alternative.

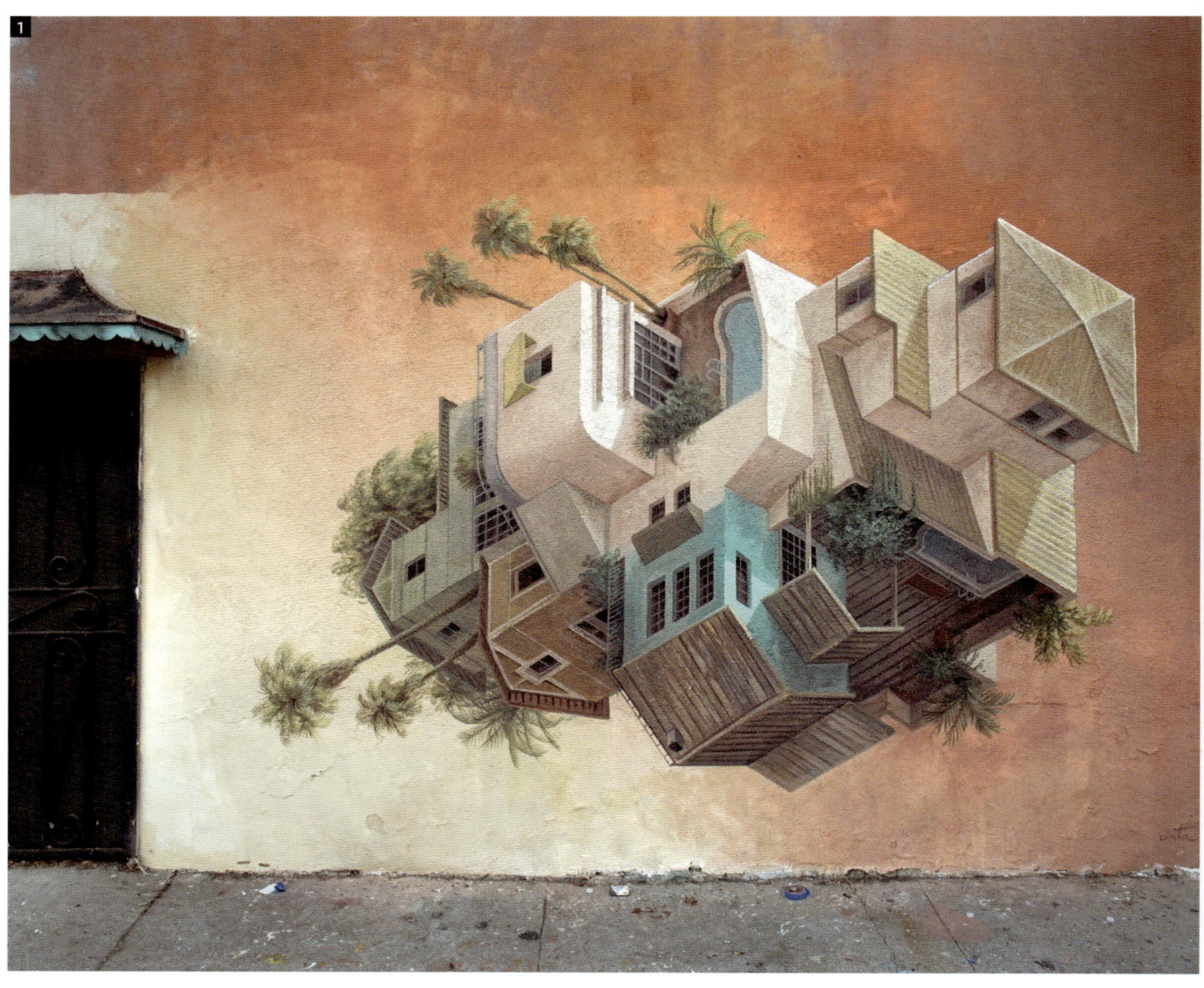

1 /
Culver City, California, USA, 2016
PHOTO BY THE ARTIST

2 /
Hong Kong, China, 2018
PHOTO BY THE ARTIST

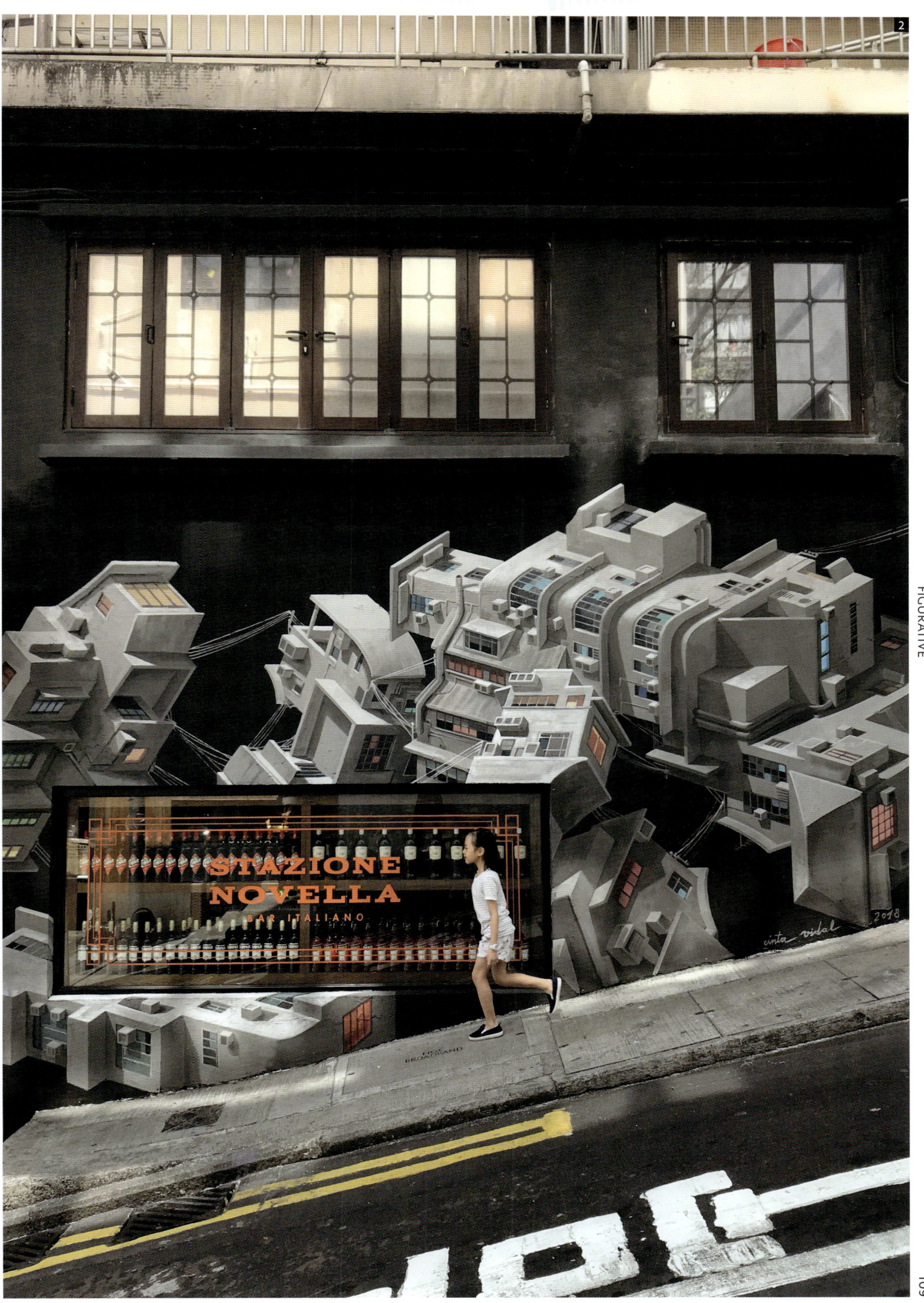

2

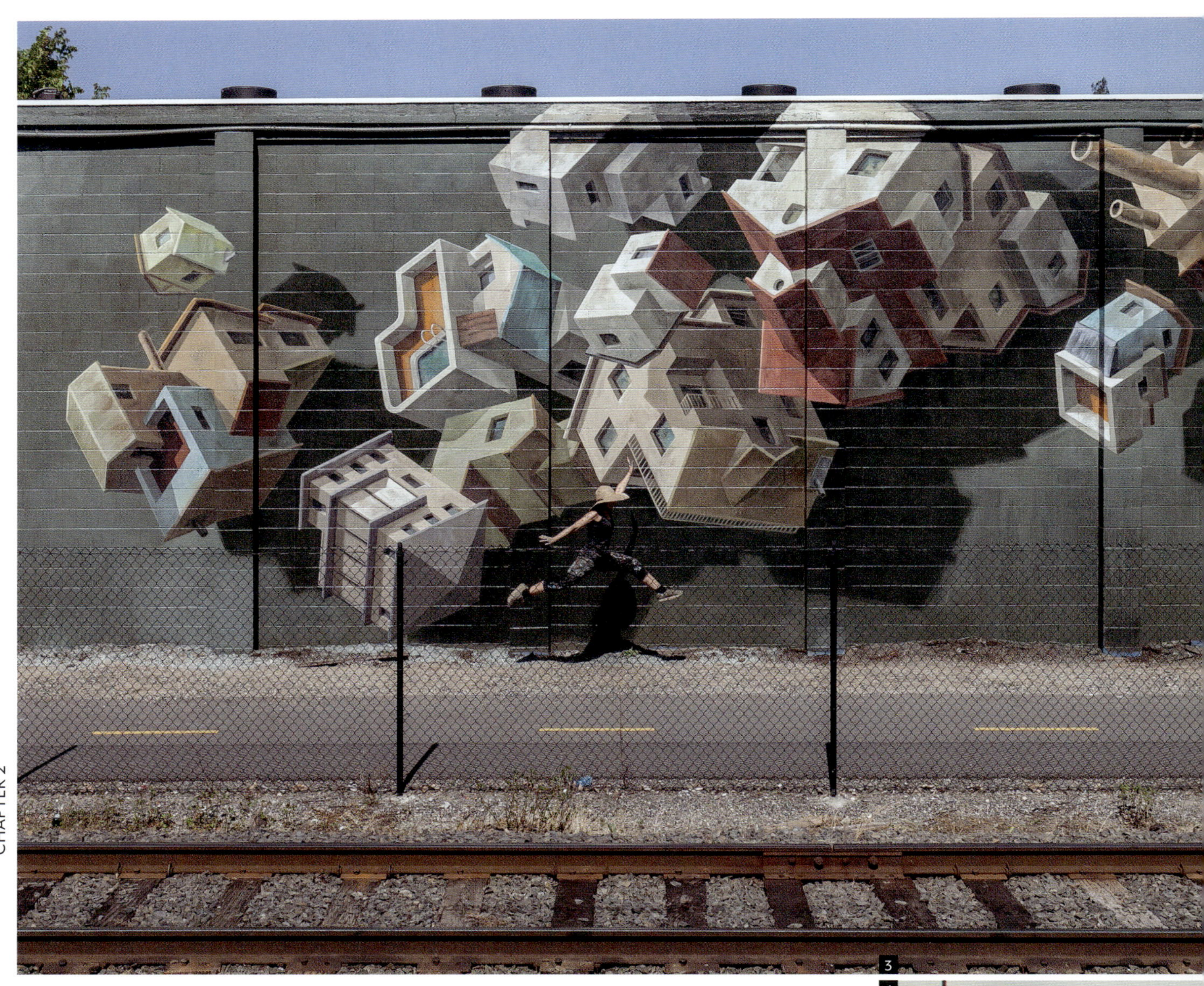

3

4

3 /
Napa, California, USA, 2017
PHOTO BY THE ARTIST

4 /
Long Beach, California, USA, 2016
PHOTO BY THE ARTIST

Her quirky landscapes seem familiar, yet hint playfully at a possible but outlandish alternative.

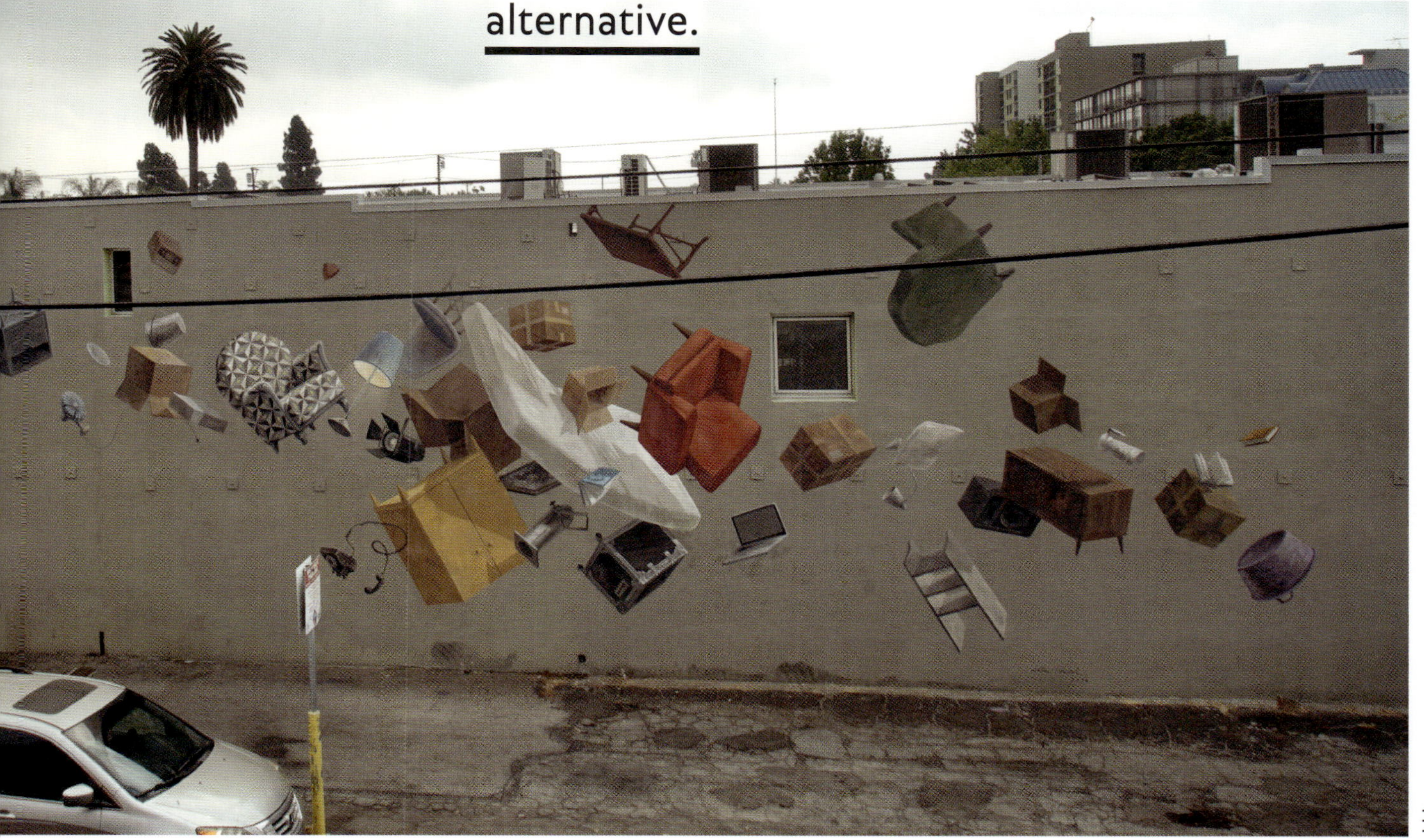

1

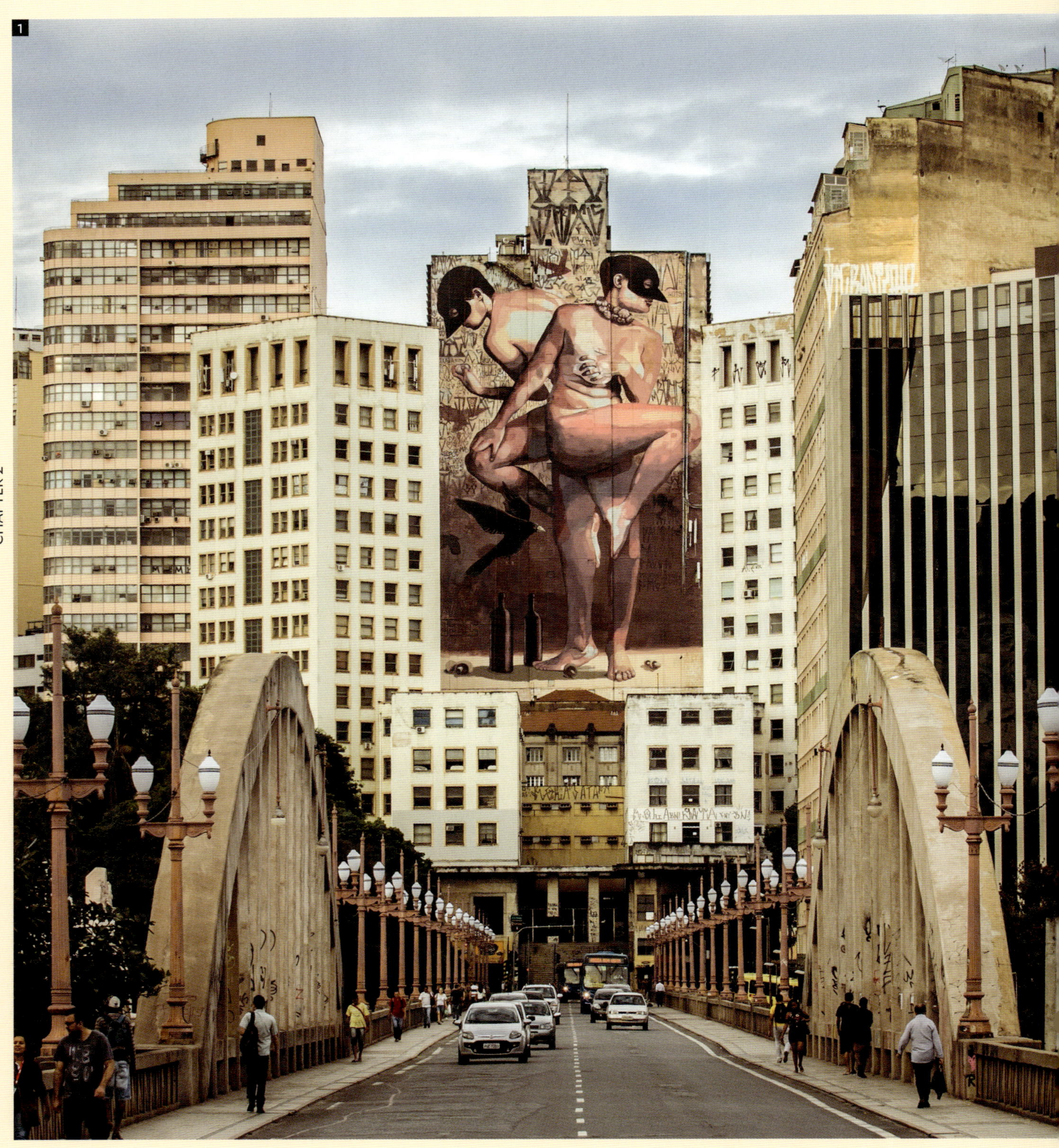

MILU CORRECH

/ Buenos Aires

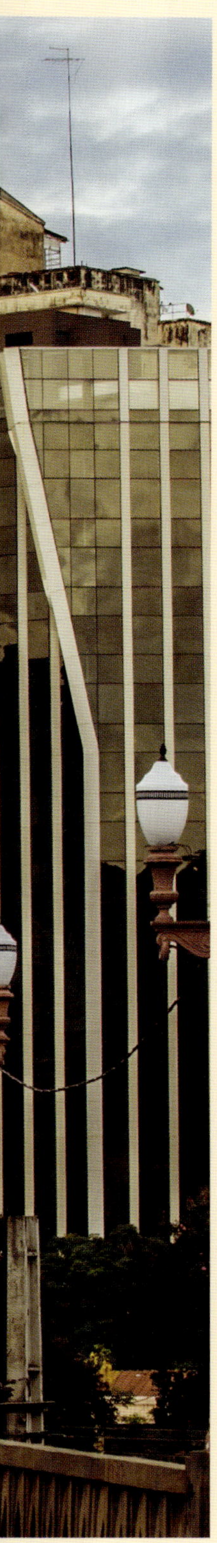

You painted your very first mural in 2011. How has your work evolved since that time?
There have been a lot of changes. For my first walls, I started doing portraits of singers: Mercedes Sosa, Omara Portuondo, Latin singers.
The challenge was to get the eyes right. If you saw the portrait, it had to be an accurate representation.
I didn't paint before I started on murals. First, it was just to get an image, and then it was more about colours. After my technique evolved, it was more about: what do I have to say?
Right now, I think about how my art impacts and interacts with the power relations in each context. How the image I create expands the images we are usually exposed to and how it plays with the other images around. My work's evolution has been about adding layers and challenges.

At first your technique evolved, and then it was more about the message, what you wanted to say with your work?
It was not really about a 'message'; it was more thinking about how does an ingredient works with a specific context. A message has this unilateral power dynamic, you know?
I'm upstairs, you're down, and I'm giving you something. But it's more like: how can this be interpreted in this context? I put an image in the public space, and that's one of the ingredient of the dish. The rest should be added and 'cooked' by the context and the spectator.

Many younger people use their full name – in contrast to the very first generations, who often worked under an alias. Why did you choose to use your full name as an artist?
In muralism, names were always on the wall. There were no aliases; that was something that appeared later when some kids started doing

1 /
Belo Horizonte, Brazil, 2017
PHOTO BY THE ARTIST

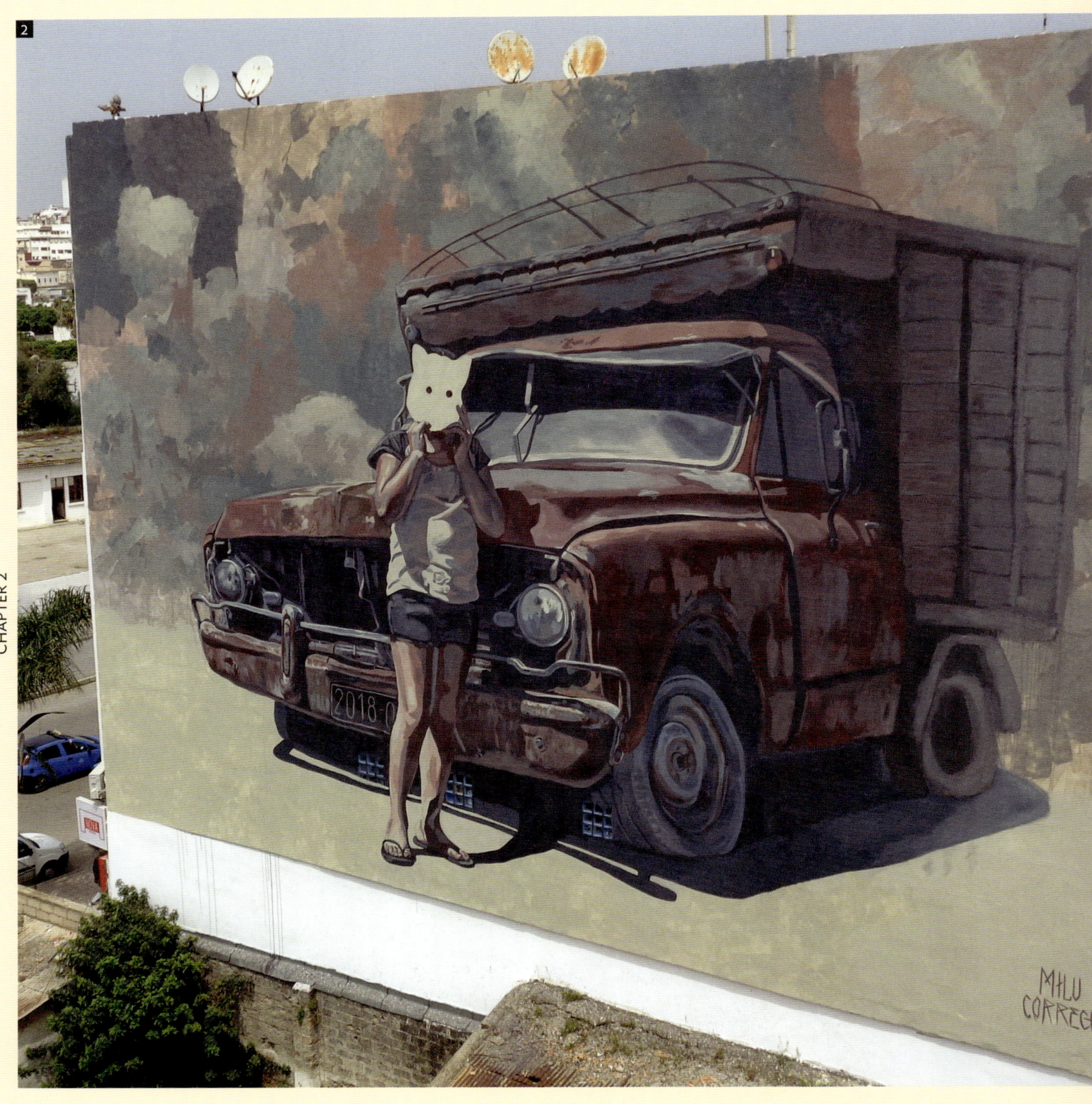

2 /
Rabat, Morocco, 2018
PHOTO BY THE ARTIST

3 /
Fanzara, Spain, 2017
PHOTO BY THE ARTIST

graffiti. This is the root of it. Legality was one of the excuses for not putting your real name. But in Argentina, and throughout Latin America, it's not illegal to paint on walls. You can do huge walls with no problem at all. I can go paint during the day and do the wall that I want, so why would I put another name?
With 'Pixo' in Brazil, they do use aliases; if those artists get caught, the punishment is brutal. Aliases make more sense to me there than using a cool name in a legal festival in Europe.

You've said there's a higher percentage of female artists in Argentina. Why is that?
I think there are lot of female muralists in Argentina and probably there is a higher percentage than in Europe, where the wallpainting tradition comes from graffiti. I do believe there is a very high amount of female painters everywhere, only they have less visibility. Organisers don't invite them to events, so they get less experience, fewer jobs; they have to work on other things too, etc.
It is a connected chain with roots in what now we call 'patriarchy'. So no, I don't know if it's higher; I don't even know if it's equal. But there is an inequality in the medium. Even among the artists sometimes you have the 'boys club' dynamic where men invite other men to projects, creating a net of power and credit with a gender base.
Curating a festival, it's hard work, and it's even harder to do it properly. The easiest, laziest thing to do to get picked up in street art news is to book the artists that are on some stupid top-ten list. But then you always have the hegemonic, the elite, the repetitive stickers. And I do believe festivals in the public space should not be just a list of names. The context should be taken into account and if we invite the

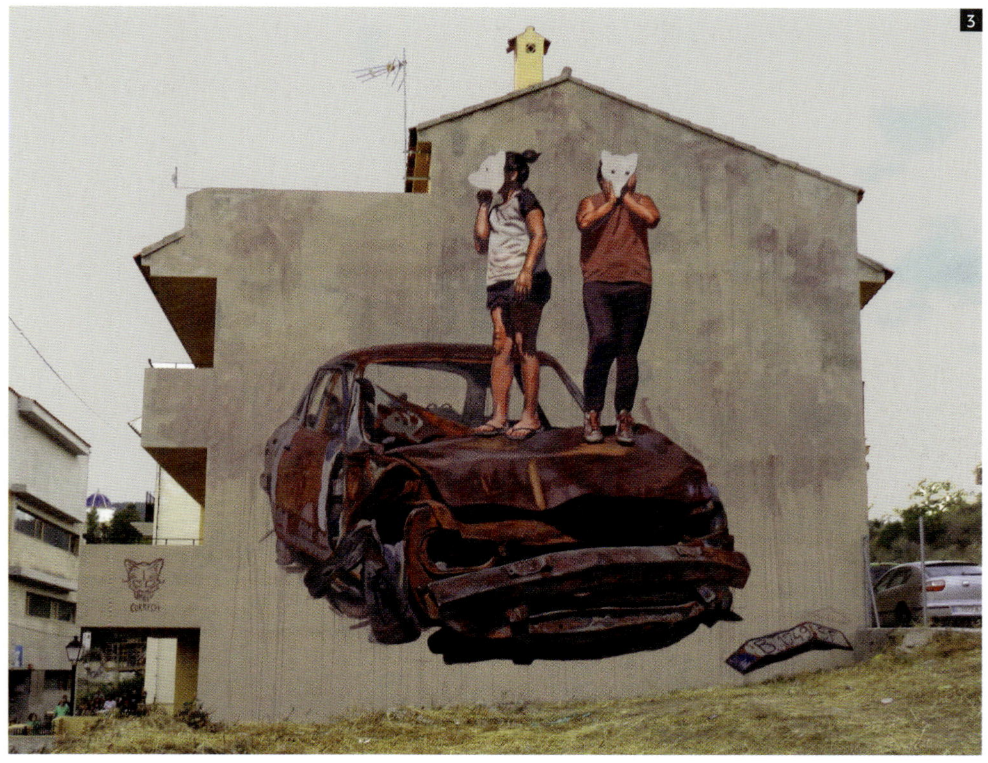

3

» /
Rabat, Morocco, 2018
PHOTO BY THE ARTIST

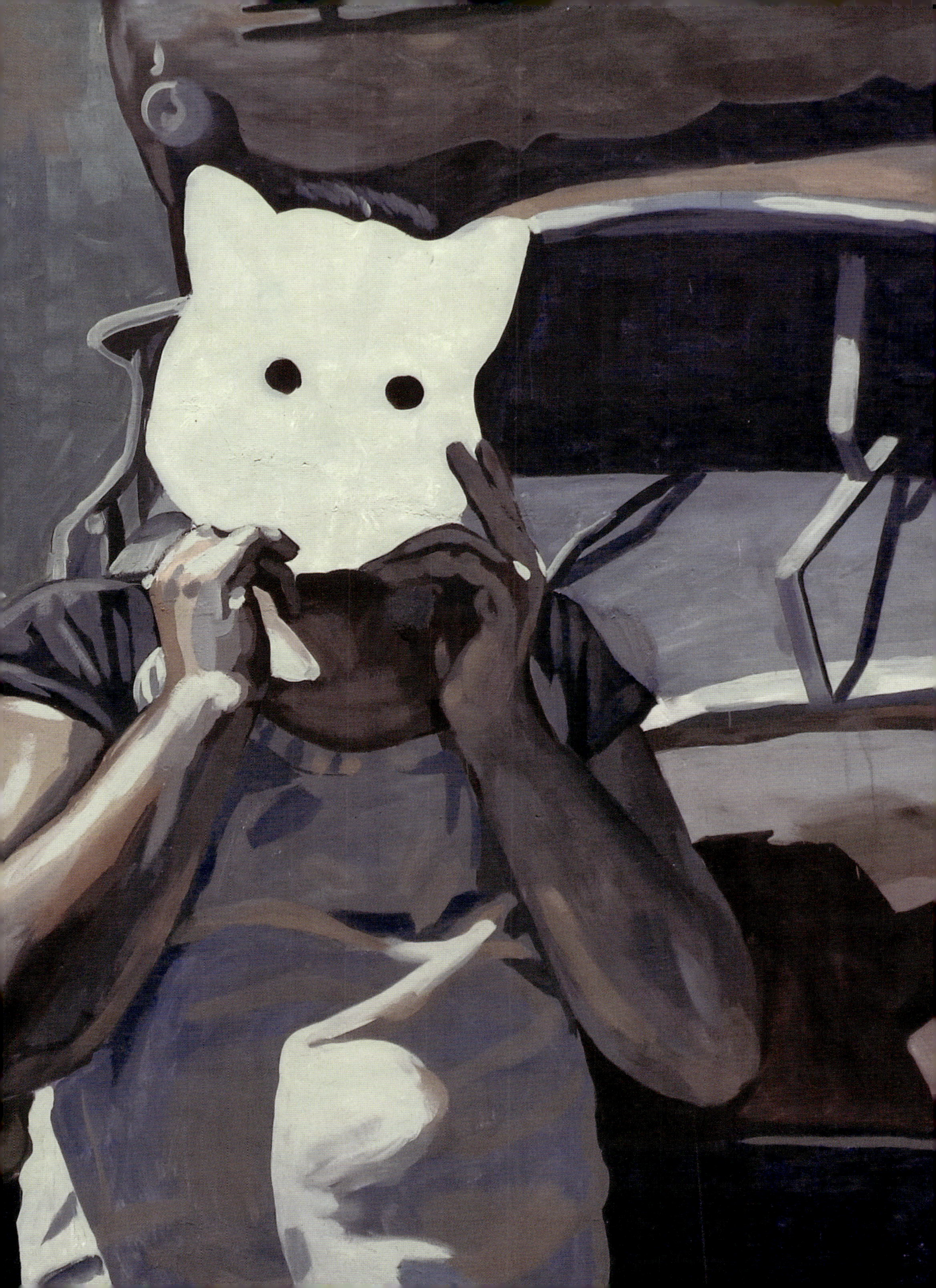

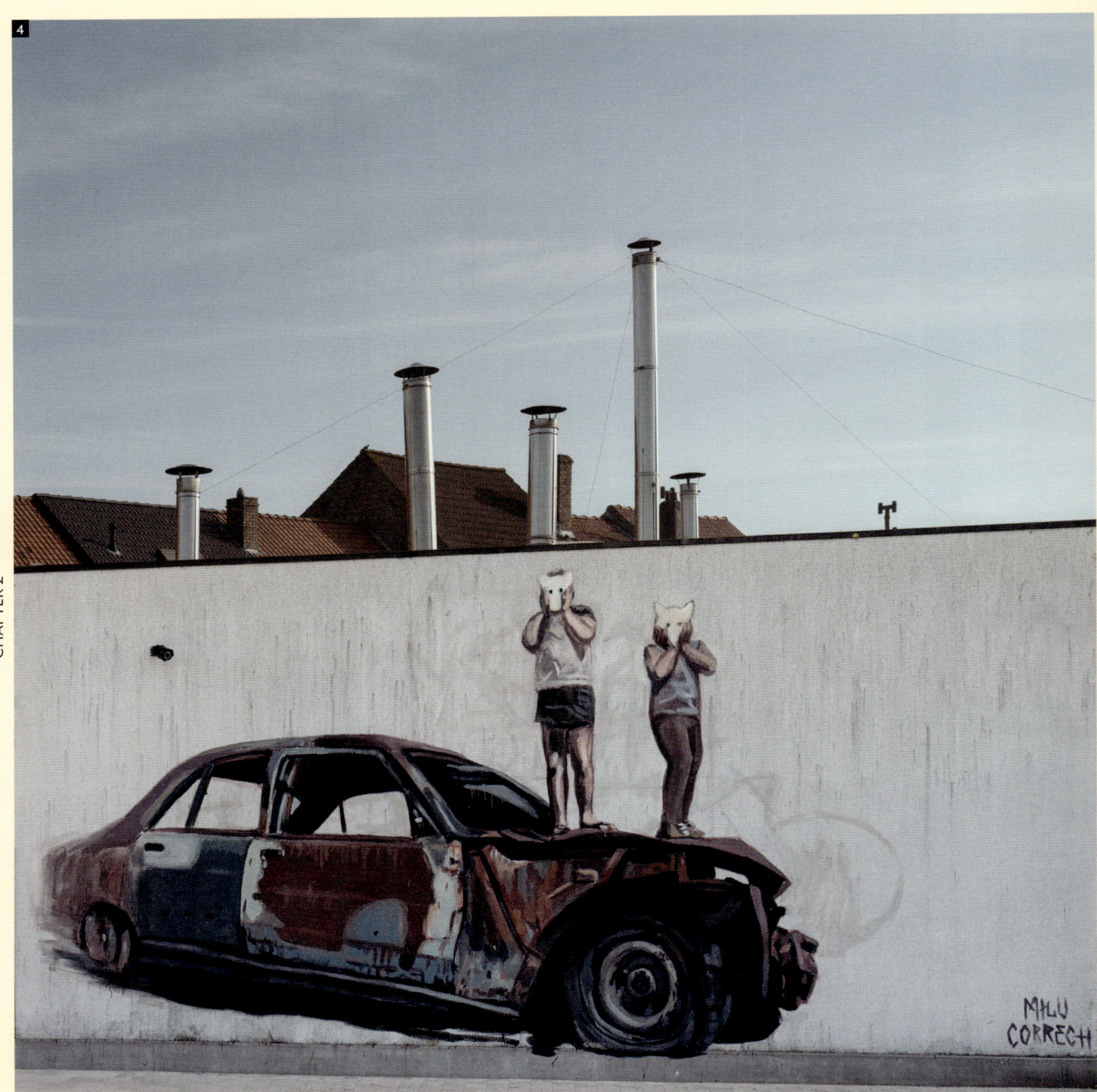

4 /
Ostend, Belgium, 2018
PHOTO BY EGMOND DOBBELAERE

5 /
Carballo, Spain, 2018
PHOTO BY THE ARTIST

6 /
Molise, Italy, 2018
PHOTO BY THE ARTIST

same people over and over again we are creating a very narrow visual speech that in theory was what painted walls came to change. It should be possible to combine, but that would imply someone really curating and doing a good job, and it's harder; I know it's harder. You have to actually go and look for all these low-visibility people and new images. If we just reproduce or repeat, then we are killing the new, fresh and unexpected that wallpainting should be all about.

Looking at your body of work, music has always been a recurring theme. Can you describe the relationship between music and art in your work?
It's more literature than music. There might be some music characters in my previous work, but I think I always had a narrative, a literature angle. All the paintings I do have a story that only I know. Maybe because my mum is a literature teacher and I read a lot of fantastic books when I was a kid. I like to create narratives that are unusual in our public spaces and to hack some normative roles in it.

You've talked about street art versus social media. An up-to-date social media profile on Instagram, Facebook, maybe Twitter, Tumblr, whatever – is that really so important for an artist?
I think unfortunately social media is very important to everyone now. The system lacks transparency and control. And even if you go all hipster, like radical hipster without social media, maybe you won't get hired because you aren't on social media. That's seen as strange now. No profile? Then you must be hiding something.

South America has a very special history and atmosphere for street art. Are there any trends or evolutions in street art over the last 10 years in South America, or more specifically in Argentina?
There's Pixacao in Brazil, and graffiti, and two types of muralism. But there are thousands and thousands of painters in Latin America, and a lot of them don't even think

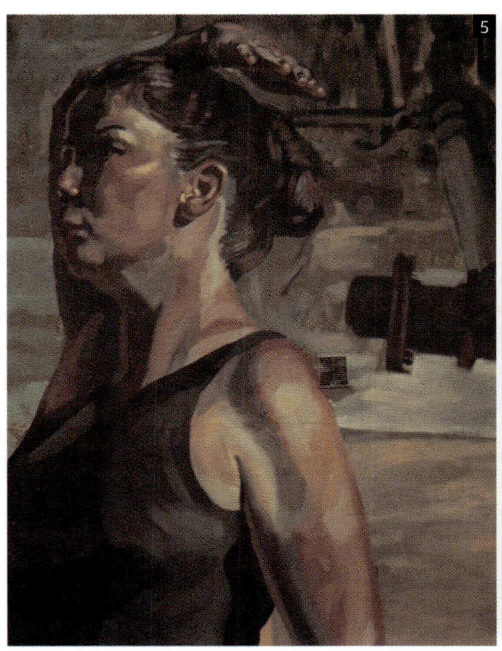
5

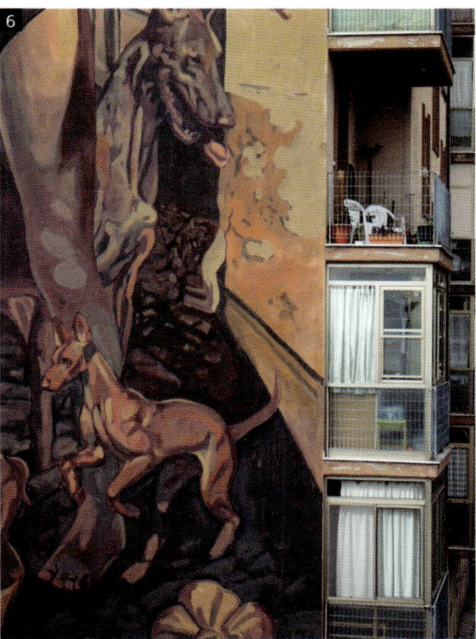
6

of Europe, or possibly outside their own city. When people say 'first generation, second generation' or whatever they think street art definition is, I always try to emphasise that these are Eurocentric concepts, and there's a whole world outside those stupid borders. Here in Latin America, each city and small town has its own story with different locals and different themes.

Women working in art are often labelled 'female artists', rather than just 'artists'. What is an effective attitude towards the male-dominated art world?
I think we should open the discussion, and I believe in micropolitics.
So what I do is, every time I go to a project to paint, I'm like: 'Hey. You notice that I'm almost the only woman here, with maybe just one other girl? Can you see the surroundings? You should address this, don't you think?' I try; that's something that we should all do. If we're the only women there, it's not because we are the only women talented enough to be there. It's basically about patriarchy, and we should address this.
Of course, it's a bigger risk when a female artist raises the issue. I do believe we shouldn't rely only on women to address this issue, and everyone should start opening the discussion and addressing this issue as do many others in the 'wallpainting' scene.

So first we have to open the debate; it doesn't have to be taboo, we have to talk about it. Second, we should go and talk to the curator or organiser and say: 'Look, I'm the only female artist here. You can do this differently.'
We should do that all the time with the organisers. And we have to learn how to talk with artists. Art is such an individual thing, and artists aren't used to criticising each other.
I do believe strongly in critics; last week I provided a print for someone to criticise my work. We have to start giving each other constructive criticism. Art should be a debate, not just buyers and friendship and stuff. We can criticise each other's work without getting personal, without getting hurt or whatever.
As painters, we have to ask curators to manage the system. Curators should debate with other curators and painters should debate with other painters. This shouldn't just be left to female artists and curators; male curators and male painters should also step up, because they do not run the same risks as female painters, who have less visibility and less power in this context. The higher you go in privilege, the more discussions you could open – and that doesn't only apply to women.
Once you start living by that principle, there are things to consider.
I do work for free sometimes: in Argentina, when there is a small project in an outside neighbourhood. But I try not to participate for free in a gentrification project, and I try not to accept less than a certain amount of money for projects that have a big production budget. We shouldn't; it's exploitation.
And make it a discussion. I believe painters and curators should elevate the conversation a bit. Move on from the small talk, like, 'hey, where are you from?'. We should be more like: 'Hey what do you think about this project? What do think about what we're painting? What do you think about the inequality in the line-up?'
I don't know if initiating a discussion is the right approach for everyone, but at least it is for me.

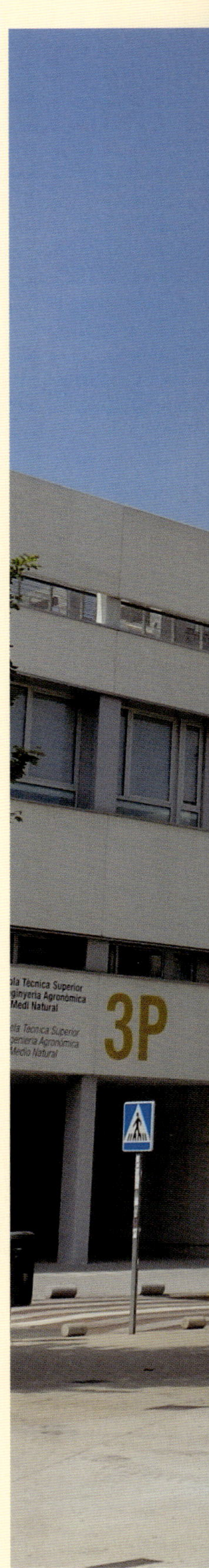

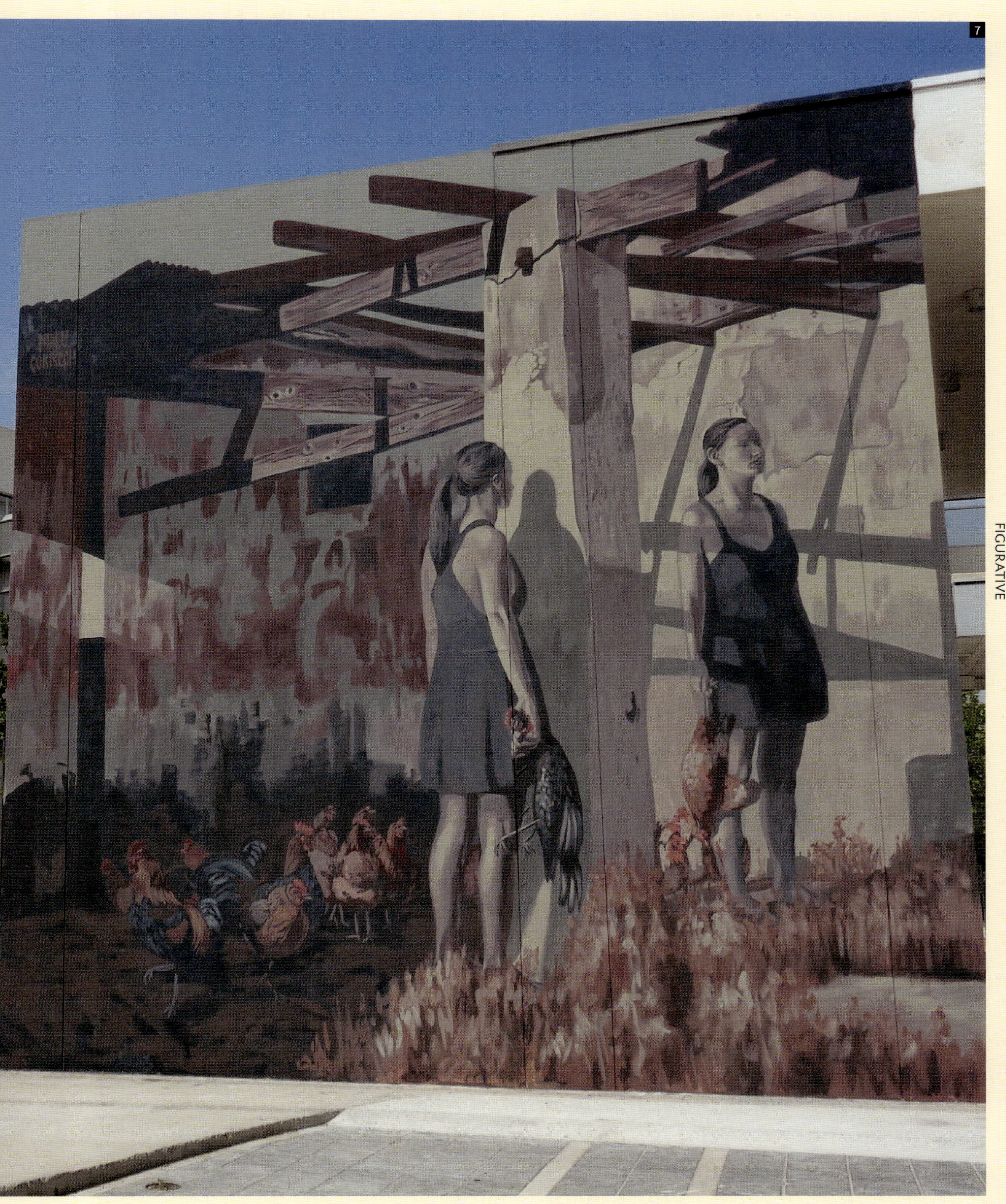

7 /
Valencia, Spain, 2018
PHOTO BY THE ARTIST

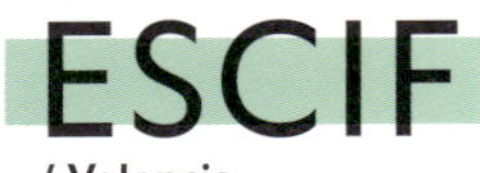

ESCIF

/ Valencia

For many years, Escif has established a solid reputation in the art world, with his not-so-subtle political commentary splayed over large-scale mural projects, exhibitions, collaborations and online commentary. Since appearing in the previous edition of *Street Art Today*, Escif has focused on themes of neoliberalism, immigration and most notably the civil war in Congo fuelled by coltan mining for the tech industry.

Recent exhibitions at the Palais de Tokyo in Paris and Brussels' MIMA museum also saw him integrate elements of augmented reality into his work. In collaboration with Félix Artagaveytia, he has gone on to develop apps like 'Graffiti Yoga' and the 'Magic Piano' installation, allowing his paintings to come to life with live animation and sound.

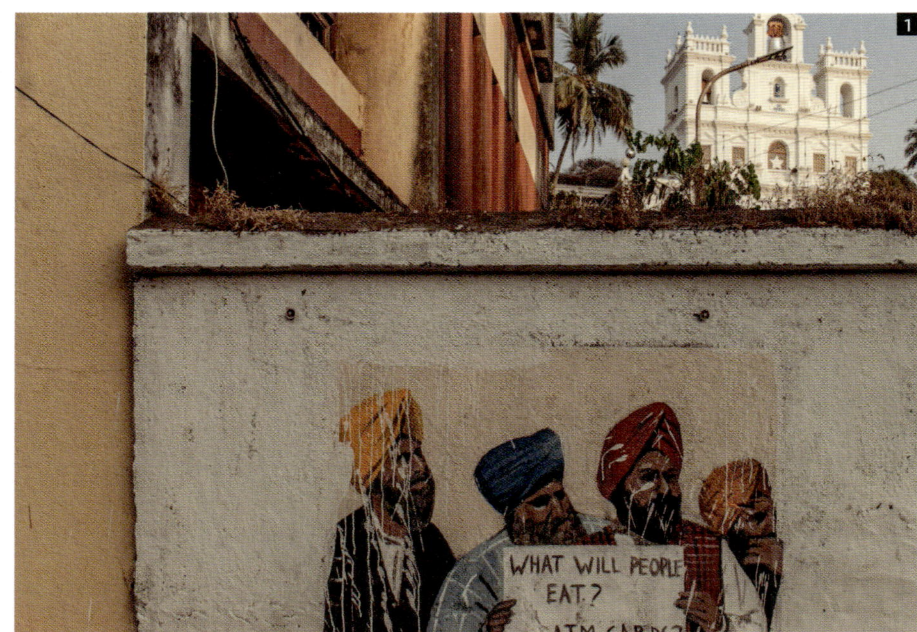

1

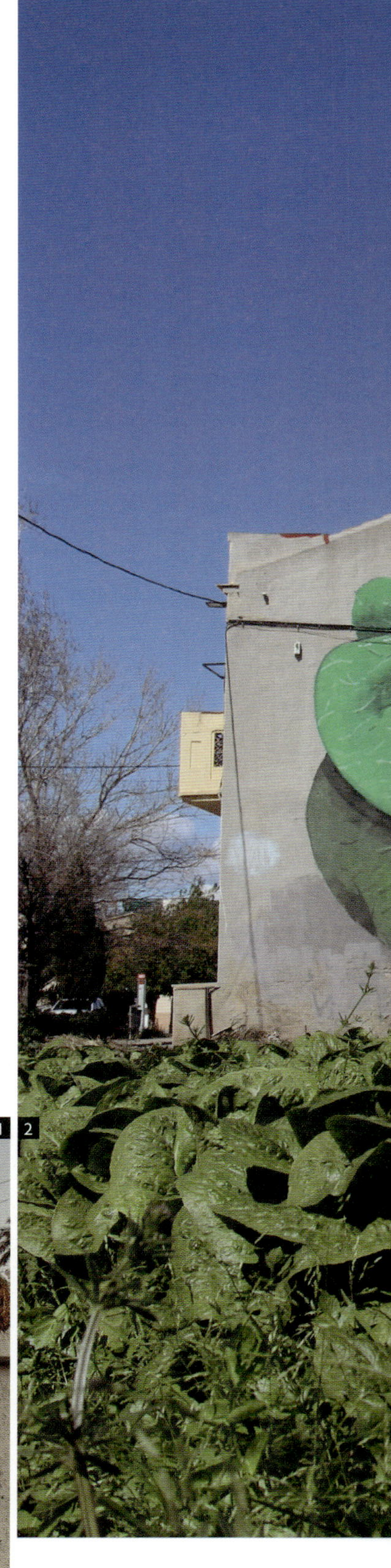

2

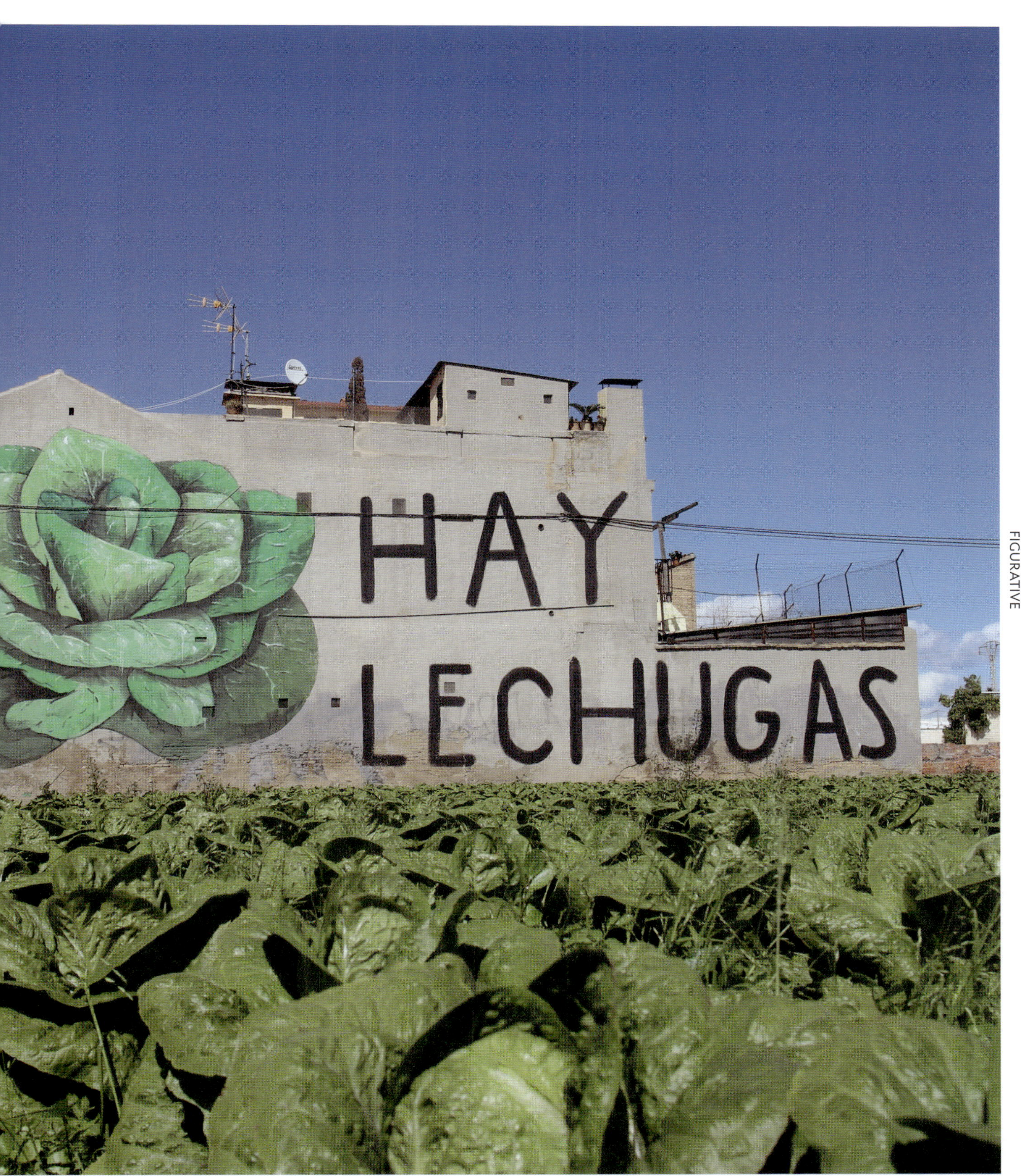

1 /
Panjim, India, 2017
PHOTO BY THE ARTIST

2 /
La Punta, Spain, 2018
PHOTO BY SASHA BOGOJEV

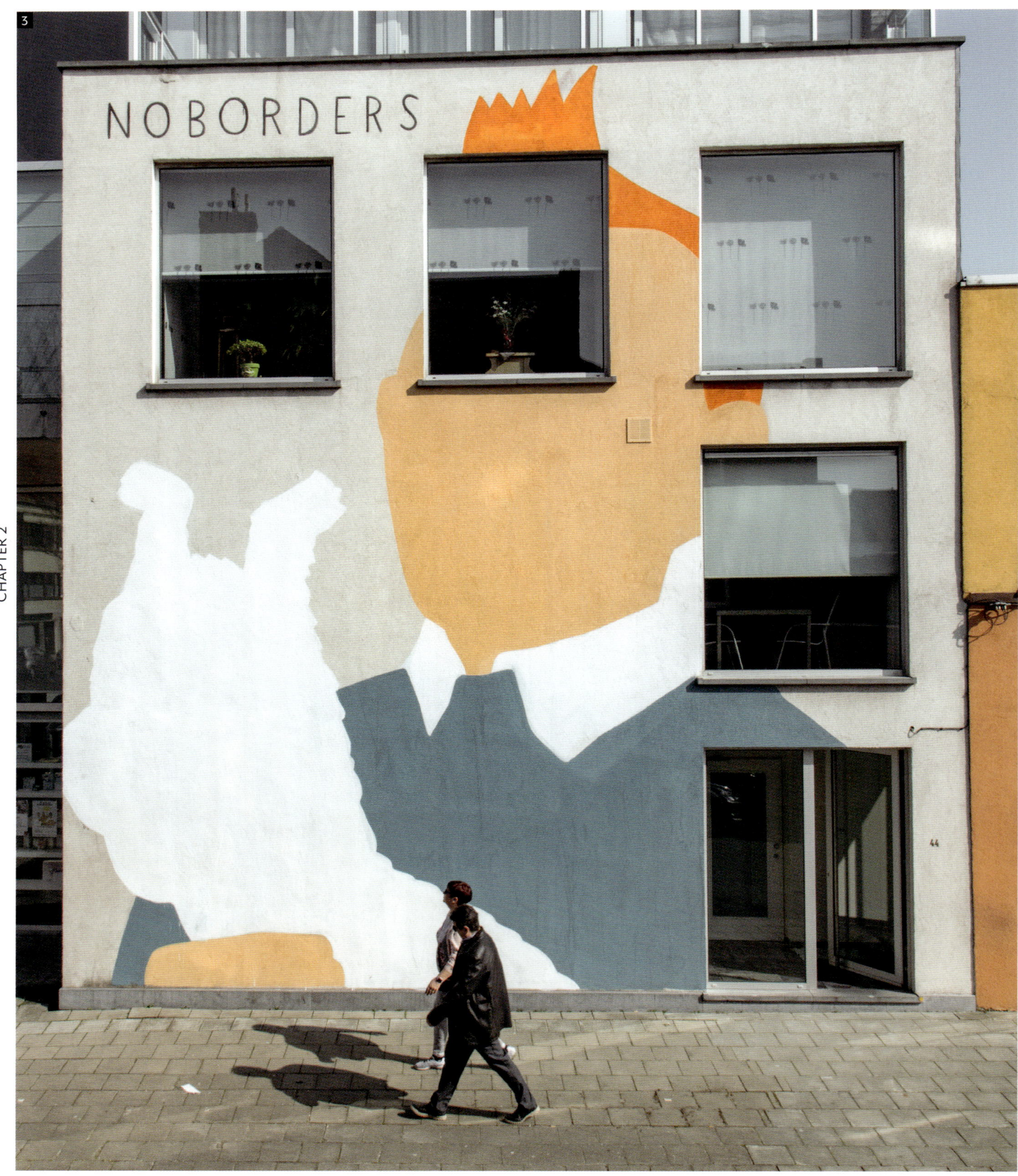
3
NOBORDERS
44

Escif has focused on themes of neoliberalism, immigration and most notably the civil war in Congo.

4

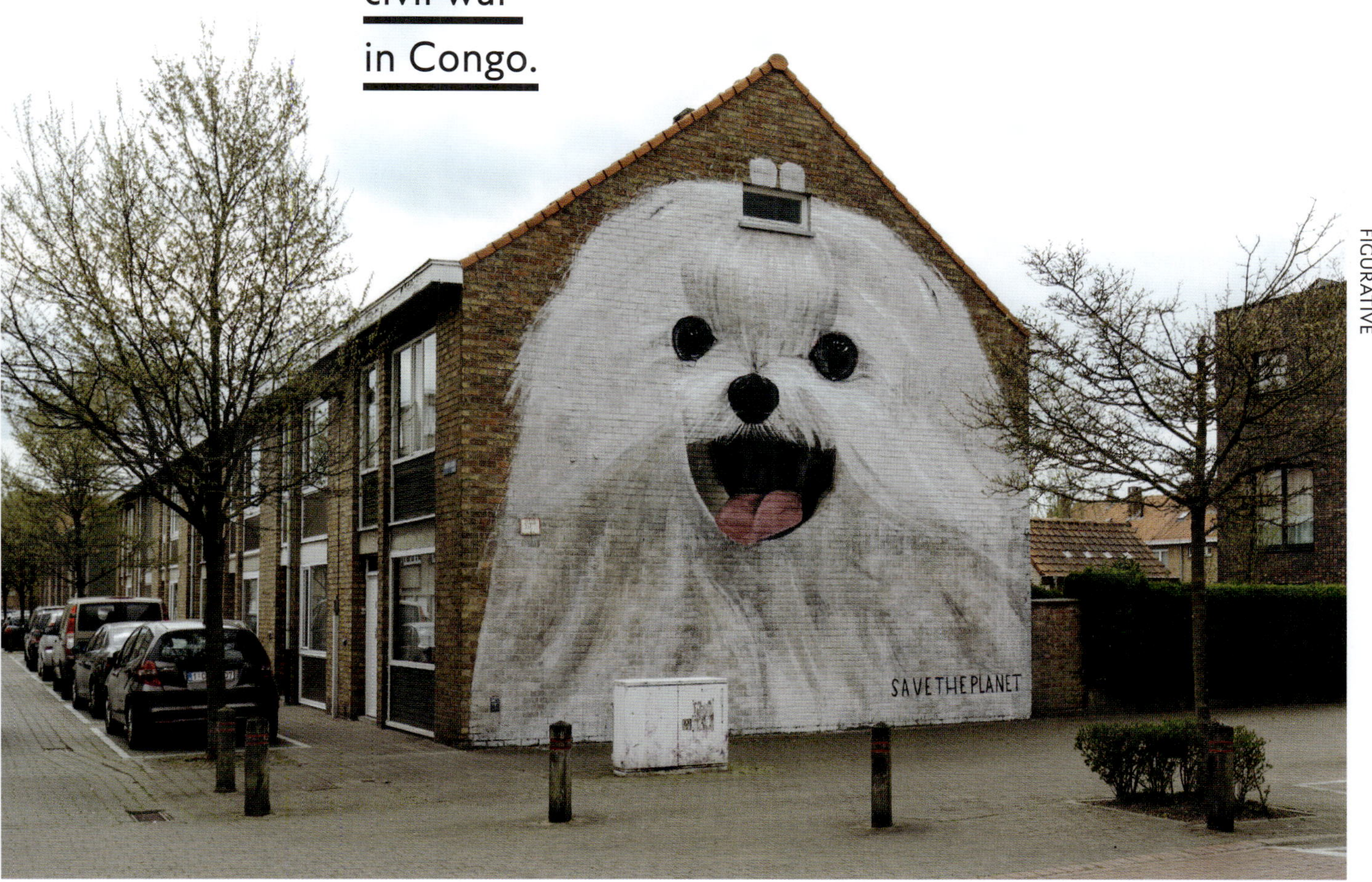

3 /
Ostend, Belgium, 2019
PHOTO BY THE ARTIST

4 /
Ostend, Belgium, 2019
PHOTO BY THE ARTIST

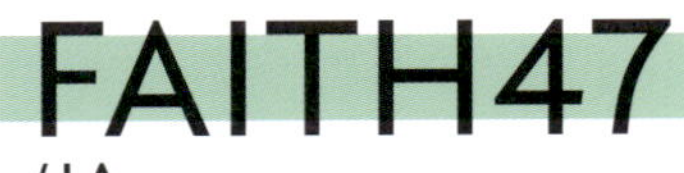

FAITH47

/ LA

Hailing from South Africa, Faith47 has been critically acclaimed by peers and the public for many years. With hundreds of urban artworks and nearly 15 years of exhibitions, she is often quoted as a reference artist for emerging and established generations of creatives.

Since being featured in the previous edition of *Street Art Today*, Faith47 has shifted in recent years from a predominantly mural-based practice to developing in new media and exploring new collaborative forms. Examples include the immersive holograms entitled 'Mysterium Tremendum' and 'Astronomia Nova', created with artists Inka Kendzia and Lyall Sprong.

Deeply concerned with paradigms of geopolitics and social (in)justice, her work is recognisable for its poetic intimacy, examining complexities and 'the interconnectedness of the human condition'. Unconstrained by medium, she has mastered muralism as well as a studio practice of drawing and sculpture, supplemented by new media, installation, virtual reality, lighting and performance production.

Her work is recognisable for its poetic intimacy, examining complexities and the interconnectedness of the human condition.

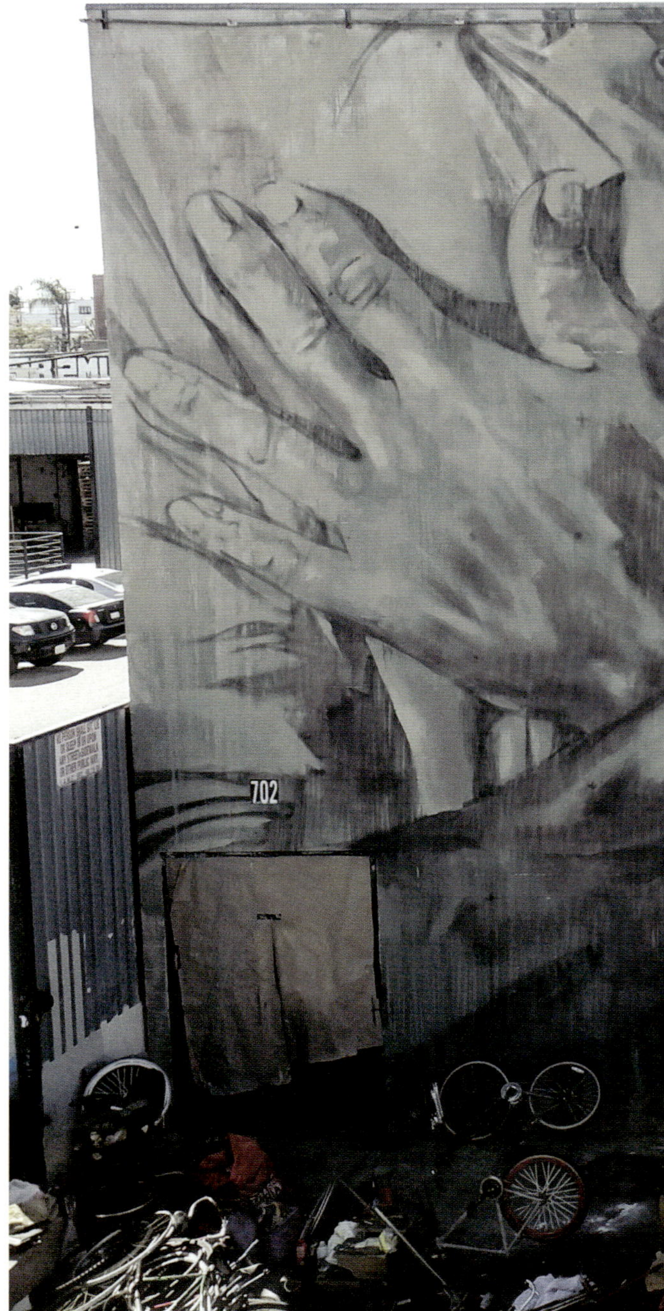

1

1 /
Los Angeles, USA, 2018
PHOTO BY THE ARTIST

2

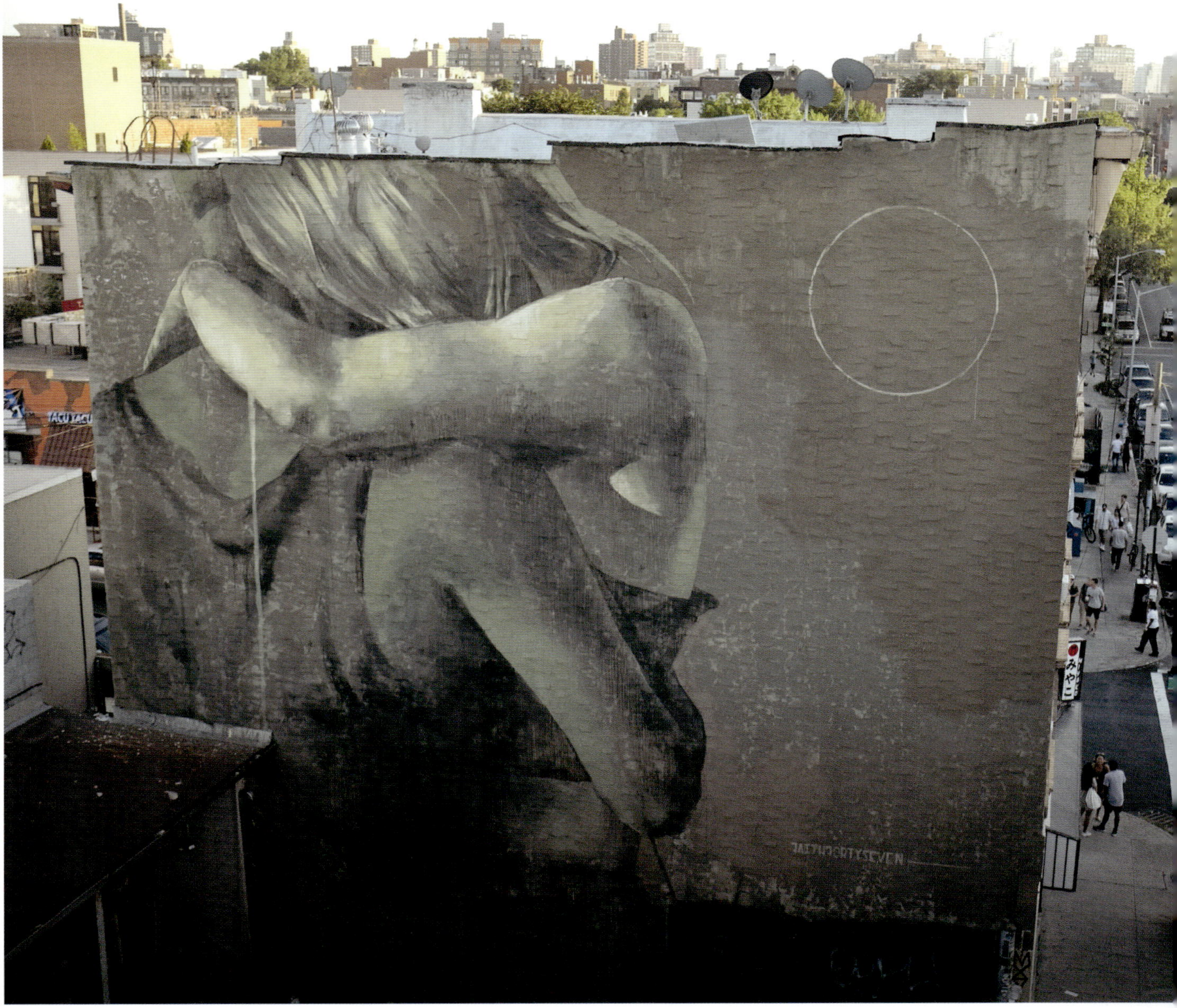

2 /
New York, USA, 2015
PHOTO BY THE ARTIST

3 /
Athens, Greece, 2016
PHOTO BY THE ARTIST

4 /
Faith47 & Lyall Sprong
Värmland, Sweden, 2017
PHOTO BY THE ARTIST

4

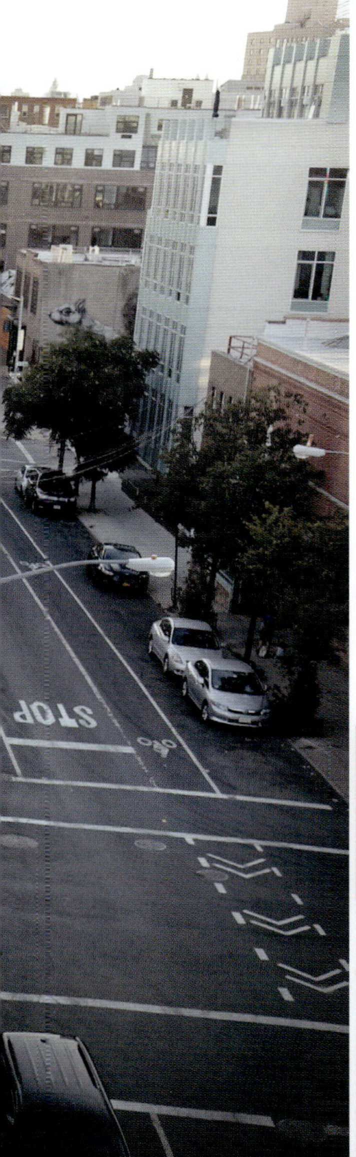

Faith47 is often quoted as a reference artist for emerging and established generations of creatives.

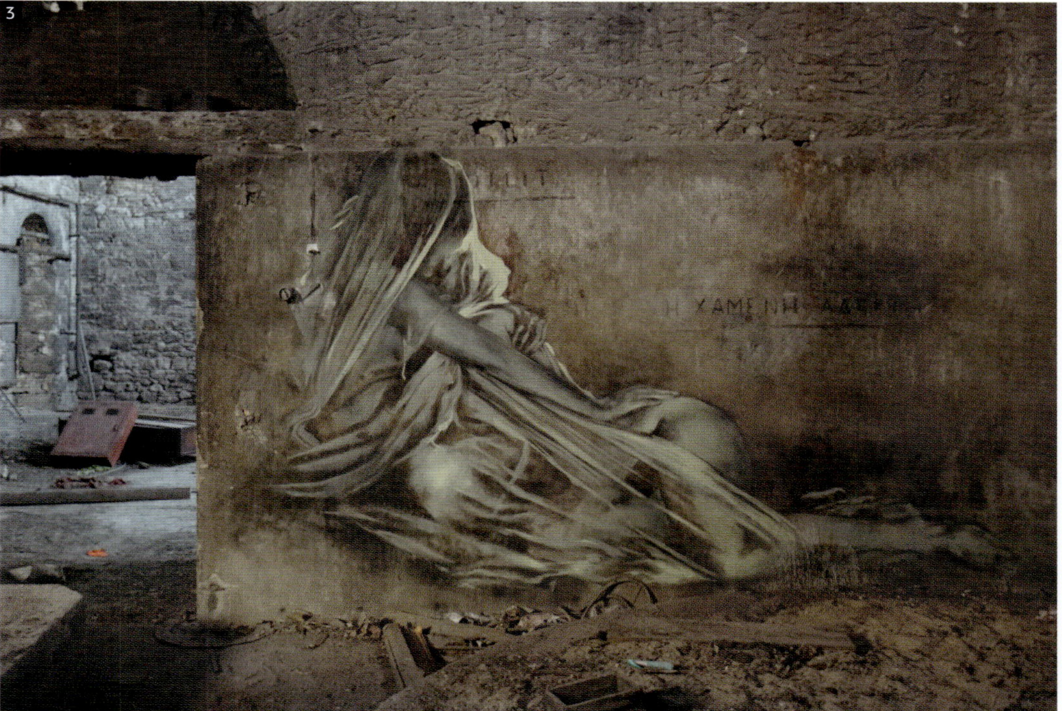
3

FINTAN MAGEE

/ Sydney

One of the most prolific Australian street artists today, Fintan Magee does not shy away from heavy political or social thematics, often taking the opportunity in his large-scale murals to open up conversations regarding economic and political injustice, climate change, and criticism of capitalist ventures.

Highly respected in the street art community for his incredible mastery of realism, his portraiture often integrates layers of visual fields and meanings. Often incorporating cues reminiscent of surrealism, Magee considers himself a 'social realist' with an imaginative style, extending the story beyond the figures portrayed.

1

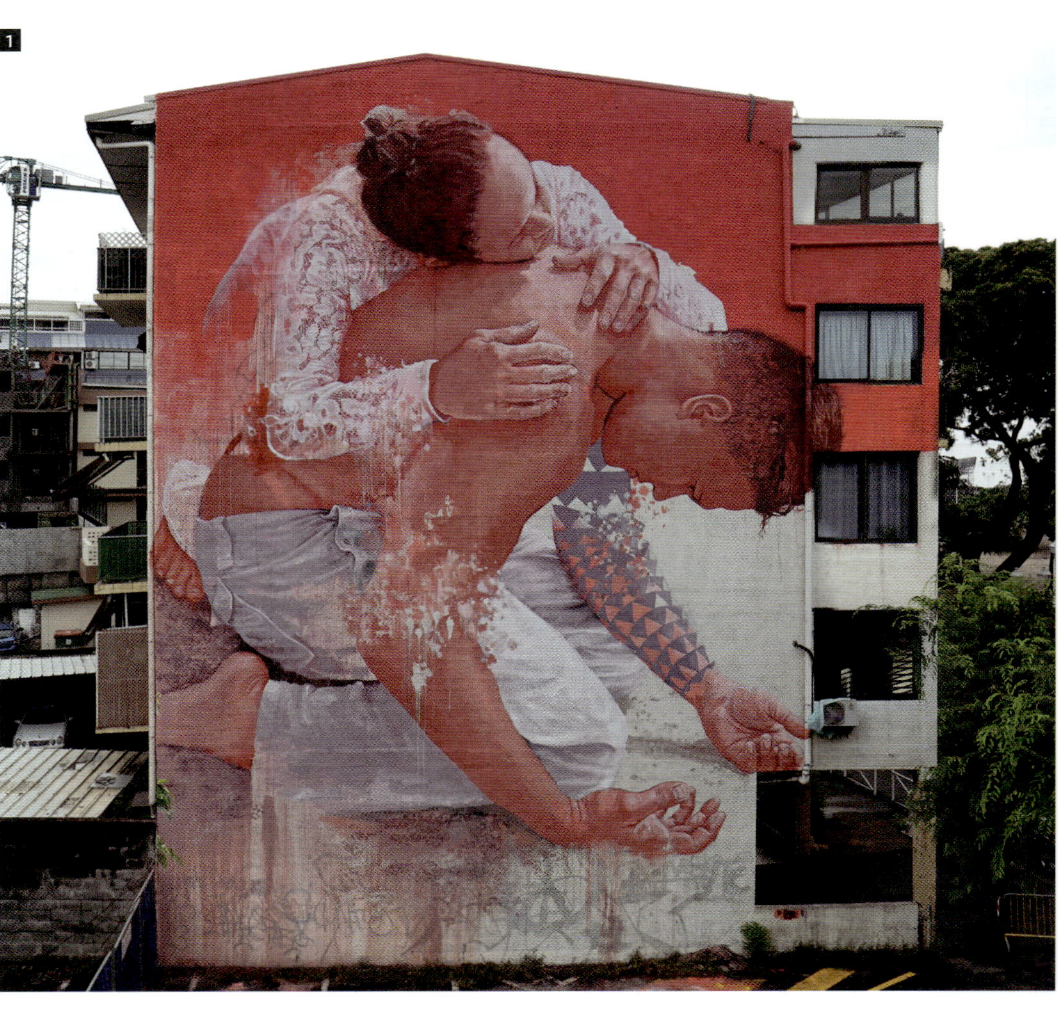

1 /
Pape'ete, French Polynesia, 2019
PHOTO BY THE ARTIST

2 /
Goa, India, 2019
PHOTO BY THE ARTIST

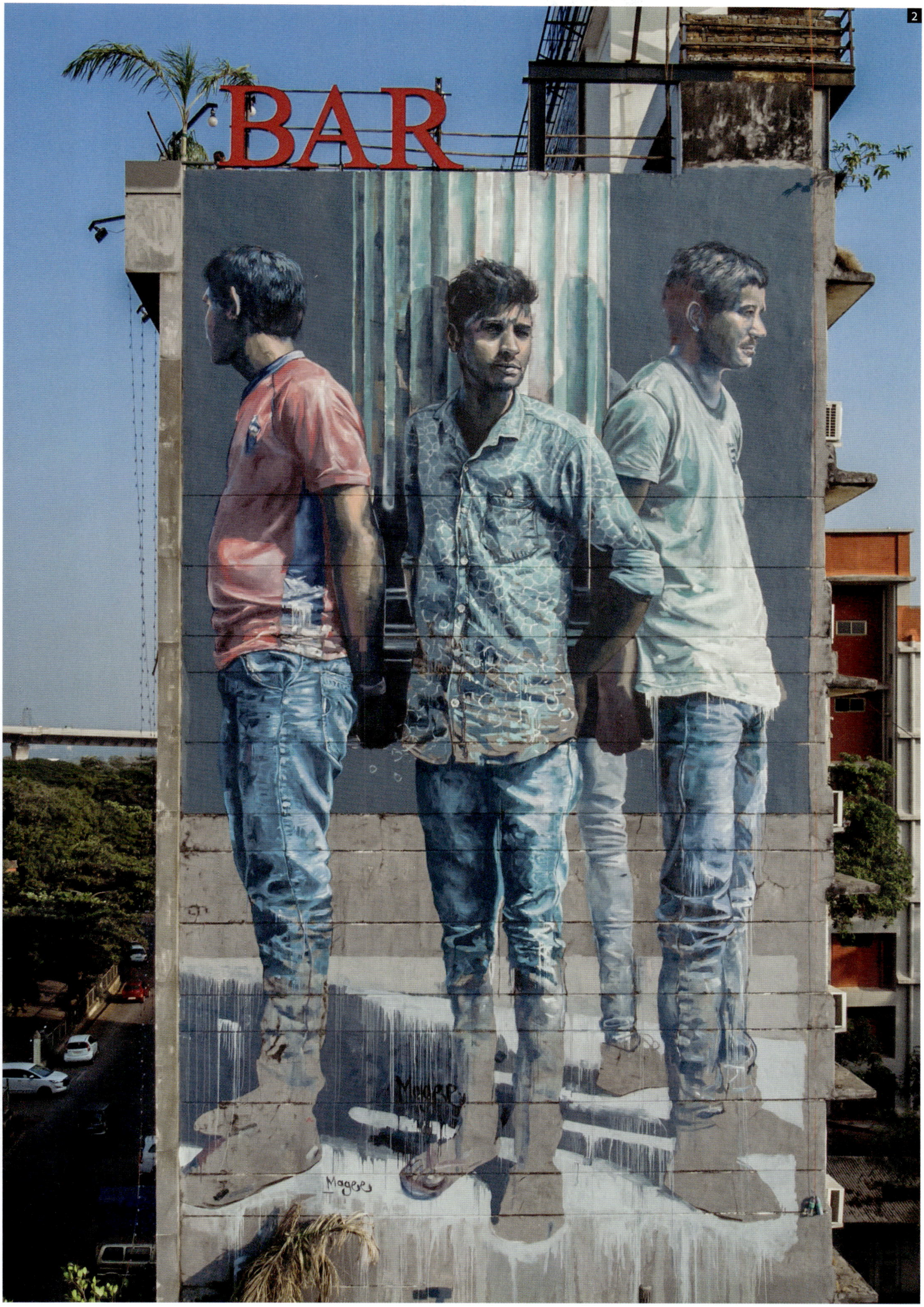

2

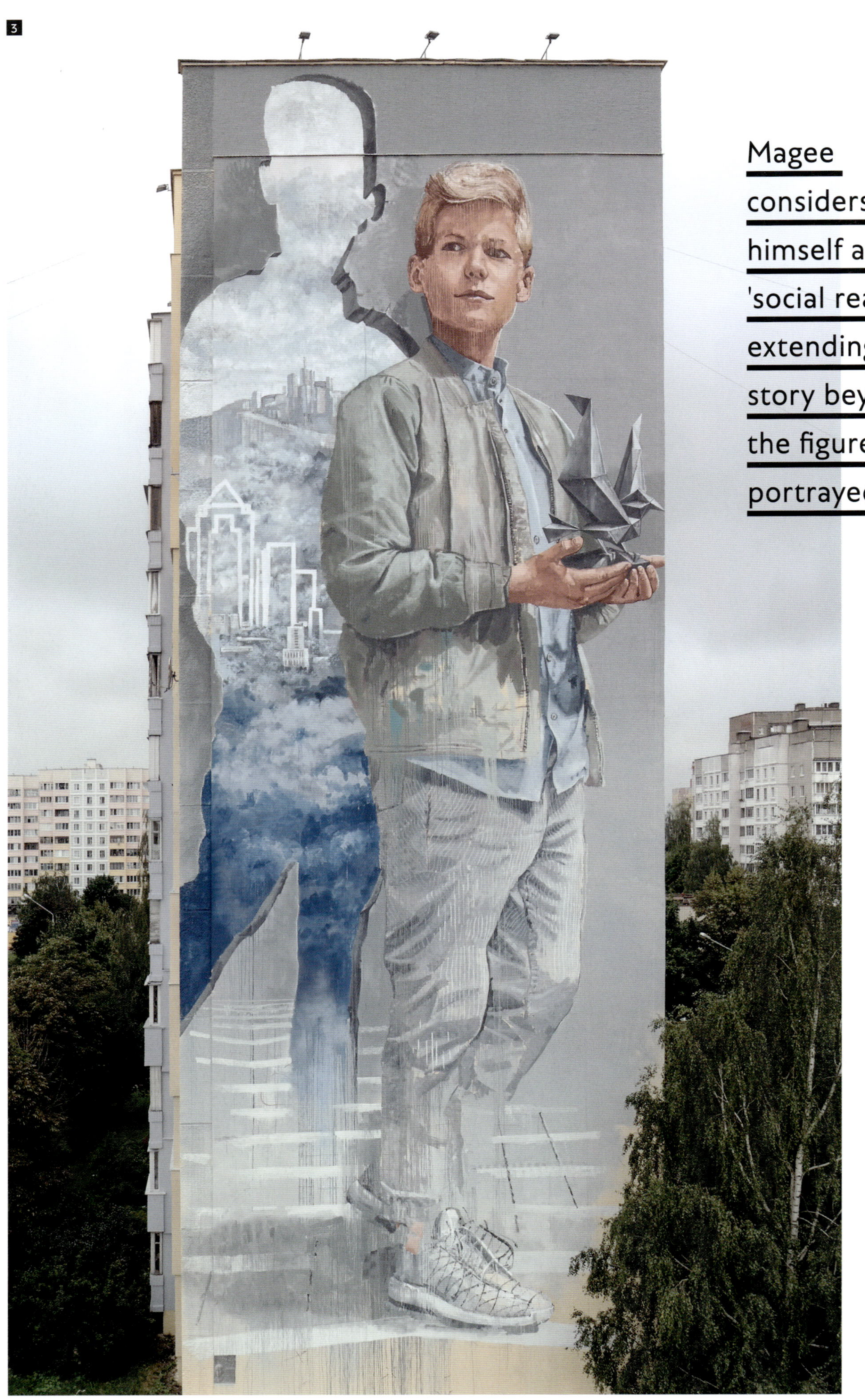

Magee considers himself a 'social realist', extending the story beyond the figures portrayed.

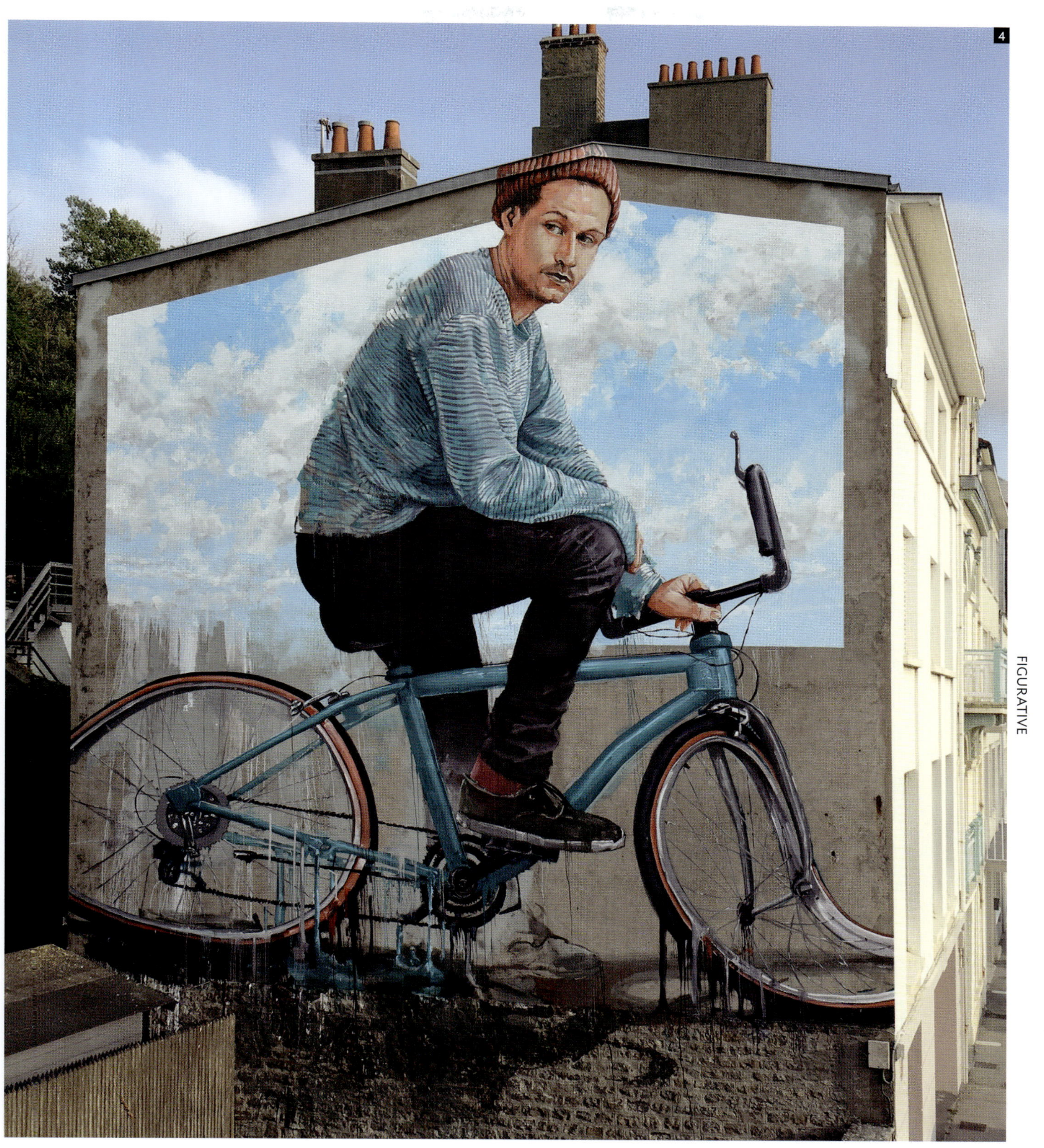

3 /
Minsk, Belarus, 2018
PHOTO BY THE ARTIST

4 /
Boulogne-sur-Mer, France, 2018
PHOTO BY THE ARTIST

HERAKUT

/ Germany

German duo Herakut joined forces in 2004 after having both traversed the paths of education in graphic design. Hera (Jasmin Siddiqui) and Akut (Falk Lehmann) balance their radically different styles to create a universe reminiscent of a dark fairy-tale. In what could be described as a contemporary fresco process, the pair combine, divide and layer their individual specialities. Hera structures and accentuates the images with dynamic lines and gestures, allowing Akut's photorealistic elements to add an impossible reality to the imagery.

This game of composition pushes and pulls our perspective, making their dreamlike landscape of characters seem ever so close to our reality.

The duo balances their radically different styles to create a universe reminiscent of a dark fairy-tale.

1

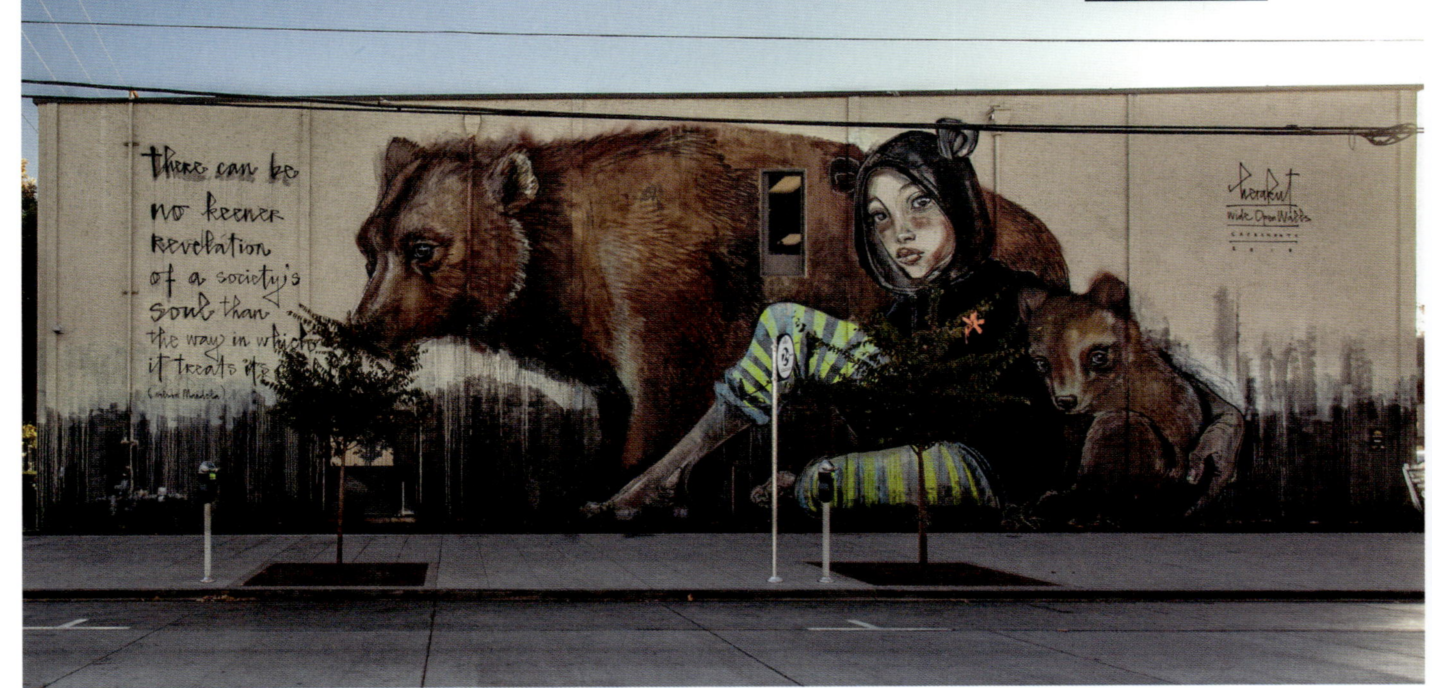

1 /
Sacramento, California, USA, 2018
PHOTO BY VINNY CORNELLI

2 / 3
Los Angeles, USA, 2018
PHOTO BY BIRDMAN

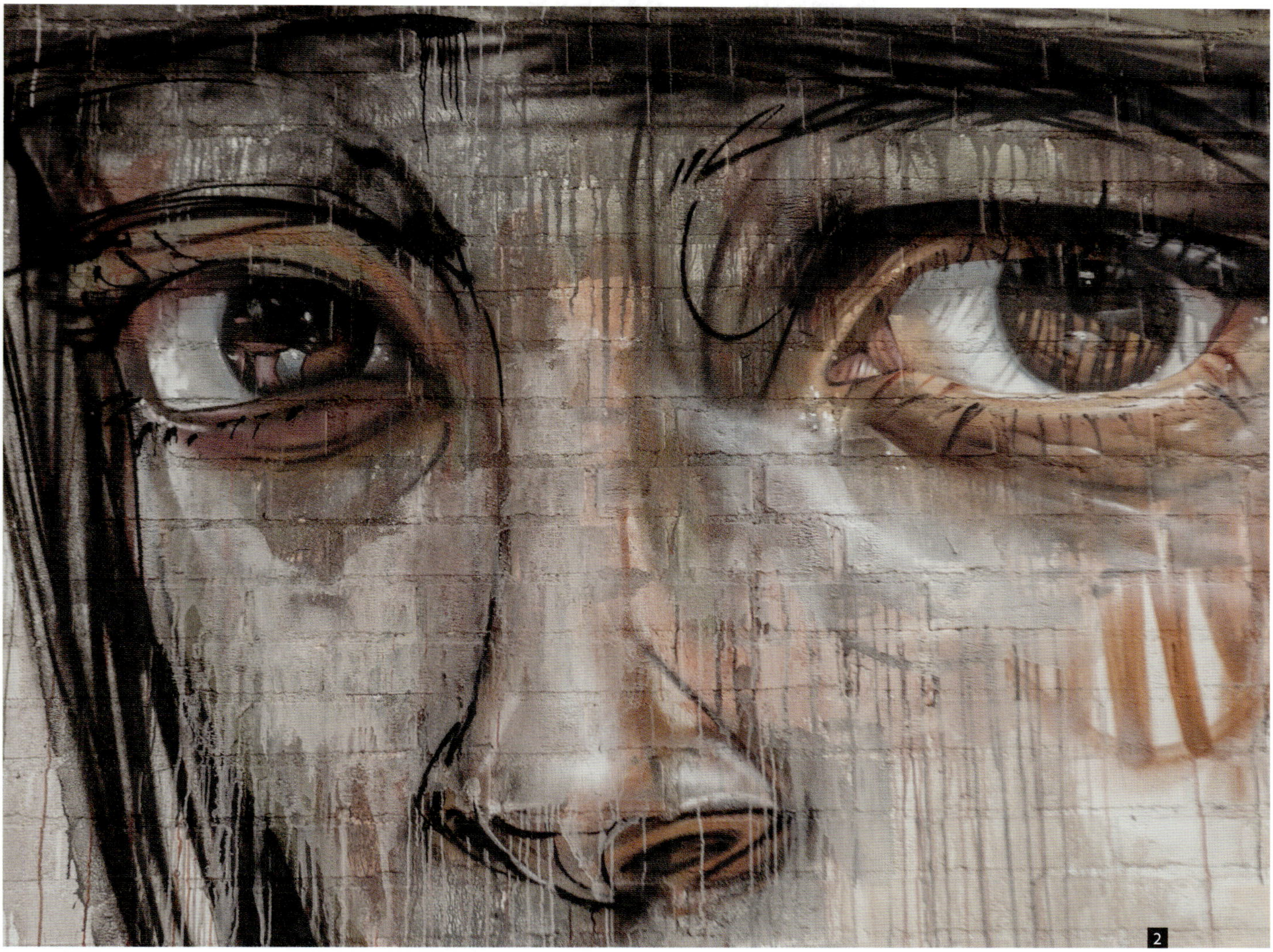

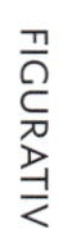

2

3

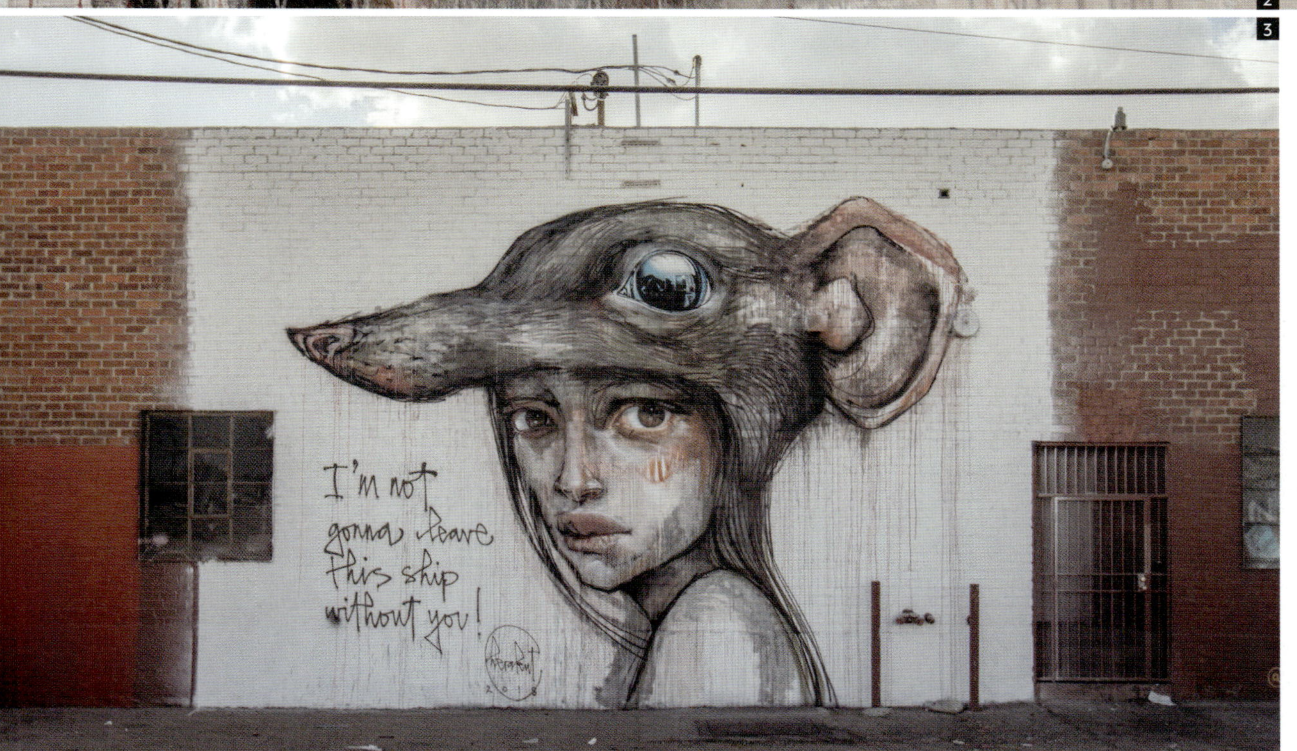

4

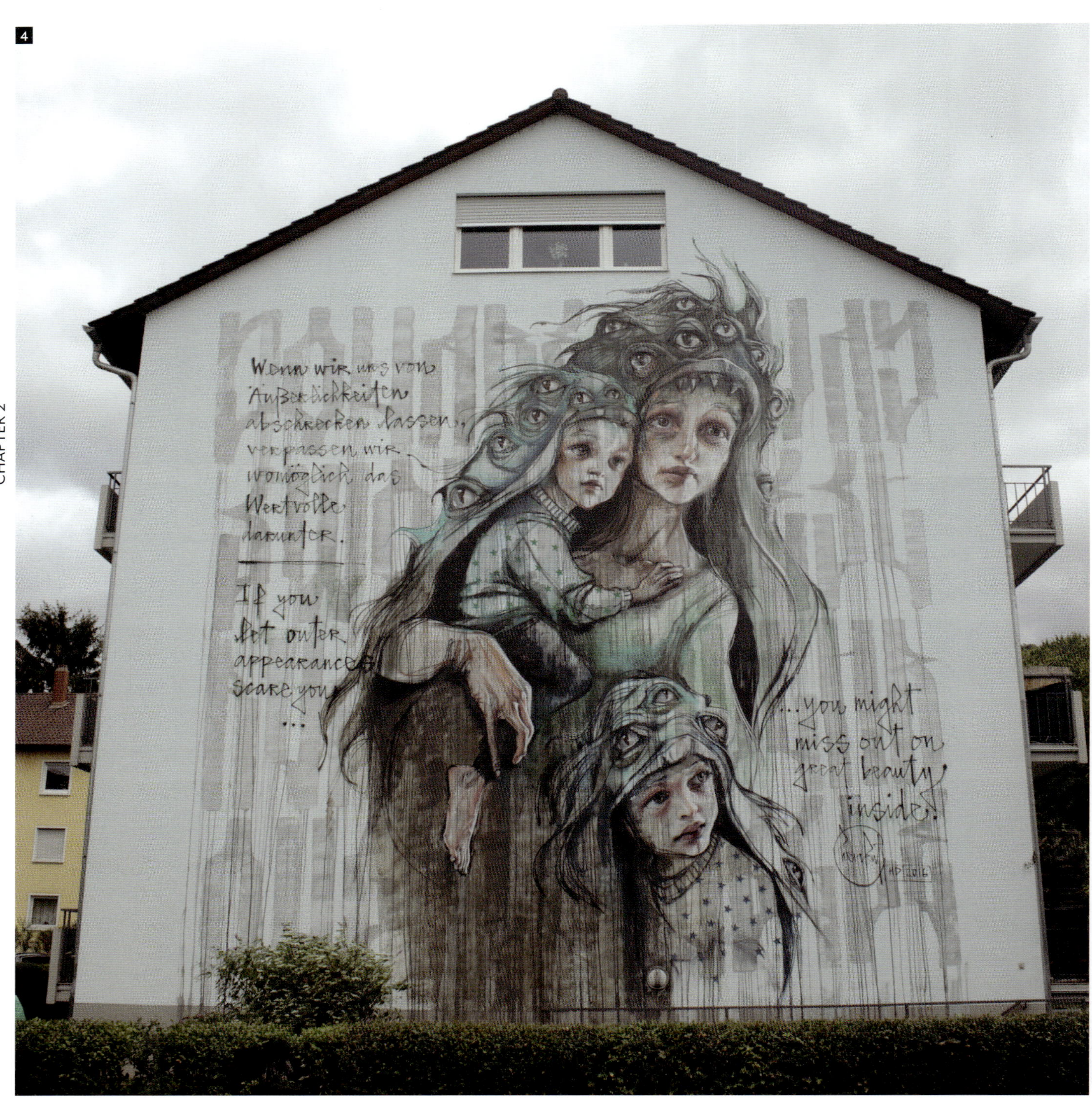
Wenn wir uns von
Äußerlichkeiten
abschrecken lassen,
verpassen wir
womöglich das
Wertvolle
darunter.
If you
let outer
appearances
scare you
...
...you might
miss out on
great beauty
inside!
HD 2016

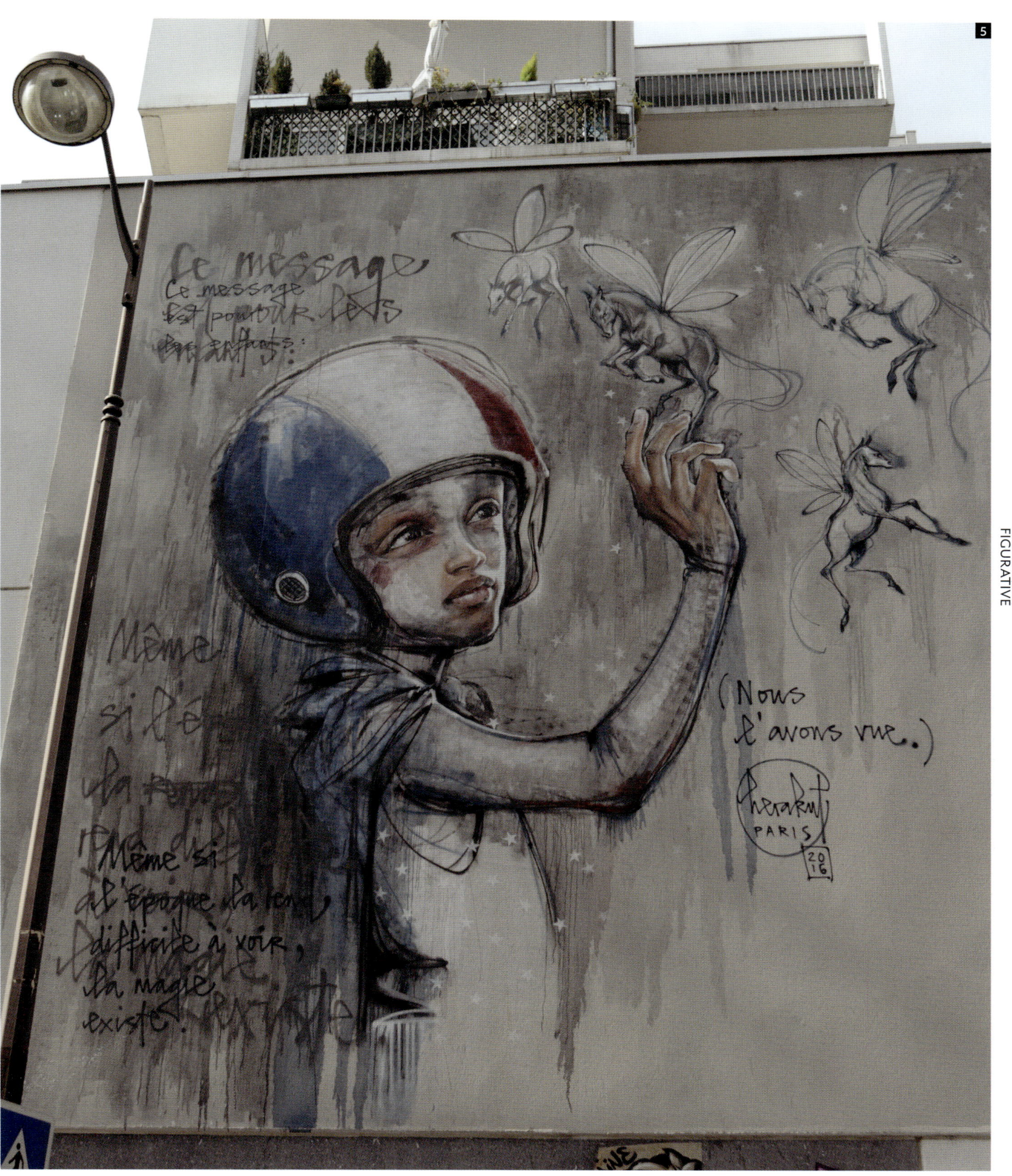

4 /
Heidelberg, Germany, 2019
PHOTO BY TIM JENTSCH

5 /
Paris, France, 2016
PHOTO BY TIM JENTSCH

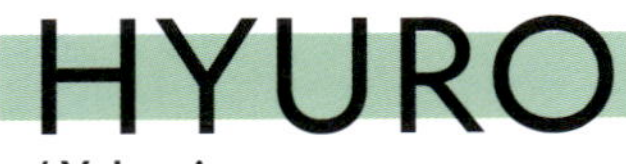

/ Valencia

Argentinian-born, Hyuro is best known for blending social issues into surrealist and dreamlike compositions. As an artist, her visual language is very poetic and often features women in challenging situations. The way she depicts the portraits in combination with her subtle palette of colours often results in an uncomfortable feeling, providing an ideal way to present socio-political topics to the world.

For Hyuro, painting in public spaces comes with responsibility. Street art can be a tool to provoke change, communicate, and share ideologies – a way to build bridges, break down boundaries and inspire dialogue. It is her way of contributing to society.

The visual language is very poetic and her work often features women in challenging situations.

1

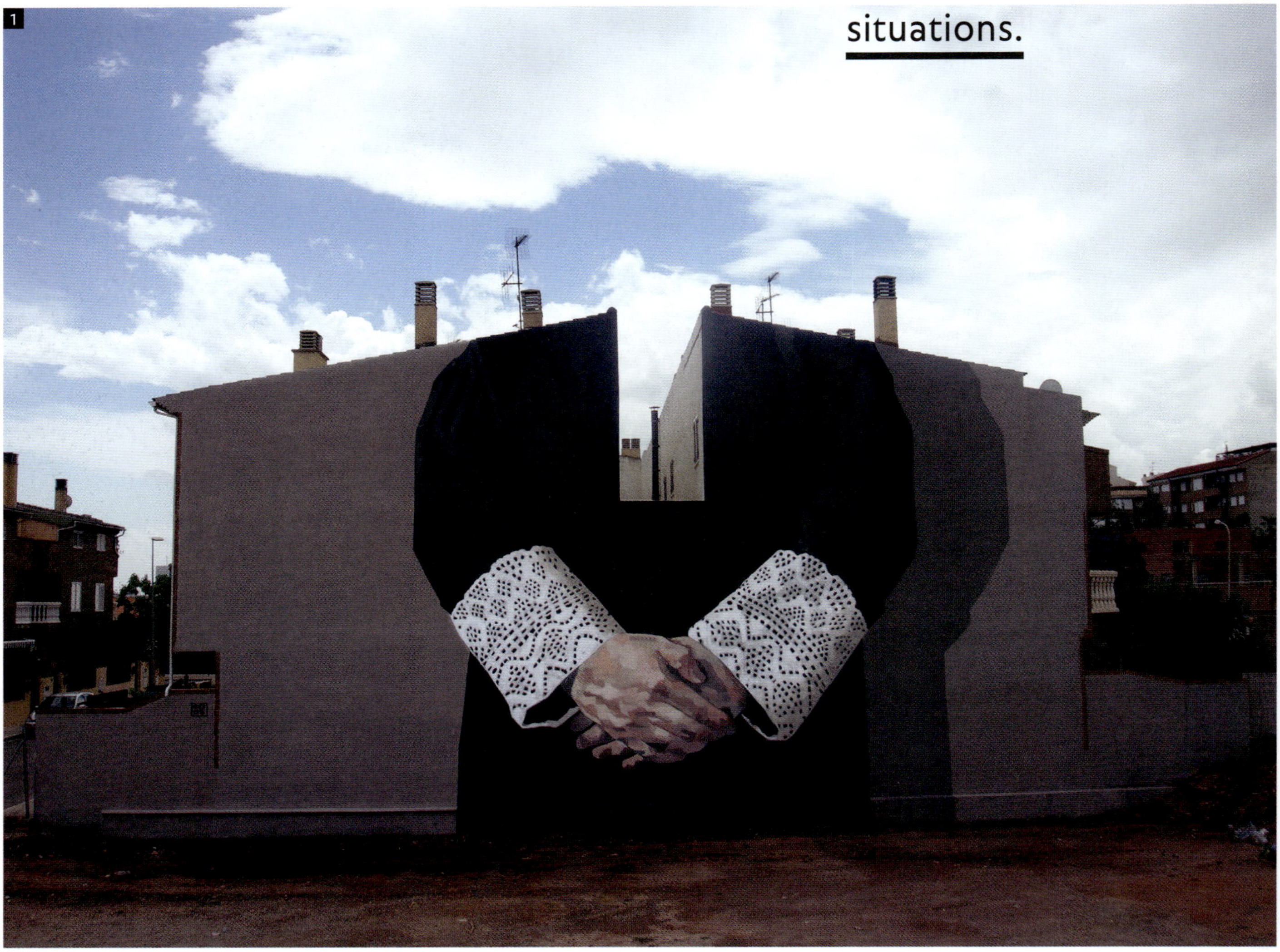

1 /
Vila-real, Spain, 2018
PHOTO BY THE ARTIST

2 /
Ragusa, Italy, 2016
PHOTO BY THE ARTIST

2

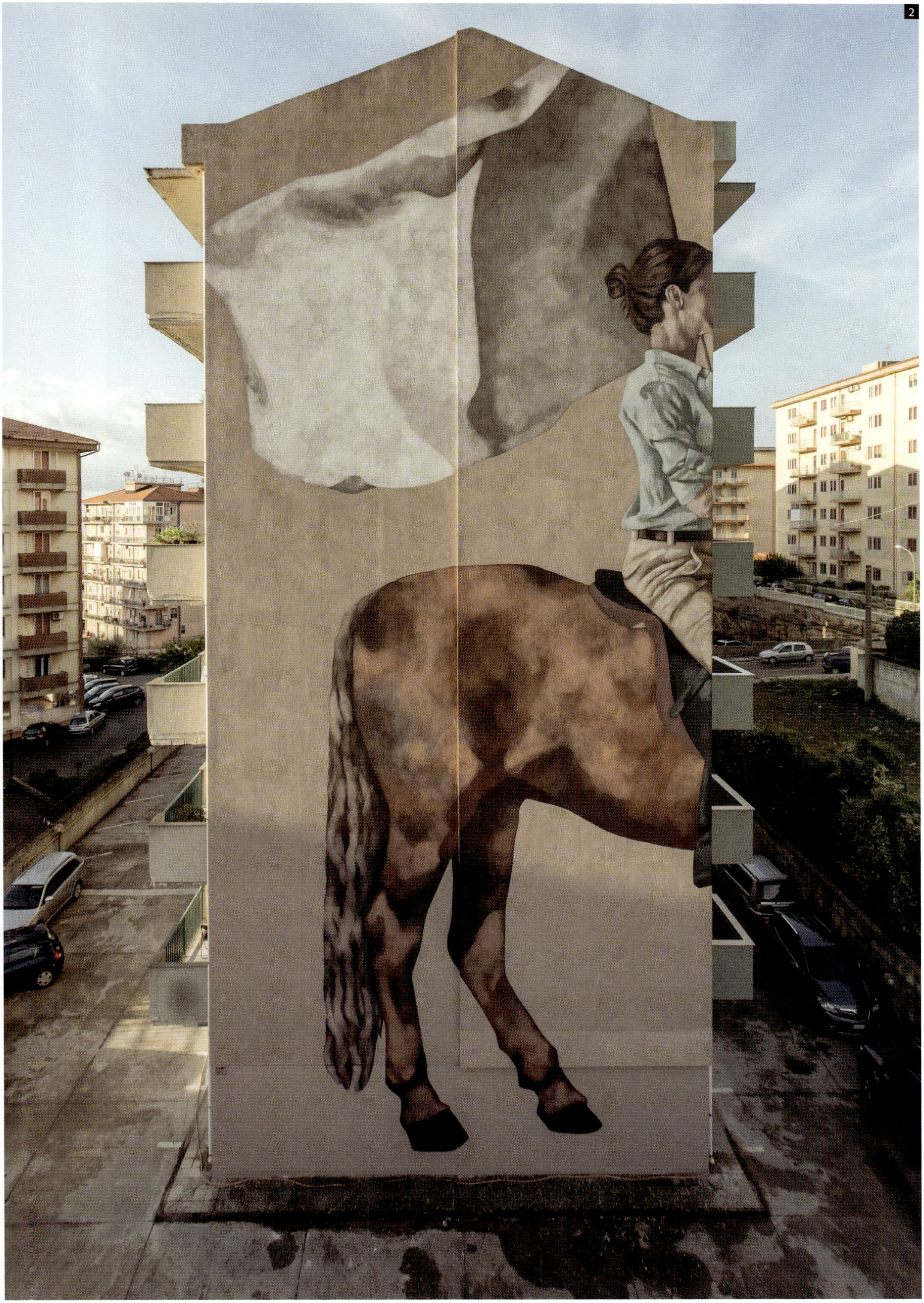

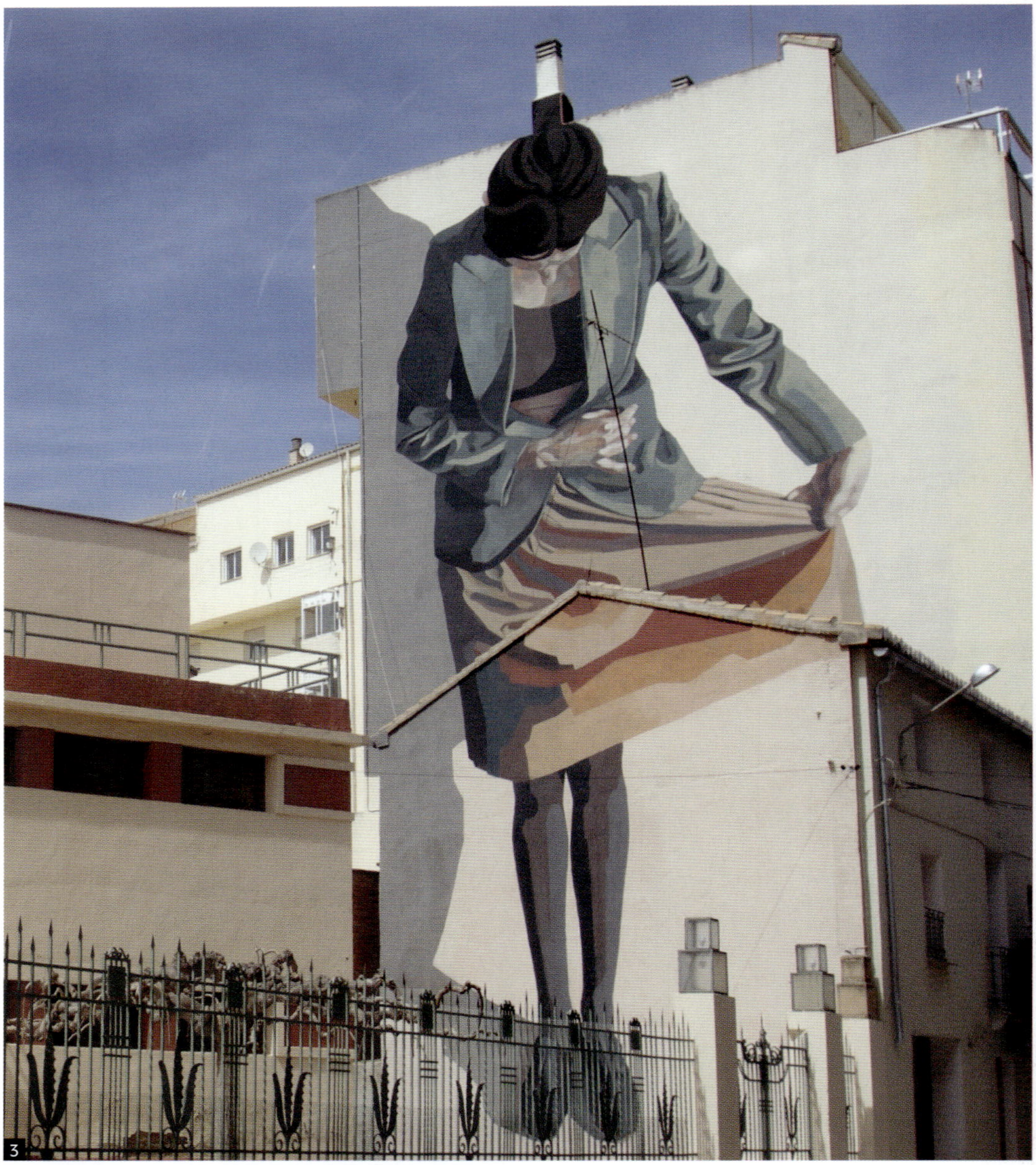

3

4

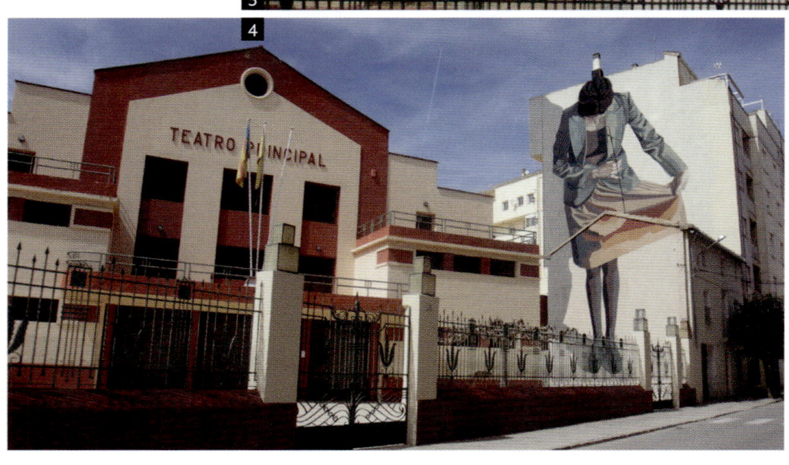

3 / 4
Requena, Spain, 2018
PHOTO BY THE ARTIST

5 /
Ostend, Belgium, 2017
PHOTO BY THE ARTIST

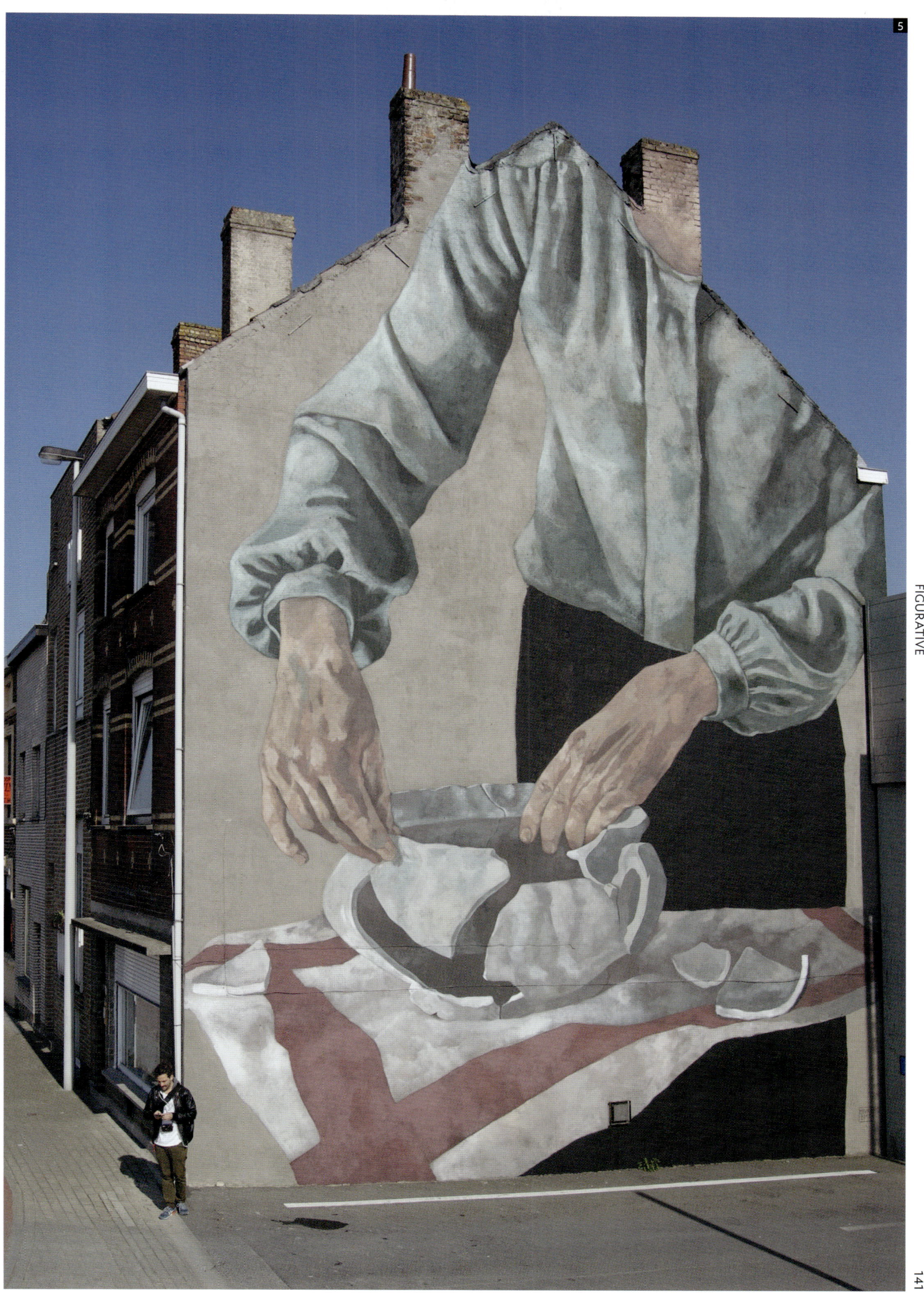

5

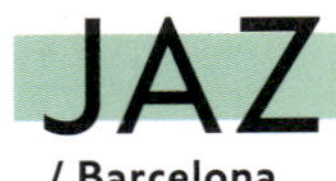

JAZ

/ Barcelona

Discussions of the work of Argentinian artist Jaz, aka Franco Fasoli, regularly include words like 'conflict', 'struggle', 'confrontation' and 'duality'. In pieces often represent human or animal figures, Jaz is interested in exploring the multiplicity and tension in individual and collective identity, particularly in the Latin American context.

With large-scale murals spread across the urban landscape, he hopes to open a public dialogue on society's norms, inherent in popular culture and subcultures world-wide. Interestingly, his education as a scenographer gave him a keen interest in materiality. He questions the ephemeral and permanent by producing mixed-media collages and bronze sculptures. Jaz shows us the inner, outer, individual and common struggle of which we are all part, consciously or not.

1

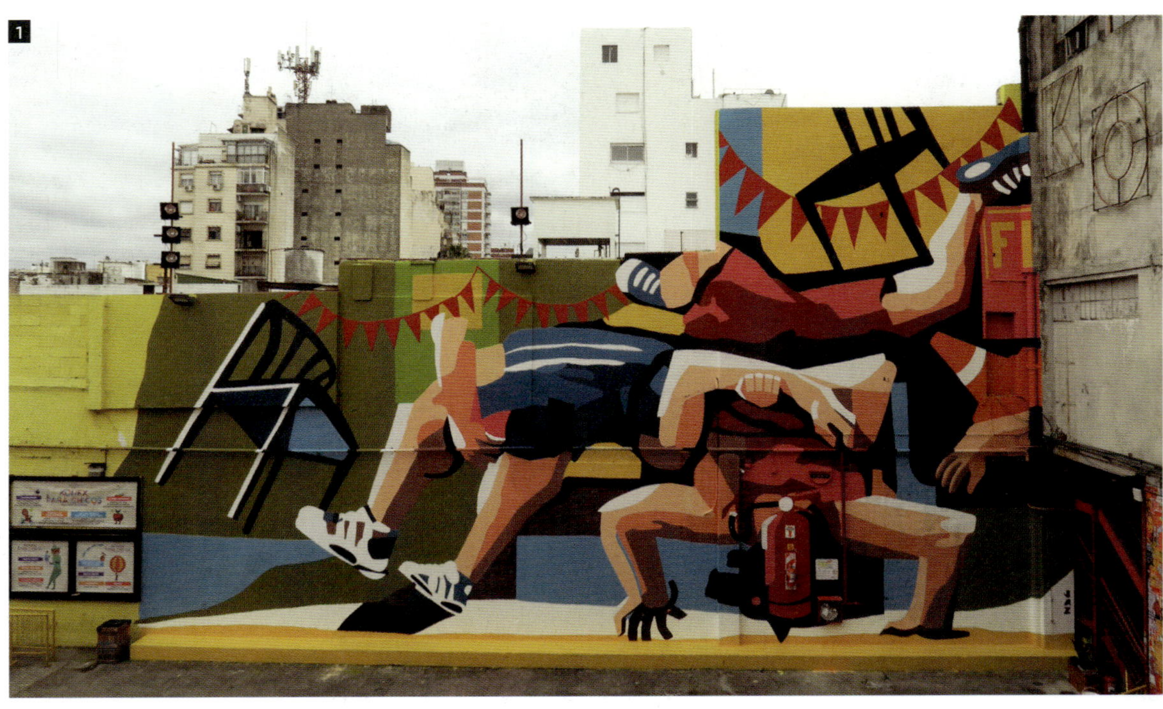

1 /
Buenos Aires, Argentina, 2018
PHOTO BY THE ARTIST

2 /
Rabat , Morocco, 2015
PHOTO BY THE ARTIST

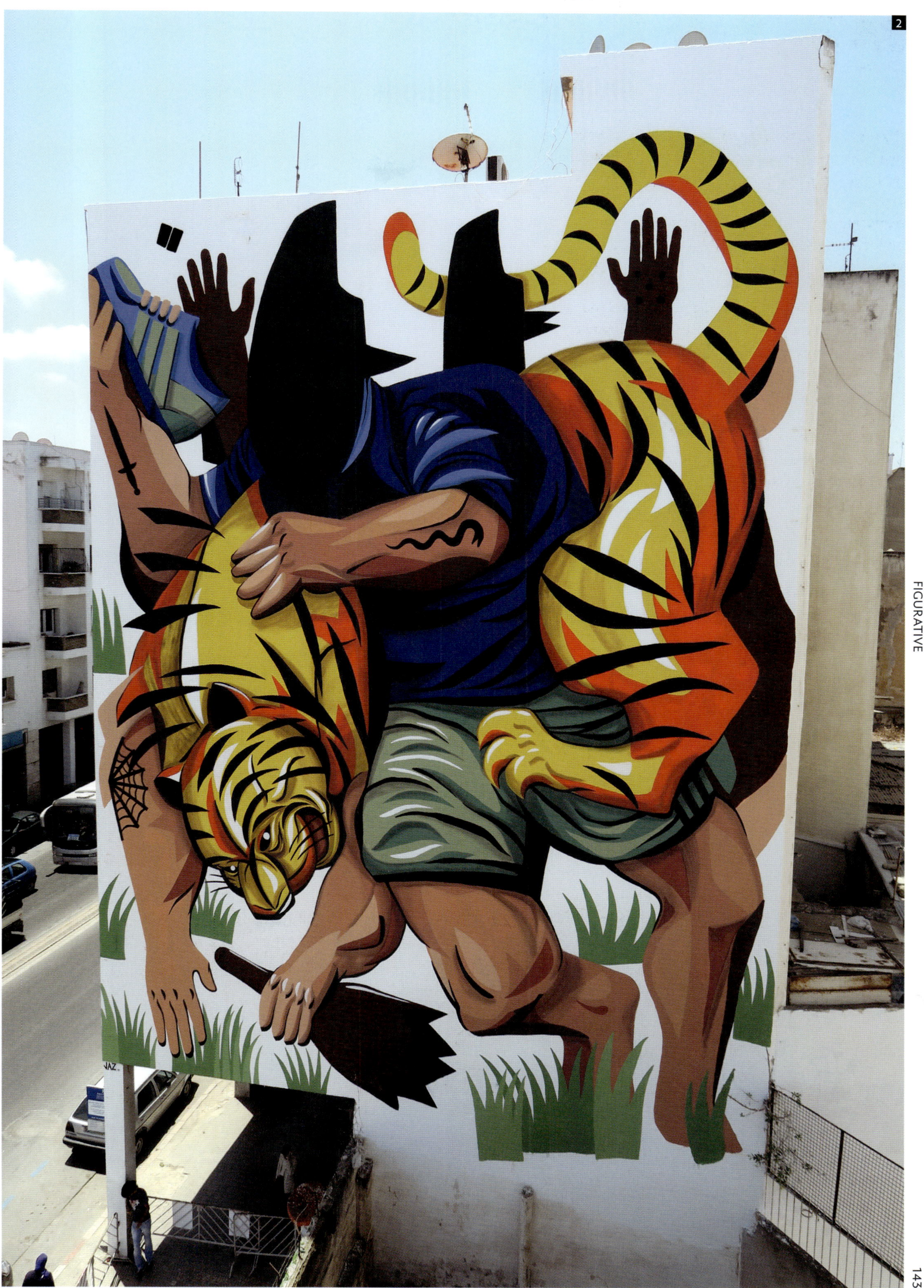

2

3

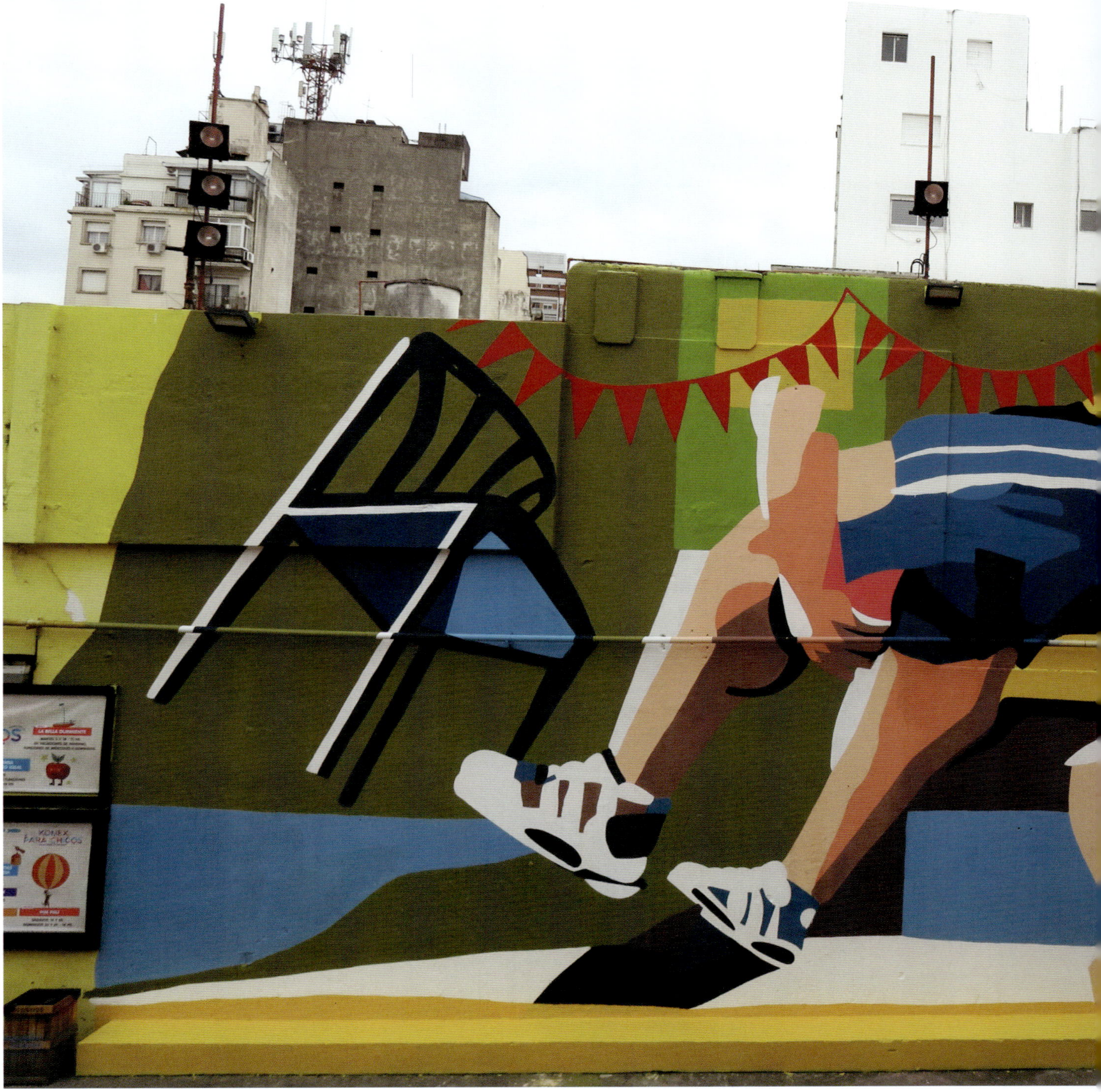

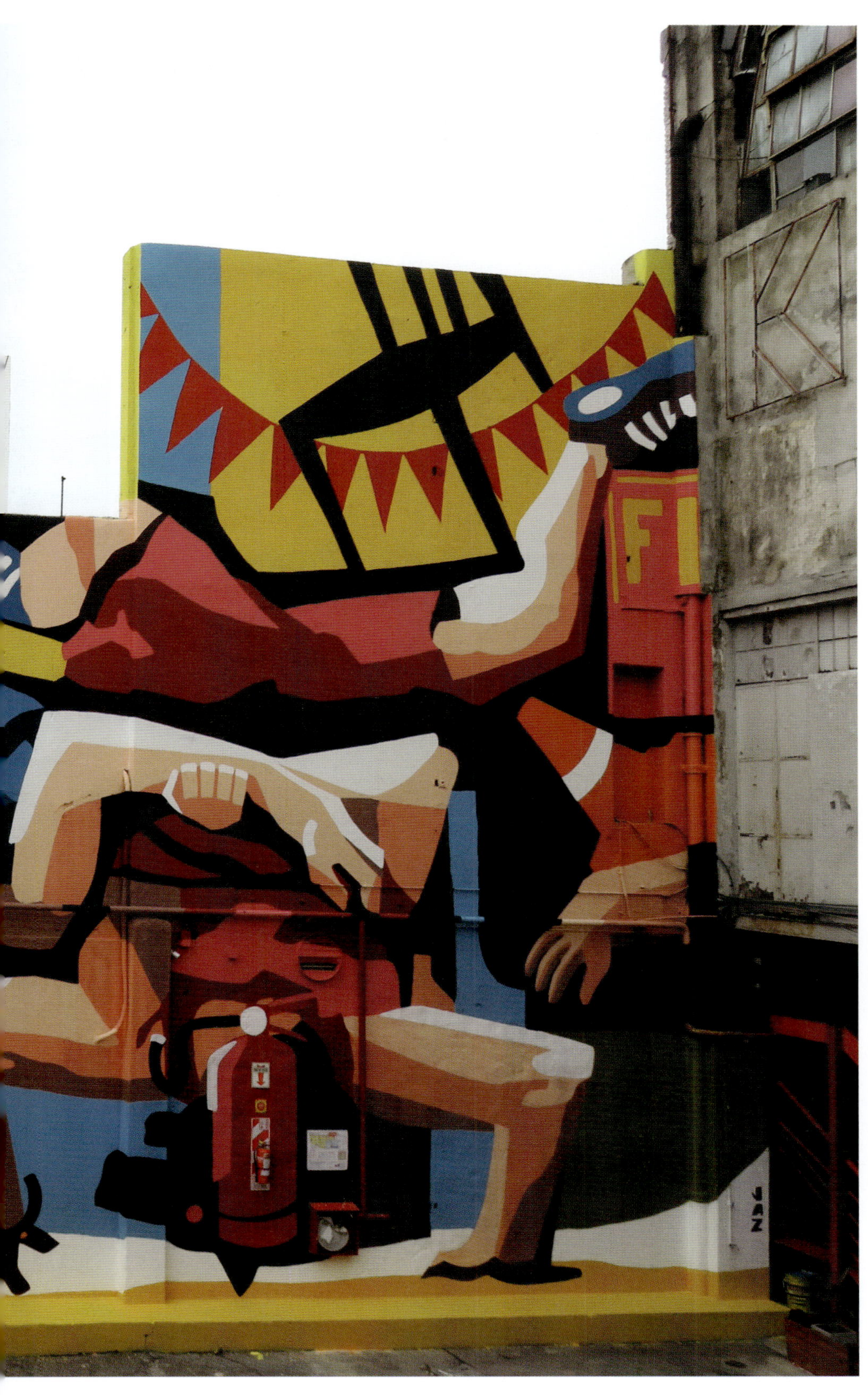

Jaz shows us the inner, outer, individual and common struggle of which we are all part.

3 /
Konex, Buenos Aires, 2018
PHOTO BY THE ARTIST

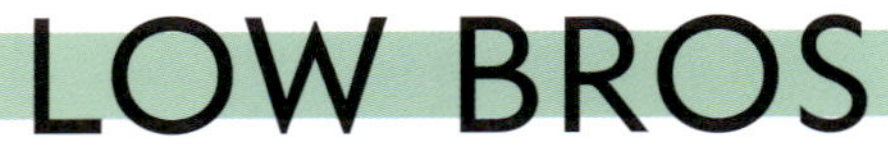

/ Berlin and Hamburg

Christoph and Florin Schmidt are German Post-Graffiti artists and collaborate under the name of "Low Bros". Having famously coined the term 'retro-futuristic' to describe their work, they clearly put forward a cheeky ambivalence that runs throughout their productions. A very peculiar balance, layering pop-culture references of the past and the slick synthetics of an imagined future, creates their timeless universe. With inorganic geometry forming planes of space and floating, animal-like characters, they create a strangely nostalgic yet surreal world.

Unsurprisingly, their work may be found not only in the public space, but also in many contemporary art galleries and design projects across the globe.

The Low Bros create a strangely nostalgic yet surreal world.

1

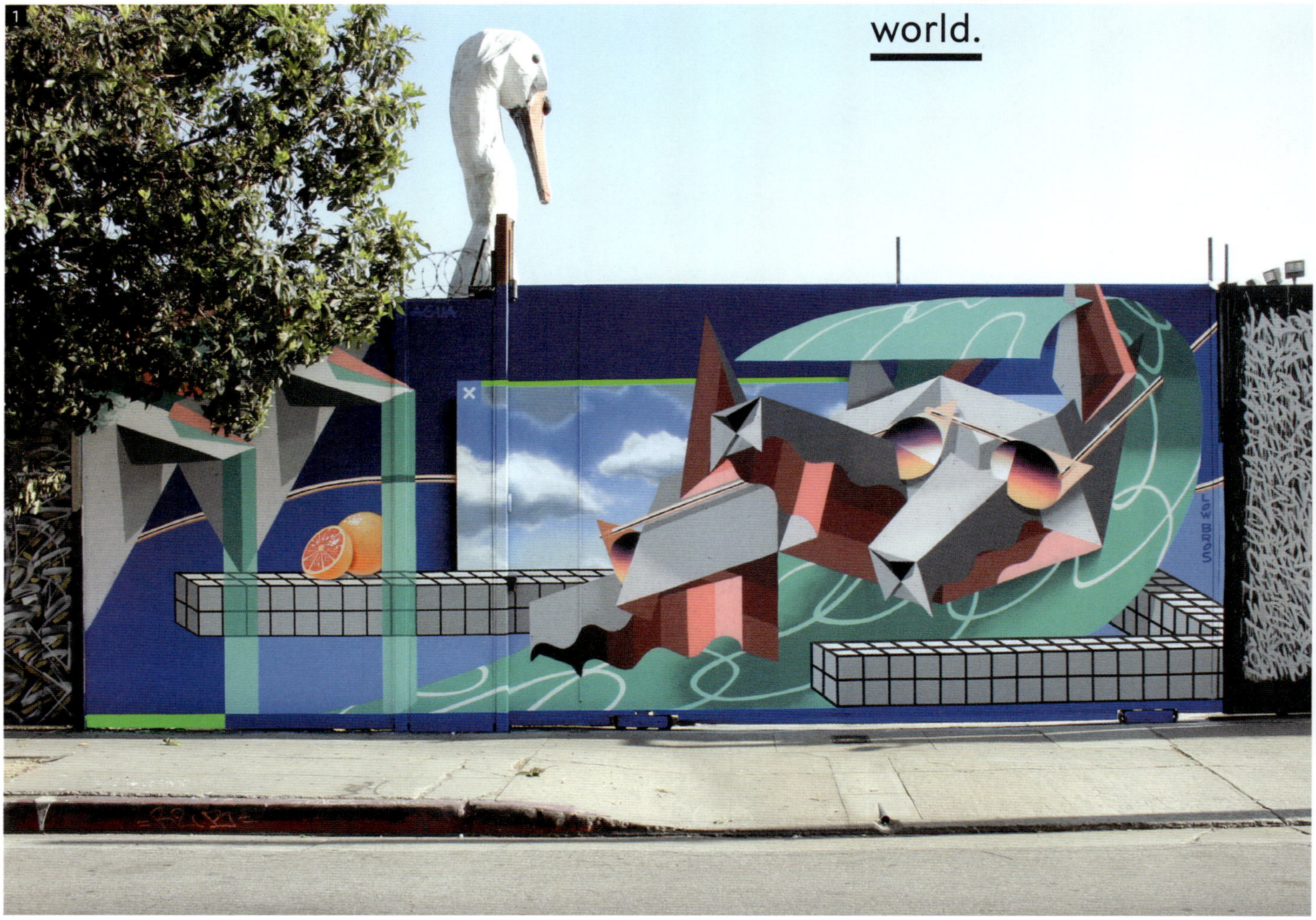

1 /
Los Angeles, USA, 2018
PHOTO BY THE ARTIST

2 /
Warsaw, Poland, 2018
PHOTO BY THE ARTIST

2

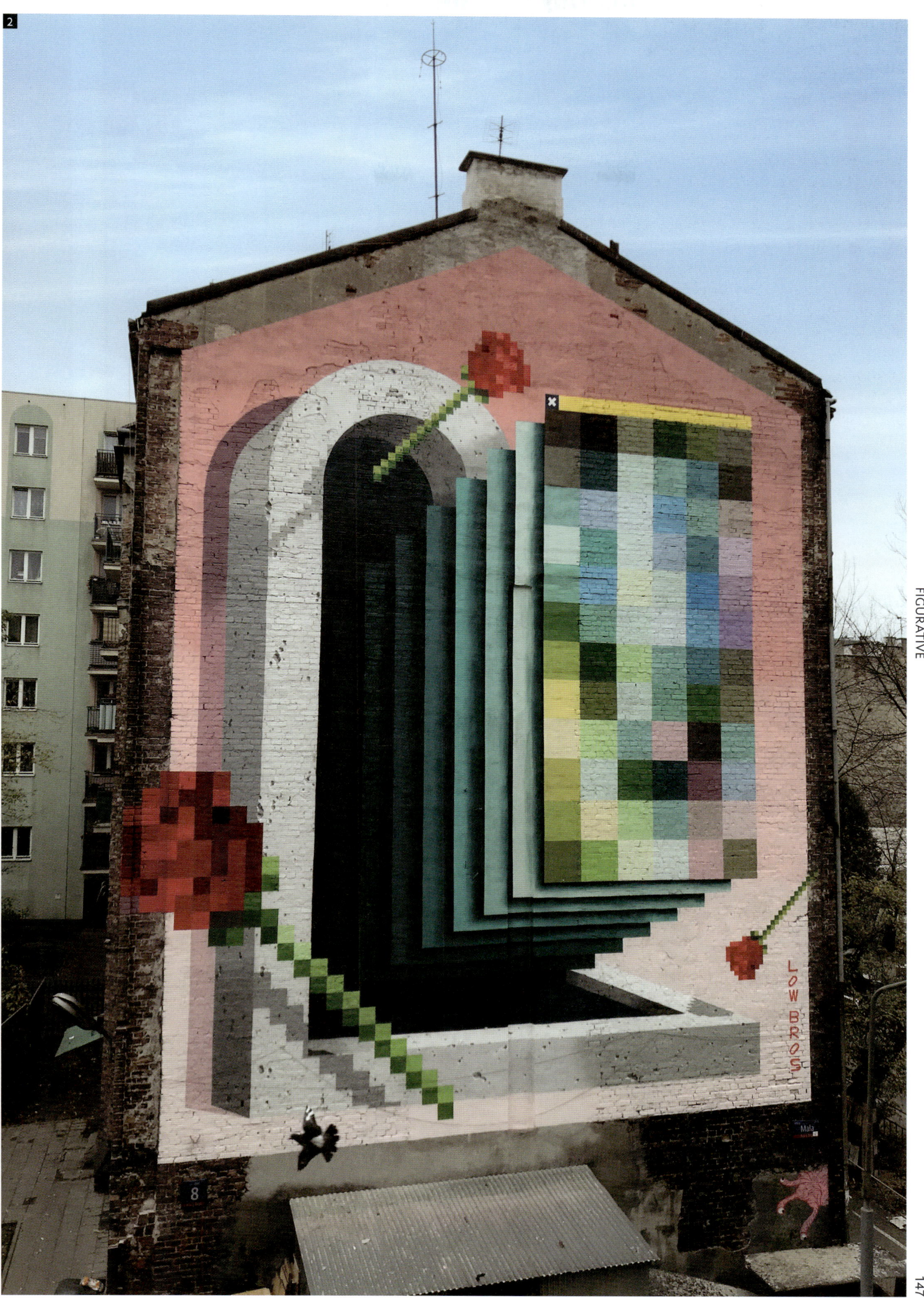

There is a very peculiar balance, layering pop-culture references of the past and slick synthetics of an imagined future.

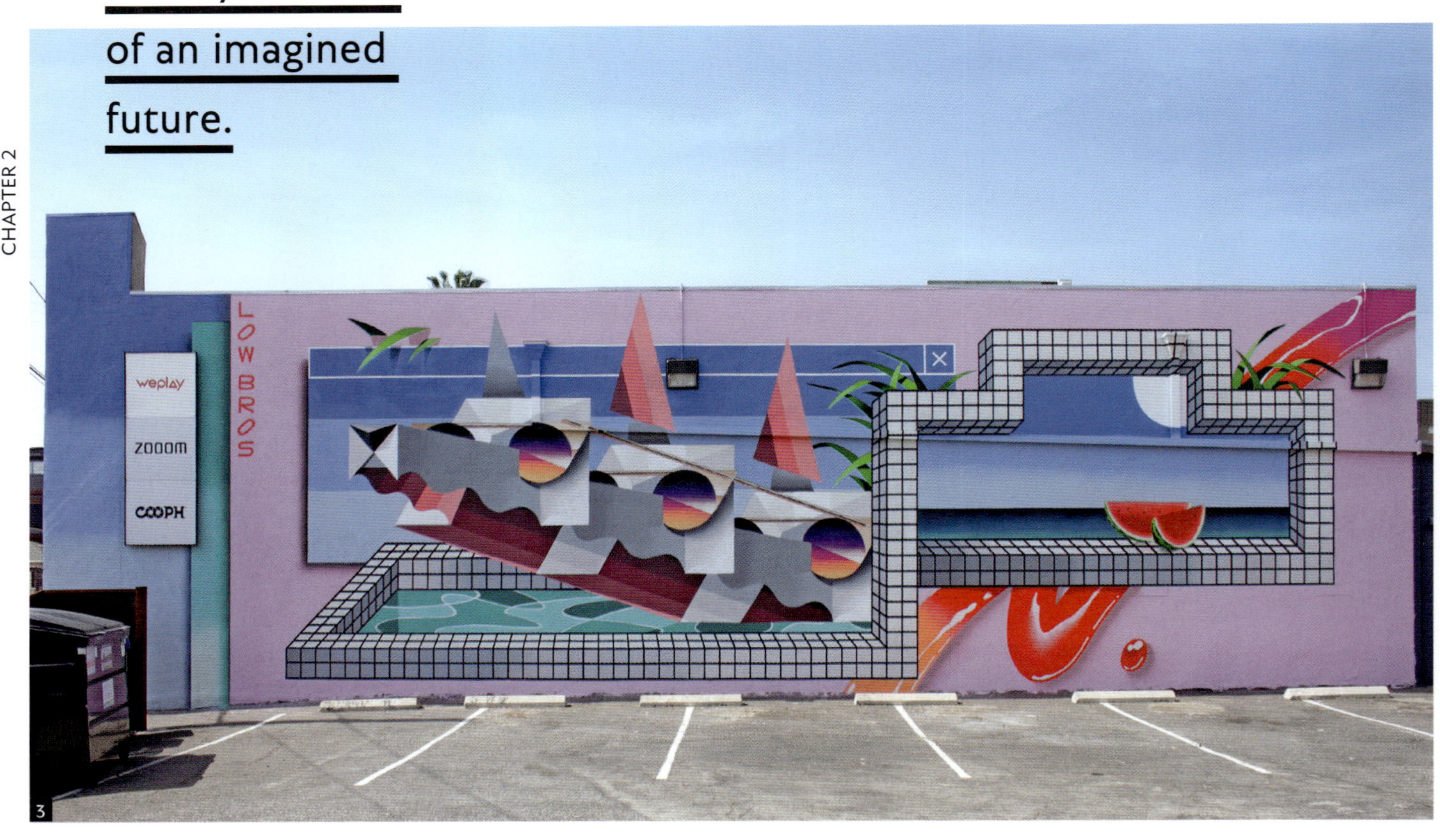

3 /
Venice Beach, California, USA, 2018
PHOTO BY THE ARTIST

4 /
Mannheim, Germany, 2017
PHOTO BY THE ARTIST

4

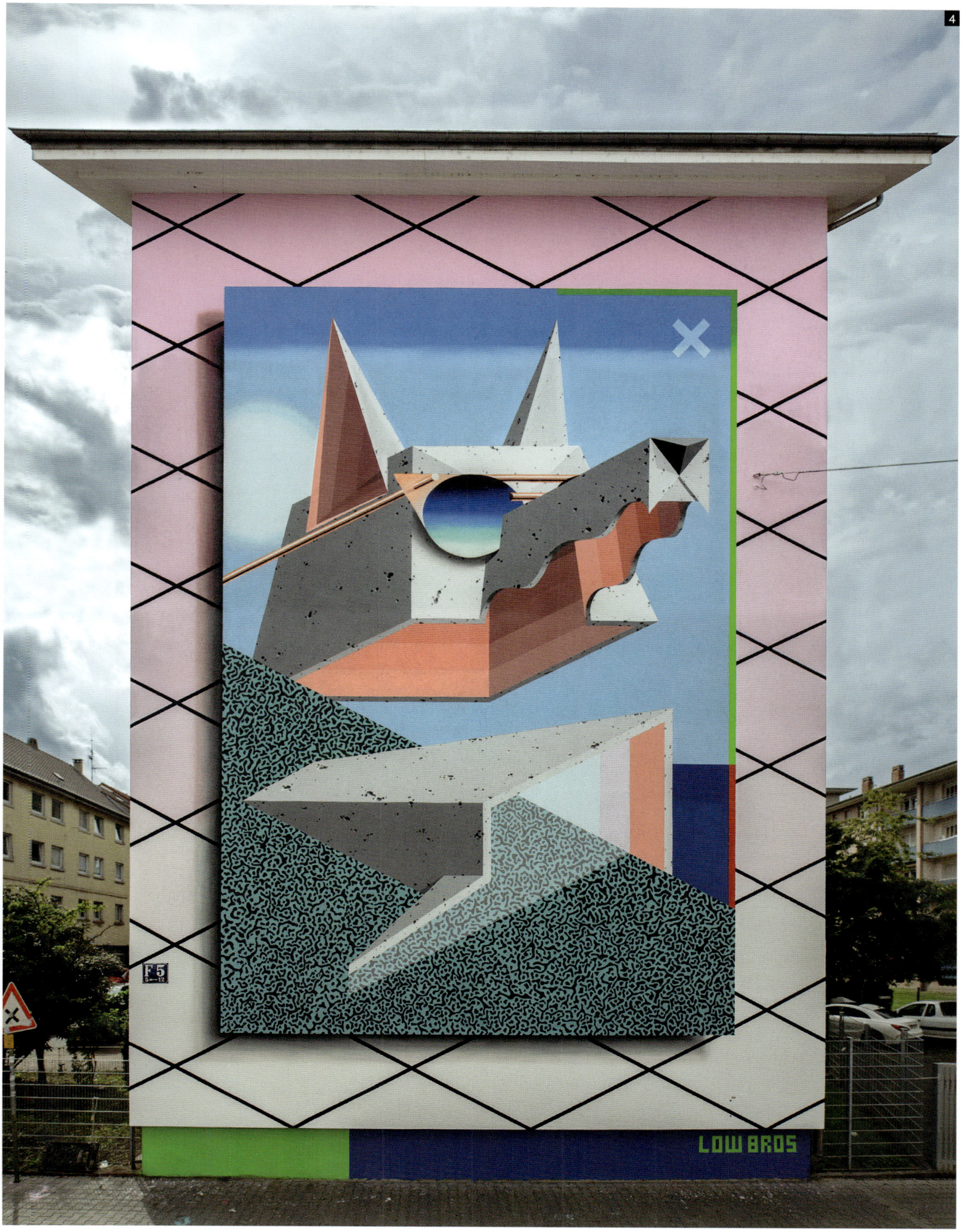

PAOLA DELFIN

/ Mexico City

Drawing and doodling for as long as she can remember, Paola found a natural voice in the visual arts from a very young age. Her works gravitate around themes of feminist beauty and identity, often cited as being particularly engaged in spreading awareness of gender issues in the street art industry as well as more universally.
Her investment in public space is born of a will to evolve through communication, using large-scale works to open up the discussion about her concerns regarding social issues.

Influenced in part by Mexican mural painters of the 1950s, she seeks to voice and discuss the aesthetics of her context and generation.

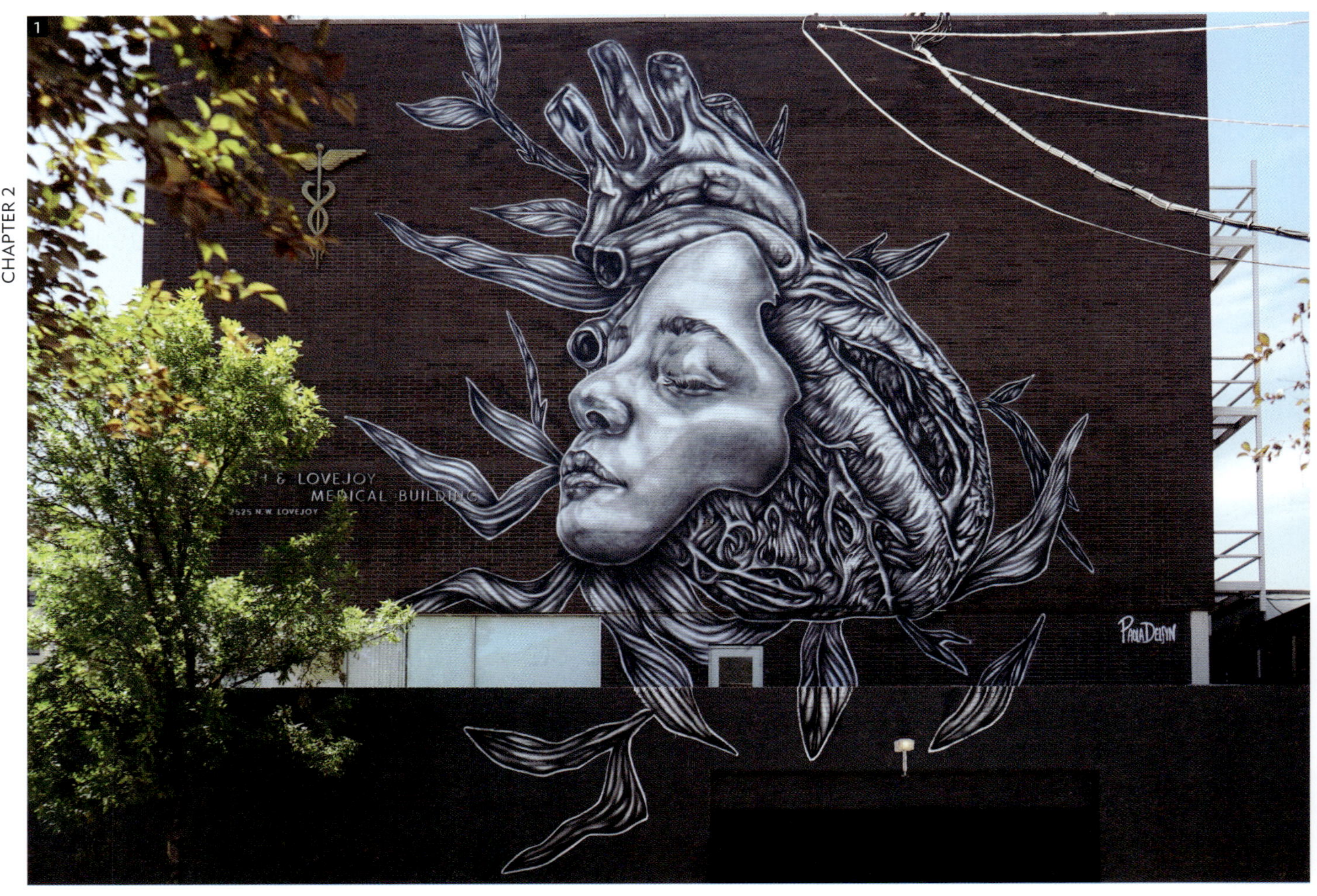

1 /
Portland, Oregon, USA, 2017
PHOTO BY THE ARTIST

2 /
Ostend, Belgium, 2019
PHOTO BY THE ARTIST

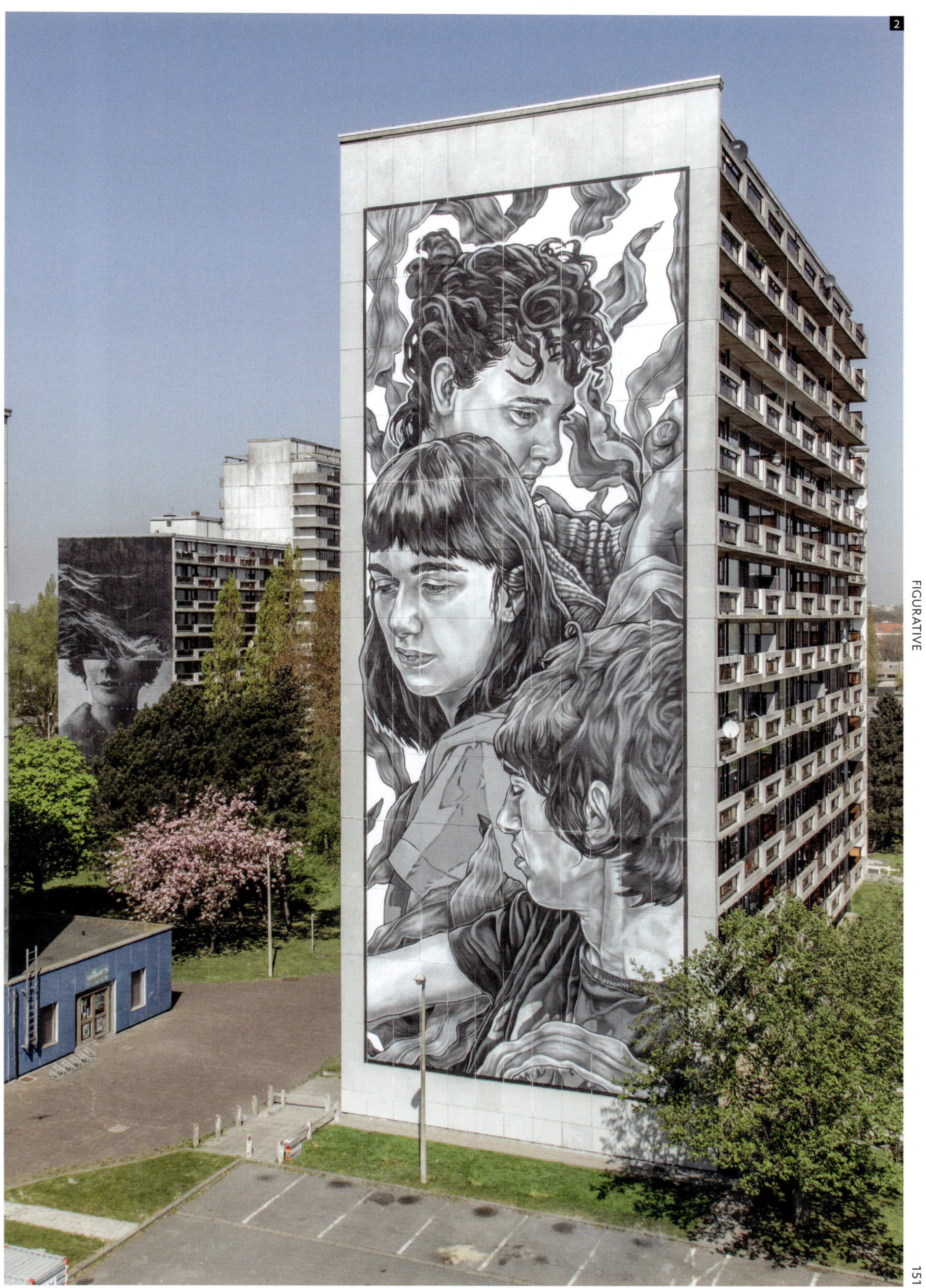

2

3

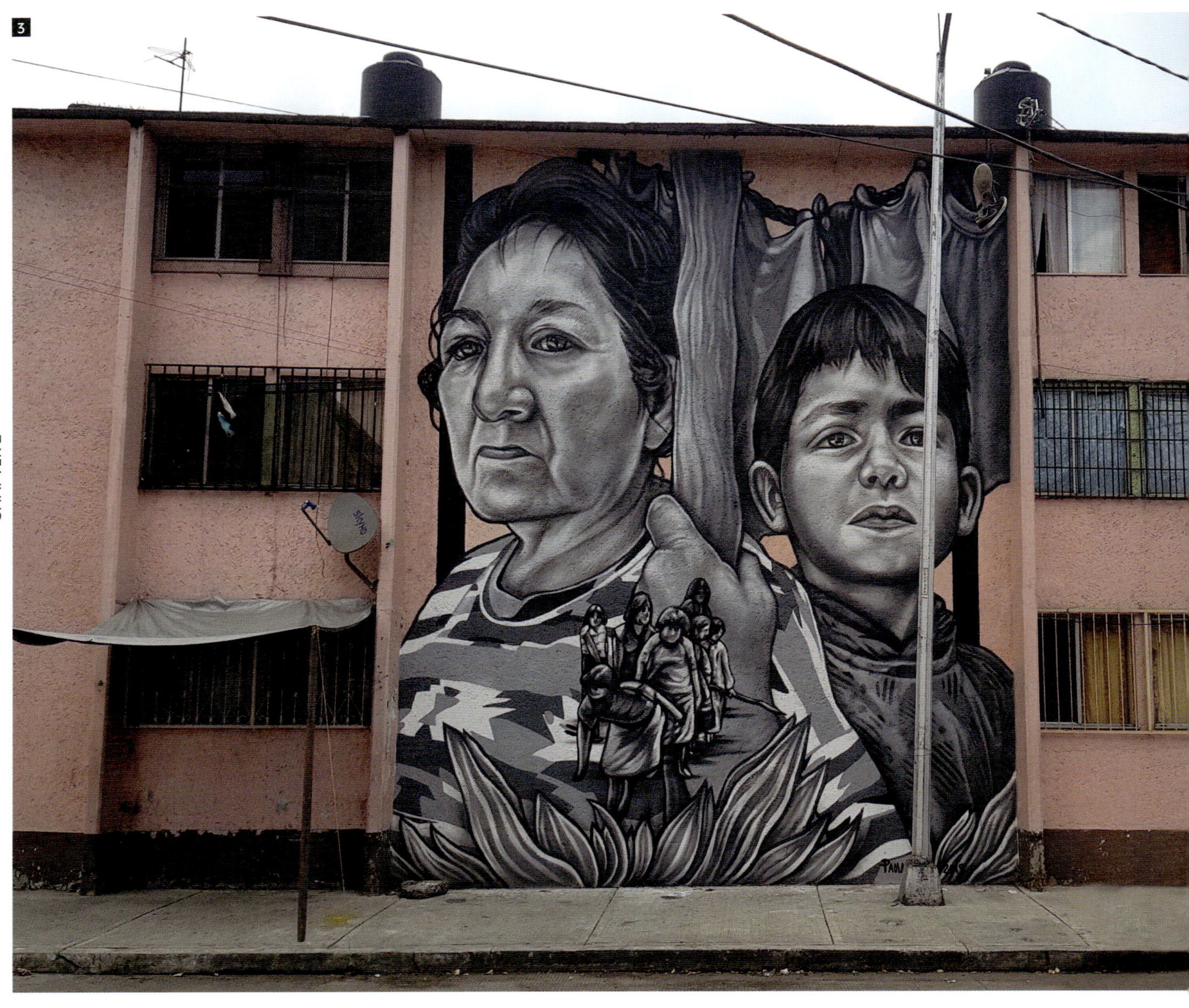

Her works gravitate around themes of feminist beauty and identity.

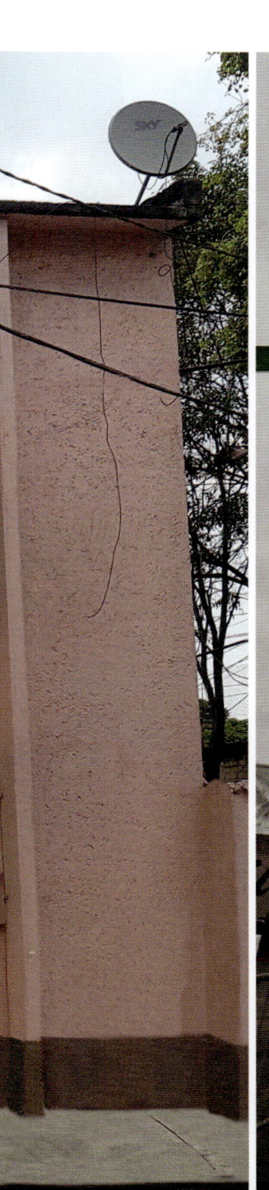

4

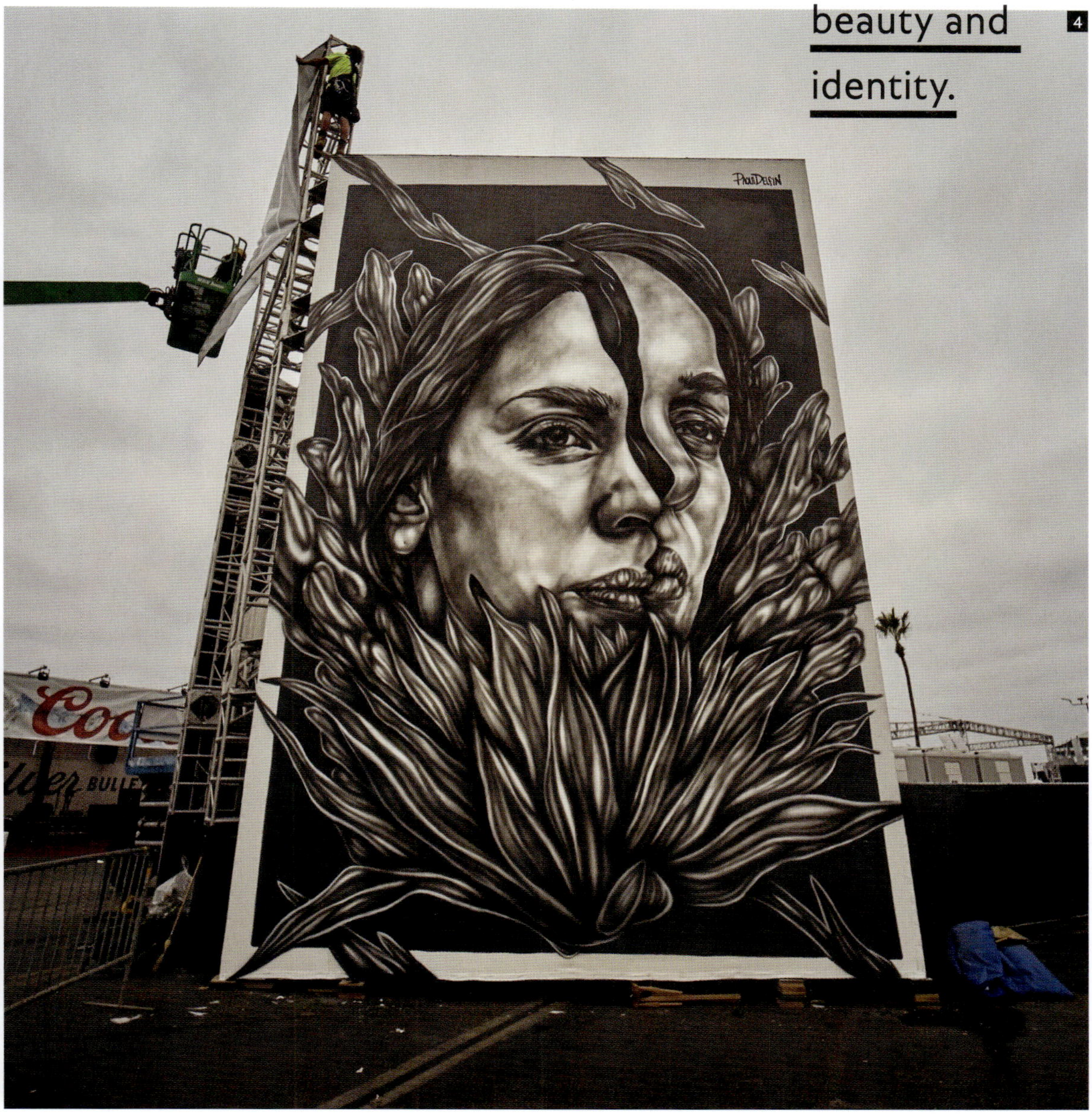

3 /
Mexico City, Mexico, 2019
PHOTO BY THE ARTIST

4 /
San Diego California, USA, 2017
PHOTO BY THE ARTIST

SAINER
/ Gdynia

Polish-based artist Sainer established his reputation in the street art world as one-half of the duo Etam Cru, a continued collaboration with fellow Łódź Academy of fine arts graduate Bezt. Since moving to different cities, the past few years have seen the two develop their individual oeuvres with solo gallery shows and separate mural commissions.

Sainer has continued to create portrait-based works, although his experimentation with landscaped backgrounds also brings forth influences from natural environments and classical painters. This sometimes minimalistic approach leans towards a certain abstraction, the details lost in an attempt to capture the light and atmosphere of a space.

The sometimes minimalistic approach leans towards a certain abstraction.

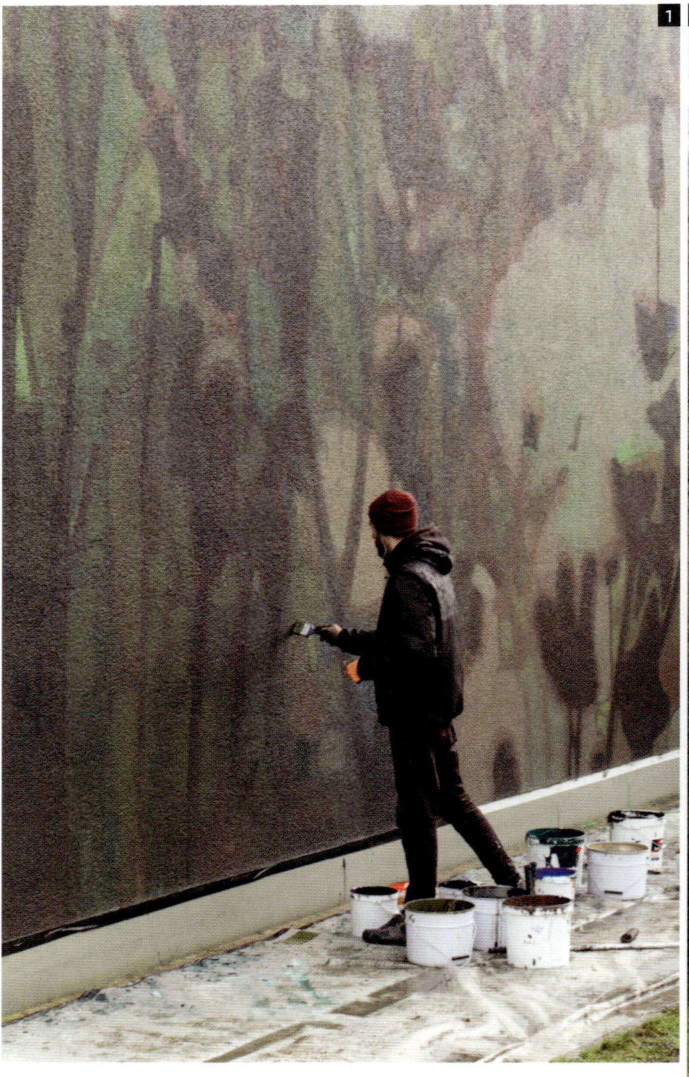

1 / 2
Ostend, Belgium, 2018
PHOTO BY HENRIK HAVEN

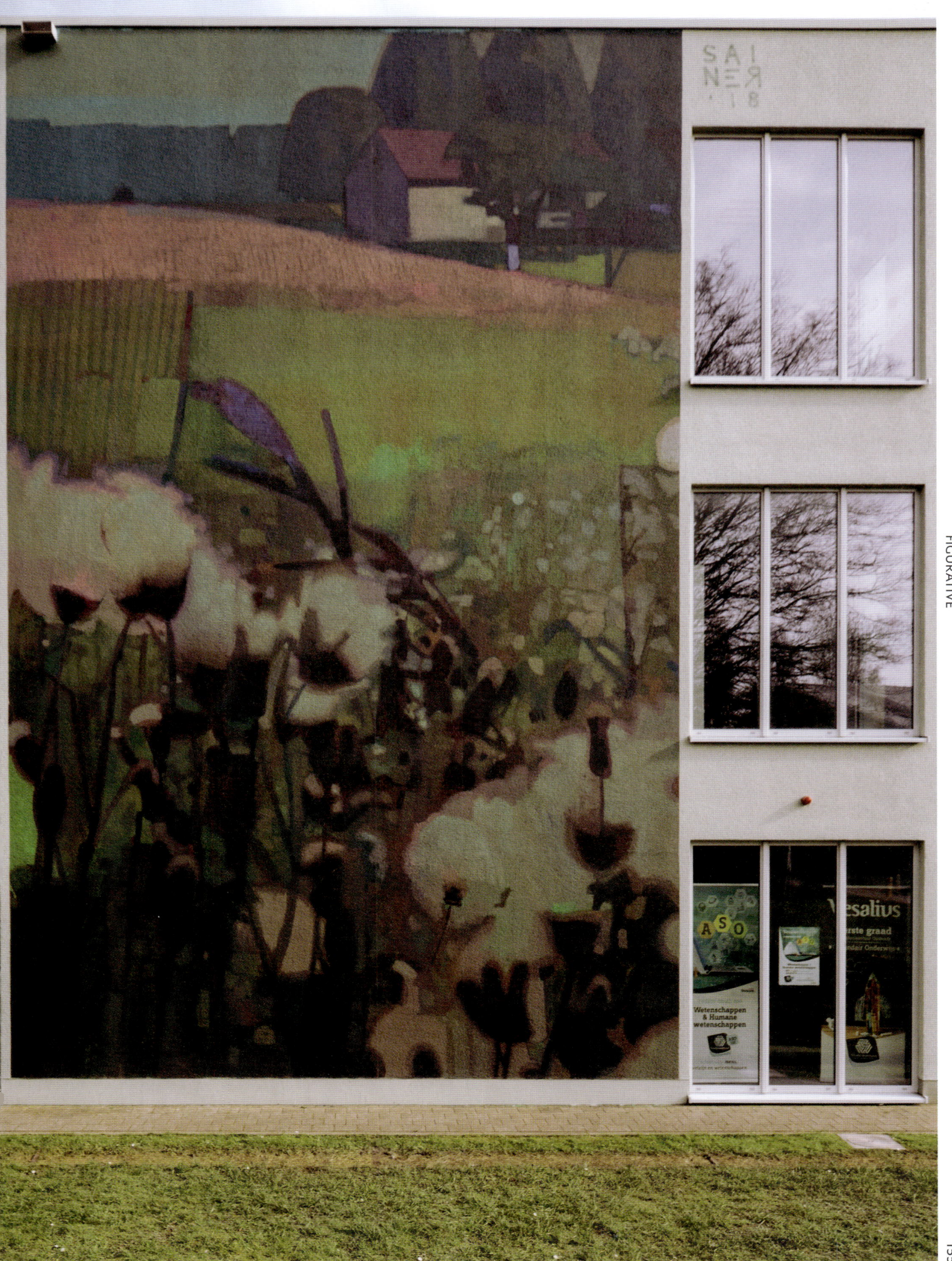
Vesalius
ASO
Wetenschappen
& Humane
wetenschappen

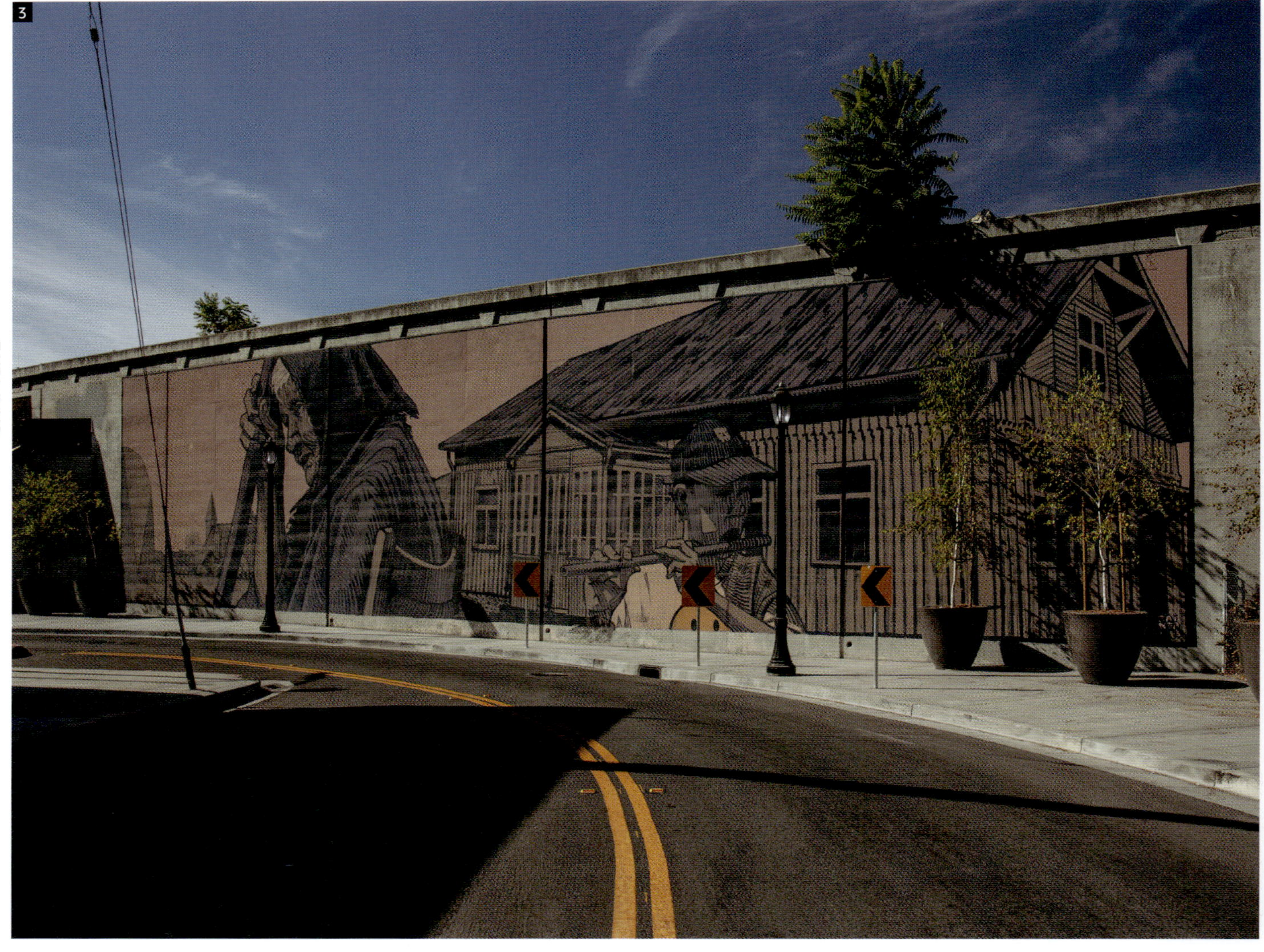
3

4

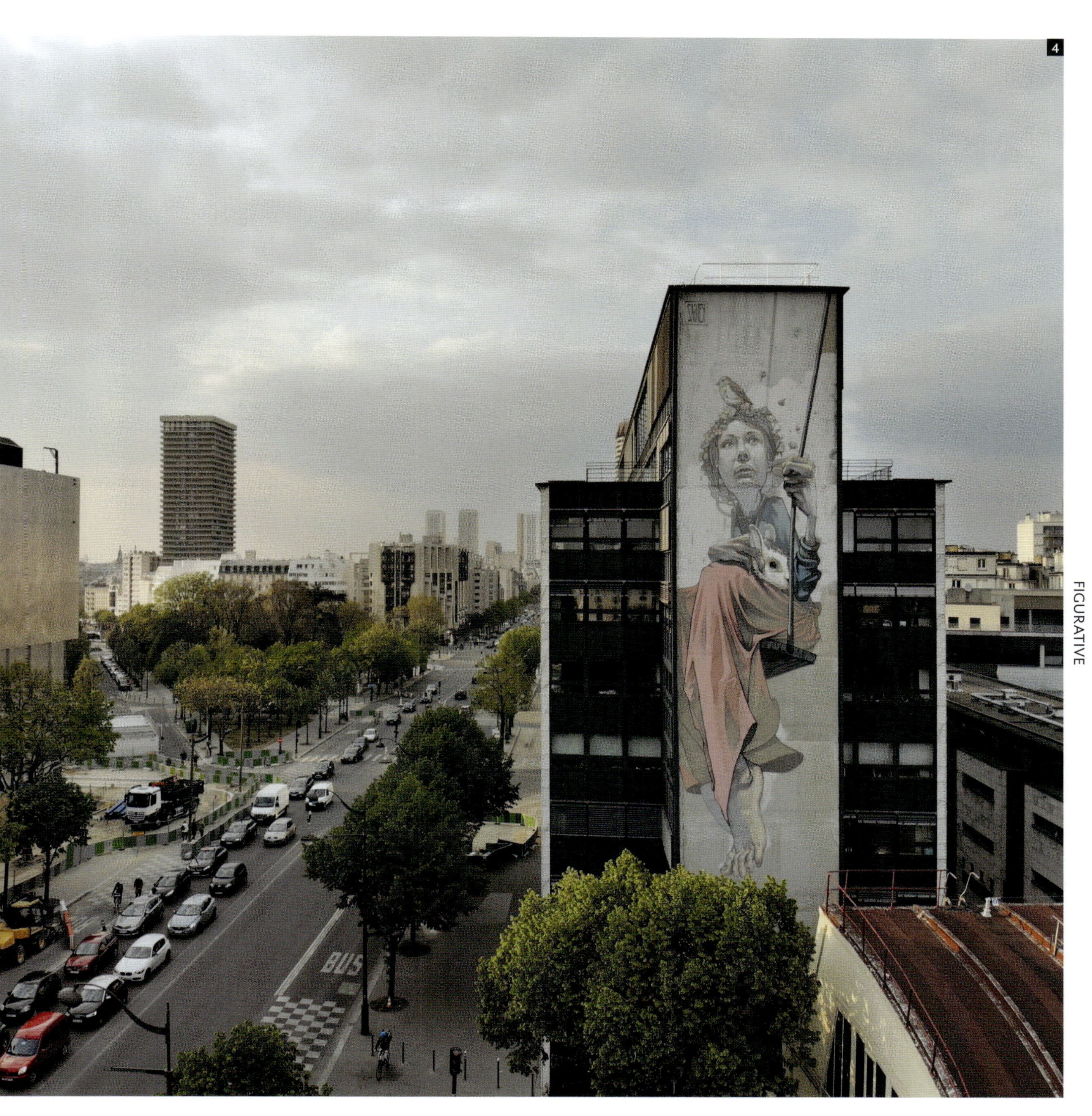

3 /
San Jose, USA, 2016
PHOTO BY VINNY CORNELLI

4 /
Paris, France, 2014
PHOTO BY TIM JENTSCH

SETH GLOBEPAINTER

/ Paris

French artist Julien Malland, aka Seth Globepainter, has continued to nourish his body of work with projects across the globe. Dividing his time between Europe, Asia and the Caribbean over the past few years, he has been further developing his universe of surreal children in eerie, playful contexts. This constant thematic presents us with a global language, referencing the importance of youth and the child in every adult.

Over the years, Seth has been focusing more and more on issues surrounding the loss of cultural heritage due to the rise of a consumer society and growing individualism. Seth often depicts children masked with traditional and playful headwear. When describing his intention, Seth says it is 'to keep our child's soul. To make someone remember his culture. That imagination is a priceless treasure.'

He has been further developing his universe of surreal children in eerie playful contexts.

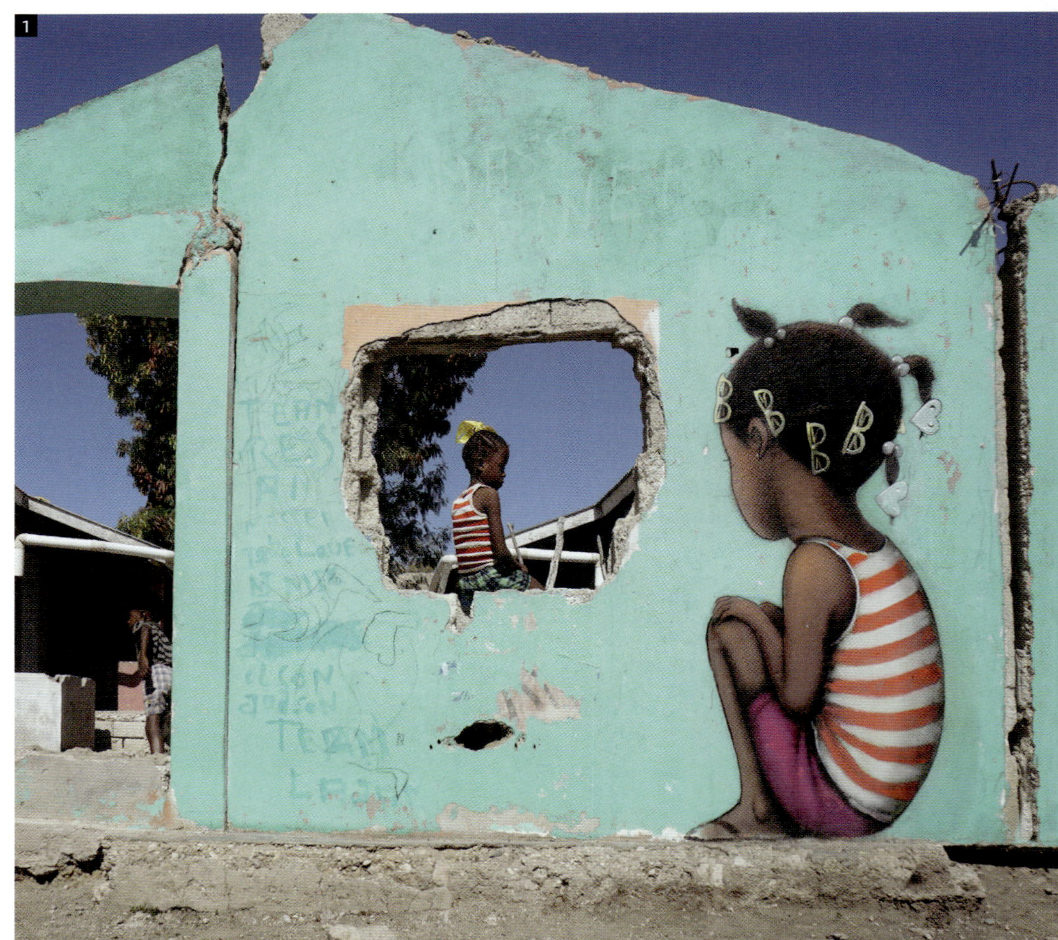

1 /
Indonesia, 2019
PHOTO BY THE ARTIST

2 /
Haiti, 2019
PHOTO BY THE ARTIST

3 /
Paris, France, 2018
PHOTO BY THE ARTIST

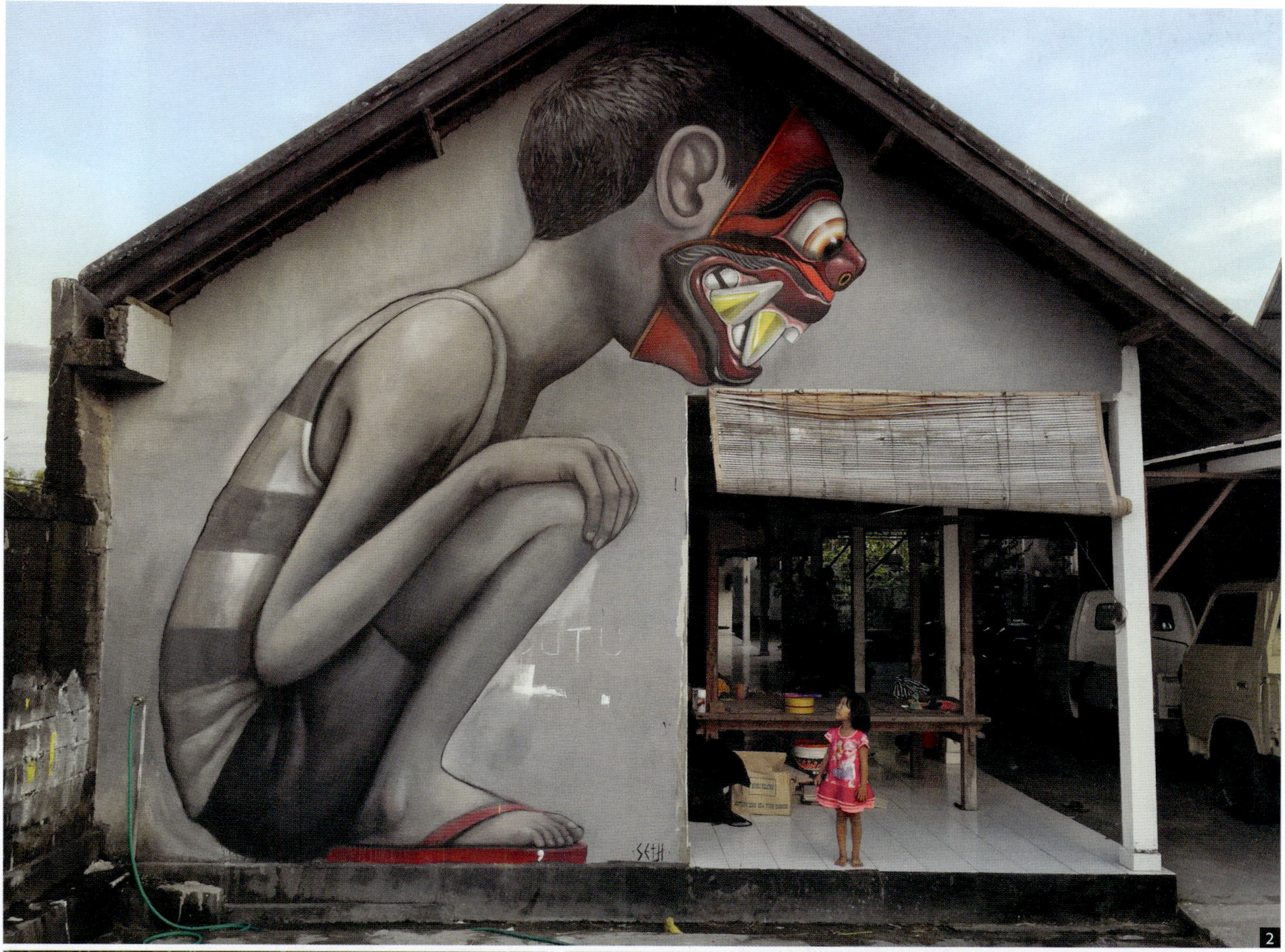

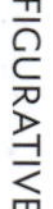

FIGURATIVE

2

3

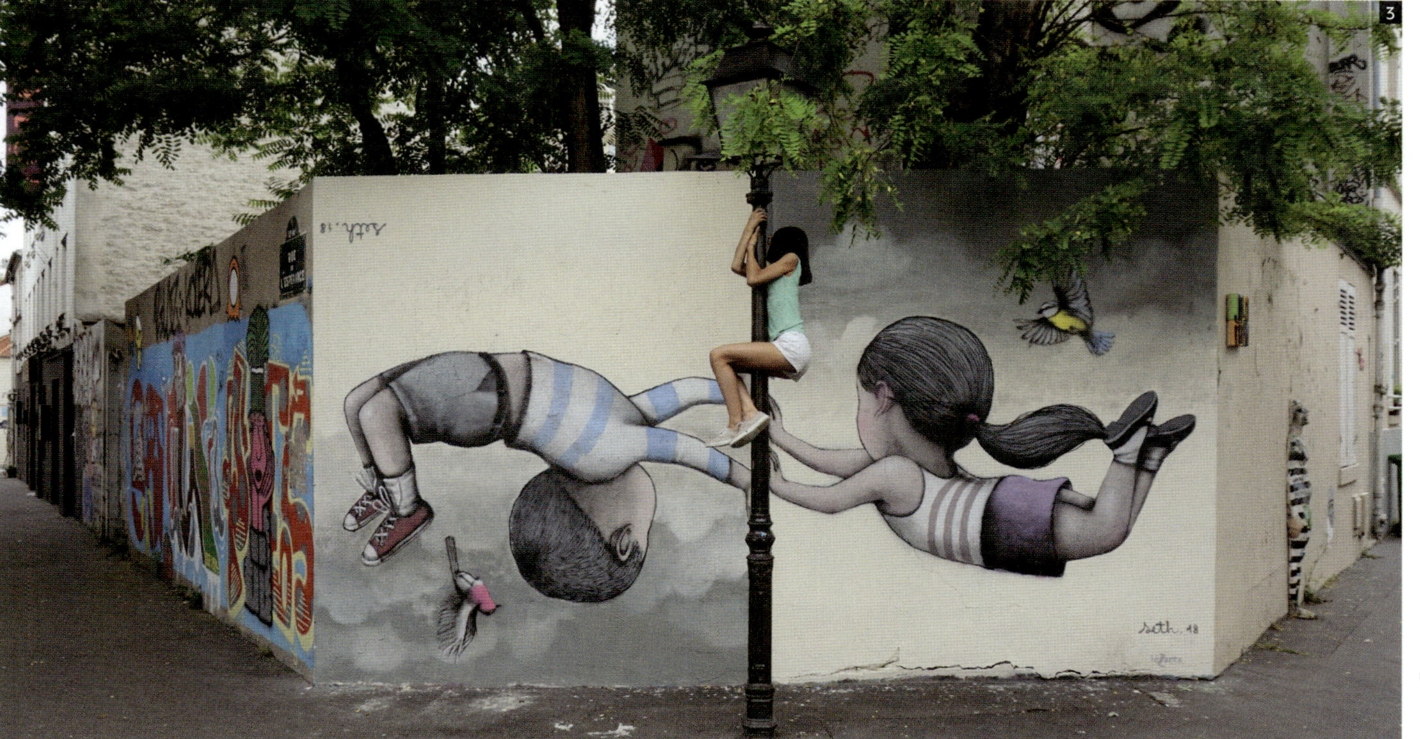

» /
Grenoble, France, 2017
PHOTO BY THE ARTIST

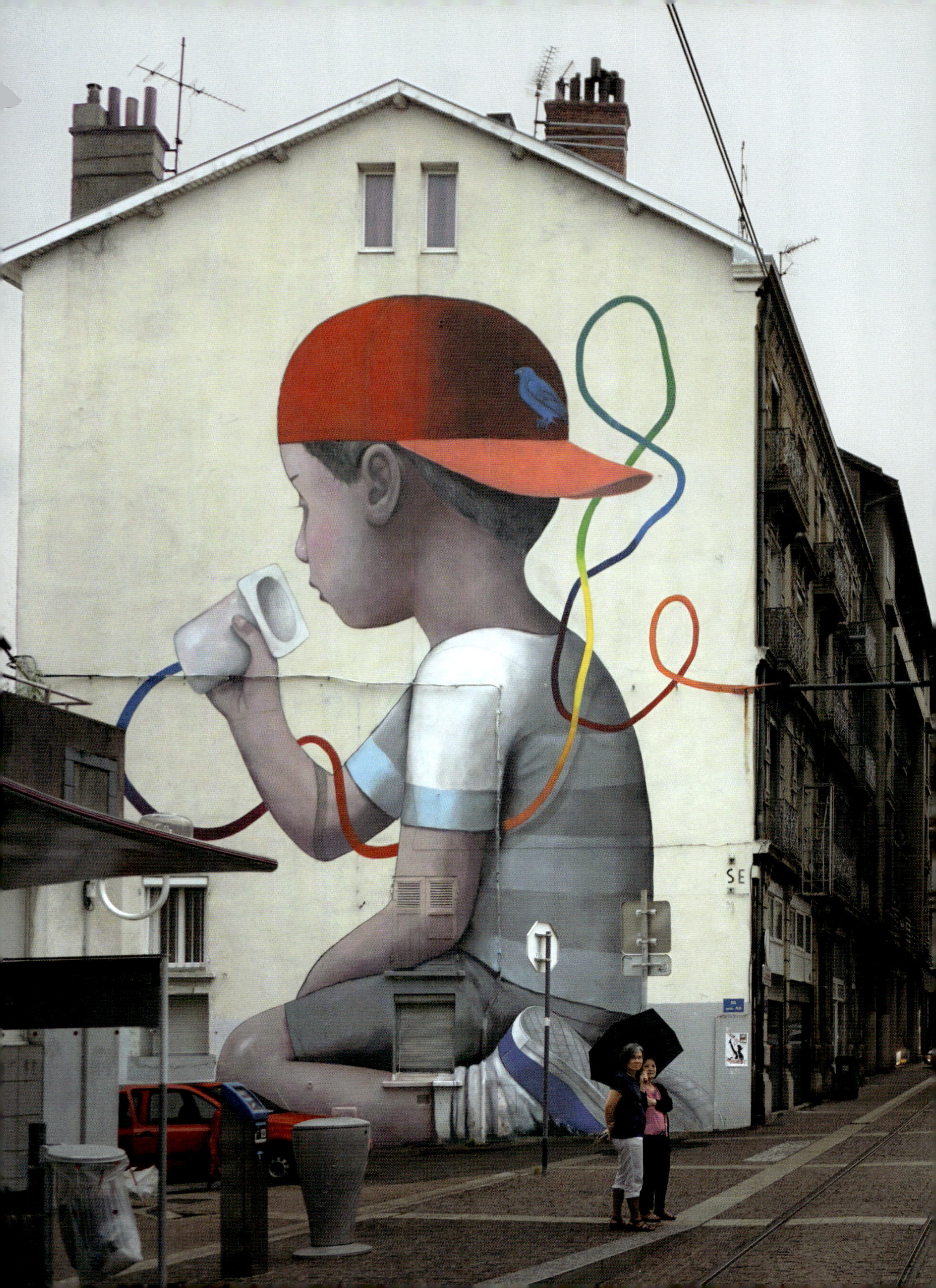
SE

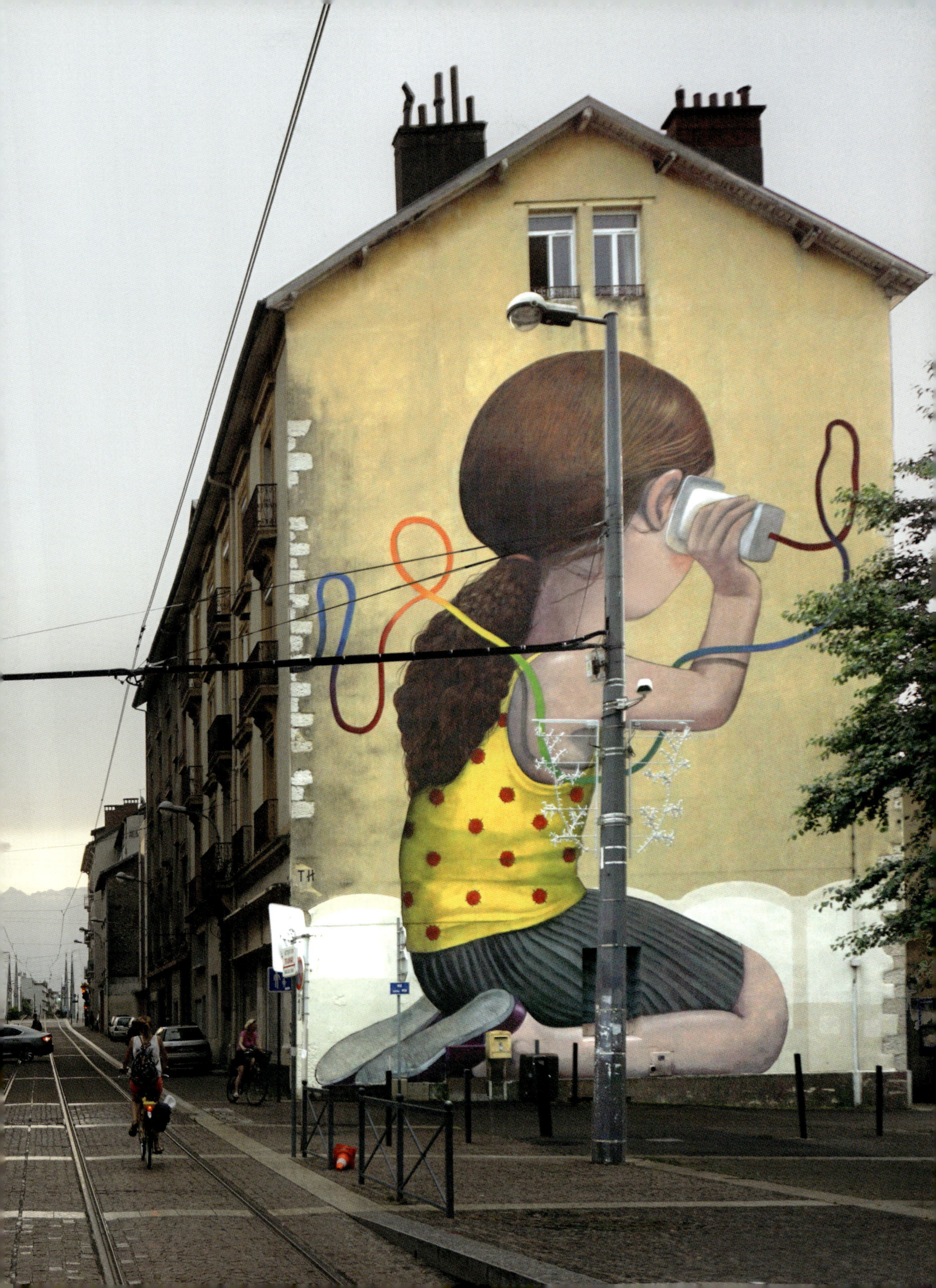

SHERYO & YOK

/ New York

Artist duo Sheryo & Yok, hailing from Singapore and Australia respectively, share a love for the subversive sub-cultures of skating, tattooing, surf and the world of illustration. Their styles of expression mostly overlap, with an exquisite corpse-like way of contributing to each piece. After having met in Singapore and spending a stint in Cambodia, the two are now Brooklyn-based, creating their illustration-style characters over murals, in zines, and in sculpture, adopting a consciously reduced colour choice to suit their travel-bug lifestyles. Working and competing as a team, their playfulness shines through with their tongue-in-cheek world of joking monsters.

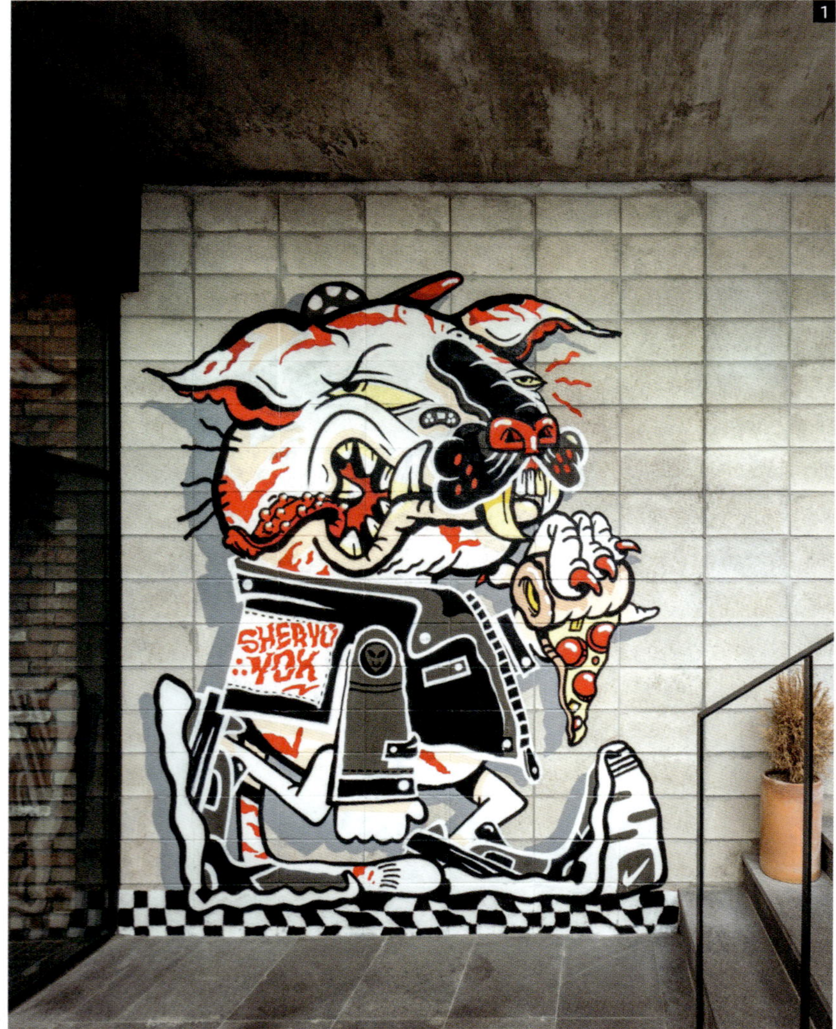

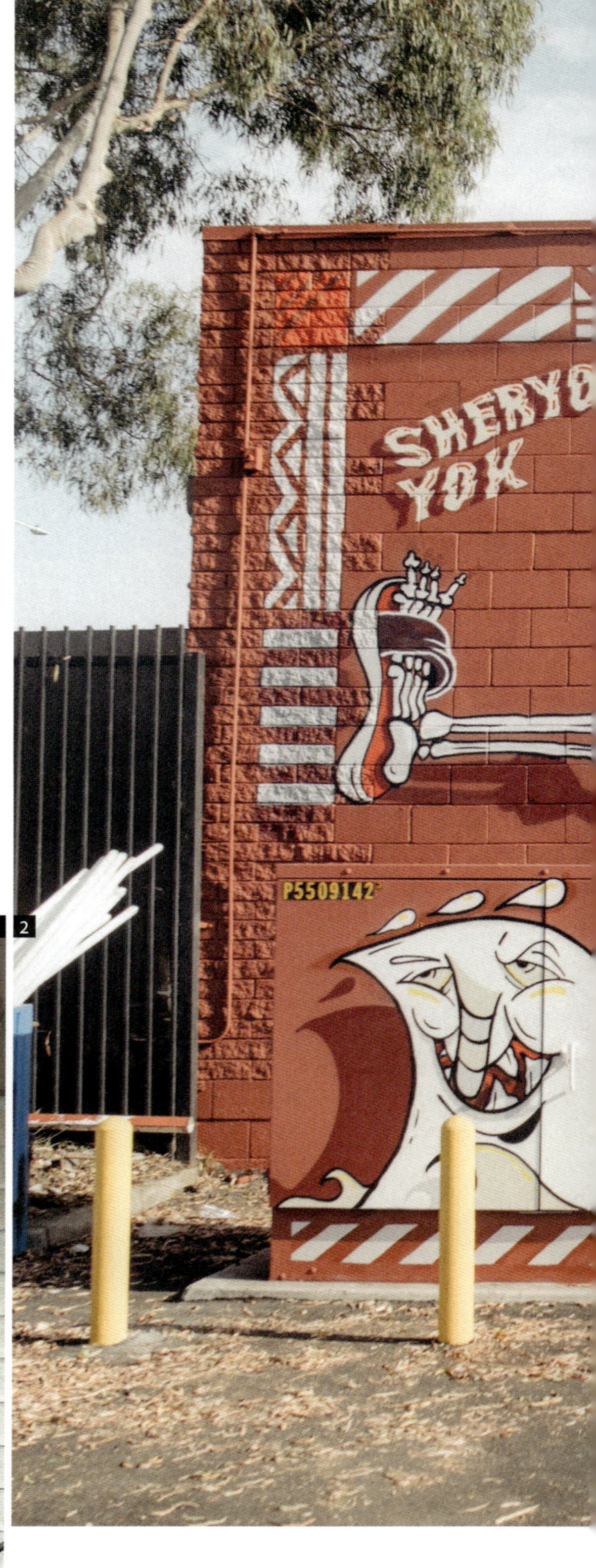

1 /
Seoul, Korea, 2017
PHOTO BY BRANDON SHIGETA

2 /
Costa Mesa, California, USA, 2018
PHOTO BY THE ARTIST

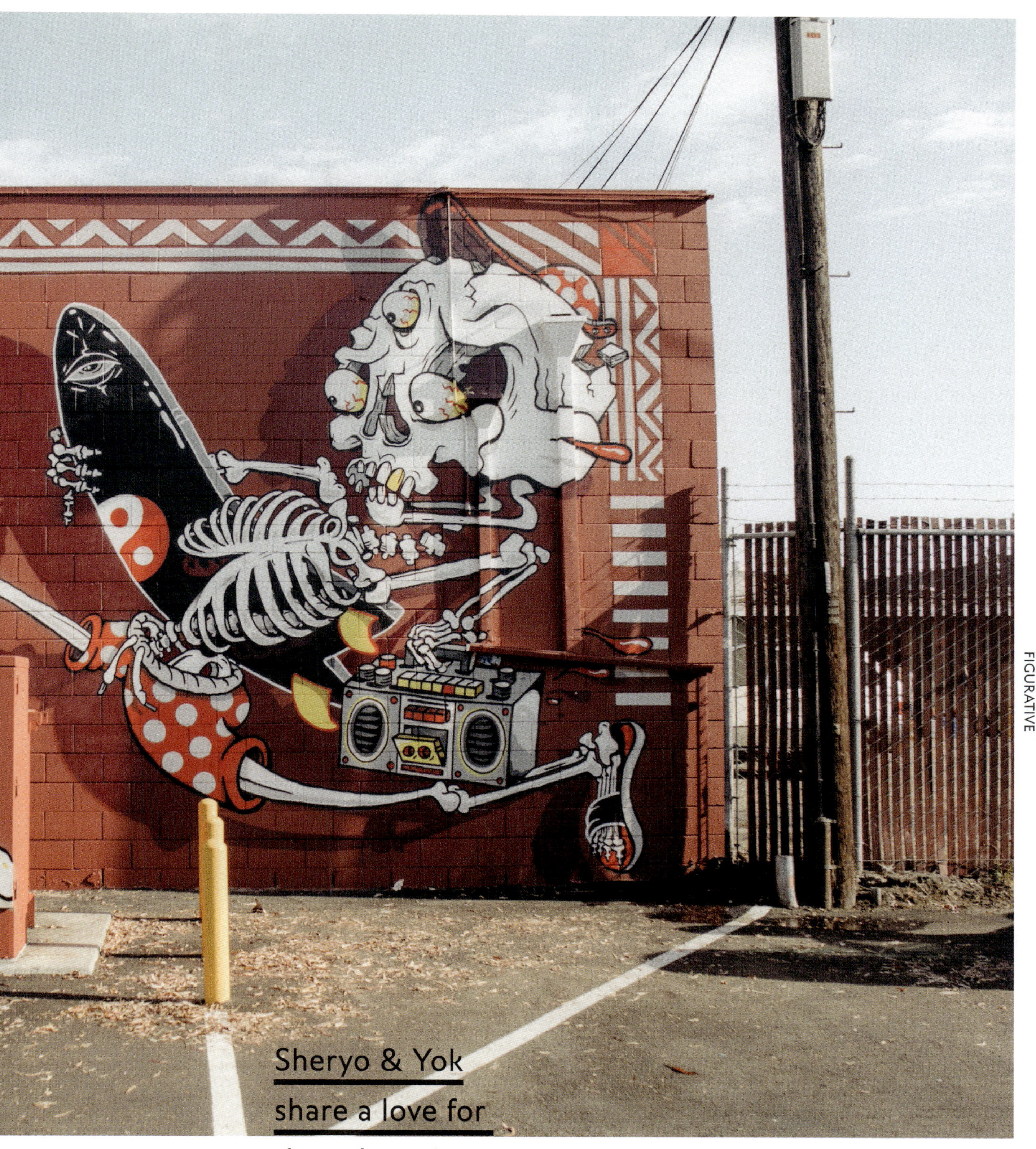

Sheryo & Yok share a love for the subversive subcultures of skating, tattooing, surf and the world of illustration.

3

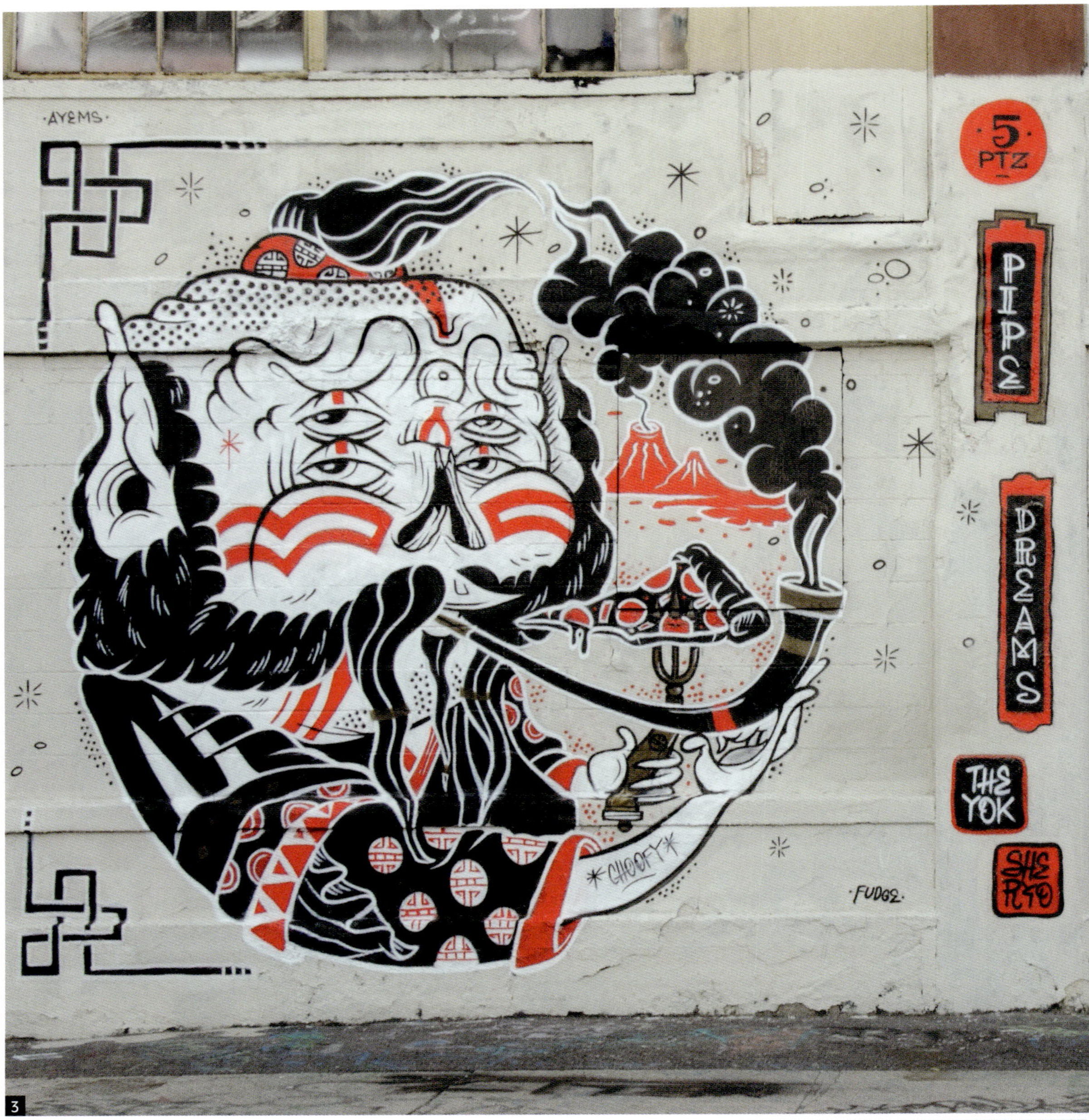

4

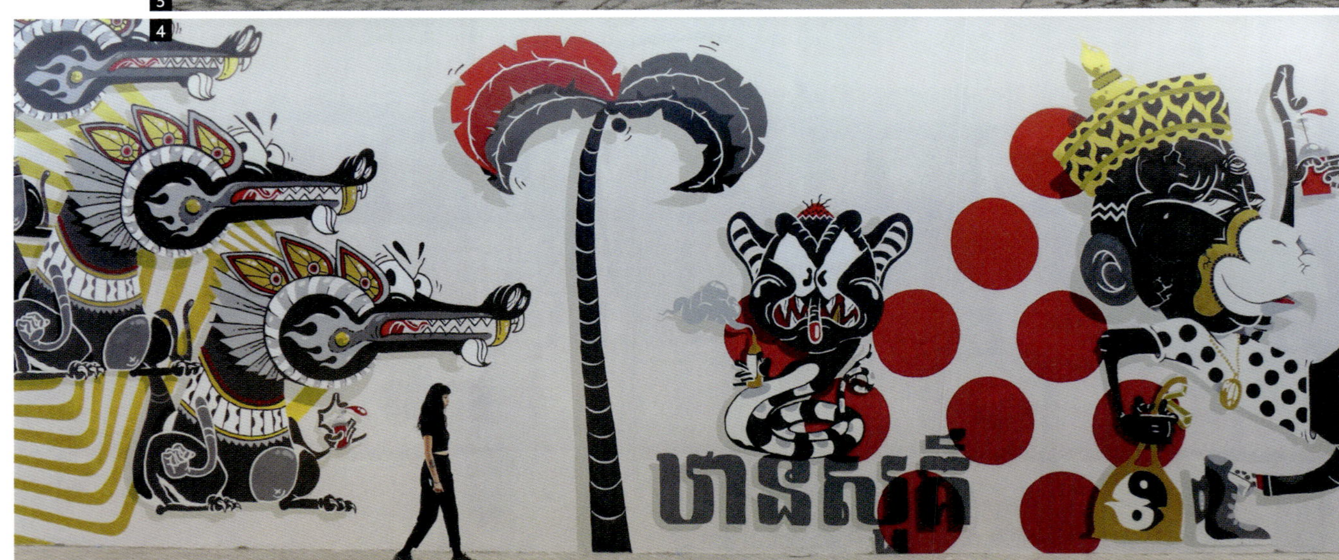

3 /
New York, USA, 2013
PHOTO BY THE ARTIST

4 /
Phnom Penh, Cambodia, 2018
PHOTO BY THE ARTIST

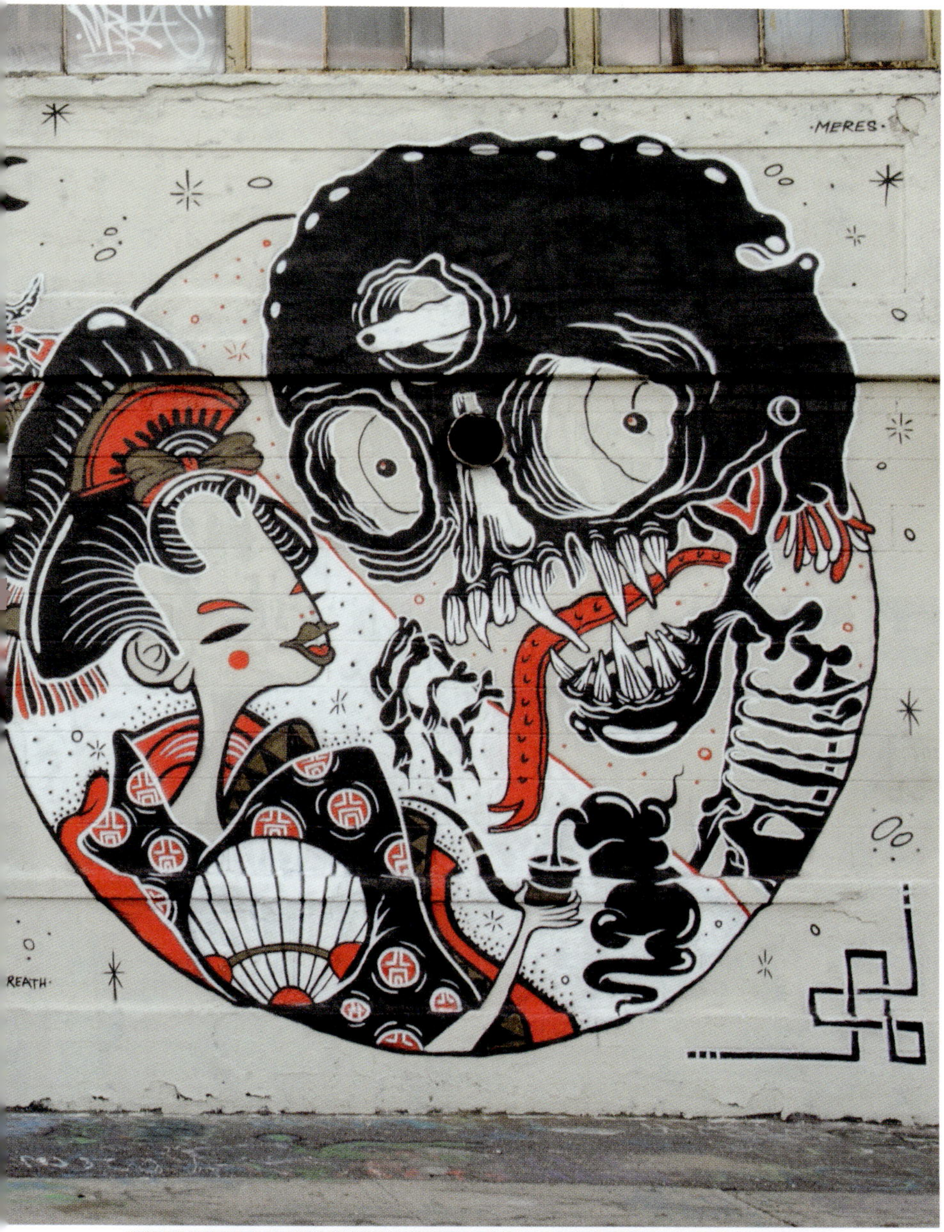

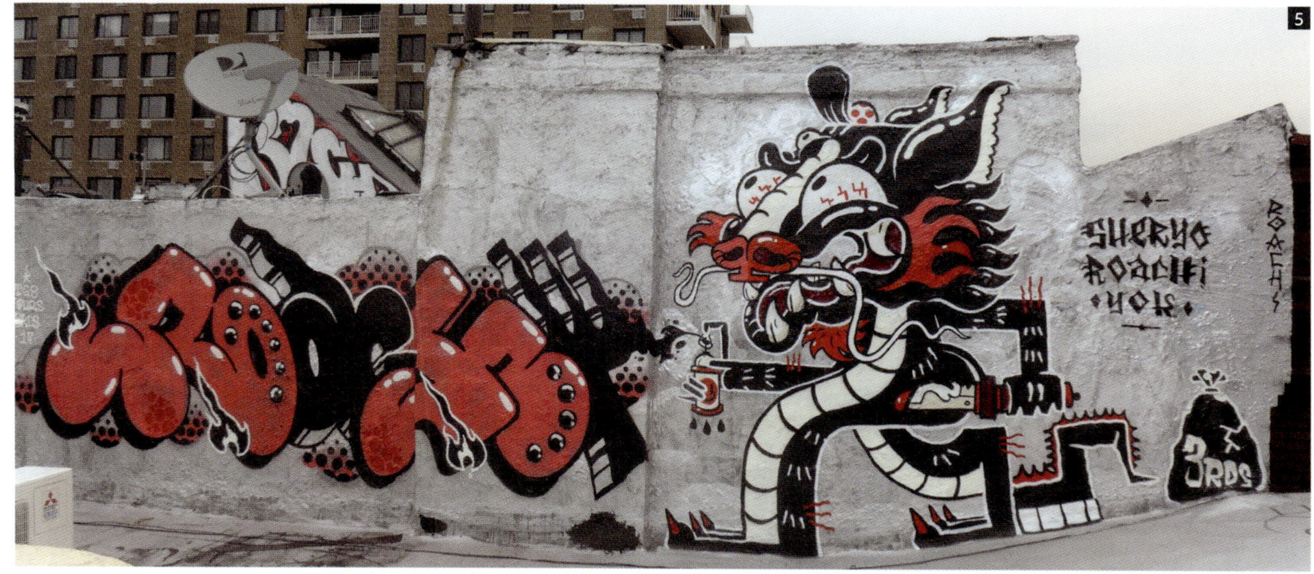

5 /
New York, USA, 2017
PHOTO BY THE ARTIST

3/

AXEL VOID
BOSOLETTI
CASE MACLAIM
GUIDO VAN HELTEN
LONAC
SEBAS VELASCO
ZOER & VELVET

REALISM

IN THE PREVIOUS EDITION of *Street Art Today,* we dedicated a chapter to the starring artists specialising in hyper-realism techniques. This very specific process and relationship with photography has always been a focal genre in public art, as artists and audience continue to admire painters who have honed their skills to such a point that realistic detail can be replicated exactly, using the seemingly brash materials of paintbrush and spray can. A few years on, though we do still believe in the overwhelming and specialised talent of the artists featured, many appearing in this publication series for the second time, we also want to highlight the importance of their oeuvre beyond a simple mastery of technique.

Here, we rename the chapter 'Realism', removing the hype and opening up the conversation with this incredibly strong collection of artists that can be seen to continue in the vein of the French art movement put forward after the populist revolution in the 1840s. Realist artists rejected the exaggerated drama of the romantics, wanting to focus on real subject, on real people and real situations. The sometimes harsh realities and unashamed truths of everyday life are portrayed and embraced, rejecting the preconceived notions of beauty and elitism that are so often depicted now in commercial or contemporary art.

As the world of street art moves, in many ways, towards a virtual and global network of representation and consumption, realism and realist painters simultaneously celebrate and damn the realities of their everyday with general gravitation towards unspectacular colour palettes and imagery of silences. With this group, we are far from the neon-pop colours and eye-catching geometry, welcome views of relatable landscapes and characters allowing for a more human perspective.

Through Guido van Helten's work, we can clearly see a proposition valorising the personalities of the everyday. His honest and invested interest in the lives of the often-disadvantaged local communities in which he works gives an important voice to individuals and groups involved in real-life struggles. The younger artists in this group, such as Sebas Velasco and Bosoletti, can be seen to portray more personal contemporary subjects, popular football players, loved girlfriends, buskers and fellow painters. Their portrayal of the world around them seeks blatant honesty and unashamed insignificance. A talented group of artists significantly – and interestingly – portraying the everyday in spectacular fashion.

AXEL VOID

/ Miami

Haitian-Spanish-American artist Alejandro Hugo Dorda Mevs has a long-established reputation as an inspiring and talented artist, working under the name of Axel Void. With a perfect balance of rebellious pragmatism mixed with technical mastery, his work - though self-described as pessimistic - reaches out to audiences globally.

The past few years have seen him invest energy in curatorial activities, organising exhibitions and pop-up events in Miami as well as launching Void Projects, a series of international itinerant events inviting artists to create in unconventional spaces. The series fosters a sense of community in creative practice and further opens up the dialogue between artist and audience. A welcome conversation with the 2018 Creença residency in Catalonia attracted over 50 artists for over two months of co-creation in an abandoned convent.

With a perfect balance of rebellious pragmatism mixed with technical mastery, his work reaches out to audiences globally.

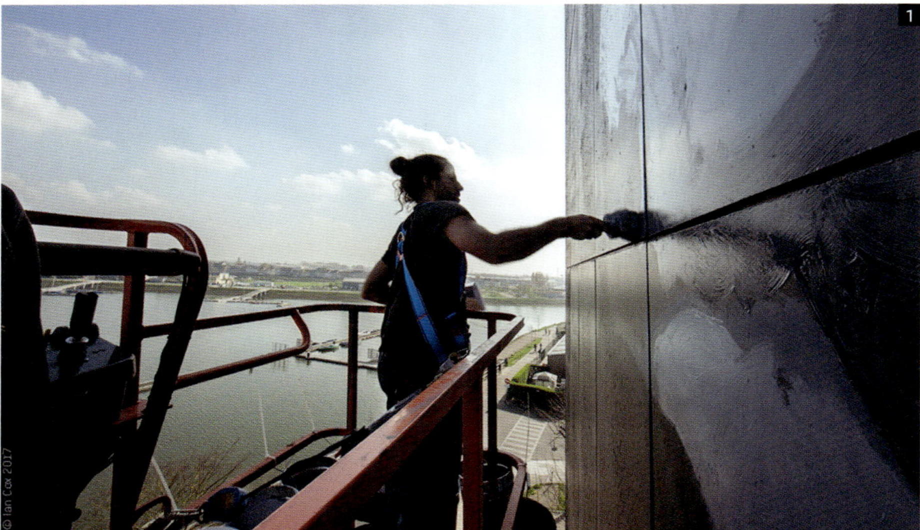

Photo © Ian Cox 2017

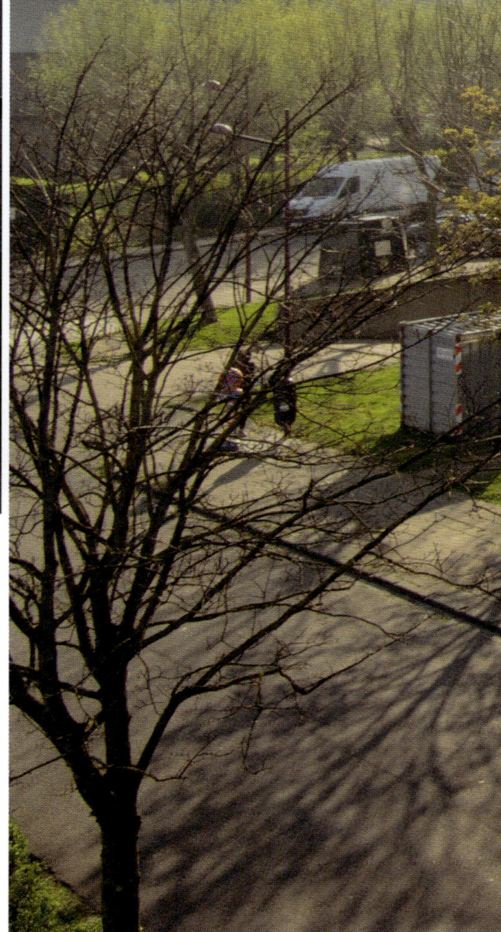

1 /
Ostend, Belgium, 2017
PHOTO BY IAN COX

2 /
Ostend, Belgium, 2017
PHOTO BY IAN COX

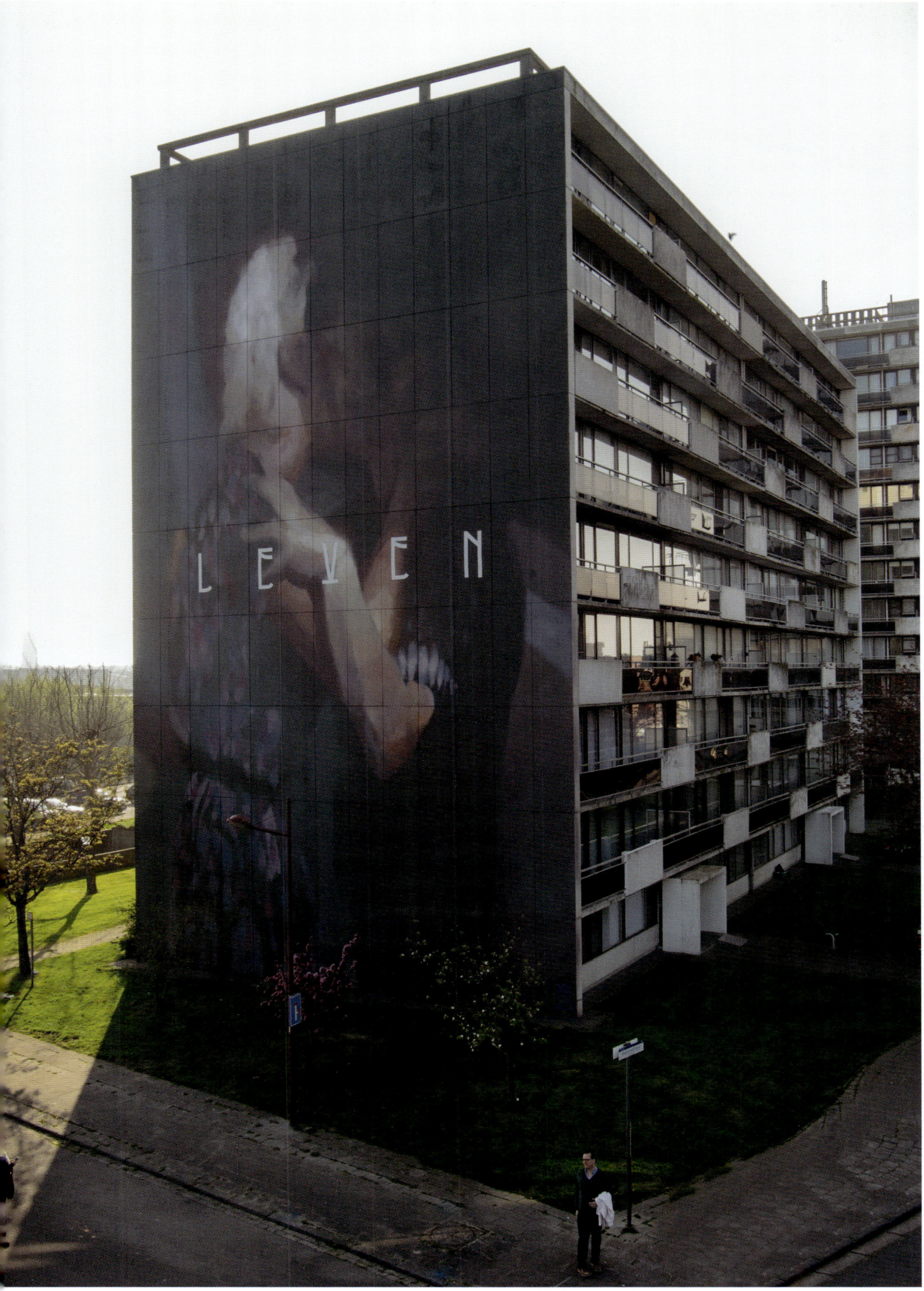

LEVEN

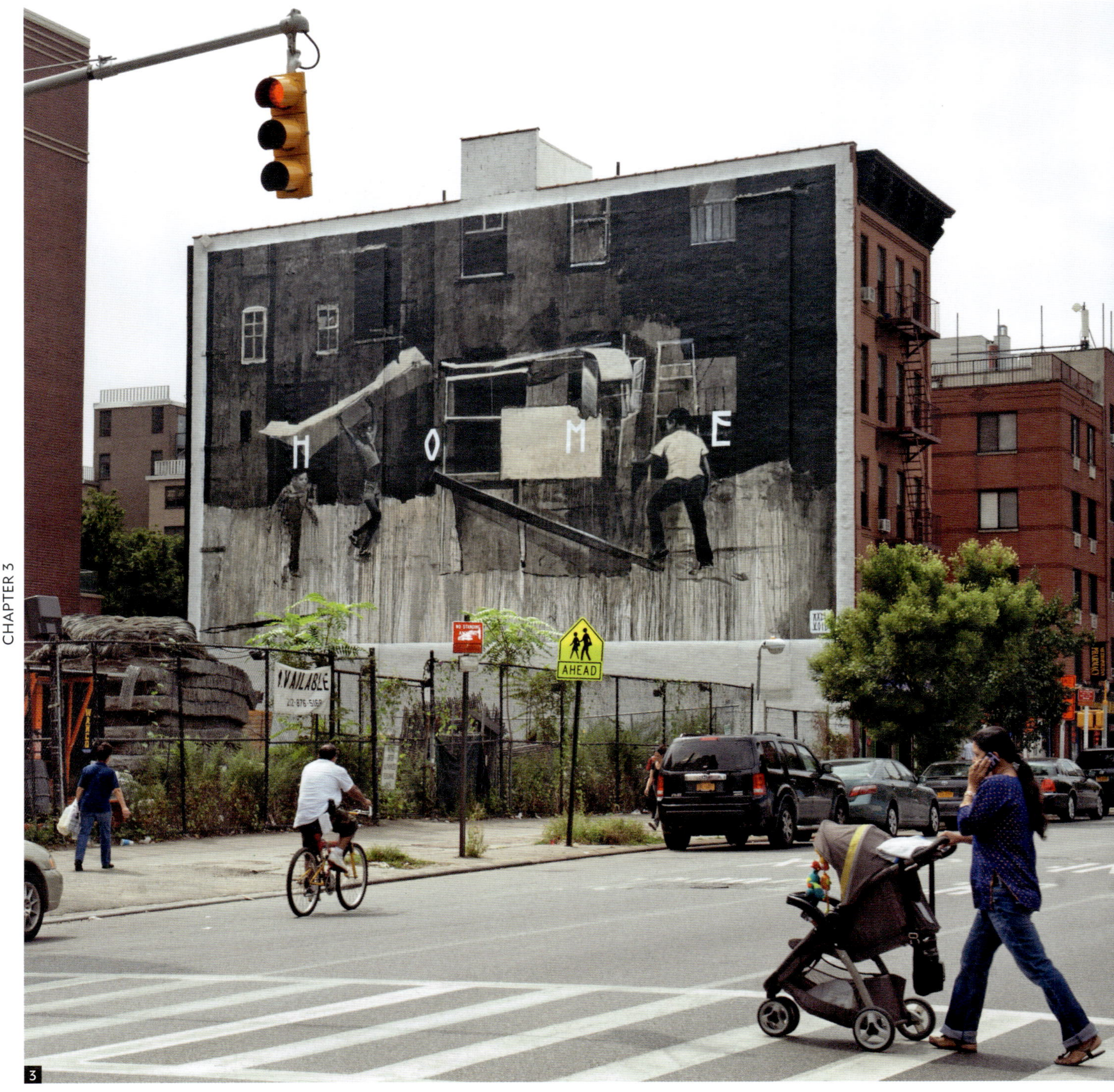

3 /
New York, USA, 2013
PHOTO BY MARTHA COOPER

4 /
London, UK, 2016
PHOTO BY THE ARTIST

5 /
Montreal, Canada, 2015
PHOTO BY THE ARTIST

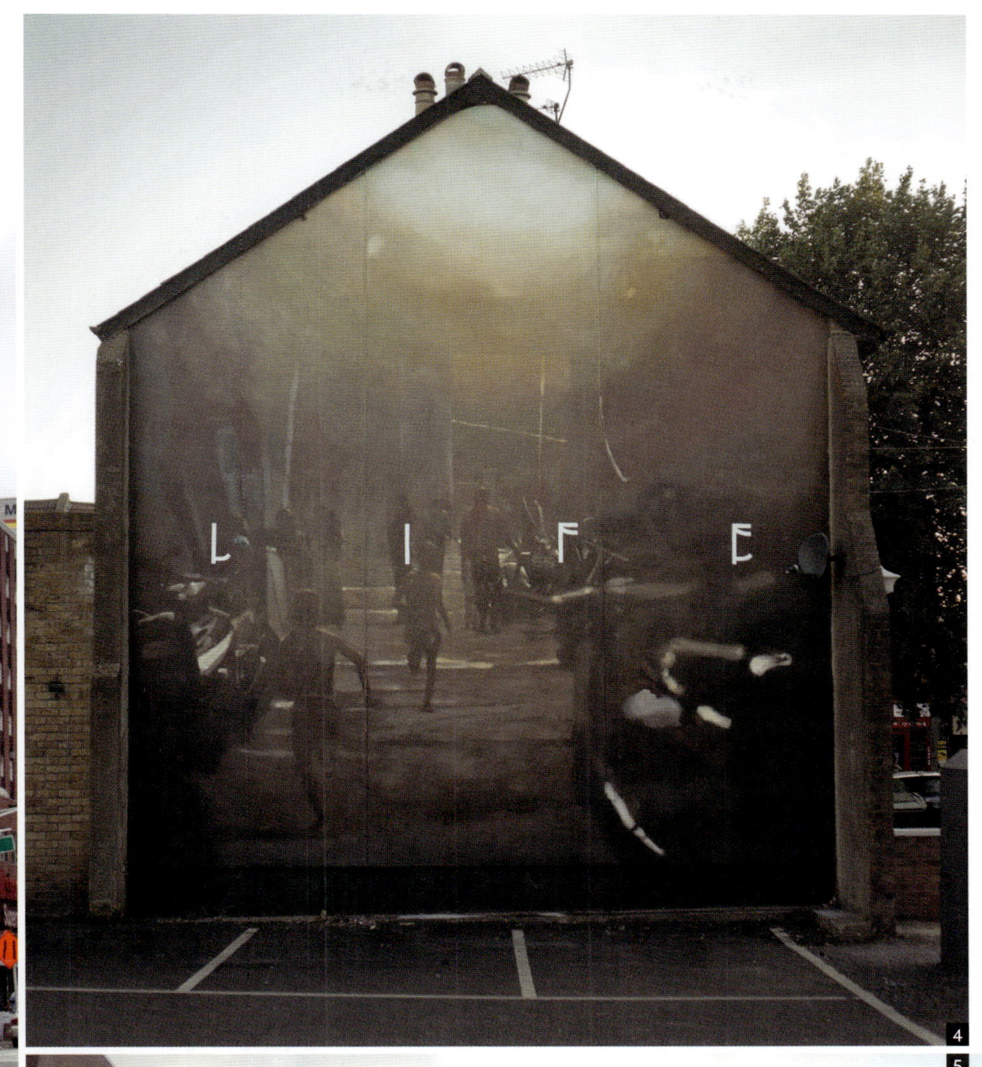

4

5

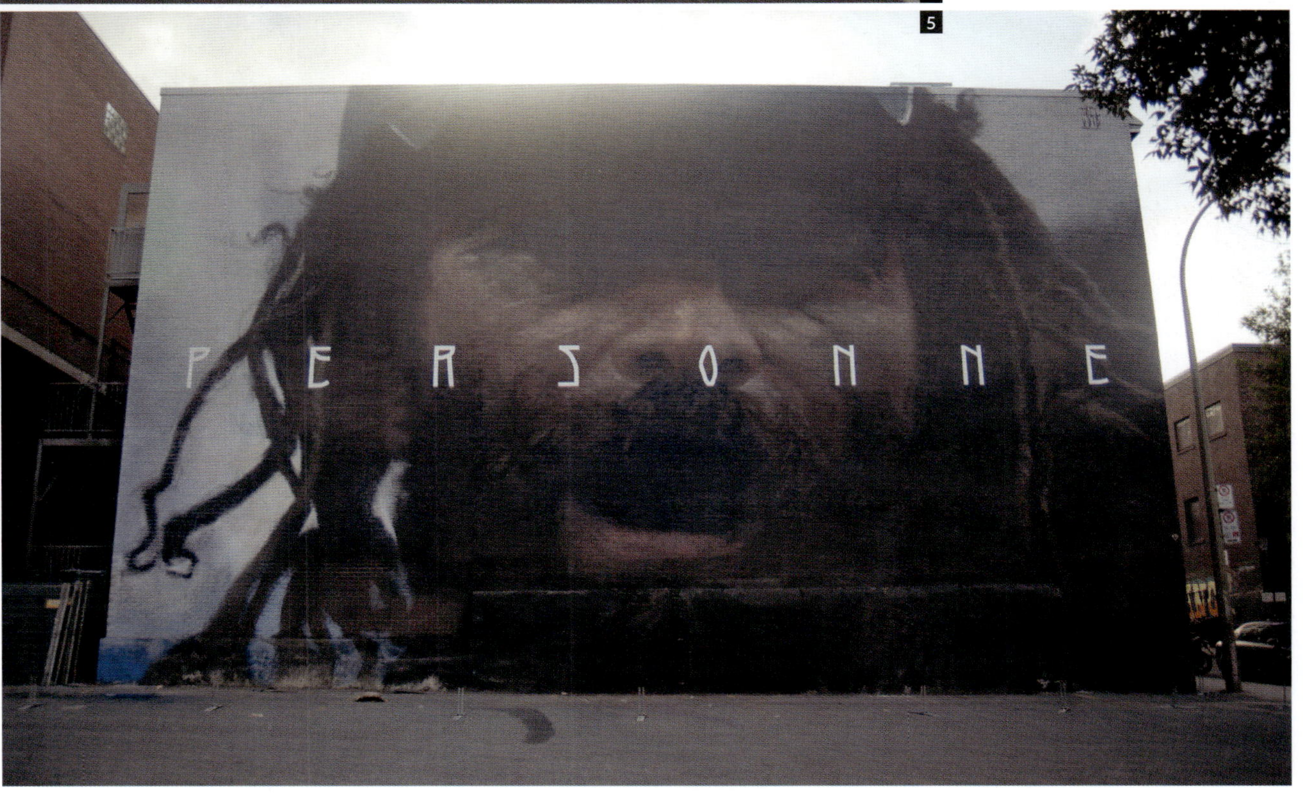

BOSOLETTI

/ Armstrong

Argentinian-born Francisco Bosoletti has travelled through various art education processes before arriving at the signature style we see today. From a background in classical painting as well as illustration and graphic design certificates, his work has evolved and morphed. In recent years, the young painter has been focusing on a unique style of large-scale negative portraiture.

The finished works resemble photo negatives, similar in aesthetic to pinhole camera imagery, where a simple smartphone filter can be used in order to see the 'correct' image,. This technological element is not Bosoletti's focus, however. Rather, his body of work comments on hidden realities, filters of perception and the generation of deeper interest in the surrounding landscape.

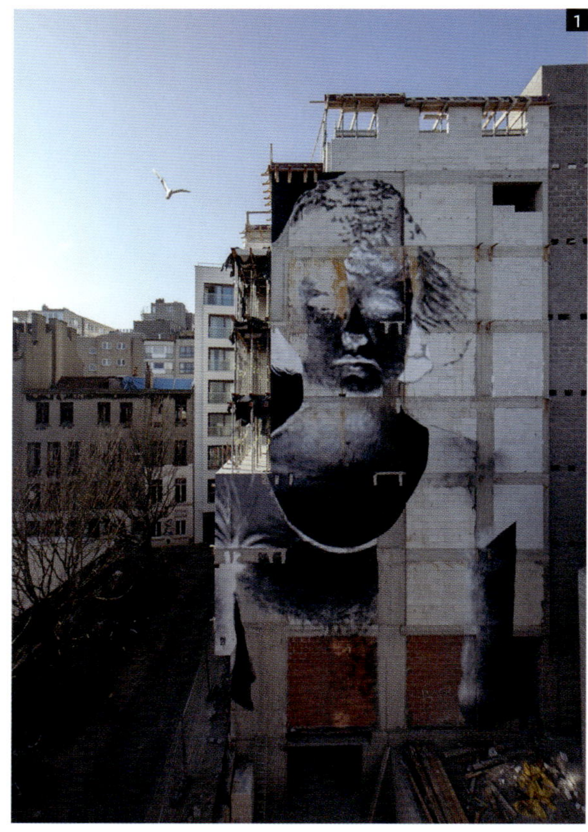

1

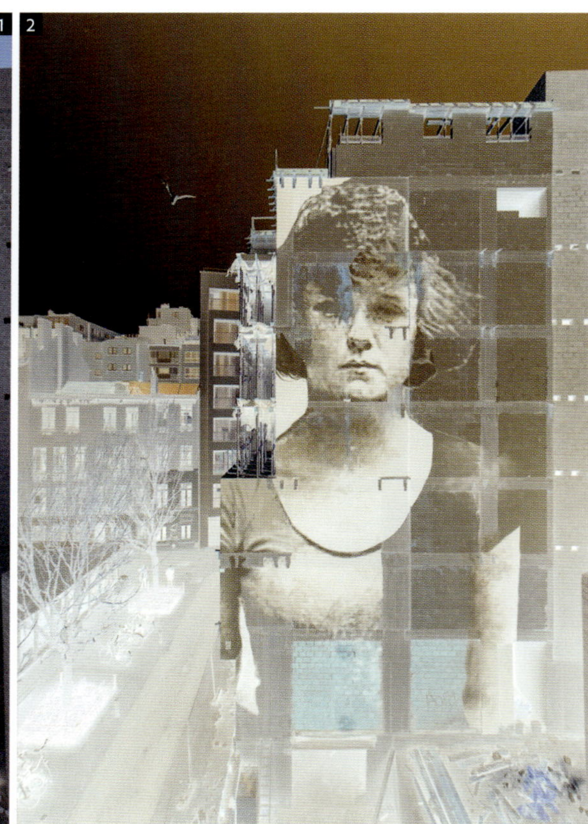

2

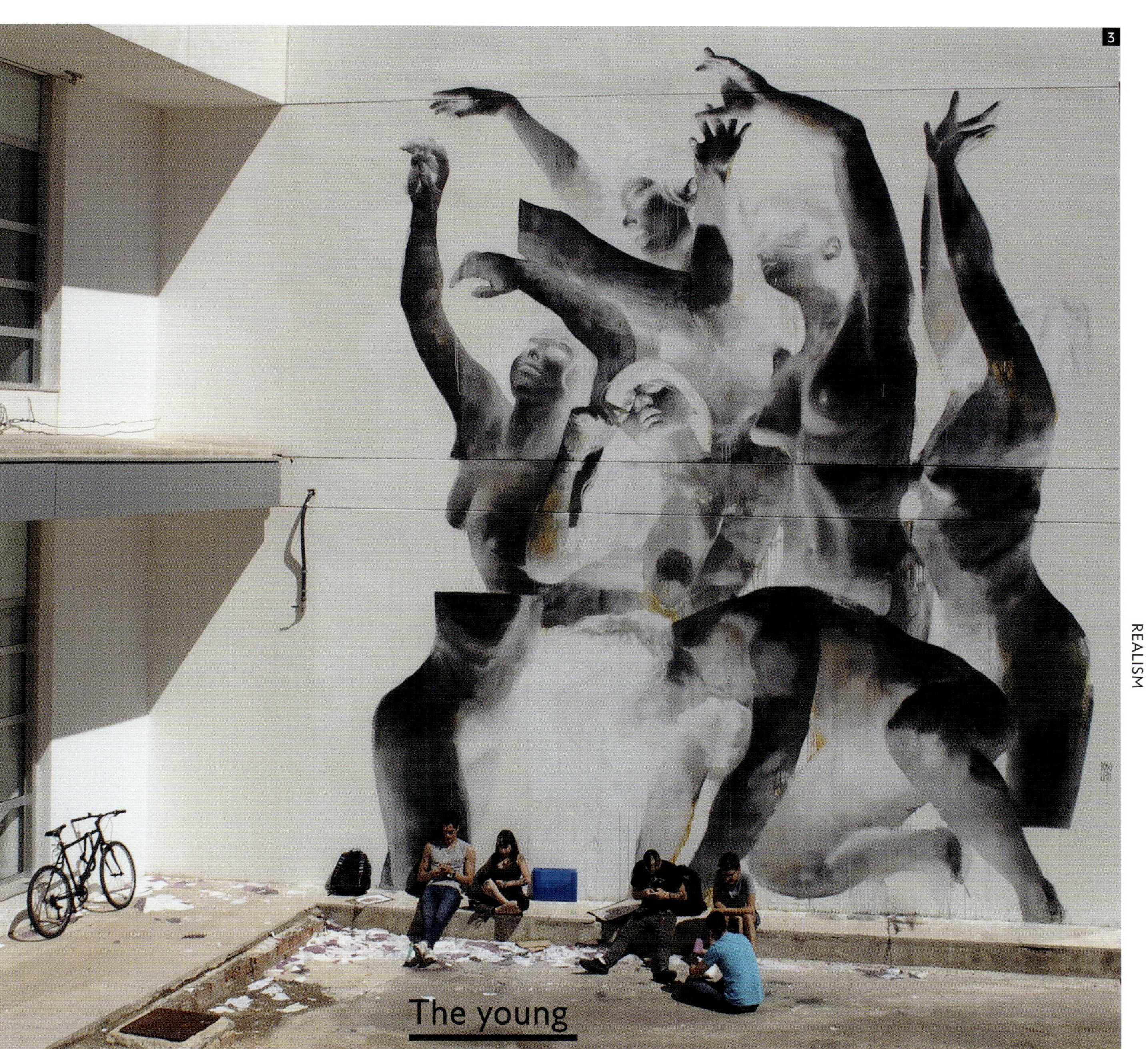

The young painter has been focusing on a unique style of large-scale negative portraiture.

1 / 2
Ostend, Belgium, 2017
PHOTO BY THE ARTIST

3 /
Valencia, Spain, 2018
PHOTO BY THE ARTIST

4

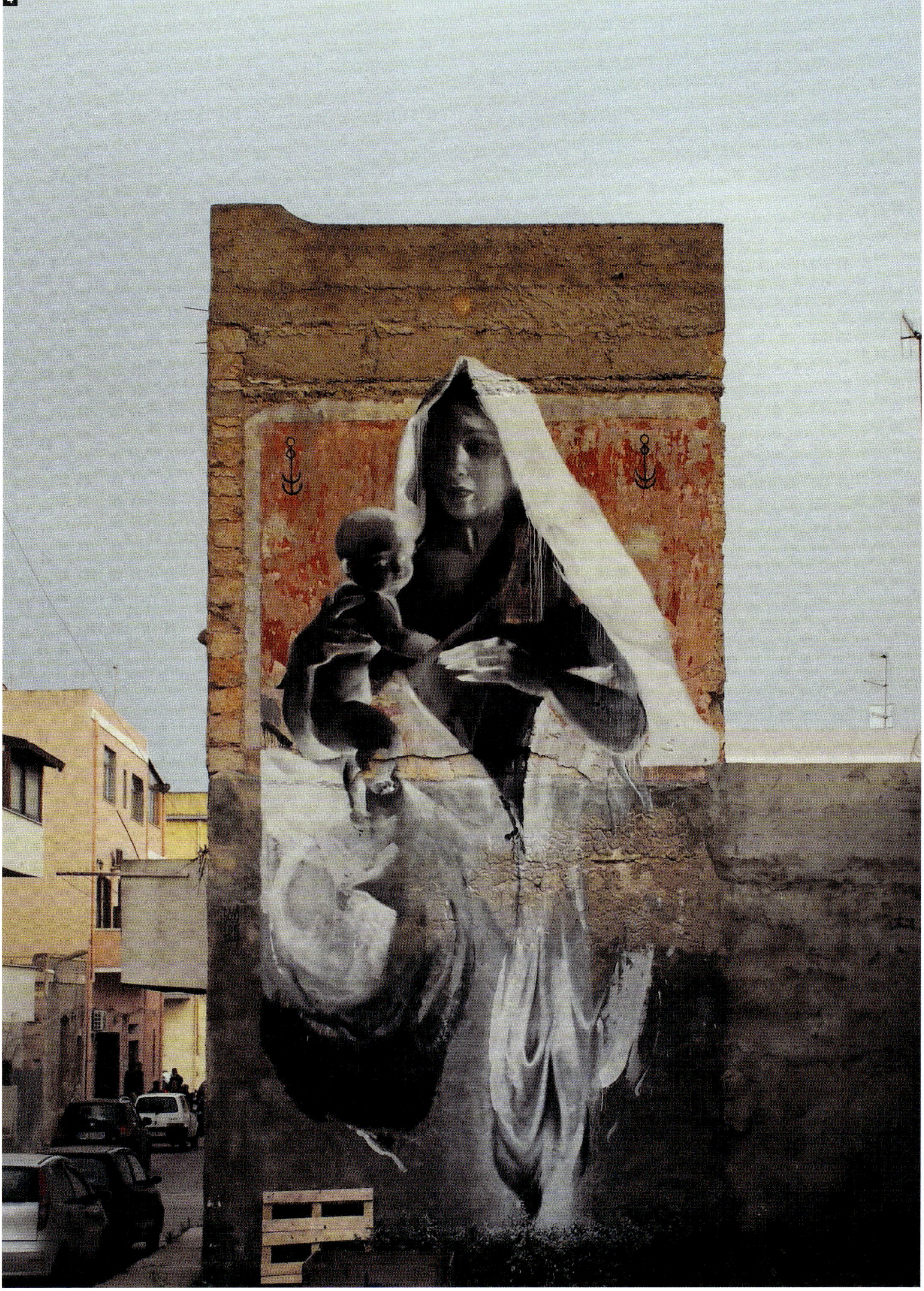

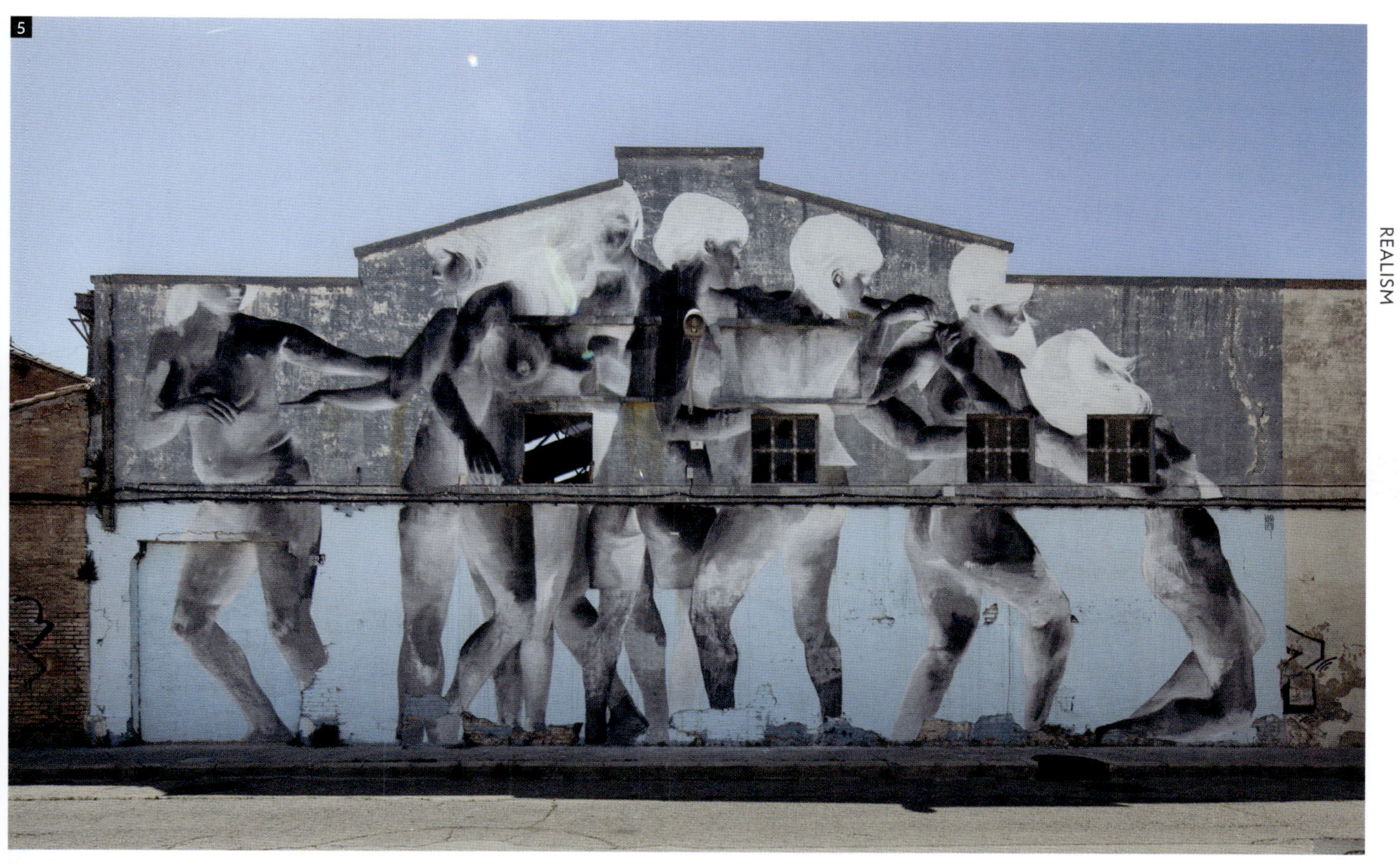

4 /
Lampedusa, 2019
PHOTO BY IAN COX

5 /
El Cabanyal, Spain, 2017
PHOTO BY IAN COX

CASE MACLAIM

/ Frankfurt

East German painter Case Maclaim, aka Andres Von Chrzanowski, has been painting streets since the mid-1990s. A true old-schooler, he has continued to evolve his technique and discourse, keeping him firmly in the arena of star artists. While his mastery of photorealistic technique previously set him amongst the pioneering painters of the genre, Case has continued to refine his craft with larger, more detailed representations.

Recent years have also seen Case become more involved with socially engaged projects, particularly valorising disadvantaged youth in the Dominican Republic and Haiti, based on his long-standing motto of 'The power of movement'.

His mastery of photorealistic technique sets him amongst the pioneering painters of the genre.

1

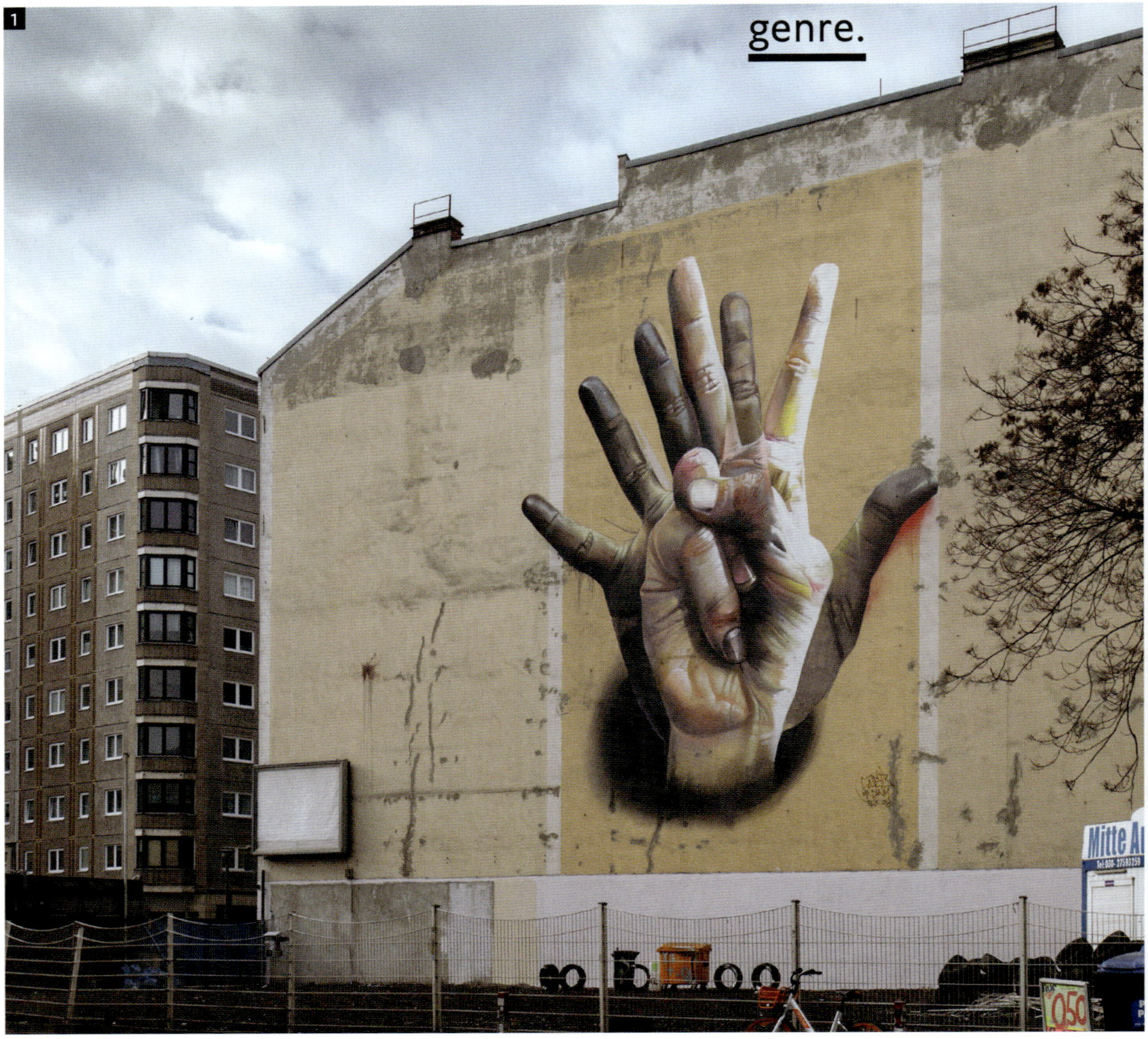

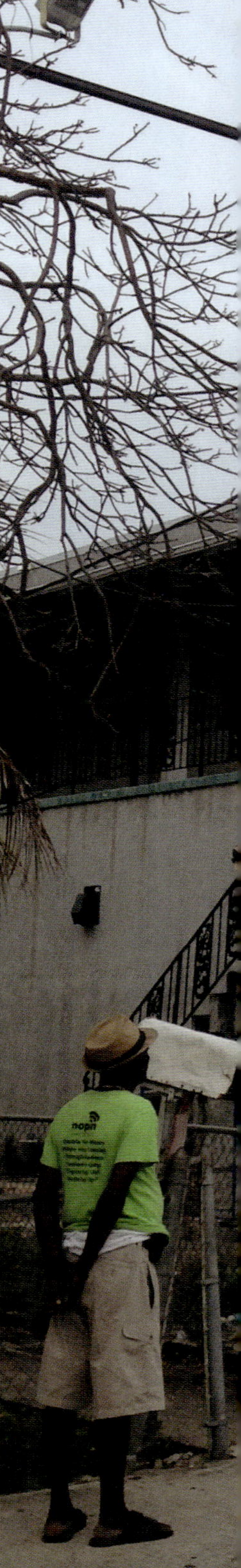

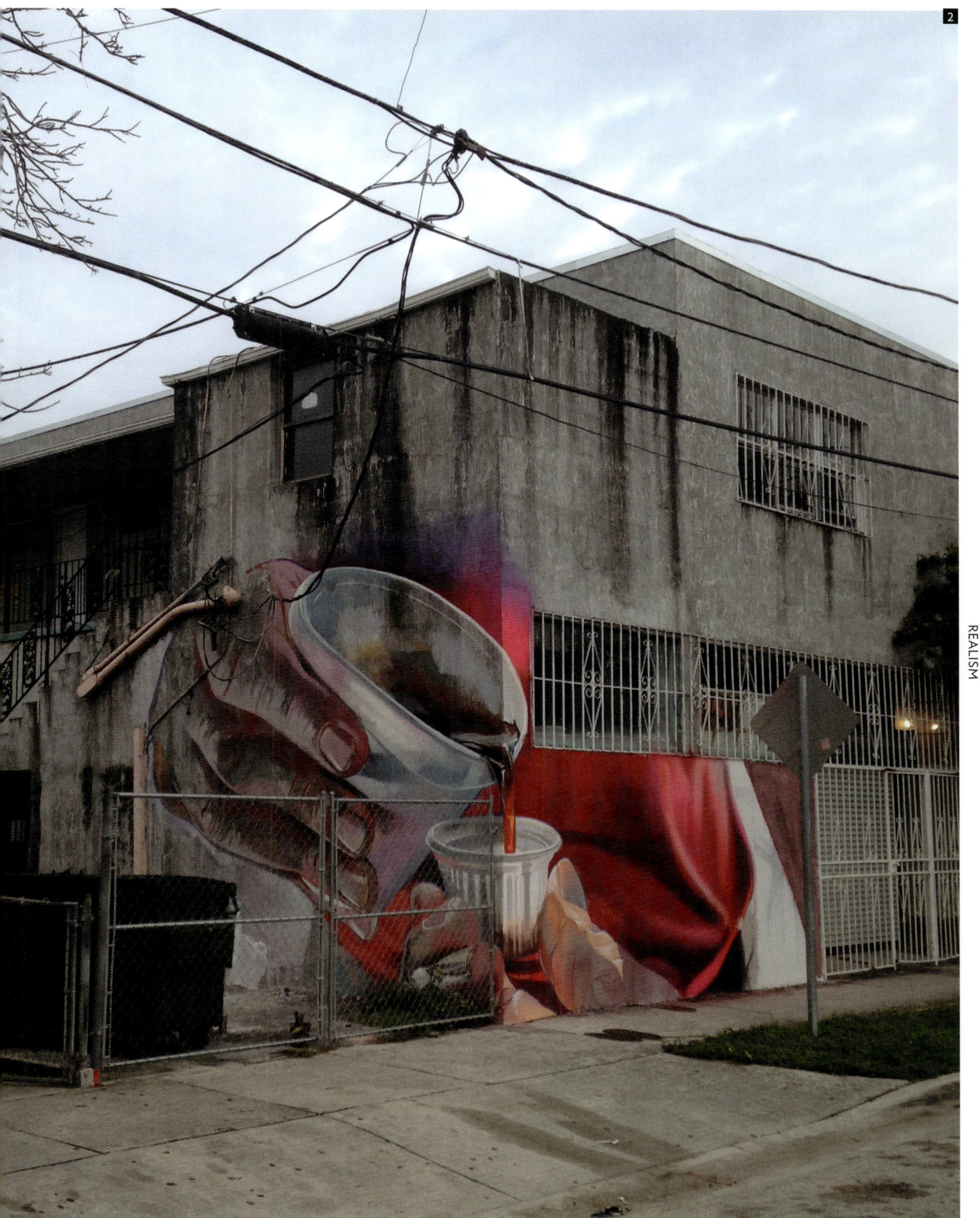

1 /
Berlin, Germany, 2015
PHOTO BY THE ARTIST

2 /
San Pedro de Marcoris, Dominican Republic, 2016
PHOTO BY THE ARTIST

3

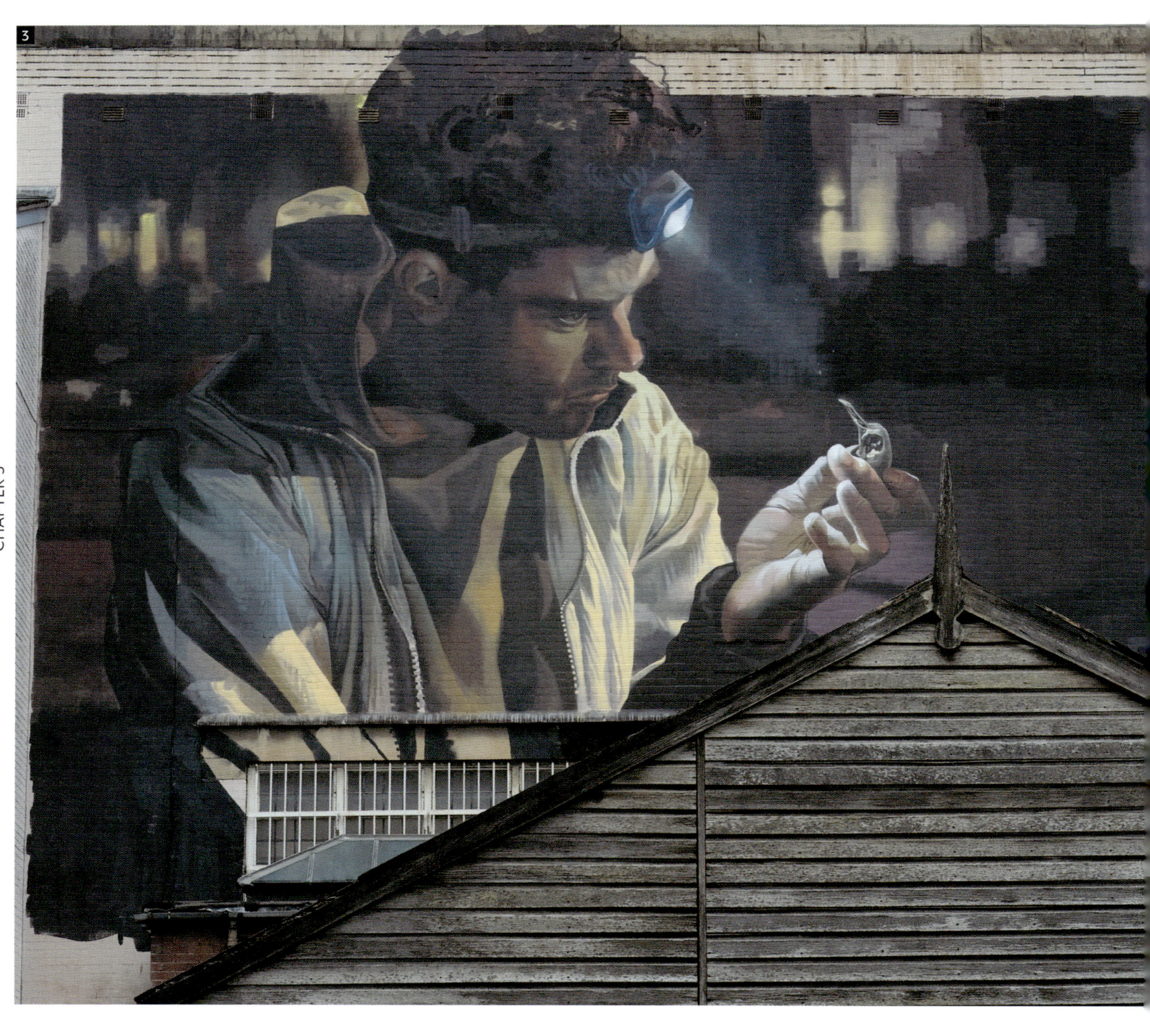

3 /
Blackburn, UK, 2019
PHOTO BY THE ARTIST

4 /
Boulogne sur Mer, France, 2017
PHOTO BY THE ARTIST

5 /
San Pedro de Marcoris, Dominican Republic, 2016
PHOTO BY THE ARTIST

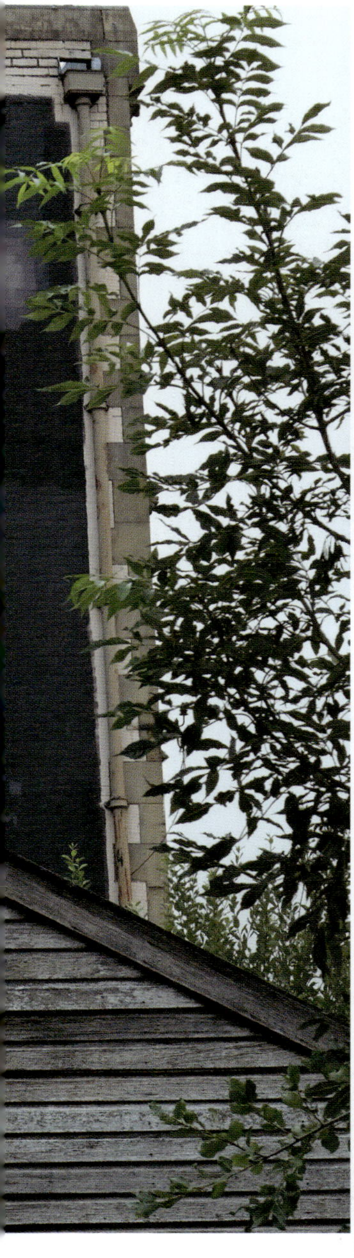

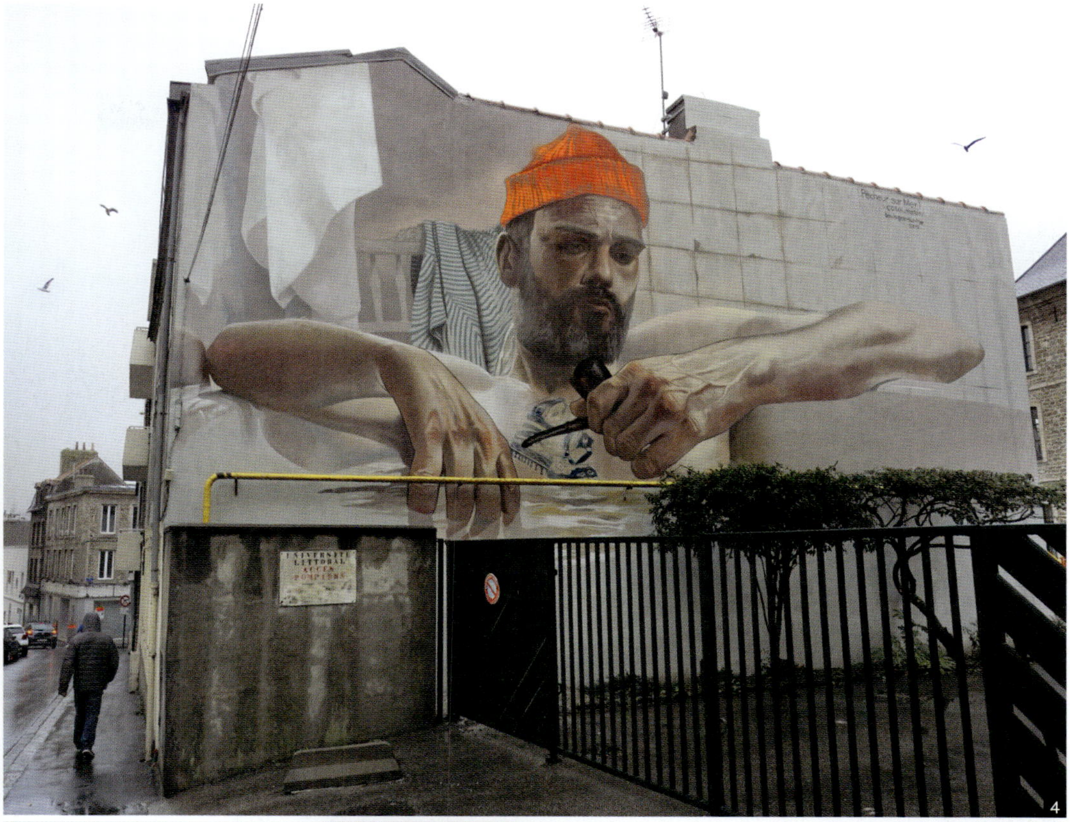

4

5

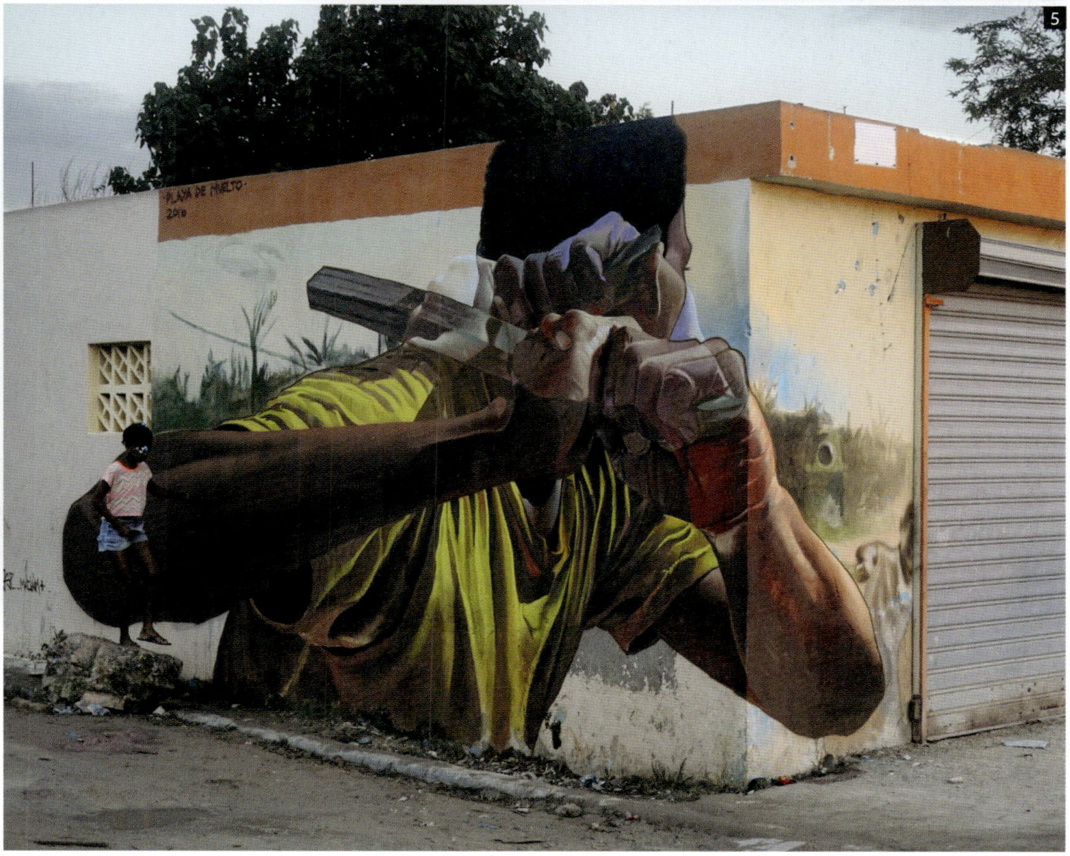

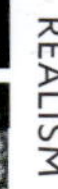

GUIDO VAN HELTEN

/ Brisbane

Best known for his large-scale, site-specific murals, Guido van Helten is a highly talented Australian artist whose breath-taking monochromatic portraits adorn walls around the world. Working in a photorealistic style, he creates delicate and elegant pieces that have an overall atmosphere of melancholy and a deeply sentimental quality. His work is often informed by photographic reference material that is socially important to the area he is working in. Guido always pays special attention to detail and tries to incorporate specific local elements into his pieces.
Guido's work can be found everywhere: from Australia to the United Kingdom, from Eastern Europe to Mexico. His portraits of un-idealised faces of ordinary men, women and children in a stunning, realistic manner are striking in their ability to capture all the emotions of their subjects. Amongst his large-scale pieces, the artist also creates studio works.

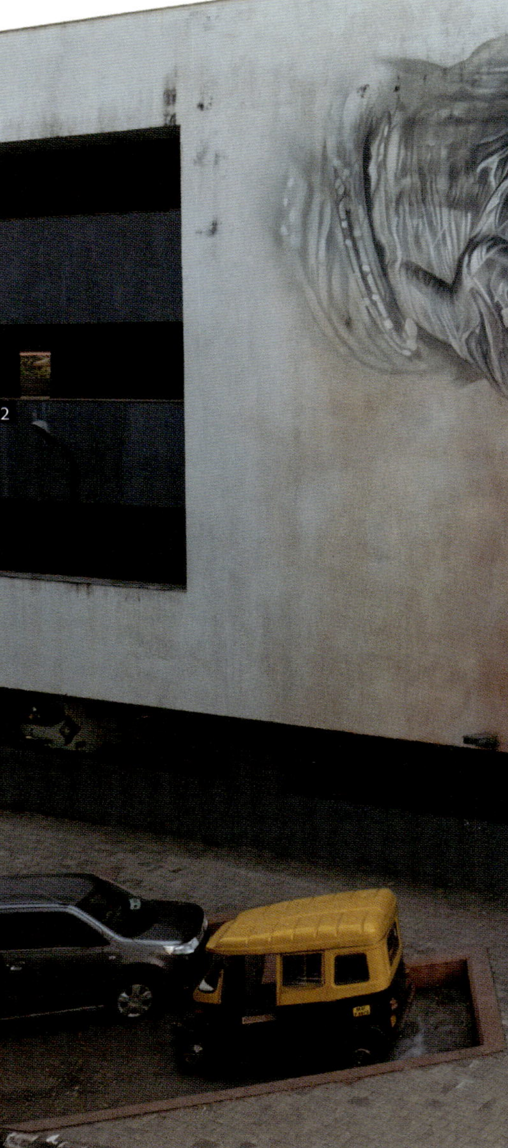

1 2

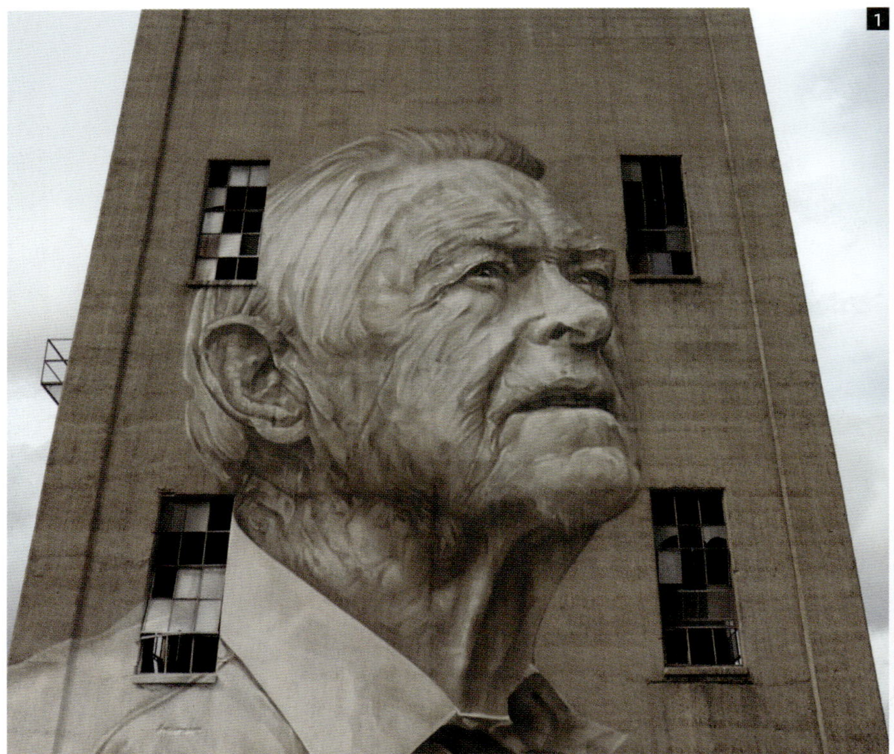

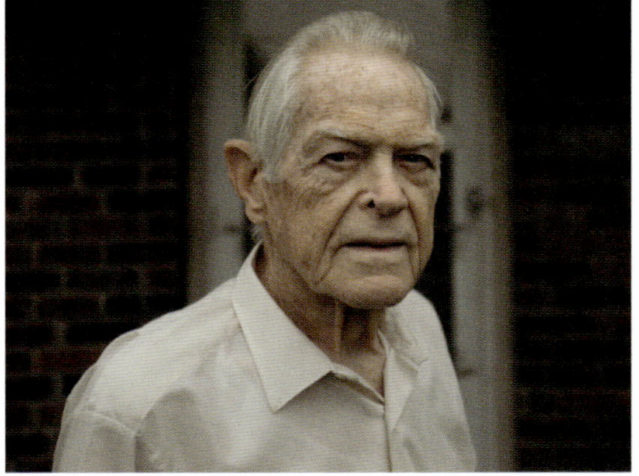

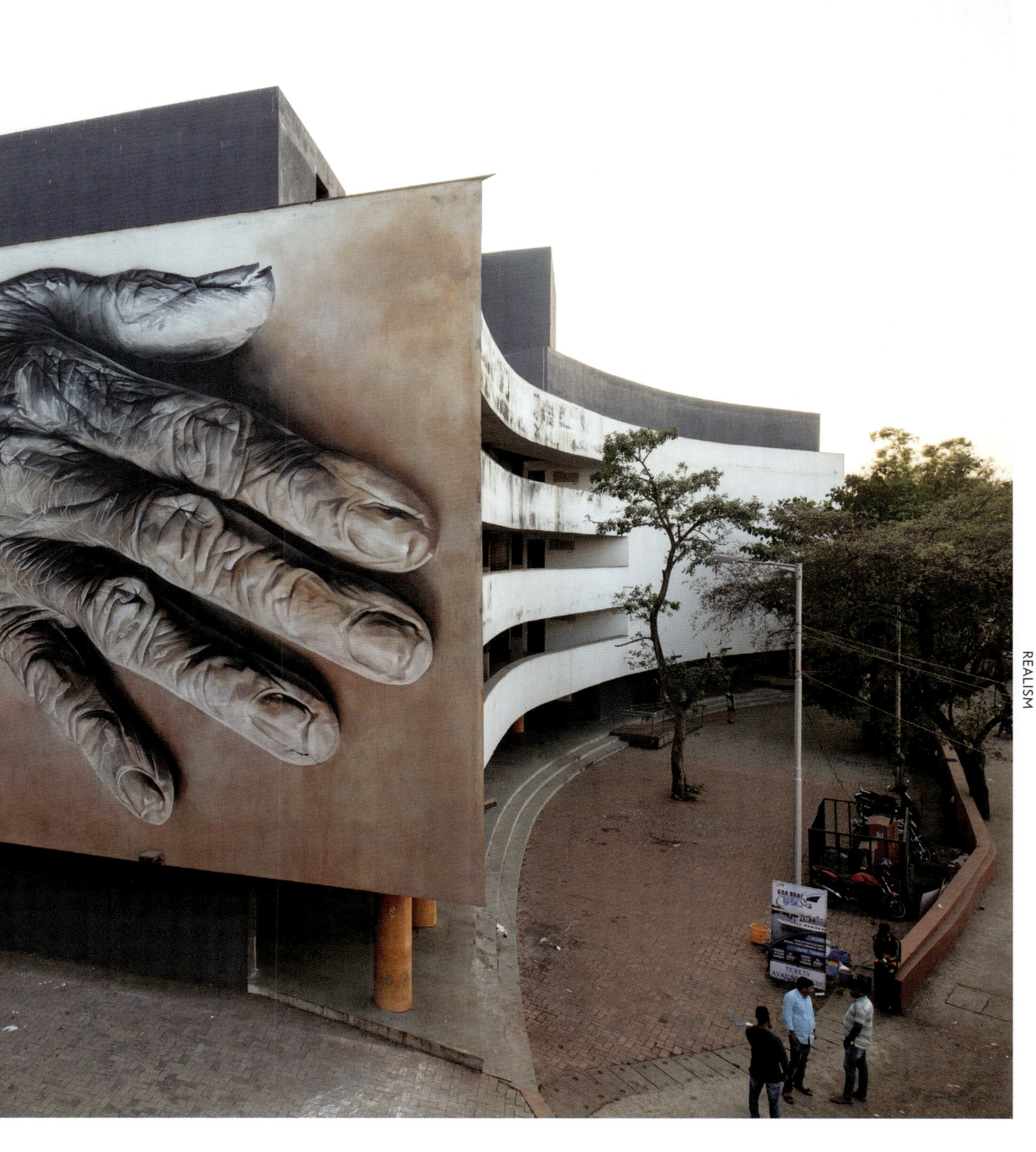

1 /
Urbandale Nations, Nashville, Tennessee, 2017
PHOTO BY THE ARTIST

2 /
Panjim, Goa, India, 2018
PHOTO BY THE ARTIST

3

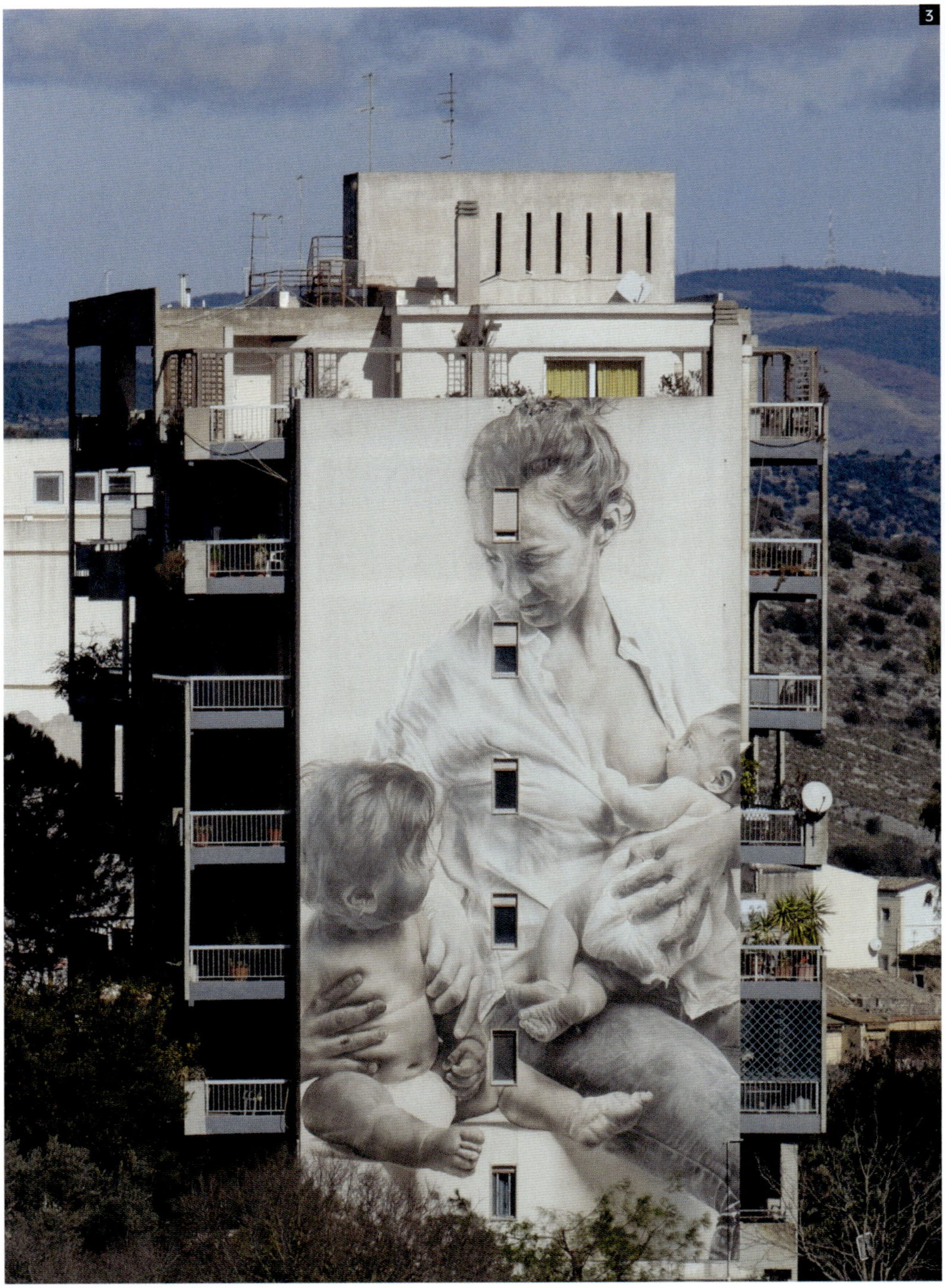

4

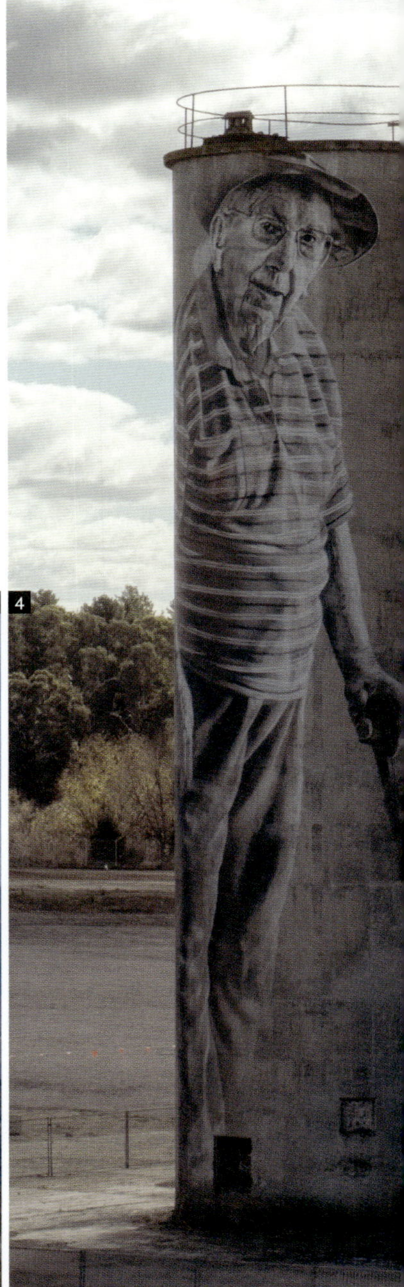

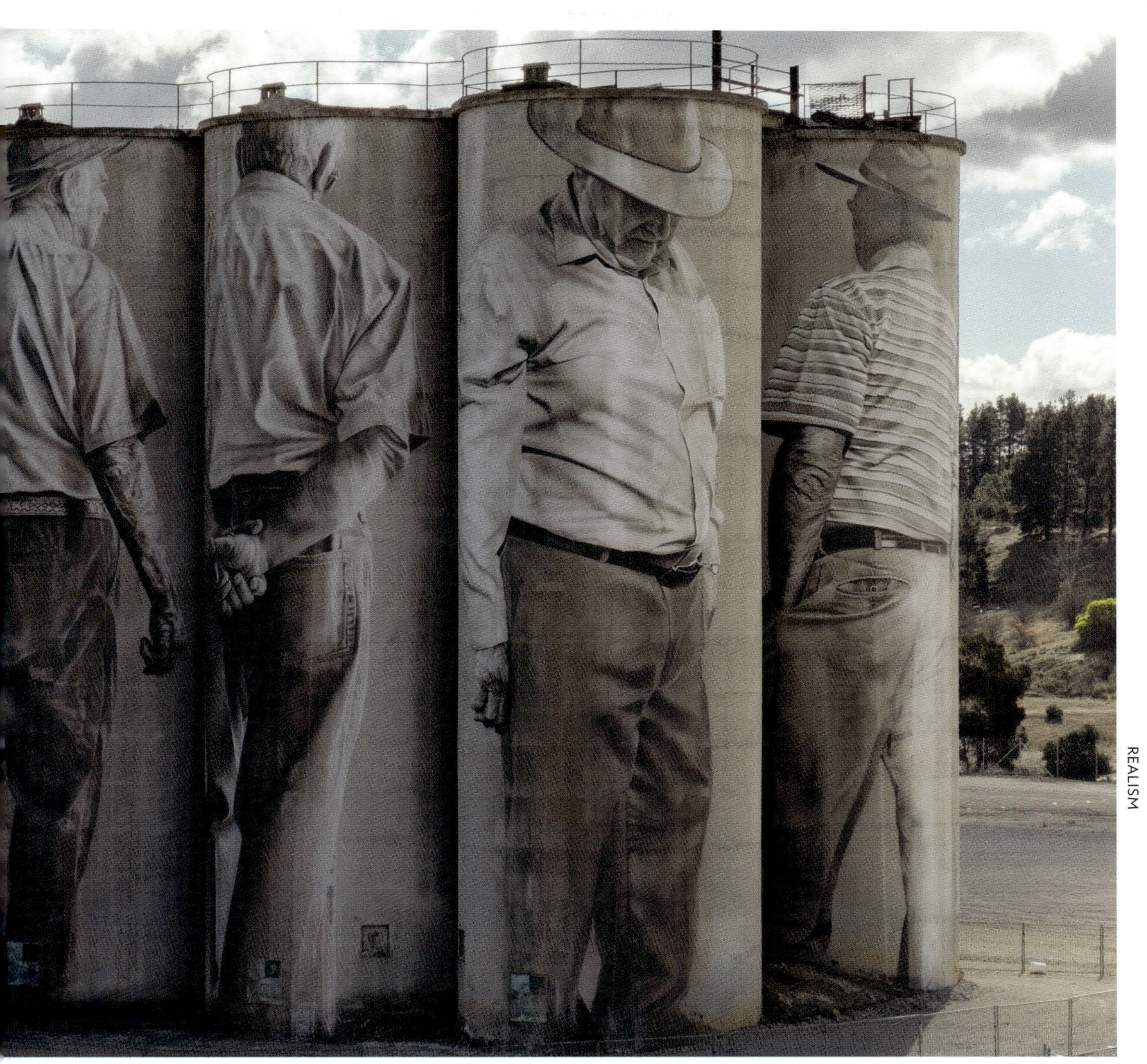

Guido always pays special attention to detail and tries to incorporate specific local elements into his pieces.

3 /
Ragusa, Italy, 2019
PHOTO BY THE ARTIST

4 /
Portland, Australia, 2018
PHOTO BY THE ARTIST

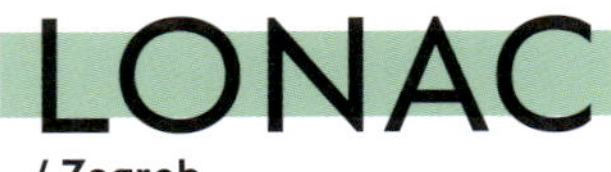

LONAC

/ Zagreb

Young Croatian artist Lonac (a name meaning 'cooking pot' in his own language) seems to be in a seething battle against all that is mundane in the world. A truly creative being - he cites influences from the subcultures of skate and graffiti - as well as pop culture through comics, movies and music. An impressive grasp on hyper-realist technique is counterbalanced with surreal content. 'Moving boundaries in that way is fun, turning things around a bit, opening people to new stuff.'

Desperately trying to show the world how important it is to express your inner child, he portrays scenes of the everyday-ludicrous and the impossible-imaginary. As he continues to develop his realist technique, it is exciting to see Lonac evolve into a master of (sur)realist imagery.

An impressive grasp on hyper-realist technique is counterbalanced with surreal content.

1

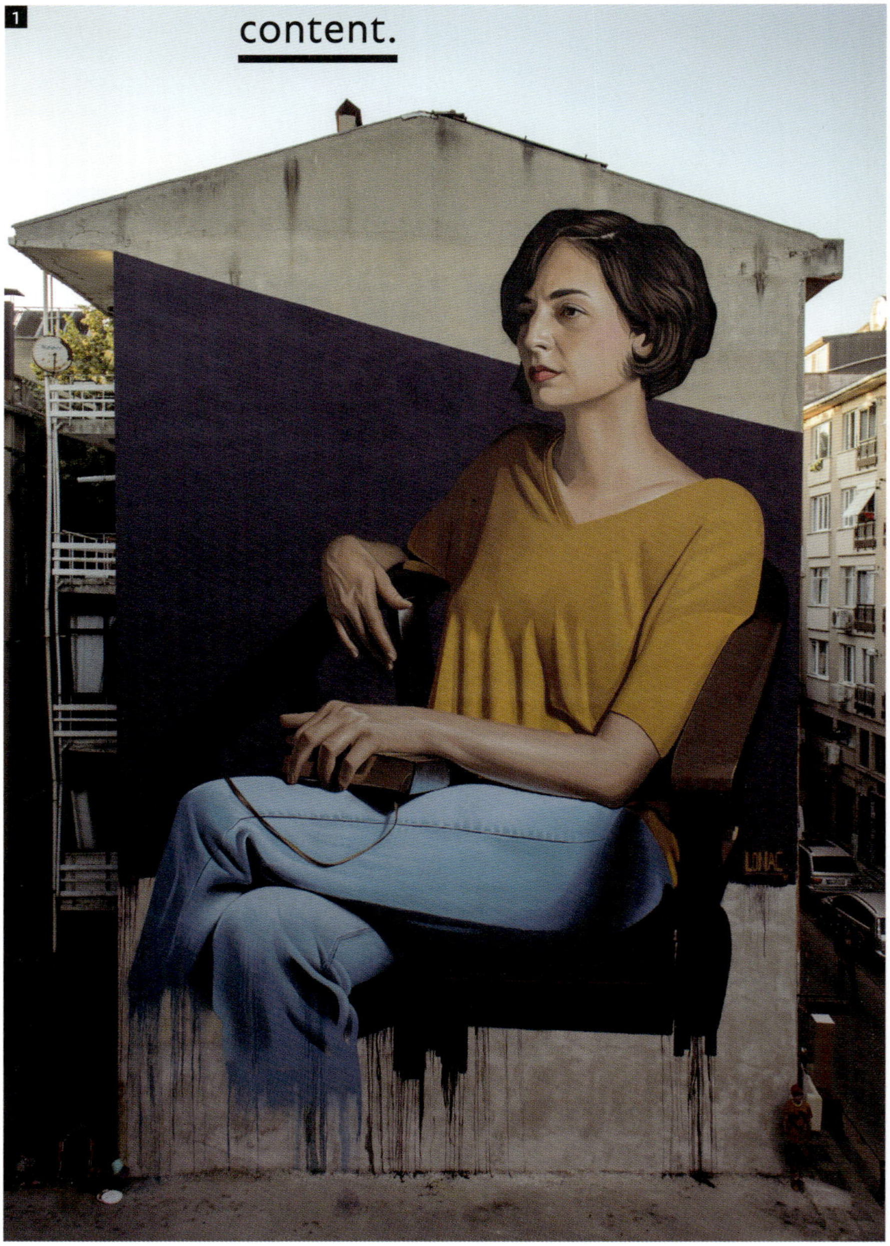

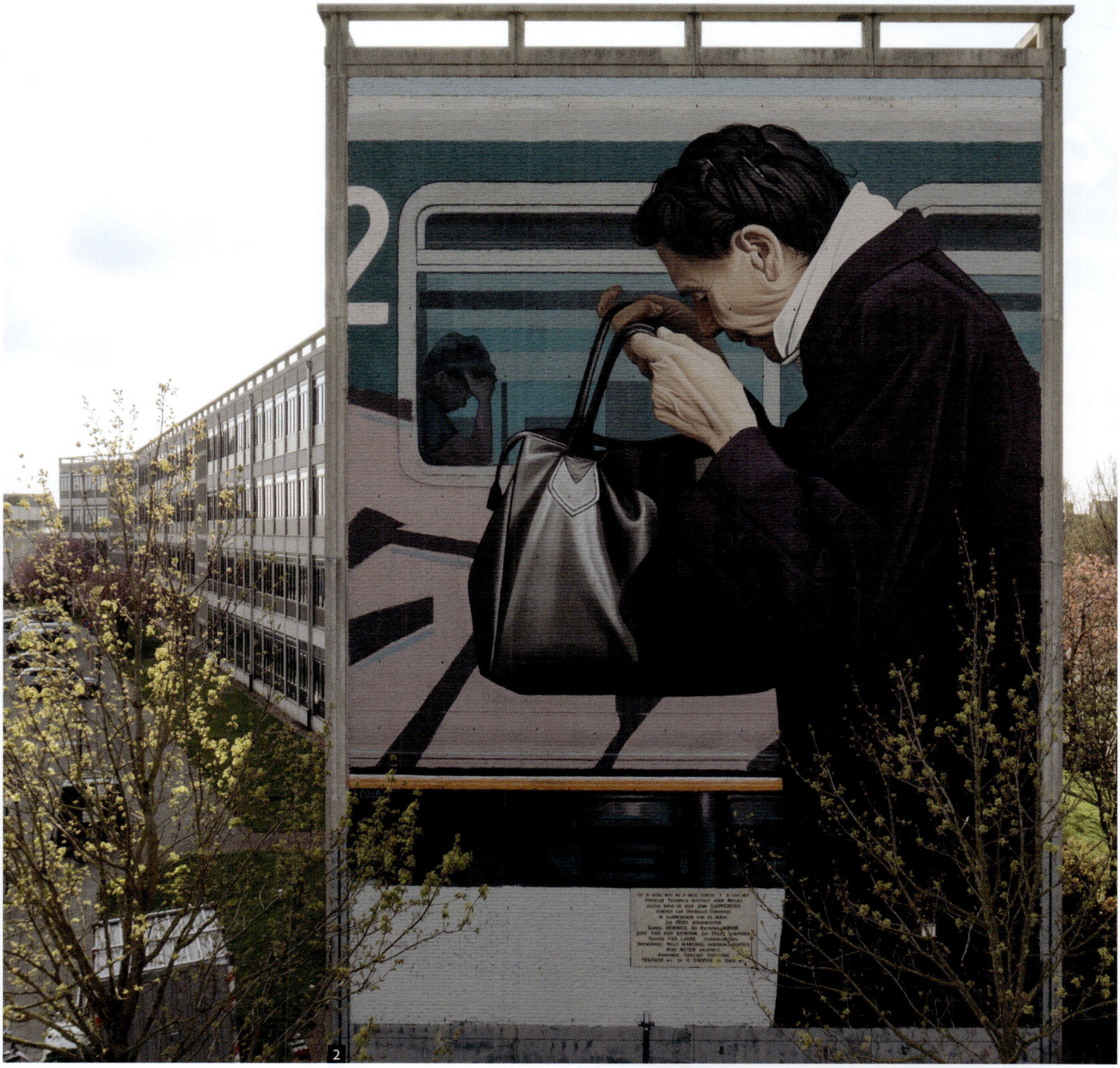

2

3

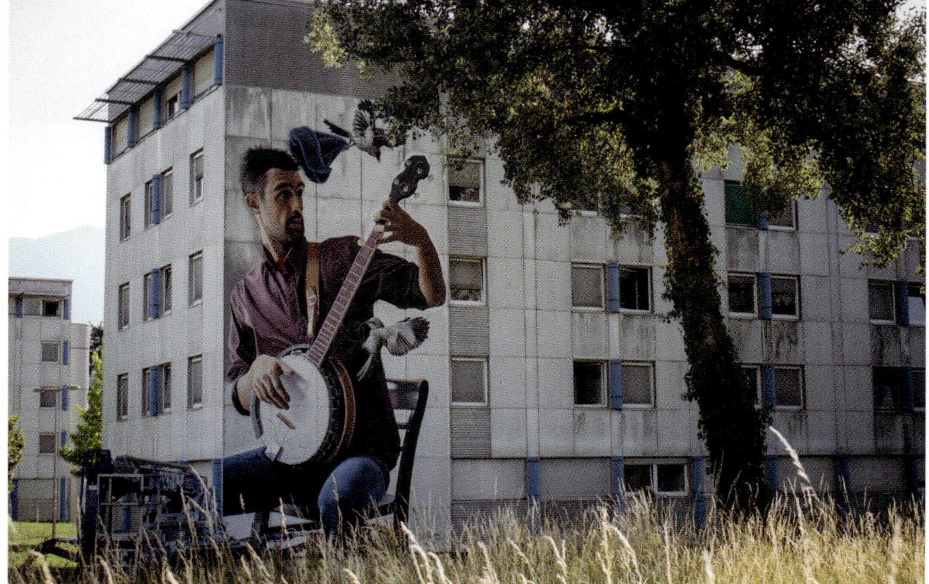

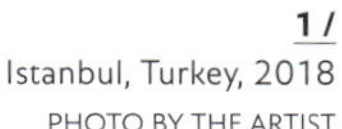

1 /
Istanbul, Turkey, 2018
PHOTO BY THE ARTIST

2 /
Ostend, Belgium, 2019
PHOTO BY THE ARTIST

3 /
Rijeka, Croatia, 2016
PHOTO BY THE ARTIST

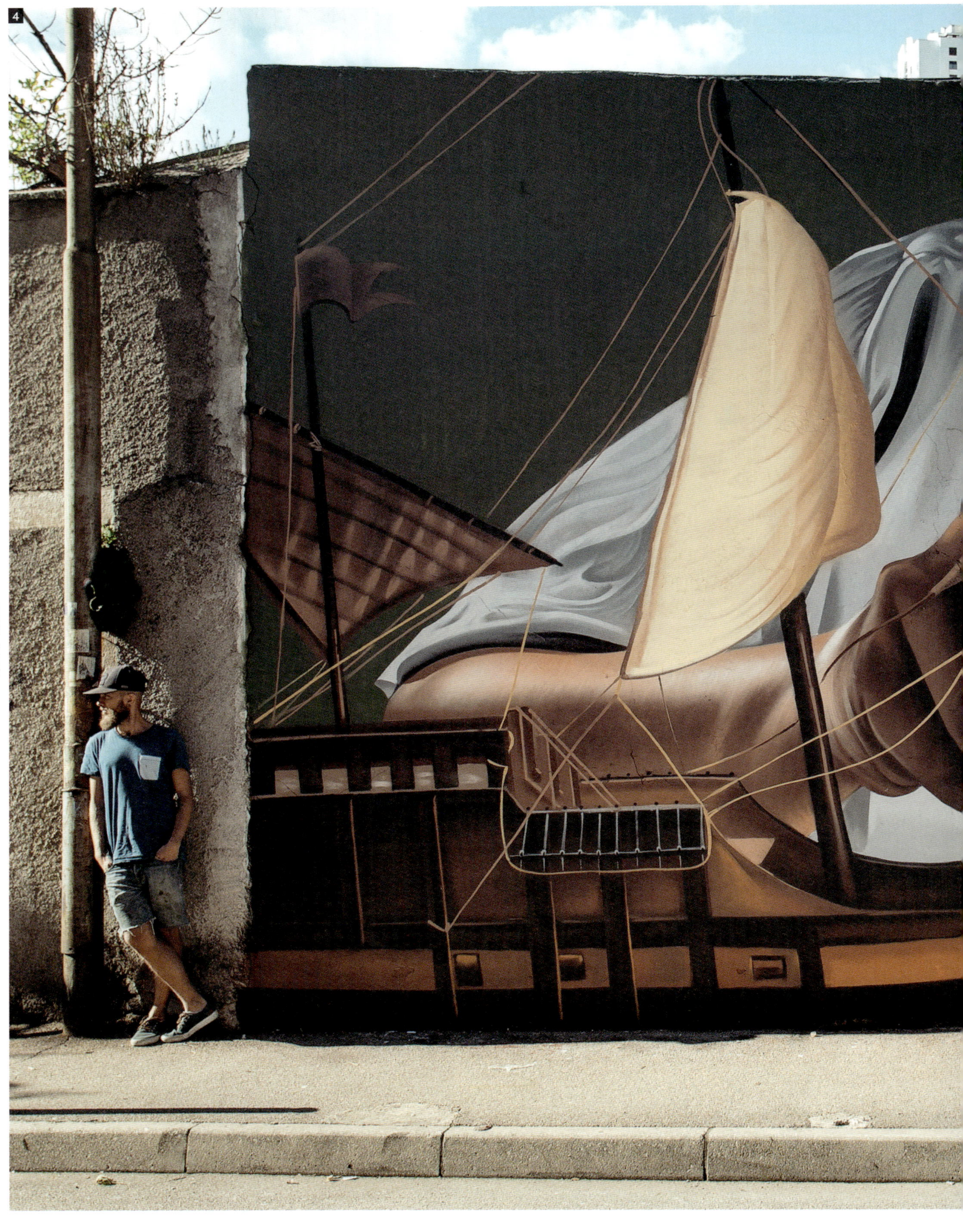

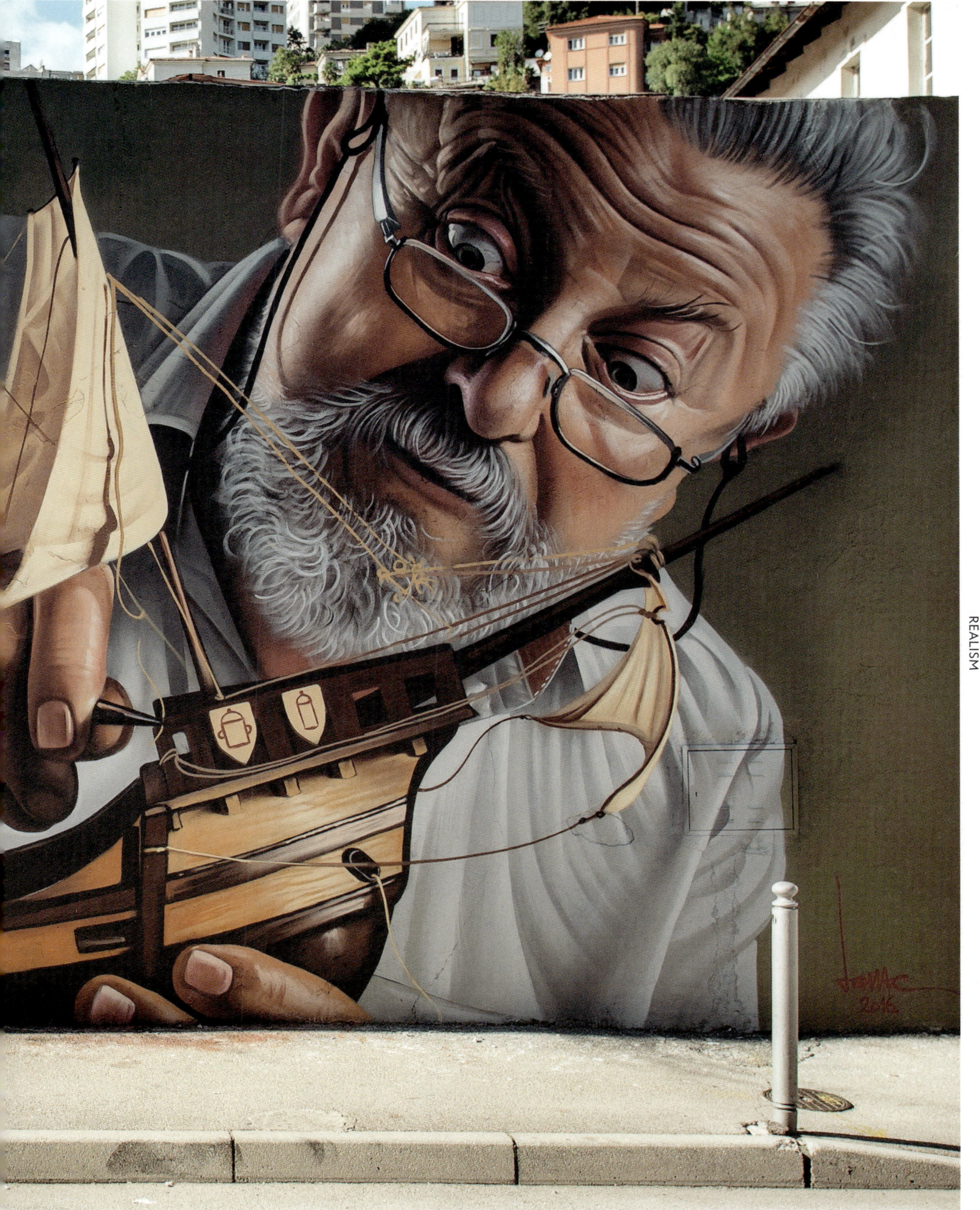

4 /
Rijeka, Croatia, 2016
PHOTO BY THE ARTIST

SEBAS VELASCO

/ San Sebastian

In a scene that often gravitates towards eye-catching pop art colours, Sebas Velasco's stern colour palette and painterly style are a refreshing celebration of the art of painting. Contemporary urban landscapes and realist portraits are portrayed with the eye of a romantic rationalist; Sebas cites a range of Old Masters as guiding influences.

Having drawn and painted from a very young age, Sebas uses a mix of materials and techniques in his mural work, including oils, spray paint and pencil. His interests in portraiture and architecture's influence on society are strongly present in his work, in which he gravitates towards scenes of nocturnal solitude in urban landscapes.

Sabas has the eye of a romantic rationalist.

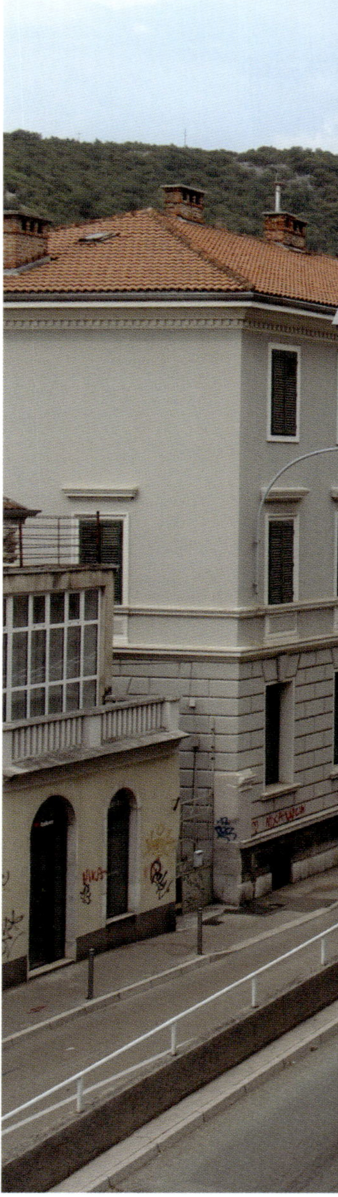

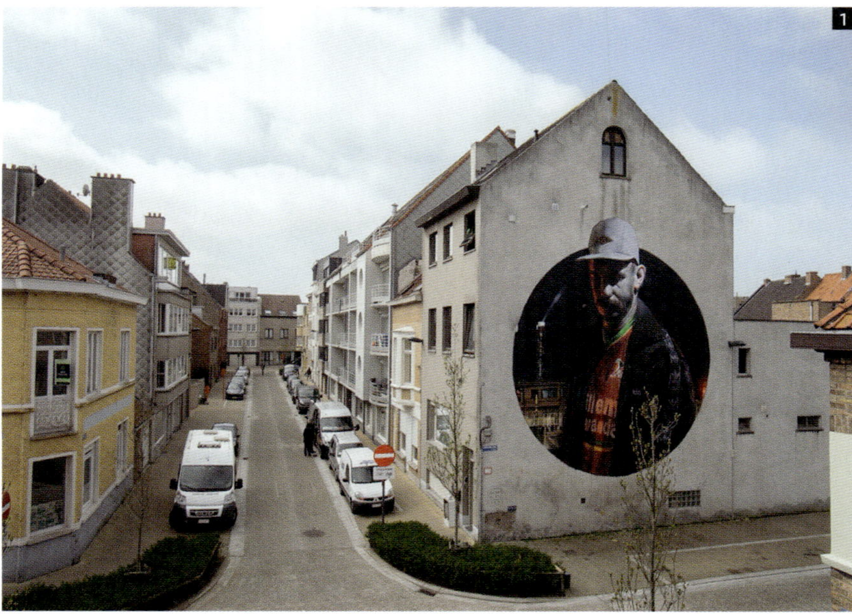

1 /
Ostend, Belgium, 2017
PHOTO BY IAN COX

2 / 3
Ostend, Belgium, 2017
PHOTO BY THE ARTIST

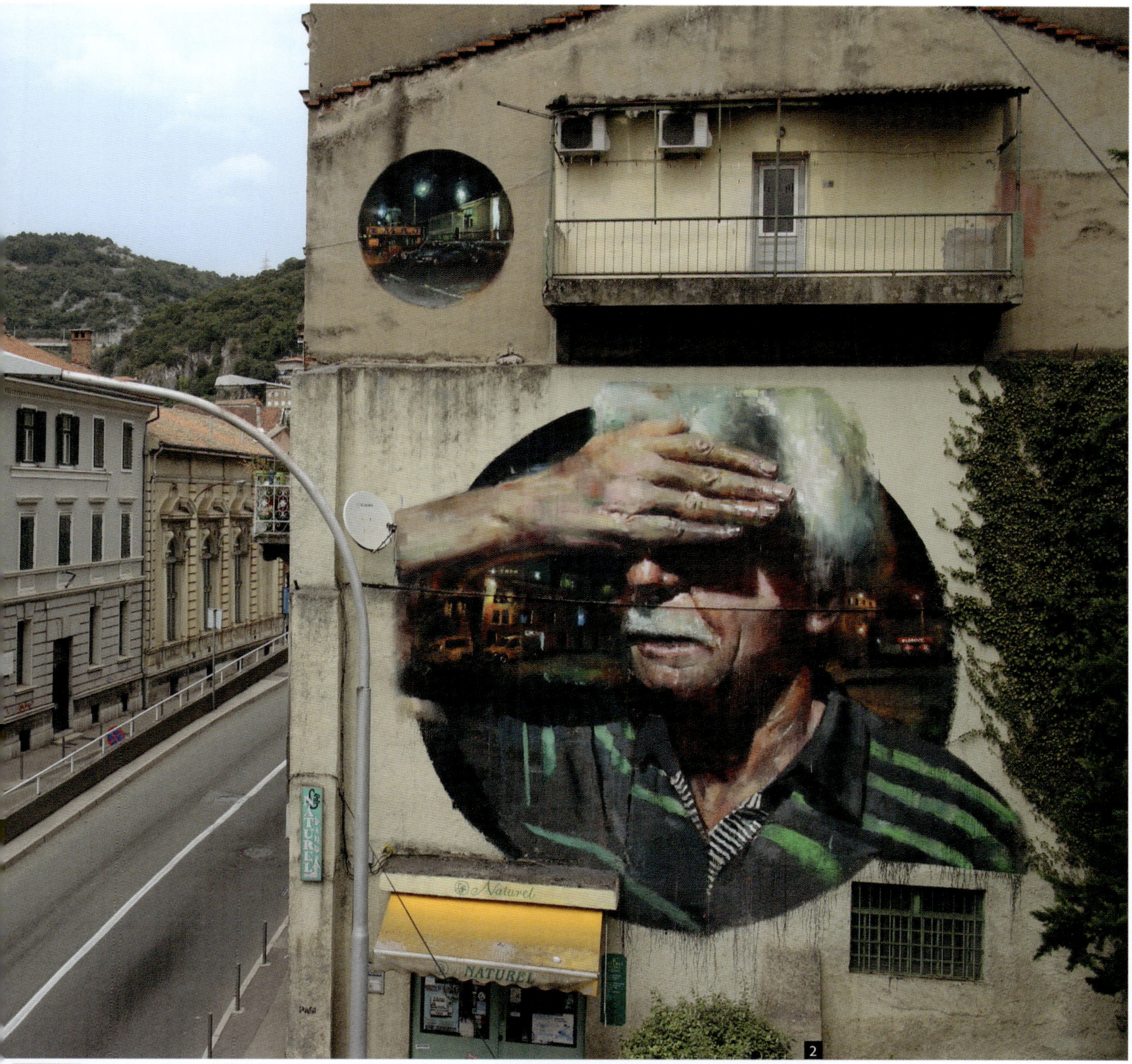

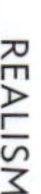

2

3

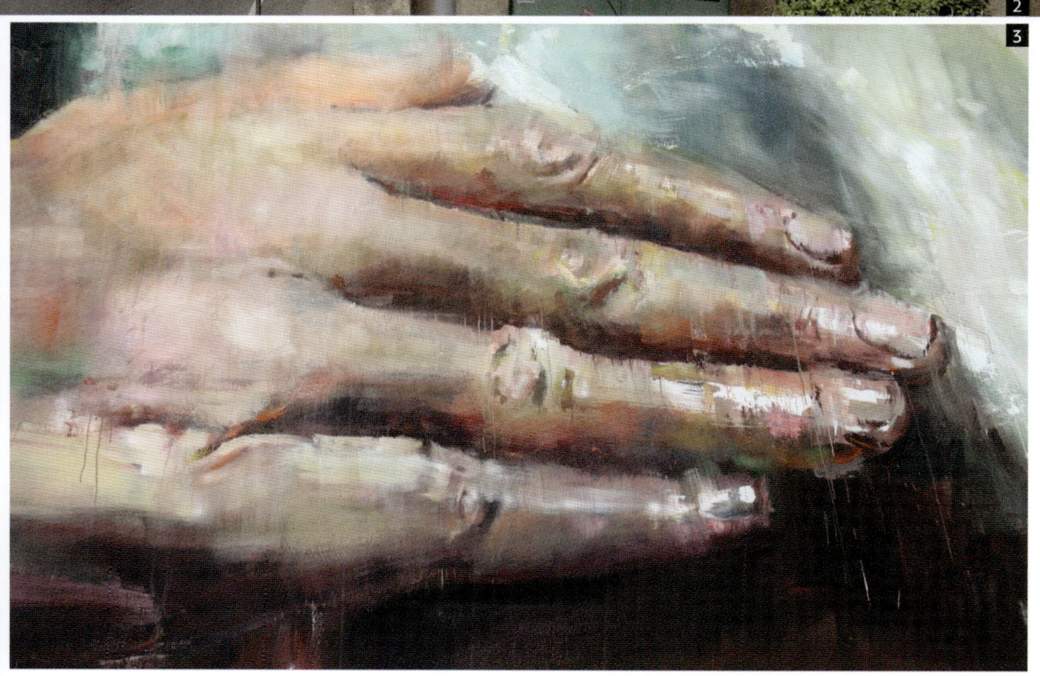

» /
Ragusa, Italy, 2017
PHOTO BY THE ARTIST

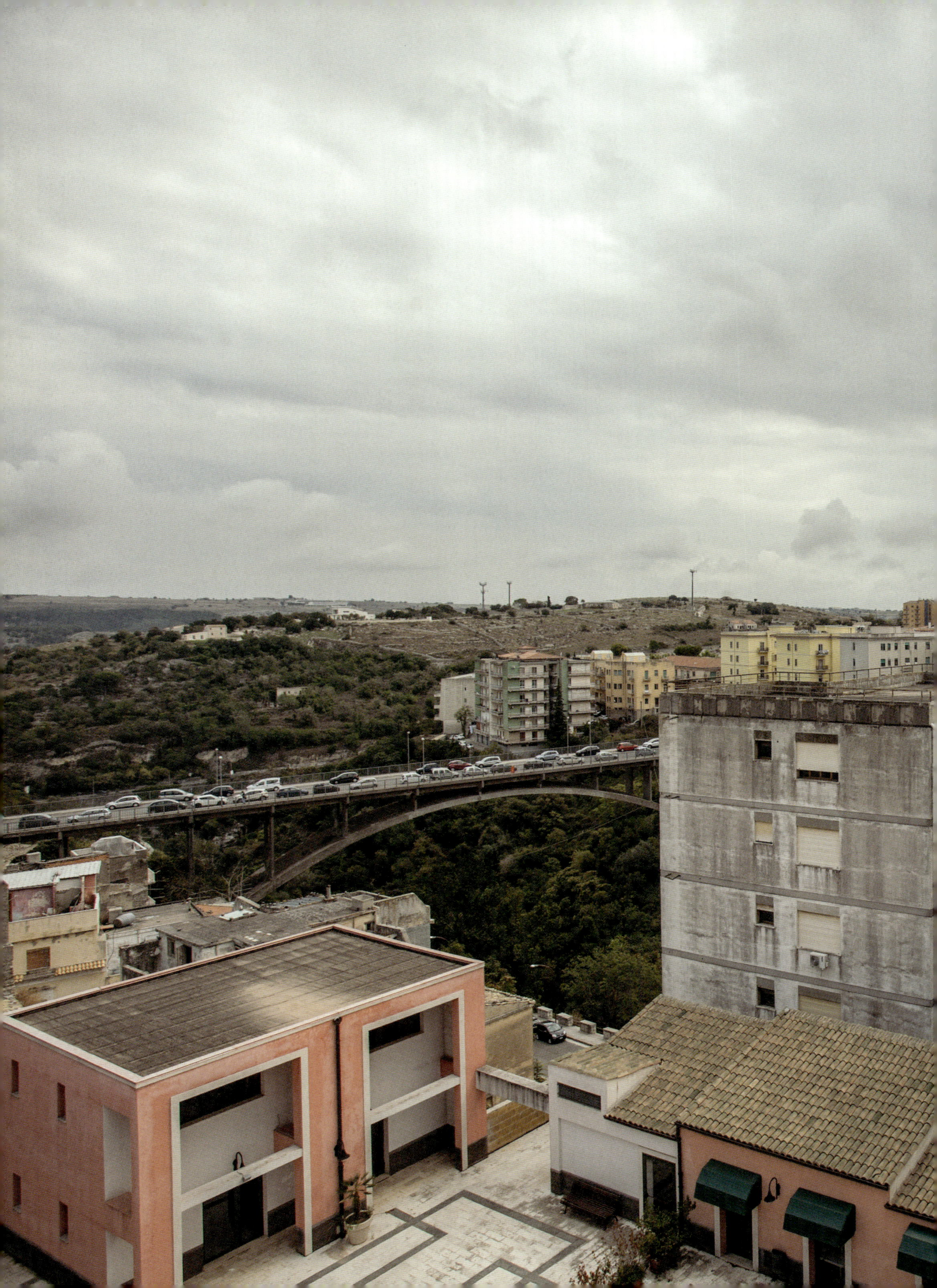

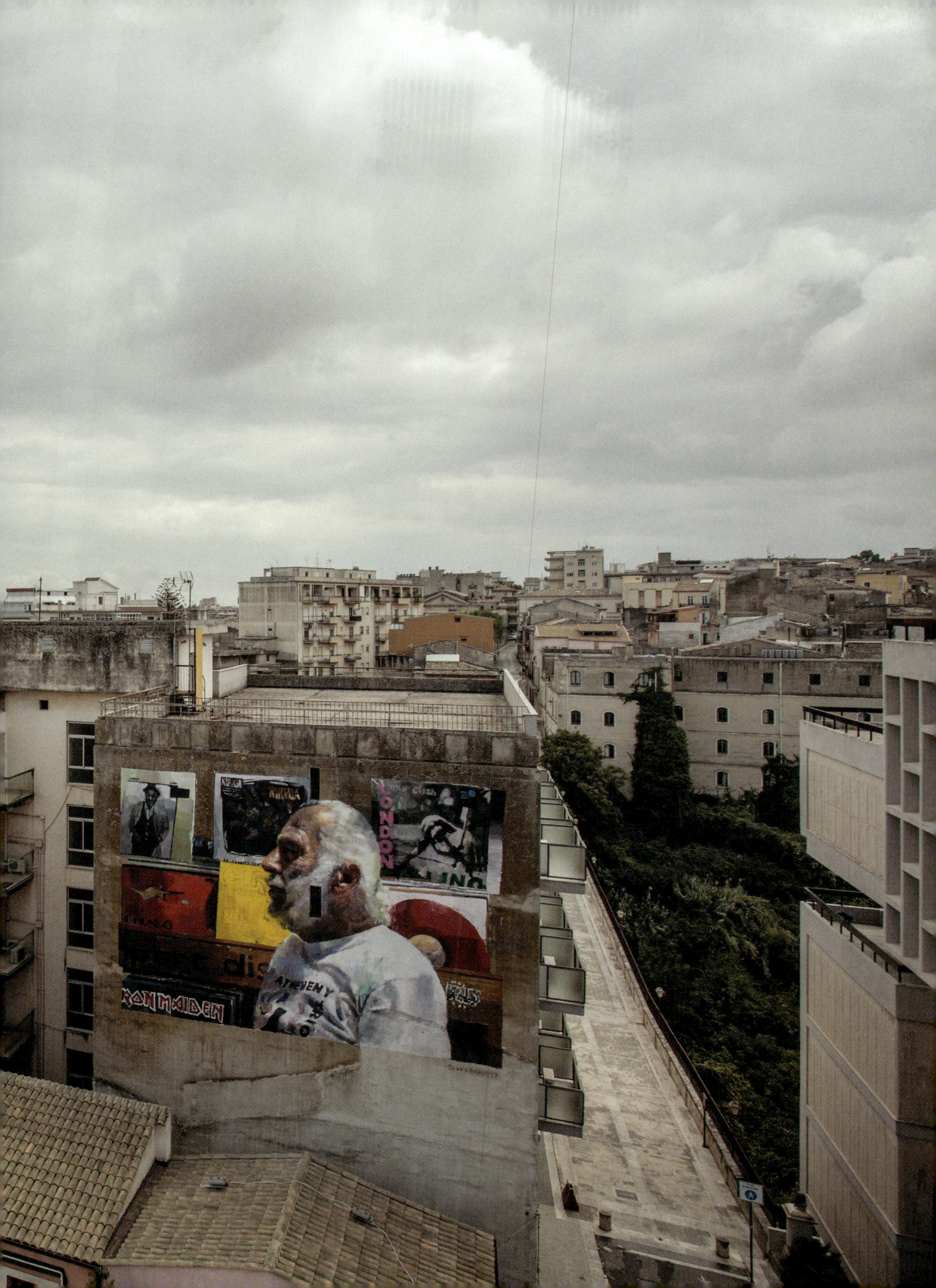
LONDON
RON MAIDEN

1

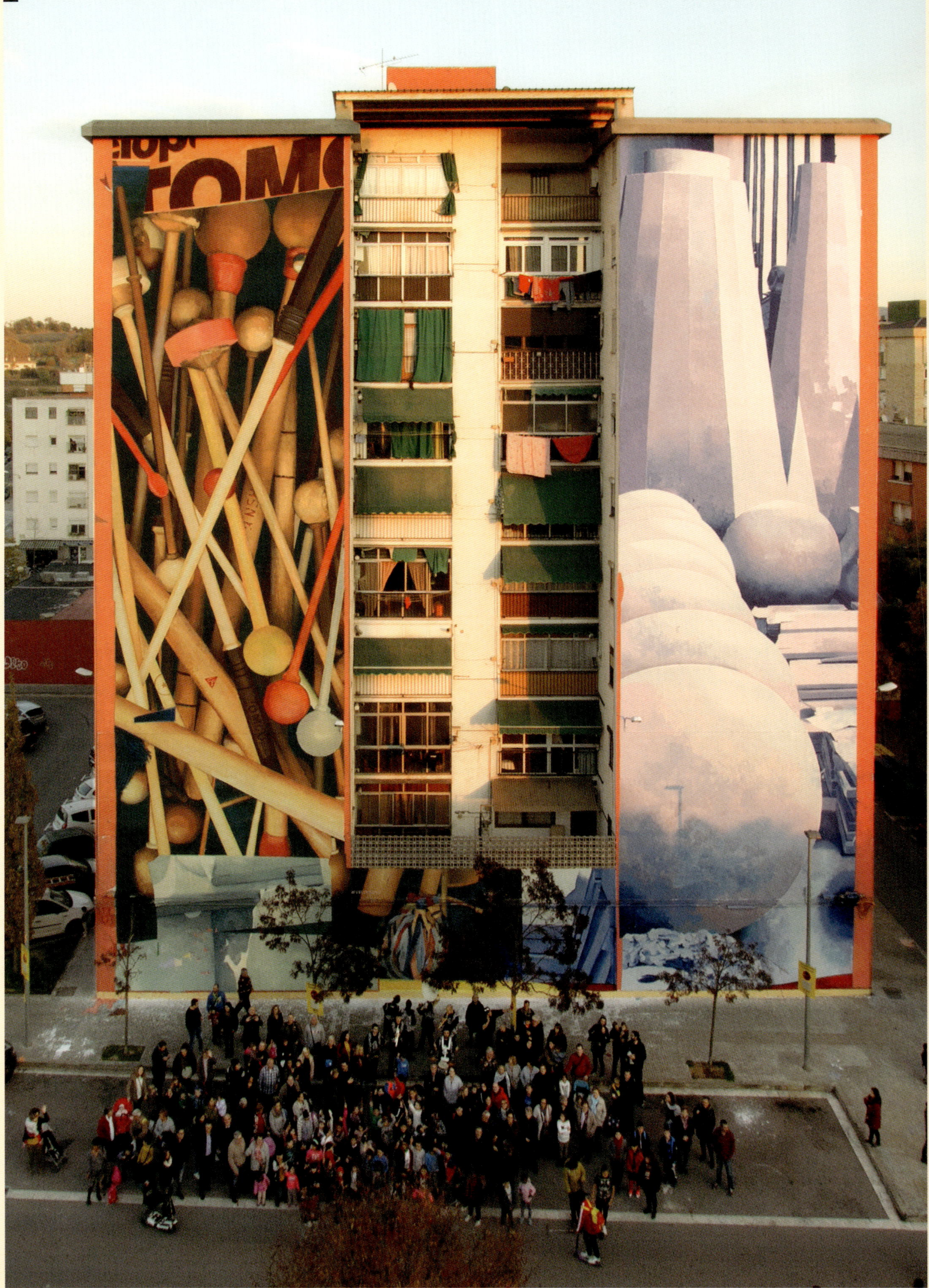

ZOER & VELVET

/ Grasse & Bordeaux

During all the years we've been working together, we have always been looking for new concepts, new forms, very curious to see what could be next.

Your body of work spans multiple visual media, from painting to installations, from murals to design. What was your educational background and how did you guys meet?
We met at school, while studying industrial design in Paris. We sat next to each other the first day of school, during the introduction speech for the courses. We quickly discovered that we had a lot in common, not least a shared attraction to objects, and to graffiti as well. Matthieu was already very much into graffiti, very passionate and at a very high level of mastery, which impressed me a lot.
During all the years we've been working together, we have always been looking for new concepts, new forms, very curious to see what could be next. We've been working together as product designers and graffiti artists, and then as mural artists and painters. We have always tried to bring inspiration and interactions from these universes to feed into the others.

Nostalgic images of objects, vehicles and houses are often featured in your paintings. Can you explain why these objects are an ongoing source of inspiration?
I think both of us have a natural attraction to human creations, architecture and industrial objects. However, aside from the formal or technical aspect of these things, I think it is mainly the human behaviour behind the objects that we like to observe or describe. Objects and architecture are nothing more than the expression of how the humans contemplate how to live, circulate and to interact, exchange, in some defined times.
I have a kind of nostalgic feeling, yes; that's why I am often trying to find explanations, ways of understanding or comfort zones along with the ancient productions. I also see it as an expression of both fear

1 /
Zoer & Velvet
Granollers, Spain, 2017
PHOTO BY THE ARTIST

2

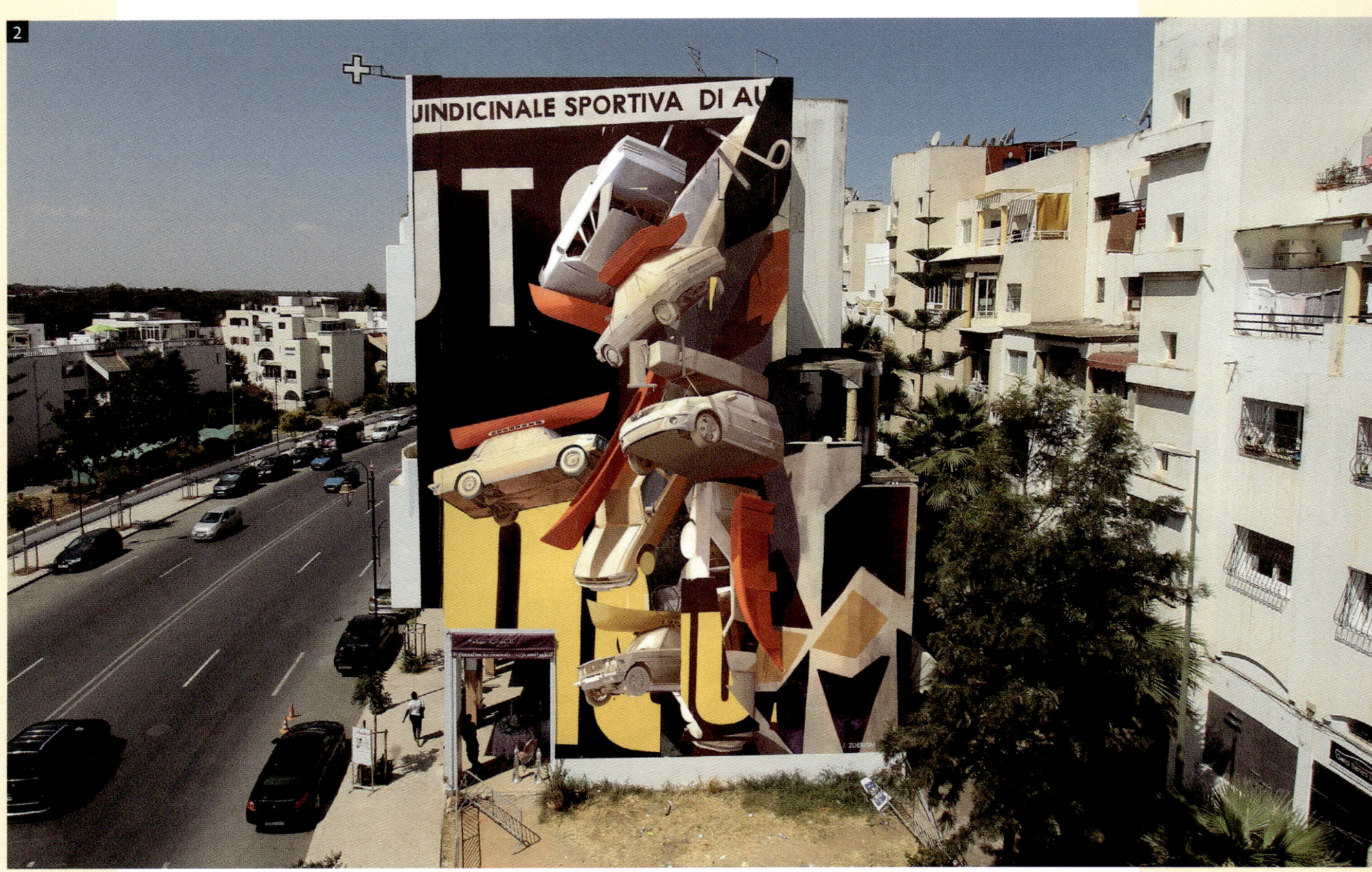

and intense attraction to the passage of time.

The colours, light and shading of your work are reminiscent of French impressionism. Is this a conscious decision?
My approach to colour was first strongly influenced by the vintage aspect of the things and objects, so my trend was naturally to go into breaking-colour schemes. Colours that cause you to question whether the painting is old or recent, used or deliberately patinated. But then I realized that if you don't have a strong knowledge of colour theory and how colours interact, this approach could lead to a 'world of grey': bland sepia tones that have little to no impact, that do not elicit any feeling of reality, or at the very least are struggling to approximate to.
I was often very fascinated by impressionism, but at times I felt that I did not yet understand the colours enough to experiment with direct connections between complementary colours or shades that work really well next to each other.
Then Matthieu started to progress rapidly in his approach to colour, slowly relinquishing the full and detailed aspect of the shapes to go deeper into colour theory and how to describe the aspect of the materials, surfaces and grounds. I realised how interesting this exercise was,

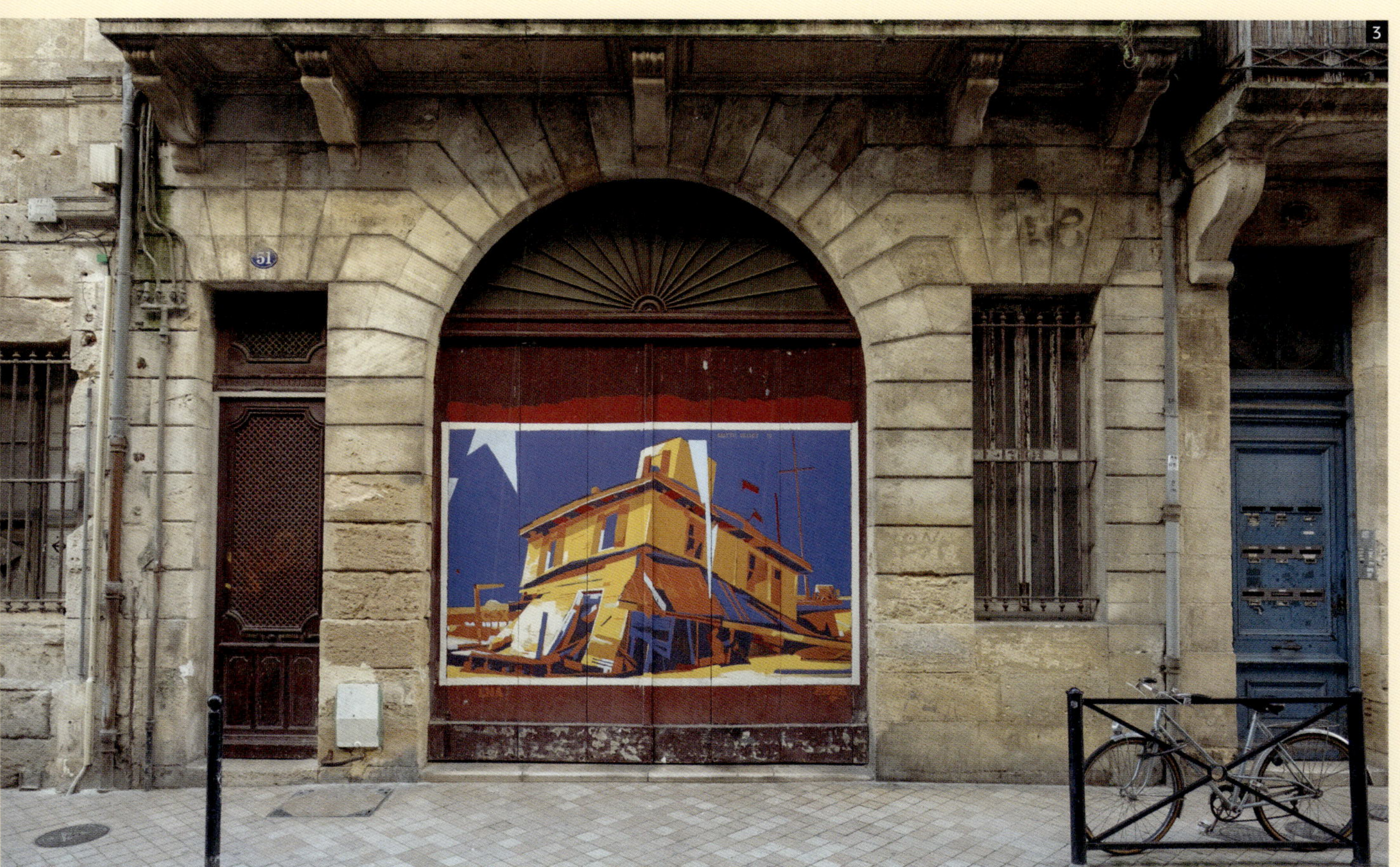

2 /
Zoer
Rabat, Morocco, 2018
PHOTO BY THE ARTIST

3 /
Velvet
Bordeaux, France, 2019
PHOTO BY THE ARTIST

» /
Velvet
Bordeaux, France, 2019
PHOTO BY THE ARTIST

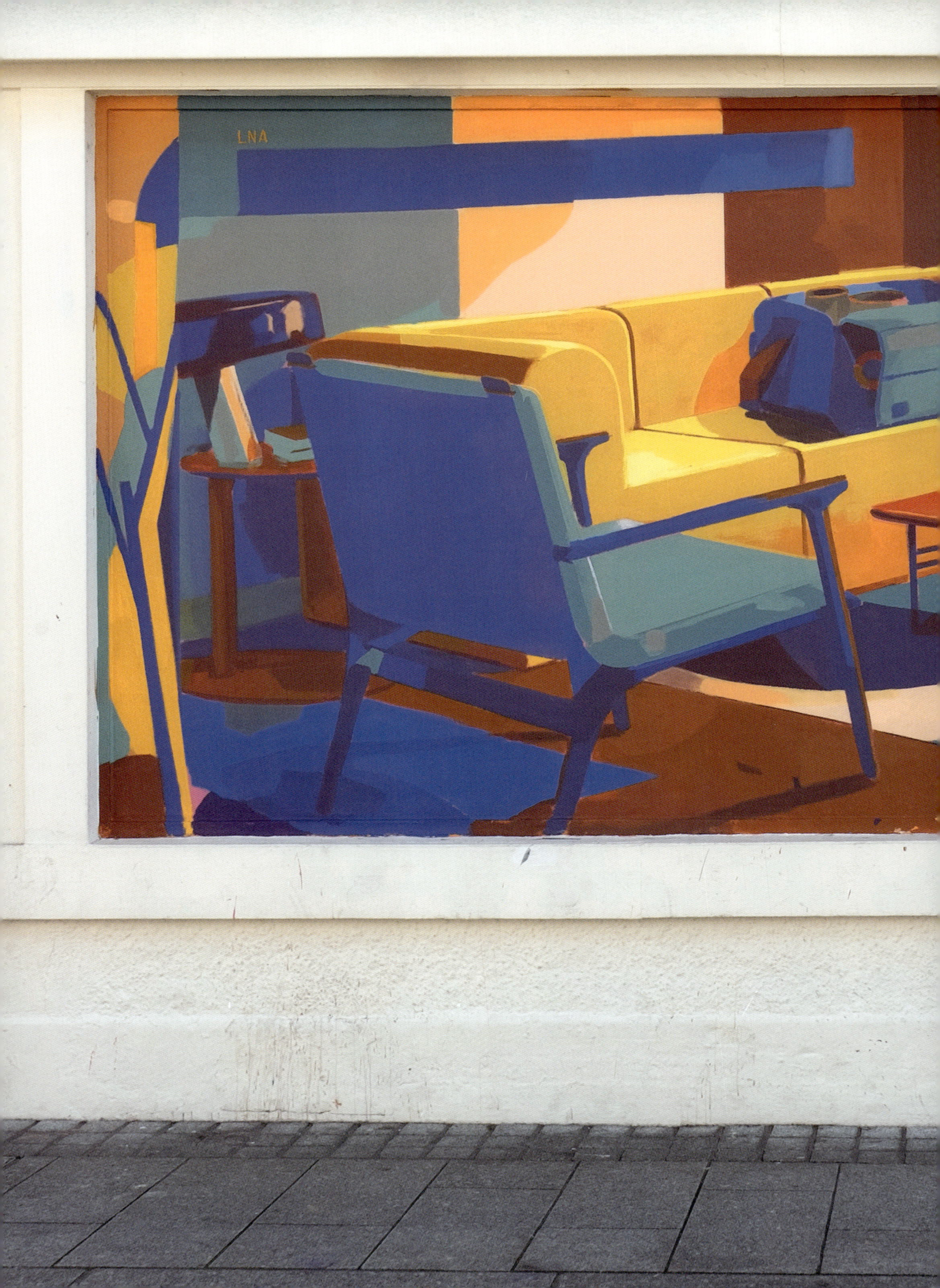
LNA

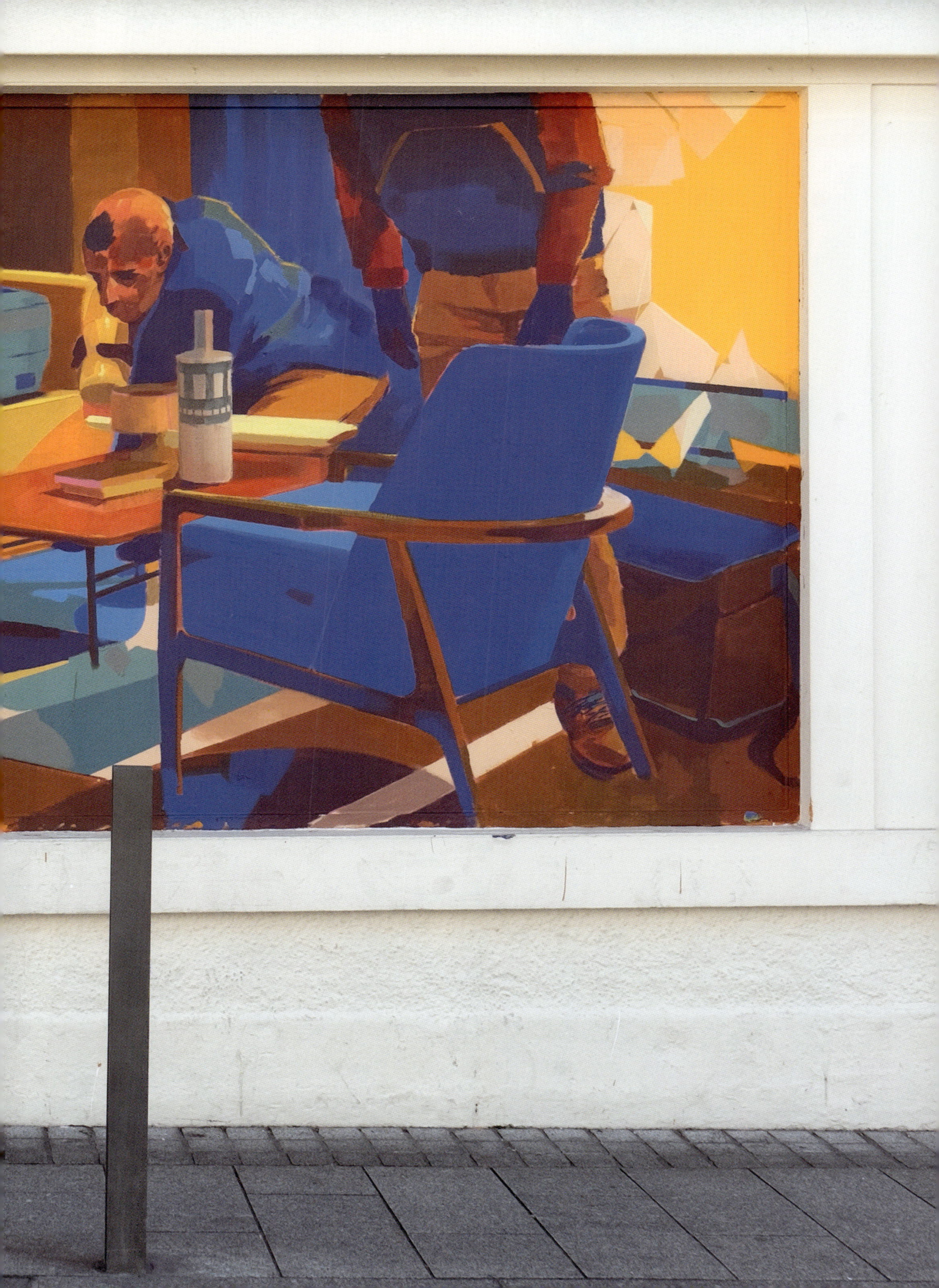

5

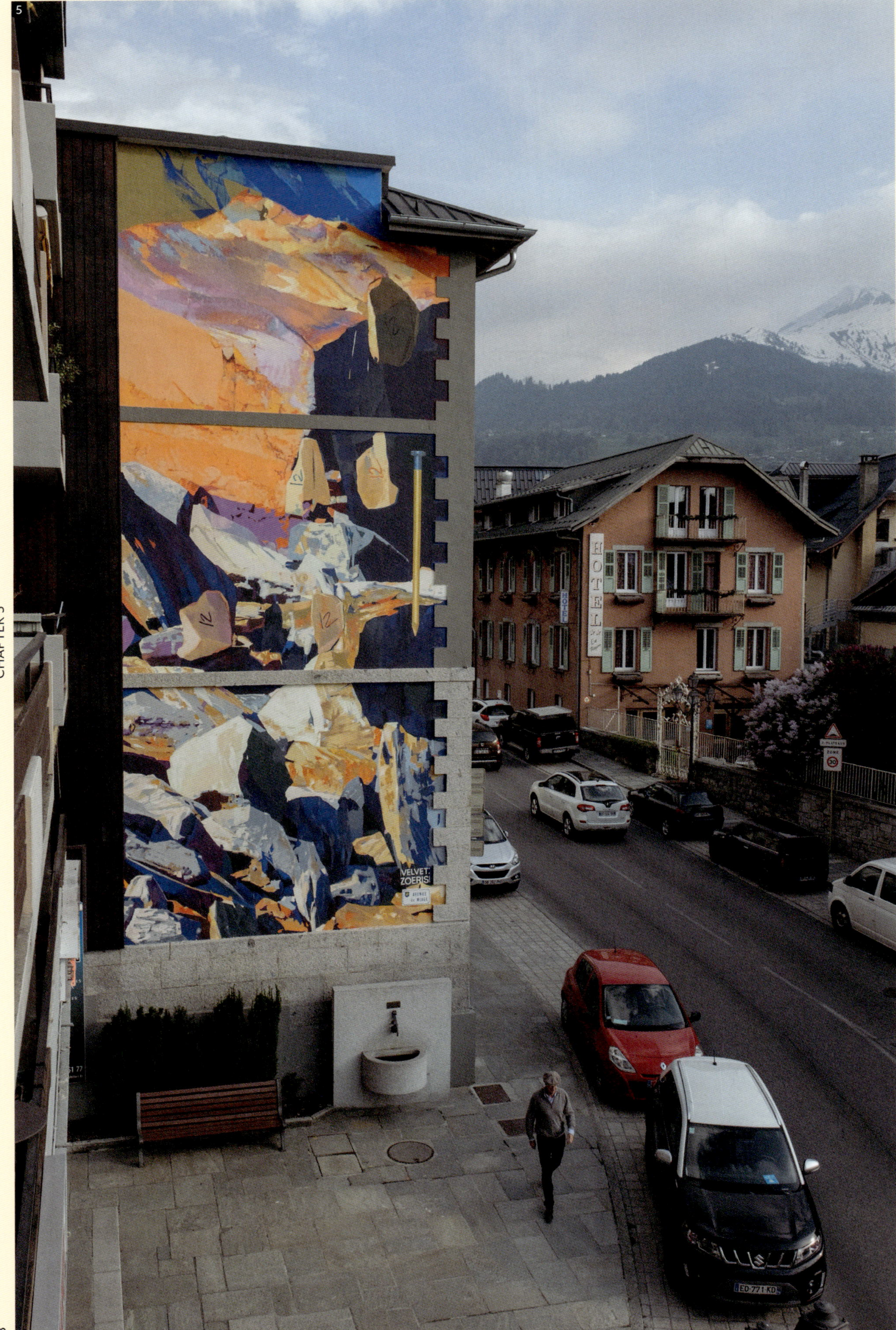

CHAPTER 3

and we started to work with sophisticated shades of colour on murals. I should note that I had decided to completely give up spray cans around this time, to focus on acrylic and oil painting, so I started to learn how to paint once I discovered techniques using a brush and real paint. This rebirth was in 2013, after a trip to Mexico where I had the chance to encounter the vernacular mural culture. I tend to wonder about how far I can take abstraction within a figurative approach.

With works popping up all around the globe, it seems you have an insatiable travelling spirit. What travelling experiences have strongly influenced your work?
Mexico, mainly; Mali when I was younger, and later Japan... All these experiences have been really different and constructive. But for sure, when you have the chance to be welcomed in a country that has a very strong connection with painting and art, or at least a very different vision from the basic Western market perspective, then it really makes things magical. It depends; some places have been very appealing due to their urbanism and architecture, some because of their freedom. Others were really instructive in how cold and unfeeling a creative context can be, focused solely on production with no room for emotions; conversely, some cultures are totally devoted to and open-minded about art.

Each practice is feeding into the other. The point is to be able to produce pieces that make sense.

Both of you seem to straddle the worlds of street art and contemporary art. Is there a context you prefer? How do you divide your production between fine art and street art?
Right now, I don't feel that there is much difference between what I am doing. I mean, each practice is feed-

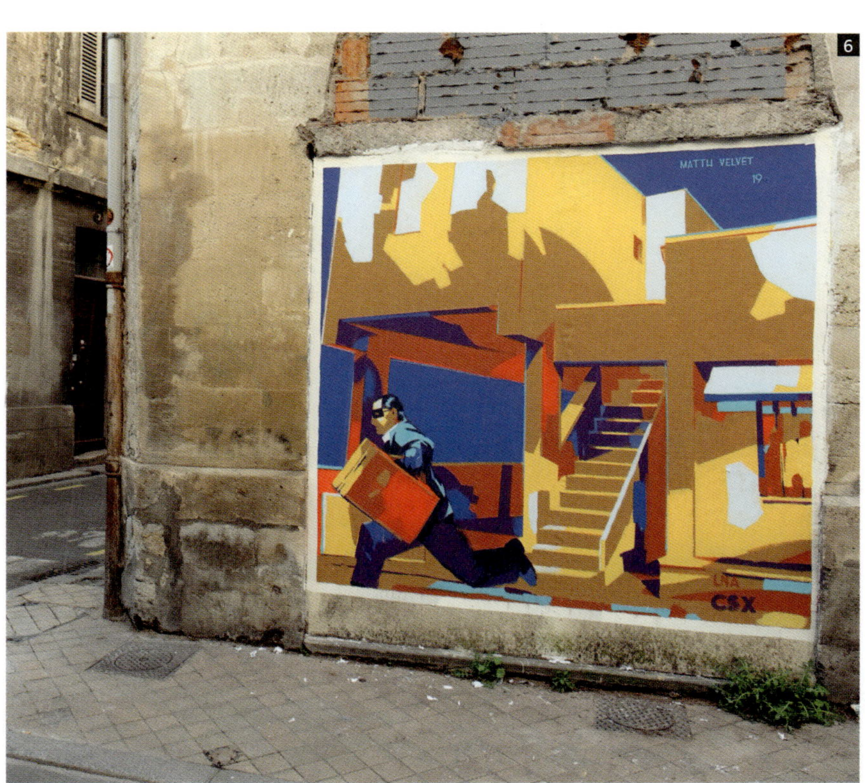

5 /
Zoer & Velvet
Rhône-Alpes, France, 2018
PHOTO BY THE ARTIST

6 /
Velvet
Bordeaux, France, 2019
PHOTO BY THE ARTIST

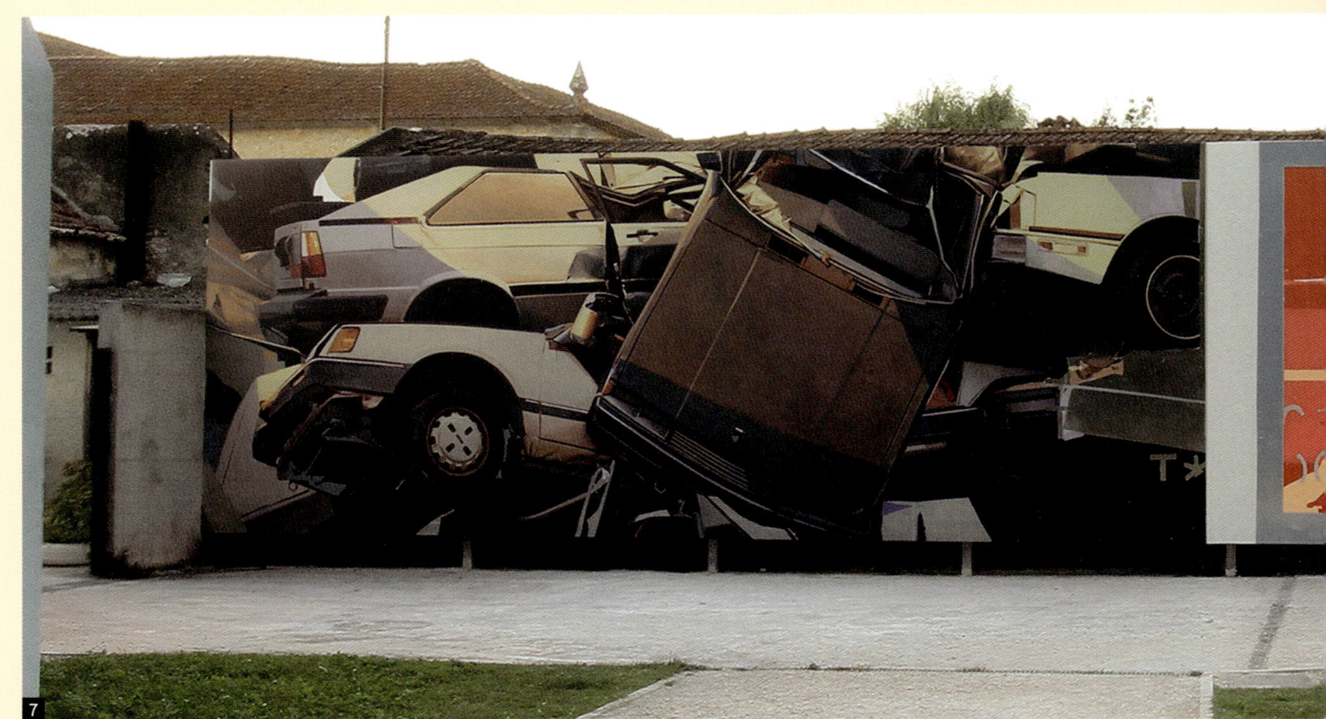
7

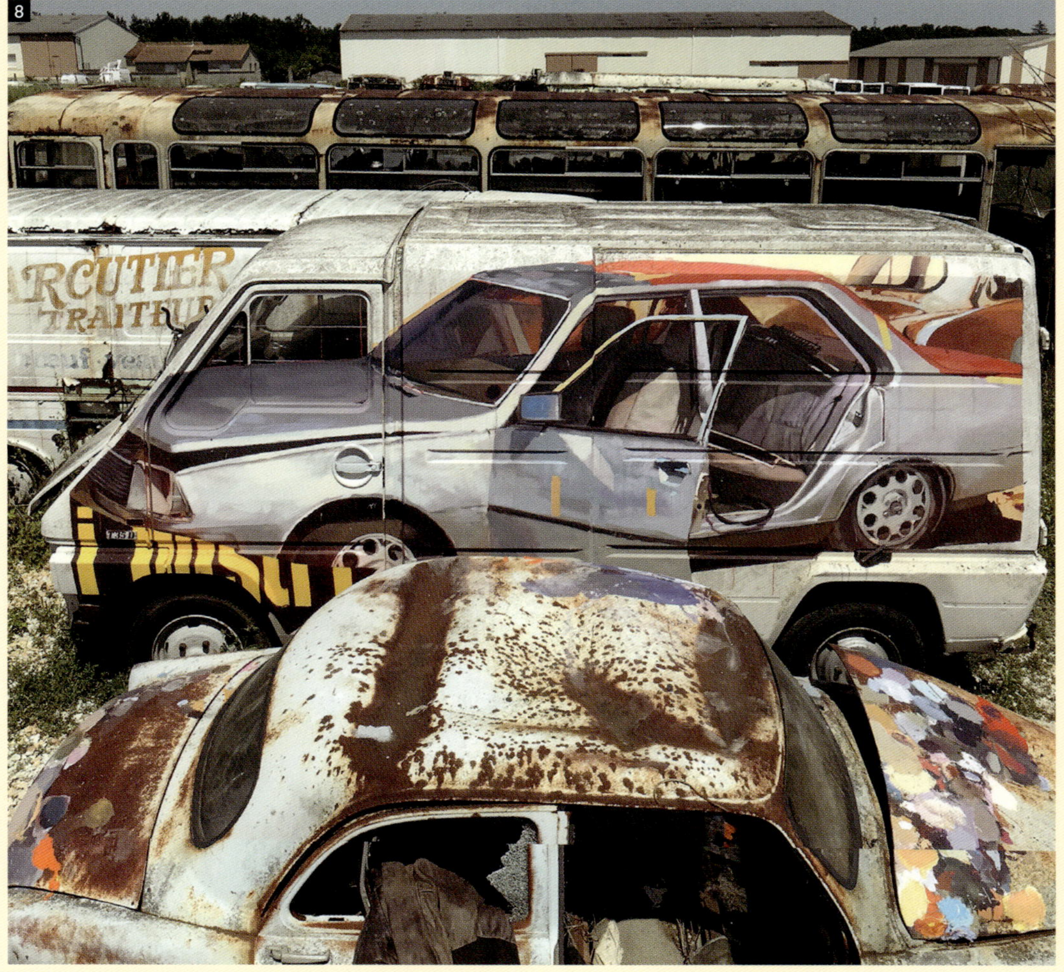
8

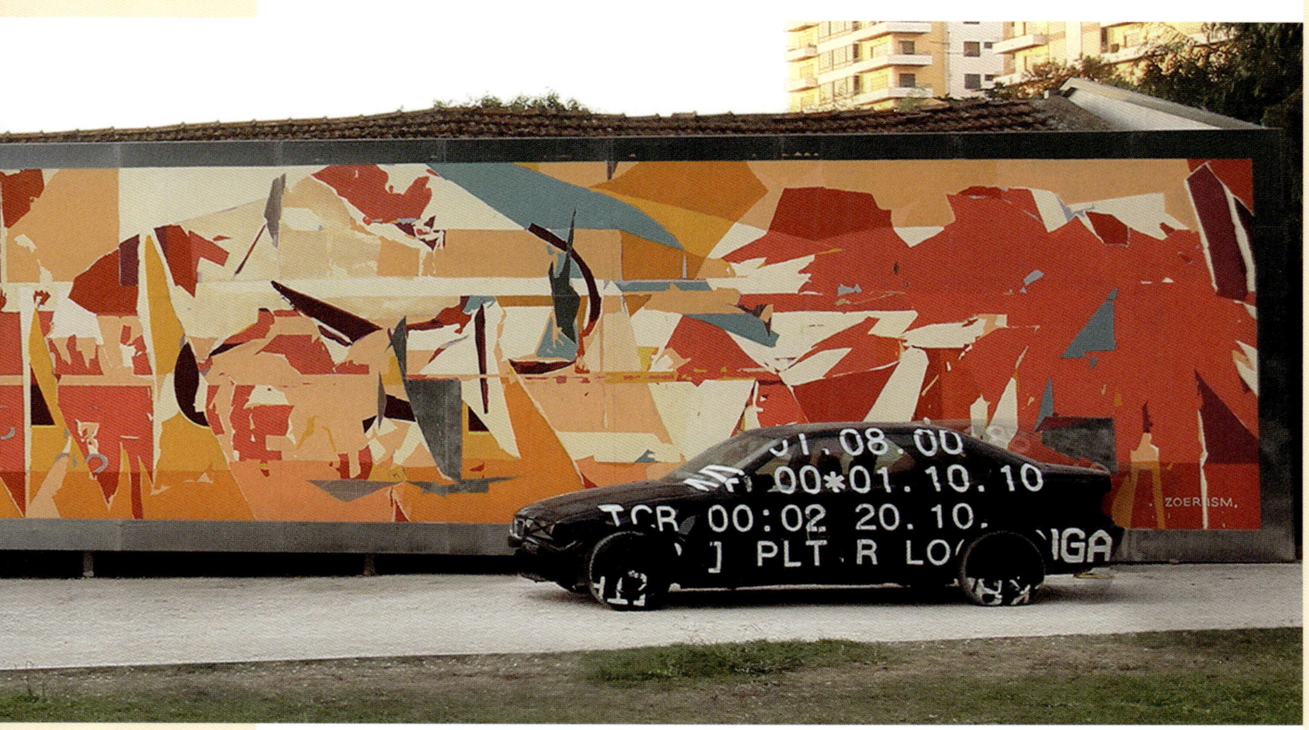

Street art has become an industry, an easy way for cities to obtain approval from young people.

ing into the other. The point is to be able to produce pieces that make sense, either on small, 'transportable' pieces or on very big urban plans or plain murals that definitely have a major impact on their surroundings. In the end, it is all about significance, about how to develop an issue or purpose that is expressed in specific ways depending on what I would call the host surface.

This publication focuses on art in public space over the past three years. What major changes or important projects have you observed recently?
Mainly the fact that this street art thing has become an industry, an easy way for cities to obtain approval from young people. Now that anyone can decide to become a 'street artist' at any time, just by watching YouTube tutorials and doing a couple of workshops or courses, adding it to their professional skills on LinkedIn, big cities are becoming a bit too crowded, saturated by this 'official' street art that doesn't really promote more significance, let alone sensitivity. But I've had a couple of discussions with friends from the same field; we always end up concluding that we have to renew the practice.

What does the future hold for Zoer & Velvet? What projects are you looking forward to?
Right now we are each working on our own personal path, our own course of development. I am about to release an in-situ project about the concept of the wreck and the disappearance of the material object. The scale of the project is really interesting to me, as I am trying to think about the intersecting consequences and social impacts of individual actions and consumption. The colour relationships will be the main axis of this project.

7 / 8
Zoer
Leiria, Portugal, 2018
PHOTO BY THE ARTIST

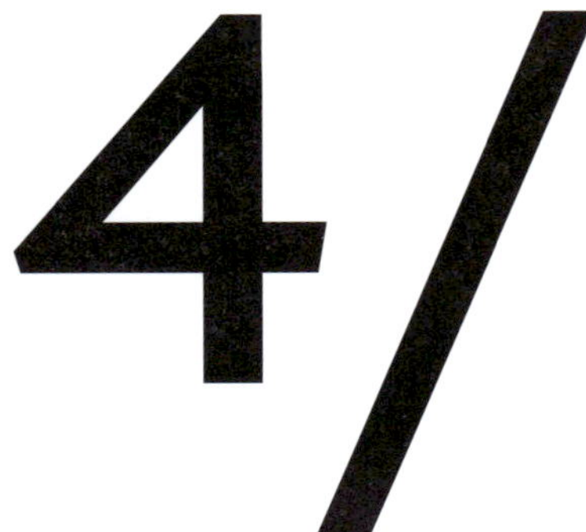

URBAN INTER-VENTION

AMPPARITO
BANKSY
CRYSTAL WAGNER
ERNEST ZACHAREVIC
ICY & SOT
ISAAC CORDAL
JAUNE
JR
LEON KEER
PEJAC
SHEPARD FAIREY
SPY
STROOK
SWOON
WASTED RITA

THROUGH A MIX of different materials, a close scrutiny of architectural and community surroundings, and a strong sense of humour that often includes a cynical twist, the artists gathered in this particular chapter are potentially the most globally visible and also the most politically challenging. With a strong semblance in their scrutiny of contemporary society - be it elements of individualism, capitalist mentality or questioning of immigration policies and freedom of speech - these artists firmly control their voices, often seeking to contribute to a greater good.

Banksy, JR, Swoon, Shepard Fairey – clearly the best-known urban artists – have an international following of thousands, their studios running with teams of assistants, their projects commissioned by national institutions and huge commercial companies, and their works selling for substantial amounts even by contemporary art standards. These superstars of the street art scene were able to set standards in the spectacular, with projects taking over entire buildings, entire blocks, crossing borders and sprayed all over the internet. Thankfully their reach has allowed for a certain empowerment in the voice of the artist. And as creative minds see the potential impact of their work, many have taken to adapting their role to one of social responsibility and activism.

The year 2016 saw Iranian brothers Icy & Sot release 'Let Her Be Free', not only a collection of their works but a commentary on the imbalance in freedom of speech rights which is present globally. In 2017 Ernest Zacharevic collectively launched the 'Splash and Burn' project, an awareness campaign proclaiming the damage caused by unregulated farming practices in Indonesia's palm-oil industry. And the list goes on, with Banksy creating work during the London global warming protests, Shepard Fairey commenting on the American racial divide, and Swoon continuing her community-based practice. As artists in this field explore different languages of materiality, they seek also different tactics of communication, reaching out to a wider audience – often, thankfully, with messages of positive social engagement.

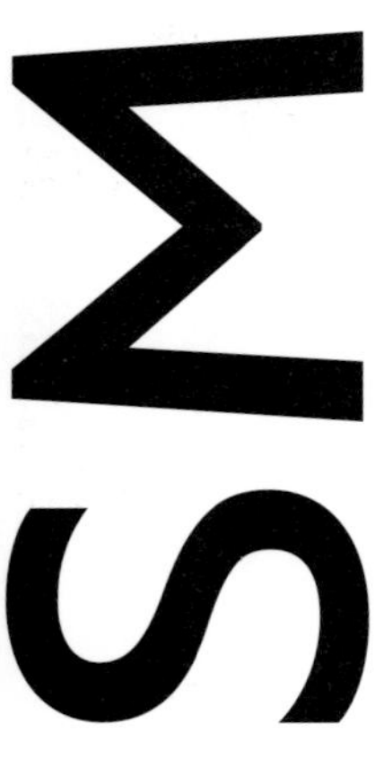

AMPPARITO

/ London

Hailing from Madrid and currently calling London home, young artist Ampparito uses urban intervention, sculpture and mural work to spread his cheeky voice across the globe. Installing impossible hopscotch, trick soccer goals and infinity roundabouts, based on simple lines and unassuming colours, he winks at you, turning public space into a temporary playground.

In 2017 his project 'Asalto' in Saragosse, Spain, used subtly varied shades of blue to create the illusion of disappearing walls. With this simple intervention, he raises the question of points of view, inviting the public to observe the wall from different angles in order to match the sky. The project reflects on differences in public opinion. Reacting to the neighbourhood complaints about the wall's graffiti, he asks the community to re-evaluate their perspective, and therefore their attitude to creativity in the public arena.

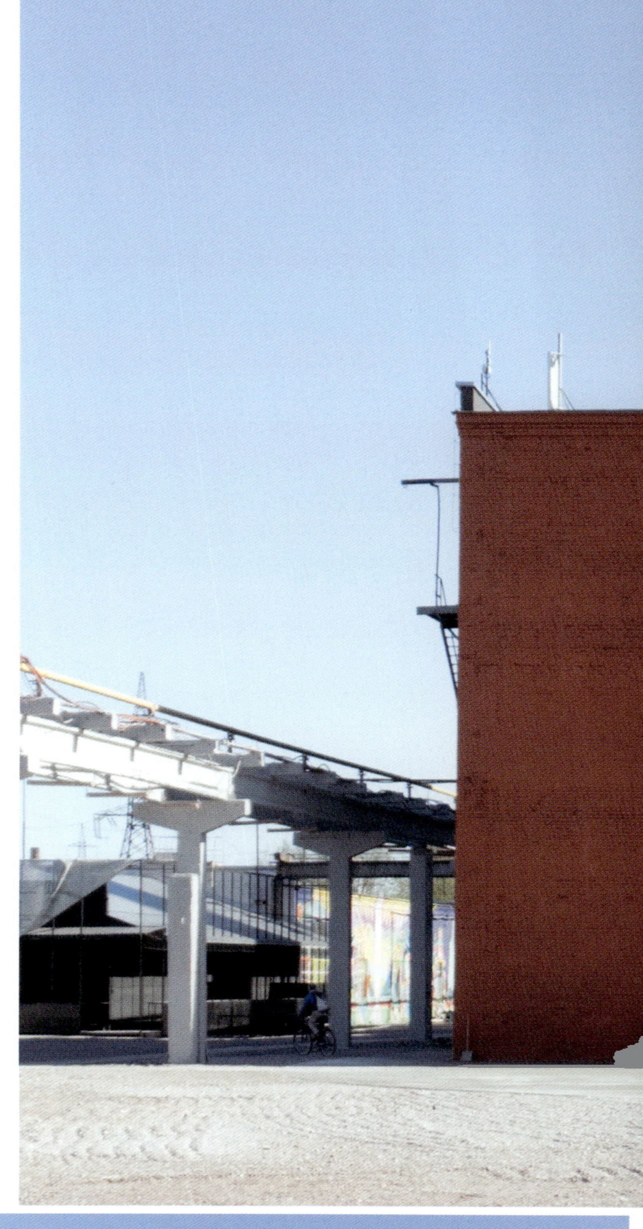

Ampparito winks at you, turning public space into a temporary playground.

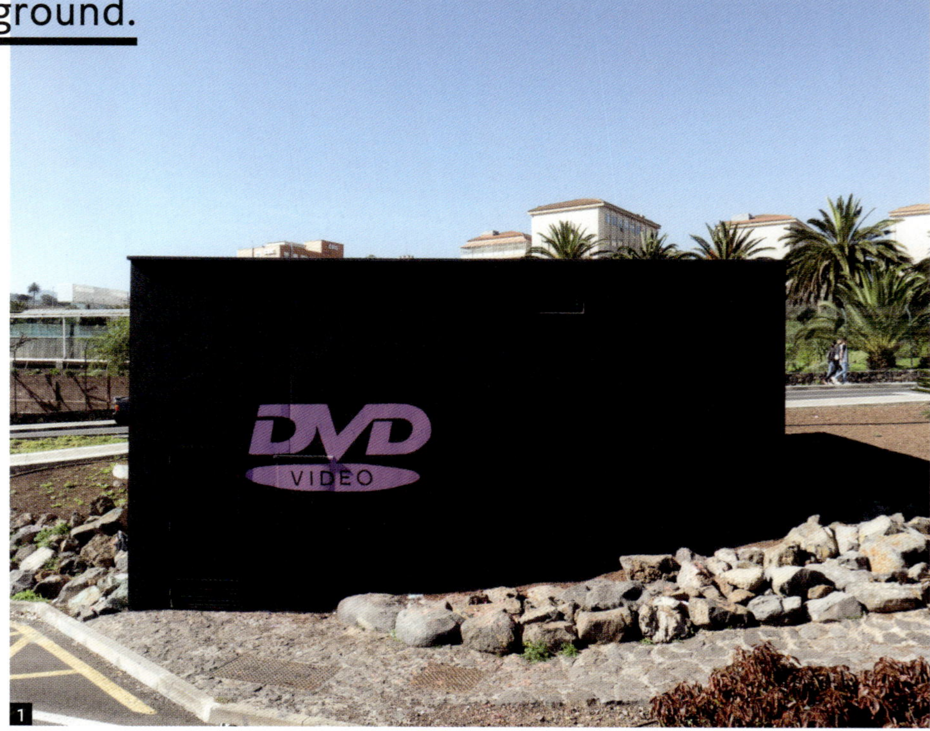

1

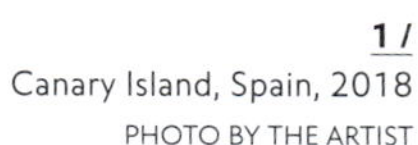

1 /
Canary Island, Spain, 2018
PHOTO BY THE ARTIST

2 /
St Petersburg, Russia, 2018
PHOTO BY THE ARTIST

3 /
Milan, Italy, 2018
PHOTO BY THE ARTIST

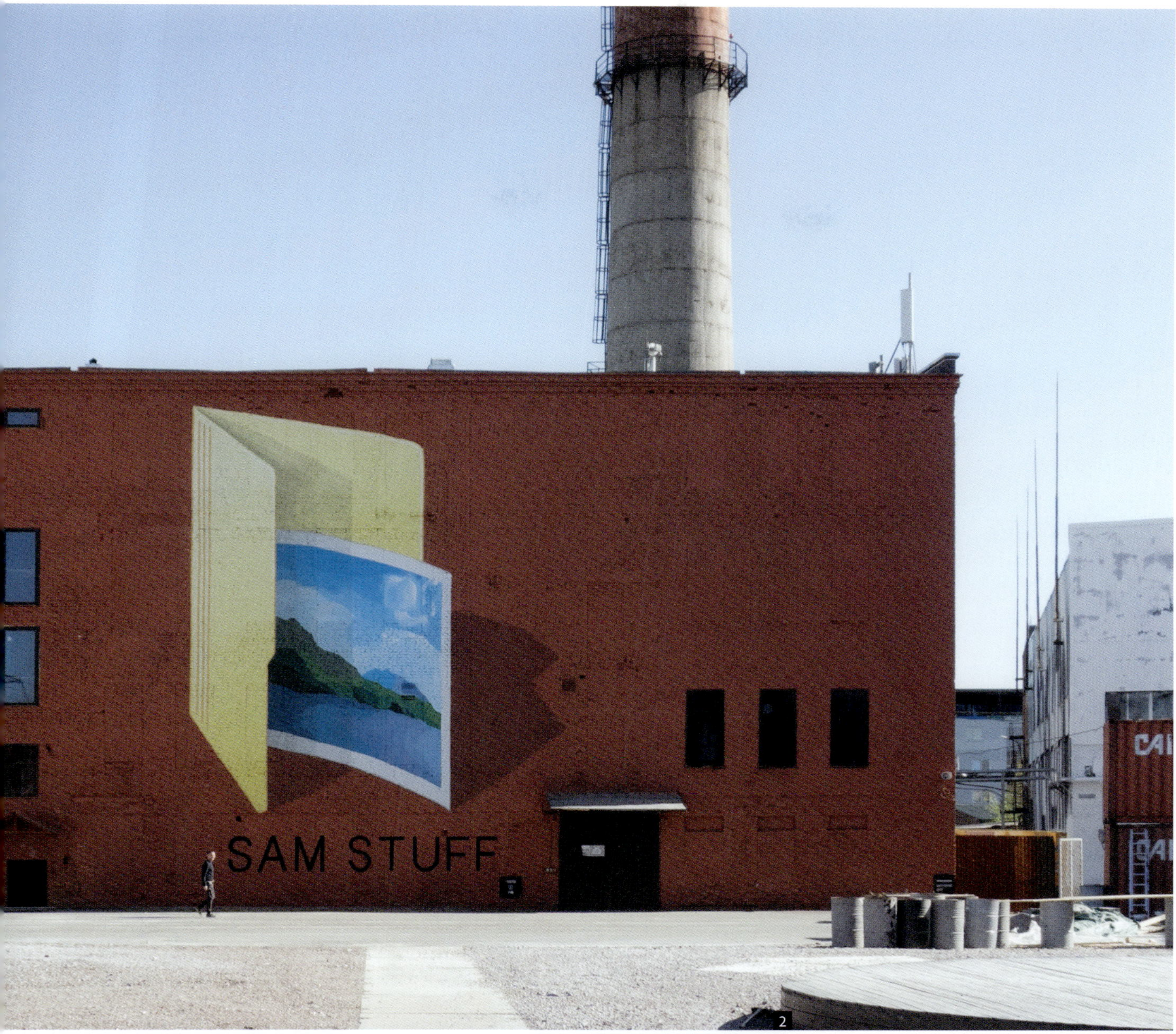

2

3

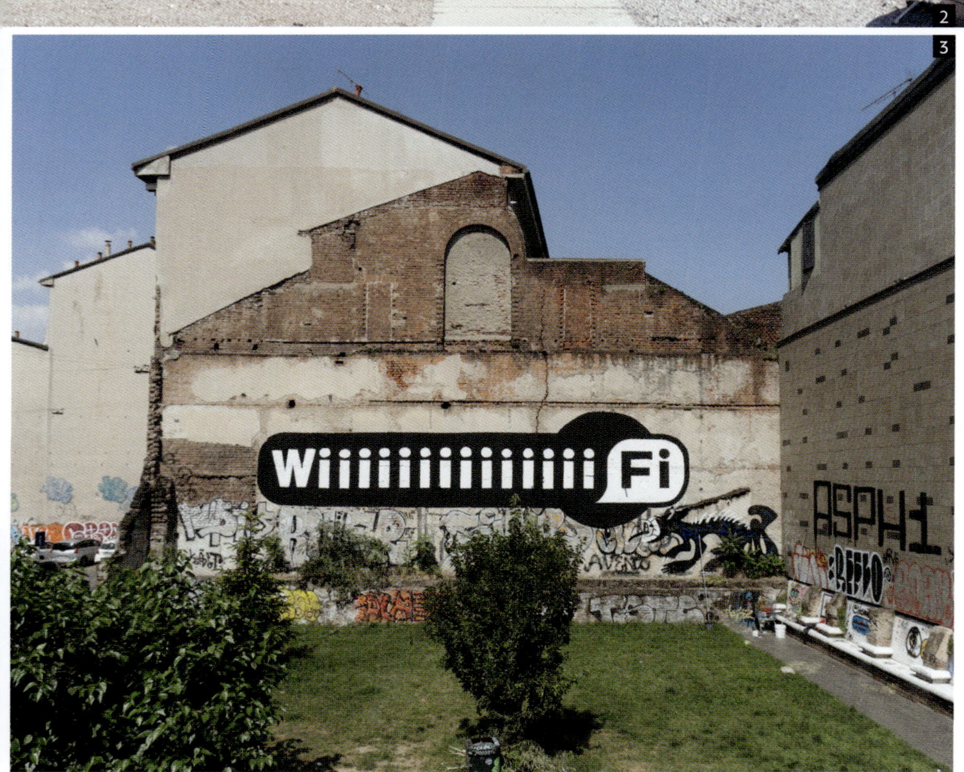

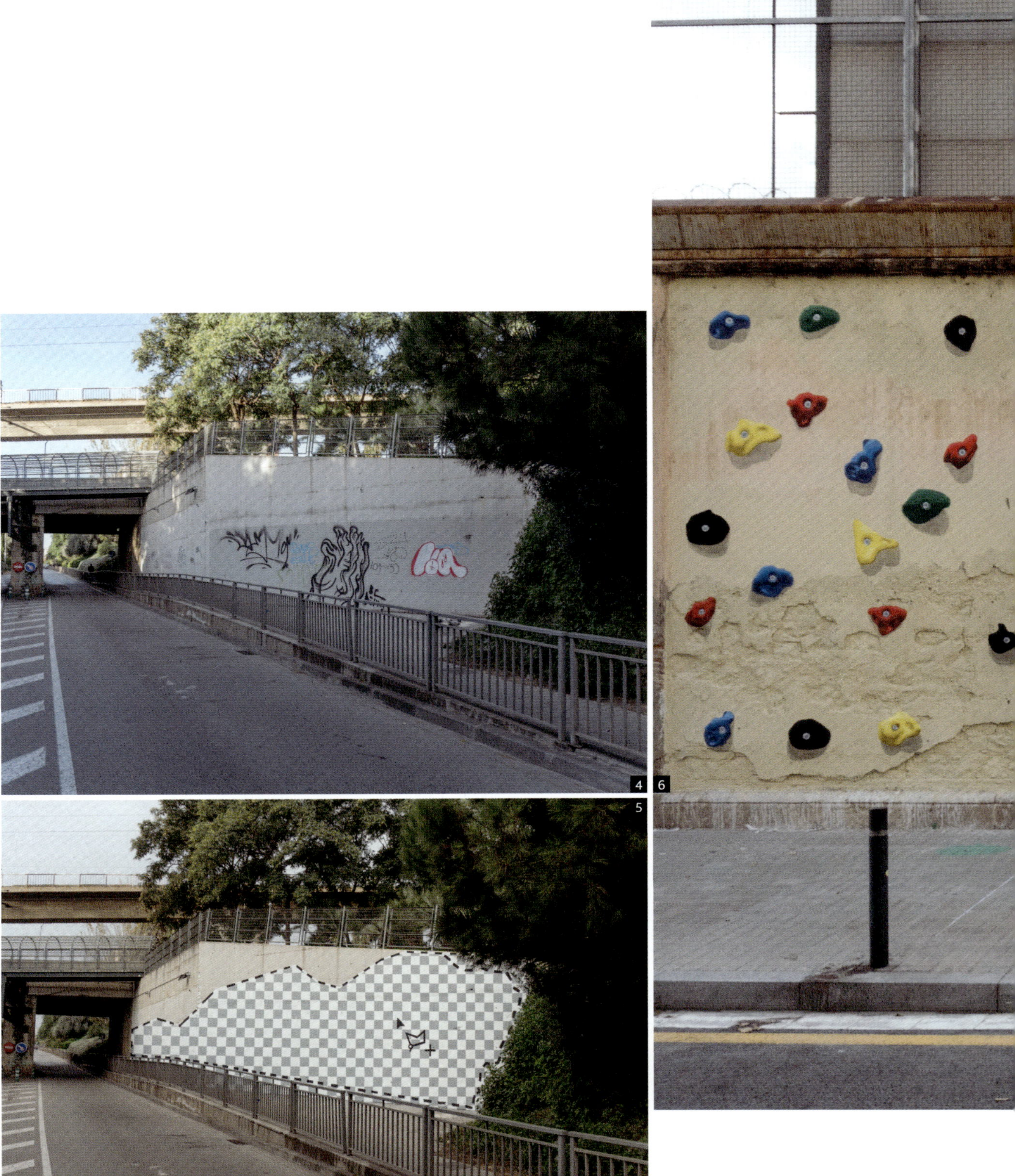

4 / 5
Hospitalet, Spain, 2018
PHOTO BY THE ARTIST

6 /
Barcelona, Spain, 2018
PHOTO BY THE ARTIST

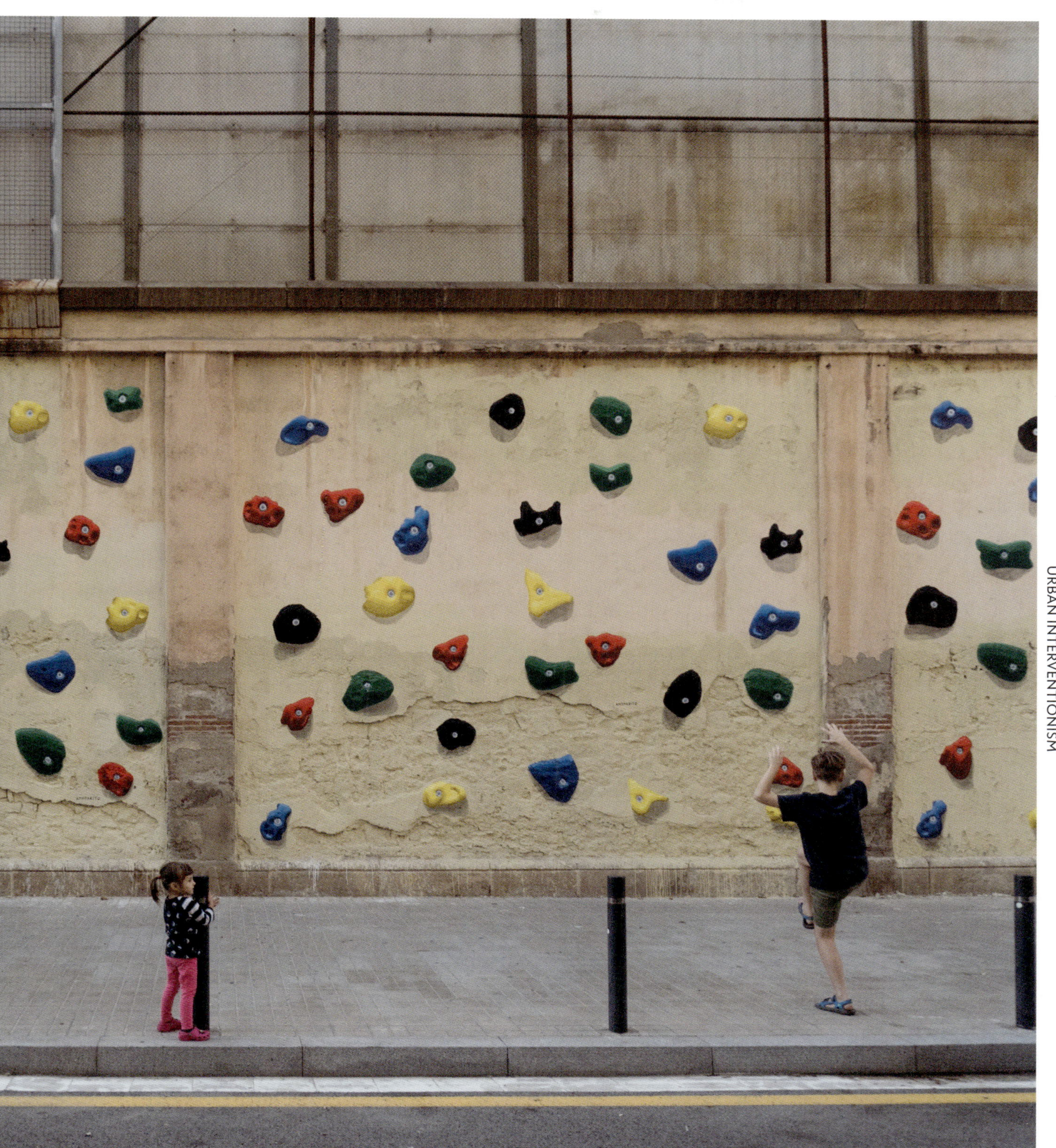

BANKSY

/ London

It's impossible to write a book on public art without featuring Banksy. The myth, the legend, the joke: whatever it is you believe about the artist(s?) behind the works, he has managed grippingly, through the fame and followers, to keep us intrigued. Since the 'Dismaland' project in 2015, Banksy has notably funded the 'Walled Off' Hotel project in Bethlehem, marking the hundredth anniversary of British control in Palestine. He also hilariously pranked the art world with a self-destructing print on sale at Sotheby's, and was again involved in controversy when his recent piece in Wales, entitled 'Season's Greetings', sparked backlash due to its over-popularity. The owner of the property claimed he was losing sleep and struggling to deal with the pressure of responsibility: 'It is an arts treasure, and it's just too much for me'.

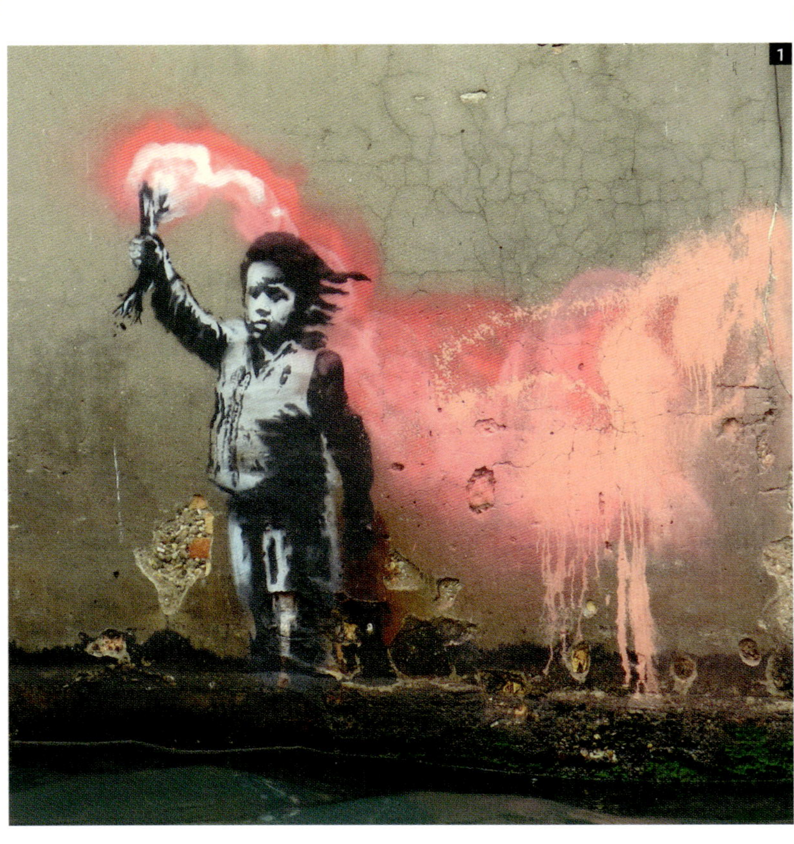

1

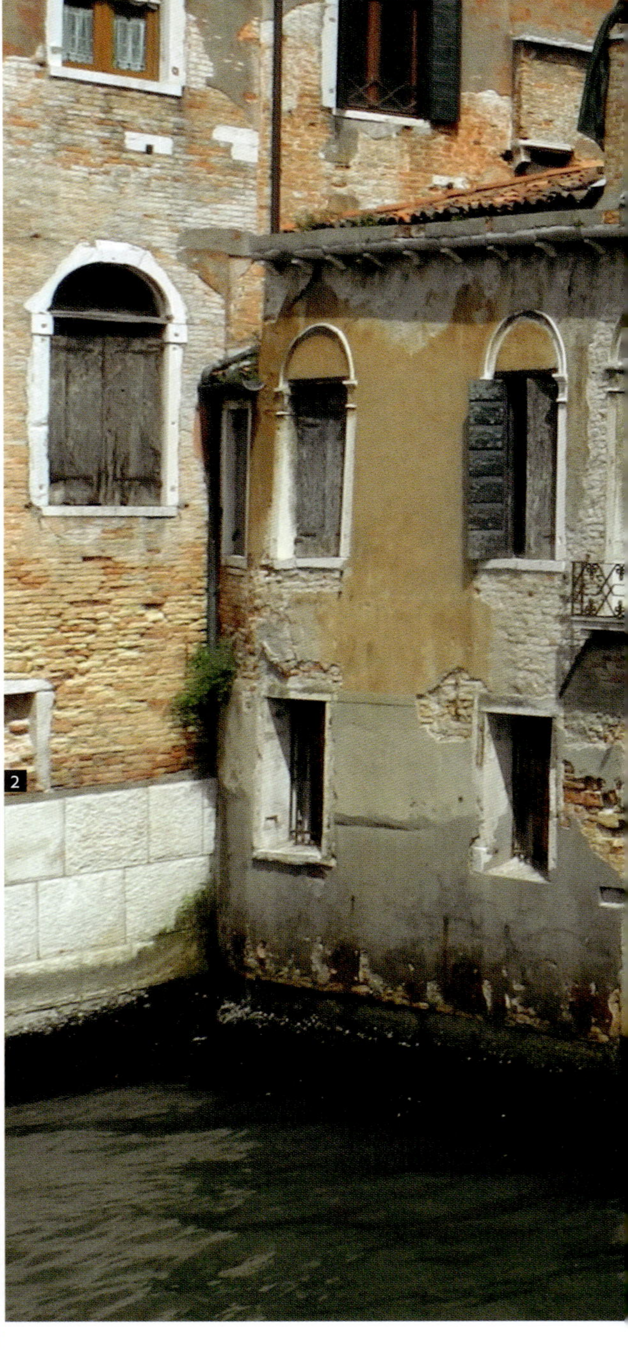

2

1 / 2
Venice, Italy, 2019
PHOTO BY BUTTERFLY ART NEWS

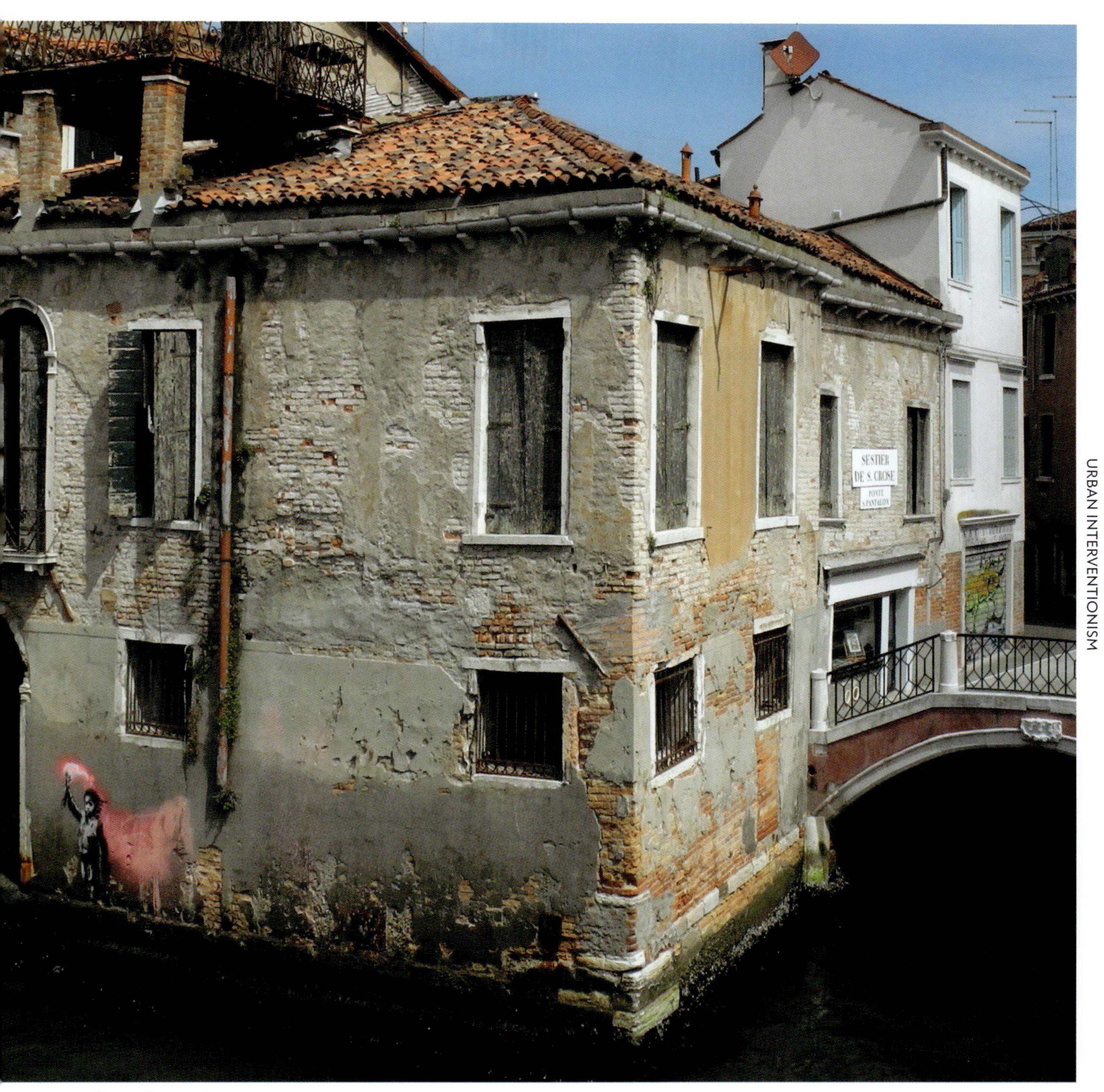

Banksy has managed grippingly, through the fame and followers, to keep us intrigued.

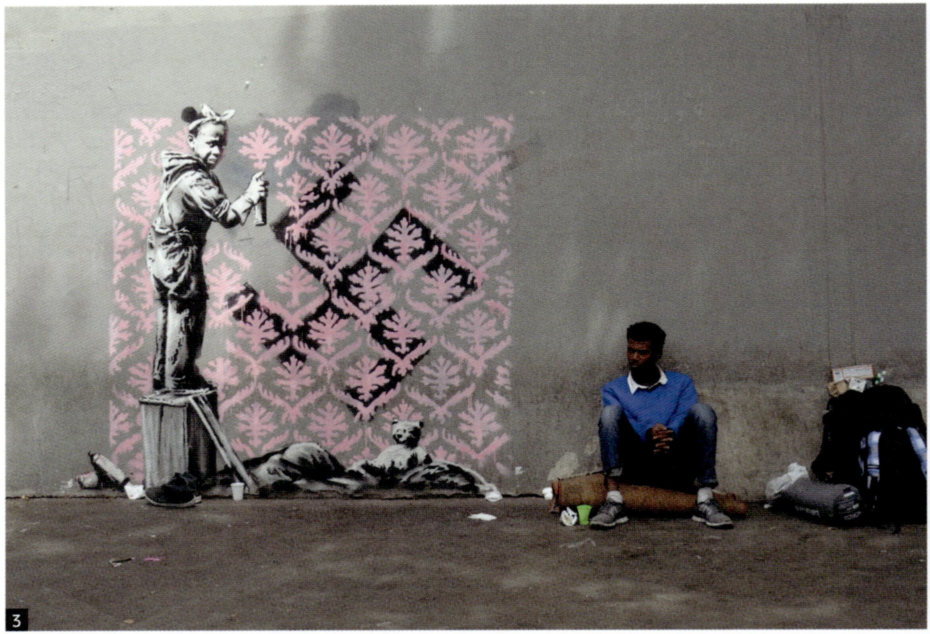
3

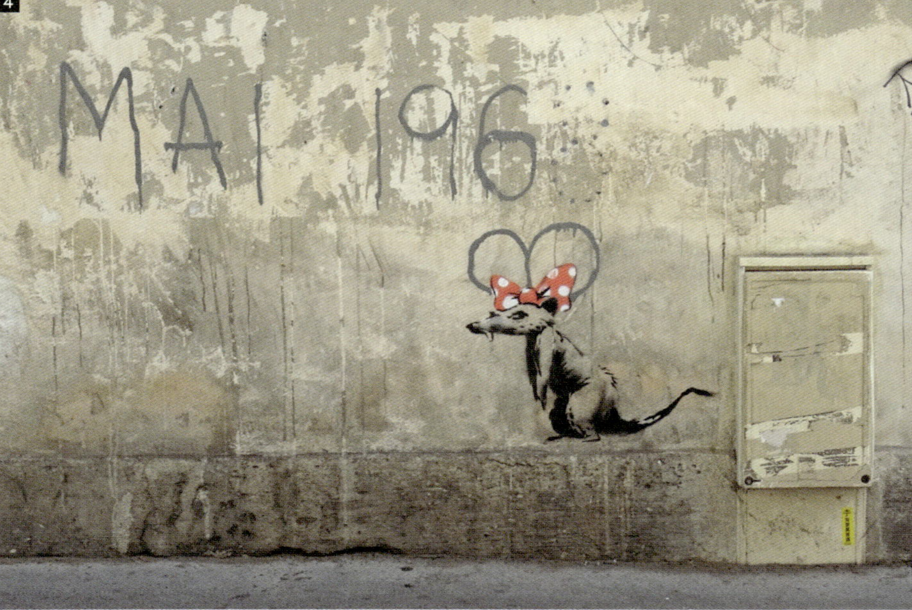

4

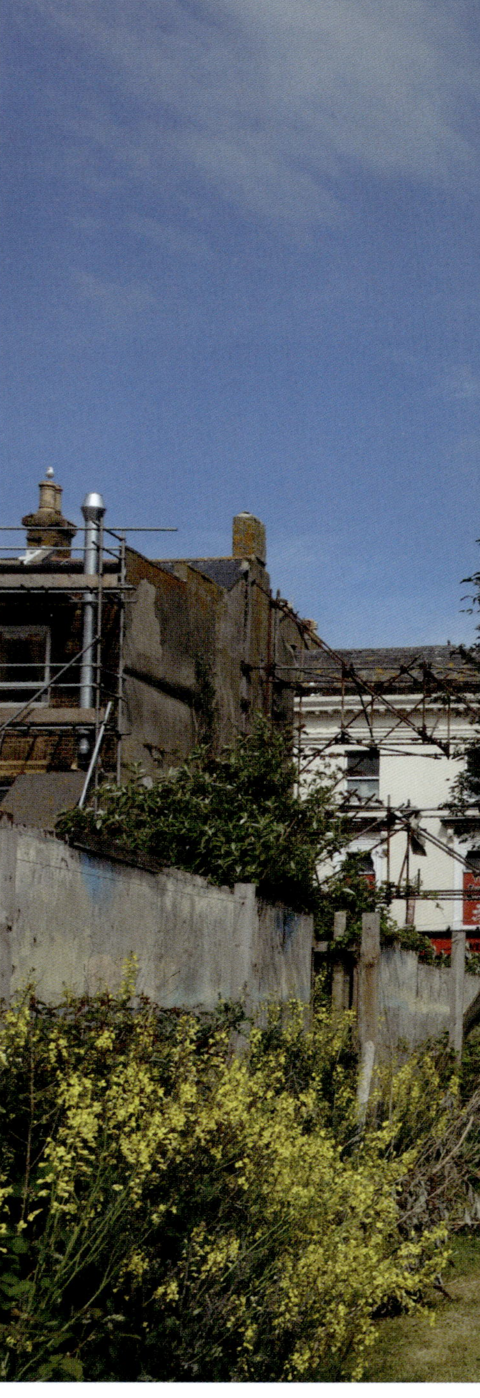

3 /
Paris, France, 2018
PHOTO BY BUTTERFLY ART NEWS

4 /
Paris, France, 2018
PHOTO BY BUTTERFLY ART NEWS

5 / 6
Dover, UK, 2017
PHOTO BY BUTTERFLY ART NEWS

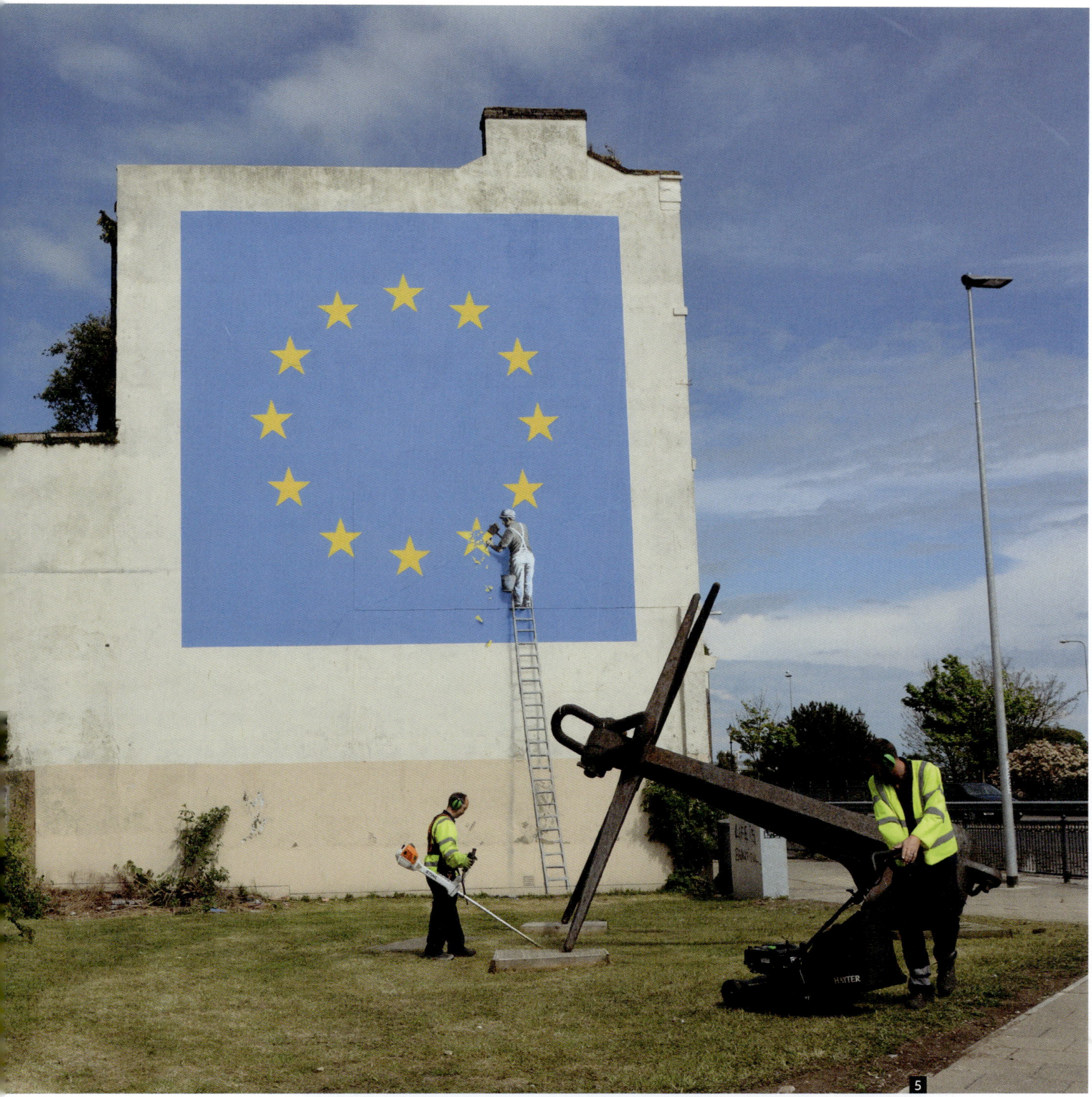

5

6

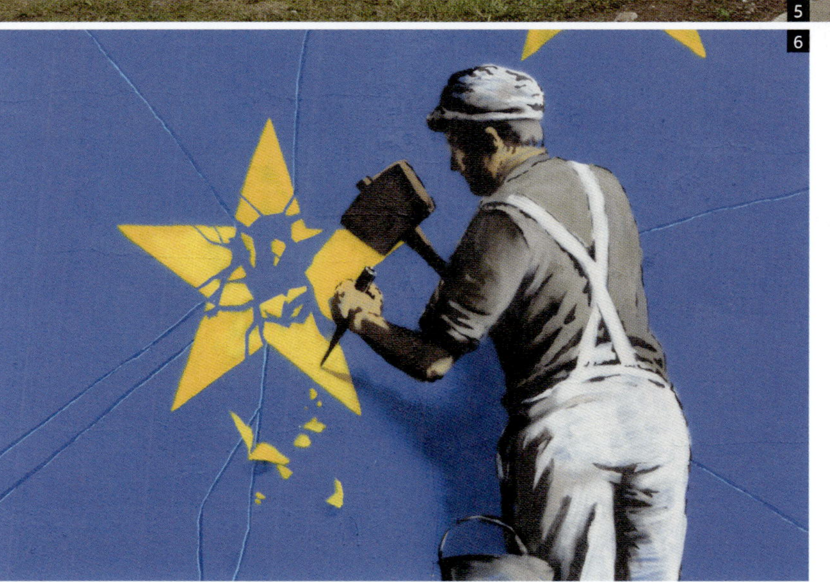

CRYSTAL WAGNER

/ Philadelphia

Highly acclaimed contemporary artist Crystal Wagner integrates a variety of media in her practice, though her works are united by an expressive bursting of colour. She is interested in the relationship between dimensions, the interaction of sculpture with architecture, with material and form, and forms that can be seen as simultaneously abstract and organic.

After abandoning her academic career to concentrate on her studio practice, she has exhibited her work worldwide, not only on meticulous gallery walls but also spilling over and through buildings. In 2019, the façade of the Chateau Belcastel in France will see her Ignis Fatuus installation transform the castle exterior into a hybrid of historic architecture and playful, abstract forms.

1

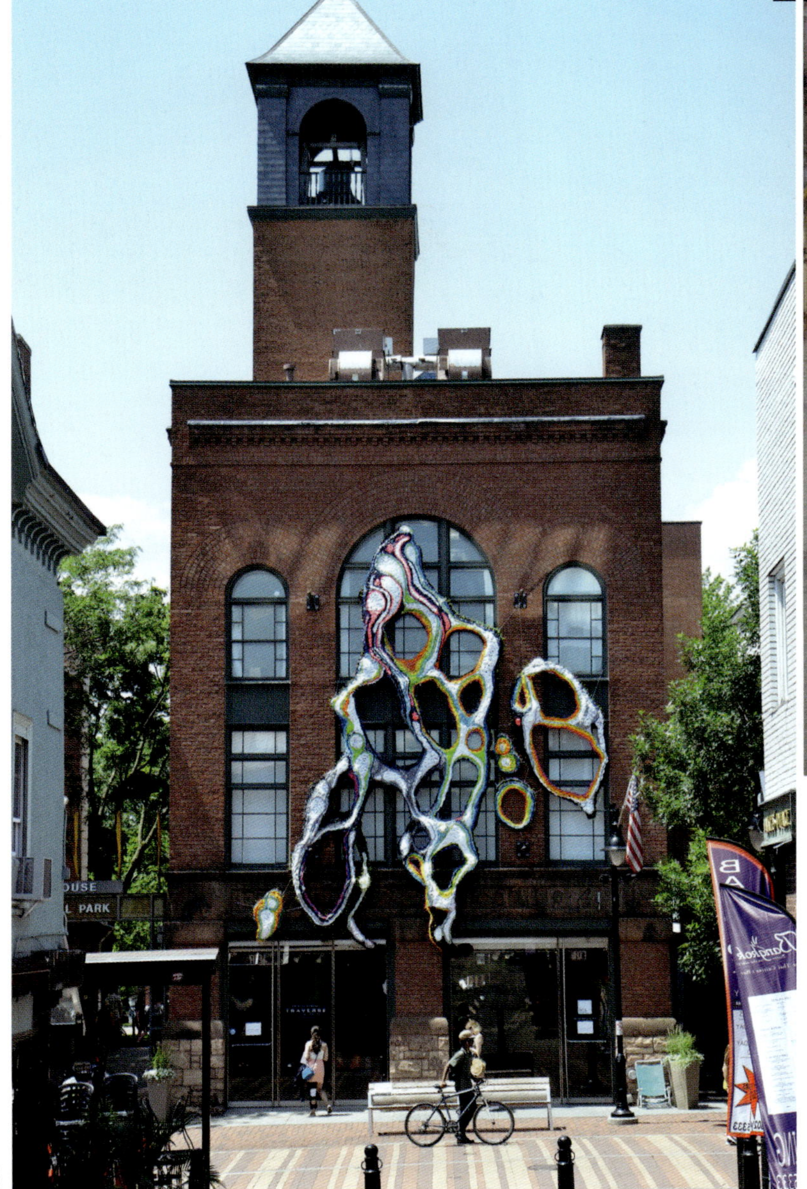

2

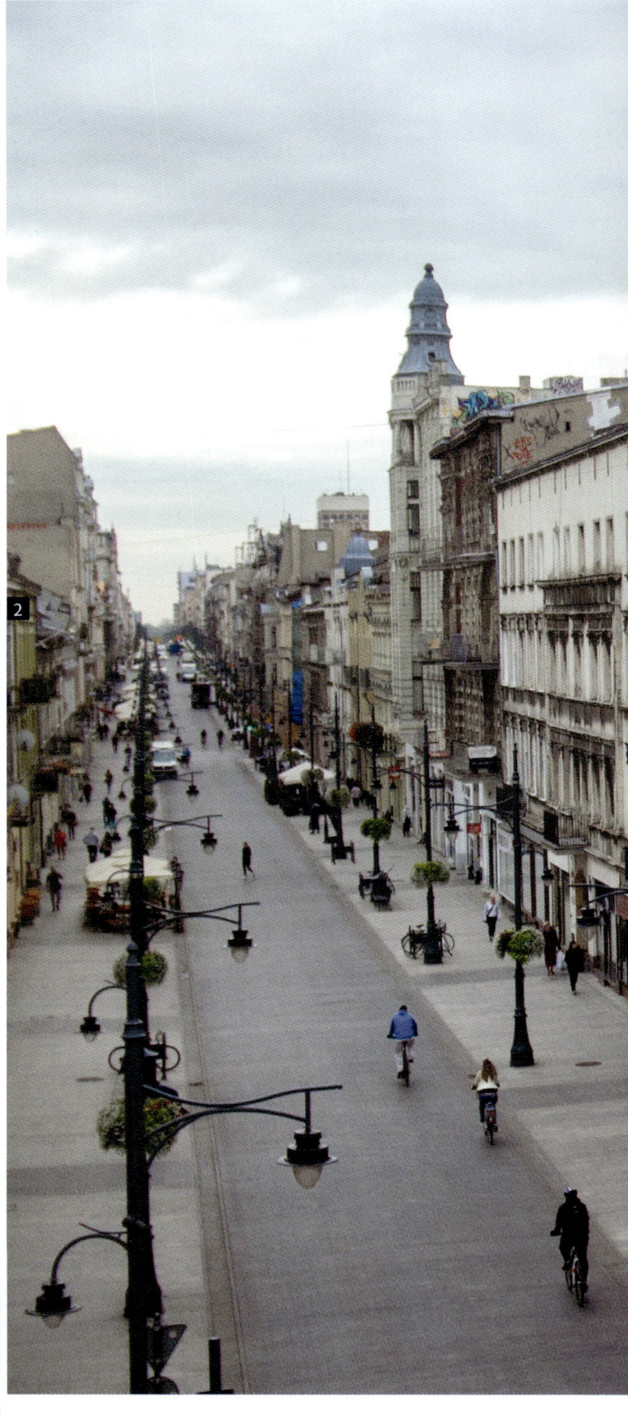

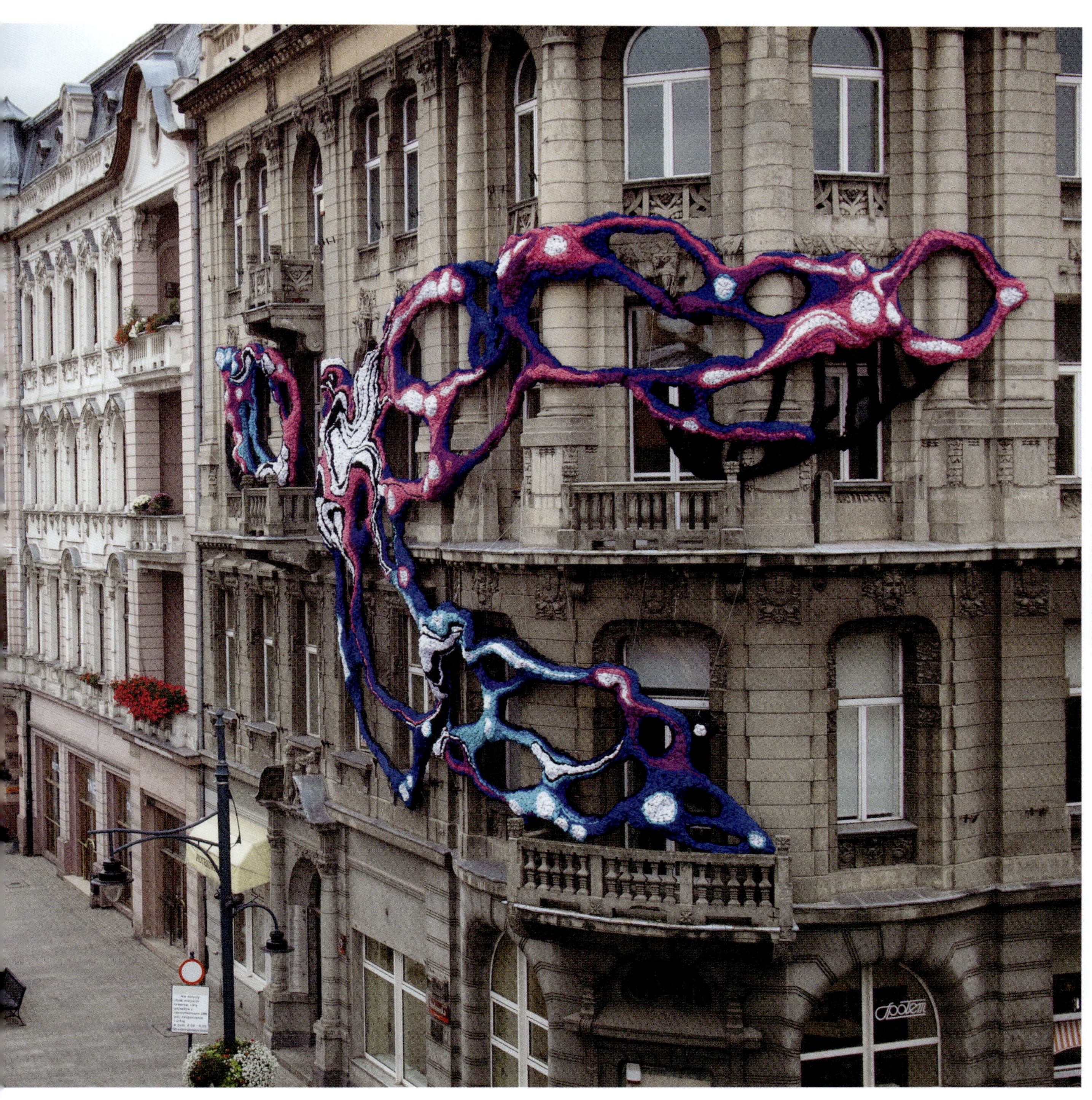

1 /
Burlington, Vermont, USA, 2017
PHOTO BY THE ARTIST

2 /
Łódź, Poland, 2016
PHOTO BY THE ARTIST

All the works are united by an expressive bursting of colour.

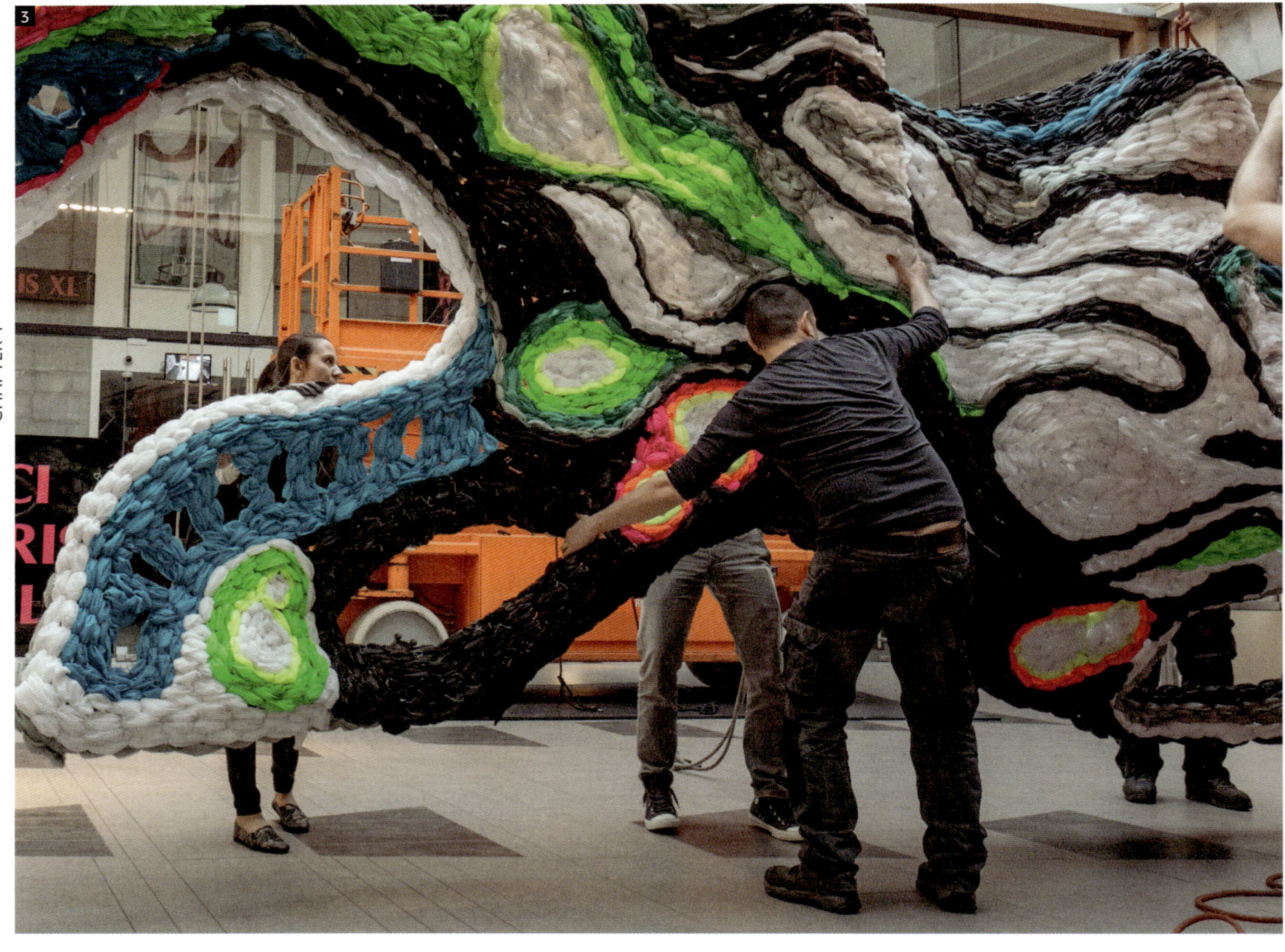

3 /
Ostend, Belgium, 2019
PHOTO BY EGMOND DOBBELAERE

4 /
Fort Smith, Arkansas, USA, 2017
PHOTO BY THE ARTIST

5 /
Aveyron, France, 2019
PHOTO BY THE ARTIST

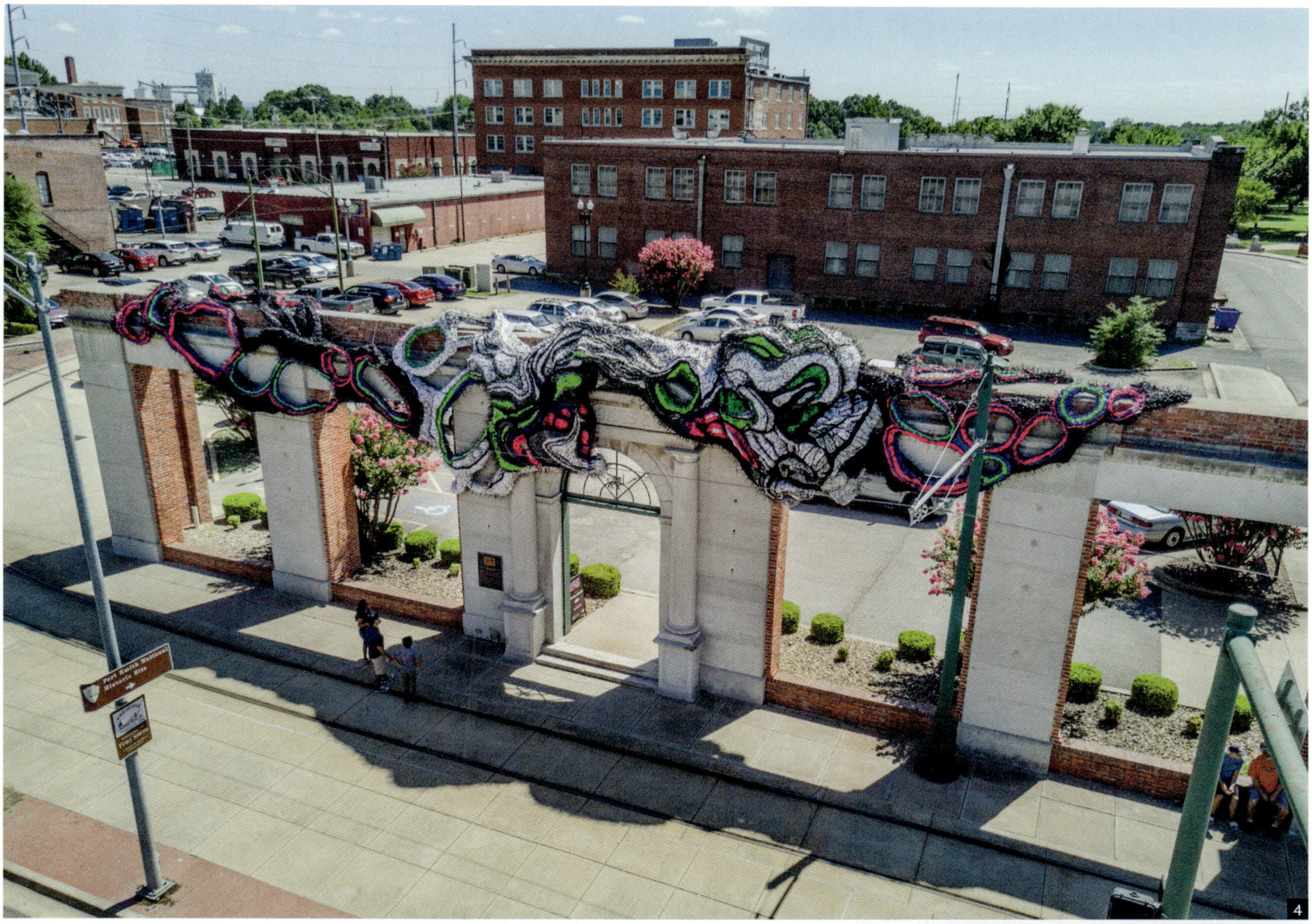

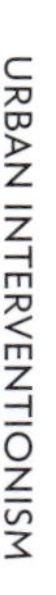

4

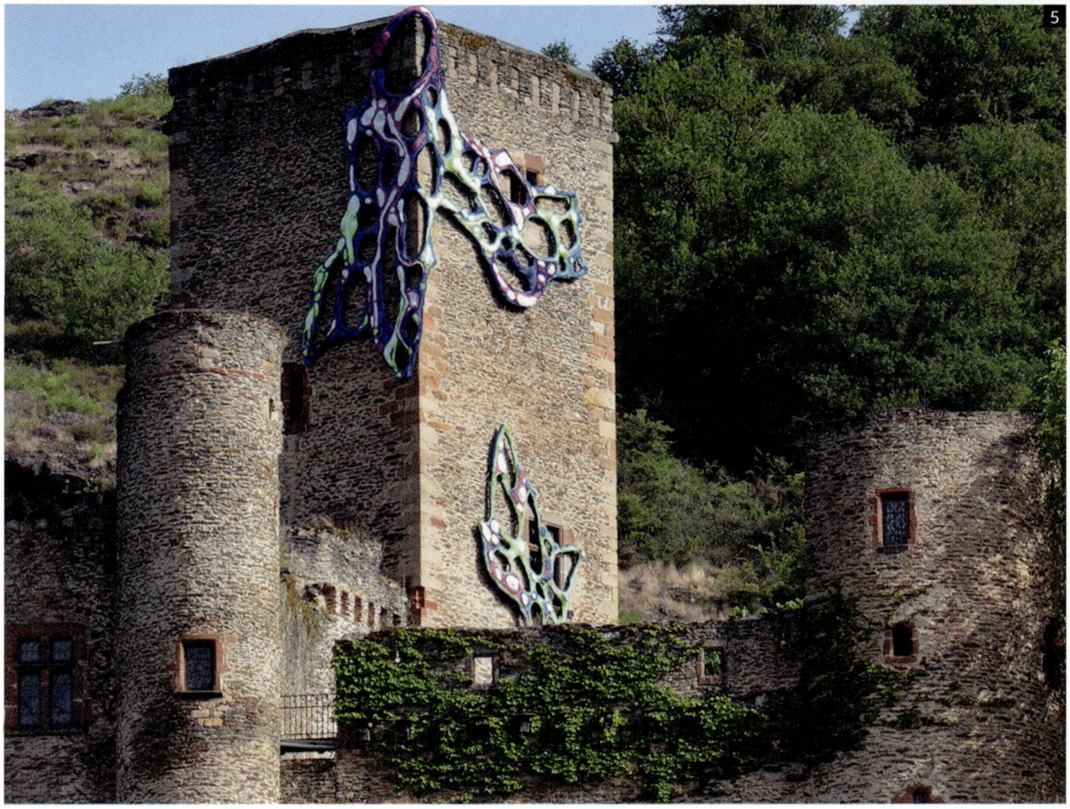

5

ERNEST ZACHAREVIC

/ Penang

Ernest Zacharevic is a Lithuanian-born artist combining fine art techniques with a passion for creating art outdoors. Experimentation lies at the heart of Ernest's style, with the only constant being the dedication to his ever-changing concepts. With ideas leading the way, he removes the restriction of artistic boundaries, moving freely between the disciplines of oil painting, stencil and spray, installation and sculpture, and producing dynamic compositions both inside and outside the gallery space.

Ernest's primary interest is in the relationship between art and the urban landscape, with concepts often evolving as part of a spontaneous response to the immediate environment, the community and culture. A good example is the 'Splash & Burn' project, an awareness campaign curated by Ernest as a creative response to unregulated palm-oil farming practices in Indonesia. Murals, sculptures and interventions throughout Sumatra tackle issues such as the transboundary haze, deforestation, and human and animal displacement.

1 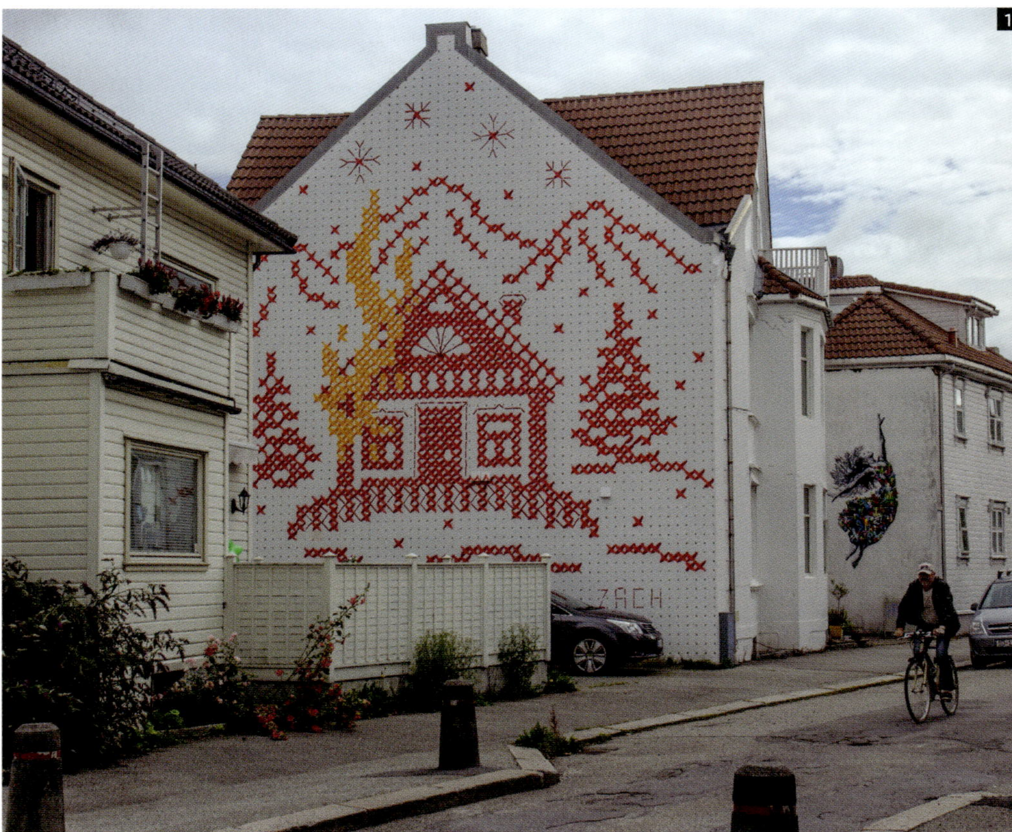

2 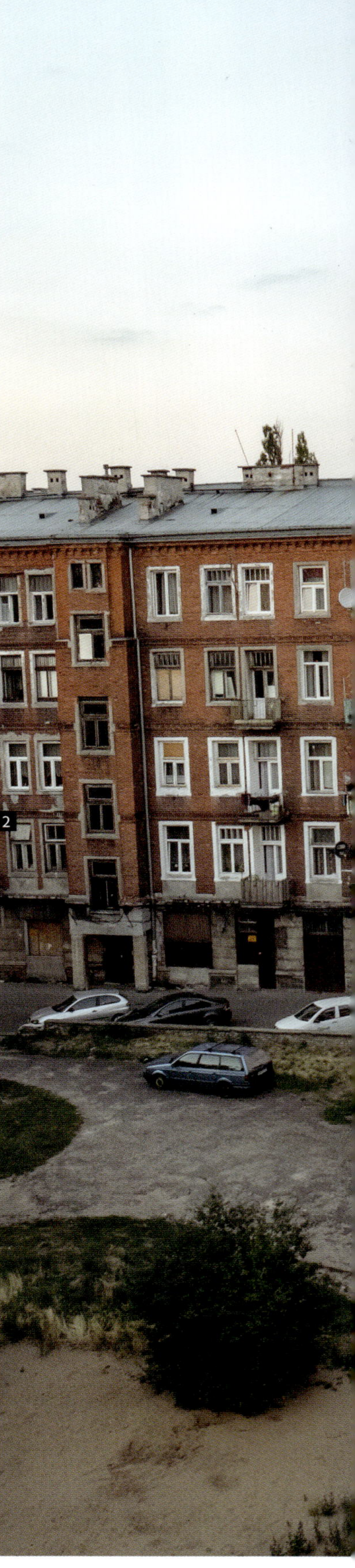

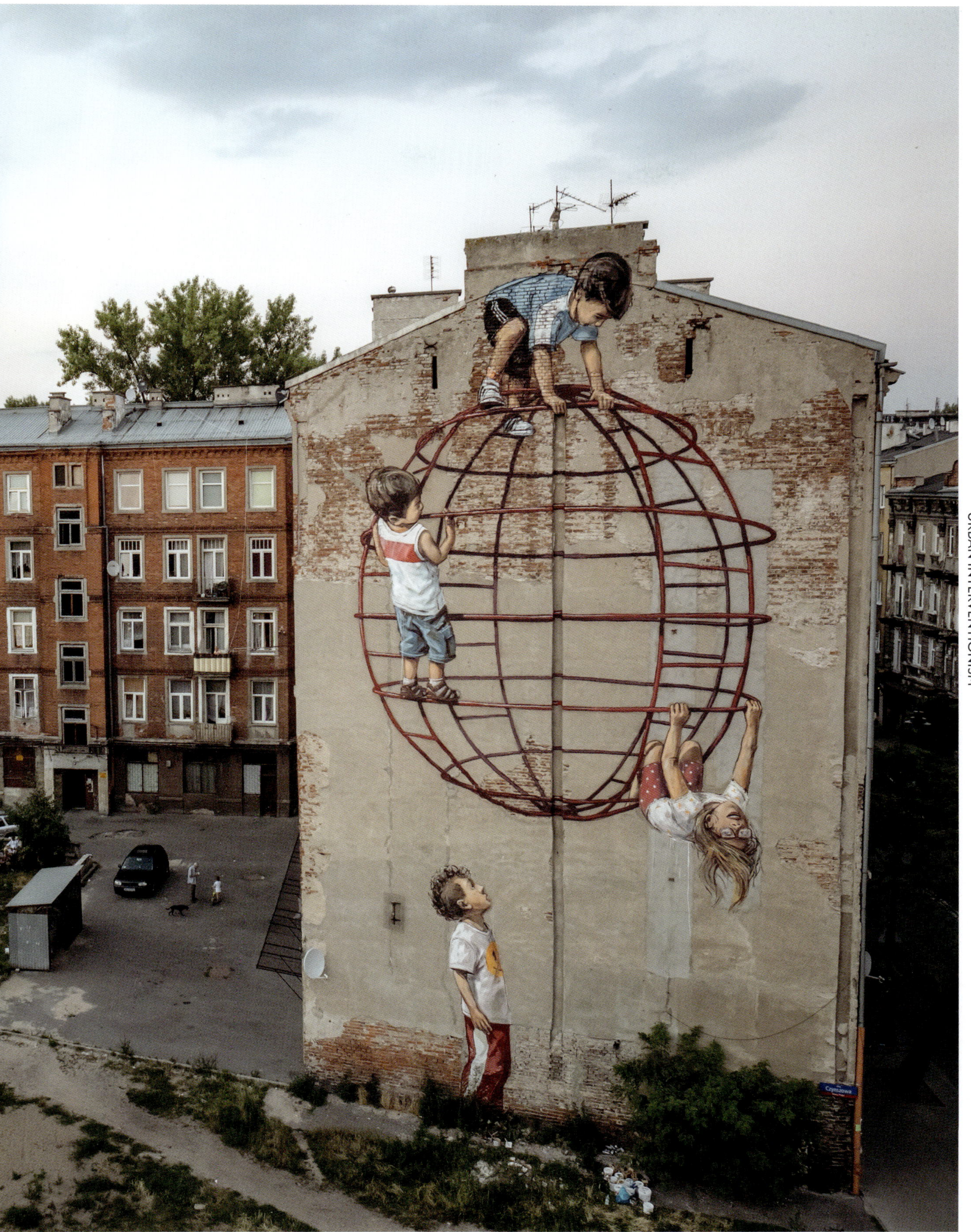

1 /
Stavanger, Norway, 2015
PHOTO BY THE ARTIST

2 /
Warsaw, Poland, 2015
PHOTO BY THE ARTIST

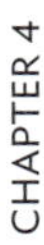

3

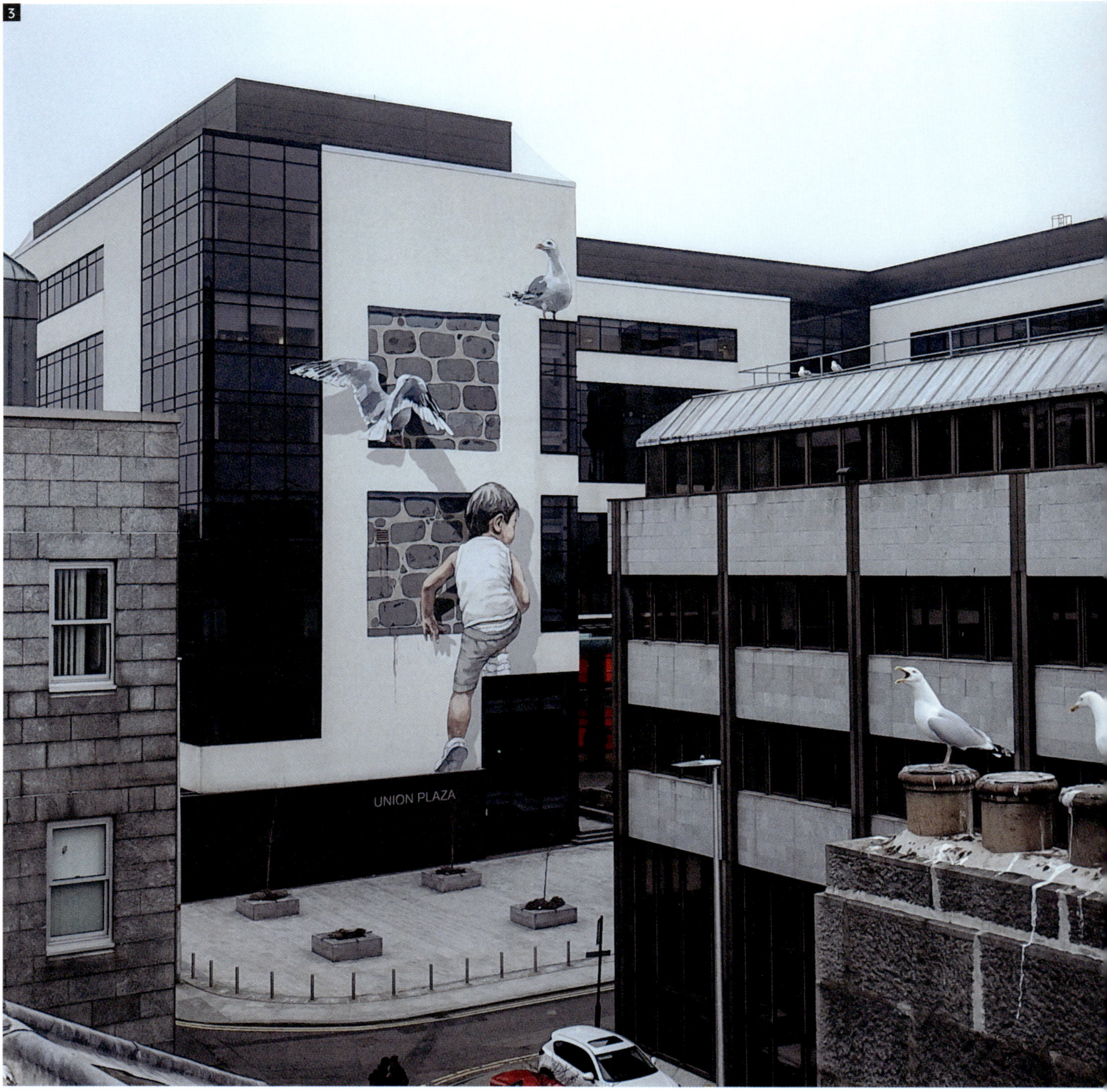

3 /
Aberdeen, Scotland, 2018
PHOTO BY THE ARTIST

4 /
Penang, Malaysia, 2016
PHOTO BY THE ARTIST

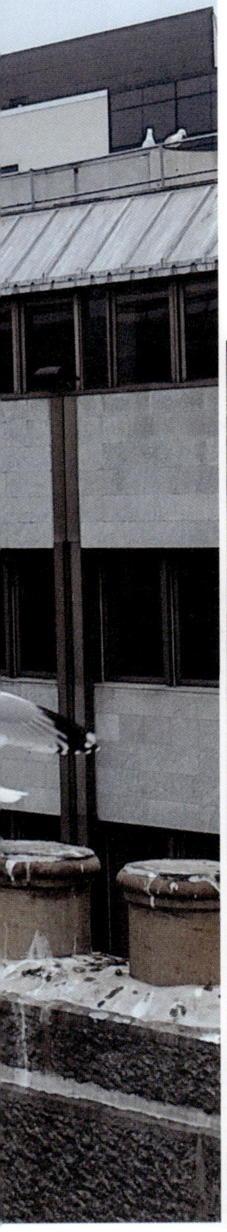

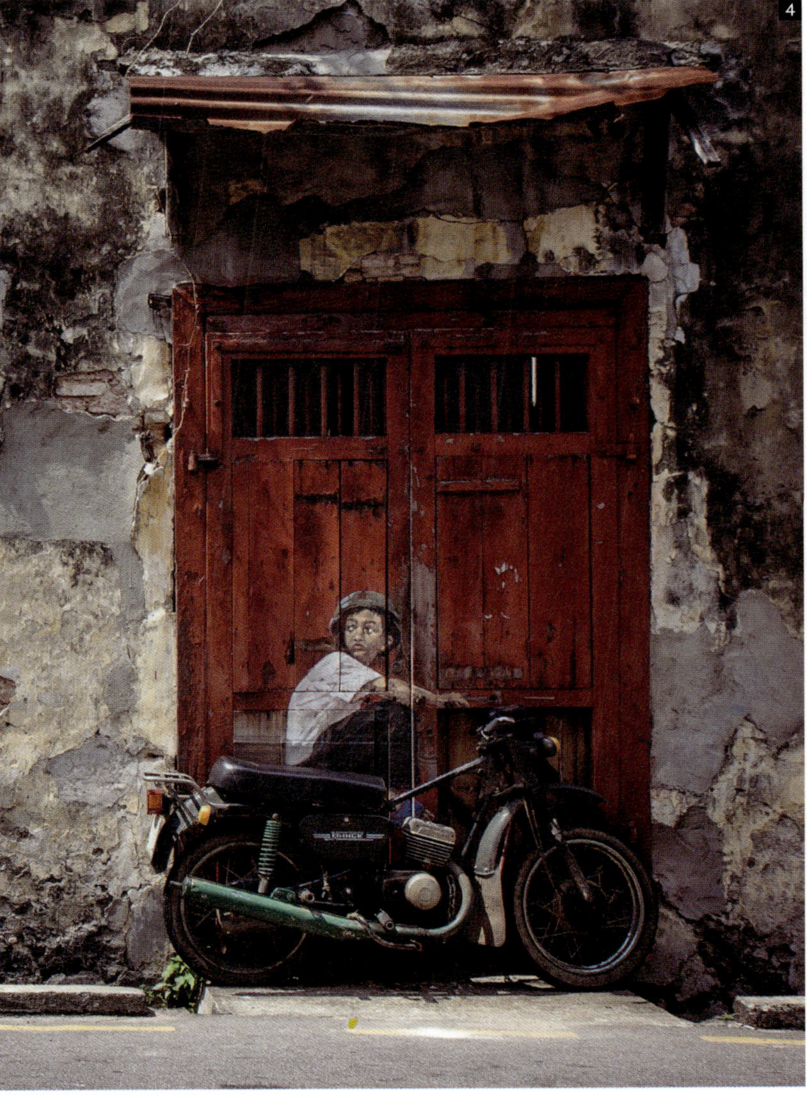

4

The artist moves freely between the disciplines of oil painting, stencil and spray, installation and sculpture.

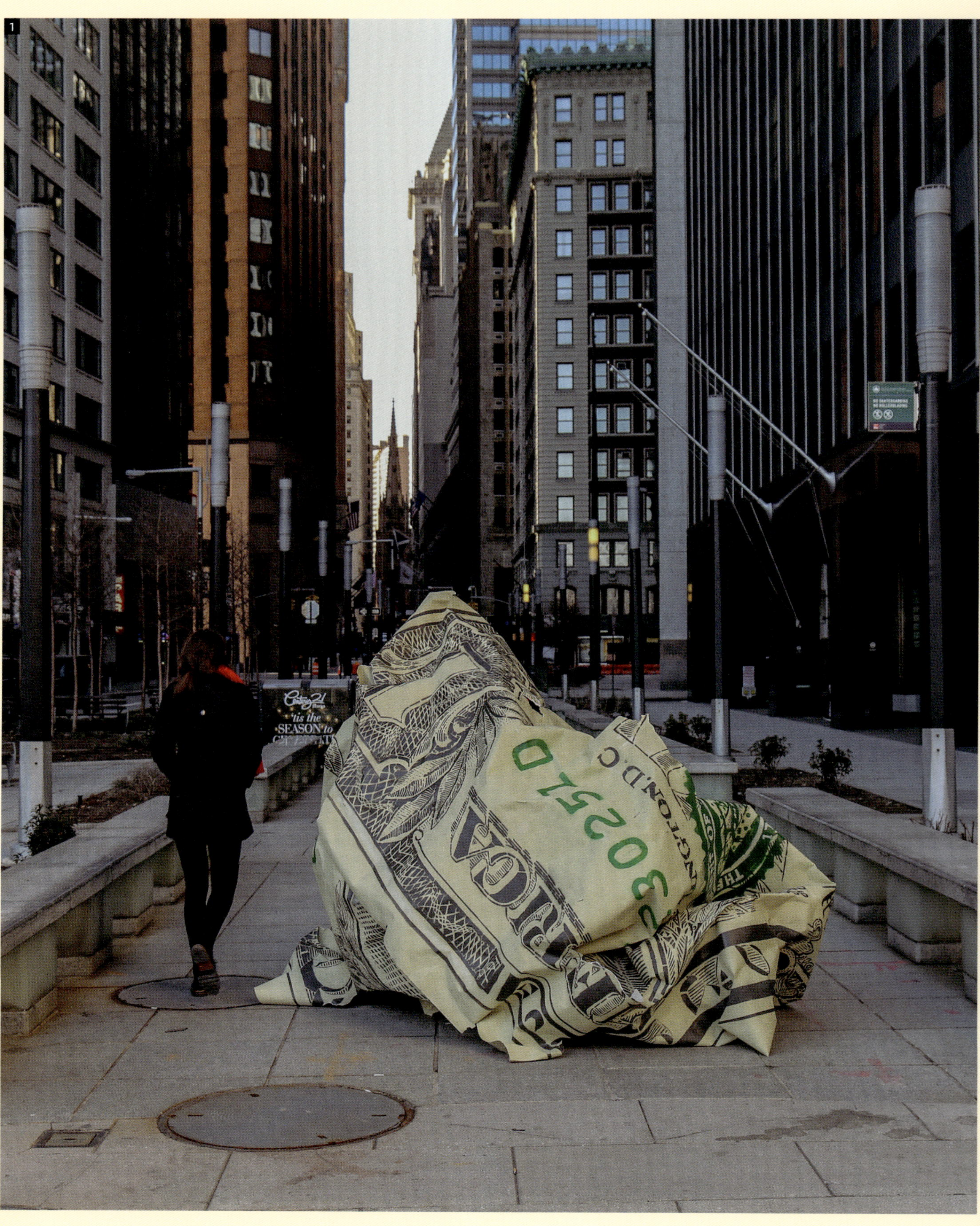
'tis the
SEASON to

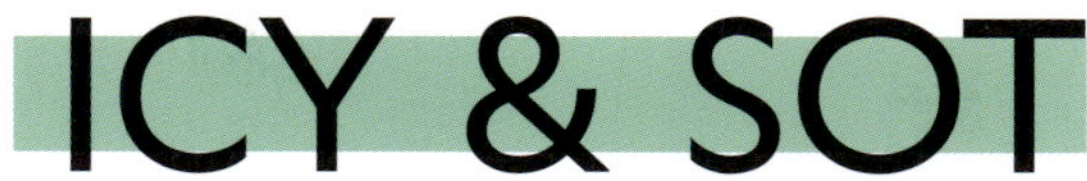

ICY & SOT

/ New York

Online presence and videos is how we spread our word and raise awareness. We think it's really important in the process of creating our work.

It is clear that you both see the role of an artist as a position of social responsibility. What issues do you think art has the most power to address?
The contemporary issues! Art has always been an important part of change in society. We believe that the role of the artist is to advocate for the freedom and the hope of the general public, and to raise awareness about the issues happening in their time.

Over the past few years, there have been many political, ecological and economic changes in society – many for the worse. What are the main concerns that your work focuses on? Have you ever encountered backlash for expressing your political views?
We always try to ensure that our work conveys a message. In recent years, we have focused more on immigration issues, the refugee crisis, climate change and social justice.

Yes, we have encountered backlash for some of our works about gun violence and borders in the United States, but for the most part we have gained an amazing response from our viewers. Sometimes people even engage with some of our projects. For example, we made a sculpture entitled 'Human Reflection on Nature', depicting humans damaging the environment. We were so happy to see an amazing response! Many volunteers and community members started to clean all the plastic trash from the river. They made sculptures inspired by our piece and installed them along the river the hope of motivating people to care about the environment.

Iran is not a very well-known urban art scene. Can you describe the street culture there?
It was always a small scene, even from the beginning, because it has been always riskier for the street

1 /
New York, USA, 2018
PHOTO BY THE ARTIST

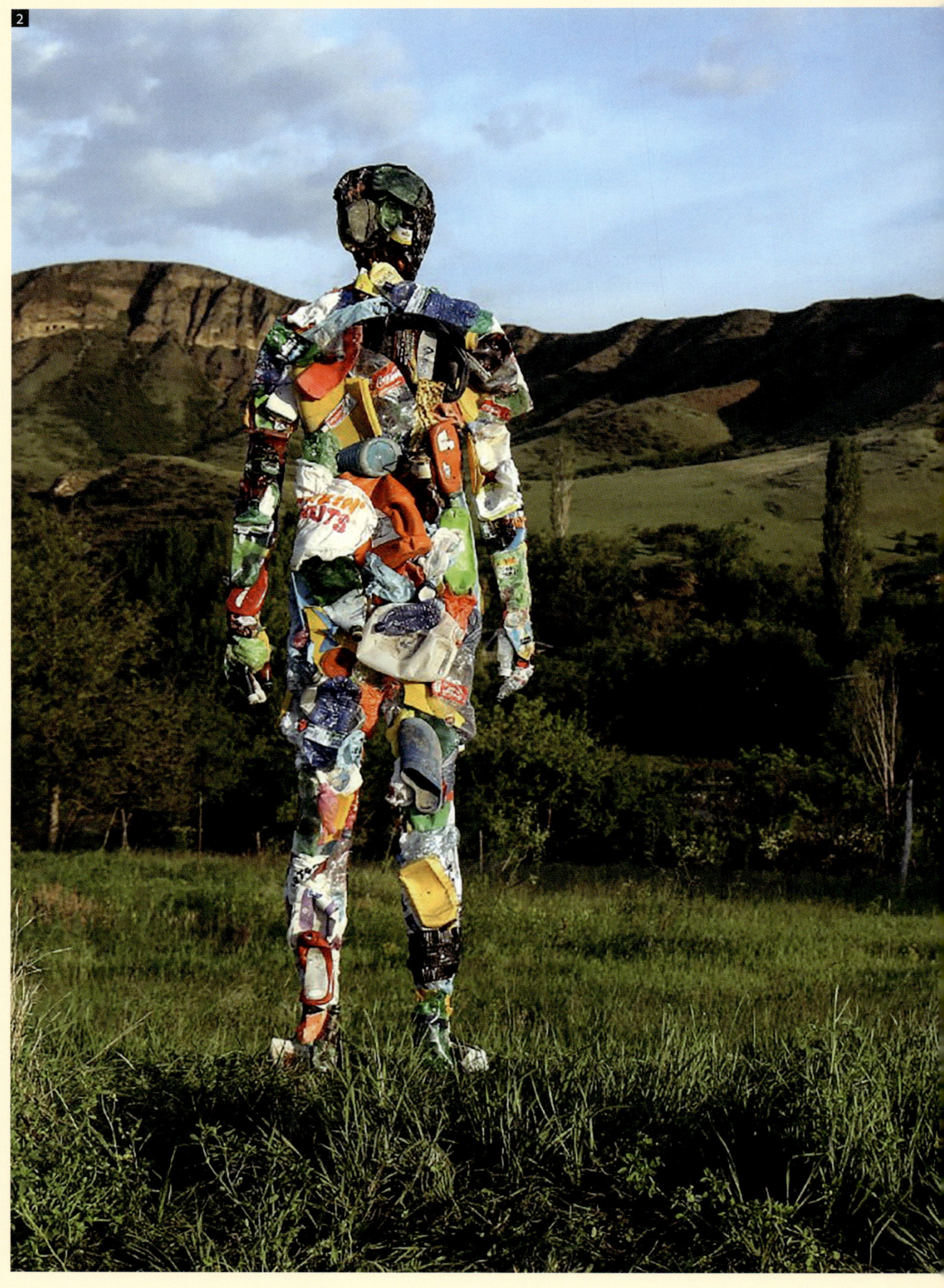

2 /
Tbilisi, Georgia, 2017
PHOTO BY THE ARTIST

3 /
San Jose, California, USA, 2018
PHOTO BY THE ARTIST

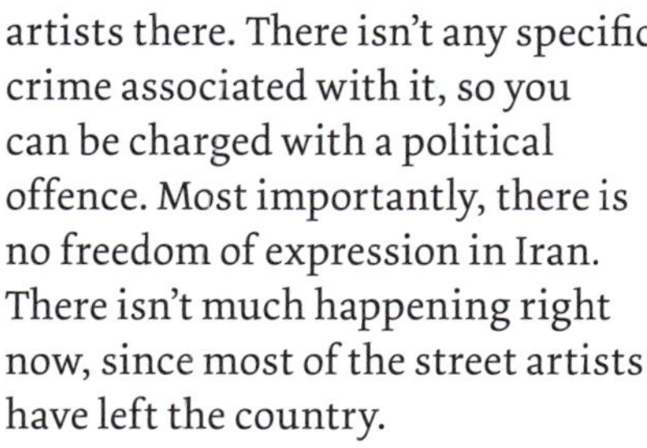

artists there. There isn't any specific crime associated with it, so you can be charged with a political offence. Most importantly, there is no freedom of expression in Iran. There isn't much happening right now, since most of the street artists have left the country.

The move to New York must have been a huge change in both of your lives. How did it influence your artistic production? What do you think of this myth of the 'Land of the Free'?
Being able to have freedom of speech and not work under so much stress has been very important. Being able to travel has also influenced us a lot. I think we would say that we have evolved so much as artists in the past 5 years.
Land of the Free? Not sure about that. There has always been racism, Islamophobia, homophobia, gun violence... So many crazy things are happening here, and it's too sad to see that those influences are growing now.

Can you tell us a little about the 'Let Her Be Free' publication?
The book *Let Her Be Free* pretty much covers all of our work from the beginning until 2016. Half of the book shows 6 years of our career in Iran, while the other half shows 4 years of our work in New York and internationally.
Oscar van Gelderen, publisher of our books, contacted us about collecting our work. Since then, we have become close friends. He has helped us in our careers in so many ways; he even organised a solo show for us in Amsterdam, although we couldn't attend it ourselves at the time.
We always stayed friends, keeping in touch through the internet.
In 2012, when we moved to NY, he came here to help us with our show. That was when we finally met. He had always told us that he wanted to publish our book, but we waited until we had enough work to fill a book. Eventually, we decided to work on the book in 2015.

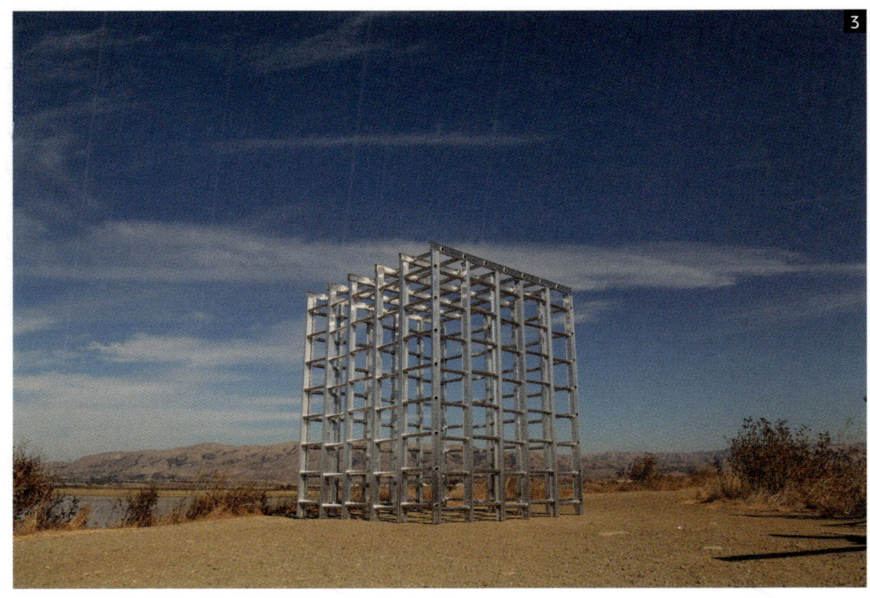

3

4

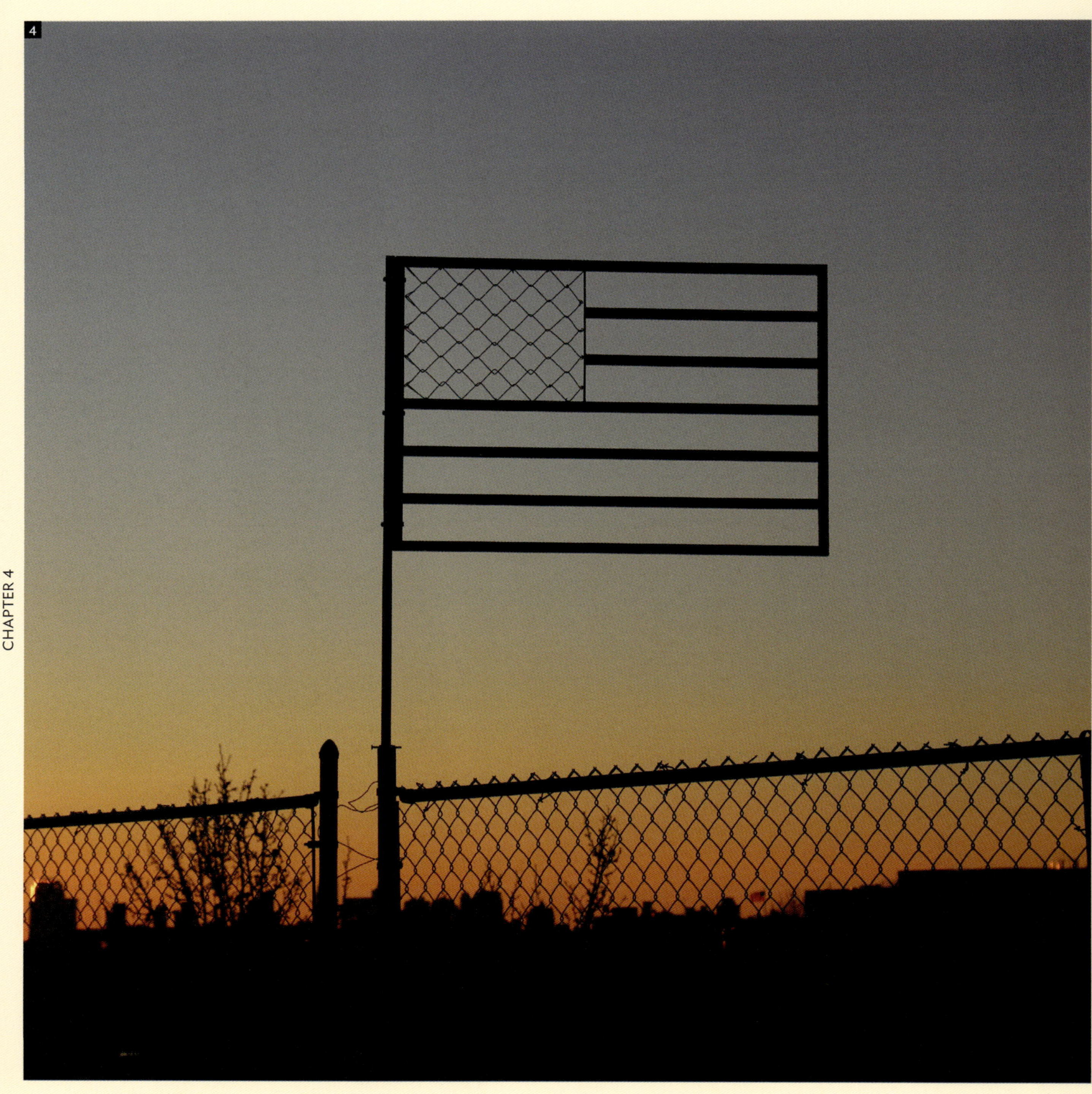

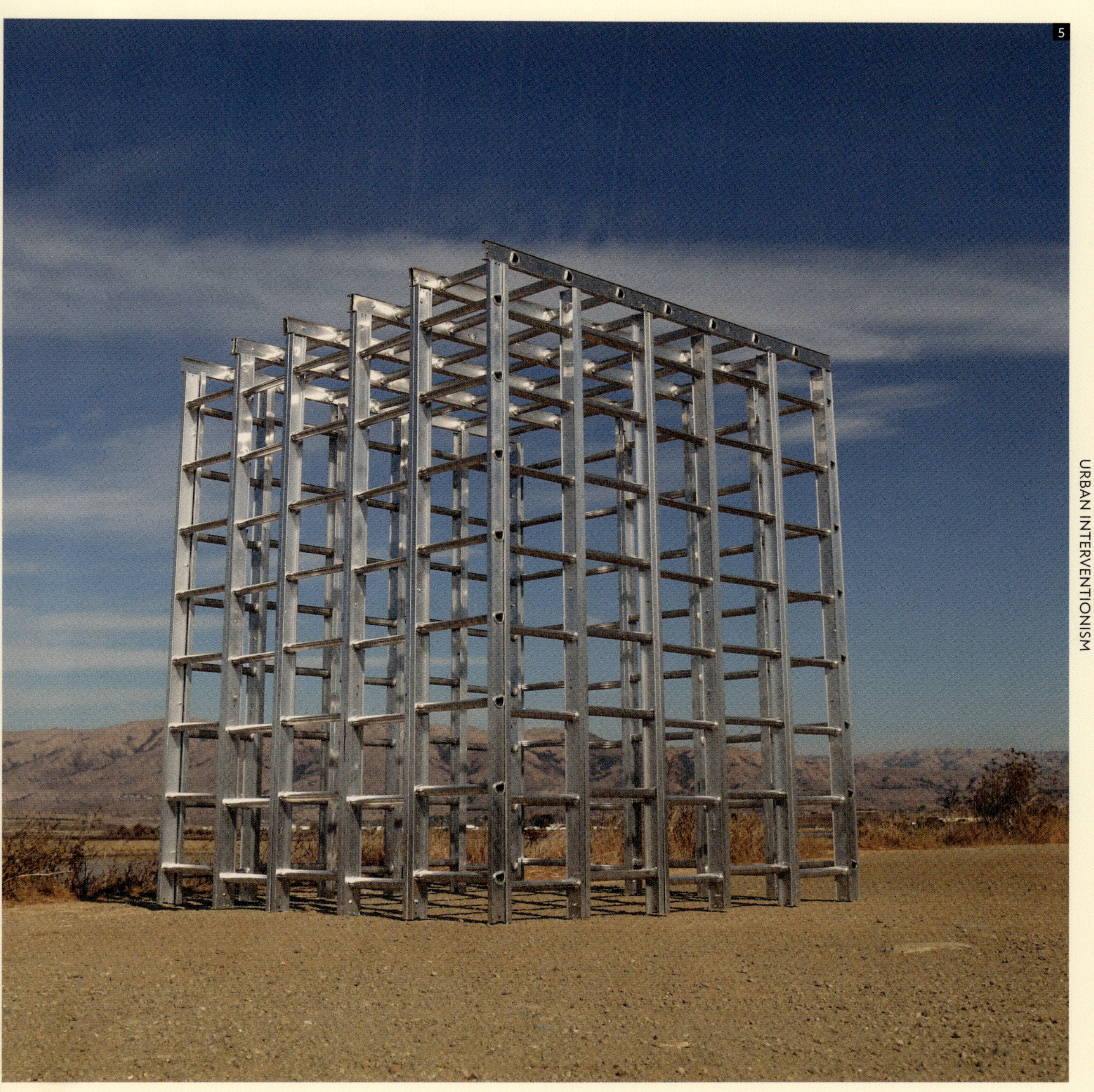

4 /
Brooklyn, New York, USA, 2018
PHOTO BY THE ARTIST

5 /
San Jose, California, USA, 2018
PHOTO BY THE ARTIST

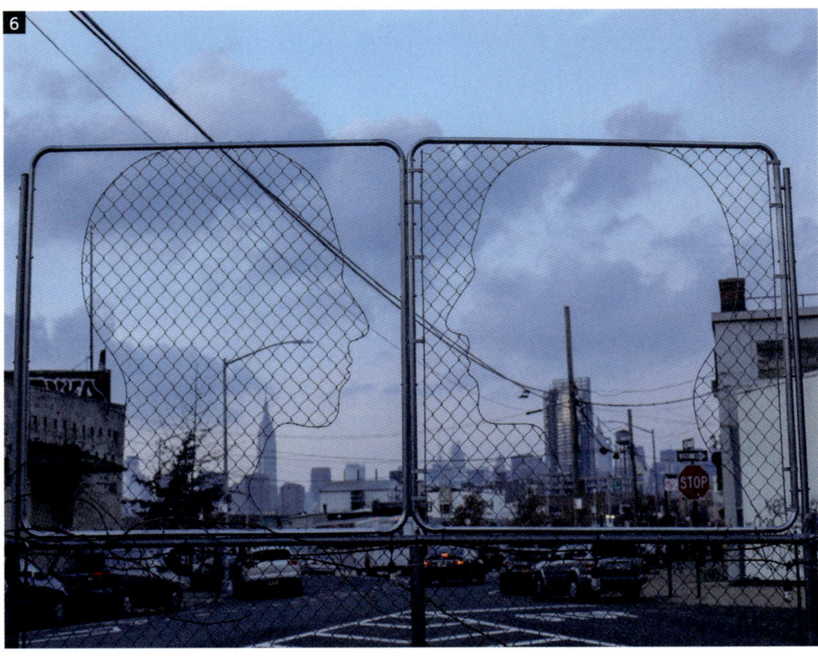

6

Sometimes it can be difficult to integrate a working relationship with a family member. How is it working as a duo of brothers?
We have been working together for so long that we don't even need to use words sometimes, to actually talk to each other. We both have the same thoughts and the same taste. It's amazing to share our ideas and combine them. That close connection also makes the production so much faster!

You seem to increasingly document your work through the medium of video. How important are the virtual world and the internet in your work process?
Sometimes we have ideas that need to be a video piece: either a complete performance or a short video clip. Obviously, the virtual world plays a big role in modern society. That online presence, those videos: that's how we spread the word and raise awareness, so we think it's really important in the process of creating our work.

How do you see your work evolving in the next few years? Do you have any projects you are excited to be working towards?'
We always try to experiment with new materials and techniques. Starting about 3 years ago, we have been doing more sculptural and installation works. We have also been mixing objects and subjects. We have more freedom to share our ideas now, but one thing that is still the same in our work is its simplicity. Everyone can connect with the work. It has always been exciting for us to try new stuff, so we are especially looking forward to finding out what we will be making in the next couple of years. We do have some exciting projects coming up, but they are still in the early stages.

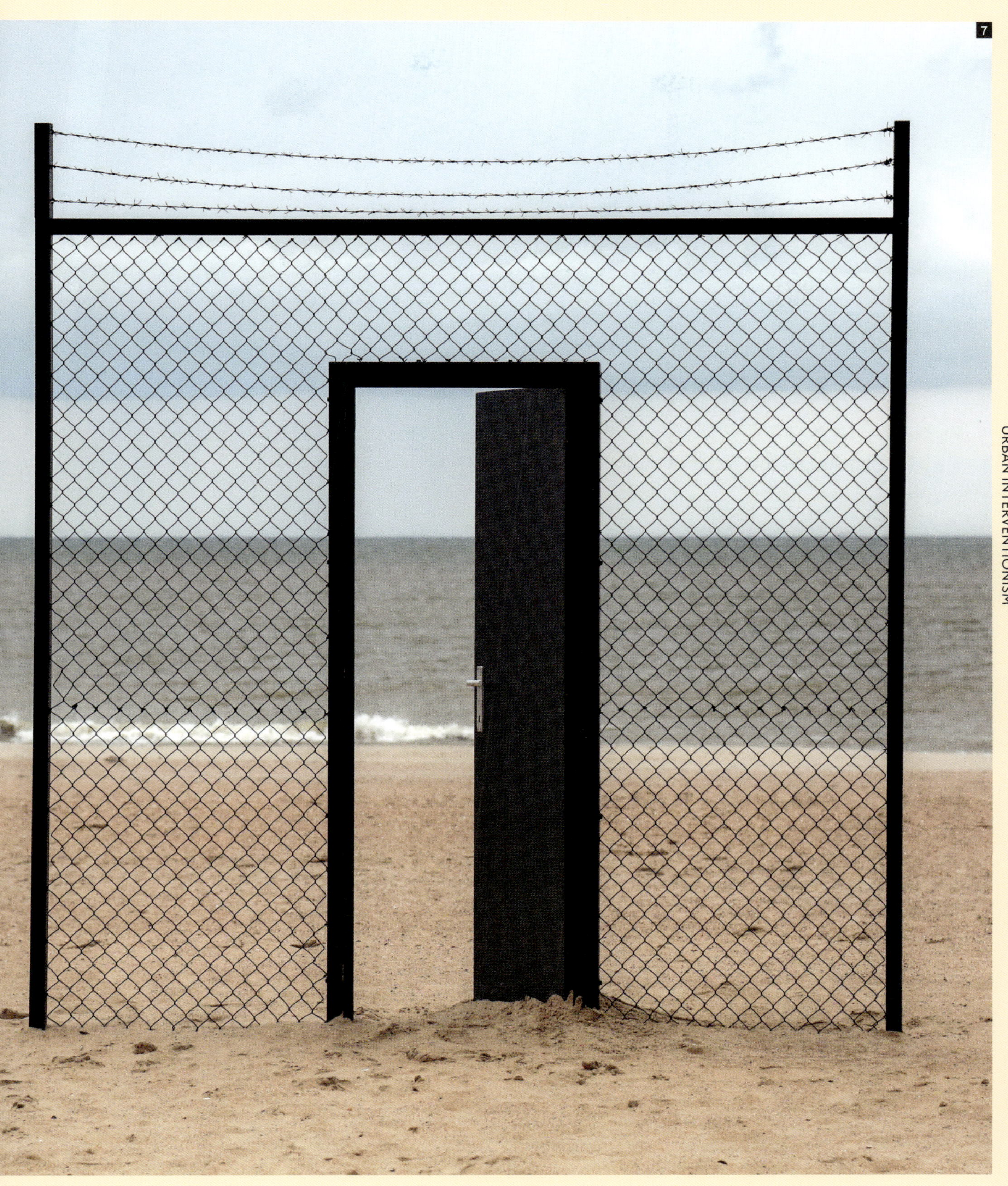

6 /
Brooklyn, New York, USA, 2017
PHOTO BY THE ARTIST

7 /
Ostend, Belgium, 2018
PHOTO BY THE ARTIST

» /
Brooklyn, New York, 2017
PHOTO BY THE ARTIST

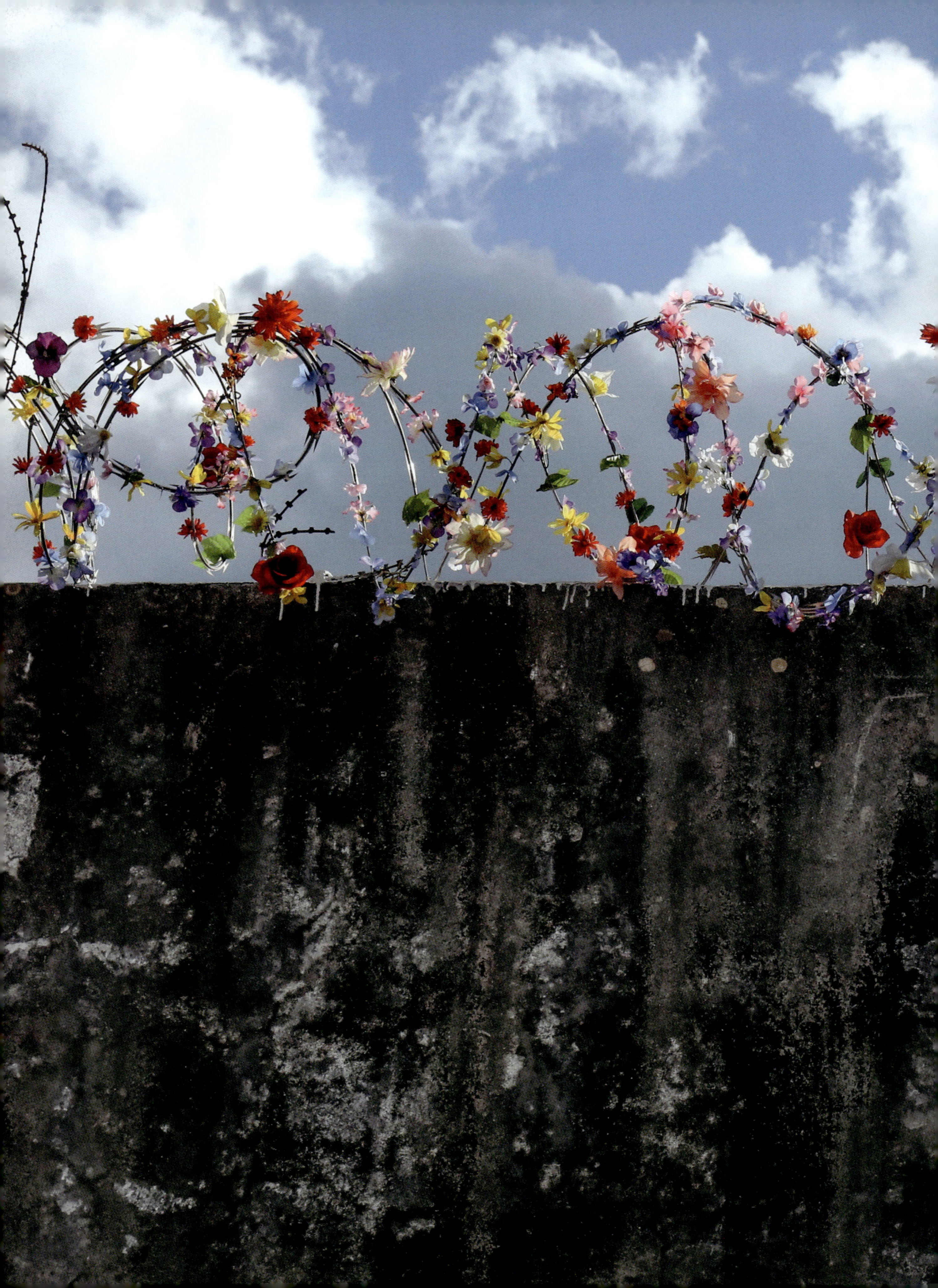

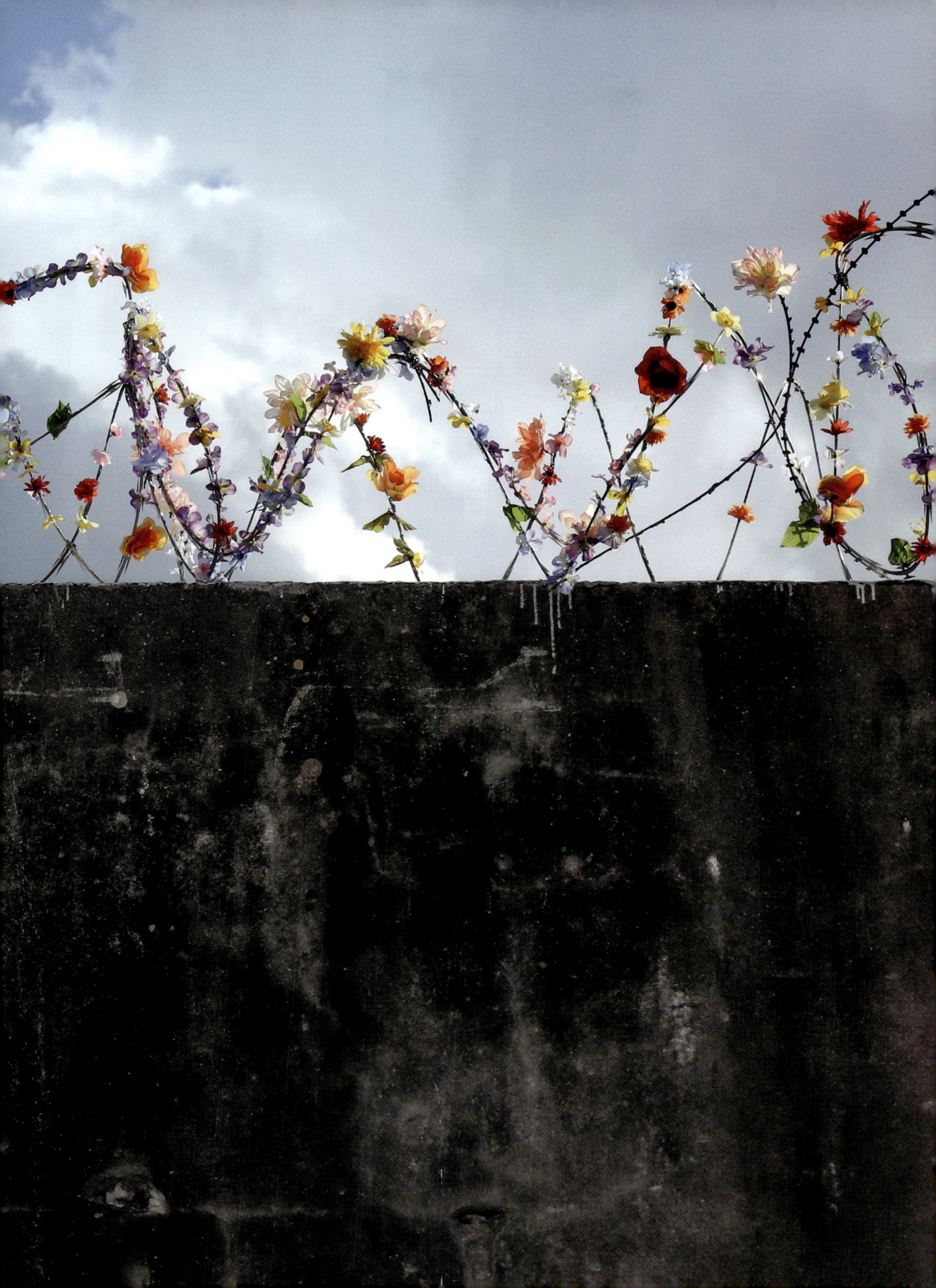

ISAAC CORDAL

/ Brussels

An active creator for over a decade, Spanish artist Isaac Cordal continues to dot the world with his miniature sculpted characters. He places his carefully staged scenes of social and political commentary in discreet nooks of the urban landscape.

The cement figurines are intended to be a critical reflection on humanity's idea of progress. Often choosing businessmen as his protagonists, he openly criticises the implications of capitalism on the individual scale, as well as the impending deterioration of our ecological environment. Famous in the urban art world, his critical acclaim and global appreciation prove that size does not matter.

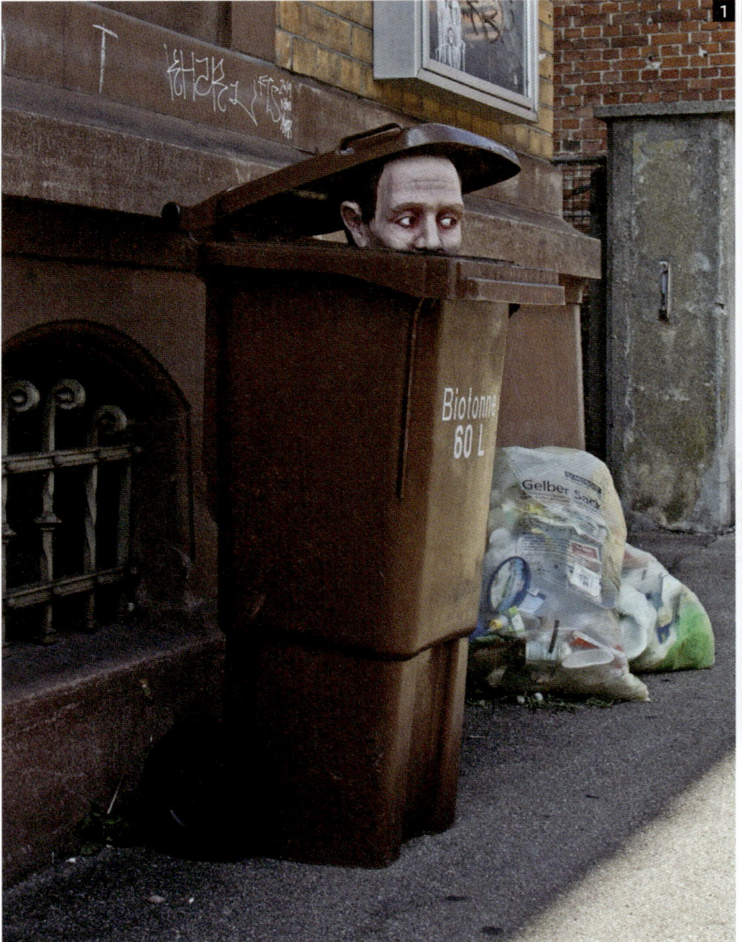

1 2

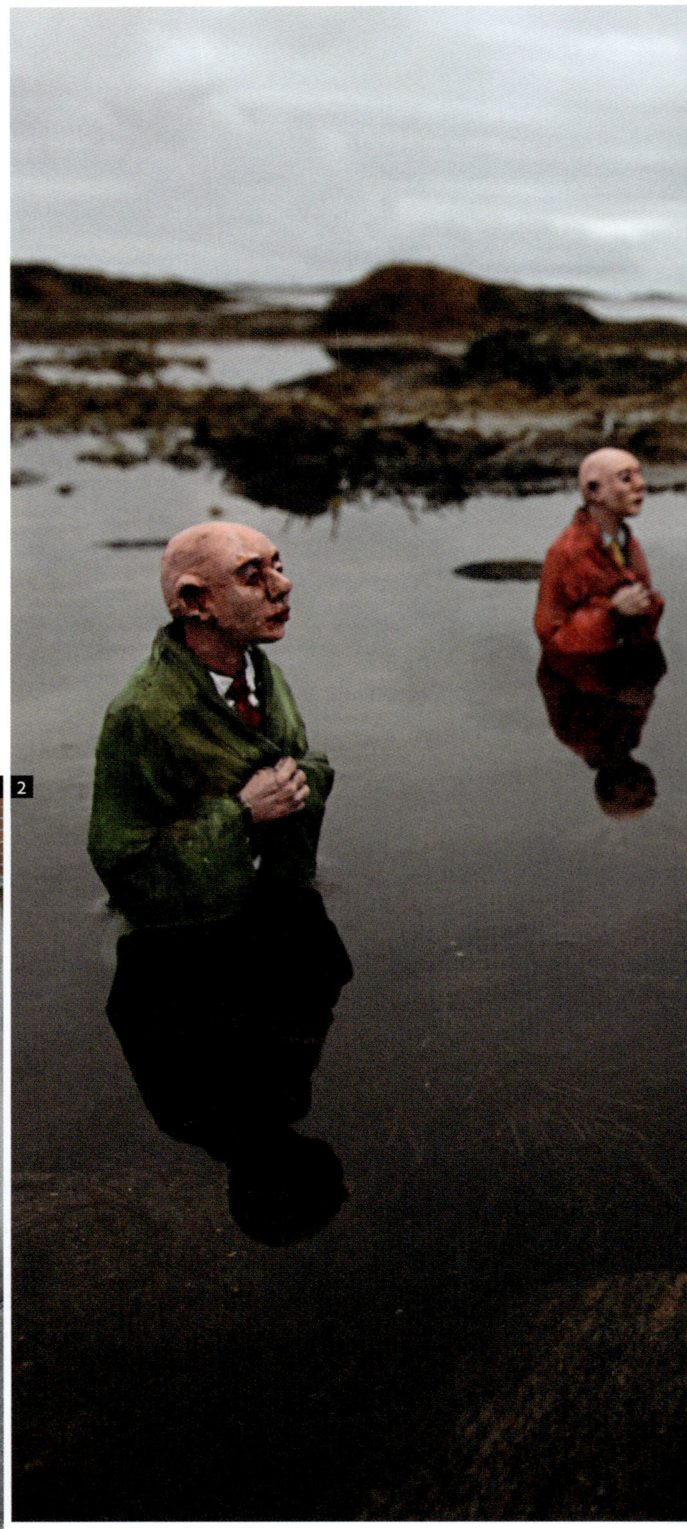

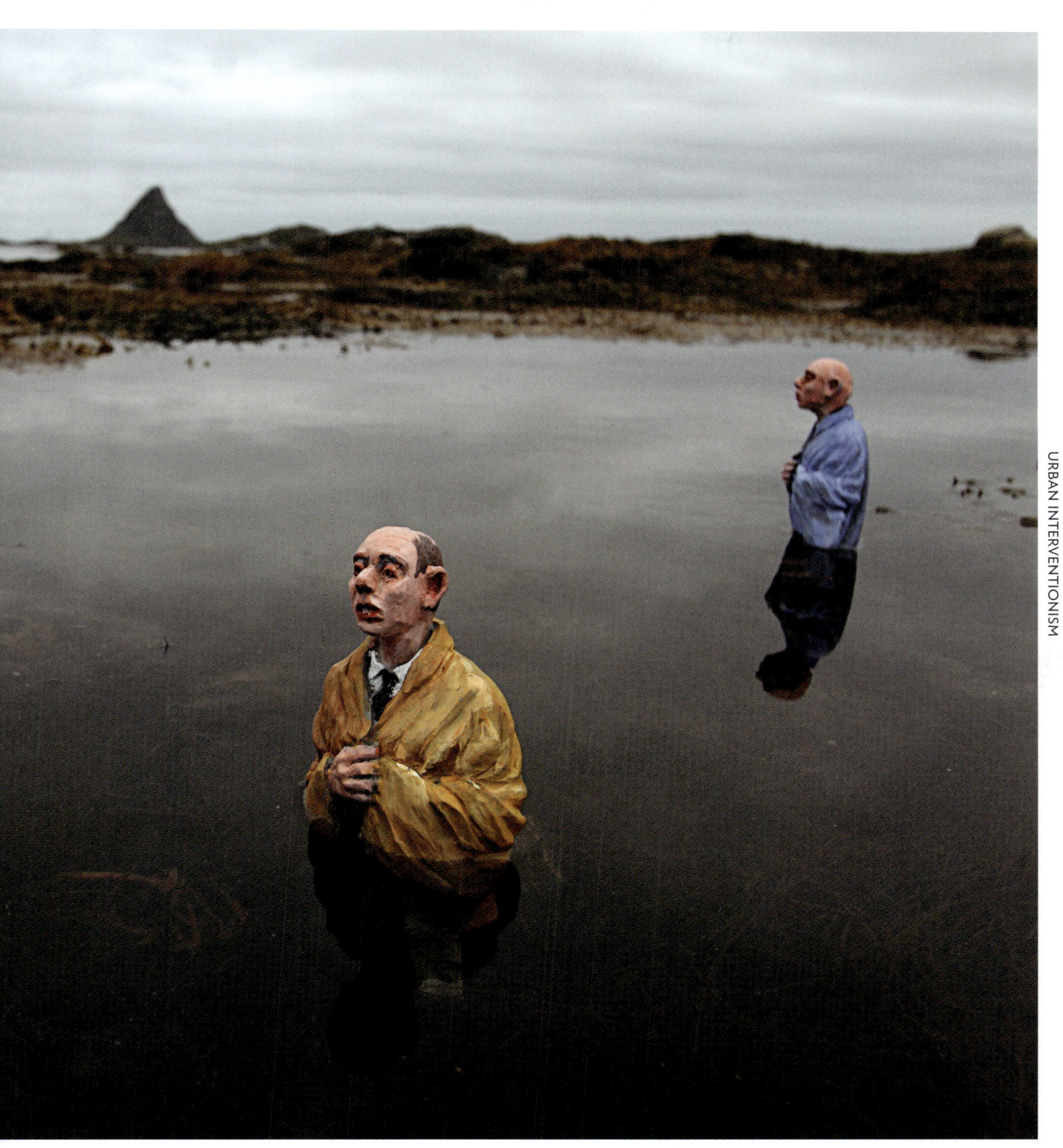

1 /
Ulm, Germany, 2017
PHOTO BY THE ARTIST

2 /
Rost, Norway, 2017
PHOTO BY THE ARTIST

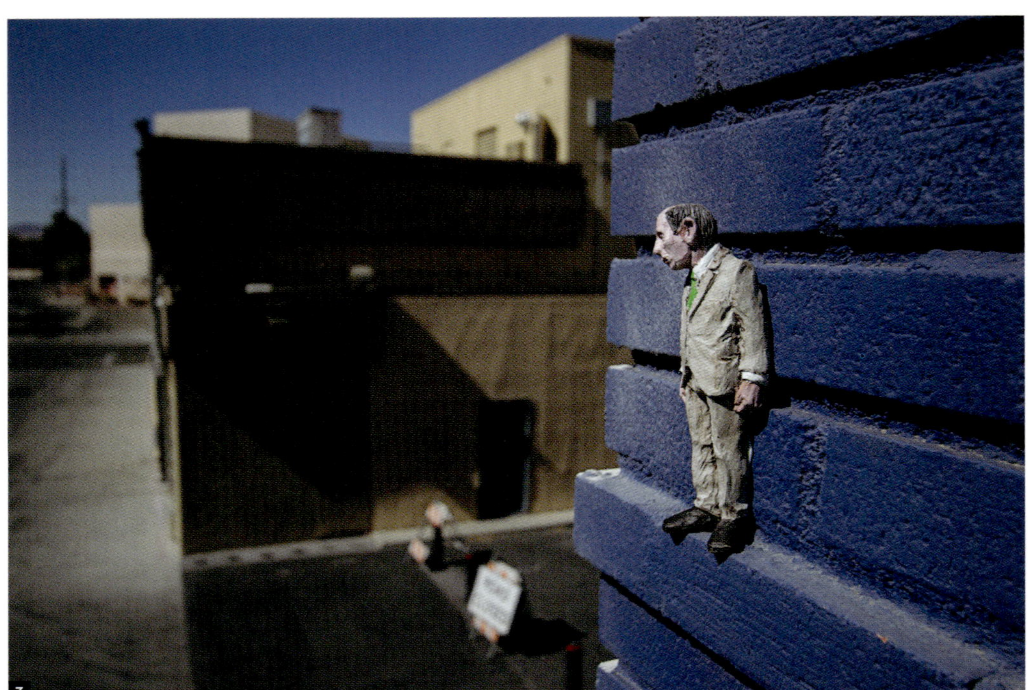
3

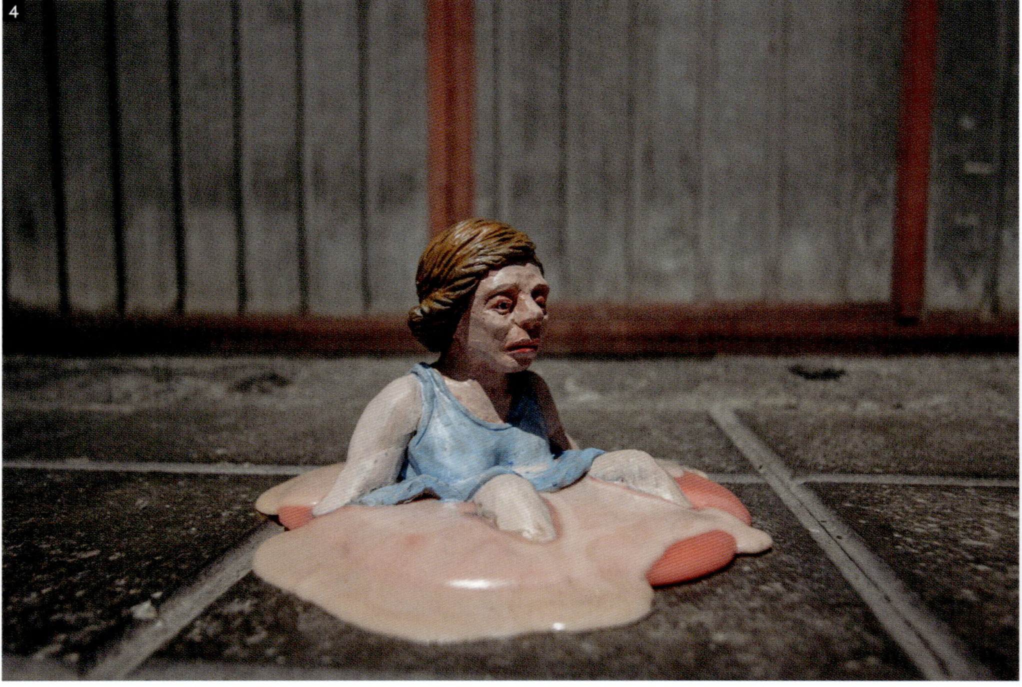
4

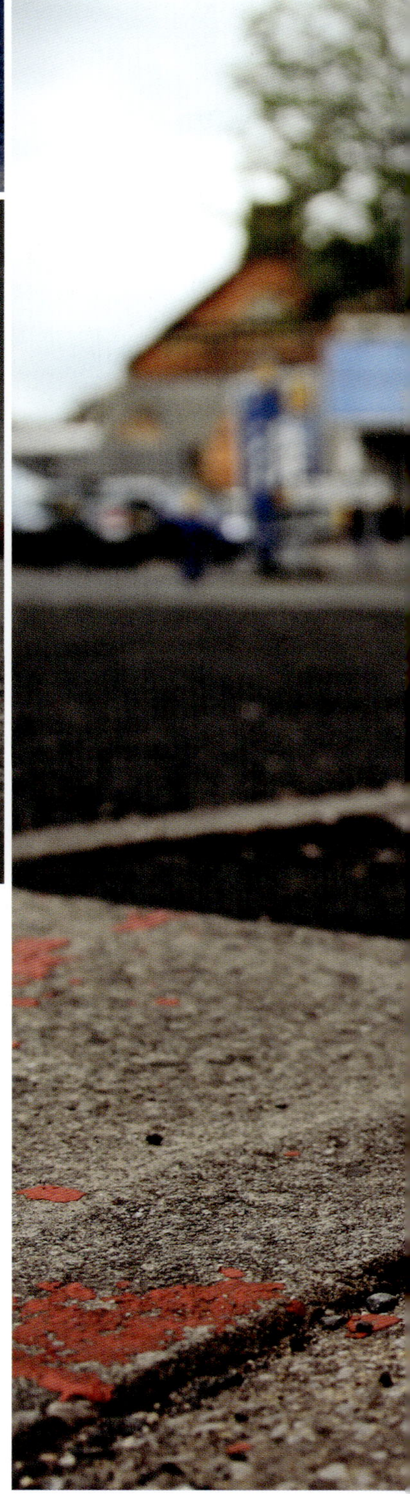

3 /
Lancaster, California, USA, 2018
PHOTO BY THE ARTIST

4 /
Bilbao, Spain, 2018
PHOTO BY THE ARTIST

5 /
Blackburn, UK, 2017
PHOTO BY THE ARTIST

Often choosing businessmen as his protagonists, he openly criticises the implications of capitalism.

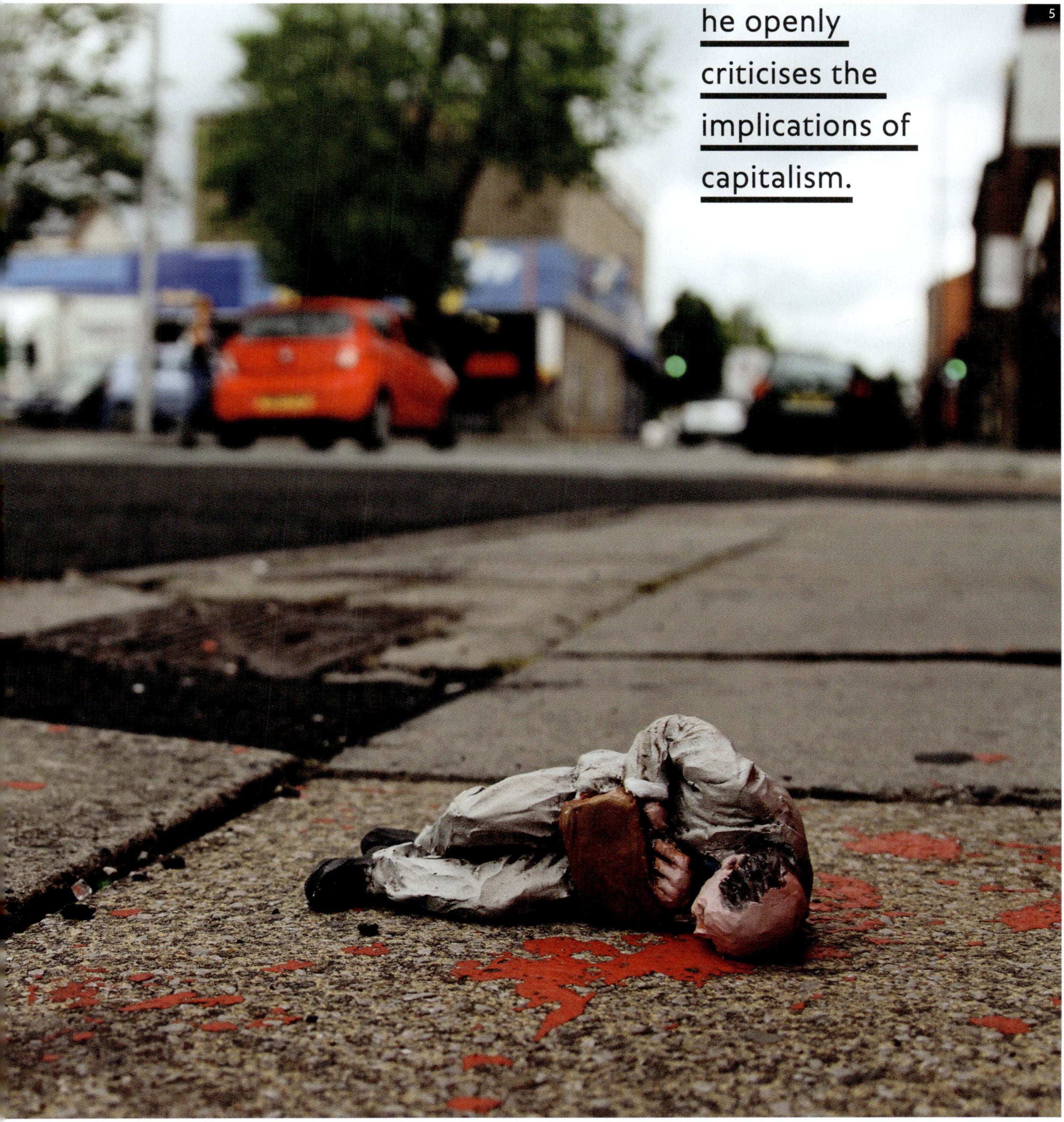

5

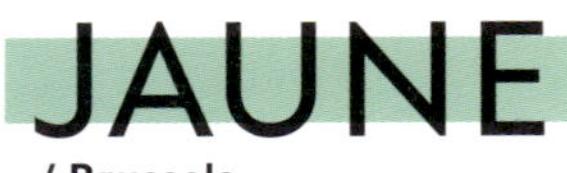

JAUNE

/ Brussels

Working as a waste collector in Belgium led Jaune to reflect on the nature of the city and the position of such workers in society. As fluoro-clad humans become part of the urban landscape, he questions social perceptions and visual doctrines. What if these workers were not cleaning the streets but climbing on walls, dancing and making a mess?

Primarily using stencil techniques to create his hilarious scenes, Jaune continues this game of the visible and invisible. His cheeky characters, hidden in the most obvious of places, encourage his audience to rethink their urban world and not to forget the possible playground that surrounds them.

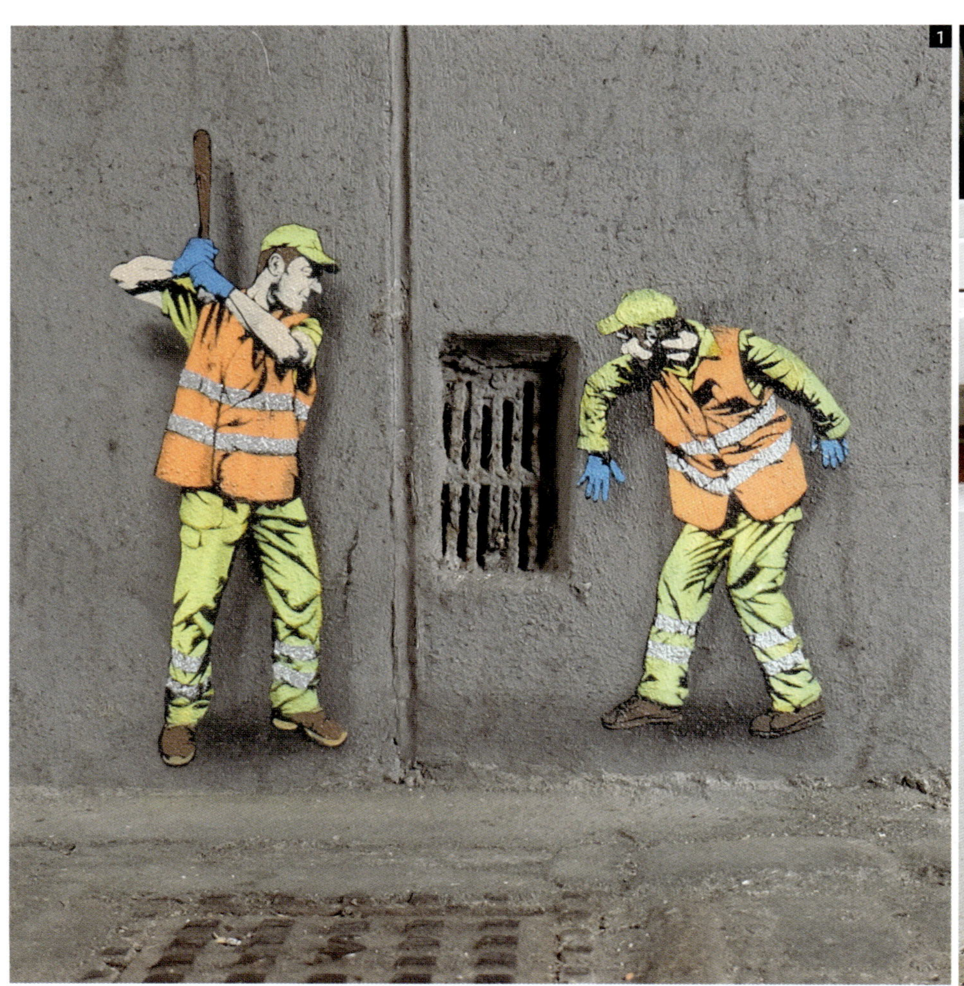

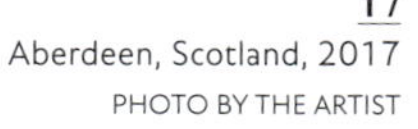

1 /
Aberdeen, Scotland, 2017
PHOTO BY THE ARTIST

2 /
Dendermonde, Belgium, 2018
PHOTO BY THE ARTIST

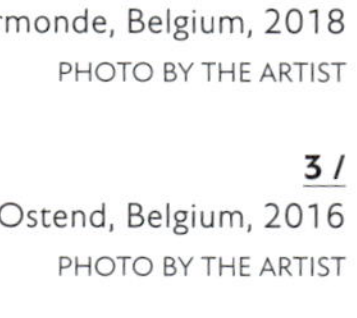

3 /
Ostend, Belgium, 2016
PHOTO BY THE ARTIST

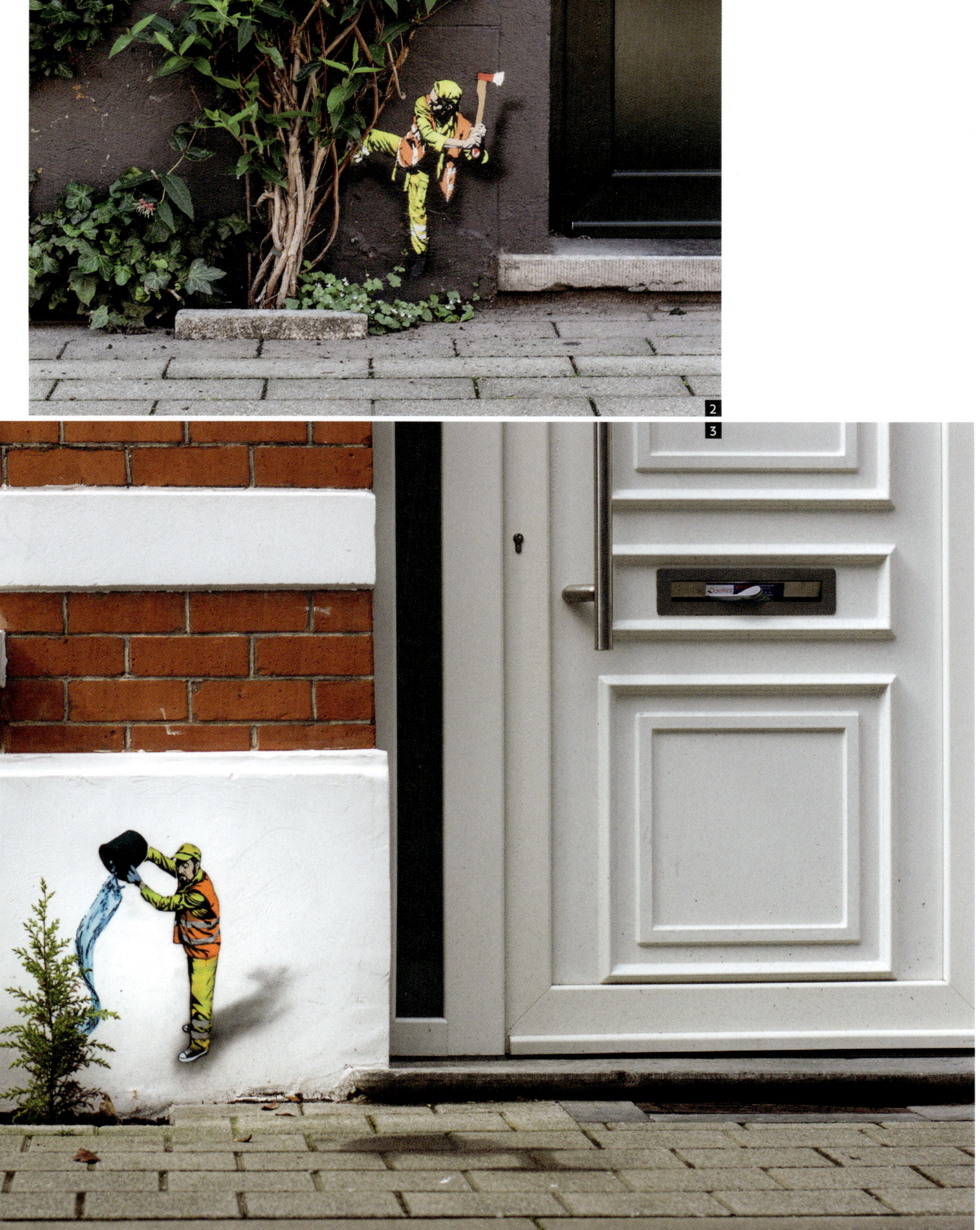

2

3

Jaune encourages his audience to rethink their urban world.

4

5

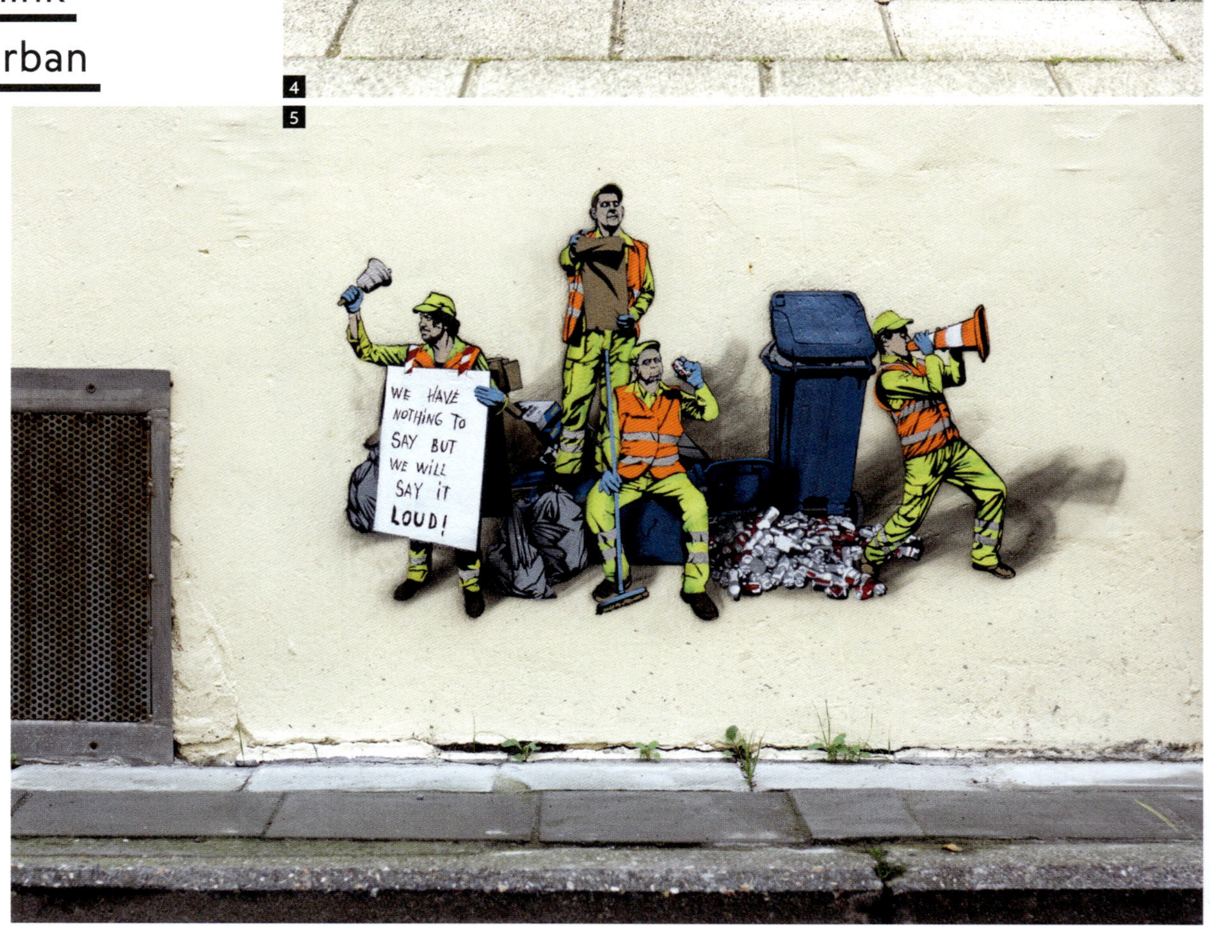

4 / 5
Ostend, Belgium, 2016
PHOTO BY THE ARTIST

6 /
Gaeta, Italy, 2019
PHOTO BY THE ARTIST

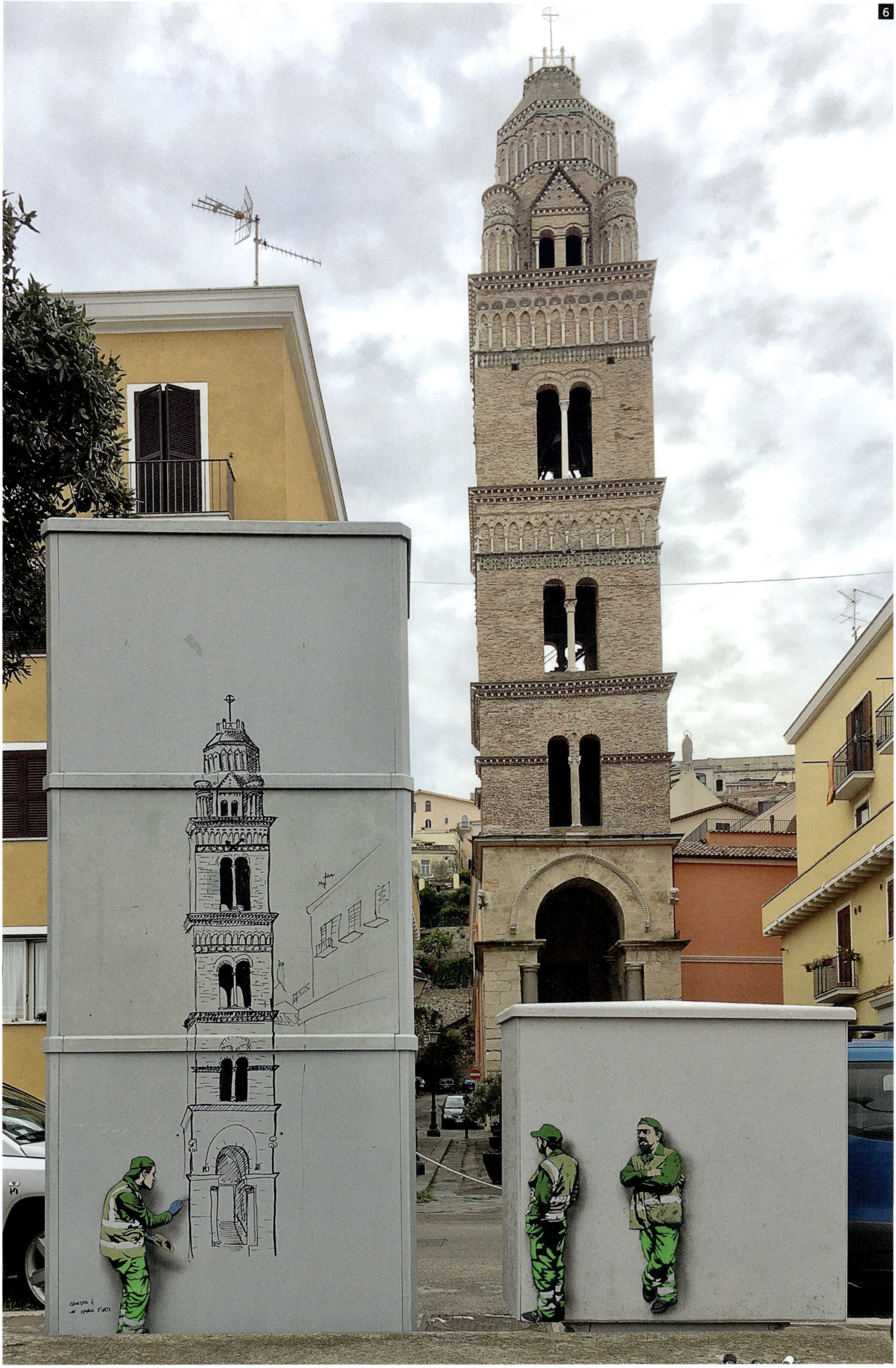

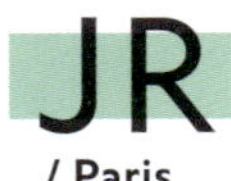

JR

/ Paris

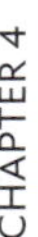

It would be close to impossible not to have heard of JR in the past few years. Although he had already made a name for himself through art activism, we have seen him grow bigger, more innovative and more socially engaged. During the 2016 Olympic Games in Rio, JR created two artworks in the city, adopting a completely novel material in its realisation: a massive installation on scaffolding, adding a third dimension to his work. To celebrate the 30th anniversary of the Louvre Pyramid, in an initiative that earned him the cover of *Beaux Art* magazine, he worked with hundreds of volunteers to create his largest installation to date, using paper and flour paste to reimagine the pyramid with an ephemeral optical illusion in 3D. On a slightly smaller, yet equally impressive, scale, 2017 saw JR react to the issues of border politics between Mexico and the United States by installing a playful yet powerful image of Kikito, a Mexican child from Baja, California, who is unable to enter the USA for immigration policy reasons.

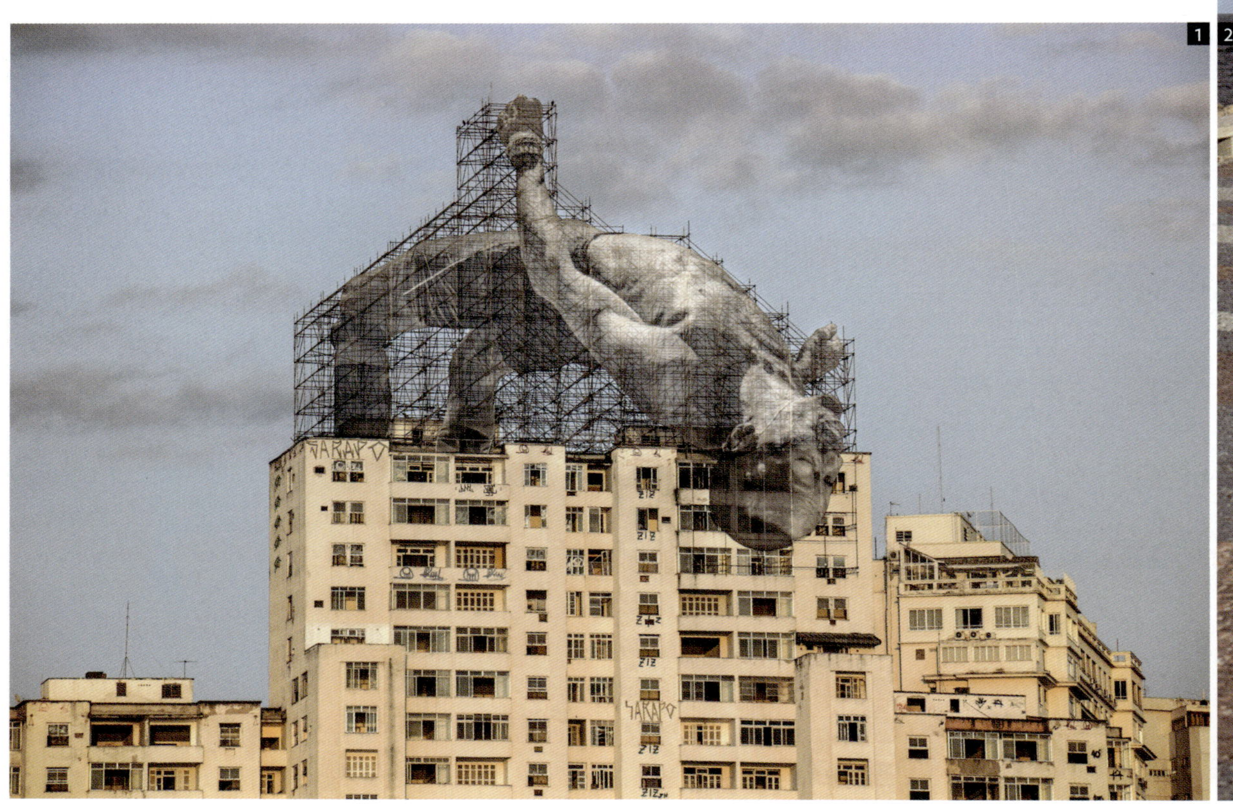

1 2

1 / 2
Rio de Janeiro, Brazil, 2016
PHOTO BY AGENCE VU

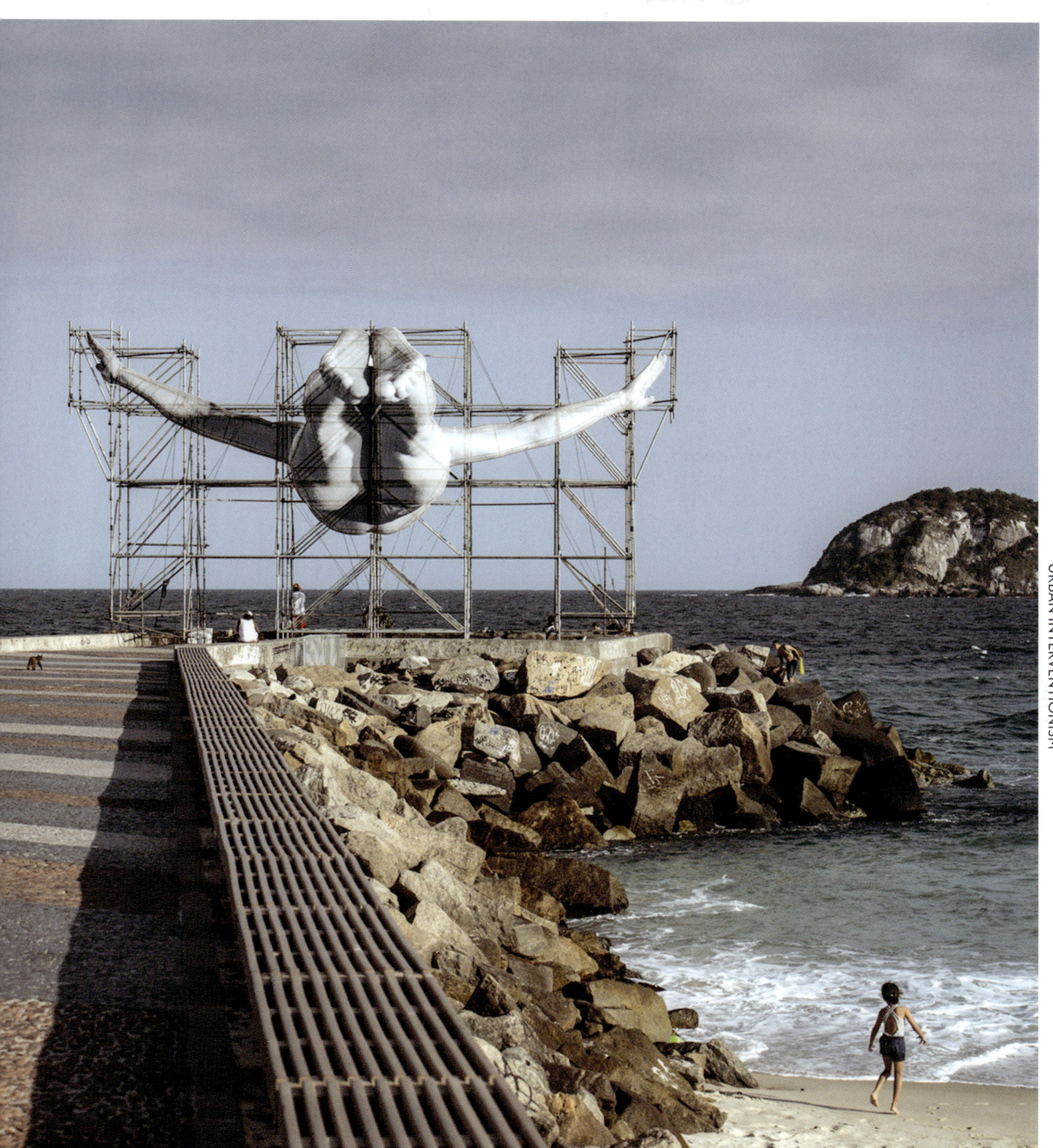

3

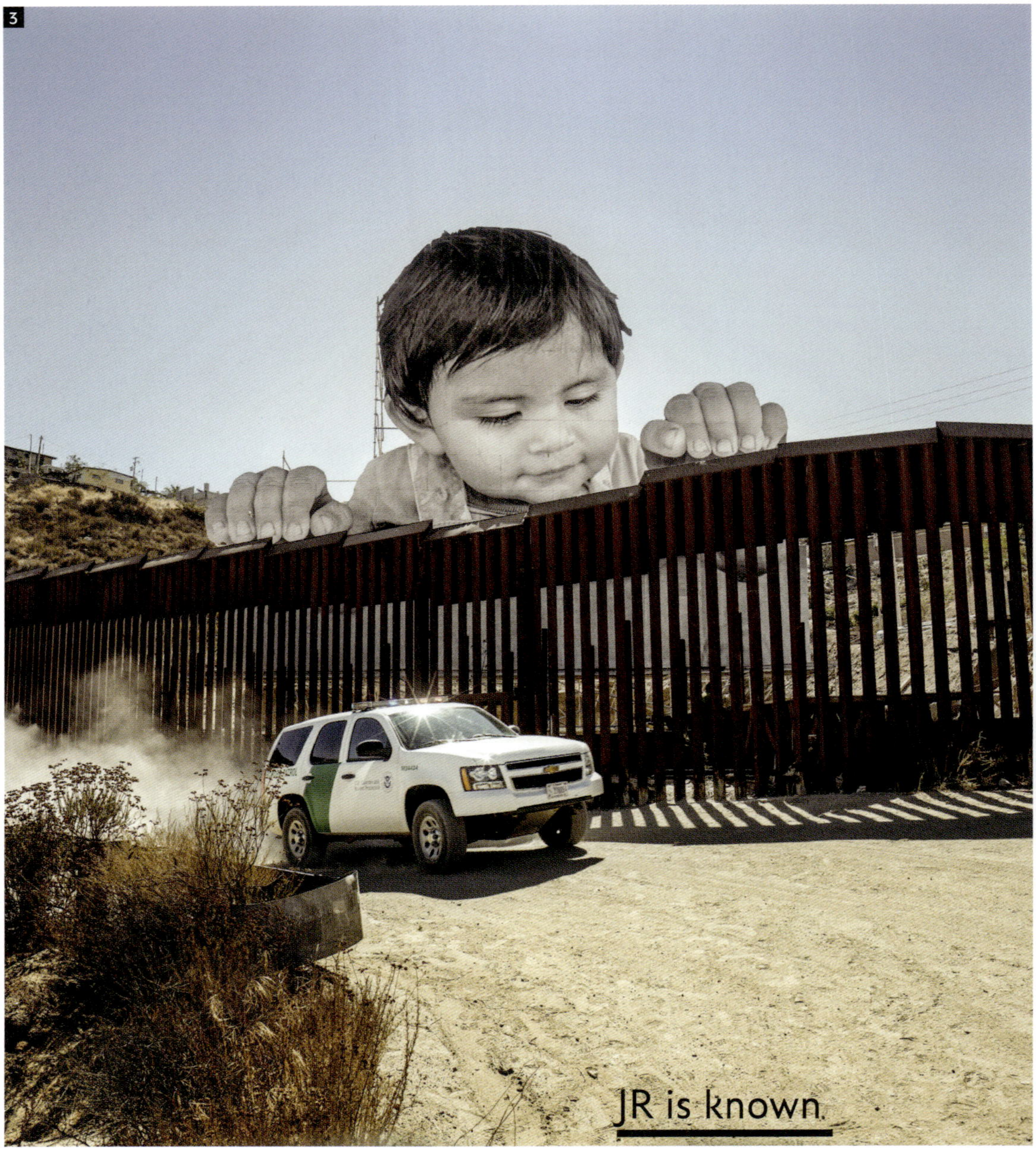

JR is known for adding an amazing third dimension to his work.

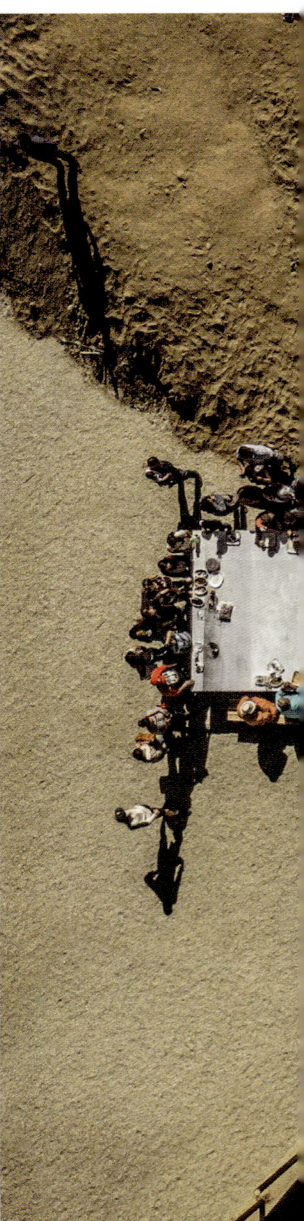

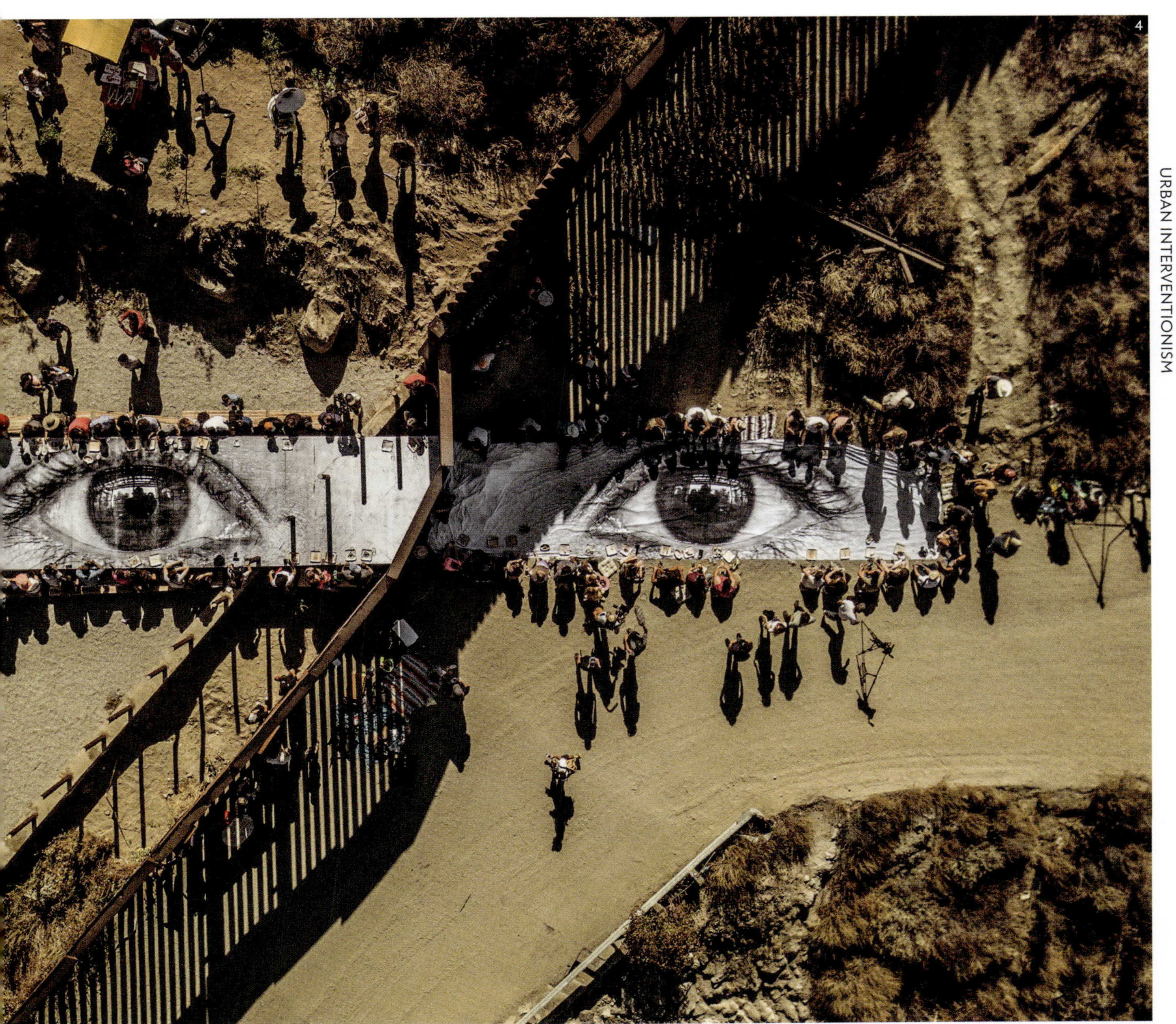

3 /
Tecate, Mexico, 2017
PHOTO BY AGENCE VU

4 /
Tecate, Mexico, 2017
PHOTO BY AGENCE VU

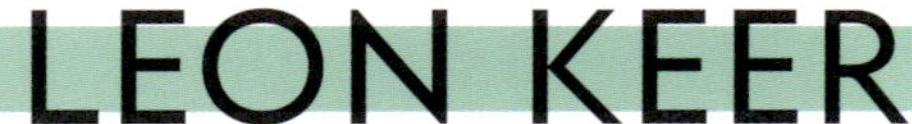

LEON KEER

/ Utrecht

Leon Keer is widely known as one of the pioneering artists in anamorphic street art. The technique, said to date back to the 15th century, distorts an image in such a way that the viewer must be placed in a very specific viewpoint in order to see the 3D visual appear. Keer has mastered this technique and is now commissioned to complete large-scale mural and indoor work around the world.

However, he is especially known for his pavement chalk drawings, decorating the streets with fictional landscapes. His illusions are attention grabbing. As viewers move around the work, a new world is formed and dissolves again, not only through perspective but due to a certain sense of 'uber-temporality' imposed by Keer's use of ephemeral chalk.

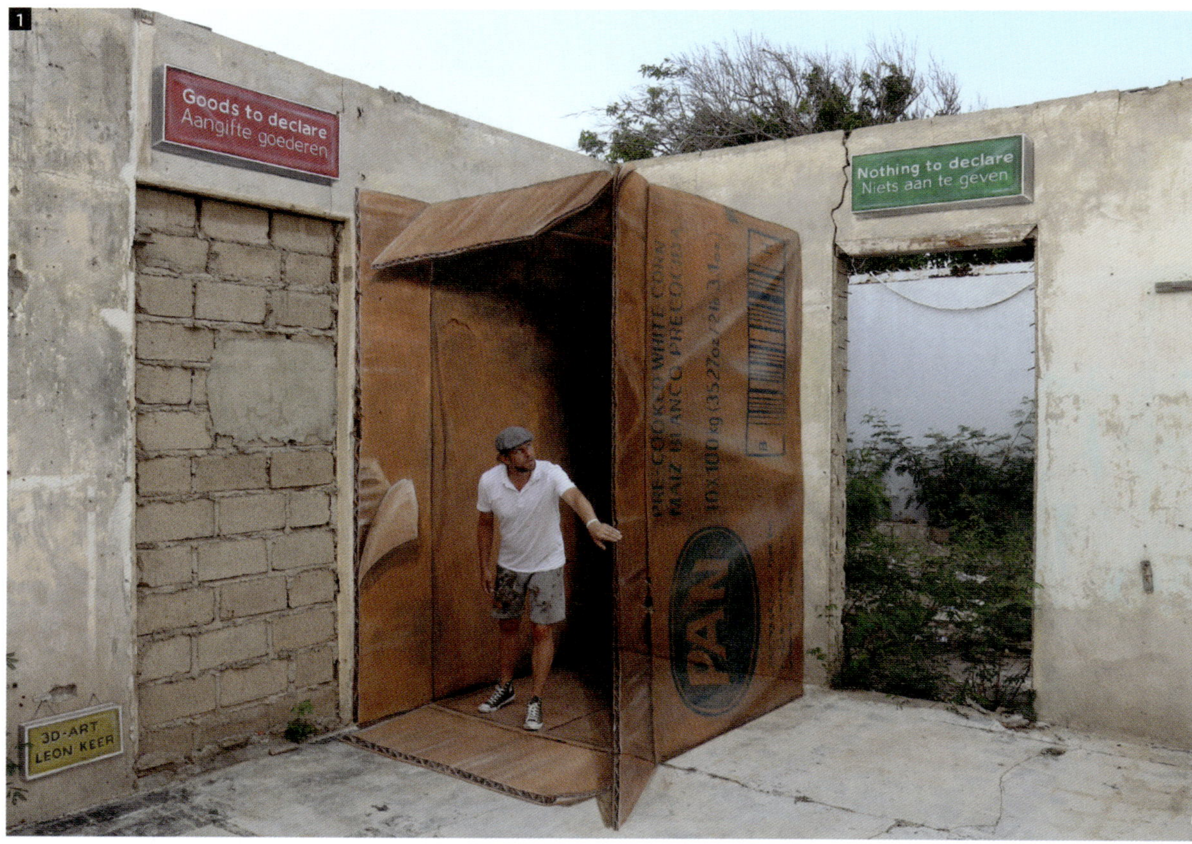

1 /
Sint Nicolaas, Aruba, 2016
PHOTO BY THE ARTIST

2 /
Mogilovo, Bulgaria, 2016
PHOTO BY THE ARTIST

3/
Miami, Florida, USA, 2018
PHOTO BY THE ARTIST

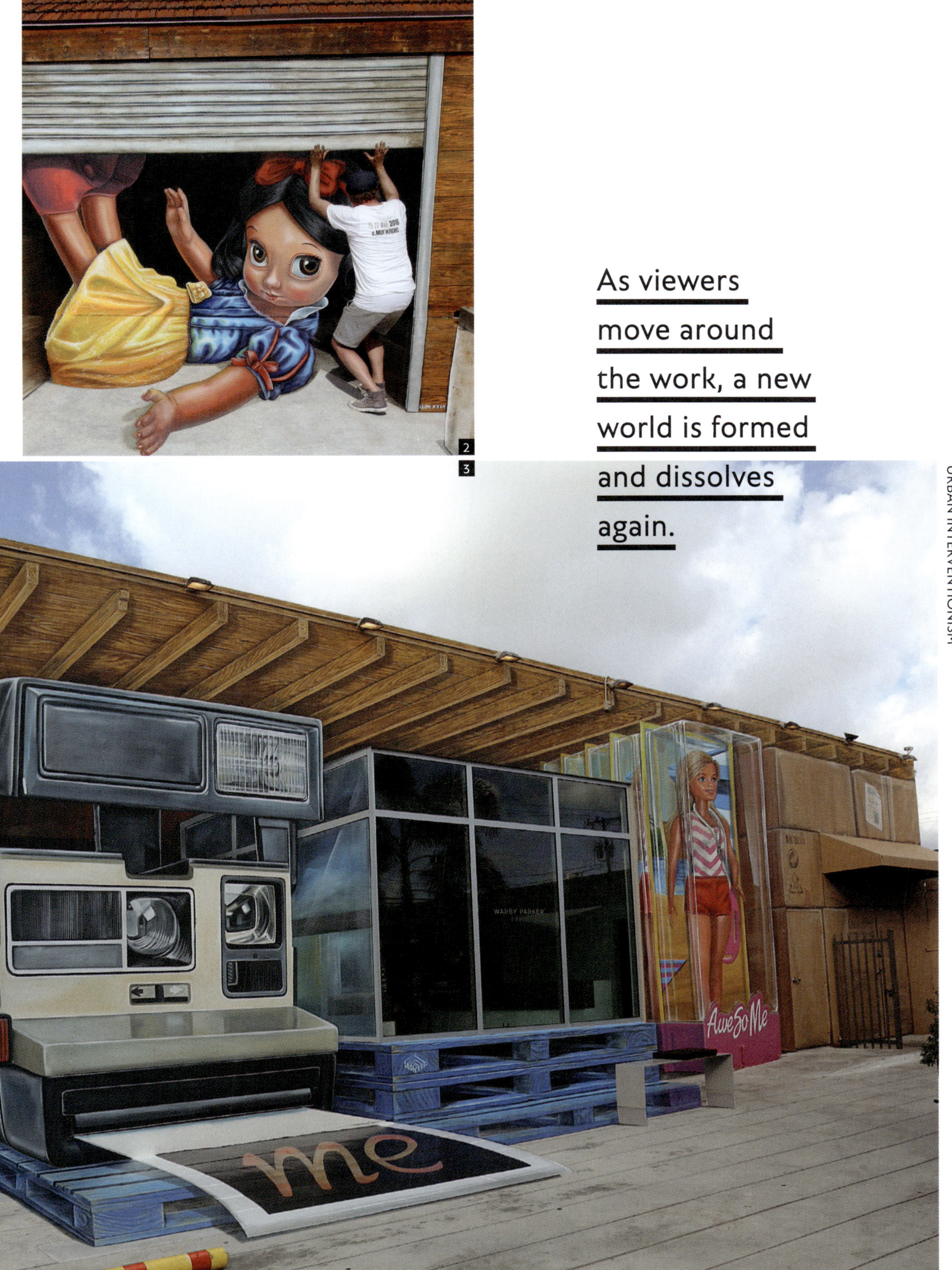

2
3

As viewers move around the work, a new world is formed and dissolves again.

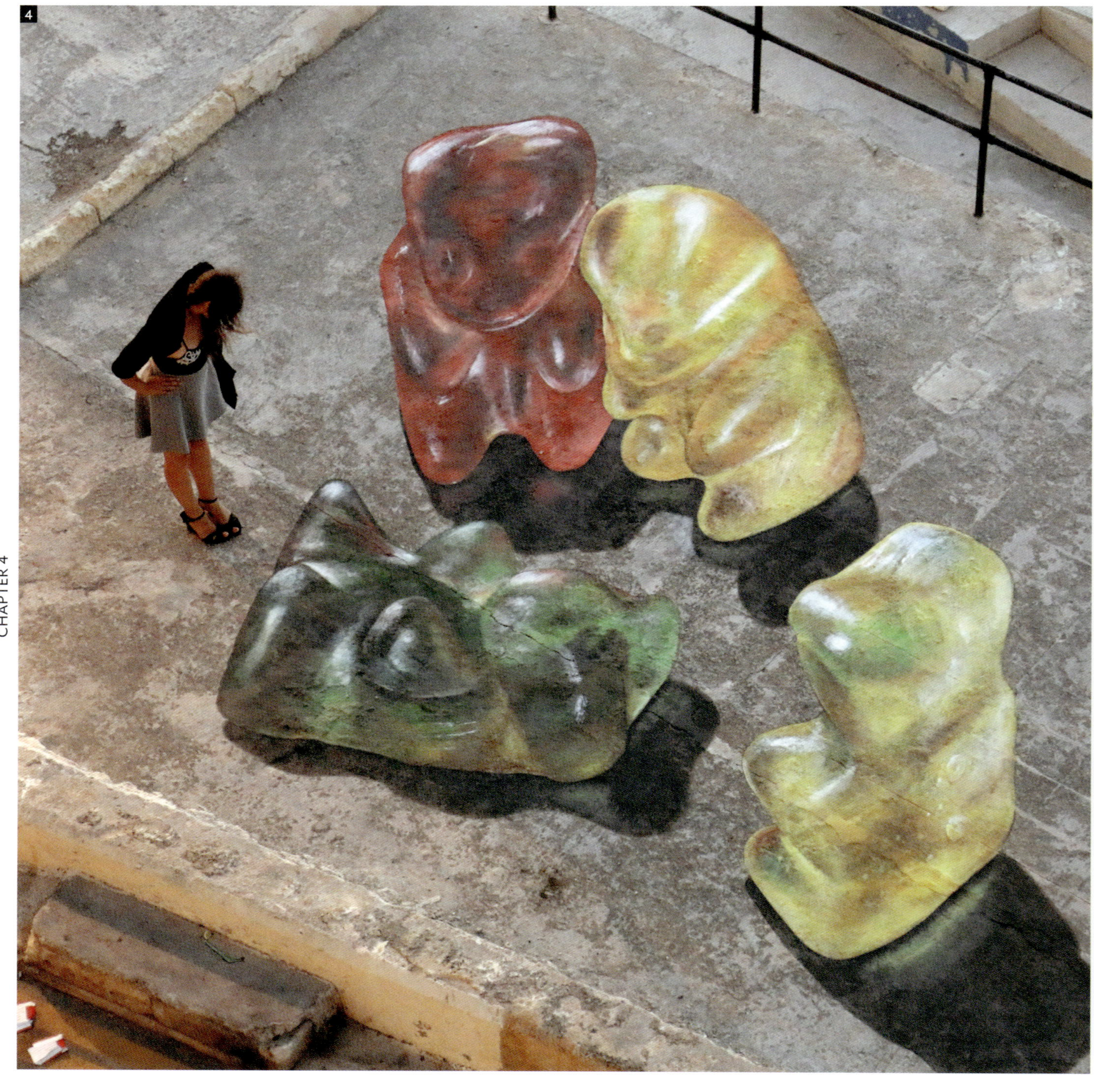

4 /
Malta, 2015
PHOTO BY THE ARTIST

5 / 6
Ostend, Belgium, 2019
PHOTO BY THE ARTIST

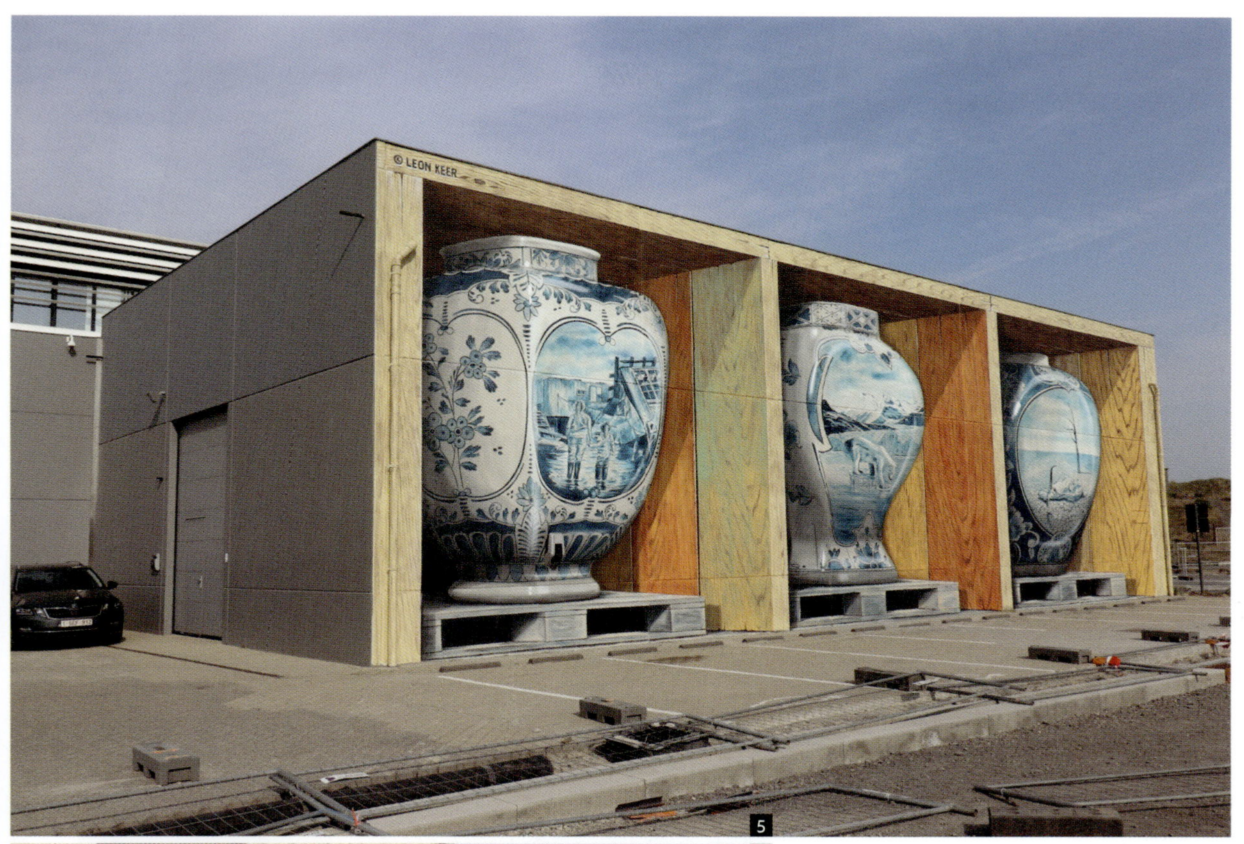

5

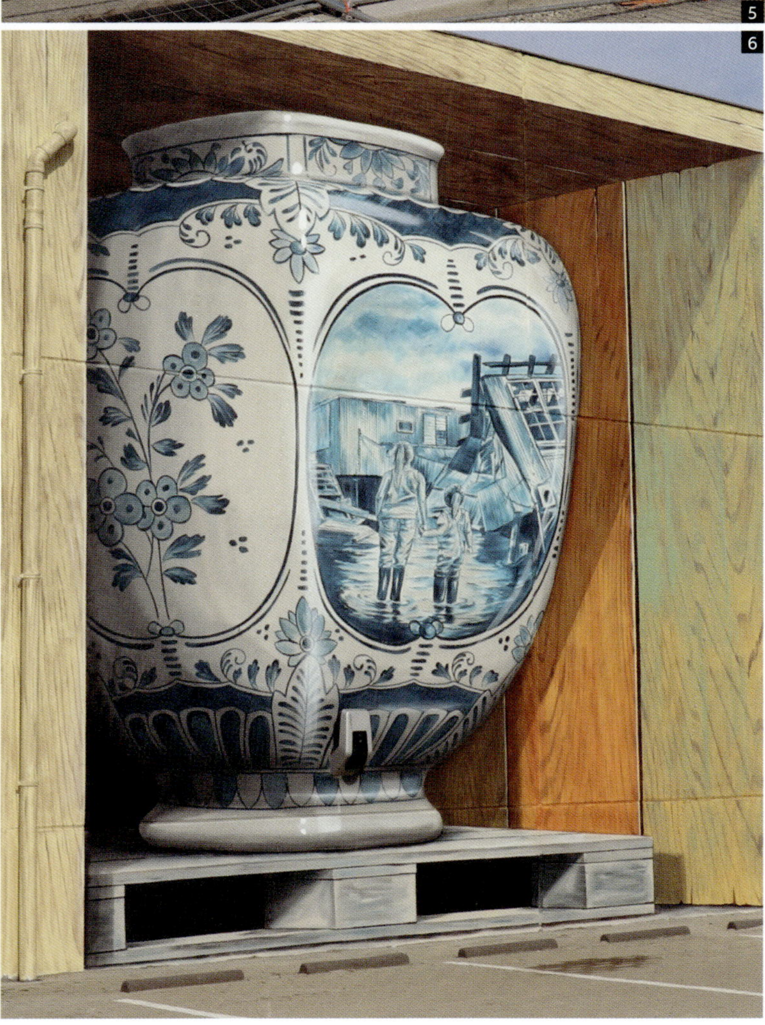
6

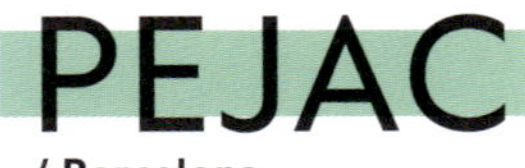

PEJAC

/ Barcelona

Since appearing in the previous edition of *Street Art Today*, Spanish artist Pejac has taken leaps forwards, evolving his practice to include a now-impressive repertoire of intervention techniques, moving on from the minimal black-and-white or trompe-l'oeil imagery for which he was originally known. He has stayed true to socially and environmentally engaged themes, with notable works bringing creativity to the Palestinian and Syrian refugee camps in Jordan. Pejac believes in art's inherent power as a tool of communication, stating: 'For me, art it is not a way to escape from the world conflicts, but to actually connect with them.'

1

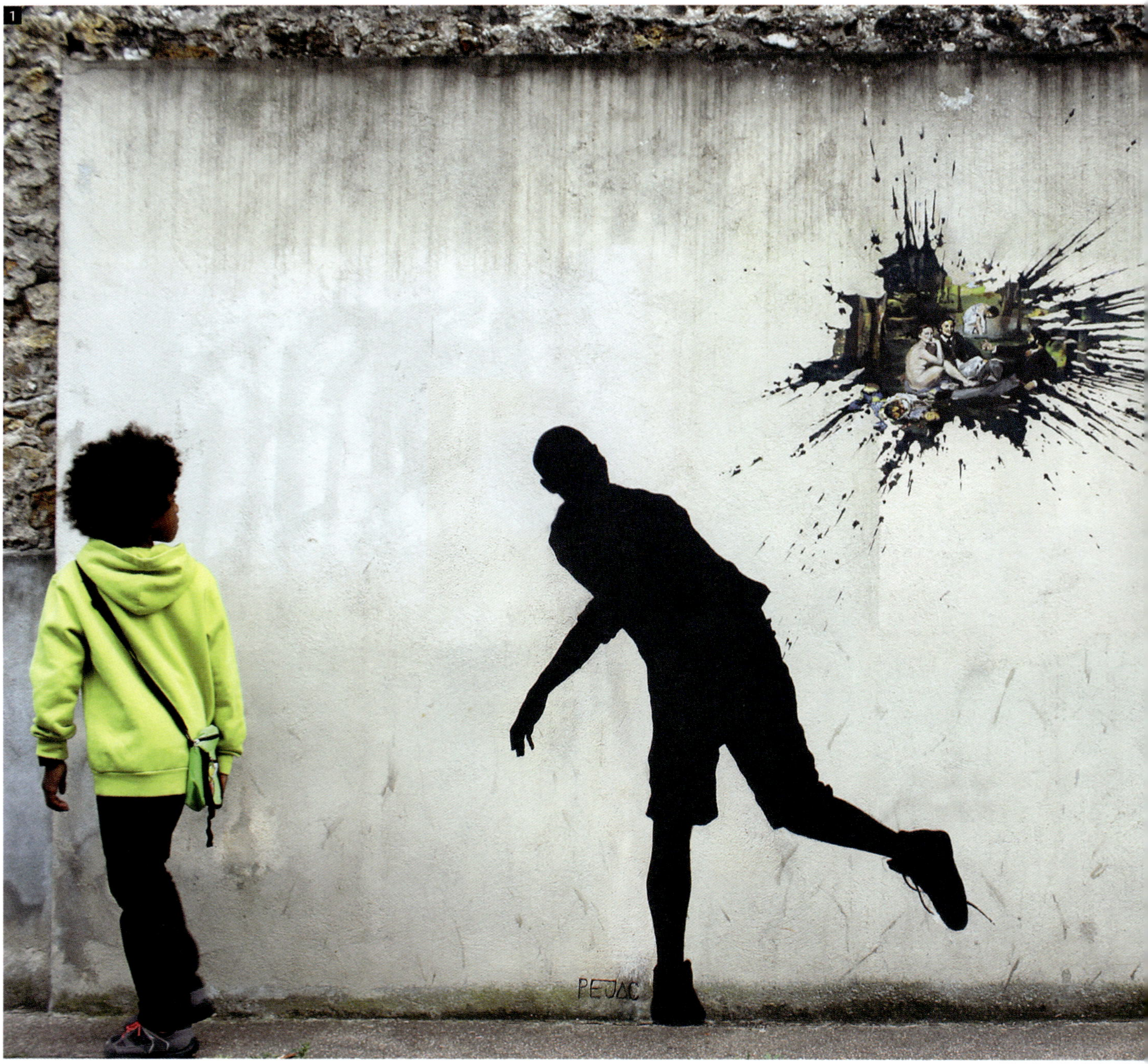

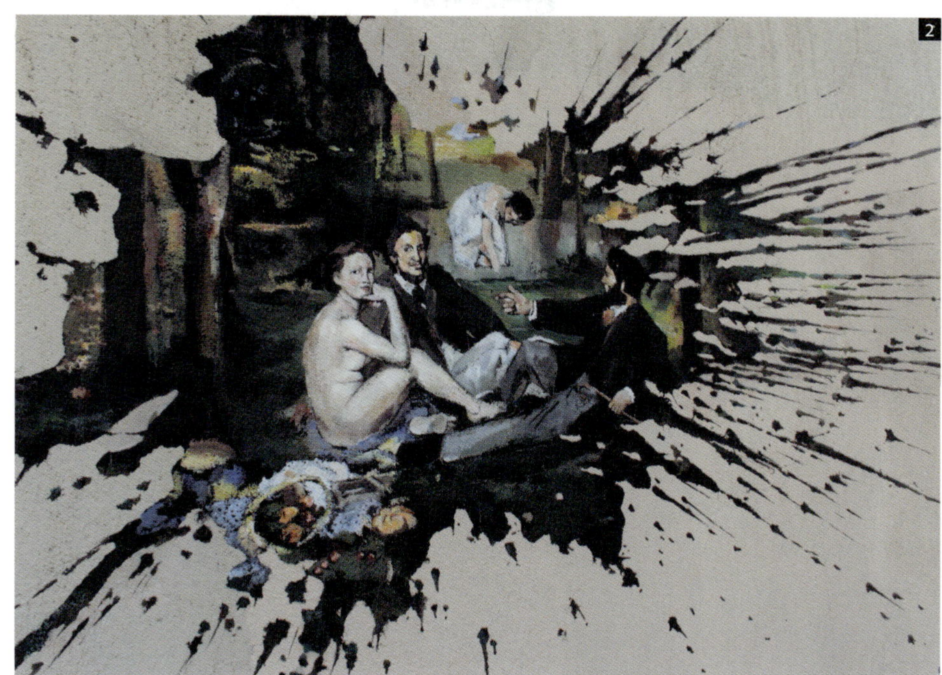

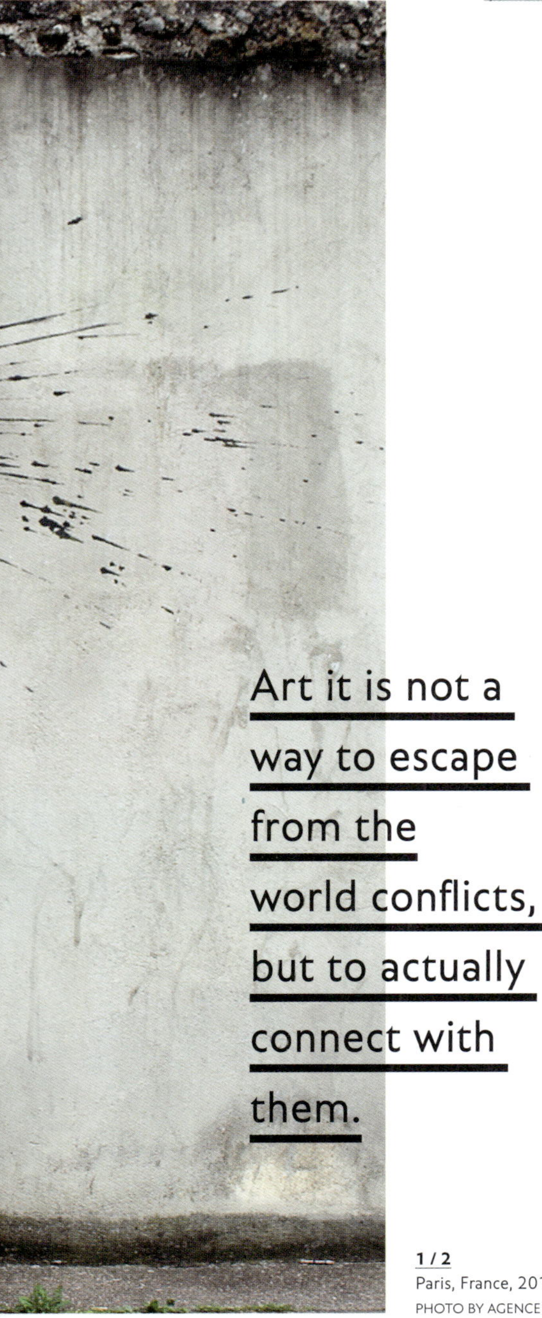

Art it is not a way to escape from the world conflicts, but to actually connect with them.

1 / 2
Paris, France, 2014
PHOTO BY AGENCE VU

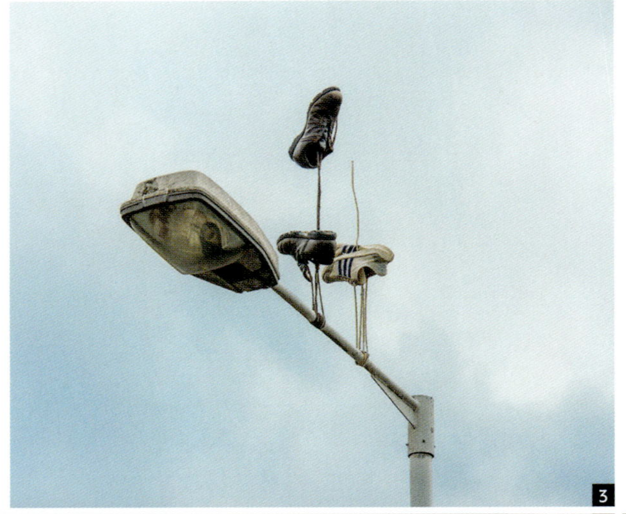

3

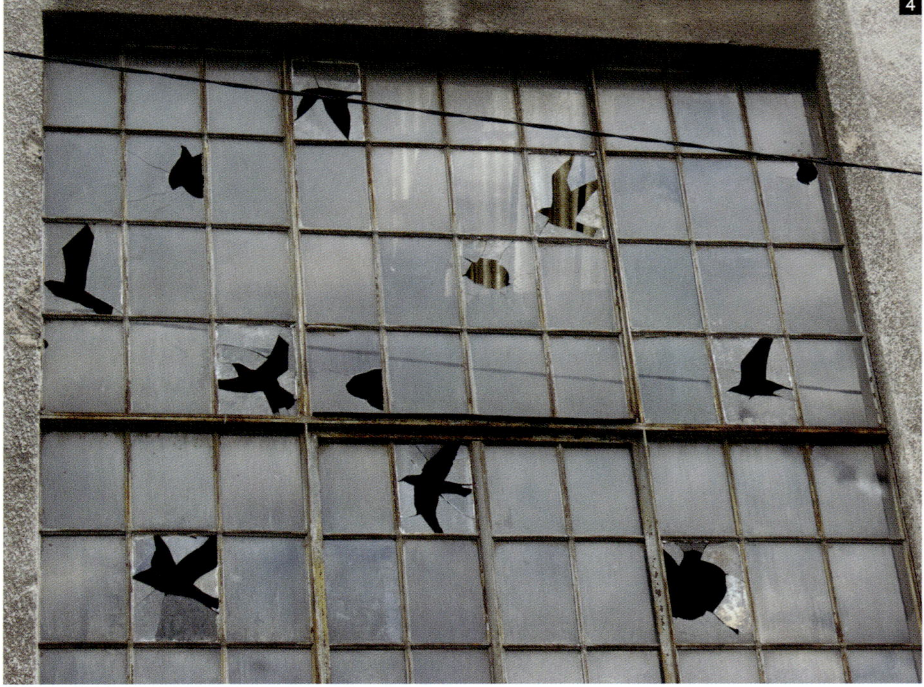

4

5

3 /
London, UK, 2016
PHOTO BY THE ARTIST

4 /
Rijeka, Croatia, 2016
PHOTO BY THE ARTIST

5 /
New York, USA, 2018
PHOTO BY THE ARTIST

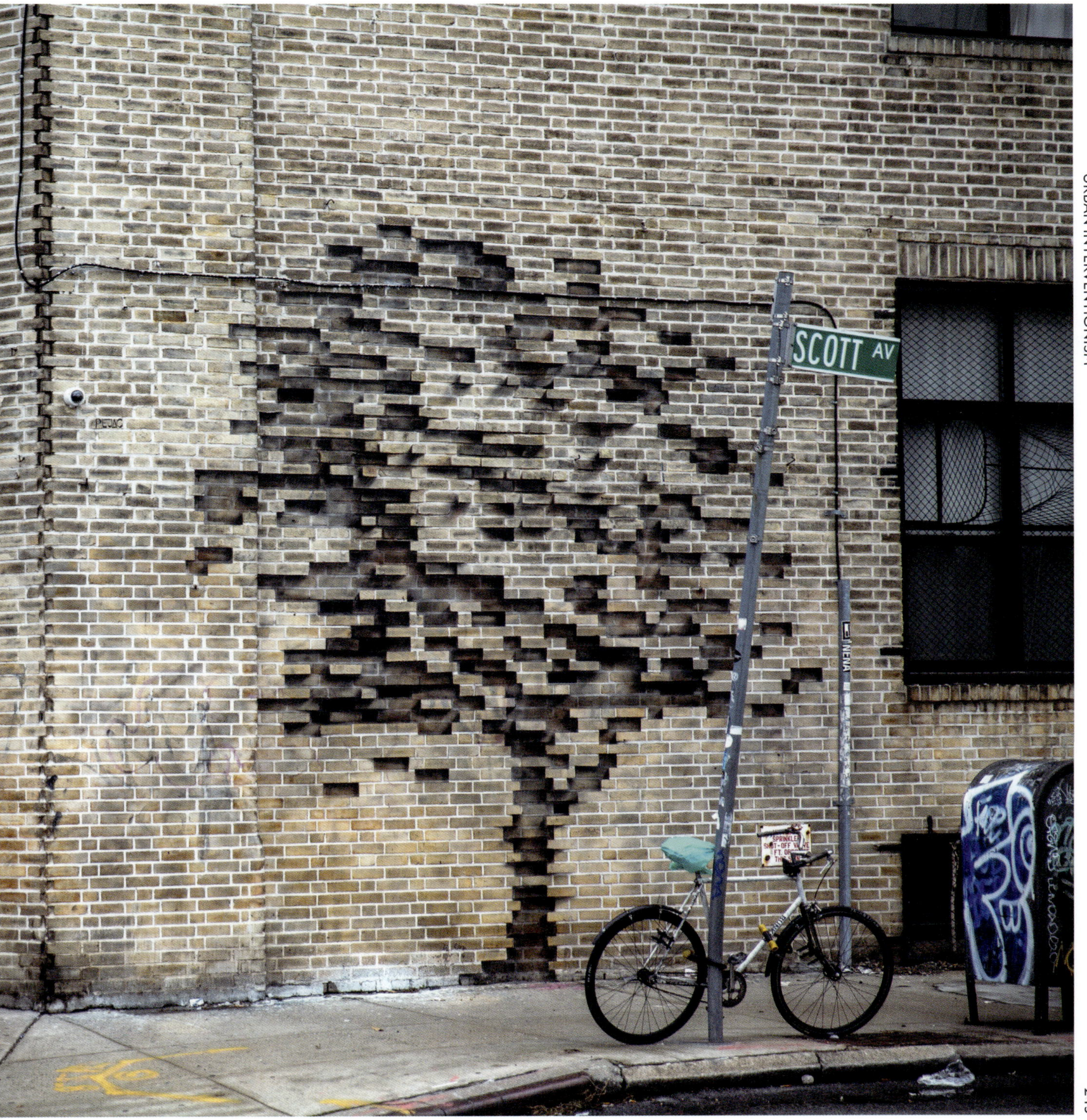
SCOTT AV
PEJAC

SHEPARD FAIREY

/ LA

Celebrating the 30th anniversary of the 'Obey the Giant' series this year, Shepard Fairey is now sitting pretty atop the brand commonly known as OBEY. With over one million followers on Instagram and a near-daily Twitter feed, he is known to aggressively promote the values he holds dear. A true believer in punk rock, and unashamed political activist, Fairey achieves studio output like an unheeding factory, with works pouring out at all times of the year.

From where he started out in stickers and flour paste, the sheer scale of his works has evolved to colossal heights. With imagery covering huge buildings, billboards and urban landscapes worldwide, he seems to have achieved his original goal: generating interest, reclaiming the streets and fighting the Giant.

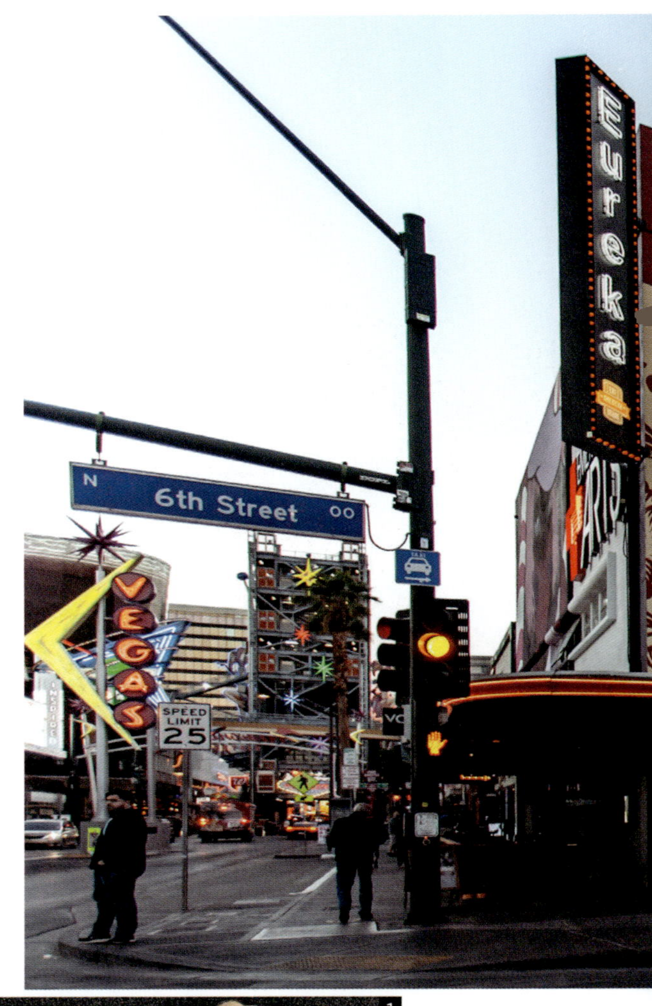

Shepard Fairey seems to have achieved his original goal: generating interest, reclaiming the streets and fighting the Giant.

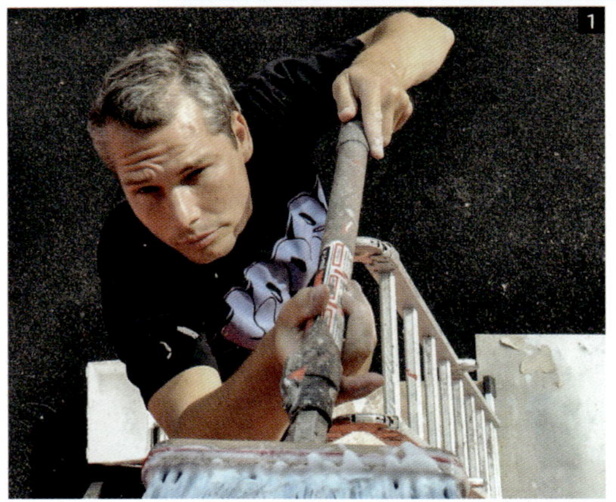

1 /
Shepard Fairey
PHOTO BY HENRIK HAVEN

2 /
Las Vegas, Nevada, USA, 2016
PHOTO BY VINNY CORNELLI

3 /
Berlin, Germany, 2014
PHOTO BY HENRIK HAVEN

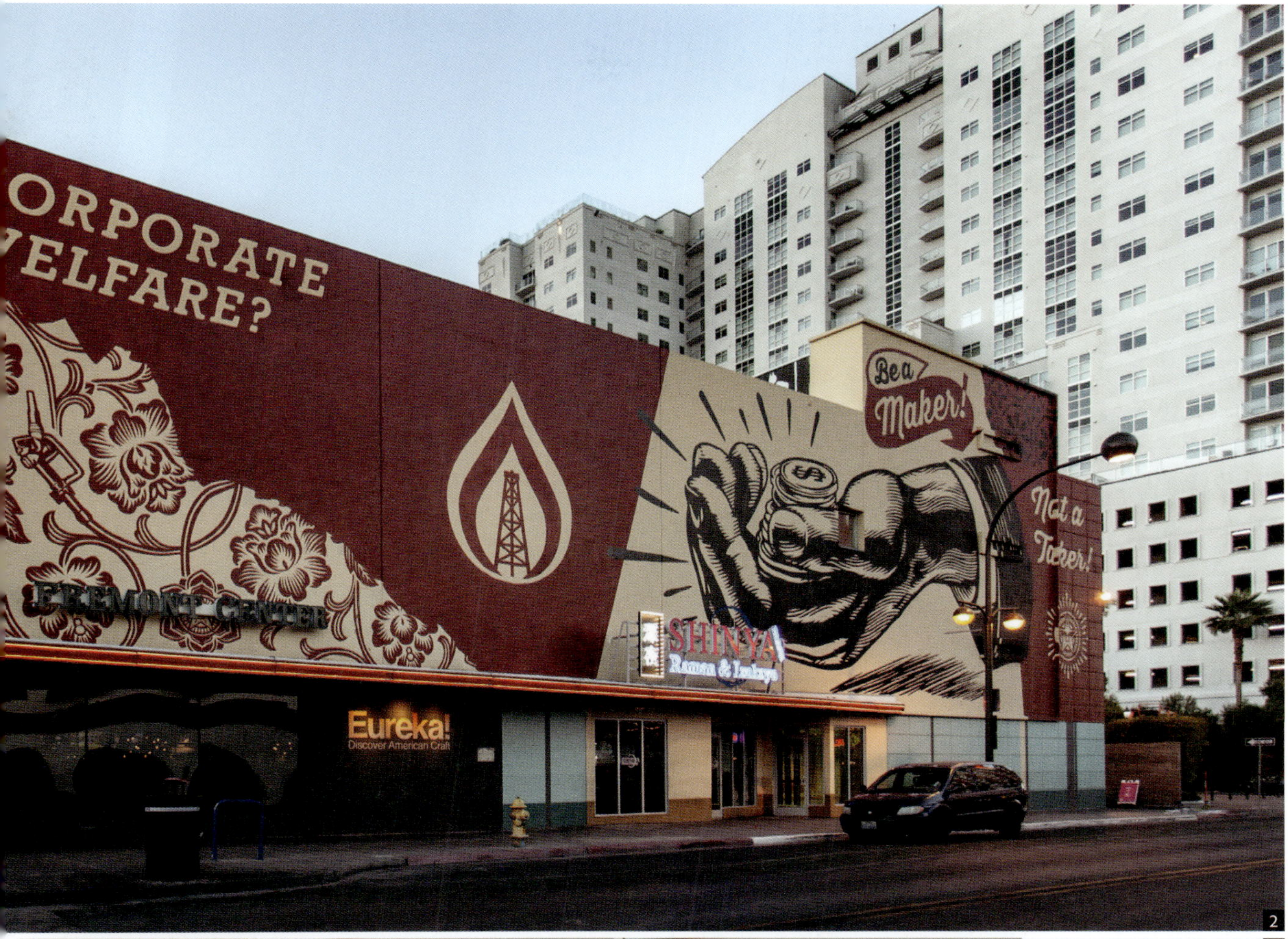

2

3

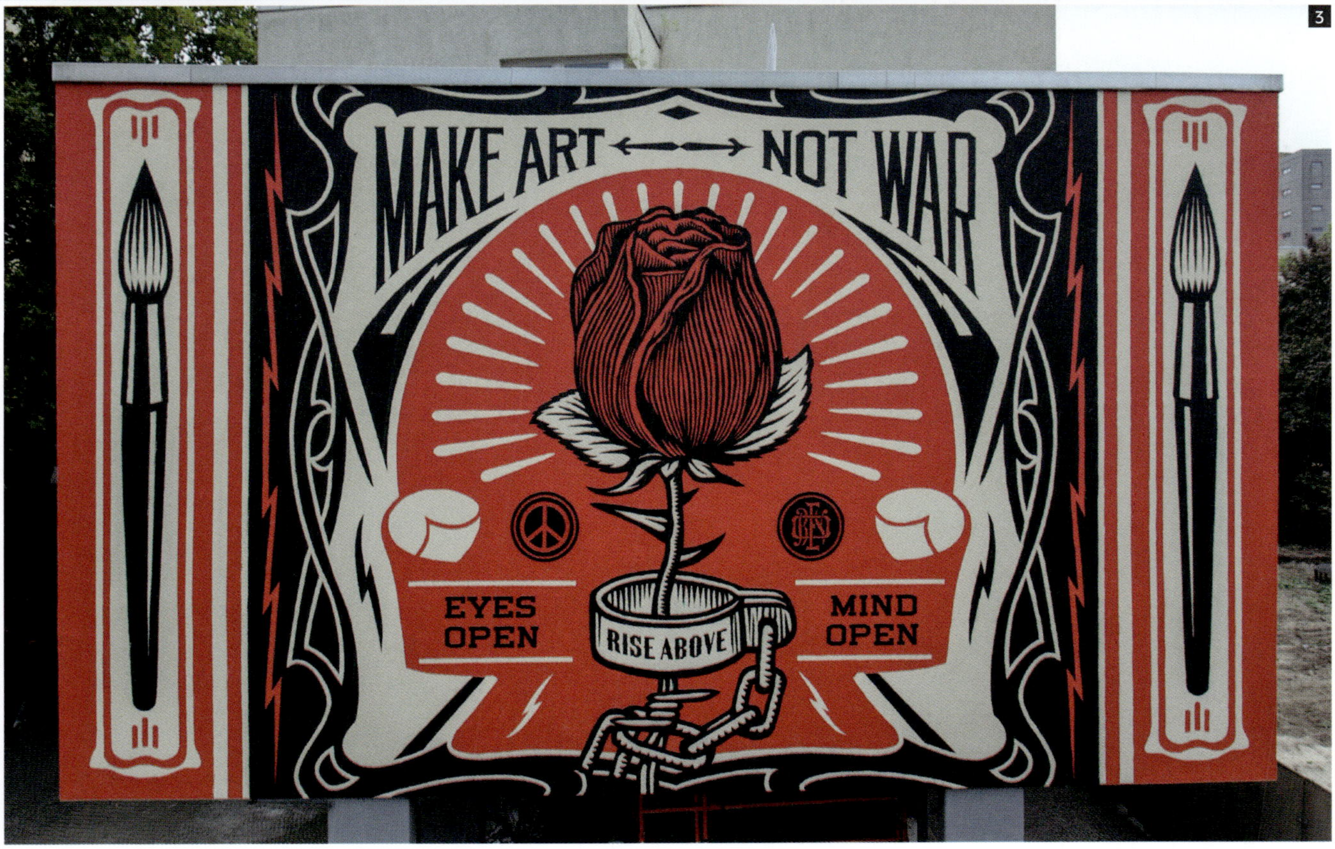

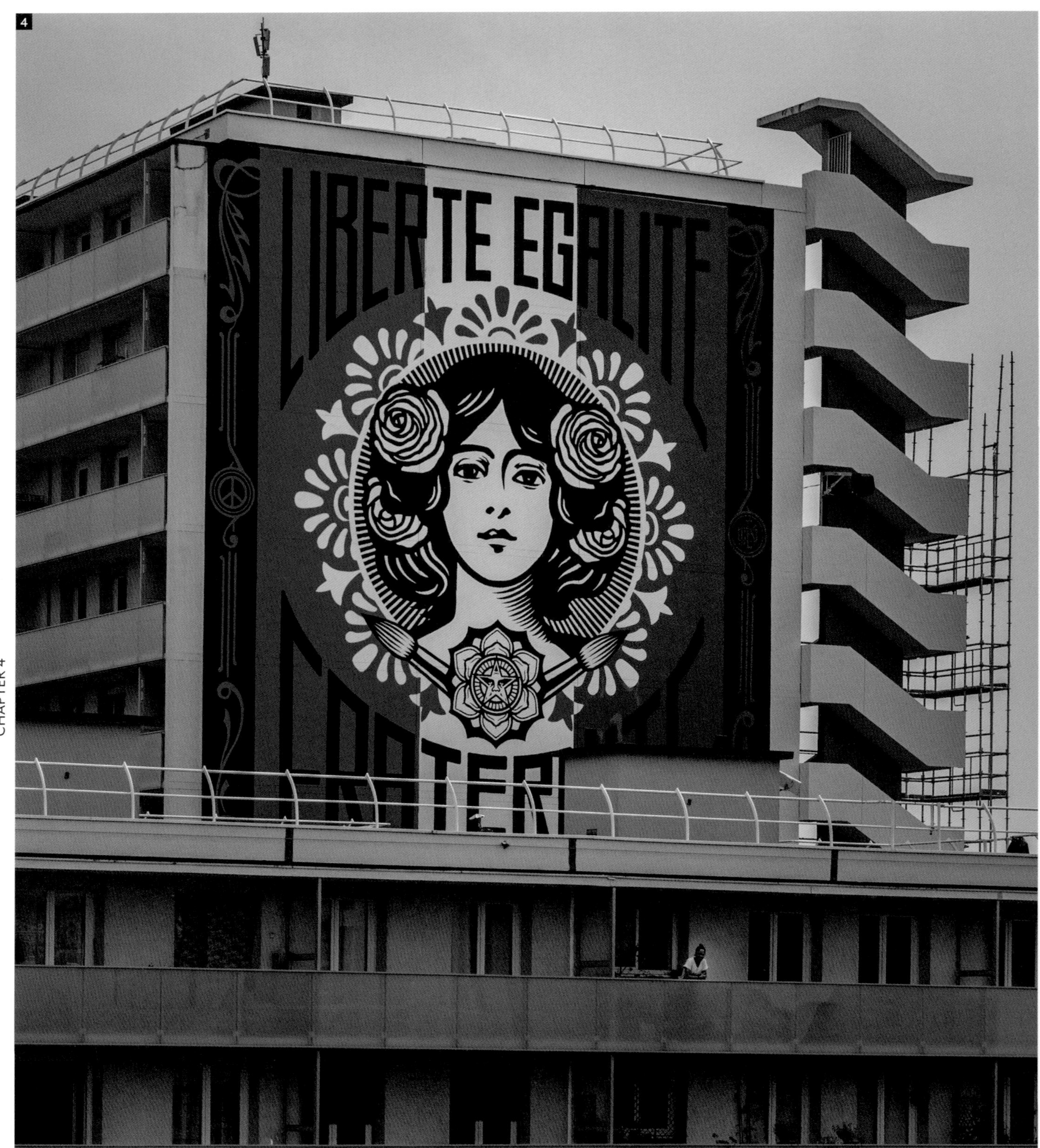

CHAPTER 4

4 /
Paris, France, 2018
PHOTO BY VINNY CORNELLI

5 /
Las Vegas, Nevada, USA, 2017
PHOTO BY HENRIK HAVEN

6 /
Seminyak, Bali, 2015
PHOTO BY VINNY CORNELLI

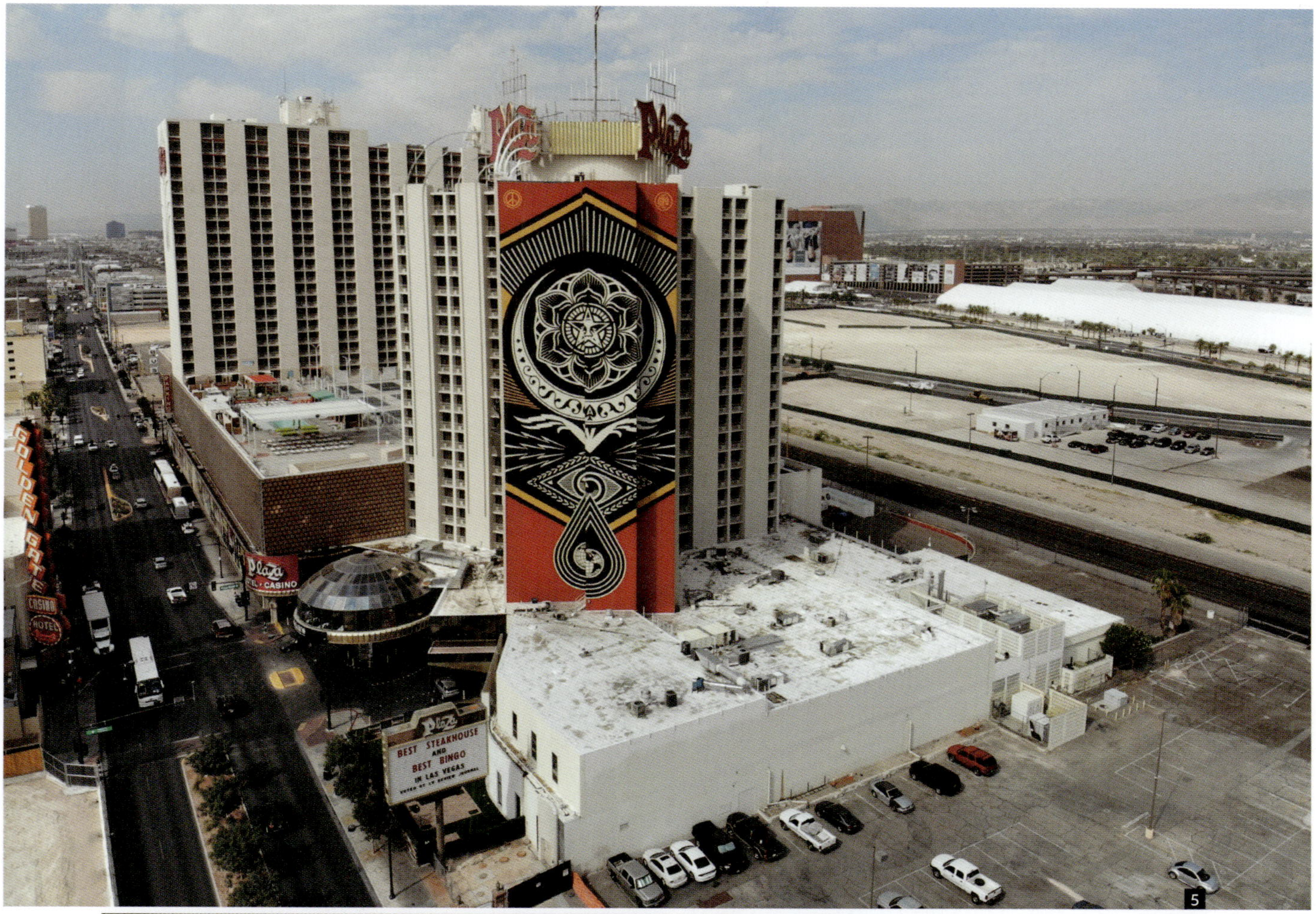

5

6

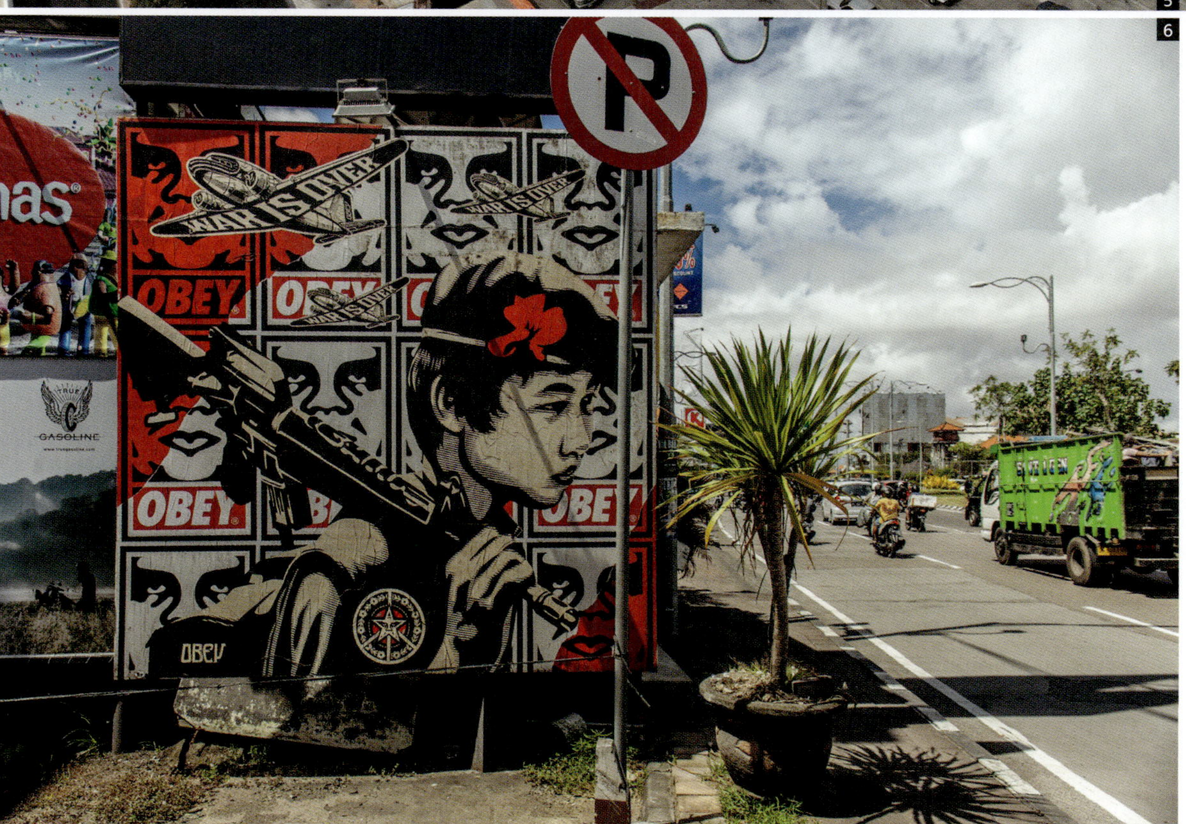

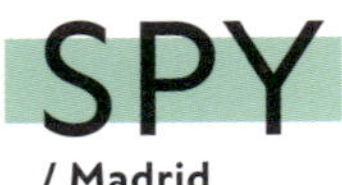

SPY

/ Madrid

One of the founding influencers of Madrid's graffiti scene, SpY has been producing in urban contexts for over 30 years, influencing several generations of Spanish and international creatives. The tongue-in-cheek urbanite regards the city landscape as his palette and architectural elements as his canvas, with found objects rearranged as sculptural compositions. Unbound to any particular medium or material, his works may be made from anything from barriers to chewing gum, grass to gold, light to paint, with clever humour and questioning commentary as his constant. SpY proposes simple yet unique gestures that allow us to rethink the human-in-city concept with honest yet critical playfulness.

Unbound to any particular medium or material, his works can be made from anything.

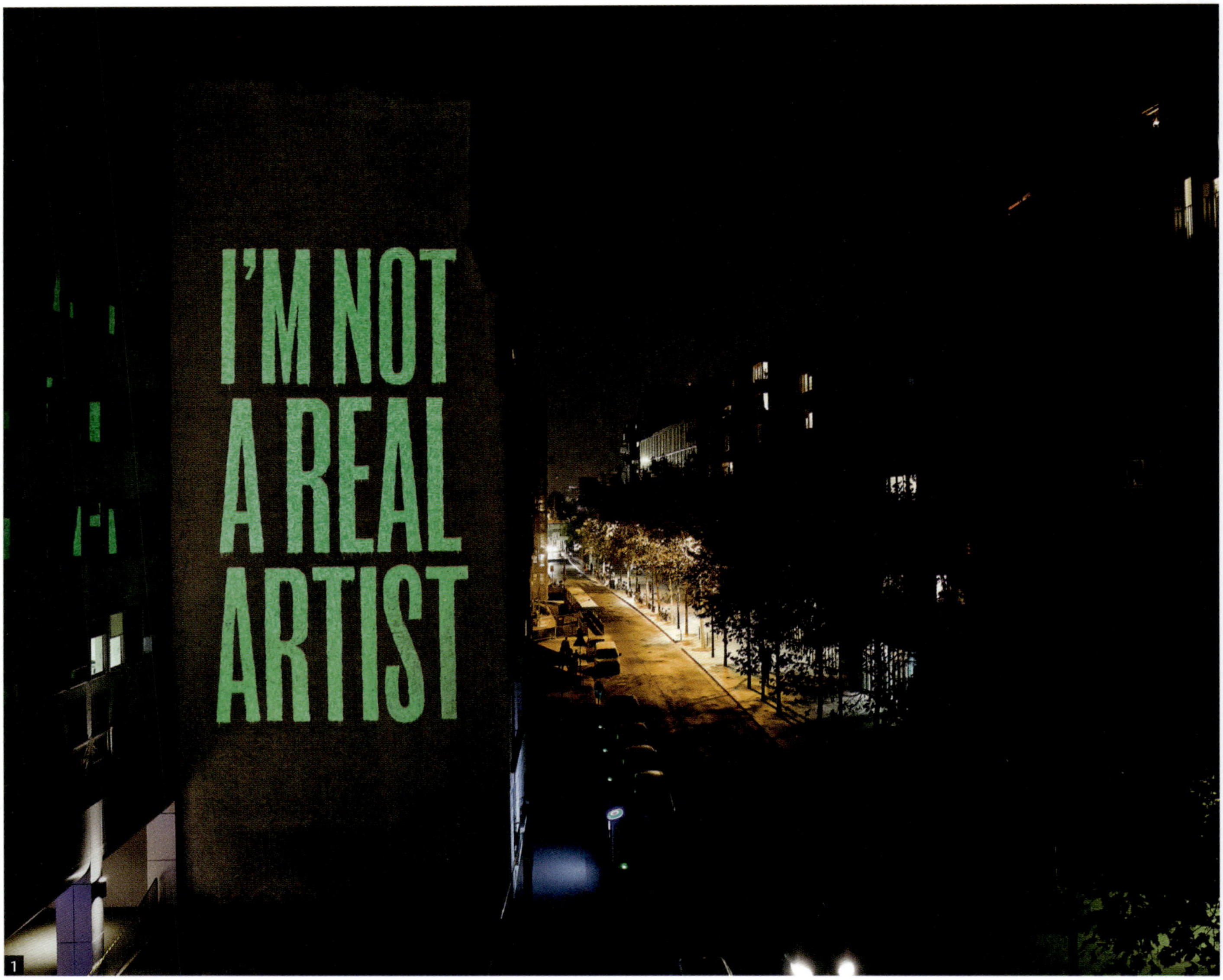

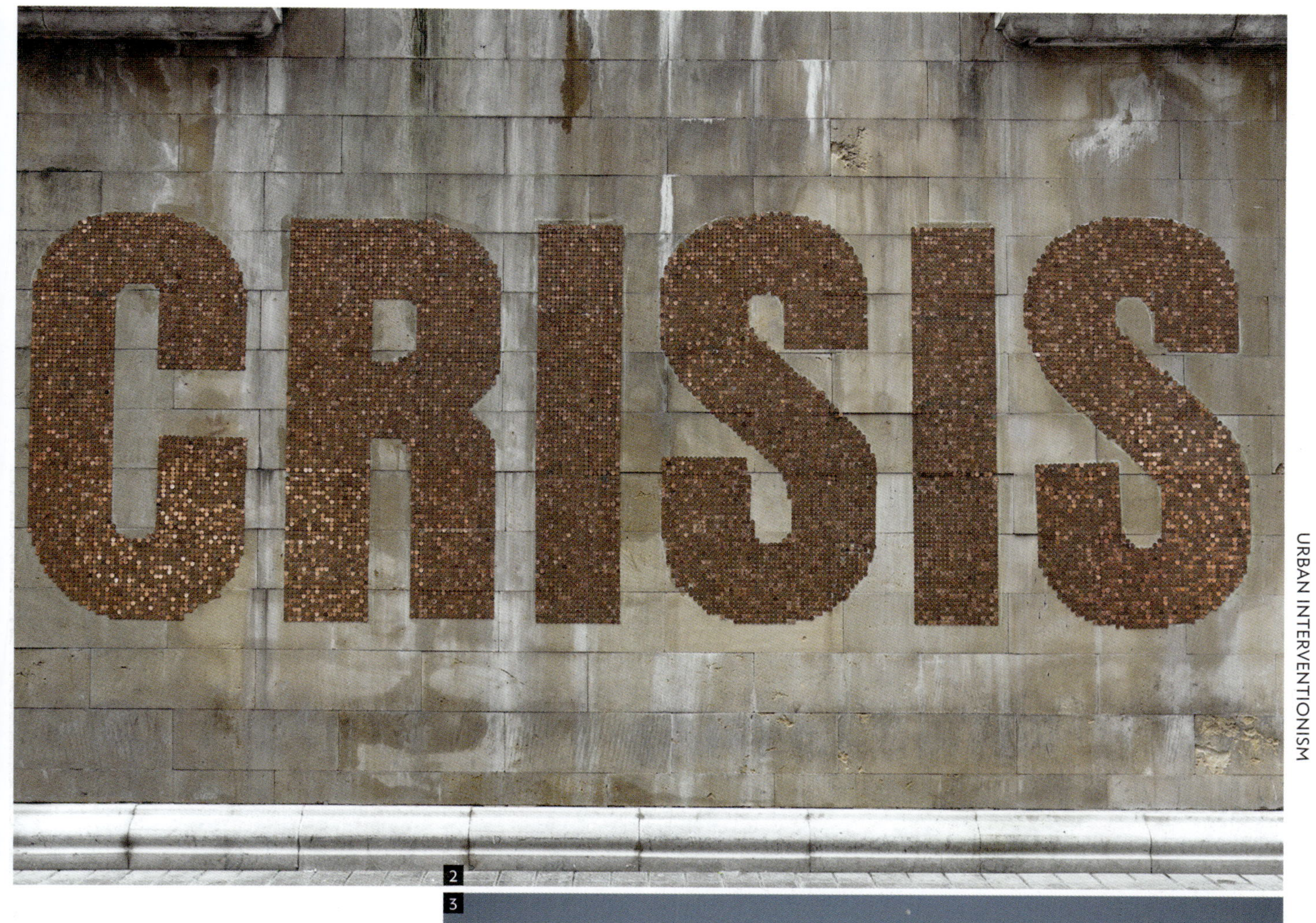

2

3

1 /
Paris, France, 2014
PHOTO BY THE ARTIST

2 /
Bilbao, Spain, 2015
PHOTO BY THE ARTIST

3 /
Ostend, Belgium, 2017
PHOTO BY IAN COX

4

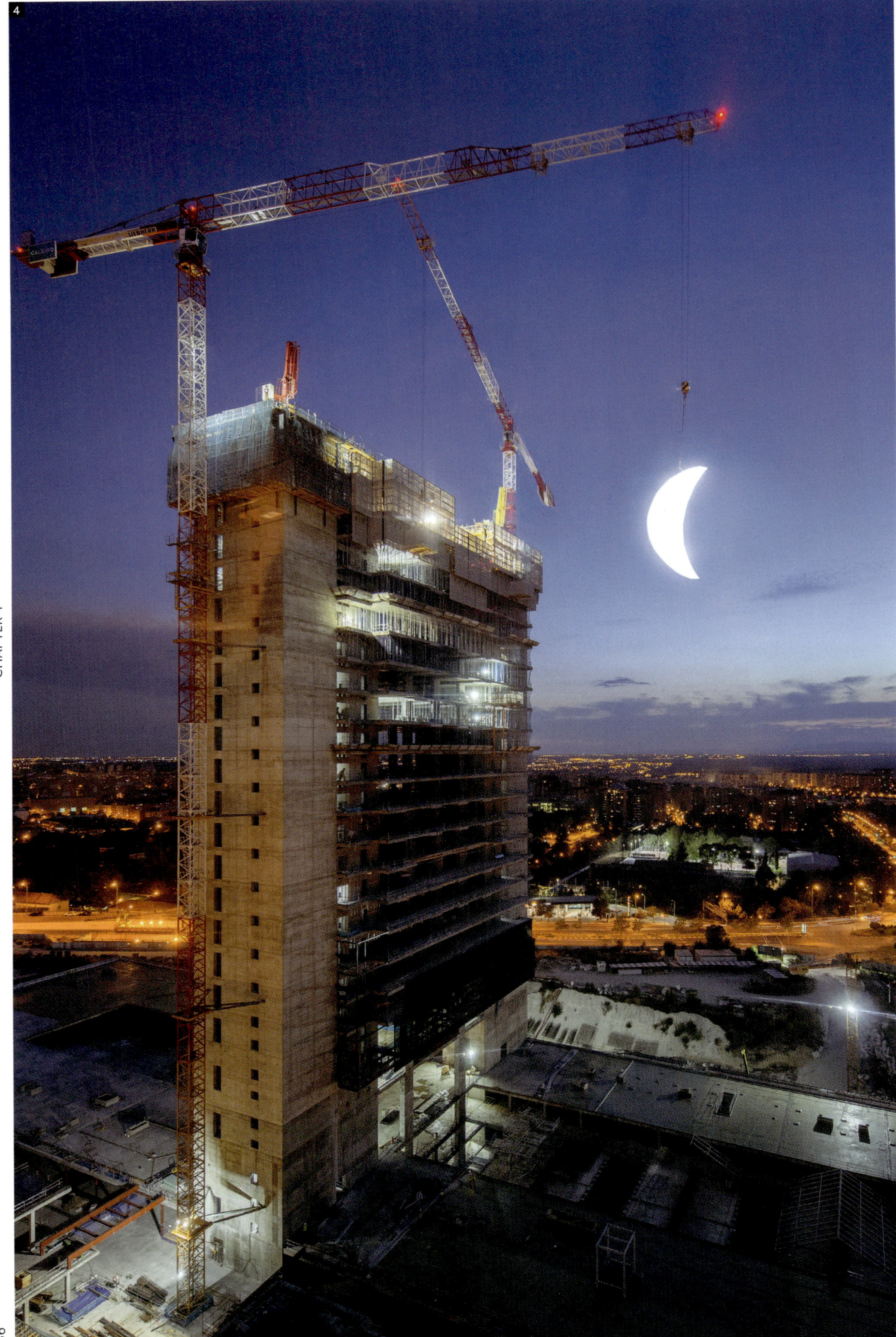

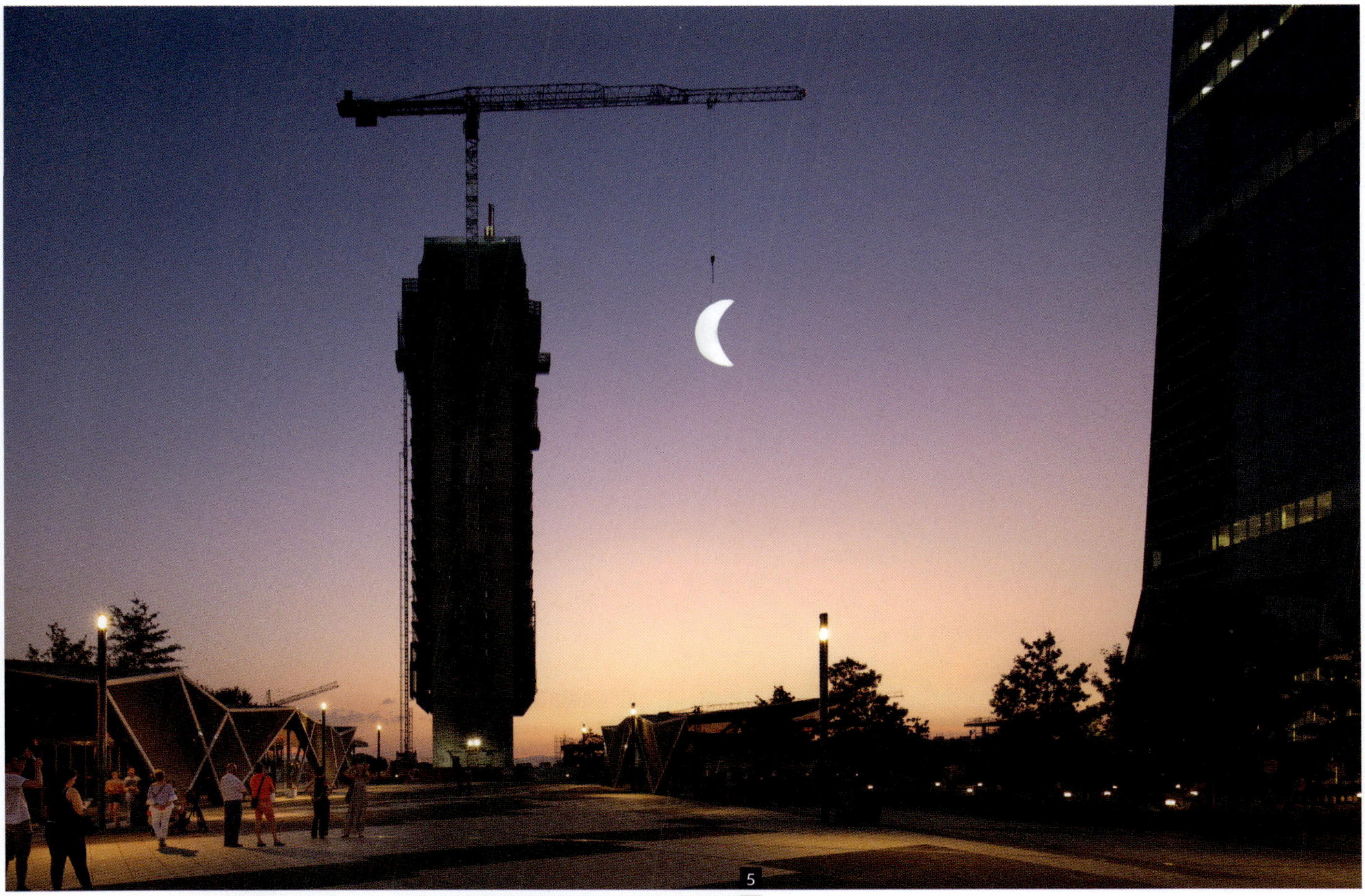

5

6

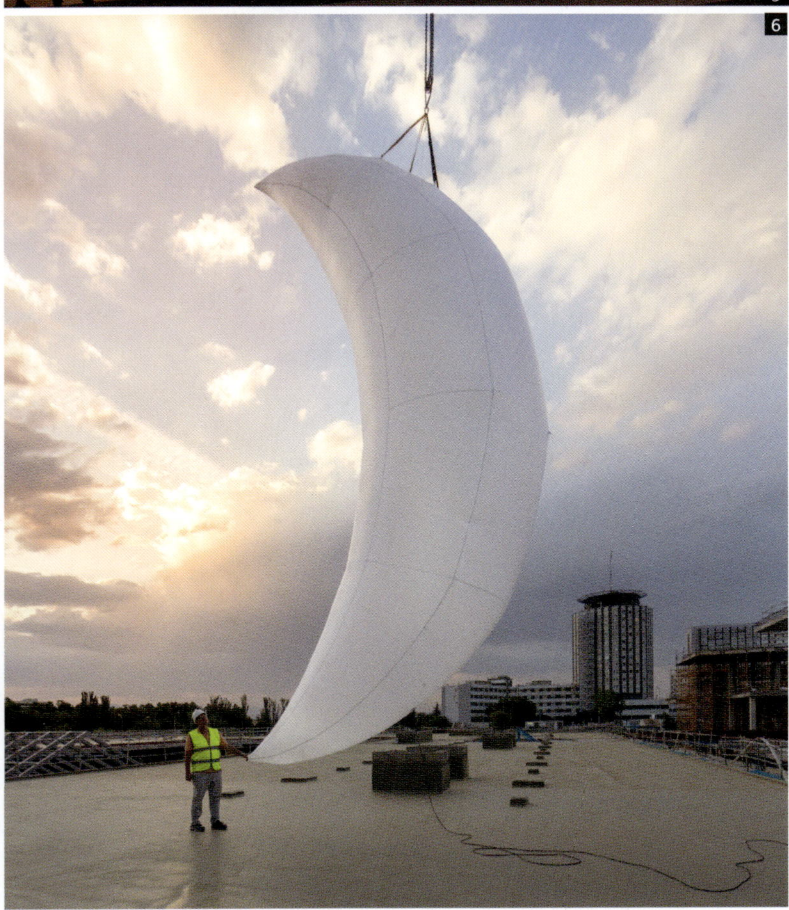

4 / 5 / 6
Madrid, Spain, 2019
PHOTO BY THE ARTIST

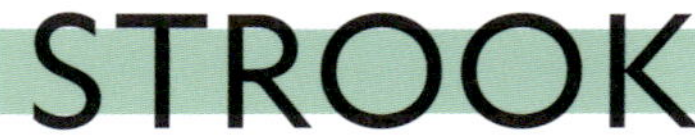

STROOK

/ Bruges

Belgian artist Stefaan De Croock creates large-scale mural interventions as part of the project 'Strook'. A graphic designer by education, his interest lies in the narrative transcribed through materials and textures. His geometric paned portraits are composed of found materials that he 'harvests' from construction sites and abandoned spaces. Mostly made of wood, these objects and their organic surfaces and shades inspire his work, comprising a narrative of place and history with simple yet precise linear compositions that come together to form portrait busts.
For Stefaan, each weathered board, each wind-worn panel, is testament to a unique past, readable and precious in our shared narrative of place.

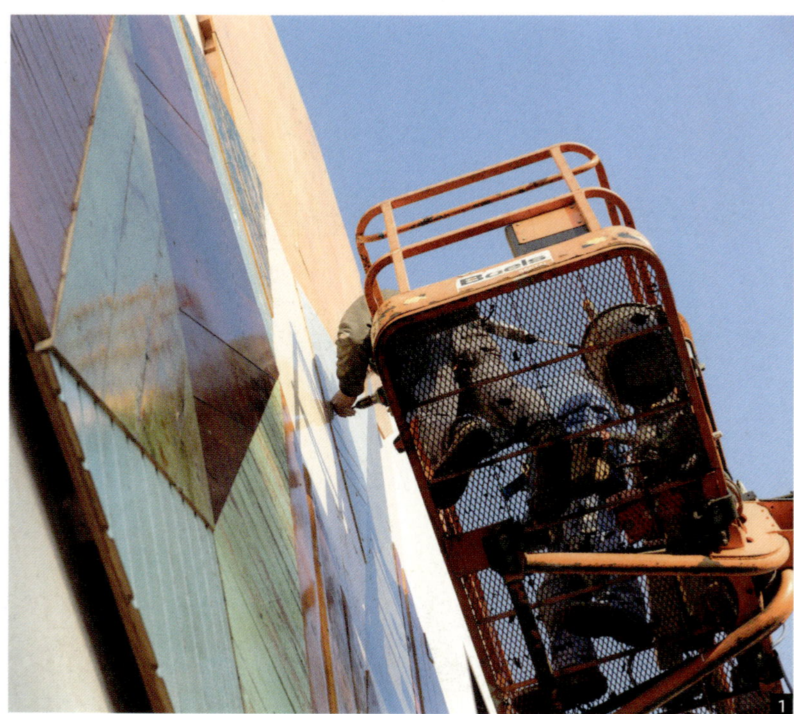

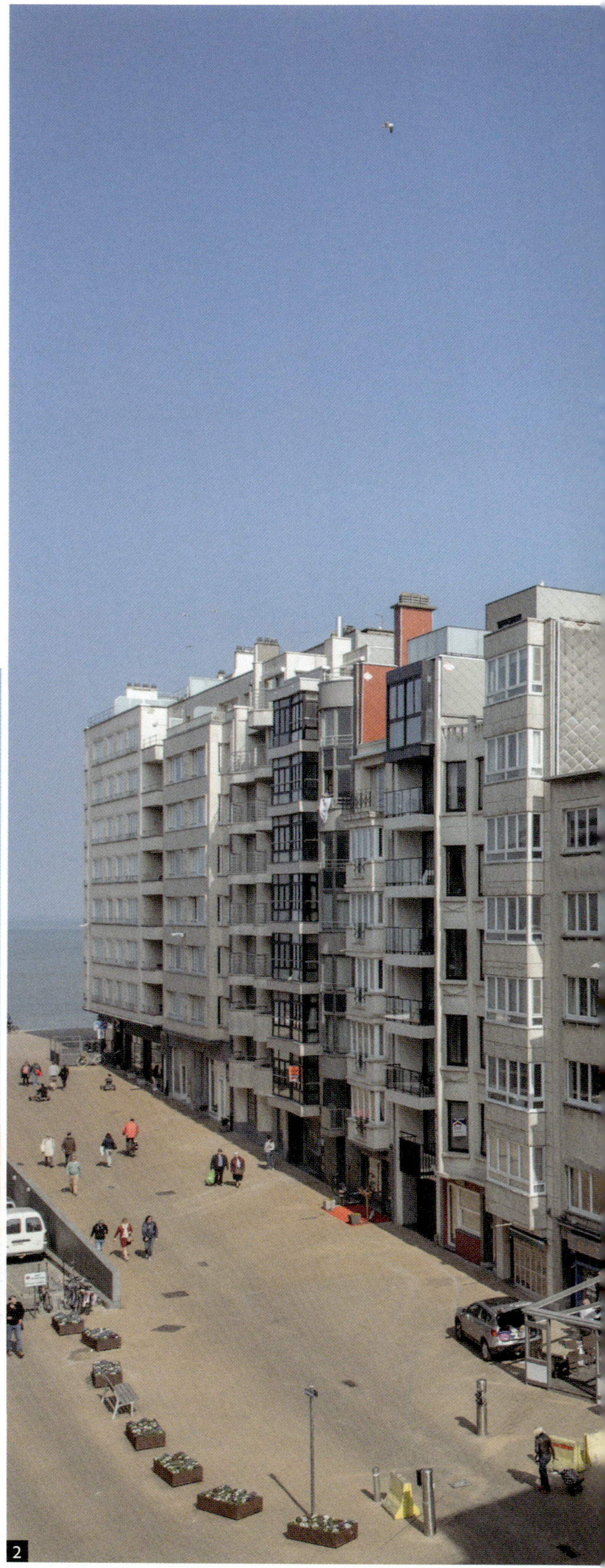

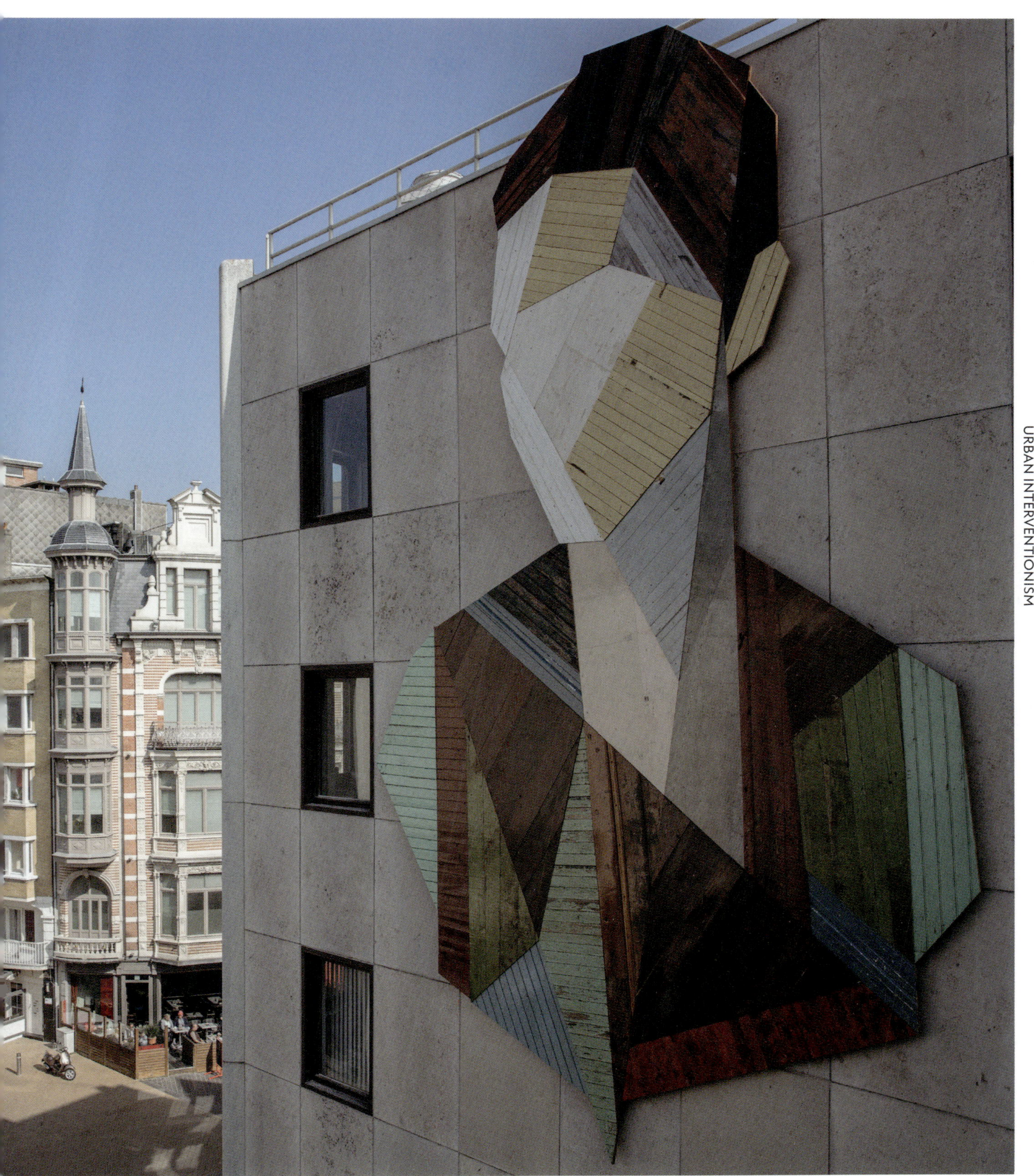

1 / 2
Ostend, Belgium, 2017
PHOTO BY IAN COX

3

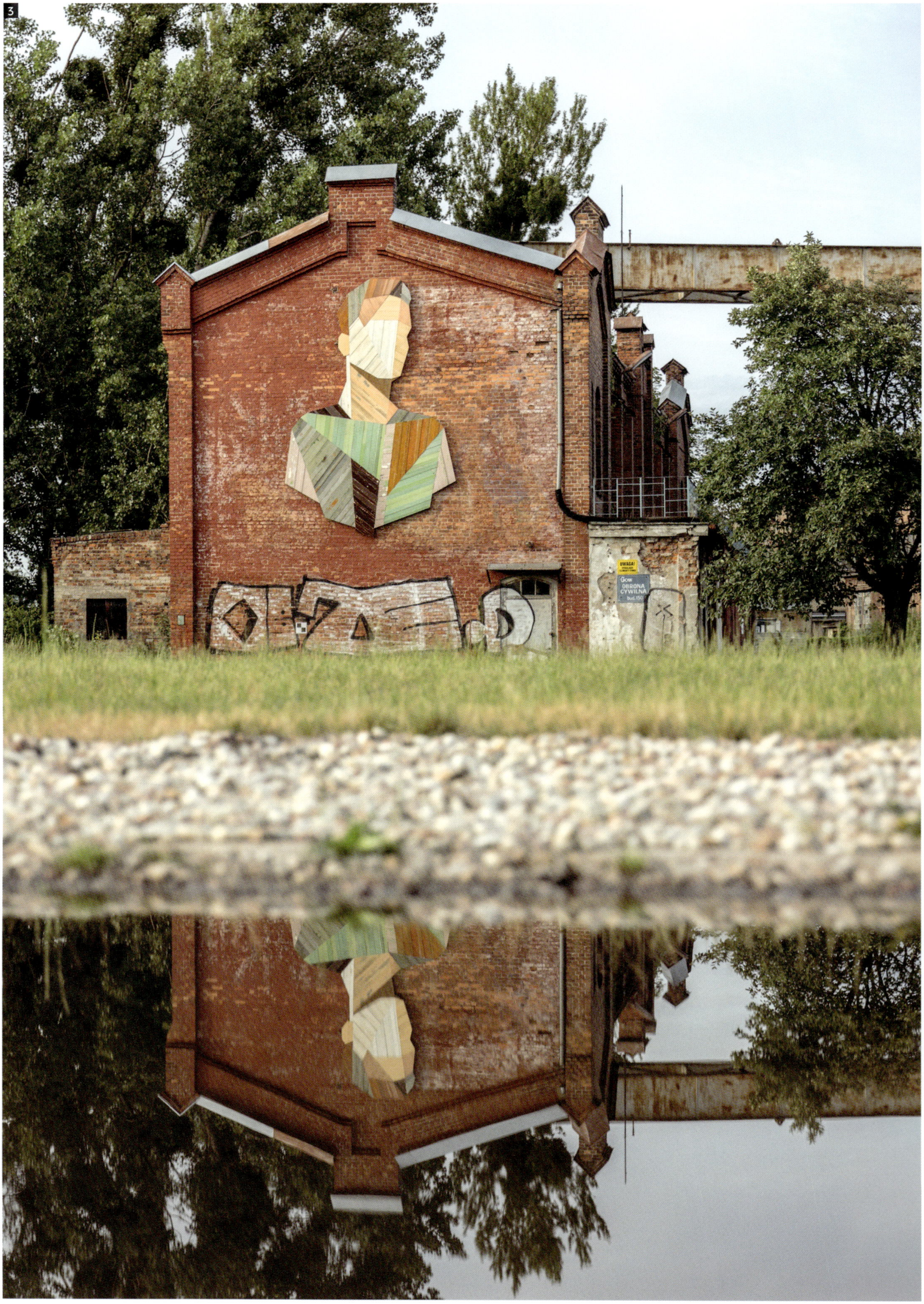

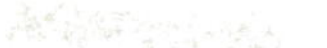

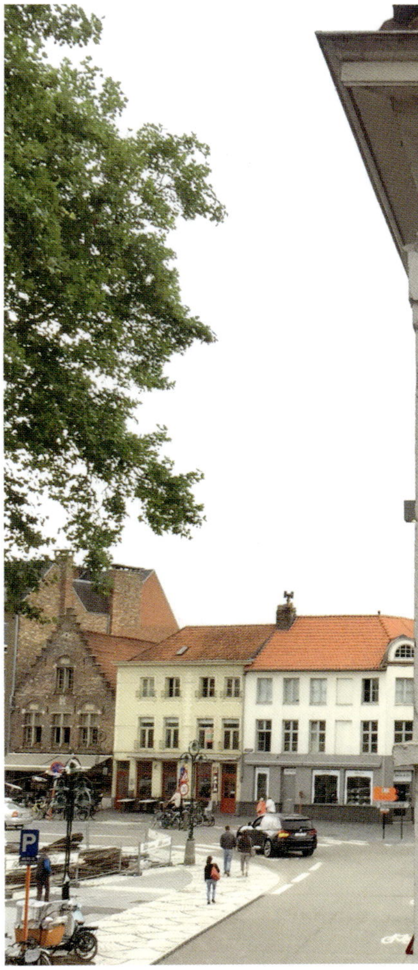

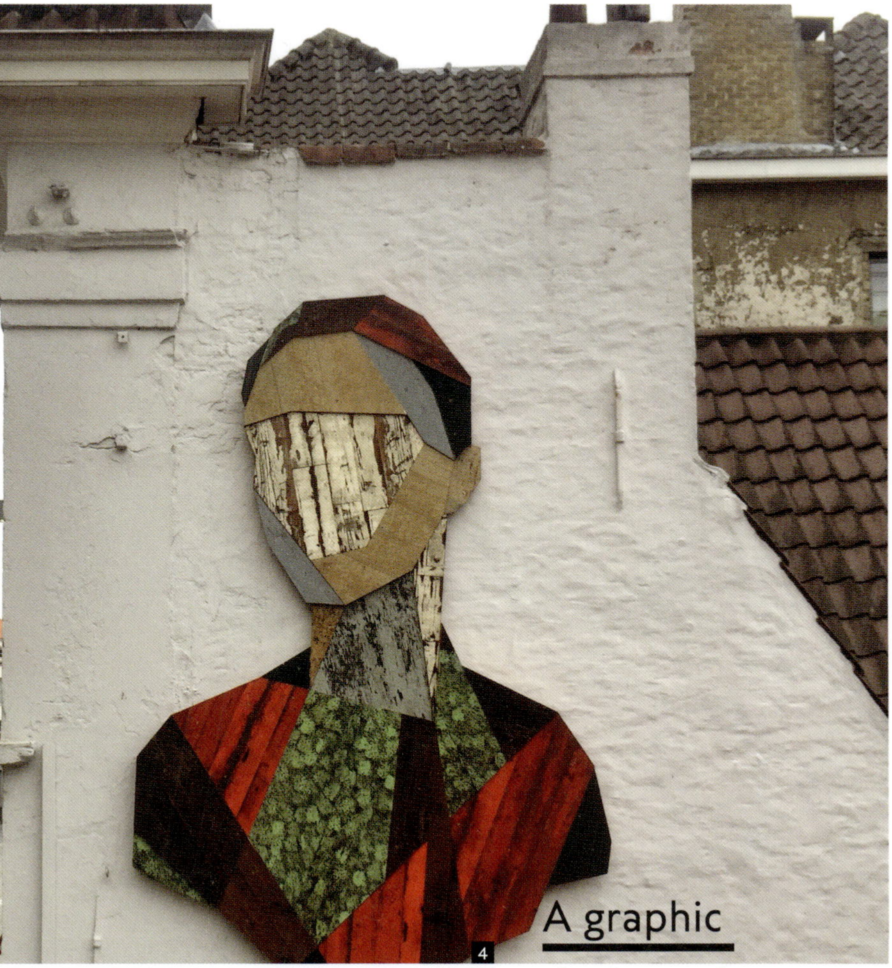

4

5

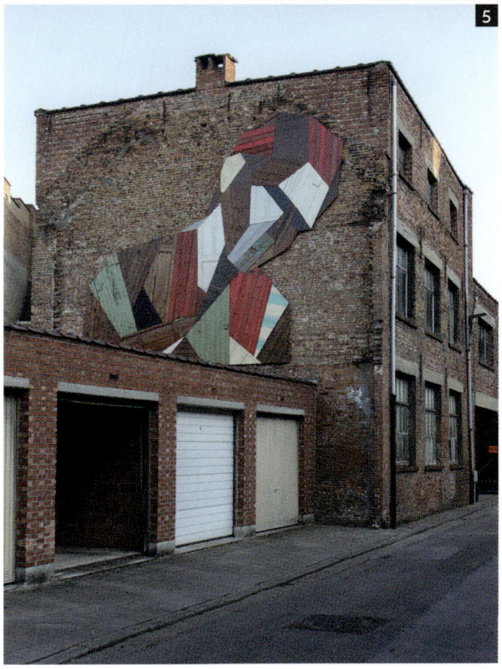

A graphic designer by education, his interest lies in the narrative transcribed through materials and textures.

3 /
Gdańsk, Poland, 2018
PHOTO BY THE ARTIST

4 /
Bruges, Belgium, 2017
PHOTO BY THE ARTIST

5 /
Mechelen, Belgium, 2015
PHOTO BY THE ARTIST

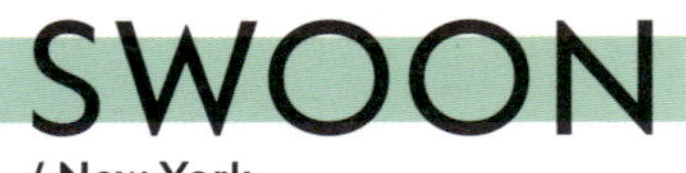

SWOON

/ New York

New-York-based Caledonia Dance Curry aka Swoon may well be the urban artist with the most institutional recognition. With a list of museum exhibitions and a long-running mentor mentee relationship with famous curator Jeffrey Deitch, since her graduation she has continued to star in important exhibitions at the Tate, the Brooklyn Museum, and the LA MOCA, to name a few.

With a grounding interest in community and social development, not only does she incorporate themes of engagement in her work, she is also the founder of the Heliotrope Foundation, a community-building initiative, and an active spokesperson raising awareness of issues surrounding mental health.

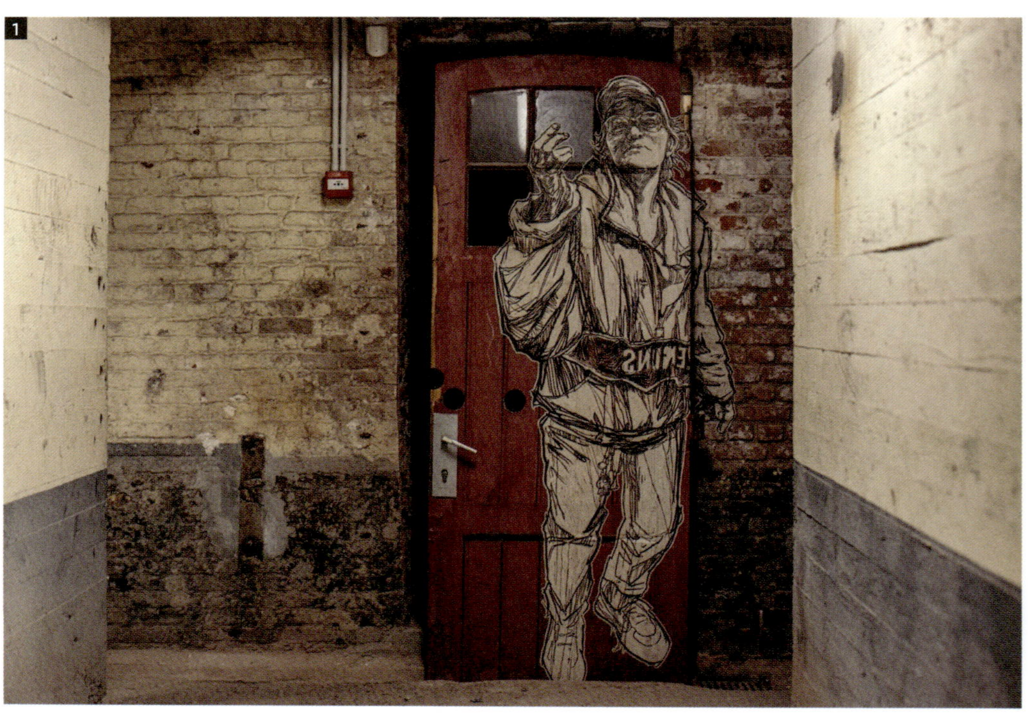

1 /
Brussels, Belgium, 2016
PHOTO BY VINNY CORNELLI

2 /
Brussels, Belgium, 2016
PHOTO BY VINNY CORNELLI

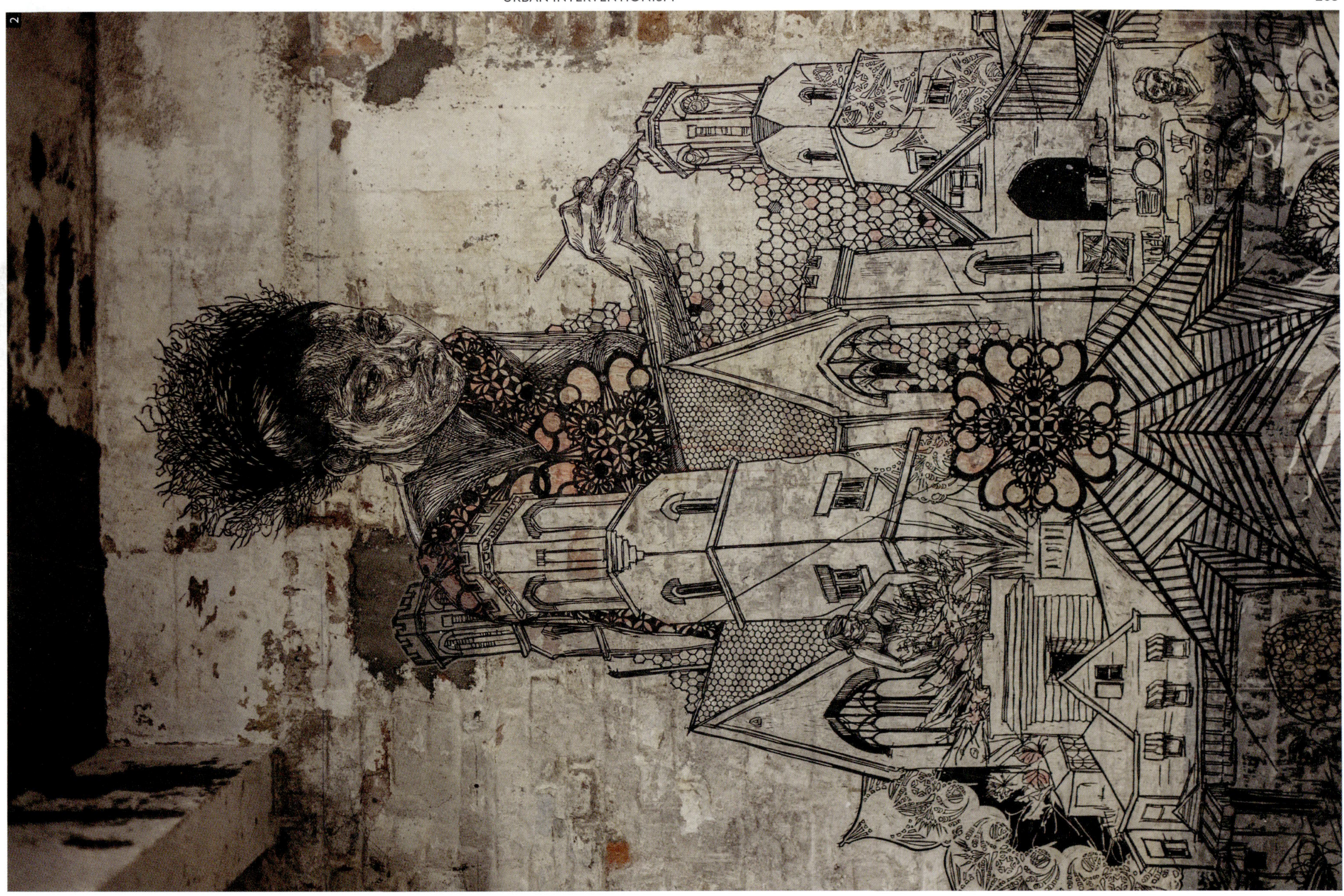
2

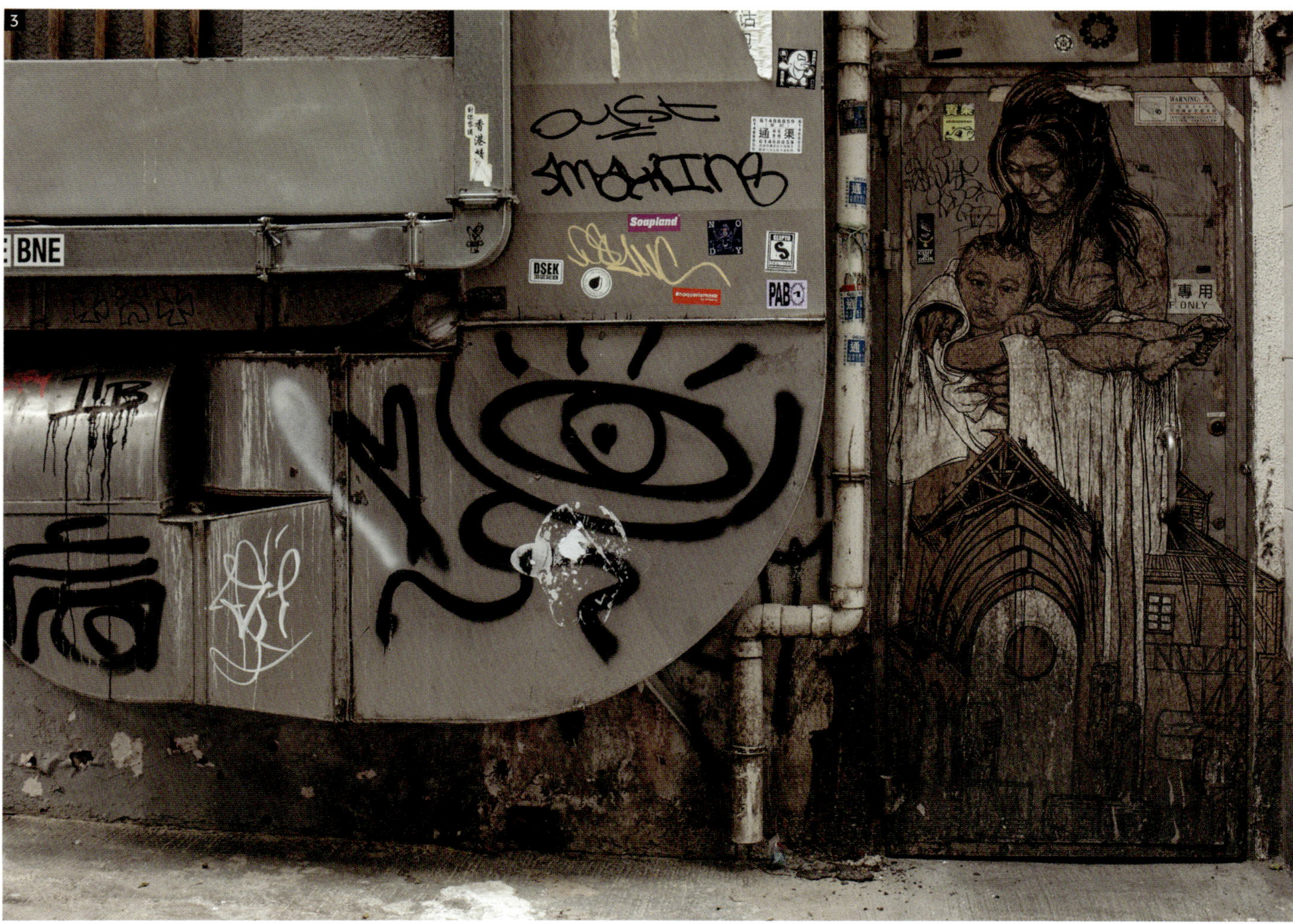

Swoon may well be the urban artist with the most institutional recognition.

3/4/5
Brussels, Belgium, 2016
PHOTO BY VINNY CORNELLI

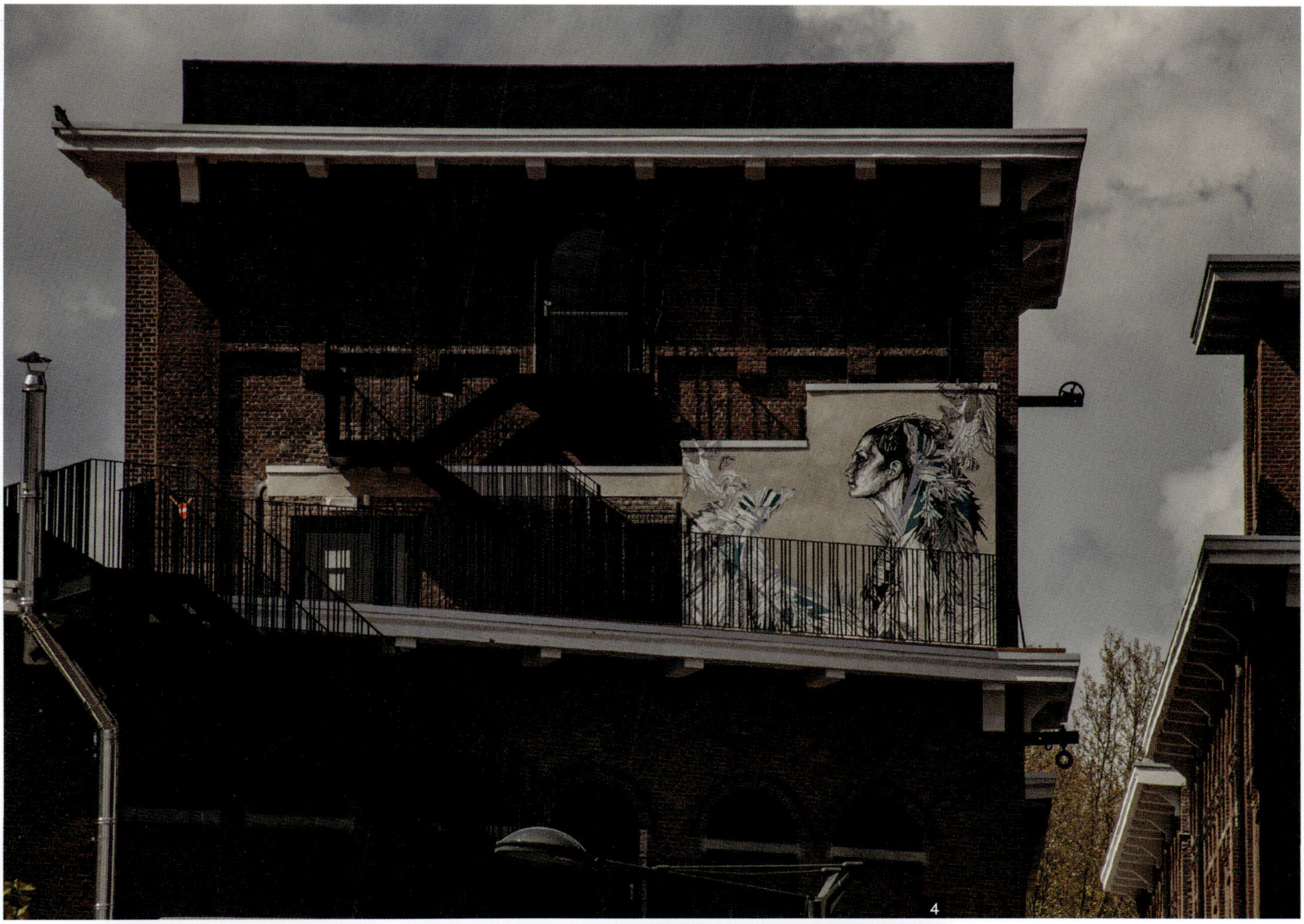

4

5

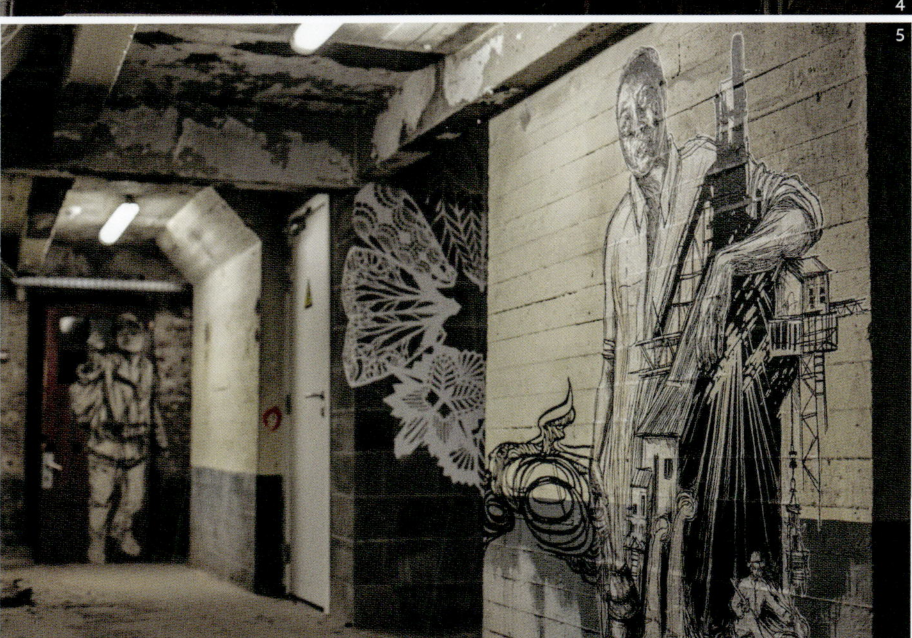

WASTED RITA

/ Lisbon

Since the beginning of her online blogging fame, young Portuguese illustrator and visual poet Wasted Rita has filled our cynical hearts with joy through her few-liner fist-shaking. Writhing in angry and honest clichés of contemporary life, she is much loved for her simple, short posters, reaching out to the frustrated punk in us all. Celebrated as an illustrator as well as a visual artist and poet, she exhibits her work through online platforms as well as design collaborations, publications, exhibitions and of course public spaces around the world.

With punk rock as her biggest influence, she critiques – perhaps unwittingly – issues of gender and individualism, with a bashed-up romantic heart, declaring things like 'I miss you. The same way I imagine hell might miss decent people'.

Wasted Rita fills our cynical hearts with joy through her few-liner fist-shaking.

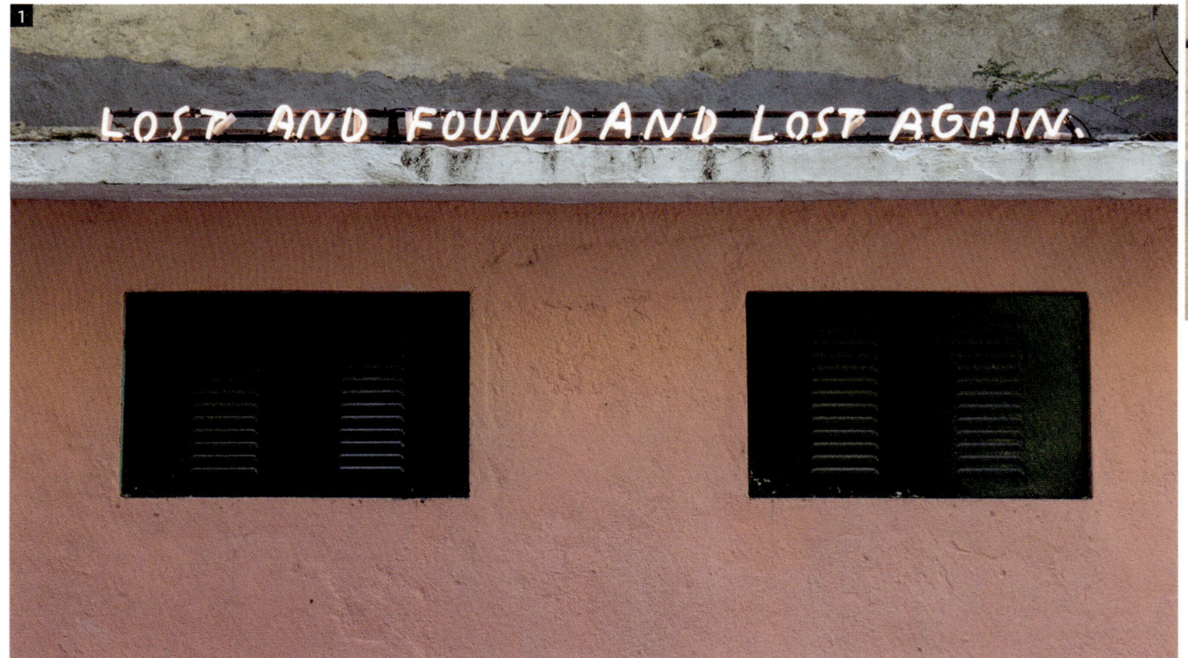

1 /
Lisbon, Portugal, 2016
PHOTO BY THE ARTIST

2 /
Ostend, Belgium, 2019
PHOTO BY HENRIK HAVEN

3 /
Ostend, Belgium, 2019
PHOTO BY EDMOND DOBBELAERE

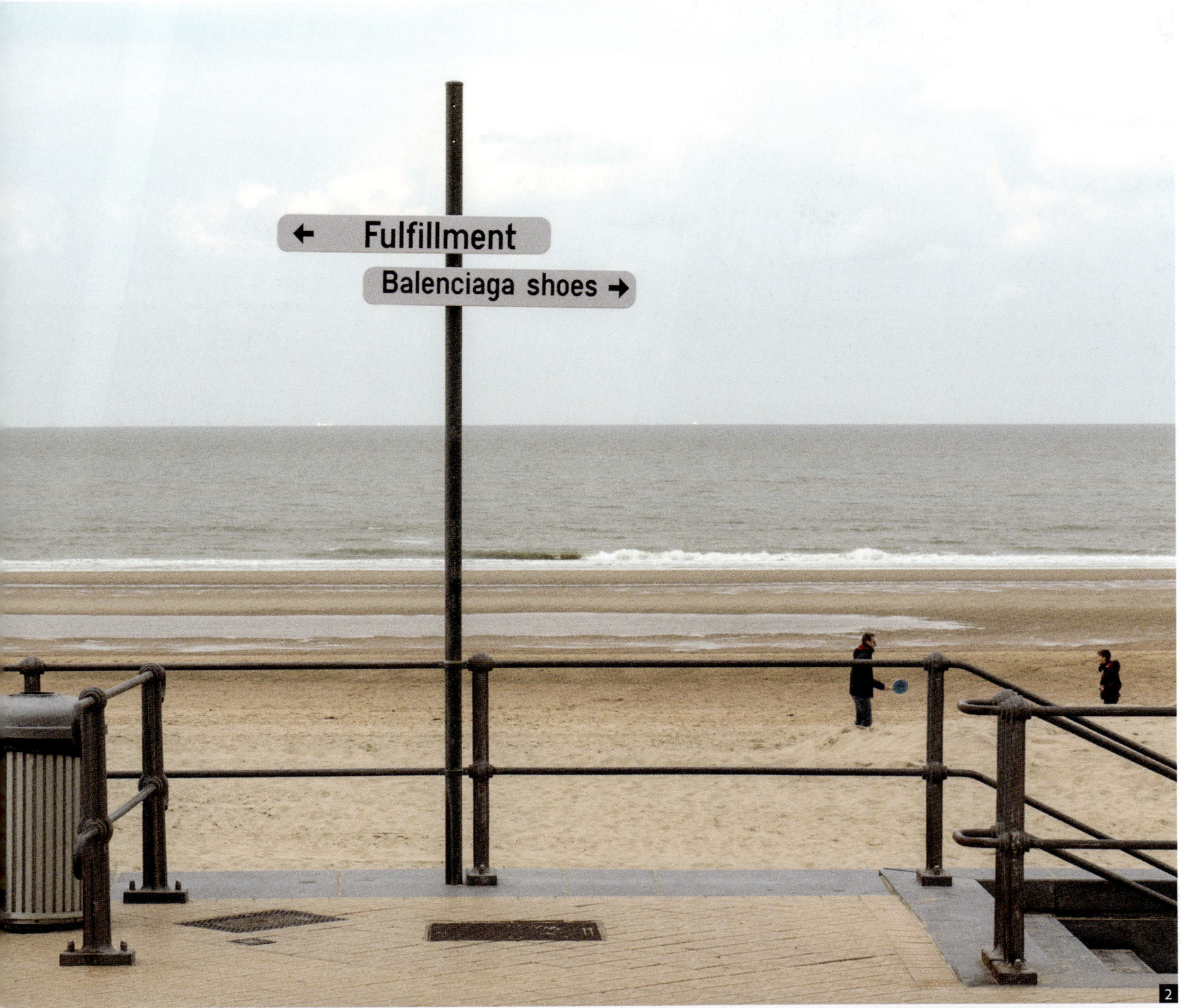

← Fulfillment
Balenciaga shoes →

2

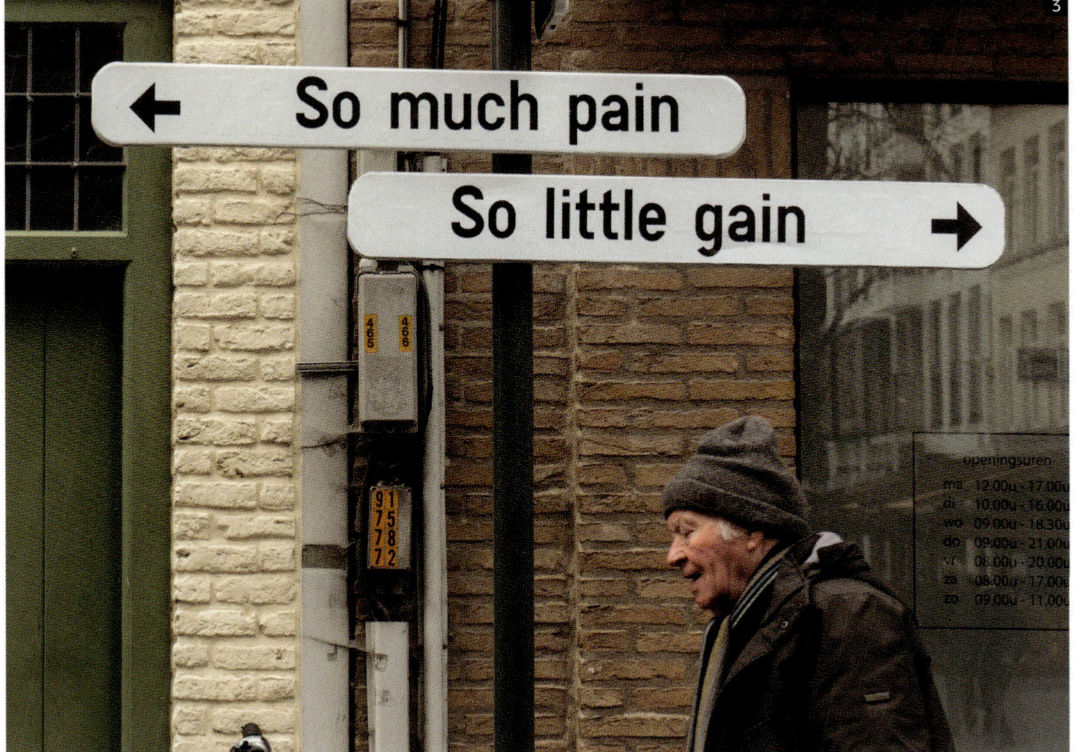
← So much pain
So little gain →
openingsuren

3

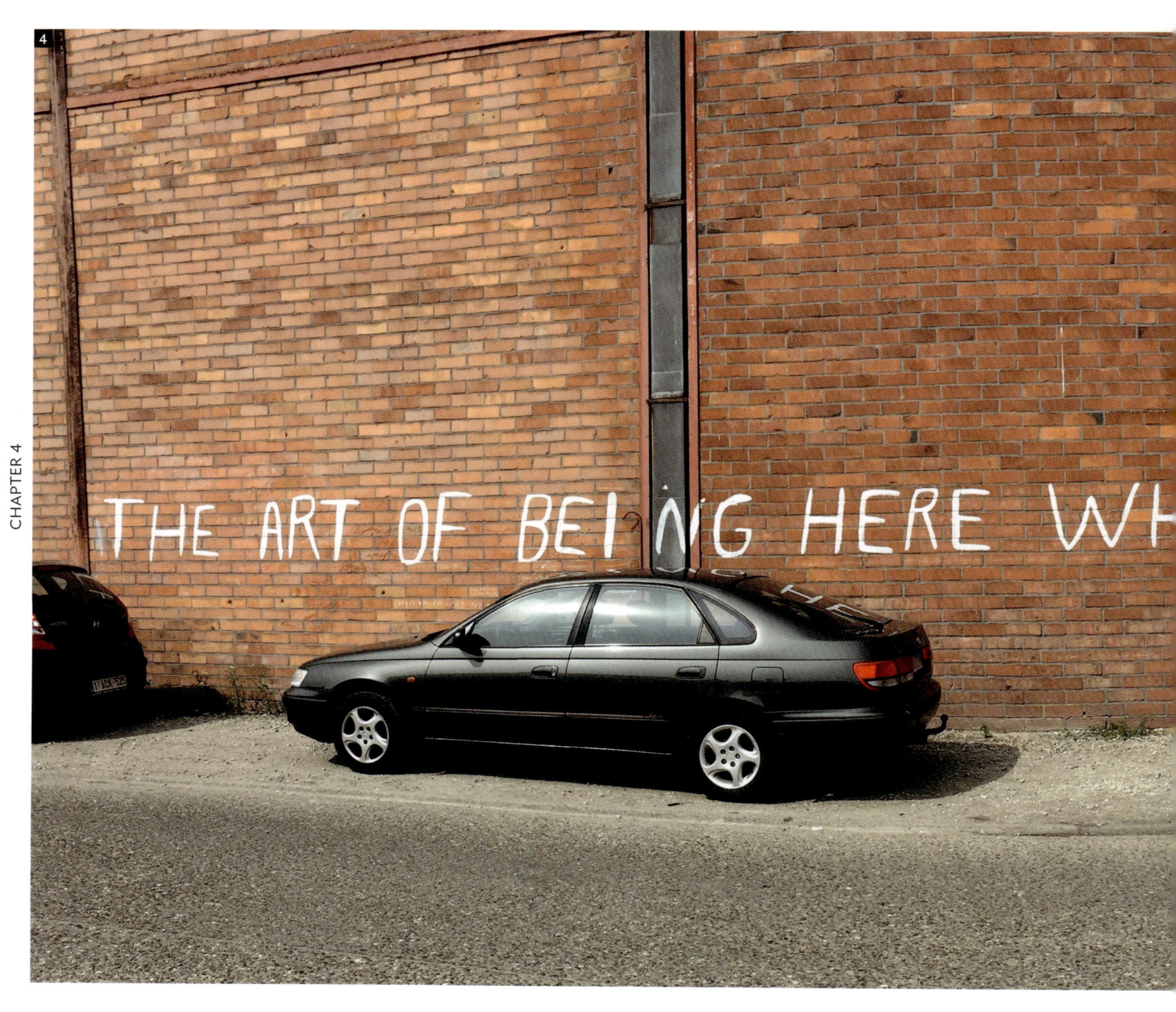
4
THE ART OF BEING HERE WH

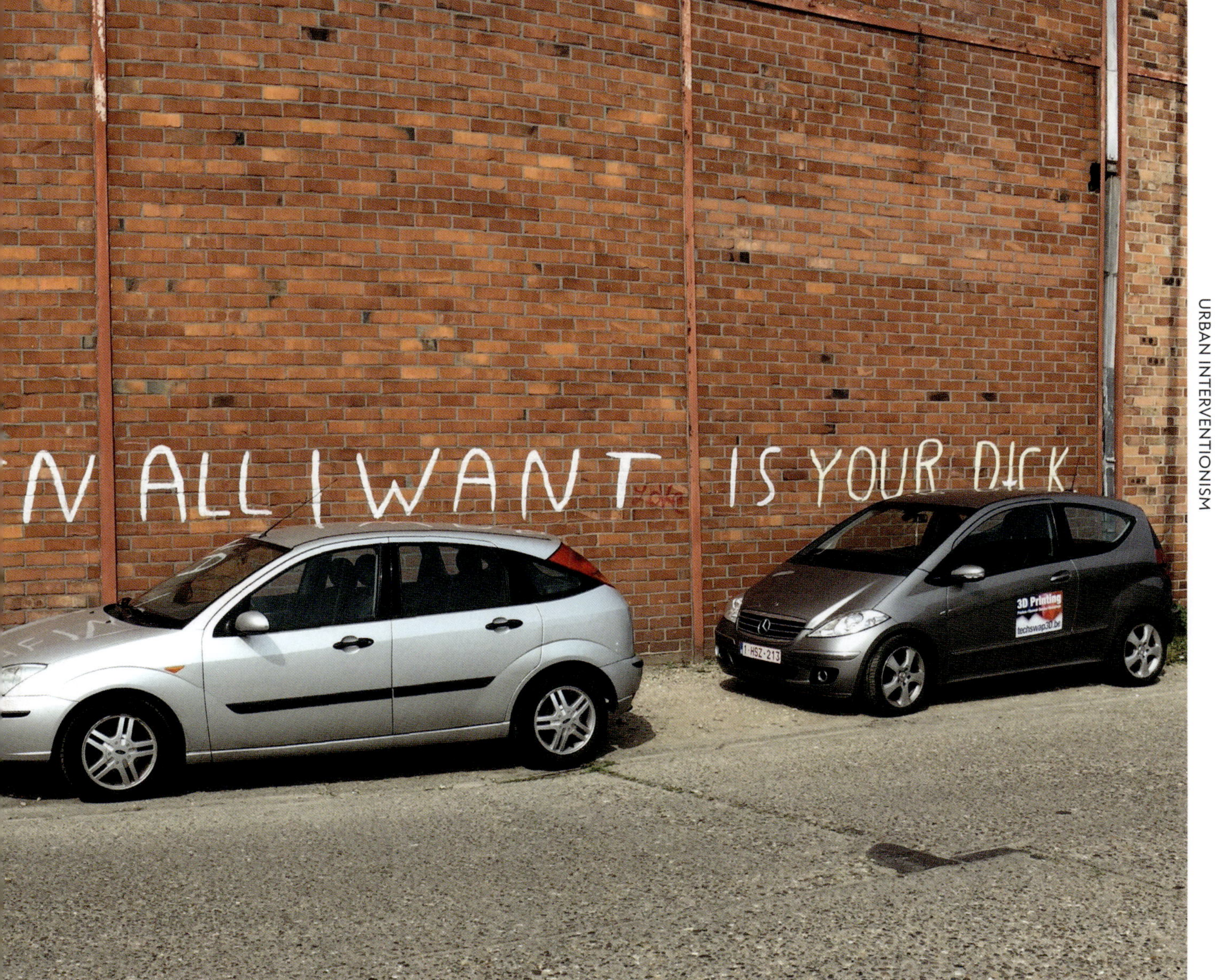

4 /
Hasselt, Belgium, 2015
PHOTO BY THE ARTIST

THANK

NOTHING SHORT of a miracle brought this publication together, due mostly to the help of some fantastic humans along the way. Thank you to the Lannoo team: Viktoria and Astrid for their gentle pushes in the right direction, Niels for taking the time to support us, Sarah for convincing me this could be a good idea and Sanny & Tim for the super-fresh imagery.

To my close friends and family who support me always (listed in alphabetical order): Annemie Bernaerts, An Van Dijck, Ben Van Alboom, Chloë Van Hamme, Elise Sandra, Elke Leemans, Elke Reynaert, Eric Van Poucke, Evy Vermeir, Helene D'Haeseleer, Jasmine Roemendael, Jolien Hapers, Lana Bauwens, Leentje Brands, Lou De Buck, Maika Pieters, Sander Buyck, Sebastian Daley, Thierry Dubois, Vincent Van Malderen and Wilfried Leemans.

And of course, three years on from the last edition, we never tire of being inspired by the generosity of the creatives who share their work on our streets. Thank you for being the reason behind all of this.

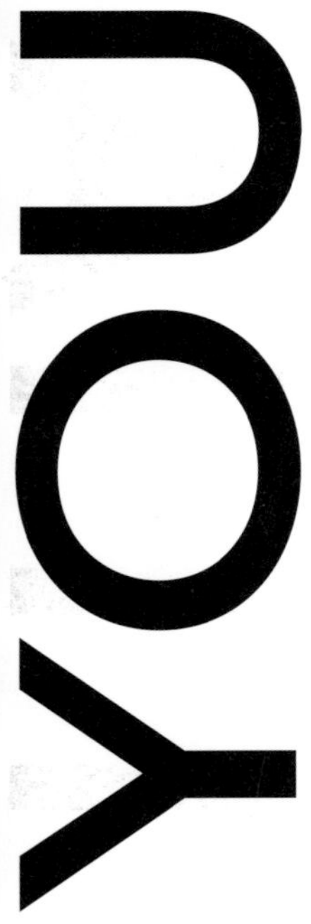

COLOPHON

AUTHOR
Bjørn Van Poucke

COPY-EDITING
Joy Philips

BOOK DESIGN
Oeyen & Winters

Elise Luong drafted all texts in this edition excluding the artist interviews, the introduction and preface.

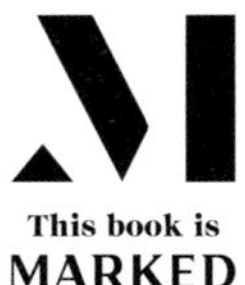

MARKED is an initiative by Lannoo Publishers
www.markedbylannoo.com

JOIN THE MARKED COMMUNITY
on @markedbylannoo

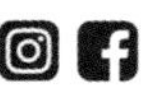

Or sign up for our MARKED newsletter with news about new and forthcoming publications on art, interior design, food & travel, photography and fashion as well as exclusive offers and MARKED events on www.markedbylannoo.com.

If you have any questions or comments about the material in this book, please do not hesitate to contact our editorial team: markedteam@lannoo.com

D/2019/45/582 – NUR 640
ISBN: 9789401461597

#AREYOUMARKED